CANADIAN PRISONS

CANADIAN PRISONS

Understanding the Canadian Correctional System

CARLA CESARONI

OXFORD
UNIVERSITY PRESS

Oxford University Press is a department of the University of Oxford.
It furthers the University's objective of excellence in research, scholarship,
and education by publishing worldwide. Oxford is a registered trade mark of
Oxford University Press in the UK and in certain other countries.

Published in Canada by
Oxford University Press
8 Sampson Mews, Suite 204,
Don Mills, Ontario M3C 0H5 Canada

www.oupcanada.com

Library and Archives Canada Cataloguing in Publication
Title: Canadian prisons : understanding the Canadian correctional system / edited by Carla Cesaroni.
Names: Cesaroni, Carla, editor.
Description: Includes bibliographical references and index.
Identifiers: Canadiana (print) 20200245155 | Canadiana (ebook) 20200245228 | ISBN 9780199034048
(softcover) | ISBN 9780199034055 (ebook)
Subjects: LCSH: Prisons—Canada. | LCSH: Corrections—Canada.
Classification: LCC HV9507 .C358 2020 | DDC 365/.971—dc23

Cover image: Bruce Rolff/Shutterstock.com
Cover design: Sherill Chapman
Interior design: Sherill Chapman

Oxford University Press is committed to our environment.
Wherever possible, our books are printed on paper which comes from
responsible sources.

Printed and bound in Canada

1 2 3 4 — 23 22 21 20

Dedication

To Nawal Ammar, Michele Peterson-Badali, and Anthony N. Doob for your mentorship, and Iain McPherson for everything else.

Brief Contents

Part IV • Current/Emerging Issues

Contents

3   Canadian Criminal Justice Policy and Imprisonment: Understanding What Is Uniquely Canadian   37

Anthony N. Doob and Cheryl Marie Webster

Part II • Doing Time

Part III • Special Populations

8 Women, Crime, and Criminalization in Canada: Understanding the Canadian Correctional Landscape for Incarcerated Women   147

Jennifer M. Kilty and Rebecca Jaremko Bromwich

9 Colonialism and Cultural Disruption: Intergenerational Pathways to Incarceration for Indigenous Peoples   169

Christopher Mushquash, Jessie Lund, Elaine Toombs, and Chris Grol

Part IV • Current/Emerging Issues

16   Religious Services in Canadian Prisons   313

Davut Akca, Mehmet F. Bastug, and Nawal Ammar

Acknowledgements

Thank you to Amy Gordon at Oxford University Press whose guidance, support, and wisdom helped this book come to fruition. Thank you also to all my co-authors for your willingness to contribute to this volume. Thanks to the reviewers whose feedback helped inform this volume: Alana Abramson, Kwantlen Polytechnic University; Cynthia Booth, Cambrian College; Liam Kennedy, King's University College, Western University; Zachary Levinsky, University of Toronto Mississauga; Eva Silden, Camosun College; Cindy Whitten, Memorial University of Newfoundland; and those who wished to remain anonymous. Finally, thank you to all those working and living within corrections who have made our research possible over the years.

Contributors

Davut Akca (Ph.D. in forensic psychology, MA in criminology) is a research officer in the Centre for Forensic Behavioural Science and Justice Studies at the University of Saskatchewan. Dr. Akca's research interests fall within the domains of investigative interviewing, risk terrains of criminal events and crime mapping, radicalization, Islamophobia, hate crimes, and criminal network analysis. Before his graduate studies, he served as a ranked police officer and crime analyst in the Anti-Organized Crimes Department of the Turkish National Police for five years.

Nawal Ammar is dean of the College of Humanities and Social Sciences and professor of Law and Justice at Rowan University in New Jersey. Previously, she served as dean of the Faculty of Social Science and Humanities and professor of Criminology at the Ontario Tech University. She also has served as associate dean in the College of Arts and Sciences and director of the justice studies graduate program and women studies undergraduate program at Kent State University in Ohio. Dr. Ammar has worked with the United Nations and researched and written about topics including elder abuse, violence against immigrant women, issues of Muslim women, and Muslims in prisons.

Mehmet F. Bastug is a lecturer in the criminology program at Lakehead University. His research primarily focuses on extremism, terrorism, cyberterrorism, radicalization, and deradicalization with an emphasis on prisoner radicalization and rehabilitation of extremists. He received his Ph.D. from Rutgers University. He continued his post-doctoral research at the University of Cincinnati's Criminal Justice Research Center and Institute of Crime Science, and then at Ontario Tech University. He has also worked as a police officer and criminal intelligence analyst. He is a member of the Canadian Network for Research on Terrorism, Security and Society and the Canadian Practitioners Network for Prevention of Radicalization and Extremist Violence.

Eric Beauregard is a professor in the School of Criminology at Simon Fraser University. He obtained his Ph.D. from the University of Montreal while he was working for Correctional Service Canada. Dr. Beauregard was responsible for the assessment of individuals convicted of sexual crimes. His main research interests concern sexual violence, homicide, the crime-commission process, and decision making. He has published more than 100 peer-reviewed articles in the field of sexual violence.

Rebecca Jaremko Bromwich is a lawyer and legal scholar with an LLM and LLB from Queen's University and a Ph.D. from Carleton University. She is now a senior research fellow with Restorative Justice for All in London, England. She also serves as the manager for diversity and inclusion for Canada and Russia at the international law firm Gowling WLG. She is an adjunct professor with Carleton University in the Department of Law and Legal Studies, where she also teaches at the Sprott School of Business. Her research interests include gender, diversity, equality, and law with a particular interest in corporate accountability and corporate social responsibility viewed through an equality lens.

Carla Cesaroni earned her Ph.D. from the Centre of Criminology and Sociolegal Studies at the University of Toronto. She currently is an associate professor of criminology at Ontario Tech University. Her main research focus has been on the experiences and adjustment of incarcerated young people. Recently, this has meant work on the trauma and masculinities of incarcerated adolescent boys and young men and comparative cross-national research on prison systems for young adults in Canada and Scotland. She has completed policy work for the Department of Justice; the Ministry of Children, Community and Social Services (Ontario); the Ministry of the Solicitor General (Ontario); the Office of the Provincial Advocate for Children and Youth (Ontario); and the Scottish Prison Service. She is a research associate with the Scottish Centre for Crime and Justice Research.

Raymond R. Corrado is a professor and director of the Institute on Violence, Terrorism & Security in the School of Criminology at Simon Fraser University (SFU) and was the associate director of research, associate faculty member in the Psychology Department and the Faculty of Health Sciences at SFU. He is a visiting fellow at Clare Hall College and the Institute of Criminology, University of Cambridge, and he is a founding member of the Mental Health, Law, and Policy Institute at SFU. Dr. Corrado was also a former co-director of the BC Centre for Social Responsibility and former director of the Centre for Addictions Research British Columbia, SFU site. He also was visiting professor, Faculty of Law, University of Bergen. He is on the editorial boards of eight major criminology and forensic mental health journals. He has co-authored nine edited books, including *Multi-Problem Violent Youth, Issues in Juvenile Justice, Evaluation and Criminal Justice Policy*, and *Juvenile Justice in Canada*, as well as having published over 200 articles, book chapters, and reports on a wide variety of theory and policy issues, including terrorism, youth/juvenile justice, violent young offenders, mental health, adolescent psychopathy, Indigenous victimization, and child/adolescent case management strategies. Currently, Dr. Corrado is a principal investigator and co-principal investigator of several research projects, including three large-scale studies on incarcerated serious and violent young offenders, a comprehensive risk management instrument for violent children and youth, and early childhood aggression. He has conducted policy research and advised governments at national and regional levels in Canada as well as Australia, Italy, and Norway. He received his Ph.D. from Northwestern University in Chicago.

Karla Dhungana Sainju is an assistant professor of criminology in the Faculty of Social Science and Humanities at Ontario Tech University. Her research focuses on the use of technology within corrections and community corrections. Specifically, her work examines the impact and effectiveness of electronic monitoring technologies to supervise pre-trial and post-conviction populations. She is also engaged in research on the topic of bullying and cyberbullying. Prior to joining Ontario Tech University, Dr. Dhungana Sainju was a senior research associate at the Pew Charitable Trusts in Washington, D.C., and produced sentencing and corrections briefs, reports, and policy evaluations. She has completed a Congressional Fellowship on Women and Public Policy in the US Congress and handled a legislative issue portfolio covering the judiciary, women's issues, and child exploitation interdiction. She earned her Ph.D. from Florida State University where she also worked as a researcher at the Center for Criminology and Public Policy Research.

Anthony N. Doob is a professor emeritus of criminology at the Centre for Criminology and Sociolegal Studies, University of Toronto. He graduated from Harvard in 1964 and received his Ph.D. (in psychology) from Stanford University in 1967. He is a fellow of the Royal Society of Canada and was named a member of the Order of Canada in 2014. He was one of the members of the Canadian Sentencing Commission from 1984 until 1987. He has carried out research and written on a wide range of topics related to the youth and adult justice systems. His current work focuses largely on the development of Canadian criminal justice and youth justice policy. In addition, however, he has been working with Cheryl Webster and Jane Sprott (Criminology, Ryerson) on bail, court delay, and the use of imprisonment and parole.

James Gacek is an assistant professor in the Department of Justice Studies at the University of Regina. He has lectured in criminology and criminal justice at the University of Manitoba and the University of Winnipeg. While his research interests are many, they can generally be categorized into three broadly conceived groupings: (1) institutional and community corrections; (2) green criminology and environmental justice; and (3) sexual regulation and the law. With Richard Jochelson, he has co-authored *Criminal Law and Precrime: Legal Studies in Canadian Punishment and Surveillance in Anticipation of Criminal Guilt* (Routledge, 2018) and co-edited *Sexual Regulation and the Law: A Canadian Perspective* (Demeter Press, 2019).

Christopher Grol is currently a Métis Masters Criminology candidate at Ontario Tech University. His research interests include youth justice, policing, Indigenous masculinity, Indigenous overincarceration, traditional Indigeneity and cultural methods of intervention, and Indigenous research methods. The focus of his research has been on the exploration of colonial impacts on Indigenous masculinity and identity. Specifically, he exams pre- and post-colonial Indigenous masculinities and how Indigenous masculinities have been represented and interpreted by Indigenous and non-Indigenous peoples. The research attempts to understand how changes in the perception of what it means to be an Indigenous man can impact how Indigenous men, notably young men, engage with the criminal justice system, ultimately contributing to the overrepresentation of Indigenous peoples in the Canadian criminal justice system. Christopher has worked in many different fields, most notably as an Aboriginal youth mental health and addictions worker and an Indigenous student development specialist, and he has also worked in various roles spanning multiple levels of government. Christopher graduated from Ontario Tech University with an Honours BA in forensic psychology with a minor in legal studies and continues to pursue his MA in criminology.

Kelly Hannah-Moffat is a full professor, former director of the Centre of Criminology and Sociolegal Studies, and a vice-president at the University of Toronto. She conducts interdisciplinary research on risk, human rights, solitary confinement, gender, punishment, and diverse populations. She has published numerous books and articles and conducted an extensive amount of independently funded research on various aspects of Canadian and international penal policy. She has served as a policy consultant and expert witness on several legal cases involving risk assessment, segregation, and gender-based penal reform. She was a policy advisor for Madame Justice Arbour on the Commission of Inquiry into Certain Events at the Prison for Women in Kingston (the Arbour Commission) and was an expert witness for the Office of the Ontario Coroner in the Ashley Smith inquest, as well as several other recent cases related to the use of segregation and conditions of confinement. She works with several government and not-for-profit organizations on issues related to criminal justice reform. She is co-editor-in-chief for *Punishment and Society*, as well as a member of several international editorial advisory boards.

Adelina Iftene is an assistant professor at the Schulich School of Law, Dalhousie University, where she teaches, conducts research, and publishes in areas related to criminal law, prison law, and evidence. Dr. Iftene's major research work explores issues related to prison health and access to justice for prisoners. Her book, *Punished for Aging: Vulnerability, Rights and Access to Justice in Canadian Penitentiaries* was published by University of Toronto Press in July 2019. Dr. Iftene is also actively engaged in prison policy and advocacy work. She has consulted with provincial governments on correctional legislation, has appeared before and made submissions on vulnerable prison groups to the Standing Senate Committee for Human Rights, and has partaken in various governmental consultation groups on criminal justice. Dr. Iftene serves on the Prison Law Advisory Committee for Legal Aid Ontario, on the Executive Board for the Canadian Prison Lawyers Association, and on the Regional Advocacy Committee for the East Coast Prison Justice Society.

Jennifer M. Kilty is an associate professor in the Department of Criminology, University of Ottawa. She is the author of numerous articles and book chapters in the fields of criminalization, gender, and mental health, and her edited and authored books include *Demarginalizing Voices: Commitment, Emotion and Action in Qualitative Research* (2014, UBC Press), *Within the Confines: Women and the Law in Canada* (2014, Women's Press), *Containing Madness: Gender and "Psy" in Institutional Contexts* (2018, Palgrave), and *the Enigma of a Violent Woman: A Critical Examination of the Case of Karla Homolka* (2016, Routledge).

Jihyun Kwon is a doctoral candidate in criminology and sociolegal studies at the University of Toronto. Her research interests include accountability, transparency, and administrative governance of law enforcement—such as policing and corrections—and their oversight mechanisms. The focus of her research has been on the structural and functional dynamics that lead to coordination or fragmentation of various oversight initiatives and agencies, which affect the fulfillment of their mandates. Jihyun completed her BA at McGill University with first class honours in sociology and finished her MA in criminology at the University of Toronto where she received the John Edwards Award for graduating with the most outstanding performance. She is a Vanier CGS scholar and a recipient of the Delta Kappa Gamma World Fellowship and two Ontario Graduate Scholarships. She is currently working with Professor Kelly Hannah-Moffat at the Ministry of the Solicitor General to enforce and oversee the implementation of a Human Rights Consent Order in Ontario prisons.

Jessie Lund is a Ph.D. student in clinical psychology at Lakehead University. Her research focuses on the psychological and social sequelae of traumatic experiences. Her dissertation research examines the interrelationships among adverse childhood experiences, executive functioning, and substance use in First Nations adults seeking treatment for substance-use problems in northwestern Ontario. Jessie collaborates with First Nations community-based organizations on projects aimed at supporting First Nations adolescents and adults experiencing substance-use problems, mental health difficulties, and housing instability. Jessie is supported by a Joseph-Armand Bombardier SSHRC Doctoral Scholarship.

Katharina Maier is an assistant professor of criminal justice at the University of Winnipeg. She holds a law degree from the University of Muenster (Germany) and a Master's degree and Ph.D. from the Centre for Criminology & Sociolegal Studies at the University of Toronto. As an interdisciplinary scholar, her research lies at the intersection of four subfields: law and society; punishment and prison law; urban poverty and public health; and comparative law and criminal justice. She has conducted research on prisoner re-entry, halfway houses, and penal supervision and is currently conducting a project on the role of "crisis" in shaping criminal justice and public health work. Her work has been supported by the Vanier Canada Graduate Scholarship, SSHRC, and other funding sources and has been published in *Theoretical Criminology, Punishment & Society*, and other outlets.

Kelly Struthers Montford is an assistant professor of sociology in the Irving K. Barber School of Arts and Sciences at the University of British Columbia, Okanagan. Previously, she was a postdoctoral research fellow in punishment, law, and social theory at the Centre for Criminology and Sociolegal Studies at the University of Toronto, and received her Ph.D. from the University of Alberta in 2017. Her research bridges settler colonial studies, punishment and captivity, animal studies, and law and has been published in *Radical Philosophy Review*, the *New Criminal Law Review, PhiloSophia*, the *Canadian Journal of Women and the Law, Societies*, and *PhaenEx: Journal of Existentialist and Phenomenological Theory and Culture*, among other venues.

Dr. Christopher Mushquash, Ph.D., C.Psych., is a Canada research chair in Indigenous mental health and addiction, an associate professor in the Department of Psychology at Lakehead University and the Division of Human Sciences at the Northern Ontario School of Medicine. He is the director of the Centre for Rural and Northern Health Research at Lakehead University. He is the interim executive vice president of research at the Thunder Bay Regional Health Sciences Centre and chief scientist of the Thunder Bay Regional Health Research Institute. In addition to his academic appointments, Dr. Mushquash is a registered clinical psychologist providing assessment, intervention, and consultation services for First Nations children, adolescents, and adults at Dilico Anishinabek Family Care. Dr. Mushquash is the recipient of numerous awards for his work, including the Canadian Psychological Association President's New Researcher Award; Lakehead University Outstanding Alumni Award; the Northwestern Ontario Visionary Award; the Ontario Ministry of Research, Innovation and Science Early Researcher Award; the Clinical Psychological Association Clinical Section Scientist-Practitioner Early Career Award; the Lakehead University Indigenous Research Partnership Award; the Ministry of Health and Long-Term Care Achievement, Collaboration, and Excellence Award; and the Canadian Alliance on Mental Illness and Mental Health 2020 Champions of Mental Health Award. In 2017, Dr. Mushquash was inducted into the Royal Society of Canada's College of New Scholars, Artists and Scientists. He is currently the vice-chair of the institute advisory board for the Canadian Institutes of Health Research, Institute of Indigenous Peoples' Health. He is a board member of the Ontario Psychological Association and the Canadian Foundation for Innovation. Dr. Mushquash is Ojibway and a member of Pays Plat First Nation.

Allison O'Donnell is a master of arts student in the criminology program at Ontario Tech University, researching Indigenous corrections. She is a former project assistant at the Correctional Service of Canada's National Headquarters. At CSC, she gained knowledge and understanding of the legislation governing corrections and experience in applying and revising CSC policy.

Adrienne M.F. Peters is an assistant professor and the liaison and co-coordinator of the Police Studies Program in the Department of Sociology at Memorial University. Her research interests include youth offending; serious and violent offending; mental health/well-being and its association with the justice system; justice system programming and intervention; the

Youth Criminal Justice Act and young offender policy; policing; police training and education; police–community partnerships; and community-based research. She has presented at conferences and co-authored publications in each of these areas. Dr. Peters has worked on several related research projects; for example, she is the principal investigator of the *Longitudinal Study of the Reoffending Outcomes of Serious-Violent, Gang-Involved, Mentally Disordered, and Sexual Offenders Supervised on Specialized Youth Probation* in Vancouver, British Columbia, and is currently leading studies examining the youth justice system in Newfoundland and Labrador and exploring the training/education of police officers with the Royal Newfoundland Constabulary. Dr. Peters has worked and volunteered for a number of community-based organizations designed for individuals involved in the justice system. She is a program facilitator for 7th Step Society Newfoundland, a peer-support prisoner group, and is the board chair of the fasdNL Network, educating and advocating for fetal alcohol spectrum disorder supports. She received her Ph.D. from Simon Fraser University.

Michele Peterson-Badali is a professor in the Department of Applied Psychology and Human Development at the University of Toronto's Ontario Institute for Studies in Education (OISE) and OISE's associate dean, Research, International & Innovation. Her teaching, research, and service have strong connections to communities and organizations related to the rights and well-being of children and youth. Her research focuses on children's and adolescents' developing knowledge, reasoning, perceptions, and experiences of the youth justice system; their understanding of rights; and their evolving legal capacities. Current foci include implementation of the risk-need-responsivity framework in community-sentenced youth, mental health and youth criminal justice, and Indigenous youth. One of the guiding principles of her research program over the past 30 years has been to provide an evidence basis for youth justice policy and practice. In addition to scholarly dissemination of her work, Michele is actively engaged in bringing her research findings into the spheres of public policy and practice.

Jim Phillips is a professor in the Faculty of Law at the University of Toronto and is cross-appointed to the Department of History and the Centre for Criminology and Sociolegal Studies. He is editor-in-chief of the Osgoode Society for Canadian Legal History. His research is principally on Canadian legal history, although he has also written on US legal history, British imperial history, and the law of property and trusts. He has published two monographs, seven edited and co-edited books, and some 65 journal articles and book chapters. In 2018 he published *A History of Law in Canada: Volume 1: Beginnings to 1866* with Philip Girard and Blake Brown, and is currently working on Volume 2, which will cover events from 1867, with the same co-authors.

Justin Piché, Ph.D., is associate professor in the Department of Criminology and director of the Carceral Studies Research Collective at the University of Ottawa. He is also a researcher for the Carceral Cultures Research Initiative, co-founder of the Criminalization and Punishment Education Project, and co-editor of the *Journal of Prisoners on Prisons*.

Kylie Reale is a Ph.D. candidate at Simon Fraser University in the School of Criminology. Her research interests include sexual violence, sexual homicide, crime scene behaviours, detection avoidance strategies, criminal careers, and offence specialization.

Rosemary Ricciardelli is a professor of sociology, the coordinator for criminology, and co-coordinator for police studies at Memorial University. Elected to the Royal Society of Canada, she is also an associate scientific director of the Canadian Institute for Public Safety Research and Treatment (CIPSRT) and has additional affiliations and appointments that include Ontario Shores Centre for Mental Health and Toronto Rehabilitation Institute. Her research is centred on evolving understandings of gender, vulnerabilities, risk, and experiences and issues within different facets of the criminal justice system. Beyond her work on the realities of penal living and community re-entry for federally incarcerated men in Canada, her current work includes a focus on the experiences of correctional officers and police officers given the potential for compromised psychological, physical, and social health inherent to these occupations. Her sources of active research funding include Correctional Service Canada, the Social Sciences and Humanities Research Council of Canada, the Canadian Institute of Health Research, Memorial University's Office of the Vice-President Research, and the Harris Centre.

John Rives holds bachelor degrees in both geology and history from the University of Toronto. He has published three book-length collections of poetry, beginning with his first, *Dead Time: Poems from Prison* (1989). His award-winning poetry and writing on justice issues has appeared widely in periodicals in Canada, the United States, and the United Kingdom, and he has lectured widely at secondary schools, colleges, and universities. John was convicted of second degree murder and attempted murder in 1982 and was sentenced to life in prison with parole eligibility set at 10 years. He was granted full parole in 1992. For 20 years John worked with the St. Leonard's Society LifeLine In-Reach program as an In-Reach worker and team leader. In that capacity, he advised, encouraged, and assisted Lifers and long-term offenders as they struggled to come to grips with the reality of their situations and worked to earn some form of conditional release, including parole. He has represented over 600 individual prisoners at National Parole Board hearings. In conjunction with his colleagues and agency partners he developed, co-authored, and provided training for the Lifer Resource Strategy (Part 1, Adaptation) for Correctional Service of Canada. Serving on the board of directors of the John Howard Society of Ontario since 1994 and as a member of the board of Kingston Community Chaplaincy, he is dedicated to the successful transitioning and integration of ex-prisoners into the community. John currently resides in Kingston, Ontario, and will remain on parole for life.

Jarrod Shook is a research assistant for the Carceral Cultures Research Initiative and dialogue editor for the *Journal of Prisoners on Prisons.*

Elaine Toombs is a clinical psychology resident with Dilico Anishinabek Family Care, an organization that provides mental health and primary care services to Indigenous communities in the Thunder Bay area. Her doctoral research is dedicated to understanding how adverse childhood experiences affect psychological and physical health outcomes within a First Nations population seeking treatment for substance use. Elaine's additional research interests include First Nations' mental health, resilience, parenting, and the use of community-based research methods. Elaine's work is supported by a Canadian Institutes of Health Research Doctoral Award.

Kevin Walby, Ph.D., is associate professor in the Department of Criminal Justice and director for the Centre for Access to Information and Justice at the University of Winnipeg. He is also a researcher for the Carceral Cultures Research Initiative and co-editor of the *Journal of Prisoners on Prisons.*

Cheryl Marie Webster is a professor at the Department of Criminology, University of Ottawa. Her initial research examined the role of the two-tiered criminal trial courts in Canada, the use and value of the preliminary inquiry, and an investigation of case processing in the provincial and superior courts. More recently, her research has concentrated on the effectiveness of general deterrence as applied to sentencing, a comparative analysis of policies related to imprisonment in Canada and abroad, and an examination of trends in pre-trial detention. For the past several years, she has been involved in various research projects on the operation of bail courts. Beyond having published in both national and international journals, she has provided expert advice to various levels of government in Canada as well as such organizations as the Human Rights Commission of Canada, the Parole Board of Canada, and the Centro de Estudios de Justicia de las Américas.

Introduction

Prisons occupy a particular position in the psyche of most members of the public. This is likely because in most democratic countries a prison sentence is the ultimate sanction. As Erving Goffman (1961) suggested, they are "total institutions," physically separated from the community by high walls, barbed wire, and security doors. In their very design they send a message about those who reside within and those who don't. Many people in the community have never stepped inside the walls of a correctional facility and know little about the reality of prison life other than what they have gathered from popular prison shows and movies, which are, after all, fictional. Correctional issues are rarely black or white nor simple. The actors that inhabit and operate in correctional spaces are rarely anything but interesting, complex human beings. Corrections capture the very essence of humanity in the subtexts that are always just below the surface of its day-to-day operations, including punishment, redemption, hope, despair, fear, boredom, and hopefully compassion. They remain a fixture of both the public's imagination and our collective reality.

Prison writings have a rich history. Whether by academics, ex-prisoners or correctional staff, prison writings used to be a prominent feature of the criminological and sociological literature during the 1950s to 1970s—what is now referred to as the "golden era" of prison research. However, since that time, there is a more limited amount of original research being conducted in corrections and on prisons, and the output on correctional topics has largely diminished. Work continues to be produced on the criminal justice system, crime statistics, sentencing, and the courts. Research on prison life (whether on prisoners or staff), doing time, and life after prison are rarer. Much of the writing currently appears in the form of prison biographies or official reports by correctional authorities. Many countries, however, have at least one anthology of prison writings by prominent academics that are of interest to students, practitioners, and members of the public. Surprisingly, Canada has been lacking such a publication. This book is the result of a belief that such a book is an important necessity to any in-depth understanding of Canadian corrections.

Canadian prisons and Canadian corrections are often discussed in the context of the United States, particularly in terms of the number of prisons and number of prisoners. Though the United States may claim to be the innovators of imprisonment as punishment (versus public displays of physical punishment), Canadian prisons and Canadian corrections have their own unique history and legacy. Our correctional landscape is distinct for many reasons, including the fact that Canada no longer has the death penalty, nor do we have super maximum security prisons ("super jails") where prisoners are seemingly "caged."

It is difficult for a single author to attempt to capture the richness of Canadian corrections. There are some authors who have provided a broad survey of Canadian correctional issues, largely based on the available research literature. Others have focused their writings and research on single topics, such as prisoner rights or release, re-entry, and reintegration.

Each of the authors who have contributed to this volume are established researchers. A number of the authors have worked closely with the Correctional Service of Canada in various capacities. One author has experienced life inside. All share similar concerns regarding prison conditions, the overuse of prison as a sanction, special vulnerable populations, and prisoner rights, including the overuse of solitary confinement. They have provided a more focused discussion of key themes based on recent/original research.

This book is an attempt to draw the reader's attention to the many important aspects of the Canadian correctional landscape, which at its heart is about prisons. Part 1 provides an important context by which to understand Canadian prisons. It lays out the history of Canadian prisons, the current legislative and operational framework, and provides a comparative look at incarceration in Canada versus the United States, focusing on what makes us uniquely "Canadian." Part 2 is focused on the central actors in prison life and life after prison. It takes the reader through the reality of doing time, the lived experience of those who work in corrections, the challenge of release and re-entry, and the important place of mental health and well-being for correctional populations. Part 3 introduces the reader to the special populations who have additional challenges when behind bars. Part 4 is a collection of emerging/current issues that have not been synthesized previously for a Canadian audience, including prison tourism, modern technology, the use of solitary confinement, or the role of religion in prison programming and adaptation.

Corrections, ultimately, is about punishment and the treatment of our fellow human beings. Fyodor Dostoyevsky once famously stated (later paraphrased by Winston Churchill, himself once a prisoner of war) "The degree of civilization in a society can be revealed by entering its prisons." To that end, we hope that readers will find this book educational but also compelling and thought provoking. We hope it helps readers understand an important and critical part of Canadian society.

PART I

Overview

The History of Prisons in Canada

1

Jim Phillips

Learning Objectives

After reading this chapter, you should be able to:

- Appreciate the many different uses to which prisons were put before the 1830s.
- Know when and why the prison became the principal sanction used by the courts when sentencing individuals convicted of crimes.
- Describe what was novel about the prison regimes used in Canada's first penitentiaries.
- Know why Canada has two prison systems—federal and provincial—and what roles each plays.
- Explain how people in the late 1880s thought about women's prisons, and how they believed they should be run differently than men's prisons.
- Describe how the two contradictory ideas about prisons—that they must punish and reform—have long co-existed.
- Describe what has changed about prisons since World War II.

Chapter Overview

This chapter will provide a narrative of Canadian prison history. It begins with European colonial settlement, because Indigenous societies did not use prisons. It briefly discusses jails (often spelled gaols in older accounts) in New France and each of the English colonies as an accompaniment to early "state building," the move to penitentiaries and their corollary, the prison discipline system in the 1830s, and the new arrangements for control of different carceral institutions at Confederation. Subsequent sections discuss the specialized institutions for women and youth that emerged in the mid- to late nineteenth century, and the seemingly endless rounds of "reform" that punctuate prison history through the late 1800s and the 1900s. Throughout this chapter, changes in penal philosophies and techniques are linked to larger social, political, and economic transformations. One enduring question pervades prison history: Given that that history is an endless catalogue of failure of the initial grand vision, why has the ideal of the prison not been abandoned and an alternative seriously examined?

Introduction

A history of the prison in Canada must be part of and engage with three other histories. One is the fact that the history of Canada from the 1600s to the end of the 1800s comprises a number of different histories by which European settlers came to various regions of northern North America at different times for different reasons and in widely different numbers. Early prisons were thus often institutions serving fledgling communities with small populations. This was a pattern set very early in the history of European settlement with the establishment of the colony of New France in the early 1600s. That same pattern was often reproduced on later occasions—with the establishment of English colonies in Atlantic Canada in the 1700s, of Upper Canada from the 1790s, of what became British Columbia in the 1850s, of Red River and Manitoba between the 1830s and 1870, and of the Northwest Territories from around 1870. The first two sections of this chapter deal with that colonial period in Canada's prison history.

The second history reflected in the development of Canada's prison system is the political and administrative history of the regions that now make up Canada. Political change affected prison history in a variety of ways, the most notable being the central political event of Confederation, which resulted, during a long process between 1867 and 1949, in a prison system from coast to coast run partly by the federal government and partly by provincial governments. The third and subsequent sections of this chapter provide an overview of this bifurcated national system.

The third history pertinent to understanding Canada's prison development is the broadly international history of changes in penal practice that affected most states in Europe and North America from the later 1700s onwards. These changes in the role of the prison unfolded, broadly speaking, in two stages and are discussed throughout the chapter. The first stage saw the establishment of incarceration as the principal sanction for offenders, largely replacing physical punishment. The second stage saw incarceration being increasingly viewed not solely as punishment but also as a means of rehabilitation—of making the imprisoned person a more useful citizen on release than they had been on first entering the prison. Complicating such changes in penal philosophy were related changes in politics and economics, as well as changing views about gender and youth. Yet for all of the many attempts by governments, penal experts, and other groups focusing on the post-prison experience, rehabilitation through imprisonment was invariably a goal much more sought after than achieved.

This chapter offers a history of the prison in Canada that integrates each of these three perspectives, seeing it as an aspect of the building of colonial infrastructures, the political development of Canada, and the changing approaches to penal philosophy across the modern world. It does not include one aspect central to the history of Canada: Indigenous peoples. Incarceration was not a feature of Indigenous societies before European settlers came, and Indigenous peoples played no role in the establishment and spread of prisons or, until very recently, in the evolution of the philosophy of imprisonment. The influence of restorative justice derived

in large measure from Indigenous approaches to justice (Girard, Phillips, & Brown, 2018, Chapter 2) has been profound in recent decades. But until recently, Indigenous peoples' principal place in prison history has been as the subjects of imprisonment; in fact, since the 1950s they have been substantially overrepresented in the prison population (Royal Commission on Aboriginal Peoples, 1993; Sangster, 1999). That overrepresentation is the result of a complex set of factors that exacerbated the long-standing racist and culturally chauvinistic attitudes of many in settler societies. This reality places Indigenous peoples outside the mainstream of this chapter, which takes the story up to around 1970. Many of the other chapters in this book deal with the last half century in much greater detail (see Chapter 9 for a discussion of Indigenous overrepresentation).

Early Prisons to circa 1800

The first prisons in what is now Canada were built starting in the 1670s in the principal towns of New France—Montreal, Quebec, and Trois-Rivières (Cellard, 2000). Built originally of wood, they were reconstructed of stone between 1717 and 1726. Holding no more than half a dozen inmates, they played a limited role in criminal justice, used principally to hold those awaiting or under trial. Criminal justice sanctions in New France were dominated by physical punishments—death, branding, and whipping—but also included **banishment** and the public humiliation of the *amende honorable*. In 1760, Britain acquired New France (naming it Quebec) and from 1750 established new colonies of English settlement—Nova Scotia, Prince Edward Island, New Brunswick, and Upper Canada (Newfoundland already was an English colony). In Quebec, existing prisons continued to play the same role as before, and from 1777 they also held debtors (Girard et al., 2018, p. 329). Elsewhere prisons were established as part of the wider process of institution building in new colonies. Halifax was founded in 1749, for example, and the first jail was built almost immediately (Baehre, 1994). In Upper Canada, carved out of the old colony of Quebec in 1791, an act of 1792 mandated that "a Gaol and Court House shall be erected . . . in each and every District" of the colony (Upper Canada Statutes 1792, cited in Oliver, 1998, p. 5). Similar legislation came into effect in Lower Canada (now Quebec) in 1799.

Francis Vachon / Alamy Stock Photo

First Quebec City Common Gaol

The history of the prison in Canada prior to about 1800 paralleled developments in Europe and the United States. Prisons, which were institutions of local governments (towns and counties) and not the central government, played only a minor role in the system of criminal punishments. Serious crimes were punished physically—execution, whipping, or, much less frequently, standing in the pillory—or by banishment (exile from the colony; banishment was employed in all colonies as a condition of being pardoned from a capital sentence and was therefore a sanction ordered by the executive, not the criminal courts; in Upper Canada, banishment could also be ordered by the courts for any offence that brought a sentence of transportation under English law).

Prisons were nonetheless widely used in the administration of criminal justice and to support the social and economic order. Individuals accused of serious offences, from larceny on up, were confined before trial, bail being largely unavailable under the received English criminal procedure in force in all colonies. Prison terms of a few months or occasionally a year were meted out to those convicted of minor offences (Girard et al., 2018, Ch. 16; Gibson, 2015). Otherwise, most of any prison's population—prisoners awaiting trial, debtors (put there by their creditors), and individuals considered insane—were confined together. In July 1771, for example, the Halifax Jail held one debtor and five men accused of offences and awaiting trial (Nova Scotia Archives, 1771).

Prison conditions were invariably poor. Prisoners were crowded into tiny cells, which were unheated if the prisoners themselves could not afford fuel, and the inmates were dependent on their own resources for any sustenance above a few pence worth of bread a day. The jail at Halifax was drafty and dilapidated; Francis Green, high sheriff of Halifax, told the grand jury in 1786 that "the Criminals now in the Goal [sic] are in great want for the necessaries of life" (Nova Scotia Archives, 1786).

Whipping of Prisoner at Toronto Gaol by CW Jeffries

The Transformation of Penal Practices: Circa 1800 to Confederation

Three related developments of the pre-Confederation period transformed both the role of the prison within the system of criminal punishment and the nature and purpose of imprisonment itself (Girard et al., 2018, Ch. 28; Fyson, 2006). The first was the much greater use of imprisonment as the principal criminal sanction. Capital punishment had never been used widely as a criminal sanction, even though it was theoretically available for a broad range of offences other than murder. But from the early 1800s it was hardly used at all in non-murder cases, and nobody was executed for anything other than murder after the hanging of John Lee for highway robbery in Halifax in 1834. Capital punishment was still employed for political crimes, especially high treason, and featured in the government's response to the 1837–8 rebellions. Corporal punishments were also used progressively less from the 1810s onward, although their prevalence varied from time to time and place to place. For our purposes, the point is that ever-increasing numbers of individuals in all colonies were, when convicted, sentenced to prison terms that were usually less than a year but could be considerably longer (in 1817, for example, the Halifax Bridewell, discussed below, held seven men serving sentences of two years or more among its total population of over 150). As noted above, only in Upper Canada was there an alternative to prison that could be used by the courts as a sentence—banishment. Even though the prison had been around for centuries, the transition from punishing the bodies of those convicted of crimes to incarcerating most of those bodies was, in relative terms, quite rapid.

The second major development of the period was that changes were made to existing carceral institutions. Although common jails remained in place and were widely used for pre-trial confinement, short-term

Prisoners in a Local Jail

Return of the Halifax Jail, 15 July 1771, compiled by John Taylor, keeper of the jail. It lists one person in jail for debt (not named) and five suspected of crimes. The five suspected criminals consist of James Harrington and John Dounen, charged with suspicion of felony; John Bowsie and Charles Bumford, charged with murder; and William Rositer, committed on suspicion of "shop robbery," a capital offence.

prison sentences, and housing those judged insane, they were joined by new institutions that housed more inmates and whose regimes involved some segregation of them. It is often assumed that new carceral institutions led to a decline in physical punishments, but the decline in the use of the rope and the whip preceded the first wave of prison reform—it was not the result of it. The most notable of the new institutions was the Halifax Bridewell, a "house of correction" built in the 1760s and enlarged and remodelled in 1815 to house convicts sentenced to short and long terms. The Quebec City and Montreal jails, which were also expanded compared to their predecessors and opened in 1811 and 1812, respectively, were similar in scope to the Bridewell.

The establishment of new institutions and the remodelling of existing ones were in substantial part the result of an increasing interest in **prison discipline**, which included work programs, internal order, greater security, and slightly improved living conditions for inmates. The prison discipline movement of the early decades of the 1800s (elsewhere associated with the building of penitentiaries) preceded penitentiary building in the British North American colonies and affected prison policy in all colonies, including those where penitentiaries were not built. The designs of the new Montreal and Quebec City jails were based on the ideas of English penal reformer John Howard. The inmates were divided into wards, so that prisoners could be classified. In 1829 female prisoners in Quebec City were moved out of their ward and into a separate building, the first separate female prison in British North America. Also in 1829 comprehensive rules and regulations for Quebec City's jail were enforced, which among other things banned loitering, liquor, and loud talking. Reform ideas driven by the new ideas of prison discipline reached far. In 1838 Prince Edward Island legislation prescribed the separation of male and female prisoners, of those held in pre-trial custody from the convicted, and of criminals and debtors. Classification according to offence and age was mandated, visitors were limited, alcoholic drinks were banned, attendance at religious services was compulsory, and magistrates were named as overseers and inspectors. In Newfoundland, any conviction that in England brought imprisonment at hard labour could bring about the same punishment on the island; the labour was to be performed in a jail or on the public streets (or both), and during the hours of labour the convict was to wear "an iron clog, or other shackle."

The 1830s also saw the first official attempts to generate statistics on local jails (numbers of those incarcerated, personal details, prison conditions, and so on) in all the colonies, prompted by British government inquiries (Girard et al., 2018, Ch. 28).

The prison discipline and reform movement's greatest landmark, however, was the third major development of the period: the construction of Kingston Penitentiary, which opened in 1835 (Girard et al., 2018, Ch. 28; Oliver, 1998; McCoy, 2012; Baehre, 1977; Beattie, 1977). The story of Kingston's founding is well known—no development in Canadian prison history has been the subject of more extensive study. The idea of a penitentiary in Upper Canada was first publicly debated in the Legislative Assembly in 1826, and by 1835 legislation had been passed and the building opened. There was some opposition, notably from labour groups concerned about competition from prison manufacturers, but there was much broad agreement about the need for the new institution, both as an effective means of punishment for a wide range of offences and as a reformatory institution, one that would remake the convict through prayer, reflection, discipline, and labour. Inmates were to be separated from maligning influences, isolated as much as possible from other convicts, and exposed to wholesome habits by industry, reflection, and prayer. The idea that criminal punishment should do more than punish and deter—that it should also rehabilitate—was a crucial departure from the old regime.

Penitentiary development in Upper Canada drew largely on developments in the United States, where the early decades of the 1800s witnessed the embrace of imprisonment as the dominant sanction and a radical rethinking of the purpose, design, and management of prisons and prison regimes (Hirsch, 1992; Meranze, 1996; MacLennan, 2008). In the United Kingdom, imprisonment also became the dominant form of penal sanction (Ignatieff, 1978; Morris & Rothman, 1995), although for some decades the penitentiary shared the role as an alternative to physical punishments with transportation to Australian penal colonies, and as a result penitentiary development was slower and less intense than it was across the Atlantic.

The need for an effective form of secondary punishment, and the interest of some in rehabilitation, meant that there was little debate in Upper Canada about whether the colony would build a penitentiary. But there was controversy about the design and function of

Image of Kingston Penitentiary circa 1901

the new institution. Should it be fundamentally punitive, or should it also seek to rehabilitate? And if it did the latter, which type of penitentiary regime was best? Upper Canadian officials put a lot of effort into investigating penitentiary design, mostly looking at American models. They were confronted with two different systems that, in the 1820s and 1830s, engendered fierce debate among American penal reformers. The **silent system**, which housed convicts separately but allowed them to eat and work together under a regime of enforced silence, was the one employed by the prisons at Auburn and Sing Sing in the state of New York. Its rival, employed in the flagship Eastern Penitentiary in Philadelphia, was the **separate system**, where convicts were kept continually in solitary confinement, living and working alone in their cells. Kingston was based on the Auburn model, as exemplified by the regulations for the prisoners' conduct: They were "to labour diligently and preserve unbroken silence" and not "exchange looks, wink, laugh, nod or gesticulate to each other." Yet one historian has argued that Kingston was but a pale version of Auburn: "[It] contained no separate accommodation for women, no hospital facilities and . . . no permanent workshops" (McCoy, 2012, p. 39).

The optimism of reformers was undermined by funding shortages, a lack of training for guards, squabbling between the warden and the government board appointed to oversee the institution, and the fact that prison labour consisted largely of stone breaking and the construction work needed to finish building the prison. The greatest disillusionment for prison reformers were revelations that the maintenance of a regime of submission was impossible without extensive recourse to the lash, and a commission headed by George Brown of the *Globe*, which investigated the penitentiary in 1848, found the use of the whip and other physical discipline to be endemic. The Brown Commission only confirmed earlier newspaper reports. One article in the Toronto *Globe* in late 1849 included the headline "Kingston Penitentiary. Lash! Lash! Lash!" and asserted that 150 lashes a day were doled out for rules infractions. This was hardly calculated to provide moral improvement; the lash would only "harden the person whose body was torn by its infliction" (Beattie, 1977, p. 148). The Brown Commission exposed these conditions to a wide audience and also found, in a telling phrase, that the hopes of prison reformers were not met: "The Reformation of Convicts is unknown," it bluntly stated. The commission recommended much greater emphasis on reformation through education.

Other colonies experienced their penitentiary movements within a decade of Kingston's opening. In New Brunswick, legislation was passed the late 1830s for a new house of correction in Saint John, which opened in 1842 as the Saint John Penitentiary and was later renamed the Provincial Penitentiary. Its design and regime was modelled on the silent system with regulations stressing labour, silence, and moral reformation (Baehre, 1994). The new penal philosophy was also clearly articulated in Nova Scotia, where a Legislative Assembly committee in 1838 argued for a prison reflecting the "meliorating influence of Science and Christianity," one that was "humane," dedicated to "correcting but not destroying the guilty." The *Penitentiary Act* of 1840 also proclaimed that in the new institution "the punishment of Criminals ought to be applied with a view to their reformation and restoration to Society." A year later Attorney General James Boyle Uniacke, in introducing legislation to repeal many capital offences, asserted that "repentance and reformation should be the main objects in the treatment of prisoners, that in nearly every case imprisonment might supersede death as a punishment." The Halifax penitentiary was completed in 1844 and also operated on the silent system (Baehre, 1990; Girard et al., Ch. 28).

Lower Canada was alone among the major colonies in not constructing a penitentiary by name, although the new jails in Montreal and Quebec City were not dissimilar reforming institutions (Fyson, 2016, 2018). There were proposals made for a Lower Canadian penitentiary, but the rebellions of the late 1830s intervened, and after the union of the Canadas in 1841 the new Province of Canada made Kingston the penitentiary for the whole colony. In 1843 it was made possible for one institution to serve both jurisdictions by reserving penitentiaries for convicts with sentences of two years or more, with shorter sentences being served "in any [other] prison or place of confinement." However, there were always more convicts in Kingston from Upper than from Lower Canada—238 to 67 in 1858, for example (Province of Canada Sessional Paper, 1860).

Newfoundland legislated the building of a penitentiary in 1851, and the enabling statute stressed both punishment and reformation of offenders. It was not completed until 1859, and its regime emphasized silence and hard labour. Like others in the Atlantic region, the Colonial Penitentiary, as it was named, was a rather more modest enterprise than Kingston or American prisons in size, cost, and inmate numbers. At the same time, these new institutions bore witness to the pervasive influence of the "modern" values of reformation linked to punishment.

No new penitentiaries were built before Confederation, although the number of inmates doubled; there were over 400 in Kingston in the late 1840s, and twice that number by Confederation (Oliver, 1998, p. 152). The decades prior to Confederation saw some innovations in penal philosophy and methodology at all colonial penitentiaries. They all stayed with the silent system, albeit with much less use of the lash on refractory prisoners than the Brown Commission had exposed. New administrative arrangements were introduced, putting them all more firmly under government control through various official boards. During the 1850s lobbyists looking to Christianity as the foundation for rehabilitation were able to augment the numbers of chaplains and religious services offered in prisons, but this produced no effect on recidivism. Faith in prison labour to both meet the costs of incarceration and boost rehabilitation, administered through a system of private contracts, remained strong, but the results were disappointing. Many inmates were unwilling to participate, and the system never saw significant profits. The most forward-looking measures were the introduction of a "mark system" at the Halifax penitentiary, which was similar to the **Crofton system**, named after Irish prison administrator Sir Walter Crofton. Prisoners began their sentence in solitary confinement, and if they were well behaved they advanced through various forms of congregate work by earning credits (or "marks") through hard work and good behaviour (Baehre, 1990). With enough marks prisoners enjoyed minimal supervision. The Crofton system was introduced in Kingston in the late 1860s.

The pre-Confederation period also saw the segregation of some classes of inmates. From the early 1850s, convicts considered insane in Kingston were either transferred to the Provincial Asylum at Toronto (opened in 1850) or housed in a separate wing at Kingston (the "penitentiary asylum"). In 1859 legislation mandated the construction of a separate criminal lunatic facility in Kingston, which became the Rockwood Criminal Lunatic Asylum and received prisoners starting in 1862, even though it was not completed until 1870. The 1850s and 1860s also saw changes in how female and juvenile prisoners were housed. Kingston had always had a women's ward, but it never entirely segregated male and female prisoners. In the early 1850s a separate women's prison wing was opened, although it was already overcrowded by the end of the decade. There would not be entirely separate female institutions until after Confederation (Oliver, 1998).

The pre-Confederation period did, however, see the construction of separate juvenile reformatories (Hogeveen, 2003, 2005; Houston, 1972). Lower Canada was the site of the first, built on Isle aux Noix in 1858, and this was followed the next year by the Upper Canada Reformatory Prison (renamed Penetanguishene in 1879), which was built on 200 acres of land on the shore of Georgian Bay that had formerly been used as a naval facility. The latter received many of the 120 children under 21 who the year before had been housed at Kingston Penitentiary. Reformatories were needed, contemporaries insisted, because children were corrupted by two kinds of influences. The first was neglect and a lack of guidance and discipline in the home, which led them to crime in the first place, and it was God's work to "snatch from vice and ruin these poor children whose greatest crime is, not unfrequently, that of an unfortunate parentage" (Province of Canada Sessional Paper, 1860). Once convicted and incarcerated, the influence of adult prisoners ensured a future life of crime. Education, specialized training in trades, and physical and moral discipline were required for these vulnerable and impressionable inmates. Starting in the 1870s, reformatories were joined by industrial schools, which housed both those convicted of offences and those thought at risk of that fate from lack of parental control (Bennett, 1986; Neff, 1994).

General histories always tend to emphasize change over continuity, and for all the changes that occurred during Canada's colonial penitentiary age from 1835 to 1867, much remained familiar from earlier periods. Local jails still played a large role in the system; there were 31 jails in Upper Canada in 1860 and 21 in Lower Canada (Province of Canada Sessional Paper, 1860). Indeed, jails were augmented by the building of new institutions. Halifax, for example, opened a new city prison, Rockhead, in 1860, and the old Bridewell was converted to use as a regular jail (Baehre, 1990). All prisons—new and old, penitentiaries and jails—were the subject of continued complaints about bad food, poor heating in winter, exhausting or pointless work, epidemic disease, and decaying and at times insecure buildings. Such complaints were invariably met with assertions that the facility was adequate or that prison inmates did not deserve "luxury" conditions. But most tellingly, the jails were invariably said to be, in the words of one inspector's report, "schools of vice, to which novices in crime repair to receive . . . lessons in villainy." The prisons' defects were varied and of many kinds, but "there is not a single one which answers the triple objects for which they are intended, namely—to punish, to deter, and to reform" (Province of Canada Sessional Paper, 1860).

Confederation: The Federal–Provincial Division of Powers and the Origins of the National Penitentiary System

Confederation brought important changes to the political administration of carceral institutions, which had previously been the responsibility of the individual colonial governments. Section 91(28) of the British North America Act (BNA Act), the list of federal powers, included "the establishment, maintenance, and management of penitentiaries" as a federal responsibility, while section 92(6) included "the establishment, maintenance, and management of public and reformatory prisons in and for the province" as a provincial power. This demarcation had much to do with the fact that the federal government was to have power over institutions of national importance while the provinces were given control over local, municipal, and community matters. Reformatories (institutions for the young) in particular were considered something more suitable for localities to control. Financial considerations probably also played a role—penitentiaries were expensive to run. The constitution has never been rewritten to create a national prison service run by the national government, although there have periodically been suggestions for doing so.

The principal line demarcating federal and provincial power has always been the two-year rule: Those sentenced to two years or more were and are sent to a federal institution, with sentences up to two years less a day being served in provincial ones. Nothing in the constitution mandated the two-year rule, which in part reflected the distinction between reformatories and adult institutions, the belief being that shorter sentences better rehabilitated those most amenable to reformation (that is, young offenders). But equally important may have been the urge to stay with what was familiar; as noted above, the two-year rule had operated in the Province of Canada for more than 25 years. The first attempt to challenge the two-year rule was made in 1887 by Quebec at a provincial conference. The purpose of the conference was to discuss financial issues that had arisen out of the operation of the new Confederation, and prison costs were a considerable financial burden on the provinces. Quebec's motion did not pass, and the issue was not again raised in future conferences. It did re-emerge in the Archambeaux Report in 1938, which is discussed below (Needham, 1980, p. 299).

In 1868 the federal Parliament passed Canada's first Penitentiary Act (Oliver, 1998). It created three directors of penitentiaries to oversee and make regulations for all penitentiaries, but it said nothing about the purpose of the institutions. It listed only three penitentiaries, and during the 1870s an expanded federal penitentiary system was created. Kingston was its centrepiece and the only institution remaining from the pre-Confederation period. It was soon joined by the St.-Vincent-de-Paul Penitentiary in Quebec (1873), to which many Quebecers were transferred from Kingston; the Manitoba Penitentiary (later named Stony Mountain Penitentiary; 1877); New Westminster Penitentiary in British Columbia (1878); and Dorchester in New Brunswick (1880), to which prisoners from Halifax and Saint John were transferred (Baehre, 1990, 1994). The Maritimes did not need more than one such institution, so the colonial penitentiaries at Halifax and Saint John were made provincial institutions. Between 1880 and World War II three more

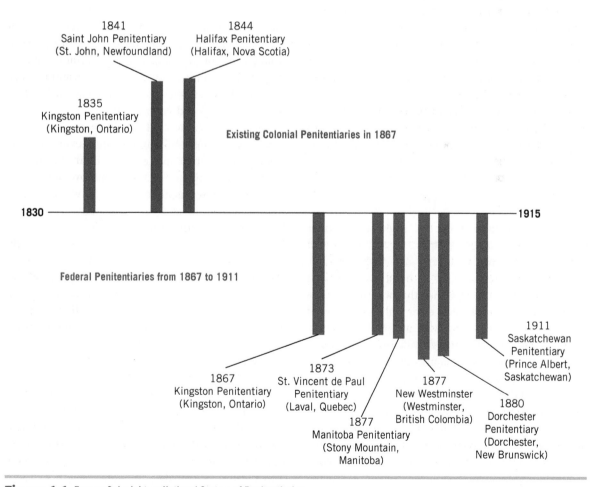

Figure 1.1 From a Colonial to a National System of Penitentiaries

institutions were added: Saskatchewan Penitentiary in Prince Albert, Collins Bay Penitentiary in Kingston, and the Montée St. François Penitentiary in Quebec (now a federal training centre). The number of federal institutions has grown exponentially since World War II; there are now more than 50.

The Confederation arrangements meant that the post-1867 history of prisons in Canada is more complicated than the earlier period. As we have seen, before 1867 different colonies operated with a range of different institutions—colonial and local, adult and juvenile—and this remained the case after 1867 in a different guise, with one authority for the major institutions (penitentiaries) and multiple authorities (the provinces) for the range of lesser institutions. Over time this has also meant that more jurisdictions had a role to play, as the country grew from four provinces in 1867 to seven in the 1870s (Manitoba, British Columbia, and Prince Edward Island were added), nine in 1905 (Alberta and Saskatchewan were created that year), and ten in 1949 (with the addition of Newfoundland). In addition, it must be recalled that the federal government has always been responsible for territorial prisons, because territories are not provinces so sections 91 and 92 of the BNA Act does not apply to them. Hence prisons in the "old" Northwest Territories were a federal responsibility from 1870 to 1905, as are prisons in the twentieth-century territories—Northwest Territories, Yukon, and Nunavut.

Territorial and Provincial Prisons from 1867

After 1870, with the addition to Canada of the former Hudson's Bay Company lands as the Northwest Territories (present-day Alberta and Saskatchewan), the federal government had to build a new prison system in the Prairie west, but that was a long time coming. To a considerable extent, the government relied on the North-West Mounted Police (NWMP, the forerunner of the RCMP) guardhouses as local jails (Skinner, Driedger, & Grainger, 1981; Bright, 2000). Two statutes of the 1870s mentioned jails in the territories: the one creating the NWMP and the Northwest Territories Act of 1876. The latter gave the lieutenant governor power to establish and manage prisons, but also stated that the guardhouses were to serve that function. In fact, serious offenders were taken to Stony Mountain in Manitoba to serve their sentences, leaving the guardhouses to house offenders guilty of liquor infractions, petty crime, bylaw violations, and the like (Skinner et al., 1981, 17–19).

The first territorial jail was opened at Regina in 1887 for all offenders with sentences of less than two years. The jail was built for both convicts and the "insane," who were segregated from each other, as were men from women. Regina and other territorial jails fell under the superintendence of the federal inspector of penitentiaries, and the Regina Penitentiary was subject to heavy criticisms in the late 1880s and early 1890s for its physical inadequacies (Skinner et al., 1981, 20–22). No such criticisms afflicted jails in what became Alberta because there were none. What little evidence we have suggests that penal institutions in Western Canada were largely unaffected by changes in penal philosophy; their dominant concerns were security and economy, so prisoners were put to work on farms to try to enhance revenue. When Saskatchewan and Alberta became provinces in 1905 the unique status of their prisons ended, although for some time this meant only that existing institutions became provincially run, not that new federally run penitentiaries were built. Administrative structures were established for Saskatchewan in the 1906 Gaols Act and for Alberta in the 1908 Gaols and Prisons Act.

After Confederation, all provinces expanded their provincial systems, building new institutions and expanding and modifying existing ones. Expansions of existing county jails or their equivalents and construction of new institutions were required in part because provincial and municipal institutions continued to perform the same functions they had before Confederation—holding people awaiting trial. In addition, the provincial systems now had to accommodate all those sentenced to up to two years in prison. The numbers of such people grew proportionately with the population. To use but one example, Manitoba's jails held 310 individuals per 100,000 population in 1918; by 1939 that number had more than doubled to 692 (Kellough, Brickey, & Greenaway, 1980; see also Ekstedt & Griffiths, 1988). Provincial prison numbers did not simply reflect population change. They rose and (occasionally) fell with changes in attitudes toward what was seen as the disorder and moral dangers brought on by increasing urbanization and by immigration from regions that had not previously been a feature of Canadian immigration, like southern

Europe. Convictions for prostitution, drunkenness, vagrancy, and other public order offences filled the provincial prisons, more in some times and places than in others, because such offences are always susceptible to moral panics (Boritch & Hagan, 1990; Oliver, 1998, p. 374). In addition, provincial jails served social service functions, both formally and informally, as refuges for the poor and homeless in the winters (Marquis, 1986; Phillips, 1990).

Not enough scholarly attention has been paid to the regimes and conditions in provincial prisons, but the evidence we do have makes it clear that institutions in all provinces attracted adverse comments. There was little or no classification of prisoners. As E.A. Meredith, one-time chair of Ontario's Board of Prison Inspectors, told a commission in 1891, all talk of classification in the province's county gaols was "illusory," and "the association of prisoners which now goes on in our gaols" was an "indulgence . . . to the degraded and hardened prisoner," an "injustice to the . . . novice in crime," and a corrupting influence to all (Ontario Prison Commission, 1891, p. 788). There was also not much in the way of work programs, poor food and unsanitary living conditions, overcrowding, and often a lack of security (Skinner et al., 1981, Ch. 2; Ontario Prison Commission, 1891). Provincial prisons were everywhere the victims of government parsimony. Where labour was required of inmates, many provincial institutions operated prison farms as a way to both fund the institution and as a form of rehabilitative work (Skinner et al., 1981, Ch. 2). Some provincial prisons adopted regimes not dissimilar to the Auburn-style penitentiary, including congregate work and a silent system. The 1943 regulations for Saskatchewan's jails, for example, which largely dated from 1915, stated that prisoners "must preserve silence except when spoken to by an officer," conversation between inmates being "not allowed except by permission of the Officer." While at work a prisoner was not to "suffer his attention to be taken from his work to look at any person," and when journeying between work, meals, and cells, they had to walk single file (Skinner et al., 1981, pp. 47–8). All provincial institutions had at minimum a separate women's wing, and over time most provinces added purpose-built institutions for women. Saskatchewan was perhaps the last province to do so, opening the Pine Grove women's prison as late as 1967, although women prisoners had been housed in an old high school at Battleford from 1931 to 1941 (Skinner et al., 1981, Ch. 2).

The late 1800s did, however, see two important new innovations in Ontario. Both the Andrew Mercer Reformatory for Women, opened in 1880, and the Ontario Central Prison were established to be intermediate institutions between the local jails and the national penitentiaries. Both entailed classification, prison labour, and a system of discipline geared at remaking the convict. The two new institutions shared the same broad origins but were designed to be radically different prisons. The Mercer Reformatory was Canada's first women's prison, inspired in part by local dissatisfaction with the jails and with the increasing prevalence of a female criminal underclass that was perceived as evidence of the breakdown of social and moral order that accompanied large-scale urbanization and industrialization (Oliver, 1994, 1998; Strange, 1985). But a crucial part of its intellectual origins was the American women's prison movement, which in the post–Civil War period was highly influential south of the border. Ontario's Prison Inspector, John W. Langmuir, made this very clear in seeking to persuade the John Sandfield Macdonald provincial government of the value of building such an institution: "Respecting the advisability of combining both sexes in the same prison, the very highest authorities in the specialty of prison administration have declared themselves in favour of separate establishments for women." These authorities included the 1870 declaration of the National Conference on Penitentiary and Reformatory Discipline, held at Cincinnati in 1870. As Langmuir continued, the women's prison should be "an industrial reformatory for women, with the official staff attendants, keepers and instructors of the same sex" (Oliver, 1994, pp. 523–4). When the Mercer Reformatory finally opened in 1880, it was indeed a prison for women staffed by women.

The Mercer's operation broadly reflected the ideas of the emerging feminist movement of the period, which historians have dubbed "separate spheres" or "maternal feminism." Its leaders were middle- and upper-middle-class women, believers in both the idea that women and men were different and that women had an important role to play in society as mothers and caregivers—the nurturers of society. Maternal feminists, among other things, campaigned against sexual violence, drunkenness, and general immorality. Most of the women sent to Mercer had been convicted of prostitution, drunkenness, or vagrancy (which were often interchangeable terms in this period) and needed to be trained in religion, sobriety, and domesticity. As Langmuir put it, only in a women's-only prison run on firm but kindly lines "will women be fully able to exercise and wield their great power and influence, in practical ways towards reclaiming the criminal and fallen of their sex" (Oliver, 1994, p. 524). As it turned out, the Mercer Reformatory did not always practice what it preached. There was little classification of inmates beyond a rough division between "hardened offenders" and younger inmates, there was no earned remission system, and most of the inmates had committed many offences and been in and out of the local jails. Historians do not doubt the sincerity of the women who ran Mercer, but those women were unable to truly appreciate the reality of the lives lived by their charges, who were women with entirely different class backgrounds.

The other major Ontario prison initiative of the period was the Ontario Central Prison, opened in 1874 and holding only male inmates with sentences of less than two years (Berkovits, 1994; Oliver, 1988, Ch. 11). It was conceived of as a local variant of the national penitentiaries, an industrial prison that would reform inmates through labour, the work being organized and run by a private contractor. Like Kingston some 40 years before, the prison would not only reform its inmates, it would operate at a profit; its leading historian neatly calls it "capitalism's . . . brilliant meeting with confinement" (Berkovits, 1994, p. 478). It stayed in operation until World War I, and all accounts deem it a failure. The first labour contractor was the Canada Car Company, a manufacturer of railroad cars, and it went bankrupt within a year. The prison was repurposed for other manufacturing ventures, which too often failed and certainly never turned a profit for the province. Most importantly, there is no evidence that the prison reformed those sentenced to it. Prisoners either did not work or worked with resentment and engaged in myriad small acts of rebellion, received no education that would serve them on the outside, and were subject to harsh physical punishments for rules violations, including the dark cell, bread and water diets for weeks (sometimes months) on end, and extensive floggings. Not surprisingly, recidivism rates were high. The only thing the Central Prison did well, argue its principal

historians, was to inculcate fear at the prospect of entering it (Oliver, 1998; Berkovits, 1994).

Federal Penitentiaries from 1867 to circa 1935

Although after Confederation Canada had a national penitentiary system subject to central government control, there was little consistency in any aspect of penal philosophy and prison administration between 1867 and World War II. Indeed, there was only one major national investigation of penal policy during that time (Royal Commission on Penitentiaries, 1914). In the broadest sense, there was a basic dichotomy in the thinking of the two principal groups of people involved in managing prisons—prison professionals and politicians. There were men among the professionals who were optimistic and liberal minded about both the goal of rehabilitation and the possibility of its achievement. James George Moylan, the sole inspector of penitentiaries from 1875 to 1895, and Samuel Bedson, warden of Stony Mountain, advocated for changes that would ameliorate prison conditions, including better staff training, the expanded use of the Crofton system, specialized institutions, and reductions in the use of corporal punishment for inmate infractions. But other prison officials had a pessimistic view of whether criminals could be rehabilitated, especially repeat offenders, "hardened criminals" who were seen as unreformable (Oliver, 1965+; Gibson, 1965+). One historian's study of Kingston notes the problems caused by "the feuding and often incompetent penitentiary officers" (Neufeld, 1998, p. 97), while another concludes that "punitive policies" were the "enduring reality" of the penitentiary (Oliver, 1998, p. 280). Yet another author has said that this period was "rich in rhetoric but impoverished regarding its application" (Zubrycki, 1980, p. 74; see also Calder, 1985). There is no evidence to refute these conclusions, perhaps because there has not been a sustained academic study of the federal penitentiary system as a whole, but more likely because, from the evidence we do have, they are irrefutable.

What, then, can be said about penitentiaries between 1867 and the 1930s? While lip service was always paid to the idea that prisons should reform offenders, there was little by the way of a serious institutional commitment to ways of achieving that goal. Prison labour was mandated in the 1868 Penitentiary Act, for example, but only briefly and without reference to "training": Convicts were to be "kept constantly at hard labour, the kind of which shall be determined by the Warden." The purpose was clearly to make prison time harder. As one inspector noted in 1891, Kingston kept "a much greater number of men at stonebreaking than our needs . . . require," adding that "there is certainly no reformation in that task" (Neufeld, 1998, p. 111).

Punishments for infractions of prison rules are another area in which we can examine penitentiary practice. Although whipping was used much less than in the period prior to 1850, it remained an aspect of prison discipline throughout the 1800s and well into the twentieth century. While whipping was increasingly seen as undesirable, other physical punishments took its place, such as having fire hoses turned on the recalcitrant as well as isolation for long periods and reduced diet (Gosselin, 1982). One of the innovative new physical punishments was the Oregon boot, which involved a shackle strapped around the ankle of a prisoner and attached to a boot that weighed 28 pounds, and prisoners were made to walk around with it; this extremely painful practice was used in the Kingston and Manitoba penitentiaries (McCoy, 2012, pp. 243–4). Penitentiaries continued to be run on the separate system and, as much as possible, by the silent

rules. The 1868 Penitentiary Act saw separation as a linchpin of both punishment and reformation, although the statute clearly implied that the latter was a subordinate clause: "[N]o system of discipline in a Penitentiary can be effectual for punishment, or for reformation of the criminal, unless it be combined with strict separate confinement during some period of the time of his imprisonment."

The one reform-focused innovation of the Penitentiary Act was to institutionalize those aspects of the Crofton system, discussed above, that had been introduced to Kingston before 1867. Prisoners could even earn early release (up to a sixth of their sentences) through good behaviour and exemplary work, the first time such a statute for any Canadian jurisdiction had included such a provision. Parole was first legislated by the Ticket of Leave Act of 1898, which allowed a person sentenced to time in a penitentiary to serve part of the time in the community under supervision (Miller, 1976, p. 379). Yet while remission stayed in place, the Crofton system of earning promotion to different grades was never fully implemented. Overall punishment was the primary goal, and punishment required misery and discomfort. No less a person than Sir John A. Macdonald believed this: "Happiness and punishment cannot and ought not to go together.

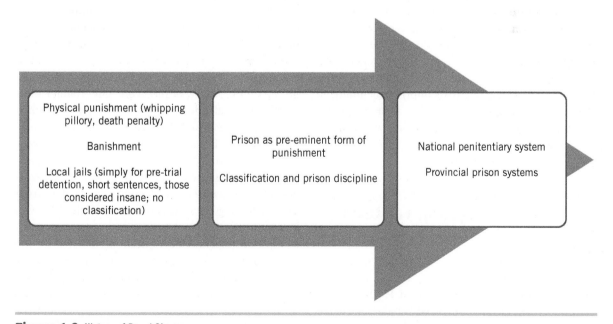

Figure 1.2 History of Penal Change

There is such a thing as making a prison too comfortable and the prisoners too happy" (quoted in Oliver, 1998, p. 310). Not surprisingly, the late 1800s and early 1900s saw a number of prison riots and other forms of protest (Neufeld, 1998). Public concern about conditions inside penitentiaries was manifested in the first national penal conference, held in Toronto in 1892, which included a wide range of participants: churches, the Salvation Army, the YMCA, childrens' aid societies, the Trades and Labour Council, and the Prisoners' Aid Society. That same year the John Howard Society of Quebec was founded, the first prisoners' aid society in Canada (Edmison, 1976, p. 366; Kirkpatrick, 1976, p. 445).

Outside lobbying could not move those who set penitentiary policy, however, and the new century brought little change: Most penitentiaries at least tried to enforce the rule of silence, prison labour consisted mostly of stonebreaking, rules infractions were punished rigorously, and there were no programs aimed at meaningful rehabilitation. As one author has put it, prison authorities "lost hope of treating and rehabilitating the inmates" and instead "concentrated on guarding and punishing them" (Cellard, 2000, p. 16). Riots were far from uncommon, partly a response to a two-thirds increase in the number of inmates across the country. The Archambault Report, discussed below, found that between 1925 and 1936 there had been 20 "disturbances . . . of a more or less serious character" across the country. There had also been numerous lesser incidents—fires, strikes, and physical assaults that did not result in full riots (Archambault Report, 1938, pp. 69–73; see also Gosselin, 1982). The one notable change in women's imprisonment during this period was the opening of a separate prison for women within Kingston Penitentiary (Hannah-Moffett, 2001; see also Chapter 8).

Signal Moments: The Archambault (1938), Fauteux (1956), and Ouimet (1969) Reports

In the quarter century between the mid-1930s and 1961 three major investigations inquired into the state of the penitentiary system. The first was chaired by Joseph Archambault, a judge of the Quebec Superior Court (Archambault Report, 1938). The commission's extensive mandate included investigation of the treatment of convicted persons in penitentiaries, the classification of offenders, prison punishments, prison labour, conditional release, aid to prisoners upon release, and a variety of other related subjects. The commission members visited a wide range of institutions, including provincial institutions and prisons in the United States and the United Kingdom. It also heard evidence from, among others, the superintendent of penitentiaries.

The Royal Commission Report on Penal Reform in Canada, to give the Archambault Report its full title, contained 88 recommendations that collectively comprised substantial changes to the penitentiary system. The 32-chapter report argued that prisons should not just be for the temporary protection of the public, but should also serve to prevent crime and rehabilitate prisoners. Reform and rehabilitation of prisoners had been recognized as a responsibility of the state for a century, but, the report insisted, it had not been effectively executed and should be a priority. Prison conditions also needed to be reformed. Archambault recommended improving the education programs in prisons and the scientific classification of prisoners. He also proposed a wholesale reform of the internal management of penitentiaries, one that gave equal weight to the protection of society, inmate safety, humane but strict discipline, and the reform and rehabilitation of offenders. Discipline was envisioned as fundamentally different from punishment and something that applied to staff as well as inmates. Generally, the report recommended a focus on the "treatment," not just punishment, of offenders. One chapter dealt with habitual offenders, prisoners the report described as having "adopted a life of crime" and as being incapable of reform; it was recommended that they be kept in separate prisons.

Archambault also paid attention to juvenile delinquents, family courts, and training schools. It asserted that it had long been the consensus that children who break the law should be dealt with differently than adults, but recommended nothing more than the need for more training schools and reformatories. Archambault also devoted one chapter to female inmates in federal penitentiaries, all of whom in 1936 were confined at Kingston. Its principal recommendation was that all female inmates should be housed in provincial institutions and be the responsibility of provincial governments. A notable feature of the report was the attention paid to the International Standard Minimum Rules, which had been drawn up by the International Penal and Penitentiary Commission in 1929. Archambault concluded that not all of the rules were followed in Canadian prisons, but they should be. Pursuing the same idea of uniformity, the report also recommended a genuinely national system—all Canadian corrections should be handled by the federal government, which would be more economical and allow the consistent implementation of the rehabilitative philosophy. The Archambault Report was significant. Although many of the things it said with reference to rehabilitation had been said before (and often), its emphasis on that goal appeared to presage a new era.

The federal government did little in response to the report, in part because World War II distracted attention from almost all other policy questions. Nonetheless, the Archambault philosophy remained influential and through the 1950s there was a broad consensus on prison policy, one that focused on rehabilitation as the principal goal.

That consensus was reflected in the next major investigation, the Fauteux Report of 1956. Apparently more narrowly focused than Archambault—its mandate was to investigate parole—it ranged more broadly than that and the key element of the report was the use, for the first time, of the concept of treatment. The inmate was to be considered a person with a treatable disorder. The emphasis was on the need for more concentration on rehabilitation, including more institutions devoted to different levels of security and specialized treatment facilities for those addicted to alcohol and those suffering from mental diseases. The Fauteux Report (1956) also pointed to the extent of overcrowding, which impaired classification, a policy that was still necessary. It also discussed sentence length, arguing that a sentence should be long enough to give enough time to rehabilitate but short enough to allow the offender to maintain hope of spending an appreciable amount of his or her life outside. Fauteux therefore recommended more vocational training and specific pre-release and post-release programs. Most notable about this report was its recommendation to hire more and better-trained personnel. Guards needed

to be augmented by psychiatrists, psychologists, and social workers.

Perhaps the most significant legal change to emerge from the Fauteux Report was a new Parole Act, passed in 1959 to replace the Ticket of Leave Act. Under the aegis of the Act, the National Parole Board was established. Another consequence of the report were amendments to the Penitentiary Act, including a plan to build 10 new penitentiaries across the country. Seven were built in the 1960s in locations where there had not been such an institution before (Gravenhurst and Trent Hills, Ontario; Drumheller, Alberta; Springhill, Nova Scotia; Cowansville and Laval, Quebec; and Agassiz, British Columbia). A further three new penitentiaries were built on the same grounds as, but separate from, existing institutions in Kingston (two new penitentiaries) and Stony Mountain. These 10 new institutions included a number of minimum security penitentiaries in which attention could be paid more to what went on inside (that is, programming) and less to the basic task of keeping people there. The same number of new penitentiaries were added in the 1970s.

The last in the triumvirate of major investigations into the federal prison system, and perhaps the most important, was the report issued by the Special Committee on Corrections, a non-parliamentary committee appointed by the minister of Justice in 1964 (Ouimet Report, 1969). Chaired by Quebec Superior Court judge Roger Ouimet, it notably included two of five members who were not involved in law enforcement or penal policy: G. Arthur Martin, a leading criminal defence lawyer, and Dorothy McArton, executive director of the Family Bureau of Greater Winnipeg, a social service organization. Its terms of reference were wide: "[T]o study the broad field of corrections, in its widest sense and to recommend . . . what changes, if any, should be made in the law and practice relating to these matters." The 500-page Ouimet Report argued that there should be co-operation among law enforcement, the judiciary, and penal services and offered a more negative view of the prison than any previous inquiry. Chapter 2 of the report listed eight "main principles" that prioritized rehabilitation over punishment; rehabilitation, it said, did more to protect society, which was the only "justifiable purpose" of criminal justice. The report condemned in the strongest terms the use of corporal punishment and argued that prison did not achieve its rehabilitative function mainly because inmates were removed from their families, communities, and employment. The Ouimet Report was the first government document to propose serious consideration of alternatives to incarceration. Somewhat inconsistently, Ouimet defended the two-year jurisdictional split and argued that the federal government should have a leadership and coordinating role, but at the same time it asserted that a single, centralized system was unworkable.

Either Ouimet changed official thinking profoundly, or it caught an already popular wind of dissatisfaction. In the short term its recommendation that corporal punishment be abolished was accepted in 1972. In the medium term, the Law Reform Commission of Canada stated in 1975 that the prison was not the place to look for rehabilitation, and in the following year a report named for then Minister of Justice Mark McGuigan baldly opined that the prison failed in both its principal purposes—those of protecting society and rehabilitating those sentenced.

Conclusion

The modern history of the prison in Canada dates from the early to mid-nineteenth century, when prisons stopped being buildings for confining those awaiting trial, debtors, men and women judged to be insane, and those sentenced to short periods of incarceration. Many local jails retained this role, but from the turn of the nineteenth century they were joined by institutions whose primary goal was to house those sentenced for longer periods for more serious crimes. From the 1830s this transition was accelerated by the construction of penitentiaries, whose aim was both to punish and reform the offender. Rehabilitation has been a goal of the penitentiary system since then, at some times more so than others, but it has never been more than an ambition: The prison has punished, but it has rarely rehabilitated. The prison has always been an enigma, committed in part to what in hindsight appears to have always been an impossible dream.

Review Questions

1. How was the penitentiary different from previous prisons?
2. Why does Canada have a federal and a provincial prison system, and why are some prisoners sent to one and some to the other?
3. What ideas about gender differences motivated the people behind early separate prisons for women?
4. How important in reshaping ideas about how prisons should be run was the Archambault Report?
5. How important in reshaping ideas about how prisons should be run was the Ouimet Report?

Critical Thinking Questions

1. How does an understanding of the history of the prison enhance your thinking about the present state of prisons in Canada?
2. Why do you think the idea of incarcerating people has resisted reform for so long?

Multimedia Suggestions

Secrets from Canada's Most Famous Prison: The Kingston Penitentiary

CBC documentary on the history of the Kingston Penitentiary upon its closing in 2013: https:// www.youtube.com/watch?v=aGprGP1GcVQ& feature=share&fbclid=IwAR0b_OjXYOhjEFgW4NTs 5hYAIkyDGgxhhkDCI4wWW6KZyyfSfZm 3Az1CVc0

Canada's Penitentiary Museum

Mostly based on Kingston's various facilities, but also featuring various "interesting facts" on the history of Canadian penitentiaries, and various photos: https:// www.penitentiarymuseum.ca

"Kingston Penitentiary's Storied History Full of Notorious Inmates, Riots, and Escapes," Amy Dempsey

Toronto Star **article on famous stories from Kingston Penitentiary, including a photo of a 1954 riot in the yard: https://www.thestar.com/news/crime/2013/09/29/ kingston_penitentiarys_storied_history_full_of_ notorious_inmates_riots_escapes.html**

"Beyond the Bars: Former Inmates at the Kinston Prison for Women Return in Fight for Recognition," Elizabeth Renzetti

Globe and Mail **article on Kingston's Prison for Women, including a brief history: https://www .theglobeandmail.com/canada/article-beyond-the- bars-former-inmates-at-the-kingston-prison-for- women/**

References

Archambault Report. (1938). *Royal Commission report on penal reform in Canada*. Ottawa, ON: Queen's Printer.

Baehre, R. (1977). Origins of the penitentiary system in Upper Canada. *Ontario History, 69*, 185–208.

Baehre, R. (1990). From Bridewell to federal penitentiary: Prisons and punishment in Nova Scotia before 1880. In P. Girard & J. Phillips (Eds), *Essays in the history of Canadian law: Vol. 3. Nova Scotia*. Toronto, ON: Osgoode Society for Canadian Legal History and University of Toronto Press.

Baehre, R. (1994). Prison as factory, convict as worker: A study of the mid-Victorian Saint John Penitentiary, 1841–1880. In J. Phillips, T. Loo, and S. Lewthwaite (Eds) *Essays in the history of Canadian law: Vol. 5. Crime and criminal justice*. Toronto, ON: Osgoode Society for Canadian Legal History and University of Toronto Press.

Beattie, J. (1977). *Attitudes towards crime and punishment in Upper Canada, 1830–1850: A documentary study*. Toronto, ON: Centre of Criminology.

Bennett, P. (1986). Turning bad boys into good citizens: The reforming impulse of Toronto's industrial schools movement, 1883 to the 1920s. *Ontario History, 78*, 209–32.

Berkovits, J. (1994). Prisoners for profit: Convict labour in the Ontario Central Prison. In J. Phillips, T. Loo, & S. Lewthwaite (Eds), *Essays in the history of Canadian law: Vol V. Crime and criminal justice*. Toronto, ON: Osgoode Society for Canadian Legal History and University of Toronto Press.

Boritch, H., & Hagan, J. (1990). A century of crime in Toronto: Gender, class and patterns of social control, 1859–1955. *Criminology, 28*, 567–99.

Bright, D. (2000). Life in Alberta's mounted police jails. *Alberta History, 48*, 10–16.

Calder, W.A. (1985). Convict life in Canadian federal penitentiaries, 1867–1900. In L.A. Knafla (Ed.), *Crime and criminal justice in Europe and America*. Waterloo, ON: Wilfrid University Press.

Cellard, A. (2000). *Punishment, imprisonment and reform in Canada, from New France to the present*. Ottawa, ON: Canadian Historical Association.

Edmison, J.A. (1976). Some aspects of nineteenth-century Canadian prisons. In W.T. McGrath (Ed.), *Crime and its treatment in Canada* (2nd edn). Toronto, ON: Macmillan.

Ekstedt, J.W., & Griffiths, C.T. (1988). *Corrections in Canada: Policy and practice* (2nd edn). Toronto, ON: Butterworths.

Fauteax Report. (1956). *Report of a committee appointed to inquire into the principles and procedures followed in the remission service of the Department of Justice in Canada*. Ottawa, ON: Queen's Printer.

Fyson, D. (2006). *Magistrates, police and people: Everyday criminal justice in Quebec and Lower Canada, 1764–1837*. Toronto, ON: Osgoode Society for Canadian Legal History and University of Toronto Press.

Fyson, D. (2016). Prison reform and prison society: The Quebec gaol, 1812–1867. In L. Blair, P. Donovan, &

D. Fyson (Eds), *From iron bars to bookshelves: A history of the Morrin Centre*. Montreal, QC: Baraka Books.

Fyson, D. (2018). Experiencing Howard from within: Prison reform and everyday life in Quebec's City's common gaol, 1760–1867. In J. Christiaens et al. (Eds), *Experiencing justice: Researching citizens' contacts with judicial practices*. New York, NY: Springer.

Gibson, D. (2015). *Law, life and government at Red River: Vol 1. Settlement and governance, 1812–1872*. Montreal: Osgoode Society for Canadian Legal History and McGill-Queen's University Press.

Gibson, L. (1965+). Samuel Lawrence Bedson. In *Dictionary of Canadian Biography* (Toronto, ON: University of Toronto Press). Accessed online at www.biographi.ca

Girard, P.V., Phillips, J., & Brown, R.B. (2018). *A history of law in Canada: Vol. 1. Beginnings to 1866*. Toronto, ON: Osgoode Society for Canadian Legal History and University of Toronto Press.

Gosselin, L. (1982). *Prisons in Canada*. Montreal, QC: Black Rose Books

Hannah-Moffett, K. (2001). *Punishment in disguise: Penal governance and federal imprisonment of women in Canada*. Toronto, ON: University of Toronto Press.

Hirsch, A. (1992). *The rise of the penitentiary: Prisons and punishment in early America*. New Haven, CT: Yale University Press.

Hogeveen, B. (2003). "Can't you be a man?" Rebuilding wayward masculinities and regulating juvenile deviance in Ontario 1860–1930. Doctoral dissertation, University of Toronto.

Hogeveen, B. (2005). "The evils with which we are called to grapple": Élite reformers, eugenicists, environmental psychologists, and the construction of Toronto's working-class boy problem, 1860–1930. *Labour, 55*, 37–69.

Houston, S. (1972). Victorian origins of juvenile delinquency: A Canadian experience. *History of Education Quarterly, 12*, 254–80.

Ignatieff, M. (1978). *A just measure of pain: The penitentiary in the industrial revolution, 1750–1850*. London, UK: Penguin.

Kellough, G., Brickey, S.L., & Greenaway, W.K. (1980). The politics of incarceration: Manitoba, 1918–1939. *Canadian Journal of Sociology, 5*, 253–71.

Kirkpatrick, A.M. (1976). After-care and the prisoners' aid societies. In W.T. McGrath (Ed.), *Crime and its treatment in Canada* (2nd edn). Toronto, ON: Macmillan.

MacLennan, R.M. (2008). *The crisis of imprisonment: Protest, politics and the making of the American penal state, 1776–1941*. Cambridge, UK: Cambridge University Press.

Marquis, G. (1986). A machine of oppression under the guise of the law: The Saint John police establishment. *Acadiensis, 16*, 58–77.

McCoy, T. (2012). *Hard time: Reforming the penitentiary in nineteenth century Canada*. Edmonton, AB: AU Press.

Meranze, M. (1996). *Laboratories of virtue: Punishment, revolution and authority in Philadelphia, 1760–1835*. Chapel Hill: University of North Carolina Press.

Miller, F.P. (1976). Parole. In W.T. McGrath (Ed.), *Crime and its treatment in Canada* (2nd edn). Toronto, ON: Macmillan.

Morris, N. & Rothman, D.J. (Eds). (1995). *The Oxford history of the prison: The practice of punishment in Western society*. New York, NY: Oxford University Press.

Needham, H.G. (1980). Historical perspectives on the federal provincial split in corrections. *Canadian Journal of Corrections, 22*, 298–306.

Neff, C. (1994). The Ontario Industrial Schools Act of 1874. *Canadian Journal of Family Law, 12*, 171–208.

Neufeld, R. (1998). Cabals, quarrels, strikes and impudence: Kingston Penitentiary, 1890–1914. *Histoire Sociale/Social History, 31*, 95–125.

Nova Scotia Archives. (1771). Report of John Taylor, jailer. Record Group 34-312, Series J, Vol. 4.

Nova Scotia Archives. (1786). Record Group 5, Series A, Vol. 2, Nos. 42 and 57.

Oliver, P. (1965+). James George Moylan. In *Dictionary of Canadian Biography* (Toronto, ON: University of Toronto Press). Accessed online at www.biographi.ca

Oliver, P. (1994). To govern by kindness: The first two decades of the Mercer Reformatory for Women. In J. Phillips, T. Loo, & S. Lewthwaite (Eds), *Essays in the history of Canadian law: Vol. V. Crime and criminal justice*. Toronto, ON: Osgoode Society for Canadian Legal History and University of Toronto Press.

Oliver, P. (1998). *Terror to evil-doers: Prisons and punishments in nineteenth-century Ontario*. Toronto, ON: Osgoode Society for Canadian Legal History and University of Toronto Press.

Ontario Prison Commission. (1891). *Report of the commissioners appointed to inquire into the prison and reformatory system of the Province of Ontario*. Toronto, ON: Queen's Printer.

Ouimet Report. (1969). *Report of the special committee on corrections: Toward unity, criminal justice and corrections*. Ottawa, ON: Queen's Printer.

Phillips, J. (1990). Poverty, unemployment and the criminal law: The administration of the vagrancy laws in Halifax, 1864–1890. In P. Girard & J. Phillips (Eds), *Essays in the history of Canadian law: Vol. III. Nova Scotia*. Toronto, ON: Osgoode Society for Canadian Legal History and University of Toronto Press.

Province of Canada Sessional Paper. (1860). Sessional Paper 32, *Preliminary report of the board of inspectors of asylums, prisons, etc.* Kingston, ON: Province of Canada Assembly.

Royal Commission on Aboriginal Peoples. (1993). *Report of the Royal Commission on Aboriginal Peoples, Aboriginal Peoples and the Justice System: Report of the National Round Table on Aboriginal Justice.* Ottawa, ON: Queen's Printer.

Royal Commission on Penitentiaries. (1914). *Report of the Royal Commission on Penitentiaries.* Ottawa, ON: Queen's Printer.

Sangster, J. (1999). Criminalizing the colonised: Ontario Native women confront the criminal justice system. *Canadian Historical Review, 80,* 32–62.

Skinner, S., Driedger, O., & Grainger, B. (1981). *Corrections: An historical perspective of the Saskatchewan experience.* Regina, SK: Great Plains Research Centre.

Strange, C. (1985). The criminal and fallen of their sex: The establishment of Canada's first women's prison, 1872–1901. *Canadian Journal of Women and the Law, 1,* 79–92.

Zubrycki, R.M. (1980). The establishment of Canada's penitentiary system: Federal correctional policy 1867–1900. Master's thesis, University of Toronto, Toronto, Ontario.

Understanding Corrections in Canada

A Framework

Allison O'Donnell

2

Learning Objectives

After reading this chapter, you should be able to:

- Define "corrections."
- Describe the tension that exists in corrections.
- List the pieces of legislation that govern Canadian corrections.
- Describe the difference between federal and provincial corrections in Canada in terms of their mandates, supervision, and prisoner populations.
- Describe the role of the correctional investigator of Canada.
- Discuss alternatives to incarceration.

Chapter Overview

This chapter will begin by defining what we mean by "corrections." It will provide an overview of the purpose, key legislation, and the framework that guides the day-to-day operations of federal and provincial prisons as well as community corrections. It also includes a discussion of alternatives to incarceration. Finally, the chapter concludes with a review of correctional oversight in Canada.

What Is "Corrections"?

Corrections, along with the police and the courts, are an integral part of the **criminal justice system**. Though many people equate prisons with corrections, prisons are only one part (albeit a key part) of a correctional system. All correctional systems have both non-institutional programs and services delivered in the community as well as those that are delivered in institutional settings (Griffiths & Murdoch, 2018). There are more correctional personnel, offenders, and programs in community corrections than there are in correctional institutions, since most convicted persons are not sent to correctional institutions. For example, a large majority of adults (80 per cent) under correctional supervision in the provinces and territories in 2015–16 were under community supervision, such as on probation or serving conditional sentences. The remaining 20 per cent were in custody (Reitano, 2017).

Corrections comprises facilities, government policies, and programs delivered by the government and community organizations that are designed to punish, treat, and supervise individuals convicted of criminal offences. As noted previously, this may take place in correctional institutions or in the community. Not-for-profit organizations and members of the public are part of the delivery of correctional services, both in custodial institutions and the community. There are numerous not-for-profit and non-governmental organizations that provide support and services for offenders at all points when they interact with the correctional system, as well as advocate on their behalf. Correctional Service Canada

(CSC) has contracted with a number of these agencies to better assist offenders throughout their reintegration process (CSC, 2008). Examples of these not-for-profit organizations are more fully described in Chapter 6.

In defining corrections, it is important to understand one of the central tenets of corrections: Corrections has the mandate to maintain the delicate balance between individual freedoms and rights and the maintenance of social order. In other words, correctional policy is a balancing act that creates a tension between keeping the public safe and protecting the rights of the individual offender.

Note that corrections does not determine a sentence—it does not determine how long a sentence will be or whether it will be served in the community or a correctional facility. That is up to the courts. Corrections, as noted previously, is a set of institutions and services that attempt to punish, treat, and supervise individuals convicted of criminal offences. A key role of corrections is to *administer* a sentence: It carries out the conditions laid down by a judge and influences what happens to an offender in prison (including which prison they go to and which programs they receive).

Correctional Ideology

Corrections and other components of the criminal justice system have as their primary mandate the protection of society. There is often disagreement, however, on how this should be accomplished. Two views dominate. The "get tough" approach suggests more severe sanctions (more arrests, more convictions, and longer sentences). However, critics of this approach note that it hasn't worked, and what is needed is a focus on why offenders commit crime in the first place, not just a reaction to criminal behaviour. This second approach suggests a focus on the treatment needs of the offender to eliminate future criminal behaviour. The persistence of these two views of the goals of corrections—punishment for the protection of society versus treatment of the offender—is the basis of the "split personality" or "tension" of corrections that has been described previously.

As Chapter 1 suggests, correctional changes are often linked to larger political, social, and economic transformations. Prisons were initially believed to be a more humane alternative to the death penalty. The philosophy of the time was that periods of imprisonment and prison conditions such as isolation would foster feelings of remorse in offenders and lower the overall crime rate (CSC, 2014). Early ideas regarding punishment practices began to be challenged in the late 1930s in Canada.

The *rehabilitation ideology* first emerged as a dominant ideology shortly after 1935. Correcting offenders first began to emerge as a science with trained specialists taking control of the correctional system—including correctional managers, psychologists, and psychiatrists. To achieve the goal of rehabilitation, better-trained personnel were employed to offer a new array of treatment programs. But old coercive punishment practices remained, creating the paradox of "Should corrections treat or control?" As outlined in Chapter 1, a series of commissions and reports lead to improvements in the quality of institutions and the quality of programs. The focus of the correctional system continued to be the incarcerated individual's personal and emotional rehabilitation.

The 1970s was a decade of unrest and violence in penitentiaries across Canada, including strikes, riots, murders, and hostage takings. During this time of great social unrest, the emphasis shifted to the relationship between conditions in society and criminal behaviour, and the *reintegration ideology* emerged. Its focus was on the importance of keeping the offender in the community and keeping them connected to their community.

Today, correctional policy and practice places a high value on proactive intervention in the lives of offenders and the involvement of community social justice agencies in responding to crime.

Throughout its correctional history, Canada's correctional ideology has been a balancing act between three different focuses: punishment, treatment, and prevention (see Figure 2.1). What do you think each of these three central tenets attempt to achieve?

The Purpose of the Canadian Correctional System

Mandate

As noted previously, the Canadian correctional system is responsible for administering the sentences of all individuals who have been sentenced to a period of incarceration or supervision in a court of law. As suggested previously, the correctional system acknowledges the importance of public safety as well as the supervision and rehabilitation of offenders. The mandate of the

Punishment	Treatment	Prevention
• *Retribution*: Offenders are punished because they have done something wrong, they are blameworthy, and therefore deserve to be punished. • *Deterrence*: Based on a mechanism of fear of the consequences of committing a crime. Focus is on deterring the offender being sentenced, though individuals also can be made an example of. • *Incapacitation*: Offenders must be removed from society so that they cannot do more harm.	• *Medical model*: The offender is seen as having a condition that can be cured • *Rehabilitation and reintegration models*: Individual interventions meant to build an offender's skills and resources in order to improve outcomes upon re-entry into society	• *Primary:* Broader crime prevention focus dealing with poverty or inequality. • *Secondary:* Assisting high-risk individuals, high-risk communities or high-risk families. Much more targeted than primary prevention. • *Tertiary:* Criminal justice initiatives like an increase in the use of community sanctions, or repealing criminal legislation such as death penalty.

Figure 2.1 The Three Tenets of Canadian Correctional Ideology

federal correctional system acknowledges its role in contributing to the safety of the Canadian public through its control of offenders and assistance in their rehabilitation. The CSC (2012a) specifically states that this mandate is upheld through the use of reasonable, safe, secure, and humane control of the offenders under its supervision. As discussed previously, the two key parts of this mandate creates an important tension. The provincial and territorial correctional systems acknowledge similar mandates. As an example, the Ministry of the Solicitor General (Ontario) (formerly the Ontario Ministry of Community Safety and Correctional Services until June 2019) identifies its responsibilities as the support and protection of communities through law enforcement, adult correctional facilities, probation offices, and assistance in offenders' rehabilitation.

Programming

Both the federal and provincial and territorial correctional systems acknowledge their responsibility in aiding offender rehabilitation through the use of programming. During the intake process at a federal institution, a **correctional plan** is created for each offender that includes recommendations for treatment and rehabilitation. The CSC provides offenders with numerous correctional, educational, and vocational programs,

as well as work opportunities within the institution. These programs are intended to provide offenders with knowledge and skills that will assist in their rehabilitation and successful reintegration to the community.

CORCAN is one of the rehabilitative programs made available to prisoners by the CSC while incarcerated and for a short period of time upon their release from a CSC institution. CORCAN offers prisoners on-the-job and third-party certified vocational training with the goal of providing them with employment and employability skills that can be used after their release (CSC, 2018b). The training provided to prisoners falls along four business lines: manufacturing, textiles, construction, and services. CORCAN aims to provide prisoners with a number of hard and soft skills that are essential when entering the workforce upon their release into the community (CSC, 2018b).

As part of an offender's correctional plan, provincial and territorial correctional facilities provide offenders with programs aimed at reducing **criminogenic risk factors**. For example, The Ministry of the Solicitor General (Ontario) provides offenders under its supervision with life skills as well as rehabilitative, educational, and work programs. These programs are developed and implemented to hold offenders accountable and address the actions and behaviours that lead to their offending. Correctional programs will then be provided based on the needs outlined in the correctional plan (CSC, 2012b). Federally, offenders in custody are paid for their participation in program and work assignments within the institution. A prisoner's pay level is dependent on their participation in their assignments, active participation in meeting the goals included in their correctional plan, and their overall institutional behaviour.

The Structure of the Correctional System in Canada

As prescribed by the Constitution Act, the Canadian correctional system is divided into two levels: federal and provincial and territorial. In total, adult corrections in Canada cost over $4.7 billion in the 2016–17 fiscal year. This figure is attributed to the incarceration of an average of 39,873 adult offenders on any given day and the supervision of over 100,000 adult offenders in the community (Malakieh, 2018). This section provides a description of the operations, population sizes, and associated costs of federal, provincial and territorial, and community corrections.

Federal Incarceration

The federal correctional system in Canada is established and operated by the CSC. The CSC is responsible for the administration of court-imposed sentences that are two years or longer, as well as the supervision of offenders who are in the community on conditional release (CSC, 2012a). As of 2019, the CSC operates 43 federal correctional institutions in five regions across the country: the Pacific, Prairie, Ontario, Quebec, and Atlantic regions. This includes eleven **clustered sites**, five **minimum security institutions**, nine **medium security institutions**, and six **maximum security institutions**, as well as twelve **multi-level institutions**. Included within these 43 institutions are five multi-level institutions

Courtesy of Correctional Service Canada

Offenders have the opportunity to gain marketable job experience while participating in work assignments through CORCAN during their incarceration in a CSC institution. CORCAN is a special operating agency within the CSC that aims to prepare prisoners for work upon release.

for women and four CSC-operated **Indigenous healing lodges** (three minimum security lodges for male offenders, and one that accommodates minimum and medium security female offenders; CSC, 2017b). As of 2016, 63 per cent of federal prisoners were classified as medium security, followed by 22 per cent as minimum security and 15 per cent as maximum security (Segel-Brown, 2018). The classification and characteristics of each institution level can be found in Table 2.1.

Approximately 4 per cent of all offenders who enter the correctional system in Canada will be under the supervision of the federal system. In the 2016–17 fiscal year, Statistics Canada reported that the CSC was responsible for the supervision of an average of 14,425 in federal custody on any given day (Malakieh, 2018).

There are significant costs associated with the federal correctional system in Canada. In the 2016–17 fiscal year, the total cost associated with federal incarceration

Table 2.1   Classification of CSC Federal Correctional Institutions

Institution Security Level/Type	Characteristics of the Institution
Federal Maximum Security	• Have a well-defined, secure, and controlled perimeter surrounded by barbed-wire fencing and armed correctional officers. • Firearms are permitted within the institutions and may be deployed. • Movement of prisoners within these institutions is strictly regulated and usually monitored. • Prisoners are expected to interact effectively under frequent monitoring and display a basic interest in participating in their correctional plan. • In female institutions, maximum security prisoners are incarcerated in a secure unit in closed pods or cells.
Federal Medium Security	• Have clearly defined perimeters that are secure and controlled by barbed-wire fencing. • Correctional officers are not armed, but firearms are available within the institution. • Movement of offenders within medium security institutions is regulated and typically monitored. • Prisoners are expected to interact effectively with regular monitoring and show interest in participating in their correctional plan. • In female institutions, medium security prisoners are incarcerated in a living unit.
Federal Minimum Security	• Have clearly defined perimeters, but these perimeters are not secure or directly controlled. • Firearms are not used by CSC staff, except when permitted in states of emergency. • Offenders in minimum security institutions receive little monitoring and may organize their own schedules. • Prisoners are expected to interact effectively with other prisoners with little monitoring and display a high level of motivation. • In female institutions, minimum security prisoners are incarcerated in a living unit.
Federal Indigenous Healing Lodge	• Similar to minimum security institutions, healing lodges for both men and women have clearly defined perimeters that are not secure or directly controlled. • Firearms are not used by CSC staff in healing lodges, except when permitted in states of emergency. • Prisoners in healing lodges are expected to actively participate in their correctional plan, respect Indigenous healing concepts, and participate in Indigenous programs and ceremonies.

Source: Adapted from Correctional Service Canada, 2018a, paras. 4–12, 19–27; Segel-Brown, 2018, p. 4.

was more than $1.3 billion, which includes CSC staff salaries, operations of CSC institutions, and the costs associated with the supervision of offenders. This significant figure averages out to approximately $105,286 per prisoner each year, or $288 per day (Malakieh, 2018). However, the cost per offender significantly varies by type of supervision and institution security level. For example, male offenders in minimum security institutions each cost approximately $47,000 a year to supervise, while supervision of offenders in Indigenous healing lodges costs approximately $122,000 per offender per year (Segel-Brown, 2018).

Provincial and Territorial Incarceration

As dictated by the Constitution Act, the provincial and territorial correctional system in Canada is responsible for the supervision of offenders who receive a sentence equal to or less than two years less a day.

Offenders who are in **remand custody**, as well as those who are being held for immigration purposes, are also detained in provincial and territorial facilities. Similar to federal corrections, provincial and territorial correctional facilities are also classified as minimum, medium, or maximum security institutions, and offenders are classified based on their level of risk and need. The Ministry of the Solicitor General (Ontario) specifically states that offenders are classified at intake to ensure their custodial and programming needs are able to be met in the facility in which they are incarcerated.

During 2016–17, Statistics Canada reported that 96 per cent of all offenders sentenced to a period of incarceration fell under the provincial and territorial jurisdiction. In the same report, it was stated that on an average day during 2016–17, approximately 25,448 offenders were under supervision within a provincial or territorial facility. It was also reported that the

Healing Lodges in Canadian Federal Corrections

Prior to the establishment of Indigenous healing lodges in Canadian federal corrections, there was a great deal of concern expressed from the Indigenous community that correctional programs were not meeting the unique needs of Indigenous offenders. This concern, coupled with the increasing severity of the overrepresentation of Indigenous offenders in corrections, led to a need to take action in combating these issues (CSC, 2019).

The plans for the first five healing lodges were developed in 1990. It was decided at that time that four of the institutions would be minimum security sites for male offenders, while the fifth would be a minimum/medium security site for women. The first healing lodge, Okimaw Ohci Healing Lodge for women, opened in 1995, while the most recent healing lodge opened in 2011 (CSC, 2019). The facilities were created with the intent to provide Indigenous offenders with access to culturally and spiritually responsive programs that facilitate healing. Prisoners residing at healing lodges also have access to Indigenous Elders and knowledge keepers, and they have the opportunity to participate in cultural ceremonies and celebrations. The intent is

that the programs and services offered, and the environment they are offered in, will encourage healing of Indigenous offenders and provide continuous support throughout the journey.

Today, there are four healing lodges that are owned and operated by the CSC, as well as an additional five healing lodges that are funded by the CSC and operated by the community. Community-operated healing lodges are legislated under section 81 of the Corrections and Conditional Release Act (CSC, 2019), which allows for an Indigenous offender to be transferred into the custody of an Indigenous community with the approval of the minister. Of these nine facilities, seven are located in the Prairie region, where the highest rates of overrepresentation of Indigenous offenders have been observed (LaPrairie, 1996; Malakieh, 2018). The remaining two healing lodges are located in British Columbia and Quebec. There are seven healing lodges for male offenders and two for female offenders (CSC, 2019). While these facilities are not limited to Indigenous offenders, any offender who requests to transfer to a healing lodge must adhere to Indigenous programming and spirituality.

Courtesy of Correctional Service Canada

Pictured on the left is Saskatchewan Penitentiary, a clustered institution with minimum, medium, and maximum security units. Pictured on the right is Okimaw Ohci Healing Lodge, an Indigenous healing lodge for female offenders that is also located in Saskatchewan.

majority of offenders currently detained in provincial or territorial facilities were on remand, meaning that the offenders were awaiting trial or a sentencing hearing (Malakieh, 2018).

The provincial and territorial correctional system's total custody costs amounted to over $1.9 billion in the 2016–17 fiscal year. However, incarcerating offenders in the provincial and territorial correctional system is less costly than in the federal system when comparing the average cost of each prisoner. The cost to incarcerate an offender in the provincial and territorial system in 2016–17 was estimated to be approximately $203 per prisoner per day, totalling approximately $77,639 per year.

Community Corrections

Though a full discussion regarding community corrections is beyond the scope of this chapter, it is important to note that the federal and provincial and territorial systems of corrections both have a community corrections sector. In the federal system, offenders under community supervision are supervised by parole officers and may be released on full parole, day parole, statutory release, unescorted temporary absences, or long-term supervision orders. Prisoners under the CSC's supervision in the community may reside in community correctional centres, community residential facilities, hostels, private home placements, or supervised or satellite apartments. The CSC (2017a) states that the purpose of community corrections is to release offenders with conditions to aid in a gradual and successful reintegration to the community. In order to successfully bridge the transition of offenders from an institution into the community, correctional plans continue through the process, and prisoners maintain access to many different programs, such as life skills and substance-use programs as well as various forms of counselling. The CSC states that "this work is essential because offenders are more likely to become law-abiding citizens if they participate in a program of gradual, supervised release" (CSC, 2017a).

Provincial and territorial community corrections are responsible for the supervision of offenders who are sentenced to probationary periods of up to three years, conditional sentences for a period up to two years less a day, and offenders serving parole, as granted by a provincial or territorial parole board. Similar to federal community corrections, offenders serving a sentence in the community in Ontario will have an individual supervision plan that includes the conditions that must be adhered to and the requirements that must be met, as well as an assessment of the offender's needs and risk of reoffending (Ontario Ministry of Community Safety and Correctional Services, 2018).

During the 2016–17 fiscal year, there were approximately 8,581 offenders on community release under federal supervision on any given day. This includes an offender granted any of the types of release that were previously mentioned. Within the provincial and territorial system, 93,135 offenders under supervision, or 79 per cent of all offenders, were serving a sentence in the community in this same time period (Malakieh, 2018).

Community corrections are much more cost effective when compared with the cost of incarceration in both federal and provincial and territorial corrections. In the 2016–17 fiscal year, federal community corrections totalled approximately $146 million, while provincial and territorial community corrections cost approximately $362 million (Malakieh, 2018).

Alternatives to Incarceration, Probation, and Parole

After Confederation in 1867, a period of incarceration was often the result of a sentencing hearing, since the courts had few alternatives to impose (Jackson & Ekstedt, 1988). As previously discussed, there was a shift from punishment toward rehabilitation as a primary goal of sentencing in the criminal justice system in the 1930s. The development of the probation system, as well as the increasing costs associated with imprisonment, both contributed to the establishment and expansion of community corrections throughout the 1970s. However, disparities in sentencing became evident, and it was acknowledged that alternatives to incarceration were not equally available or accessible across regions and provinces in Canada. The alternatives available to each individual will also vary based on the charge they have been convicted of and their specialized needs (Jackson & Ekstedt, 1988). Some of the alternatives to incarceration available across the country are monetary, custodial, and community based and include the following:

- *Fine options:* Courts can first sentence someone to a fine *(monetary)* when custody or supervision is not required. There have been cases, however, when an offender is sent to jail for not paying a fine (when they are in default of so many days given).
- *Community based:* Community-based options include conditional discharge and probation, **suspended sentence** and probation, and conditional sentence order. Conditions attached to probation orders may include restitution orders or community service work, but they are not sentences that stand on their own. (It is different for youth offenders: Attendance programs, community service, and restitution can be a stand-alone disposition for youth only.)
- *Custodial release:* Programs granted for inmates' release may include temporary absence programs and parole, but they are granted by the parole board, not the courts.
- *Intermittent sentences:* These are considered a custodial sentence but are scheduled intermittently to allow the offender to be in the community part of the week for employment or family responsibility reasons. This is not so much an alternative to incarceration but an opportunity for integration.

Drug treatment courts and **mental health courts** have also been introduced into the Canadian criminal justice system in an attempt to divert certain individuals away from the correctional system. The first drug treatment court opened in Toronto in 1988, followed by courts in Vancouver, Edmonton, Winnipeg, Ottawa, and Regina. These courts were established following the acknowledgement that a large population of prisoners incarcerated for drug offences were found to recidivate as a result of their drug dependency (Department of Justice, 2016). Participation in drug treatment court requires an individual to submit a guilty plea to receive judicially supervised treatment as an alterative to incarceration (Canadian Centre on Substance Use and Addiction, 2007).

Mental health courts have been established across the country in response to the overrepresentation of people with mental illness in custody, although these courts are not mandated and therefore vary in their practices. Generally, these courts aim to improve the well-being of the individuals involved and increase their access to services while decreasing recidivism and increasing the safety of the community (Baba, 2018).

The Criminal Code, section 718.2(e), requires that a court take into consideration "all available sanctions, other than imprisonment, that are reasonable in the circumstances and consistent with the harm done to victims or to the community . . . for all offenders, with particular attention to the circumstances of Aboriginal offenders."

Legislative Framework of Canadian Corrections

There are numerous pieces of legislation that govern the criminal justice system in its entirety, as well as the correctional system specifically. Federal statutes, provincial and territorial legislation, and various policies govern everything from the treatment of offenders down to the day-to-day operations of the correctional system in Canada.

The Canadian Charter of Rights and Freedoms

The **Canadian Charter of Rights and Freedoms** outlines the legal rights and fundamental freedoms that are afforded to every individual in Canada regardless of their citizenship, unless otherwise stated. Legal and equality rights are laid out in sections 7 through 15 of the Charter, which address life, liberty, and security of the person; search and seizure; detention and imprisonment; arrest and detention; criminal and penal proceedings; treatment and punishment; self-incrimination; interpreters; and equality rights, respectively. The Charter protects the rights and freedoms of all individuals accused and convicted of a crime in Canada, except for the rights and freedoms that are forfeited as a result of imprisonment.

The Constitution Act

The **Constitution Act** (1867) distinguishes the roles of the federal government and the provincial and territorial governments in Canada. Matters that are overseen by the federal government are laid out in section 91 of the Act, while provincial matters are listed in section 92. Specifically related to the correctional system, the Constitution Act divides the system into two entities. The federal correctional system is responsible for the custody and supervision of offenders who receive a court-imposed sentence of two years or longer. The provincial and territorial correctional systems assume the responsibility of offenders who receive a sentence of two years less a day or shorter.

The Criminal Code

The **Criminal Code** is a piece of federal legislation that provides a definition of criminal offences in Canada. The Criminal Code defines an offence, when an individual is guilty of such an offence, the means by which the offence should be prosecuted, and the penalties that may be imposed upon a conviction of the charge. Offences in Canada can be prosecuted as a **summary offence**, **indictable offence**, or **hybrid offence**. For example, section 88 of the Criminal Code addresses possession of a weapon for dangerous purposes. Section 88(1) defines the offence, stating "Every person commits an

offence who carries or possesses a weapon, an imitation of a weapon, a prohibited device or any ammunition or prohibited ammunition for a purpose dangerous to the public peace or for the purpose of committing an offence." Section 88(2) states that any person who commits such an offence is guilty of (a) an indictable offence and may receive a prison sentence not exceeding 10 years, or (b) a summary conviction offence.

Corrections and Conditional Release Act (CCRA)

The **Corrections and Conditional Release Act** (CCRA) is the governing legislation of the federal correctional system. The CCRA governs both the CSC as well as the Parole Board of Canada (PBC). The Act is a "living document," meaning that it can be amended to reflect changes to legislation made by Parliament. The CCRA is divided into four parts. Part I, sections 2–98, address institutional and community corrections; Part II, sections 99–156, outline conditional release, detention, and long-term supervision; Part III, sections 157–198, defines the purpose and responsibilities of the Office of the Correctional Investigator; and Part IV, sections 199–234, addresses amendments, repeal, and transitional provisions that are coming into force.

The CCRA also addresses the needs of several vulnerable groups involved in the correctional system, including Indigenous offenders and victims of crime. The Act makes reference to Indigenous offenders in sections 79 through 84. Included within these sections are the requirements for programs designed specifically for Indigenous offenders, the ability for an Indigenous community to provide care and custody of an Indigenous offender, the formation of a National Aboriginal Advisory Committee, access to Elders and spiritual leaders, and the ability to be released into an Indigenous community. Section 142 of the CCRA outlines which offender information may be disclosed to the victim of their crime. This information includes the length of the offender's sentence, the institution at which the offender is serving their sentence, and the date of release and location of the offender should they be granted temporary absences from the institution, parole, or statutory release.

The CCRA also provides the CSC with the ability to develop and enforce policies governing the day-to-day functioning of federal corrections, known as **commissioner's directives**. These directives are required by law to be available to CSC staff, offenders, and the public.

Provincial and Territorial Legislation

Each province and territory has enacted legislation that governs its correctional system, including its purpose, goals, and functions. For example, the Corrections Act enacted by the Government of Alberta is the key legislation governing corrections within that province. Laid out within the Act are the roles, responsibilities, and powers held by officials within the Department of Justice. The Act also includes policies and procedures concerning daily operations, such as monitoring of prisoner communications, prisoner transfers, and drug testing (Government of Alberta, 2018).

International Agreements and Conventions

Canadian corrections are also governed by international agreements and conventions, including the United Nations *Standard Minimum Rules for the Treatment of Prisoners* (see Chapter 14). Now known as the Nelson Mandela Rules, these rules define the principles and practices that are widely accepted as proper treatment of offenders and prison management. They clearly state that prisoners should be treated with the respect they deserve as human beings and should not be discriminated against based on race, colour, sex, language, religion, political or other opinion, national or social origin, property, birth, or any other status (United Nations Office on Drugs and Crime, 2015).

The Youth Criminal Justice Act

The Youth Criminal Justice Act (YCJA) came into force on April 1, 2003, replacing the former Young Offenders Act (1984–2003). This piece of legislation applies to youth in Canada between the ages of 12 and 17 who have been accused of a criminal offence. Youth younger than 12 years old who commit a criminal act in Canada cannot be convicted of an offence. This Act includes specific rights and freedoms that are afforded to youth because of their age and lack of maturity, which are laid out in the preamble and declaration of principle. Also included in the preamble and declaration of principle is the requirement that alternatives to incarceration be used when sentencing youth when a fair and proportionate alternative exists (Department of Justice, 2017). Youth sentences are referred to as dispositions, and they are sent to custodial facilities rather than prisons (see Chapter 10).

Oversight of the Correctional System

The **Office of the Correctional Investigator (OCI)** was established as an ombudsperson for federal offenders as a result of the mandate in the CCRA. The function of the OCI is "to conduct investigations into the problems of offenders related to decisions, recommendations, acts or omissions of the Commissioner (of Corrections) or any person under the control and management of, or performing services for, or on behalf of, the Commissioner, that affect offenders either individually or as a group" (Office of the Correctional Investigator, 2013). In fulfilling its mandate, the OCI assesses and reviews federal correctional practices and policies, and responds to individual offenders' complaints. It is the responsibility of the OCI to take an objective approach to its work and make informed decisions when discerning right from wrong and developing effective recommendations for the CSC. Each year, the OCI produces a year-end report that includes significant findings and a list of recommendations. It is up to the CSC to resolve the issues that have been identified. While the OCI is granted special authority in regards to accessing information, the report and its recommendations are simply that—recommendations. The CSC is not legally obligated to follow up on the issues or adhere to the recommendations made.

Similar to the OCI, provinces and territories have ombudspersons that operate as third parties who are separate from government and political parties. The priority of the ombudsperson is to oversee government actions, services, and policies and ensure that the government is being held accountable. For example, the Nova Scotia Office of the Ombudsman "provides independent, unbiased investigations into complaints against provincial and municipal government departments, agencies, boards, and commissions" (Nova Scotia Office of the Ombudsman, 2014). The objective of the office is to investigate cases where individuals feel they have been treated unfairly by members of municipal or provincial governments in Nova Scotia, which would therefore include complaints from offenders who feel they have been mistreated by correctional staff. Reports produced as the result of investigations are provided to both government employees and the public (Nova Scotia Office of the Ombudsman, 2014).

Recommendations from the Office of the Correctional Investigator

Each year since its establishment, the OCI has produced a fiscal year-end report summarizing the topics and issues they have investigated. The report concludes with a list of recommendations on how the CSC can improve policies and day-to-day operations within institutions.

In the first annual report produced by the office in 2003–4, the OCI identified significant issues caused by the prisoner pay system in place in federal corrections. The highest level of pay that an offender could be awarded was $6.90 per day. This had been calculated based on the disposable income of minimum-wage-earning Canadians at the time (OCI, 2014). In addition, in order to increase offender accountability, the CSC imposed 30 per cent deductions from offenders' pay to assist with the costs of room and board and the inmate telephone system. This resulted in little money left over each pay period to be saved, resulting in very few funds saved for an offender's release. In their report, the OCI contested that releasing an offender with little savings reduces the chances of successful reintegration (OCI, 2014).

Since the first acknowledgement of this issue, prisoner pay has been a reoccurring topic in numerous OCI annual reports. In 2013, a prisoner's day's worth of pay prior to deductions would not be enough to purchase a number of prisoner canteen items. In this report, the OCI noted that limited funds were found to be a source of tension within institutions. Further recommendations for a review of the prisoner pay and allowance system were included within the 2015–16 (OCI, 2016) and 2016–17 (OCI, 2017) annual reports.

Summary

This chapter discussed what we mean by "corrections." It reviewed the purpose of corrections and key pieces of legislation that guide the day-to-day operation of corrections in Canada. It also reviewed alternatives to incarceration. Finally, it discussed the role of the Office of the Correctional Investigator in overseeing the correctional system in Canada.

Review Questions

1. What is the definition of "corrections"?
2. What piece of legislation governs the Correctional Service of Canada?
3. What is the purpose of the Office of the Correctional Investigator?

Critical Thinking Questions

1. Do you think there is a tension in Canadian corrections between protecting society and the rights of the offender?
2. This chapter discussed the role of the Office of the Correctional Investigator, as well as provincial ombudspersons within the correctional system. While these offices can

review policies and practices and investigate issues, correctional entities are not obligated to respond to or follow up on the recommendations that are made.

    a.   Do you believe that there should be a legal obligation for federal and provincial corrections entities to follow up on these recommendations? Why or why not?

    b.   What are the potential benefits and consequences of doing so?

3. Based on your knowledge of the overrepresentation of Indigenous offenders in the Canadian criminal justice system,

    a.   What are the benefits of the facilities, programs, and services provided for Indigenous offenders in federal corrections?

    b.   Are there any limitations to these facilities, programs, and services?

Multimedia Suggestions

Correctional Service Canada

For general information about the CSC, go to their website: www.csc-scc.gc.ca/index-en.shtml

CORCAN Modular Structures

Promotional video of the CORCAN program from the CSC: www.youtube.com/watch?v=VQEej4PnK40

Step Inside a Private Tour of Collins Bay

Tour of Collins Bay Institution (a federal institution) in Kingston, Ontario: www.youtube.com/watch?v=sEqIVDK6K8M

Saskatchewan Penitentiary Drone Footage

Drone footage of Saskatchewan Penitentiary: www.youtube.com/watch?v=M0kBrhXPKgY

References

Baba, S. (2018). Canadian developments in alternative sentencing: Mental health courts (Part 2). *McGill Journal of Law and Health—Online*. Retrieved from https://mjlh.mcgill.ca/2018/02/06/canadian-developments-in-alternative-sentencing-mental-health-courts-part-2

Canadian Centre on Substance Use and Addiction. (2007). Drug treatment courts FAQ. Retrieved from https://www.ccsa.ca/drug-treatment-courts-faq

Correctional Service Canada. (2008). Partners in good corrections. Retrieved from http://www.csc-scc.gc.ca/text/pblct/sb-go/06-eng.shtml

Correctional Service Canada. (2012a). About us. Retrieved from https://www.csc-scc.gc.ca/about-us/index-eng.shtml

Correctional Service Canada (2012b). The correctional plan. Retrieved from https://www.csc-scc.gc.ca/002/007/002007-0004-eng.shtml

Correctional Service Canada. (2014). Penitentiaries in Canada. Retrieved from https://www.csc-scc.gc.ca/about-us/006-1006-eng.shtml

Correctional Service Canada. (2017a). Community corrections. Retrieved from https://www.csc-scc.gc.ca//publications/005007-3008-eng.shtml

Correctional Service Canada. (2017b). CSC Statistics—Key facts and figures. Retrieved from https://www.csc-scc.gc.ca//publications/005007-3024-eng.shtml

Correctional Service Canada. (2018a). Commissioner's directive 706 classification of institutions. Retrieved from https://www.csc-scc.gc.ca/005/006/706-cd-en.shtml

Correctional Service Canada. (2018b). CORCAN. Retrieved from https://www.csc-scc.gc.ca/corcan/002005-0001-eng.shtml

Correctional Service Canada. (2019). Correctional Service Canada Indigenous healing lodges. Retrieved from https://www.csc-scc.gc.ca/aboriginal/002003-2000-en.shtml

Department of Justice. (2016). Drug treatment court funding program. Retrieved from https://www.justice.gc.ca/eng/fund-fina/gov-gouv/dtc-ttt.html

Department of Justice. (2017). The Youth Criminal Justice Act summary and background. Retrieved from https://www.justice.gc.ca/eng/cj-jp/yj-jj/tools-outils/back-hist.html

Government of Alberta. (2018). Corrections Act. Retrieved from https://open.alberta.ca/dataset/1375f189-f84a-479e-9d1e-af2e73381d8e

Griffiths, C., & Murdoch, D. (2018). *Canadian corrections* (5th edn). Toronto, ON: Nelson Education.

Jackson, M., & Ekstedt, J. (1988). Alternatives to incarceration/sentencing option programmes: What are the alternatives? Catalogue no. J23-3/5-1988E-PDF. Ottawa, ON: Department of Justice Canada, Policy, Programs and Research Branch.

LaPrairie, C. (1996). *Examining Aboriginal corrections in Canada*. Catalogue no. JS5-1/14-1996E-PDF. Ottawa, ON: Solicitor General Canada.

Malakieh, J. (2018). Adult and youth correctional statistics in Canada, 2016/2017. Catalogue no. 85-002-X. Ottawa, ON: Statistics Canada.

Nova Scotia Office of the Ombudsman. (2014). Administration. Retrieved from https://novascotia.ca/ombu/administration.htm

Office of the Correctional Investigator. (2013). Roles and responsibilities. Retrieved from http://www.oci-bec.gc.ca/cnt/roles-eng.aspx

Office of the Correctional Investigator. (2014). *Annual report of the Office of the Correctional Investigator 2013–2014.* Retrieved from http://www.oci-bec.gc.ca/cnt/rpt/annrpt/annrpt20132014-eng.aspx

Office of the Correctional Investigator. (2016). *Annual report of the Office of the Correctional Investigator 2015–2016.* Retrieved from http://www.oci-bec.gc.ca/cnt/rpt/annrpt/annrpt20152016-eng.aspx

Office of the Correctional Investigator. (2017). *Annual report of the Office of the Correctional Investigator 2016–2017.* Retrieved from http://www.oci-bec.gc.ca/cnt/rpt/annrpt/annrpt20162017-eng.aspx

Ontario Ministry of Community Safety and Correctional Services. (2018). Correctional services. Retrieved from https://www.mcscs.jus.gov.on.ca/english/corr_serv/inmate_class/inmate_class.html

Reitano, J. (2017). Adult correctional statistics in Canada, 2015/2016. *Juristat.* Retrieved from http://www.antoniocasella.eu/nume/Canada_1march17.pdf

Segel-Brown, B. (2018). Update on costs of incarceration. Catalogue no. YN5-152/2018E-PDF. Ottawa, ON: Office of the Parliamentary Budget Officer.

United Nations Office on Drugs and Crime. (2015). The United Nations standard minimum rules for the treatment of prisoners (the Nelson Mandela rules). Retrieved from http://www.unodc.org/documents/justice-and-prison-reform/GA-RESOLUTION/E_ebook.pdf

Canadian Criminal Justice Policy and Imprisonment

Understanding What Is Uniquely Canadian[1]

3

Anthony N. Doob and Cheryl Marie Webster

Learning Objectives

After reading this chapter, you should be able to:

- Describe how Canadian trends in adult imprisonment rates differ from those in the United States and England and Wales.
- Understand how Canadian policies related to imprisonment rates differ from those in the United States.
- Recognize how broad criminal justice policies in Canada have been fairly consistent over time.
- Differentiate between rhetoric about "crime and punishment" and the actual effects of policies related to crime and punishment.
- Better understand how criminal justice policies are sometimes used for political purposes rather than purposes related more directly to justice or public safety.

Chapter Overview

This chapter provides a brief overview of Canadian criminal justice policy that relates to—and may help explain—Canada's relatively stable adult imprisonment rate over the past 70 years. Trends in Canada's incarceration rate are very different from those found in the United States and England and Wales. This chapter explains the ways in which Canadian governments have understood imprisonment and how this perspective differs dramatically from that in the United States from the early 1970s onwards. Until the 1990s, Canadian policies related to the use of adult prison were not highly correlated with political ideology. Members of both dominant political parties agreed with the idea that imprisonment should be used sparingly. Indeed, many government and government-initiated reports urged restraint in the use of imprisonment. In this century, the rhetoric changed during the Harper decade (2006–15), but imprisonment rates changed very little. This chapter also explores possible explanations for this apparent incongruence. It concludes with a look to the future, particularly within

the context that little has changed since 2015 (when the Trudeau government was elected).

Introduction: Imprisonment as an Integral Part of the Canadian Criminal Justice System

If one were living in the 1970s and interested in understanding the operation of the Canadian criminal justice system, one could purchase (for $5, or about $34 in 2020 dollars) a bound copy of the 505-page Report of the Canadian Committee on Corrections entitled *Toward Unity: Criminal Justice and Corrections*, published by the Government of Canada in 1969. Commonly referred to as the "Ouimet Report" (after the chair of the committee that produced it), this document is remarkable for many reasons, beginning with its broad terms of reference. The committee was asked by the government "to study the broad field of corrections, in its widest sense, from the initial investigation of an offence through to the final discharge of a prisoner" as well as all stages between these two criminal processes, including "arrest, summonsing, bail, representation in Court, conviction, probation, sentencing, training, medical and psychiatric attention, release, parole, pardon, post-release supervision and guidance and rehabilitation" (Government of Canada, 1969, p. 1).

Clearly, the government of the day and the committee that it appointed understood, explicitly, that "corrections" should be understood within a broad context. By extension, it was believed that the issues facing corrections in Canada could not—and should not—be separated from other aspects of the criminal justice system. Hence the report contained 25 chapters dealing with matters such as the following:

- Arrest (Chapter 6)
- Bail (Chapter 7)
- Sentencing (Chapter 11)
- Purposes and origin of adult corrections (Chapter 14)
- Prisons (Chapter 17)
- The young adult offender (Chapter 21)
- The woman offender (Chapter 22)
- The significance of criminal records and recognition of rehabilitation (Chapter 23)

Typically, these chapters contained descriptions of the issue (often supported by detailed statistics) and recommendations for change. Equally important, the Ouimet Report is but one of many official statements on the Canadian criminal justice system written during the twentieth century. The committee itself noted that its report was the third major study of the Canadian criminal justice system to be carried out since 1938. Perhaps not surprisingly, these other reports also tended to have broad terms of reference.

This chapter focuses on one of the central leitmotifs running through this report. Specifically, its authors— like many others who studied the criminal justice system in Canada—were skeptical about the usefulness of imprisonment. In fact, the Ouimet Report recommended that the criminal law should not be employed "unless its incidence, actual or potential, is *substantially damaging to society*" (Government of Canada, 1969, p. 12). Furthermore, the committee stated, as one of its relatively uncontroversial principles, the idea that "The deliberate

infliction of punishment or any other state interference with human freedom is to be justified only where manifest evil would result from failure to interfere" (p. 13).

When it came to sentencing, the committee was quite clear: Imprisonment should be used with considerable restraint. In fact, this committee emphasized "the danger of overestimating the necessity for and the value of long terms of imprisonment except in special circumstances" and recommended that it be used only as a last resort when all other alternatives have failed.

This chapter will explore the central role of this notion of restraint in the use of incarceration as a defining characteristic of Canada's approach to crime and criminals. We begin with an examination of this belief as a long-standing principle guiding Canadian criminal justice policy. We subsequently juxtapose Canada's use of imprisonment with that of other comparable nations, highlighting our unique position on a world stage that is seemingly increasingly wed to imprisonment as the preferred response to crime and criminals. To better understand Canada's approach, we use the various roles that prison has been seen to play as a crime control strategy in the United States as a foil to Canada's historically entrenched conviction in the limited use of incarceration. Following this broader analysis, we examine the decade of criminal justice policy under the Harper government (2006–15) as arguably the most significant threat to Canada's belief in restraint in the use of imprisonment. Finally, we look to the future by providing some concluding thoughts on the possible direction of criminal justice policy in Canada.

Restraint in the Use of Imprisonment of Adults as a Long-Standing Principle in Canadian Criminal Justice Policy

Perhaps the most important lesson to be learned from reading the Ouimet Report more than 50 years after it was written is that it was not controversial at the time. In fact, there were reports, both before this one and after it, that recommended restraint in the use of imprisonment. Notably, these official statements began to appear on the Canadian criminal justice policy horizon as early as 1914 (with the Report of the Royal Commission on Penitentiaries) and extended to 1998 (with a comprehensive policy paper outlining what was to become the Youth Criminal Justice Act).

Perhaps more noteworthy is the sheer number of formal statements over the last century that expressed concern with the usefulness of imprisonment. In fact, at least two dozen reports endorsing restraint in the use of incarceration can be identified. The consistency of the message is difficult to deny. Report after report affirmed the need to limit the recourse to prison.

However, this principle is rooted in two separate (albeit interrelated) tenets. First, the broad belief that Canada's prisons and penitentiaries are not particularly effective in making Canadians safer is repeated, in various ways, throughout our history. A 1982 government statement makes the point in stating that "In awarding sentences, preference should be given to the least restrictive alternative [that is] adequate and appropriate in the circumstances" (Government of Canada, 1982, p. 53). More importantly, it went on to suggest that the control of crime was not going to be enhanced by the use of harsh sentences. Rather, the most effective criminal justice response to criminal activity was believed to be rooted in "improvements in preventative, investigative and prosecutorial methods and in court procedures . . . [that would increase] the certainty of detection, apprehension, convictions and punishment" (p. 28).

Notably, this document is described as "[setting] out the policy of the Government of Canada with respect to the purpose and principles of the criminal law. As such it is unique in Canadian history" (preface). More notably for our current purposes, this policy recommendation clearly recognized that harsher sanctions do not reduce crime in any significant way. By extension, this type of policy recommendation challenged any belief in the use of incarceration as a successful strategy in deterring offenders through fear of severe penalties.

However, it was not just that the federal government endorsed the view that high rates of imprisonment were not useful as a crime reduction strategy. Rather, the belief in restraint in the use of prison was also rooted in a second premise. When the issue of imprisonment rates was raised in public documents, the consensus was, for the most part, that Canada imprisoned too many people. In response, Canadian governments frequently recommended that prison—as a criminal sanction—should be restricted to a small subset of criminals and situations. Illustratively, a 1984 government policy statement on sentencing asserted that there were only "three main sets of circumstances . . . justifying a sentence of imprisonment: separation of offenders posing a threat to life and personal security; denunciation of conduct so reprehensible that lesser punishment would be inappropriate; and last resort coercion of offenders who willfully refuse to comply with other sanctions" (Government of Canada, 1984, p. 38).

A similar policy statement was made less than a decade later. Specifically, the policy paper released by the minister of Justice in 1990 entitled *Directions for Reform: Sentencing* repeated almost word for word the restrictions on imprisonment advocated by the previous government (Department of Justice, 1990). Indeed, the consistency of such statements across time is notable. However, their similarity is equally significant given their origins. While the latter (1990) recommendations were made by a majority Conservative government, the former (1984) endorsements came from a majority Liberal government. While it would be easy to assume that imprisonment policy in Canada is closely linked to larger political ideologies, this does not appear to be the case. In fact, it would seem that not only is the message of restraint in the use of prison consistent across time, it is also essentially independent of political party (at least during the twentieth century). Although there might have been some differences between the parties, they were not important ones.

Within this context, it is not surprising that the 1990 Conservative proposals on sentencing and corrections quoted the 1982 Liberal document *favourably*, which is described as a statement of the policy of the government on the purpose and principles of criminal law. Equally illustrative, one need only to compare, in this context, the following two statements, the first from a Liberal justice minister in the 1990s and the second from a Conservative justice critic in the 1970s:

> Crime prevention means recognizing connections between the crime rate and the unemployment rate, between how a child behaves at school and whether that kid has had a hot meal that day. (Allan Rock, minister of Justice, 1995)

> I want to congratulate the minister for realizing at last that crime is not just a sordid happening but rather a result of human behaviour brought about by our economic and social conditions which we have failed to change. (Conservative justice critic, Eldon Woolliams, responding to the [Liberal] solicitor general, 1972)

Notably, Woolliams was critical of the Liberals. However, the root of his criticism was not for being too liberal, but for not moving from words to actions. Indeed, this latter comparison underlines the consistency of Canada's belief in restraint in the use of prison not only over the space of roughly two decades but also across political party affiliation. But even this evidence of the uncontroversial nature of the limited recourse to incarceration can be further extended. Indeed, it was not just the federal government that endorsed the view that high rates of imprisonment were not effective or desirable. Rather, it was equally expressed by the provinces/territories.

In a series of reports addressing the problem of the growth of imprisonment that Canada experienced between the mid-1970s and the mid-1990s, a federal–provincial–territorial working group was convened to make recommendations. It noted in its 1997 report entitled *Corrections Population Growth: First Report of Progress* that the proposed strategies to counter this rise in provincial/territorial incarceration rates had achieved unanimity (Public Safety Canada, 1997). That is, the 11 recommendations contained in this document were endorsed by all federal, provincial, and territorial ministers.

Perhaps even more remarkably, two of the governments (Ontario and Alberta) that supported these proposals were known at the time to be quite conservative. Indeed, Ontario's Conservative government, led by Mike Harris, endorsed the reduction of imprisonment. Perhaps more interestingly, Ralph Klein's Conservative government in Alberta (widely recognized as Canada's most conservative province) also signed on to the proposals. In fact, his justice minister, Brian Evans, was quoted in a 1996 newspaper article as saying

> There are other ways of dealing with some of the criminal activity . . . that are more effective than putting a person in jail. Our . . . correctional facilities should be used, for the most part, for people who have committed serious and violent crime and therefore are a substantial risk to society. (Gold, 1996, p. A3)

In fact, the case of Alberta illustrates yet another important aspect of imprisonment in Canada. The manner in which the justice system is *administered* may be as important—or perhaps even more important—than the laws governing criminal justice decisions. In a period of approximately three years in the early to mid-1990s, Alberta reduced its provincial imprisonment rates by roughly 32 per cent (Webster & Doob, 2014). Notably, it accomplished this change by administrative action, not changes in the law.

In brief, perhaps the most notable characteristic of the belief in restraint in the use of imprisonment in Canada is that the unanimous agreement across the

federal, provincial, and territorial governments on ways to "counter" prison population growth was hardly newsworthy. In other words, these statements were largely uncontroversial in nature. Further, this continuity not only crosses levels of government and political parties but also time. Indeed, report after report written by governments across the entire twentieth century endorsed the same call for restraint.

However, this is not to say that all statements recommending lower imprisonment rates were uncontroversial. In 1998, the then commissioner of Correctional Service Canada (CSC) commented on the federal correctional population in an editorial in a magazine published by his own organization. At the time, roughly two-thirds of the offenders under his responsibility were in prison (the other third being supervised in the community). However, he believed—based on an analysis conducted by the CSC—that Canadians would be better served if only about half were serving their sentence in a federal penitentiary. In fact, the commissioner ended his editorial with the words "To reach a 50/50 split by year 2000 will be a professional challenge—but not at all unattainable" (Ingstrup, 1998, p. 1). More importantly, though, this statement was subsequently seen—unfavourably—as evidence that the commissioner in particular and the CSC generally were both soft on prisoners. Nevertheless, it is notable that in 1998 the commissioner of the CSC was comfortable making the suggestion that Canada would be well served if more than 2,000 federal penitentiary prisoners in "his" prisons were moved into the community on parole with supervision and support (even though he always expressed it in terms of percentage changes rather than numbers of former prisoners who would be in the community). Reading his full editorial now, it is hard to believe that he felt he was saying anything controversial.

Contrasting Canada with Other Comparable Nations: The Uniqueness of Our Overall Stability in the Use of Imprisonment

Given the consistent—and largely uncontroversial—skepticism about the use of imprisonment of adults over the last century, one might have expected Canada to have been reasonably successful at meeting its policy goals of restraint. However, this was not the case.

While the policy message was clear, actually changing Canadian incarceration rates was a different matter. Indeed, Canada has never been able to accomplish what one other country—Finland—did when it recognized that it was imprisoning too many people. Specifically, Finland decreased its imprisonment rate by 65 per cent.

Perhaps such a reduction was easier in Finland. Not only is its population considerably smaller than that of Canada, but it is a "unified" country rather than a collection of independent provinces/territories, each of which administers its own criminal justice system. But Finland also had another advantage. Lappi-Seppälä (2007) notes that there was near unanimous support by all groups working in the justice system for the belief that both the imprisonment rate was too high and that reducing it would not increase crime rates. He also points out that Finnish criminal justice policy is "exceptionally expert-oriented," which was reinforced by "close personal and professional contacts [of these experts] with senior politicians and with academic research" (p. 241). But even then, the change was slow. It took roughly 40 years to reduce the rate of imprisonment from approximately 155 (in 1960) to 55 prisoners per 100,000 residents (in 2000). Furthermore, 28 separate law reform efforts were made during this time. Lappi-Seppälä (2007, p. 234, Table 1) estimates that 23 of them were likely to reduce imprisonment.

Importantly, Finland constitutes an anomaly on the international stage. In fact, many Western democratic nations have witnessed the opposite—*increases* (often significant) in their prison populations over this same period. Within this wider context, Canada's claim to fame lies in its ability to have maintained relatively stable levels of imprisonment over the past half century (if not longer). Figure 3.1 displays our adult incarceration rates per 100,000 residents since 1951.

While there has clearly been some fluctuation over time—with a low of 81 per 100,000 residents in 1974 and a high of 116 in 1994—Canadian imprisonment rates as a whole have remained relatively constant for more than a half century. Further, this overall pattern is mirrored at both the federal (sentences of two years or more) and provincial (sentences of less than two years) levels. Having said this, two caveats to this overall assessment of relative stability should be noted.

First, it is important to remember that the provincial prison population is made up primarily of two distinct groups: sentenced prisoners and unsentenced prisoners (those in pre-trial detention plus a few who have been found guilty and are awaiting sentencing).

It is precisely the unsentenced (remand) prisoners whose trend over time diverges from the overall stable pattern. In fact, the percentage of unsentenced prisoners has increased dramatically over the last three decades. In 1978 (the first year for which we have data), 14 per cent of *all* Canadian prisoners had not yet been sentenced; by 2016, this value had increased to 39 per cent (see Figure 3.1).

Interestingly, this problem did not appear to receive much attention until 2005 when provincial prisons had, on average, more remand prisoners than sentenced prisoners for the first time ever. In 2016, 61 per cent of provincial prisoners were on remand (as opposed to serving sentences). One of the reasons that it went unnoticed for so long is that remand prisoners, if found guilty and sentenced to prison, are partially compensated for their stays in prison before sentencing by being given "credit" for time in pre-trial custody (under Criminal Code s. 719). Hence, the rate of people in *sentenced* custody decreased as the custody rate for *remand* custody increased.

Second, the variability that did occur had important consequences. The most obvious was the period from the mid-1970s to the mid-1990s during which imprisonment rates rose relatively steadily (before dropping once again). When one looks at this period, it is understandable that the provinces/territories in particular would have been concerned about their ability to cope with the increased numbers of prisoners in these correctional institutions. Not surprisingly within this context, the federal–provincial–territorial working group mentioned earlier was set up with the explicit intention of finding ways in which to reduce this prison population.

The uniqueness of Canada's overall stability in imprisonment becomes even more evident when contrasted with the trends of other comparable nations. We have opted to compare Canada's incarceration rates with those of the United States and England and Wales. Indeed, these jurisdictions arguably represent Canada's closest comparators (sharing not only similar cultures, economies, histories, geographies, and institutions, but also, broadly speaking, crime trends). Figure 3.2 presents their imprisonment rates.

The stability of Canada's adult incarceration rate stands in stark contrast to those of the other two nations. While the initial (1955 to the early 1970s) Canadian and American trends in imprisonment were similar, with both displaying relative stability over this period, dramatic differences quickly emerge.

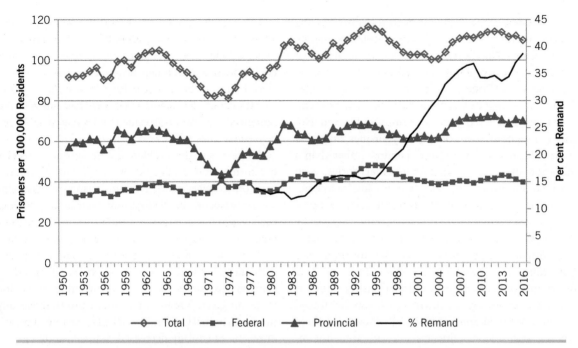

Figure 3.1 Canadian Adult Imprisonment Rates (per 100,000 Residents) and Percent of Total Prisoners in Remand

Note: Remand prisoners (prisoners not serving a sentence, largely awaiting trial) are held in provincial institutions. The provincial rates, then, include both sentenced and remand prisoners.

Source: Doob & Webster, 2006; Webster & Doob, 2018; data from Statistics Canada's CANSIM database.

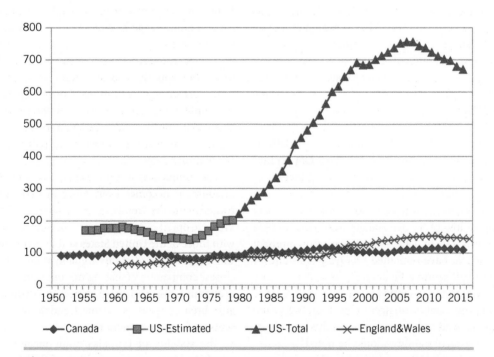

Figure 3.2 Adult Imprisonment per 100,000 Residents in Canada, the United States, and England and Wales

Note: Prior to 1980, US jail data (pre-trial detention plus those sentenced to under a year in prison) were not broadly available. As such, the US estimated rate includes estimated jail populations for this period based on the size of the jail population after 1980.

Source: Doob & Webster, 2006; Webster & Doob, 2007, 2018; Canadian data from Statistics Canada's CANSIM database; US data from US Department of Justice, 2018, and Bronson & Carson, 2019; England and Wales data from UK Ministry of Justice, 2020.

Indeed, US rates quadrupled over the next four to five decades. In fact, the scale of US imprisonment dwarfs imprisonment rates of both Canada and England and Wales. However, a careful examination of the trend in incarceration in England and Wales reveals that even in this country, the rate more than doubled over the same period. In sharp contrast, Canadian levels maintained relative stability. Indeed, rates of imprisonment in Canada changed very little, hovering around 100 (plus or minus roughly 20) per 100,000 residents for more than 50 years.

It is equally notable, however, that the overall stable trend in Canada's use of imprisonment (evident in Figures 3.1 and 3.2) does not mean there is stability in the characteristics of those who are in prison. Illustratively, there is substantial evidence that the proportion of federal penitentiary prisoners who identify as Indigenous has increased substantially since 1994. Similarly, although women constituted "only" 4.9 per cent of the penitentiary population at the end of March 2017, they represented only 2.8 per cent of the penitentiary population 15 years earlier. These two important shifts in the nature of the penitentiary population should be viewed as warning signs: Although the overall imprisonment rates might not have changed much in Canada, the rates for particular groups appear to have changed substantially.

Understanding Canadian Imprisonment Stability: The (Dramatic) Contrast with the United States as Our Closest Comparator

The comparison of Canadian trends in imprisonment with those of other comparable nations may also serve as a valuable window into the underlying explanations for our diverging patterns. We have chosen to focus on the United States. Although a similar analysis could be conducted with England and Wales, this choice is pedagogic in nature. Indeed, the United States provides the starkest contrast in terms of imprisonment trends. By extension, it offers the most effective foil in (partially) explaining Canadian stability.

In addition, the growth in American imprisonment is interesting from a number of perspectives. Most obviously, the overall increase described in Figure 3.2 reflects growth *across* the United States. Unlike Canada, in which criminal law is a federal responsibility (with the provinces being responsible for the administration of justice and only a portion of all imprisonment), US states (and local governments) are entirely responsible for most of the criminal justice system—both in making the law and administering it. The federal government in the United States has limited criminal law responsibility (and responsibility for the imprisonment of those who violate the law). In the early 1970s, federal prisoners accounted for 11 per cent of those in American prisons (not counting local jails, which house about a third of American prisoners, specifically those awaiting trial and serving sentences of less than a year). When imprisonment rates peaked at the end of the first decade of the twenty-first century, federal prisoners accounted for only 12 per cent of those serving custodial sentences (again, not including those in local jails; Webster & Doob, 2018).

Within this context, what is remarkable is that every one of the 50 states increased its imprisonment rate considerably over this period. The lowest absolute change in imprisonment (not counting jails) was for the state of Maine (increasing from 49 prisoners per 100,000 residents in 1971–5 to 150 in 2006–10). The greatest increase was in Louisiana, whose rate increased from 113 to 862. Federal imprisonment in the United States increased from 11 to 60 over the same period (Doob & Webster, 2014).

Clearly, the size of the increases across US states varied enormously, but they were all large. Further, those states with the lowest imprisonment rates in the early 1970s showed the lowest increases, and those with the highest imprisonment rates increased the most (Webster & Doob, 2018, p. 133). As such, one might suspect that increased incarceration in the United States did not "just happen." Instead, it appears to reflect something about the manner in which the less fortunate in each state are dealt with when they commit offences and are being sentenced. And, in fact, there are data that demonstrate that states with high and low imprisonment rates differ in other predictable ways. For example, high-incarceration states are more likely to have low minimum wages and restrictions on the voting rights of ex-felons (Doob & Webster, 2014; Webster & Doob, 2018). Indeed, it would seem that the use of prison also reflects much deeper notions of citizenship and an offender's status within society.

In terms of criminal justice policy, though, American responses to crime and criminals would appear to be largely rooted in a long-standing belief that crime can be controlled (if not eliminated) through criminal justice interventions. In fact, one might propose that American exceptionalism in its growth in incarceration since the early 1970s can be tied (perhaps ironically) to its penal optimism. That is, the optimism in the ability of the criminal justice system, primarily (albeit not exclusively) through recourse to prison as an instrument of effective crime policy, to control criminal activity.

American Optimism: A Long-Standing Belief in the Effectiveness of Imprisonment in Reducing Crime

For many decades, American policy would appear to suggest that the criminal justice system could reduce reoffending by those convicted of criminal offences by rehabilitating them in prison. Indeed, prison was seen as the site *par excellence* to cure or reform "lost" or "sick" offenders who would be incarcerated until such time as they were deemed to have been rehabilitated. Not surprisingly, every US jurisdiction had an indeterminate sentencing structure in the early 1970s whereby maximum and minimum terms of imprisonment might be set by the law, but the actual release was governed by parole authorities. Their decisions were essentially unregulated, since it was assumed that the paroling authorities would make valid decisions about when a person was adequately rehabilitated and could be safely released back into the community. Of course, the alternative to release is that the prisoner would remain in prison because of an administrative rather than judicial decision. But that option, too, was seen as serving the security needs of the community through selective incapacitation.

Since that time, about half of US jurisdictions have moved away from this indeterminate sentencing model (Reitz, 2012, p. 270). Equally important, the strong belief in the criminal justice system's capacity to rehabilitate offenders was also largely abandoned. This rejection of the "rehabilitative ideal" found its roots, at least to some extent, in the enormously influential Martinson Report, released in the mid-1970s (Martinson, 1974). Though its findings were somewhat more complex, it was (and still is) cited as suggesting that "nothing works" in correctional rehabilitative programming. This "empirical evidence" demonstrating that prison rehabilitation programs do not turn those who have offended into law-abiding members of society clearly undermined Americans' utilitarian optimism in the reformative properties of prison as a crime control strategy.

However, penal optimism was not destined to be abandoned in the United States. Rather, it was simply reinvented. In fact, it took the form of a strong belief in the criminal justice system's ability to reduce crime rates through brute incapacitation and deterrence. Specifically, prison was henceforth conceptualized as the ideal site to segregate offenders from society as a form of physical warehousing for as long as possible. Further, harsher penalties (in the form of longer prison sentences) were seen as a natural deterrent for those thinking about (re)offending. In brief, by turning indeterminate sentences on their head and creating long fixed-length sentences whose principal functions were to segregate and deter, imprisonment continued to be at the forefront of American responses to crime and criminals.

More importantly in explaining the dramatic increase in incarceration rates in the United States beginning in the early to mid-1970s, this new penal optimism justified, if not demanded, ever-increasing recourse to prison in the continuing belief that crime would eventually be solved. In fact, such unshakable faith in utilitarian mechanisms seemingly provides few inherent limits to the use of prison as the ultimate sanction. Further, even moral or ethical arguments were impervious to this new form of optimism. Criminals were hereafter conceptualized as "bad" or morally corrupt individuals who threatened the safety, security, and well-being of "good" people. By extension, exclusion—in the sense of the offender's complete "excommunication" from society and from the rights and protections inherent in its citizens—was justified for the good of law-abiding citizens.

An illustrative case study helps to make the point. On January 3, 1973, New York's governor, Nelson Rockefeller, explained his new approach to the use of illegal drugs with the following words:

> It is time for brutal honesty regarding narcotics addiction . . . In this state, we have allocated over $1 billion to every form of education against drugs and treatment of the addict through commitment, therapy, and rehabilitation. But let's be frank—let's tell it as it is: We have achieved very little permanent rehabilitation—and have found no cure. (quoted by Kohler-Hausmann, 2010, p. 71)

The Martinson Report was released shortly thereafter, giving Rockefeller empirical support not only to abandon rehabilitation as the principal strategy to address illegal drug use but also to advocate a new role for incarceration. Those involved in the drug trade needed to be segregated from society, and the criminal justice system was well placed to accomplish this task. Brute incapacitation became America's new saviour. As such, long prison sanctions were proposed precisely because they were believed to effectively contain—if not eliminate—drug crime. Not surprisingly, Rockefeller asked for the enactment of legislation that would make the punishment for all illegal trafficking of hard drugs a life sentence of imprisonment. As a means of ensuring that the full force of this sanction would be unavoidable, he further suggested that the law eliminate the possibility of recourse to any mechanisms that could reduce the severity of the punishment (plea to a lesser charge, probation, parole, sentence suspension, and so on; Kohler-Hausmann, 2010, p. 71).

This optimism in the ability of the state to control drug crime through sheer containment of criminals obviously neglected to consider the likelihood that an incarcerated drug trafficker might simply be replaced by another on the street. Rather, it was rooted in the simple belief that crime could be solved by locking up offenders. More importantly, this optimism was contagious, opening up the floodgates to more punitive responses to crime. In the 10 years following the passing of the Rockefeller drug laws in 1973, 48 states added mandatory minimum penalties to their drug laws (Kohler-Hausmann, 2010). Blumstein and Beck (1999) suggest that not only was the incarceration of drug offenders a major contributor to the growth in imprisonment between the early 1970s and the turn of the century, it also contributed "in an important way to the extreme representation of African-Americans in prison" (p. 54). Both phenomena, Kohler-Hausmann (2010) argues, reflect a new perception that cast drug pushers as not only "anti-citizens, but as non-humans whose fate was utterly irrelevant" (p. 82).

Canadian Pessimism: A Long-Standing Belief in the Ineffectiveness of Imprisonment in Reducing Crime

Canadian policy vis-à-vis its crime and criminals stands in stark contrast to that of the United States. For illustrative purposes, we will continue with the case study on drug crime and the role of the state in responding to it. Importantly, Canada's most prominent thinking on this issue was occurring simultaneously to the discussion of the Rockefeller drug laws in the United States. Though the use of marijuana for recreational purposes was made legal on 17 October 2018,

the most thoughtful Canadian study of its use almost certainly took place in the late 1960s and early 1970s. Predictably, it came in the form of an analysis and discussion of the matter in a Royal Commission report: the report of the Commission of Inquiry into the Non-Medical Use of Drugs (typically referred to as the Le Dain Report after the chair of the commission, Dean Gerald Le Dain).

In brief, the commissioners were not optimistic about the use of criminal law as a response to the problem of drug crime. In fact, they noted that "the effective application of the criminal law in the field of non-medical drug use is subject to many difficulties" (Le Dain Report, 1973, p. 53). After looking at the evidence that had been brought before them, the commission predictably concluded that "The rate of success with law enforcement against both distribution and simply possession (or use) is relatively disappointing . . . The actual risk of apprehension, which is the essential basis of deterrence, is not very great" (p. 54).

While the commission did not condone the non-medical use of drugs, it was concerned about the enthusiasm that some people had for "stamping out" the use of drugs with the criminal law (and ultimately the use of imprisonment). In particular, it pointed out that although prohibition might have some benefits, they were outweighed by the costs to society. These harms included creating an illicit drug market, inhibiting people from seeking treatment, distorting or limiting the messages that could be given in drug education programs, the demand that a prohibition model puts on law enforcement resources, the stigma of a criminal conviction, and the effect of imprisonment. Particularly in terms of this latter cost, the committee was clear: Prison, they suggested, "Instead of curing offenders of criminal inclinations . . . tends to reinforce them . . . These adverse effects of imprisonment are particularly reflected in the treatment of drug offenders" (pp. 58–9).

Clearly, the advice to Canada was very different from what the governor of New York and others were suggesting in the United States. For instance, the interim report of the Le Dain Commission had recommended maintaining (albeit lowering) the then-existing penalties for marijuana (for example, removing the mandatory minimum penalty for importing marijuana but still considering the act a criminal offence). However, the most notable recommendation was that Parliament repeal the prohibition against the simple possession of cannabis. Indeed, they suggested that the risks of cannabis were far outweighed by the known harms of its criminalization, particularly given that the majority of offenders were young people (Le Dain Report, p. 10).

By the time the final report was transmitted to the government of Canada (in December 1973), Rockefeller's drug bill had become law. Aside from the obvious difference between the United States and Canada, what is notable is that the Le Dain Commission saw the avoidance of imprisonment as a goal to be given substantial weight when deciding on policy regarding marijuana. Forty-five years later, in 2018, the use of cannabis by adults was decriminalized in Canada (after similar changes had been made in some US states).

The contrast between the American approach to drugs and the approach followed in Canada is important. During the 1970s and 1980s, the United States shifted from optimism that crime could be addressed through the rehabilitation of those who offended to a model based on optimism that crime could be addressed through the incapacitation of bad people and by deterring everyone else through harsh penalties. During this same period, Canadian policy never reflected American optimism that crime could be effectively addressed through the criminal justice system.

In fact, from a policy perspective, Canada's approach to crime and criminals is, in many ways, the antithesis of that in the United States. Most notably, it is rooted largely in the general acceptance that levels of imprisonment have little to do with crime rates—that is, Canadians have never held a strong or consistent belief that crime could be solved through greater recourse to the criminal justice system generally and prison in particular. On the contrary, penal pessimism—the lack of strong faith in the ability of sentencing and imprisonment to serve utilitarian goals such as rehabilitation, incapacitation, and deterrence—has been the predominant leitmotif traversing Canada's policy approach to crime since the nation's birth in 1867.

Canadian penitentiaries have been the subject of reviews and inquiries many times over the past century. Importantly, it is difficult to find any report that suggests they are very effective at either rehabilitating people or deterring potential or actual offenders (those serving sentences) from committing crimes. As such, the predominant message has generally been one of restraint in the use of incarceration. In its first report to Parliament entitled *Our Criminal Law*, the Law Reform Commission of Canada (1976) recommended the following:

> The cost of criminal law to the offender, the taxpayer and all of us must always be kept as low as possible . . . The harsher the punishment, the slower we should be to use it . . . The major punishment of last resort is prison . . . As such it must be used sparingly . . . Positive penalties like restitution and community service orders should be increasingly substituted for the negative and uncreative warehousing of prison. (pp. 24–5)

In fact, the failure of prisons to reduce criminal activity was emphasized. A year after the Law Reform Commission's report was released, a House of Commons subcommittee chaired by a future minister of justice (Mark McGuigan) was tasked with looking into the penitentiary system in Canada. Symptomatically, this document (released under a Liberal government) highlighted that despite the millions of dollars spent over the years in creating and maintaining prisons, incarceration had failed in two ways. First, it had not succeeded in "correcting" the offender, and second, it was not successful in protecting society (MacGuigan Report, 1977, p. 35).

Not surprisingly, non-custodial sanctions were recommended as a more effective means of responding to prohibited behaviour. In arguably one of the clearest statements yet of Canadian pessimism in the ability of incarceration to solve the problem of crime, the MacGuigan Report concluded as follows:

> It is apparent that the penitentiary system is not an effective means for dealing with a significant proportion of the criminality that exists in Canada. If we continue to conceive of imprisonment as a sort of universal solvent to the problems of crime in our society, we will do nothing more than repeat old prescriptions for failure.

In fact, it was strongly recommended that Canadians should only rely on the prison system to accomplish "what it is capable of doing and not be expected to accomplish the impossible task of solving complex social, behavioural and economic problems using steel bars, gas, walls, clubs, repression and isolation as its methods" (MacGuigan Report, 1977, p. 35). When assessing the impact of prison on society, it was further argued that not only the financial losses must be taken into account. Rather, the damage done to the offender's familial and social relationships, as well as to their employment future, must also be considered. Indeed, the devastating effects of imprisonment on the individual often makes it impossible for them to ever become successfully reintegrated into society (p. 36).

Nor was the message dependent on political ideology. A set of three reports—one signed by both of the ministers responsible for justice, a second focusing on sentencing, and a third focusing on corrections—were released by the Conservative government in 1990. Constituting the last major comprehensive report on Canada's (adult) justice system, this collection noted not only the importance of an integrated examination of the sentencing and corrections systems but also attempted to be honest about what was possible. At the same time, a more pessimistic view of the ability of the punishment system to reduce crime would be hard to find. As a general or overall summary of Canada's position, it was emphasized that we clearly do not currently know how to drastically reduce crime or rehabilitate all offenders. However, there are still avenues in which we can intervene. Specifically, we can seek to "mitigate the social costs of crime, punish offenders, and create programs, opportunities, and incentives for treatment for those we think might respond so that they are not an ongoing burden to society" (Department of Justice, 1990, p. 8).

This acknowledgement of the limited power of the criminal justice system in solving the problem of crime was reiterated within the context of the perceived ability of imprisonment, in particular, to reduce criminal activity. With no ambiguity, it was affirmed that "Imprisonment is generally viewed as of limited use in controlling crime through deterrence, incapacitation and reformation, while being extremely costly in human and dollar terms" (Department of Justice, 1990, p. 10).

Further, the overuse of prison was yet again condemned. In fact, we were reminded in this same document that "virtually all official reports on sentencing and corrections have declared that we rely too heavily in Canada on imprisonment as a criminal sanction" (p. 10). In particular, the report called attention to the criminogenic nature of incarceration in that it "may decrease rather than increase the chances of reforming individual offenders" (p. 8). Within this context, this formal document underlines that "We need to develop effective alternative methods for punishing and reforming offenders, and where imprisonment is used, we must better prepare offenders for safe reintegration into the community" (p. 8). As an overall approach to sentencing, the report is equally clear: "Criminal penalties should be applied in proportion to the degree of responsibility of the offender . . . On the other hand, the principle requires that punishment be limited by the requirement not to sacrifice the individual accused to the common good" (p. 12).

As Canadian governments have never, apparently, had much faith that the problem of crime could be solved through the criminal justice system, the fundamental principle of sentencing has largely been that of **proportionality**. Indeed, Canada's Criminal Code (s. 718.1) states relatively clearly that "A sentence must be proportionate to the gravity of the offence and the degree of responsibility of the offender." Notably, proportionality is also conceived as serving a limiting or restraining function. Independent of the weight that a judge might give to such sentencing objectives as rehabilitation, incapacitation, or deterrence, the resulting sentence must necessarily respect the fundamental principle of proportionality.

We might also add that the perception of offenders within Canada also restricts the type (and degree) of state response to them. In a statement made in the House of Commons in 1971, the (Liberal) minister responsible for federal penitentiaries reminded Parliamentarians that "An inmate is always a citizen who, sooner or later, will return to a normal life in our society and as such, is basically entitled to have his human rights as a citizen respected by us to the largest possible extent" (Goyer, 1971).

Further, it is important to recall that when sentencing purposes and principles were *first* incorporated into the Criminal Code, restraint in the use of imprisonment was a relatively uncontroversial part of the bill (C-41, 1st session, 35th Parliament). Though the sections have since been modified slightly, the current provisions would still appear to suggest restraint in the use of imprisonment. Section 718.2 includes two relevant paragraphs:

(d) an offender should not be deprived of liberty, if less restrictive sanctions may be appropriate in the circumstances; and
(e) all available sanctions, other than imprisonment, that are reasonable in the circumstances and consistent with the harm done to victims or to the community should be considered for all offenders, with particular attention to the circumstances of Aboriginal offenders.

Less than two years (in June 1998) after the new sentencing laws came into effect, the commissioner of Correctional Service Canada made the statement mentioned earlier, suggesting that there were too many people in Canada's penitentiaries and that they should be moved more expeditiously to the community (Ingstrup, 1998). Within this context, it needs to be remembered that most of those sentenced to prison have not been found guilty of a violent offence. In 2016–17, for example, for those courts in Canada for which data were available to Statistics Canada, only roughly 18 per cent of the custodial sentences involved violent offences. This is not terribly surprising given that only about 18 per cent of all cases in which there was a finding of guilt involved violent offences.

Stress Testing Canada's Belief in Restraint in the Use of Imprisonment of Adults: The Challenges Raised during the Harper Era

Certainly in comparison with the United States, Canadian criminal justice policy during the twentieth century might aptly be described as being rooted in penal pessimism. Successive politicians as well as numerous government-appointed bodies had little confidence that the criminal justice system (and incarceration, in particular) are well placed to control crime—either through rehabilitation, incapacitation, or deterrence. In fact, prison was largely seen as a "bad thing" whose criminogenic features are more likely to constitute a cause of crime rather than a solution to it. Further, Canadian governments repeatedly maintained that offenders remain full citizens and, as such, continue to be afforded the rights and privileges inherent in citizenship. Exclusion from society was never seen as an effective solution to crime. In brief, a strong, historically entrenched belief in restraint in the use of imprisonment was the central leitmotif guiding Canadian criminal justice policy throughout the twentieth century.

The twenty-first century, at least on the surface, would appear to constitute a break with this long-standing past. Indeed, the years leading up to as well as the 10 years in which Canada was governed by the newly branded Conservative Party of Canada under the leadership of Stephen Harper might easily be characterized as the greatest challenge to date to our belief in restraint in the use of imprisonment. There was a significant change in rhetoric during this time, in which "tough-on-crime" policies were promoted and celebrated as effective strategies for reducing criminal activity. Further, anyone who followed political happenings between 2006 and 2015 is aware that "crime" legislation was repeatedly headline news. In fact, one might aptly describe this legislative period as a virtual punishment tsunami.

By our count of government bills during the so-called Harper decade (setting aside private members' bills sponsored by individual Conservative members of Parliament that were not officially considered to be "government" bills), there were 94 pieces of crime legislation introduced into Parliament. While only 42 of these bills actually became law (including two omnibus bills, in which many bills introduced in previous sessions of Parliament were rolled into a single bill that was then reintroduced into Parliament), it is important to remember that legislative bills seem to attract the most attention when they are introduced rather than when they are passed or come into effect.

The vast majority of these bills dealt, directly or indirectly, with imprisonment. Indeed, almost all of them fit neatly into the "tough-on-crime" mantra that had been part of the Conservatives' appeal to Canadian voters. Not surprisingly, Canada witnessed a significant increase in maximum penalties for many criminal offences, the creation (or extended breadth) of several new criminal offences, and the introduction of a large number of mandatory minimum sentences—a relatively rare provision until this time. Equally notable was the virtually complete absence of any moderating forces to this type of "law and order" legislation. Indeed, the crime legislation was all in one direction: an unprecedented hardening of responses to criminal behaviour.

Within this context, it would be entirely expected that adult imprisonment rates in Canada would increase. A re-examination of Figure 3.1 (and to a lesser extent Figure 3.2) already announces the punchline. Although there has been some variation in levels of incarceration in the last 70 years, it does not appear to correlate in an obvious way with the federal party in power in Ottawa (which determines criminal law). This description would also appear to be true during the Harper decade. When this "tough-on-crime" Conservative party formed the government in 2006, the imprisonment rate was 109 prisoners per 100,000 residents; 10 years later, when they lost power in 2015, it had increased only to 112.

We would suggest that those who remember the Harper decade as a tough-on-crime era can be excused for thinking there must have been an increase in imprisonment during this period. On the one hand, the natural experiment with tough-on-crime laws being conducted since the 1970s by our American neighbours would have predicted significant increases in Canada's levels of incarceration as well. On the other hand, the Canadian prime minister himself boasted that his government had increased imprisonment and, as a result, reduced crime. Specifically, in October 2014, a year before the Conservatives lost power, Prime Minister Harper stated at a Conservative party event in Sault Ste. Marie, Ontario, that

> We said "do the crime, do the time." We have said that through numerous pieces of legislation. We are enforcing that. And on our watch the crime rate is finally moving in the right direction, the crime rate is finally moving down in this country. (Greenspan & Doob, 2014)

Notably, the then prime minister did not provide any supporting data on the implication that imprisonment ("doing the time") had increased or that "the crime rate" was *finally* moving down. But at least regarding the latter argument, it would have been easy to do so. Figure 3.3 presents the data.

The only serious problem with the former prime minister's criminological evidence is that the drop in crime in Canada started long before he became prime minister. This long-term decrease is evident in Figure 3.4.[2] The arrow marks the beginning of the Harper period.

In other words, crime had been decreasing for some time *before* Prime Minister Harper came to office, and imprisonment had, in fact, not increased substantially. It would appear that he took credit for a drop that had started years earlier and, as such, could not have been the result of his tougher crime legislation.

Why the Imprisonment Rate Did Not Increase during the Harper Decade

Harsher Political Rhetoric without Widespread Punitive Impact

Imprisonment rates in Canada did not increase appreciably between 2006 and 2015 under a government that celebrated being "tough on crime." Part of the explanation for this apparent incongruence likely resides in the actual impact of the criminal justice laws passed during the Harper era on levels of incarceration. Specifically, few of the legislated bills had a large impact on large numbers of offenders. Rather, many of the legislative changes that significantly increased the use of prison affected only a small number of those convicted.

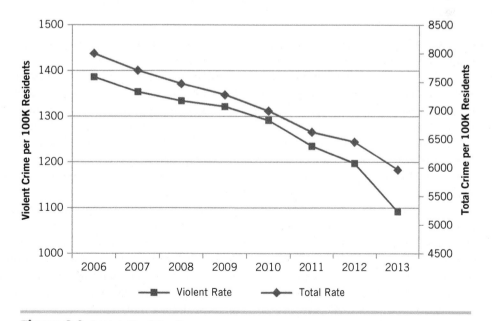

Figure 3.3 Conservative Crime Drop

Source: Doob & Webster, 2006; Webster & Doob, 2018; data from Statistics Canada's CANSIM database.

Figure 3.4 Total Reported (Non-Traffic) Crime per 1,000 Residents; Homicides per 100,000 Residents, Canada

Source: Doob & Webster, 2006; Webster & Doob, 2018; data from Statistics Canada's CANSIM database.

The "faint hope clause" is a case in point. Historically, this clause permitted those sentenced to life imprisonment for murder with a parole ineligibility period of more than 15 years the opportunity to apply to have this ineligibility period reassessed by a jury (obviously in the hopes that it would be reduced). Under the Harper government, this possibility was eliminated. Clearly, its abolition could dramatically affect those prisoners who might have been released early from prison. And, in fact, most (76 per cent) of those who had applied in the past were successful. Indeed, juries hearing from both the Crown and the prisoner had been willing to reduce parole ineligibility periods. Further, most (91 per cent) of those whose parole ineligibility periods were reduced were subsequently released by the Parole Board of Canada. Notably, though, while having a large impact this legislative change would affect a relatively small number of people. A mere 173 lifers received earlier parole eligibility between 1987 and 2017,

constituting an average of roughly six per year (Public Safety Canada, 2018, p. 105).

Another relevant example is rooted in the substantial restrictions the Harper government placed on the use of "conditional sentences of imprisonment"—a poorly constructed alternative to normal imprisonment created in the 1996 sentencing legislation (see Webster & Doob, 2019, for a discussion of this sanction). Specifically, this sentencing option was no longer available for many offences. For those offenders who would previously have been granted a conditional sentence of imprisonment (and, as such, served their time in the community rather than in prison), the impact of the reduced availability of this sanction could be non-trivial. However, conditional sentences have never been a highly used sanction. Further, restrictions on their use did not inhibit judges from using other non-prison sanctions (such as suspended sentences and probation).

Arguably more important in terms of explaining why Canadian imprisonment rates did not increase substantially during the Harper decade is the fact that other (harsher) legislative bills passed under this government would almost certainly have no discernable impact on imprisonment rates. Illustratively, the Protecting Canada's Seniors Act (which came into effect in 2012) did nothing more than add 24 words to the Criminal Code. Specifically, it now instructs judges that "evidence that the offence had a significant impact on the victim, considering their age and other personal circumstances, including their health and financial situation" (s. 718.2) is to be considered an aggravating factor. In other words, it requires judges to hand down harsher sentences when the crime is committed against vulnerable people. No judge to whom we have spoken believed this new law would make any difference, in part because judges have been instructed by the Criminal Code since 1996 that "A sentence must be proportionate to the gravity of the offence and the degree of responsibility of the offender" (s. 718.1).

Similarly, a new Criminal Code provision was enacted in 2014 in response to an incident in which a suspect, when resisting arrest, stabbed and killed a police dog. The new law made it a specific offence to wound or kill a police/military animal while it was aiding an officer. If the animal was killed, a six-month mandatory minimum penalty would apply. One expects, once again, that this legislative change would make little difference. Indeed, the man involved in the incident that triggered the new law was himself sentenced to 22 months in prison under animal cruelty laws already in existence before his offence (ss. 445, 445.1).

Perhaps the most bizarre set of harsher provisions added to the Criminal Code during the Harper decade were those relative to a subset of offences related to bestiality in the presence of a child or inciting a child to commit bestiality. Before 30 April 2008, a child was defined as a person under 14 years of age. The maximum penalty was 10 years (when the Crown proceeded by indictment) or six months (when the Crown proceeded summarily). On 1 May 2008, this offence was changed so that it covered children under 16 years of age. On 9 August 2012, a mandatory minimum of one year (by way of indictment) and a mandatory minimum of 6 months imprisonment as well as a maximum sentence of two years less a day were set for summary convictions. Finally, on 17 July 2015, the maximum penalty was raised from 10 years to 14 years.

Certainly, given these three different changes to this offence, one might naturally assume that bestiality in the presence of a child must constitute a serious crime problem in Canada. It is, of course, possible that the government has statistics that differ from those available to us. However, looking at official police data from 2012 to 2017, this criminal offence would appear not to represent a major concern. Across Canada, there were a mere *two* incidents reported to the police during this six-year period (both apparently having occurred *after* the penalties were toughened up). Notably, though, neither led to anyone being charged, much less convicted.

There were, of course, other legislative changes that would have an impact on imprisonment, though the size of the effect and the number of people affected are likely not large. The 2006 increase in the mandatory minimum penalties for certain violent offences in which a handgun or prohibited weapon (such as a machine gun) was used makes the point. Prior to these changes, there was a minimum penalty of four years in prison for committing these offences (for example, robbery) with *any* firearm (including rifles and shotguns). The Conservatives raised this mandatory minimum (for those convicted of these offences for the first time) to five years in the case that the firearm was a handgun or prohibited firearm (but not if it was a rifle or shotgun). For second offences of serious violent crimes with a handgun or prohibited weapon, the mandatory minimum sentence was raised from four years to seven years.

Two points need to be made about these changes. First, though violence is clearly a problem in many parts of Canada, relatively speaking there are not many people convicted of violent offences with firearms. Second, the commission of a robbery or other violent offence with a firearm (of any kind) has always led to fairly long prison sentences. We estimated (Doob & Webster, 2006) that when the first set of "new" mandatory minimum sentences became law as part of the 1996 Liberal firearms legislation (the law that brought in the now-defunct long gun registry), the impact on the penitentiary population would be small. As such, legislative changes of this nature under the Harper government would likely not only affect relatively few people but also have a largely muted impact.

In brief, despite the unrelenting stream of harsh-sounding legislative proposals on criminal justice matters, the Harper decade did not bring about any appreciable rise in Canadian levels of incarceration. Indeed, for a change in law to have a measurable impact on imprisonment, it would need to affect a large number of people and have a fairly large effect on them. Most of the Harper crime bills did not have both of these characteristics.

The Wider Moderating Factors of Judicial Resistance, Structural Obstacles, and Political (versus Principled) Motivation

While the legislative changes themselves obviously play a role in understanding the lack of increase in Canada's imprisonment rate under the Harper government, we suggest that this explanation might not tell the whole story. Rather, there may also be other moderating factors at play that shed additional light on why a government that advertised itself as "tough on crime" and prided itself on showing no compassion for offenders did not end up being, in practice, especially punitive.

First, Canadian criminal justice culture played an important restraining role. Most notably, some judges were clearly not sympathetic with either the apparent harshness of the new provisions or the incoherence (and interference with the process of handing down proportional sentences) brought about by the Harper government's changes. As such, they seemingly resisted legislative modifications that they saw as unjustifiably harsh or unfair by circumventing them.

As a case in point, the Conservatives restricted the credit that a sentencing judge could give to those who served time in pre-trial detention. The new legislation was clearly intended to disadvantage those who served time in pre-trial custody (see Doob & Webster, 2013). In response, courts intervened by giving creative interpretations of this law such that a just and fair sentence could still be handed down. Not surprisingly, this issue eventually made its way to the Supreme Court, which unanimously ruled in favour of a broad interpretation of one of the clauses in the new legislation, ensuring that a more fair credit could be given in virtually all cases (*R. v. Summers*, 2014).

Similarly, the Harper government made monetary **victim surcharges** mandatory even when those convicted of offences clearly would never be able to pay them. It would appear that judges were not pleased with the prospect of imposing conditions that could never be met. In response, they found innovative ways of avoiding or circumventing "mandatory" victim surcharges in cases where offenders were unable to pay. More broadly, they ensured that people were not unfairly disadvantaged.

Second, it is equally possible that there were structural obstacles to bringing about real growth in Canada's prison population. Although the Harper government may have been fully committed to introducing harsher sanctions, there may simply not have existed any obvious or easy mechanisms to accomplish this task. Most obviously, Canada does not have numerical sentencing guidelines (as is the case in some US states) that could quickly and easily increase all penalties (or at least those of a particular offence type). Further, the Harper government did not show any interest in doing a comprehensive review of sentencing procedures. As such, its move toward "harsh" treatment was piecemeal and largely ineffective in achieving "wholesale" harshness.

Equally notable, although criminal law in Canada is the responsibility of the federal government, the structure of the criminal justice system and the ways in which it is administered make it difficult to make changes. Most obviously, the divisions of responsibility among the federal, provincial, and municipal governments have meant that the government of Canada has traditionally been reluctant to legislate on criminal justice policy without a consensus. Spending money on prisons has never been particularly popular, and changes that would increase imprisonment rates (especially in provincial/territorial prisons) would be expensive.

As an instructive illustration, the Harper government set up a working group to look at penitentiaries (the Sampson committee, named after the chair, Rob Sampson). Its highly criticized report (Sampson Report, 2007; for criticism, see Jackson & Stewart, 2009) proposed that "statutory release" from penitentiaries (the automatic release, for almost all prisoners, on supervision after completing two-thirds of their prison sentence) be abolished and replaced with "earned" release on parole as the only way in which any prisoner would be released before the end of their sentence. Perhaps unsurprisingly, the government did not even introduce (much less pass) legislation that was consistent with this recommendation, likely because of concerns about its cost.

Indeed, although there is no particular reason to assume that the committee had looked carefully at parole data, they were easily available at the time and would have shown that parole (for those on fixed-length sentences) was having only a minor impact on federal penitentiary populations. In fact, Doob, Webster, and Manson (2014) suggested that the *complete* abolition of full parole for fixed-sentence federal prisoners would increase Canadian prison populations by only 4.5 per cent. Said differently, the parole board was releasing very few people on full parole. Specifically, approximately five times as many prisoners serving fixed-length sentences are released as a result of statutory release than on full parole. Assuming consistent behaviour on the part of the Parole Board of Canada, one could expect imprisonment to increase dramatically if statutory release were abolished.

Third and finally, it is equally possible that harsher sanctions (and their corresponding impact on imprisonment) were not the real goal. Rather, the Harper government may have simply used them to "look tough." Indeed, crime and punishment is an easy "wedge" issue. By appealing to the emotions of the Conservative Party's electoral base, this political pandering would likely have been effective in garnering votes.

Within this logic, it is unsurprising that this government took advantage of public concerns surrounding criminal cases that caught their attention. Symptomatically, two such cases were instrumental in changing Canada's pardons legislation. First, the possibility that Karla Homolka (former partner to and co-offender with one of Canada's most notorious offenders, Paul Bernardo) might be eligible for a pardon was used to justify one set of restrictions on the availability of pardons for those who had served their sentences. The second case involved a man who had been found guilty of serious sexual assaults that took place decades before the conviction. He received a pardon, but it was subsequently discovered that he had committed other sexual assaults (also decades earlier) that had not come to light at the time of the first set of convictions. The legislation not only restricted the availability of pardons for certain offences but also lengthened the time one had to wait before being eligible to apply. Other processes were used to dramatically increase the cost of getting a pardon.

Another indication that the motivation behind legislative change was more political than principled is that there was no attempt to even suggest that the changes being made added coherence to the punishment structure of the Criminal Code. As a case in point, it is difficult to imagine a principle that would suggest that a mandatory minimum penalty for bestiality in the presence of a child was necessary (when it was known that there were almost no cases of this offence) when many common property offences (theft and break and enter, for example) or serious violent offences (such as aggravated assault) do not normally carry mandatory minimums (unless a firearm is involved). In fact, one criminologist suggested that the pattern of changes, to use his words, demonstrated that the Harper government "really didn't give a shit about the Criminal Code and the criminal law" (Harris, 2015).

In less colloquial terms, the Harper government may simply have wanted to *look* tough. They may not have been concerned with whether the criminal justice system was coherent, principled, or harsh. *Activity* may have been what was required, not real change. Equally notable, the language used in legislative bills was often emotionally charged, and the message was frequently constructed to suggest the changes favoured the victim and took from the accused or offender. And even if it failed to favour the victim, it did not seem to matter. Similarly, the titles of many of the bills suggest the same political pandering.

As an instructive example, what might have been seen as a "technical" (and harsh) amendment was introduced by a Conservative member of Parliament rather than the government (and, therefore, was exempt from certain bureaucratic processes like cost estimates) late in the Harper government's final mandate. This bill made it considerably more difficult to get parole by extending the time period that a prisoner had to wait after being turned down and before they had the right to another parole hearing. Though it also dealt with several issues related to victims' attendance at parole hearings, one might have thought this bill would be given a title relating to parole. It was not. Instead, it was entitled An Act to Bring Fairness for the Victims of Violent Offenders (Bill C-479, 41st Parliament, 2nd session).

Looking to the Future: A New Government but Little Actual Criminal Justice Reform

In the 2015 election, criminal justice reform was not high on the agenda of any party. Though the legalization of recreational marijuana was part of the Liberal platform, few important criminal justice principles or problems were debated. Thus, not surprisingly, when the Liberals regained power in the House of Commons, little changed in the area of criminal justice. In his 2015 mandate letter to his first minister of Justice, the prime minister charged her with the responsibility of reviewing the changes made to the criminal justice system and sentencing reforms over the past decade to ensure that each provision was consistent with the objectives of the overall system.

A time traveller from 1969 might have thought that the prime minister was encouraging the minister of Justice to carry out a review analogous to that completed by the Canadian Committee on Corrections described at the beginning of this chapter. Our hypothetical visitor from 1969 would have been sorely disappointed.

The government has a website in which its progress on these promises is tracked. In January 2019 (just before the minister of Justice was replaced), the website suggested that none of those promises had been completed (fully or in modified form) but that some "actions [had been] taken, progress made" (Government of Canada, 2019). While already disappointing, it is further discouraging that the "actions" already taken are breathtakingly different from the kinds of actions that might have occurred decades earlier. According to the government as of 2019, they involved a set of roundtables in which people discussed what they thought should be done, government reviews, and various forms of consultations (including an online questionnaire). Nothing that even vaguely resembled a careful, systematic, principled, or comprehensive examination of the justice system (or even part of it) was seemingly carried out.

Completely consistent with this interpretation, 39 months into its mandate the only legislation that the government website could point to that addressed this aspect of the minister's mandate letter were some specific provisions that had been introduced into Parliament but not—at that time—passed. Clearly some legislation had passed (the legalization of marijuana, assisted dying, and the addition of the words "gender identity and expression" to two parts of the Criminal Code [ss. 318(4) and 718.2(a)(i)]). And one cannot forget the government's apparently peculiar bipartisan interest in bestiality, which translated into the introduction of a bill broadening the definition of bestiality (C-84)—an offence that accounted for a single incident of the 636,714 incidents that the police cleared by charging someone in 2017. (That bill became law in June 2019.) However, the desire for comprehensive study and reform has clearly disappeared. And imprisonment rates, as we can see in Figure 3.1, are the same as they have been for many years.

Certainly in comparison with many other Western democratic nations that have seen sometimes dramatic increases in their incarceration rates over the last several decades, Canada's long-standing belief in restraint in the use of prison continues to serve us well. Even during times in which this notion has been put to the test, Canadians have largely resisted wider punitive forces. However, it appears that broader reform will still have to wait. Certainly within the adult criminal justice system, little is likely to occur until some party does what seems today to be politically unthinkable: develop thoughtful comprehensive policy on sentencing and imprisonment. It has been many decades since any political party was daring enough to do so. Ironically, though, the task is well within our means. Indeed, Canada has shown considerable success in reducing its youth imprisonment rates (Webster, Sprott, & Doob, 2019). All that is needed is a government that has the courage to stop merely talking about restraint and start actually bringing it about. While our continuing ability to resist wider punitive pressures toward increased use of imprisonment is laudable (particularly on the international stage), the translation of our belief in restraint into actual reductions in the use of incarceration would really put us on the world (criminal justice) map.

Review Questions

1. How does Canada differ from the United States in its approach to imprisonment?
2. How have Canadian imprisonment policies changed over the past 70 years?
3. Why didn't imprisonment increase substantially during the so-called Harper decade (2006–15)?
4. How important has "party politics" been in understanding Canadian imprisonment?
5. Why has the Canadian government traditionally not favoured the use of imprisonment?

Critical Thinking Questions

1. Before 2006, there were relatively few mandatory minimum sentences. The Harper government imposed mandatory minimums on large numbers of offences. Even though a number of them have been found unconstitutional, the subsequent Liberal government repealed none of them. Why do you think this is the case?
2. The many reports urging restraint in the use of imprisonment did not generally result in explicit legislative change related to sentencing of people to imprisonment. Does this mean that they were not effective?
3. What is the value of looking at imprisonment broadly, as was done by the Canadian Committee on Imprisonment in 1969?
4. How important is imprisonment in preventing crime?
5. Why do you think imprisonment policy largely disappeared from the political agenda in the first four years following the end of the Harper decade (2015–19)?

Multimedia Suggestions

"Tory Crime Bill Cracks Down on Drug, Sex Offences," *CBC News*
   This *CBC News* article addresses the debate about the proper use of funds to address matters of crime. How do the various politicians differ and how do they reflect—or not reflect—Canadian criminal justice traditions? https://www.cbc.ca/news/politics/tory-crime-bill-cracks-down-on-drug-sex-offences-1.1003225

"Five Fundamental Ways Harper Has Changed the Justice System," Sean Fine
   This *Globe and Mail* article suggests that former Prime Minister Stephen Harper made fundamental changes to the Canadian criminal justice system. What would you say about these matters now, a number of years later? https://www.theglobeandmail.com/news/politics/five-fundamental-ways-harper-has-changed-the-justice-system/article18503381

"Lock 'Em Up and Other Thoughts on Crime," James Q. Wilson
   This 1975 *New York Times* article was written by perhaps the best known (and most articulate) academic advocate for incapacitation as a solution to the US crime problem: https://www.nytimes.com/1975/03/09/archives/lock-em-up-and-other-thoughts-on-crime-lock-em-up.html

Incarceration in America: The Inside Story
   The effects of mass incarceration are not equally imposed on all groups. In the United States, where the term "mass incarceration" was the policy, Black Americans were targeted directly: https://www.youtube.com/watch?v=Nv2lZh6NqCY

"Supreme Court Quashes Mandatory Minimum Sentences for Gun Crimes," Canadian Press
   One of the easiest ways to demonstrate being "tough on crime" is to create new mandatory minimum sentences for certain crimes. However, they do not always survive court challenges, as discussed in this article: https://www.cbc.ca/news/politics/supreme-court-quashes-mandatory-minimum-sentences-for-gun-crimes-1.3031847

Notes

1. Parts of this chapter are drawn from some of our previous writings, most notably Doob & Webster, 2006, 2013, 2014, 2016, and Webster & Doob, 2007, 2014, 2015, 2018. Preparation of this chapter was aided by a grant to Cheryl Marie Webster from the Social Sciences and Humanities Research Council of Canada. This chapter deals exclusively with adult imprisonment policies. The issues in the area of youth justice are very different (see Webster, Sprott, & Doob, 2019).
2. Statistics Canada's definition of "violence" changed in 1998; hence, comparable figures are not available for "total violence" for this full period.

References

Blumstein, A., & Beck, A.J. (1999). Population growth in U.S. prisons, 1980–1996. In M. Tonry & J. Petersilia (Eds), *Crime and justice: A review of research: Vol. 26. Prisons* (pp. 17–62). Chicago, IL: University of Chicago Press.

Bronson, J., & Carson, E.A. (2019, April). Prisoners in 2017. NCJ 252156. Retrieved from https://www.bjs.gov/index.cfm?ty=pbdetail&iid=6546

Department of Justice. (1990). *Directions for reform: A framework for sentencing, corrections and conditional release*. Ottawa, ON: Solicitor General of Canada.

Doob, A.N., & Webster, C.M. (2006). Countering punitiveness: Understanding stability in Canada's imprisonment rate. *Law & Society Review, 40*(2), 325–67.

Doob, A.N., & Webster, C.M. (2013). The "Truth in Sentencing" Act: The Triumph of Form over Substance. *Canadian Criminal Law Review, 17*(3), 365-92.

Doob, A.N., & Webster, C.M. (2014). Creating the will to change: The challenges of decarceration in the United States. *Criminology & Public Policy, 13*(4), 547–59.

Doob, A.N., & Webster, C.M. (2016). Weathering the storm? Testing longstanding Canadian sentencing policy in the 21st century. *Crime and Justice: A Review of Research, 45,* 359–418.

Doob, A.N., Webster, C.M., & Manson, A. (2014). Zombie parole: The withering of conditional release in Canada. *Criminal Law Quarterly, 61*(3), 301–28.

Gold, M. (1996, February 8). Alberta wants non-violent inmates out of jail, back to work. *Edmonton Journal*, p. A3.

Government of Canada. (1969). *Toward unity: Criminal justice and corrections*. Report of the Canadian Committee on Corrections. (Robert Ouimet, chair). Ottawa, ON: Queen's Printer.

Government of Canada. (1982). *Criminal law in Canadian society*. Ottawa, ON: Author.

Government of Canada. (1984). *Sentencing*. Ottawa, ON: Author.

Government of Canada. (2019). Mandate letter tracker: Delivering results for Canadians. Retrieved from https://www.canada.ca/en/privy-council/campaigns/mandate-tracker-results-canadians.html

Goyer, J.-P. (1971, April 20). Kingston nightmare. *Toronto Star*.

Greenspan, E., & Doob, A. (2014, December 30). Stephen Harper's scary clime bluster. *National Post*. Retrieved from https://nationalpost.com/opinion/greenspan-doob-stephen-harpers-scary-crime-bluster.

Harris, K. (2015, October 29). Liberal justice: Experts expect less punitive, more principled approach to crime. *CBC News*. Retrieved from https://www.cbc.ca/news/politics/canada-trudeau-liberal-justice-crime-marijuana-1.3292965

Ingstrup, O. (1998, June). Every day counts in our profession: Commissioner's editorial. *Let's Talk, 23*(2), 1.

Jackson, M., & Stewart, G. (2009). A flawed compass: A Human rights analysis of the roadmap to strengthening public safety. Retrieved from http://www.justicebehindthewalls.net/resources/news/flawed_Compass.pdf

Kohler-Hausmann, J. (2010). "The Attila the Hun law": New York's Rockefeller drug laws and the making of a punitive state. *Journal of Social History, 44*(1), 71–95.

Lappi-Seppälä, T. (2007). Penal policy in Scandinavia. In M. Tonry (Ed.), *Crime, punishment, and politics in comparative perspective: Vol. 36. Crime and justice* (pp. 217–96). Chicago, IL: University of Chicago Press.

Law Reform Commission of Canada. (1976). *Our criminal law*. Ottawa, ON: Ministry of Supply and Services.

Le Dain Report. (1973). *Final and Interim Reports of the Commission of Inquiry into the Non-Medical Use of Drugs*. Ottawa, ON: Information Canada.

MacGuigan Report. (1977). *A report to Parliament by the subcommittee on the penitentiary system in Canada*. Standing Committee on Justice and Legal Affairs. Ottawa, ON: Ministry of Supply and Services.

Martinson, R.M. (1974). What works? Questions and answers about prison reform. *The Public Interest, 35,* 22–54.

Public Safety Canada. (1997). Corrections population growth: Report on progress for federal/provincial/territorial ministers responsible for justice.

Public Safety Canada. (2018). 2017 Corrections and conditional release statistical overview. Retrieved from https://www.publicsafety.gc.ca/cnt/rsrcs/pblctns/ccrso-2017/index-en.aspx

R.v. Summers. (2014). SCC 26. Retrieved from https://www.canlii.org/en/ca/scc/doc/2014/2014scc26/2014scc26.html?searchUrlHash=AAAAAQANUi4gdi4gU3VtbWVycwAAAAB&resultIndex=1

Reitz, K.R. (2012). The "traditional" indeterminate sentencing model. In J. Petersiliia & K.R. Reitz (Eds), *The Oxford handbook of sentencing and corrections*. New York, NY: Oxford University Press.

Rock, A. (1995). Keynote address: Crime, punishment and public expectations. In J.M. Brisson & D. Greschner (Eds), *Public perceptions of the administration of justice* (pp. 185–94). Montreal, QC: Canadian Institute for the Administration of Justice.

Sampson Report. (2007). A roadmap to strengthening public safety. Report of the Correctional Service Canada Review Panel. Retrieved from https://www.publicsafety.gc.ca/cnt/cntrng-crm/csc-scc-rvw-pnl/report-rapport/toc-en.aspx

US Department of Justice. (2018, April). Correctional populations in the United States, 2016. NCJ 251211. Retrieved from https://www.bjs.gov/content/pub/pdf/cpus16.pdf

UK Ministry of Justice. (2020). Offender management statistics quarterly. Retrieved from https://www.gov.uk/government/collections/offender-management-statistics-quarterly

Webster, C.M., & Doob, A.N. (2007). Punitive trends and stable imprisonment rates in Canada. In M. Tonry (Ed.), *Crime and justice: A review of research: Vol. 36* (297–369). Chicago: University of Chicago Press.

Webster, C.M., & Doob, A.N. (2014). Penal reform "Canadian style": Fiscal responsibility and decarceration in Alberta, Canada. *Punishment & Society, 16*(1), 3–31.

Webster, C.M., & Doob, A.N. (2015). American punitiveness "Canadian style"?: Cultural values and Canadian punishment policy. *Punishment & Society, 17*(3), 299–321.

Webster, C.M., & Doob, A.N. (2018). Penal optimism: Understanding American mass imprisonment from a Canadian perspective. In K. Reitz (Ed.), *American exceptionalism in crime and punishment* (121–80). New York, NY: Oxford University Press.

Webster, C.M., & Doob, A.N. (2019). Missed opportunities: A postmortem on Canada's experience with the conditional sentence. *Law and Contemporary Problems, 82*, 163–97.

Webster, C.M., Sprott, J.B., & Doob, A.N. (2019). The will to change: Lessons from Canada's successful decarceration of youth. *Law & Society Review, 53*(4), 1092–1131.

Woolliams, E. (1972). Conservative justice critic, responding to the (Liberal) solicitor general. House of Commons.

PART II

Doing Time

Doing Time

John Rives and Carla Cesaroni

4

Chapter Overview

In the "golden era" of prison research (1950s–70s), prisons were at the centre of social science research. For the first time ever, social scientists attempted to explore and understand life in prison. During the current era of hyper-incarceration in countries such as the United States, we know how many people are being imprisoned and for what offences, yet we now know much less about life inside the modern prison (Simon, 2000). This is in part because access to prisoners for research has become increasingly difficult. Correctional authorities over time have become less supportive of prison research by outside investigators. Thus, much of what we currently know about prisoners and corrections is often confined to official correctional reports. The biographies and stories of ex-prisoners have therefore become even more critical in terms of understanding what it is like to "do time."

Though this chapter will include a brief summary of the rich theoretical, criminological literature on doing time, it will focus on the realities of prison life, life after prison, and being a "Lifer."[1] It will include the first author's description of the "stages" of doing time, and it will emphasize the essential alienation inherent in the experience that, for the Lifer especially, becomes a permanent condition.

Life Inside and Total Institutions

Erving Goffman (1961) contends that prisons belong to a group of institutions called **total institutions**. Goffman maintains that total institutions have barriers to the outside world that are generally built right into the physical plant, such as locked doors, high walls, barbed wire, water, forests, or moors. Other examples of total institutions could include hospitals for the mentally ill, army barracks, or a convent or monastery. Additionally, he suggests that total institutions have specific social arrangements. According to Goffman, all aspects of daily life are conducted under a single authority, with each phase of a person's daily activity being carried out in the company of a large group of others. All phases of the day are tightly scheduled with enforced activities that fulfill the single aim of the institution. There is generally a split between a managed group and a smaller group of supervisory staff. One critical aspect of total institutions is the **status degradation ceremony**, where individuals are stripped of their outside persona and forced to take on a new persona, moving from becoming an outsider to an insider. For the individual entering prison it means leaving behind

Office of the Correctional Investigator of Canada

their life as a civilian and taking on the role of a prisoner. This includes being strip-searched, issued prisoner clothing, losing personal possessions, and the end of unhindered access to the community and the outside world (Goffman, 1961).

Coping with Prison Life: A Theoretical Perspective

As Goffman suggests, life inside the prison walls should be thought of as a world set apart, one with unique cultures, demands, and processes (Clemmer, 1940). A universal attribute of prisons is the existence of a prisoner social system, often referred to as a **prison subculture**. Criminologists have attempted to determine the origins and functions of the prisoner social system, giving us some insights into prison life and the prison experience.

In 1940, Donald Clemmer first argued that every man who enters the prison undergoes the **prisonization effect**, or the process by which an individual takes on the values and norms of the prison. Inmates develop ways in which to modify their behaviour to fit and adapt. According to Clemmer (1940), those prisoners with a low level of prisonization have shorter sentences, stable personalities, and positive relationships outside of prison. They also refuse to integrate with prison groups. Those who demonstrate a high degree of prisonization tend to have longer sentences, unstable personalities, few relationships outside of prison, and are well integrated into prison groups, blindly accepting prison subculture.

Gresham Sykes's (1958) book, *The Society of Captives*, was the first to introduce one of the key theoretical models of prison adjustment: the **deprivation model**. Sykes was the first to suggest that it was the depriving conditions of the prison environment itself that caused the stress and difficulties associated with prison life and its coping mechanisms. He argued that the depriving conditions of the prison have a huge impact on a prisoner's sense of self, self-esteem, and adjustment.

Sykes (1958) was the first to coin the phrase "**pains of imprisonment**," and he suggests that all prisoners experience the pains of imprisonment by virtue of being placed in a correctional institution. He describes five specific pains of imprisonment:

1. *Deprivation of liberty:* Obviously removing a prisoner's freedom is central to prison life. Within the prison, the prisoner's movement is constricted—they must move from point to point in a military fashion and must ask for permission to leave their cell.

2. *Deprivation of goods and services:* Though a prisoner's basic material needs are meet (such as food and basic medical care), prison restricts most comforts of normal civilian life and there are few amenities. A prisoner's material possessions, which normally connect a person to their identity and sense of self, are also stripped from them.

3. *Deprivation of heterosexual relationships:* Sykes (1958) argues that being denied normal sexual contact demeans the prisoner's identity as a heterosexual male. He suggests a prisoner cannot deal with sexual needs in a way approved by society. Few prisoners are given conjugal visits. In Canada, conjugal visits are only allowed for registered married couples (including same-sex couples) or domestic partnerships of six months or more.

4. *Deprivation of autonomy:* This occurs because all daily decisions are made for the prisoner, reducing the prisoner to a state of childhood. The prisoner is subjected to a vast number of rules and commands.

5. *Deprivation of security:* Prison is an environment where no one can feel entirely safe, because prison life includes the daily pressure of being surrounded by other prisoners. The prisoner is put into an institution with men who have a history of violence and aggression. The prisoner has an understanding that they inevitably will be tested, and they have anxiety over whether they will have sufficient courage to stand up.

The prisonization effect, first described by Clemmer (1940), is described by Sykes (1958) in terms of a prison subculture. He describes two different ways that prisoners chose to adapt to life in prison. The first is to become part of the "society of captives"—to develop a cohesive, shared identity, where each prisoner is loyal and respectful to each other, where there is no friction with each other, and prisoners agree to remain oppositional to prison authorities. Under this mode of adaptation prisoners follow an understood set of norms. This is being part of the prisoner subculture. He also describes the alienative response. Under this mode of adaptation the prisoner chooses not to be part of the general subculture and instead chooses to take on a specific type of role. Sykes describes these roles as **argot roles**, which some inmates take on as a coping response to the difficulties of prison. See Table 4.1 for examples

Table 4.1 Argot Roles

Rats	Prisoners who "squeal," who betray the inmate code and who talk to officials either for personal gain or to settle a grudge or get rid of a competitor.
Square John/Straight John	Any new prisoner from a more normative social background. A prisoner with pro-social values who is positive toward staff and not involved in the inmate social system.
Right Guy or Real Men	Prisoners who do their time without confronting or acknowledging the guards; are dignified, composed, and self-reliant; are masculine; can "take it"; and do their own time.
Merchant	A prisoner who undertakes the economic exploitation of fellow prisoners by selling them contraband items and is in charge of the underground economy.
Gorilla	A prisoner who uses force to take goods from other prisoners.
Wolves	A prisoner who preys on other prisoners for sex (but are not seen as gay). They use rape as a form of power and are seen as taking the masculine role.
Punks	Prisoners who are forced into sex and forced into a feminized role.
"Fags"	A stereotype of a gay man; their encounters with other men are by choice, and they were likely gay when they came in to prison.
Hipsters	Prisoners who pretend to be tougher than they are. They shoot off their mouths a lot and show a false front and false bravery. They are always trying to get in and belong to a group where they don't fit in.

of argot roles. Sykes argues that taking on argot roles, like becoming part of the prison subculture, may help neutralize the effects of imprisonment.

The deprivation model of prison adjustment dominated most prison studies through the 1960s. A change in correctional management styles and a shift in prisoner demographics in the 1960s and 1970s, however, meant increases in inmate violence and a shift toward a new theory of adjustment. Ex-offender John Irwin and sociologist Donald Cressey (1962) proposed the **importation model** of adjustment. This model states that it is what prisoners bring into the prison that counts. They argue that prisoners' pre-prison experiences from the outside world are what is critical. According to Irwin and Cressey, inmates bring with them a ready-made set of patterns that they apply to the new situation. They argue that the manner in which prisoners adapt to prison is a function of adaptive patterns learned on the city streets and is not related to prison structure. To Irwin and Cressey, it is an individual's external behaviour patterns that predict their behaviour in prison— what one walks in with, such as past experiences, personal characteristics, and individual demographics. They suggest that there are three distinctive subcultures that are imported into the prison:

1. *Thief culture:* These are individuals who are professional and serious criminals who emphasize reliability, loyalty, coolness in the face of provocation, and moral courage. Thief culture is orientated toward a criminal life rather than the prison world itself and aims to make a sentence run as smoothly as possible, seeking out occasional luxuries to make life in prison easier.
2. *Convict subculture:* These individuals are state-raised youth with long records of confinement in juvenile institutions. They socialize within more individualistic, exploitive, and manipulative cultures. According to Irwin and Cressey, these are convicts who actively seek status and influence within the prison. Since this is the world they know, they are likely to be involved in illicit activities in prison only as a means to an end.
3. *Legitimate culture:* These are marginal, straight prisoners who hold a legitimate value system, have anti-criminal attitudes, and generally conform to institutional goals, acting in accordance with conventional, lawful principles.

Irwin and Cressey (1962) argue that prison culture as a whole is an adjustment or accommodation of these three systems within the official administrative system of deprivation and control.

iStock.com/fongbeerredhot

Additional Views on Prison Life

It is now recognized that the prison experience is too complex to be reduced to a single model and instead requires an **integrated approach**. Most modern prison scholars concede it is a combination of a prisoner's characteristics and the prison environment that shapes adjustment. In other words, both the deprivation and importation model are combined to understand prison adjustment. Arguably, prison exposes already-vulnerable people to additional risk. There is a danger, in fact, that a prisoner can become **institutionalized**, which occurs when they are prisonized to such a degree that they cannot function in the outside world.

Cooley (1992) maintains that aspects of the prison subculture still exist and that there is a prisoners' code or norms that have never gone away. These include the following: do your own time; don't rat; stay out of others' business; avoid the prison economy and stay out of debt (as that can lead to psychological intimidation or victimization); don't trust anyone; show respect to your fellow prisoner; don't be a "goof"; and don't act out, interrupt, or cause disruptions. Note that calling someone a "goof" in prison is one of the worst insults you can give someone on the inside.

According to Robert Johnson (2002), the prison is designed to be painful, but in the modern prison the pains of imprisonment are more psychological than physical. Johnson argues that corrections should teach prisoners the correct ways of coping with an inherently painful experience. He suggests that prisoners should be taught **mature coping**. Johnson (2002) suggests that mature coping involves (1) dealing with problems in the prison in a straightforward way and not resorting to denial or manipulation, (2) avoiding the use of deception or violence to address problems, and finally (3) trying to care for oneself and others.

Modern Theory on Prison Adaptation

According to Crewe (2007), there is no single pattern of adaptations to prison. Instead, he argues, prison adjustment is a complex process that must be understood through more than one framework. Prison life has been greatly impacted by the influx of drugs and gangs. Crewe maintains that there is no longer any formal organization—there is no longer any single prison norm. Instead, prison life is now loosely structured, interlocking with little formal organization or leadership, and is based on locality, religion, age, lifestyle, and prison identity. Crewe does, however, note that one thing that has remained constant is that sex offenders remain at the bottom of the prison hierarchy. In keeping with

Sykes (1958) idea of argots, sex offenders are often referred to as "skin hounds," "hounds," and "diddlers" (mostly in reference to offences relating to children).

Crewe (2007) suggests that some prisoners choose to withdraw, retreat, or regress. These prisoners, he says, focus on little beyond the immediate events around them. Their behaviour could include maladaptation, such as self-isolation and self-mutilation, but could also include less maladaptive choices, such as obsessive bodybuilding or deep absorption into art or education that allows some mental escape. Others, he contends, rebel against the prison. These may be prisoners who attempt escapes, use physical resistance, or engage in campaigns against prison conditions and practices, which sometimes include the use of violence. Finally, there are prisoners who display conformity or conversion. They are relatively satisfied with their prison experience, internalize official views, and comply with sincerity and enthusiasm to the demands of the system. Some of these are innovators, prisoners who accept official objectives but reject institutional means to obtain them. As always, there are also the manipulators.

THE CANADIAN PRESS/Paul Daly

According to Crewe (2007), the majority of prisoners find ways of coping with imprisonment that do not involve extreme resistance or complete acceptance of institutional goals. There is often support of other inmates, but within limits. Prisoners try to avoid trouble and show little enthusiasm for the regime, but they also try to avoid trouble with prison officials. Crewe notes that adaptation can include minor acts of subversion, such as group language or slang, backhand jokes, or stealing from prison supplies.

Thus far, this chapter has described prison adaptation from an academic, theoretical viewpoint. It will now turn to the first chapter author's, John Rives', experience of life on the inside and the lived reality of doing time.

An Insider's View of Doing Time

When the police finally dropped me off at the old Metro West Detention Centre that last day of January 1982, my personal transition had not just begun, it had been completed. Although I had yet to face the court proceedings that would set the seal on my life sentence, I knew that things had changed. I would plead guilty to second degree murder and attempted murder and be sentenced to life in prison with no possibility of parole for 10 years. I was a Lifer. I am still a **Lifer**. I will continue to be a Lifer until I die.

Much has been written about the prisoner (inmate, offender) culture and especially the effects of incarceration on identity and deviance. The life sentence is a powerful identifier; it is not subtle, with little variation from person to person, and it is hidden only so long as the knowledge of its imposition remains unknown. I have lived with this new identity for over 35 years—25 of those years ostensibly "reintegrated" into the community on parole. Having been told I do not fit the expected persona of the released murderer, my psyche (and parole officer) recognized a more profound reality. My person was altered in 1982, permanently and inescapably. I cannot be pardoned except through the extraordinary measure of the Royal Prerogative of Mercy, which has not been invoked for many, many years. I have acquired a new ethnicity: Lifer. When people learn of it, there is instant recognition. They treat me differently than before their eyes were opened—even if it is to express some sort of solidarity or sympathy.

I am not alone in my perception. Working in the correctional system as a LifeLine In-Reach worker with the St Leonard's Society and as a volunteer with the John Howard Society of Ontario has given me the opportunity to get to know literally hundreds of Lifers on both a professional and personal level. Within the "system" there are many labels and identities applied to prisoners. Some identities are generally embraced, such as "Aboriginal." Other labels have been actively resisted, such as "inmate." For most Lifers, the self-identification as "Lifer" takes first position. This is not to suggest that the other profound realities that shape identity, such as gender, race, or social status, have any less effect on the prison experience for individual Lifers as they make their way through the system. I have been asked to assist female Indigenous Lifers simply because I am a Lifer and, hopefully, will understand what they are going through. I should not have been surprised at this, but I was. After all, incarceration exerts such profound and often differential effects on prisoners. But prison also levels. When the doors are locked behind us, we all lose our freedom. When the guards walk the range, we are all numbers to be counted. We are housed, we are fed, we are watched. Some of us forever.

For the Lifer, this is permanent reality. But there is also a promise for the future—to walk beyond the walls and fences. Research informs us that there are four stages to a life sentence: *adaptation* to the carceral environment; *integration*; *preparation* for release; and *reintegration* into the community (see Figure 4.1). These stages do not follow a distinct timeline, and Lifers do not experience them as distinct steps. But to work one's way through the system—to access lower-security institutions and programming and ultimately to earn an opportunity to sit before the Parole Board of Canada, the arbiter of release—a Lifer will pass through these four stages.

Hope is the engine of this progression. Without hope for some possibility of improvement in your circumstances the stages become truncated, muddled, and can ultimately only lead to a path of despair. With hope, a Lifer can maintain a positive attitude under the most discouraging of circumstances, including, commonly, crushing guilt and personal revulsion. They can even begin to realistically conceive of a release in the earliest years of their imprisonment and work toward its fulfillment. Education and personal faith walks are notable in the lives of motivated Lifers.

I would like to count myself among the motivated. But despite the evidence of my actions and even

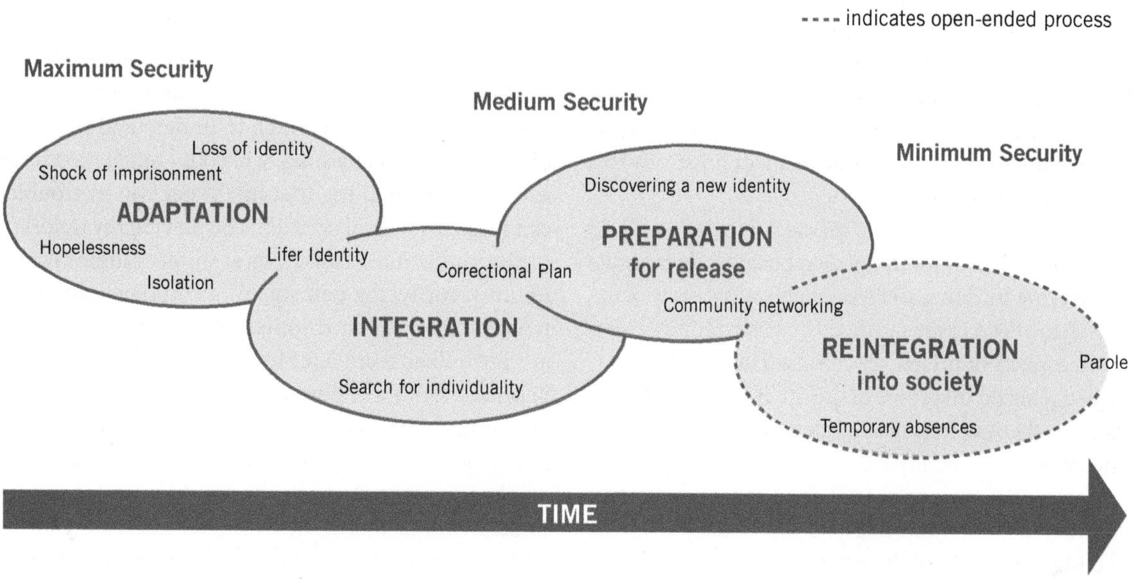

- - - - indicates open-ended process

Figure 4.1 Stages of a Life Sentence
Source: Adapted from Correctional Service Canada (1998).

significant success, embracing progress on a personal level is much more difficult in the face of a deep, abiding identity as a condemned Lifer. On reflection, I think a key to overcoming the sticky tar of imprisonment is to accept the identity in all its harsh reality and to "Keep calm and carry on." What else can you do? Well, I'd rather not think about those former options. I'm not entirely sure I have overcome. But as I once advised a close friend and client, don't beat yourself up even more because after 40 years you have failed to forgive yourself like all the nice supportive people say you should. You may never do it, but you can find a place to set that rotten jar of misery so you don't have to look at it every living moment. Be a Lifer and live.

Stage 1: Adaptation

So you have fallen down the rabbit hole. Now what? Up seems to be down, and words have unfamiliar meanings. Never say "goof" in jail unless you are willing to back up your mouth. You must adapt, but to what? Criminologists have spent a great deal of time and paper defining and debating the prison subculture. There is such a thing, but I dispute strongly that it is a criminal subculture. I, for one, did not adopt criminal attitudes and behaviours during my 10 years behind

bars. But I did learn to cope. Prison, jails, and like institutions present an inherently dangerous environment, especially to the uninitiated. Adaptation is not merely a theoretical posit to assist students in understanding the effects of incarceration. It is an imperative for survival. As in any community of human beings, culture will develop as we interact. Prison is no different and, in fact, exhibits the results of what amounts to a sort of loosely controlled venue for social interaction. It must be emphasized that the "community" of a prison is not solely composed of the incarcerated. In most modern institutions the staff (security, administration, support, health care, kitchen, maintenance, training, programming, chaplaincy, and more) will nearly equal the population of prisoners.

In truth, a newly incarcerated prisoner must adapt their behaviours to two distinct sets of expectations. There is the prisoner subculture that is founded on respect for each other and suspicion of and resistance to authority. Then there is the prison bureaucracy itself—founded on obedience to rules. Of course, respect among prisoners is a highly variable concept and subject to all sorts of contrary pressures, from gangs to personal animosity and the stress of confinement. As regards the prison bureaucracy, I soon learned that rules can be ill-conceived, ill-administered, and arbitrary. Fortunately, like most of the prisoners, the majority of prison guards and staff operate with a good dose of common sense. But common sense in Wonderland (or anti-Wonderland, if you will) has its limitations. So the question was and remains for those experiencing incarceration, how to adapt positively to a negative environment?

Right from that first night inside, I decided to (1) do as I was told and (2) mind my own business. I was quite unaware that by doing so I was establishing a way of existing that in the main satisfied the basic requirements of both aspects of prison subculture. How nice.

I also realized that some of the other prisoners in this county bucket (as we called all detention centres) were unstable and potentially dangerous. Oddly, one of the advantages that often accrete to a pre-conviction charge of murder is the notion that you are yourself unstable and dangerous. So said the newspapers, and there is no anonymity with a murder charge. I did not fully appreciate this dynamic at the time but did notice that I was given some space in the 10-cell, 30-man range and was provided soap and offered extra tobacco by some of my fellows. I did not smoke. Indeed, one of my early charitable works was to give my weekly bale to some unfortunate chain-smoker who seemed rather desperate.

There was violence on the range—some the result of angry, frustrated men packed in close quarters, some due to "differences" between co-accuseds during the court process, and some because of mere bullying behaviour. I soon took it as an axiom that one is never so far down that he cannot find someone to look down on. On a range where many of the men had mental health and addiction issues, it was not difficult for those so inclined to take out their frustrations on the weak. The illusive code (the inmate code to staff, the prisoners' code to those living it) should have mitigated these behaviours. On ranges and cellblocks where older, more seasoned cons exerted some authority, intentional or by example, life was better. More mature individuals have a vested interest in keeping their space livable and have little tolerance for "punkish" behaviour. But what was this code? Of course, it was abundantly clear the key aspect of it was not to "rat." Informing to prison staff was an absolute taboo, although self-interest and fear regularly led men to break that taboo. It also denounced certain crimes, such as sex offences and offences against children. These were not always equally applied, and "who you knew" could make a big difference on your general acceptance by the larger group.

As time passed, I began to view this essential, unspoken, and inchoate set of prisoner-driven expectations as the Three Monkey Code (my term): See no evil, hear no evil, speak no evil—with heavy emphasis on the latter. It was easy enough to understand that if you didn't see or hear anything, you could much more easily avoid saying anything that might get you in trouble. I can recall on several occasions displaying my ignorance to the authorities. In fact, later on at Millhaven maximum security, the pen squad (a combined guard and police unit) would not bother asking much of anything as they walked from door to door down a range of cells, because even if a con was inclined to say something, it was unlikely he would do so within earshot of another prisoner.

Having embraced the Three Monkey Code and understanding that it was generally operative among all prison populations, it became obvious that in most circumstances it was simply easier to "not see" than take any action whatsoever. Prisoners did and do assist during some crises, such as an overdose. However, in most circumstances the general unspoken consensus was that if it wasn't your business, it was not worth the trouble. After all, at this stage most of us were awaiting trial on very serious charges. We had enough trouble already.

Perhaps the worst advice I have ever heard shared from prisoner to prisoner was "You should get into trouble early in your bit [sentence] so you can show your parole officer how much you have changed over the years." Having been convicted of murder, I shudder to think what sort of enhanced bad behaviour would be necessary to establish a rock-bottom foundation on which to construct an "improved" self to impress decision makers. Then as now, most Lifers took a certain pride in trying to work out their own best path for doing time. So it was no contradiction that to fit into the greater prisoner group we were essentially forced into almost a hyper-state of self-consciousness. But we were in it together, and we adapted.

Stage 2: Integration

After a year awaiting trial and enduring the court process, I was transferred from the provincially administered detention system to the federal prison wherein I would serve my time. It was during these next few years I would fully integrate. At the outset, I was placed at maximum security Millhaven Institution in Kingston,

Ontario. In addition to serving the court-ordered sentence and proving yourself worthy, a Lifer must "cascade" from higher to lower security (maximum, medium, minimum) to be considered for release. As such, the phase most typically associated with maximum security is adaptation, while the issues facing a con during integration and preparation tend to cluster more in the medium and minimum security settings. However, there is much overlap and backtracking, as this journey is as diverse as the individuals taking it. Such is true for all prisoners, not just Lifers—although the former have the prospect of sentence expiration and definite release to motivate them if they so choose.

For me, it was a process of transitioning from a "straight john"—someone who came from a typical middle-class background with little exposure to Canadian justice and no experience of prison—into a con. As you will have noted, I use the terms "prisoner" and "convict" (con) interchangeably. Unless constrained by technical definition, I avoid using "inmate" and "offender." There is a reason for this. My preferred term, "con," is not only perfectly descriptive it has a strong and recognizable historical connotation. More importantly, by adding the prefix "ex" it confers a sense of progress. An ex-con is no longer under the carceral constraints of the sentence. And this notion is key to maintaining a forward-looking attitude while integrating into the prison environment and subculture. Most cons dislike the formerly official term "inmate" because it carries a notion of brokenness or sickness, such as with the inmate in a hospital or mental health facility. No one wants to be considered damaged goods, even if a certain amount of development is in order—even necessary—to earn a chance at release from prison.

Some well-meaning folks use "offender," as if this officially sanctioned terminology mitigates the stigmatization of prison. This is a pretense. Once someone is an offender, they are always an offender. My parole papers do not say I am an ex-offender: It is as if I am entirely defined by the offence for which I served time. In addition, using "offender" rather than "prisoner" denies us of a key part of our self-identification. Prison and stigmatization cannot be resisted or overcome if the reality of the situation is denied or supposedly softened by the latest mandated euphemism.

But integration is not a growing personal identification as some sort of rebel without a cause. Coping with the loss of freedom is the beginning. Locked up in a small cell for much or even all of the day during lockdowns (primarily for searches after a serious incident), subject to specific feeding (not dining, feeding) times, and always under observation is the tangible framework. The more insidious aspect of imprisonment is the inability to make decisions for oneself. Loss of choice. This can, if not actively resisted, result in the classic institutionalization where the prisoner has lost his ability to make even the most prosaic of decisions regarding his situation, even including personal care.

"It takes time to do time" is an old adage. Making every effort to exercise choice wherever and whenever possible is the key. In my case, I had the opportunity to continue my university undergraduate education while awaiting trial. This was thanks to a history professor who helped me design some independent study courses. I also became more active with my Christian faith. When I reached Millhaven, I was required to seek work or pursue an education. The snag was that the decision makers felt I had enough education and it was several months before I was placed in the prison school where I could study. A few short months later, I was handed my second bachelor's degree by the school principal. He seemed quite pleased—I was his first. Note that my family paid for this education-Correctional Service Canada gave me a place to sit. Soon after this I was accepted in to a master's program in medieval and naval history offered jointly through Queen's University and the Royal Military College, as they had professors active in prisoner support work who were willing to assist me and believed I might make an academic career.

I was active in chapel, although I was initially reluctant to leave my cell either for exercise in the yard or gym or to attend chapel service. This was out of fear. Once I grew acquainted with a few of my fellows, I became a regular for walks in the yard. On my first evening at chapel, a fight broke out between two of the guys, ostensibly over the interpretation of Paul's epistles.

Eventually upon transfer to medium security I discovered a variety of groups, including a newly formed Lifers Group. These groups had the added benefit of interaction with volunteers from the community. Literally hundreds of people volunteered at Collins Bay where I would spend the remaining 7 1/2 years of my incarceration prior to parole. These volunteers were roughly divided between university and college students, those active in their community faith groups, 12-step organizations, and those attending the various ethnically based groups.

There were no rehabilitation programs. Given the current focus on programming it is hard to conceive of a time before. Of course, everything is now considered a "program," including case management and family visits. There is less emphasis on social programs than in my day (not that these no longer exist), some of it is a practical matter. For instance, if a prisoner had a substance abuse problem in 1984, he attended AA or NA or received no treatment or counselling at all.

On the topic of "illicit substances," I was not averse to getting high on occasion with a friend who had some hash or oil papers. But it was not how I did my time. I was never comfortable with it and far too paranoid and averse to getting into trouble to make smoking drugs a habit. Others did, and still others looked to profit from the trade. And some cons used the ever-constant search for a high as a way of simply getting through another day. Endless sameness marks each and every day in prison; it is a challenge for the most sober of personalities. It was not long before I gave up even the most occasional use, even as I truly began to sense a possibility of life outside of prison sometime in the future.

I was fortunate in that I was one of a few who accessed some true psychological counselling in the early stages of my time inside. Even at that time, the psychology department of an institution was primarily tasked with risk assessments for decision makers (regarding transfers or parole recommendations) and crisis management. One particular psychologist I worked with at Millhaven had a particular interest in challenges of the life sentence and believed us Lifers could benefit from some more formal counselling. She was also transferred to Collins Bay around the same time I was, which allowed for continuity. This intervention was vital.

Through individual and later on small (three-person) group sessions, I slowly began to open up—about what I had done and why. There are no easy answers. Poetry helped, and I often shared my writing with the psychologist and others. I sought reason and discovered insight. I wished to find peace and struggled with remorse. I questioned how wretched self-esteem, repressed anger, and alcohol fuelled my previous violent behaviour. There was no cure to be found here, but I learned there is a place to rest my issue-ridden past so I could carry on with living. At times to this day something falls off a psychological storage shelf and makes a mess of my mind. But it has become a quick cleanup.

This work only lasted until our psychologist took another assignment. Yet while she was there at Collins Bay Institution, the progress I made settling my personal life had a direct impact on how I did time. I was more cognizant of how repressed anger could build up inside me. Indeed, prior to my counselling (and this sounds rather absurd) I had convinced myself that I could not get angry. That and the inhibition of alcohol make for an explosive mix. In prison I became more assertive—not in a foolhardy fashion, mind you. But along with my understanding of the basic aspects of the prison code I could more confidently manoeuvre my way through

Humanity

I was told
the punk lay bleeding
on the floor.

And though some laughed,
to break the tension
or in mocking echo of
his gurgling pleas,
most convicts stepped around his pain:
indifferent participants,
so careful not to slip
and spill their supper trays
into his steaming knifed-out guts.

Don't get involved.
Don't ever look around.

It could be you.

But would I simply go about my business?
There is some residue of action left;
I hope, I pray
through agony to outrage.

Yet, I lie
upon my bed, inside my cell,
venturing only in imagination
to the dying man.

And to avoid the risk
I turn a key,
remain entombed
for fear I'll fail another test.

Source: Rives (1989).

doing time. Being more comfortable in my own skin, I was better able to see myself as a real person and fight the alienation and separation of the environment. The group sessions also helped me access the typically hidden people behind the prisoner persona of others. Admittedly, the members of my group were friends, but this understanding certainly assisted in the ability to interact positively with a sometimes hostile group of fellow convicts. Indeed, the two men with whom I shared these sessions continue to be close friends some 30 years down the road. There were many other people in my life during these difficult years and many were, I believe, quite unaware of their significance to me.

The volunteers kept me connected. The chaplain kept me grounded in hope. But all was not well. In the middle years, imprisonment seemed to have gone on forever and would continue to do so. I stopped working out. I had to struggle just to get up and face the day. Often the guards would just quietly lock my door at work up (being called to go to work) and let me sleep. The guards who generally worked the particular cellblock where I lived—and which housed a large proportion of Lifers—were inclined to let sleeping dogs lie when things were quiet. The prisoners on this block (with first and second floor ranges of cells) were also motivated to keep things as livable as possible. In those days one had to wait to move from the somewhat wilder, often open-fronted barred cell ranges where so many younger prisoners resided. You also needed to more or less be invited by friends and certainly clear it with the senior keeper prior to any move. This sort of administration is much more programmed these days and fraught with arcane policies. But I diverge.

When I eventually discovered that I simply could not focus on my graduate studies I finally quit school. A friend found me a clerk's job in the maintenance department. Oddly enough, it was this placement behind a desk in an obscure office surrounded by maintenance shops that had the most profound positive effect on me during all my time in prison. I was treated like an employee, not an inmate. My supervisors were tradespeople; the senior clerk was the only non-uniformed

THE CANADIAN PRESS IMAGES/Lars Hagberg

Inside Kingston Penitentiary before it closed in 2013.

woman working in the main prison compound outside of the barred-off health-care area and the main administration building.

I have often been asked what the corrections service did for me. My answer is nothing. However, many of the people who *worked for* corrections did a great deal. This is common for most Lifers and prisoners serving lengthy sentences. And as often was the case, the person making the difference was in uniform. After all, the majority of our interactions with non-prisoners were with guards. I know of several men whose lives have literally been saved by guards. Now as mentioned, many other people helped me through the darkest times—family, chaplains, volunteers—but it was the day-to-day interaction with "real" people in a work environment as close as possible to those found on the street that helped me not to fall into institutionalization.

During this time, as I moved from straight john to convict, I had a peculiar advantage over some of my other uninitiated Lifers. Sure, at 24 on entering Millhaven I was actually older than most, and having been a student at the University of Toronto I was perhaps a tad more worldly, though not more mature. It was the fact that I was a very, very, straight john. It was readily apparent to anyone I met that I was not involved with anything truly criminal and knew precious little about issues that mattered in the realm of rivalries and "joint" politics. And I was polite. There were some others like me—one of my best friends to this day was also a university student when he committed murder—and we gravitated toward one another. We could not isolate ourselves, and that would not have been productive. I was not willing to seek some form of segregation, and in fact quite soon realized I preferred to be among the more potentially hazardous population than perpetually locked in a cell. We integrated into the population. We learned the ways of the institution, discovered our own paths, and helped each other when we could. Throughout this time I often reflected on something my mother told me long before: "Don't tattle on your brother!" Sound advice for a young boy with prison in his future.

Stage 3: Preparation

It is not widely known that the standard greeting at higher security prisons is "okay." Pass someone in the hall, nod, and say "okay." Passing a friend in line at canteen, "okay." I was told that this was short form for "everything is okay, isn't it?" So if you pass someone and fail to say "okay," it is a real oops moment.

As the years pile up, a Lifer feels an almost tangible desire for things to be okay. Certainly there are some who, for whatever reason, are trapped in old ways. Trouble has accumulated on them like barnacles on a whale. This is not the same as institutionalization, but it might as well be. Integrating into prison is a process. It is what you make of it. You can work to minimize the negative effects by manoeuvring through a hostile environment on its own terms, or you can immerse yourself in the human muck of it all. Of course, no one gets through completely unscathed.

During the 19 months I was at Millhaven, seven men were murdered out of a population of about 400. In addition, there were suicides and natural deaths—if any death in a cage can be considered natural. We were often locked down in our cells, sometimes for weeks at a time—occasionally with the water turned off. The four stages of the life sentence truly overlap. And the nasty thing is that you work and progress and earn the more open environments of lower security, but it can all be lost. Years later when I was working with Lifers at all levels of security, it was with a discouragement bordering on despondency that I all too often learned that a client had been "sent back." Sent back over the wall, if he had been at fenceless Frontenac minimum (camp we called it) and was caught for some infraction and transferred to stone-walled Collins Bay next door.

Progress is dangerous for Lifers. Speaking for myself, I put so much effort into moving ever forward that the thought of a return to Millhaven made me almost physically ill. Worst of all it would probably mean that I did something stupid and let everyone down. It is quite a strain to always be aware of trying *not* to be doing something stupid. This is another reason integration is so important—it teaches avoidance. Once when I was an In-Reach worker I recall an older con with a checkered institutional record recommending a younger Lifer to me with the statement, "He's a good kid. He always does what I say, not what I do." The younger prisoner eventually earned a release and is successfully on parole.

Integration never really ends so long as the prisoner remains a prisoner. Rules change, people change, and the culture changes over the course of 10, 25, or even 30 or 40 years, and the Lifer must keep current or, as I have heard it said of some elderly prisoners, "they don't know how to do time anymore." Such men look in other convicts' cells, talk out of turn to staff, or may just be irritating. During these long years, the best way to keep doing time is to keep preparing for the time when you will no longer have to: release.

Preparation is best begun early—before the Lifer has even finished adapting to his environment. I don't believe anyone can avoid adaptation even if they tried to. What they can do is avoid drowning. During the integration process, survival is the byword. But it is also during this period that all the work on the self, from addressing the criminogenic factors that brought the Lifer to prison (from alcohol to anger to family violence) to advancing education and training, must be initiated. The means to address these issues and needs must be discovered and accessed. Often the normal run of programs available will not be sufficient.

To earn the chance for a parole, a Lifer must prove to his parole officer, superiors, and most importantly the parole board that he is no longer a threat. The changes need to be made and demonstrated. In my day, it was all on the con. Even when the corrections programs were introduced just prior to my parole, Lifers were either prohibited from participating in the process or subject to endless waiting lists because priority was given to prisoners with specific release dates. No Lifer has that. Even today a Lifer who accesses programming will complete it many years before he is considered for any sort of conditional release, such as an escorted pass for a few hours. An option is to retake the programs again and again to keep them current. The best option is to continue the hard work on the self.

What this consists of will vary greatly from person to person. In my case, I wrote poetry. Yes, this began shortly after my arrest. It was therapeutic, but I did not consider it so at the time. I would bring small scraps of paper and a stub pencil with me to court appearances. I would send poems out with letters home so they could be typed up. After four years, I finally managed to get one accepted for publication in a small literary magazine, *Poetry Toronto*. I received the usual fee of a free year's subscription. In the mid-1980s I won third prize in the Salmon Arm Sonnet Contest and was interviewed on CBC radio from my parole officer's office at Collins Bay—presumably because I was the most interesting entrant from a talk show perspective despite the third-place finish. I was so nervous I had to pee several times prior to air. I had not spoken to the media after the murder, so this was my first time. In 1989, my first collection, *Dead Time: Poems from Prison* was published out of Hamilton (Rives, 1989).

Just prior to this publication, I had been granted escorted passes to spend some time in the community, initially with two uniformed guards. At that time, you had to personally arrange for the escort, and fortunately at Collins Bay there were four guards who had stated that they were willing to escort Lifers. These four (three men and one woman) were experienced hands—they also knew that Lifers were the easiest and least risky prisoners to take outside. For Lifers, actual tangible reintegration is the program for release. After so many years I needed to go slow. The guards provided a comfort zone for me during these early passes. I was beginning a process that was the purported culmination of my career as a Lifer.

Stage 4: Reintegration

Later on, once the parole board had granted me unescorted temporary absences (UTAs) I was faced with making most of my own decisions. This was not easy. I had to report to the community parole office: I didn't know where to go. I had to report to the police: same. I was falling out of the rabbit hole, and it was just as alien. I was making the first real steps into the community. I was eager and, as it turns out, better prepared than I had thought.

For all prisoners, but especially Lifers, returning to Canadian society at large consists of distinct steps. Escorted passes, which technically can be considered right from the beginning of the given sentence, lead to unescorted passes, which leads to day parole (where the parolee is out full time in the community but is strictly required to reside at a halfway house) and finally to full parole, which is as far as legislation permits. Each step requires careful decisions (the last three entirely by the parole board) and is subject to strict conditions that vary according to the needs and risks of the individual prisoner. In addition to the lengthy list of standard conditions, such as remaining in Canada, on full parole I had additional requirements to abstain from alcohol and seek psychological counselling as recommended by my parole officer. I have long since had both conditions removed by application to the parole board.

This should be the part where I write about my release on day parole. I was not released on day parole. I also did not "cascade" any further to a lesser security institution. I continued taking UTAs from medium security Collins Bay. It was a time in corrections where policy was being implemented to make every institution a releasing institution, in part to reduce the excessive and disruptive number of transfers as prisoners cascaded down on their way to release. As far as I have been able to ascertain, I was the first Lifer to be granted UTAs from medium security and the only Lifer to be released on full parole from this same institution—at least in Ontario. Other Lifers did get passes and even day parole; the current process demands a slower transition and often lengthy stays at minimum security. Everyone must prove themselves at every step.

During my UTAs I was spending 12 hours every Sunday at a local Anglican church and with the priest's family. Upon my release on full parole, I resided in their home. This was the fruit of my efforts during integration and plans during preparation for release. The network of friends and supporters I had developed during those years allowed for a more fluid transition into the community. I had community, where most prisoners do not. Just prior to my release on February 1, 1992, my second book was published. There were book launches and interviews. Former volunteers and friends were with me. This greatly reduced the sense of otherness this attention generated. I was never just a poet reading from his book; I was Lifer at a local bookstore. Given that two of the key objectives for reintegration are to combat alienation and stigmatization, being a poet on the loose posed challenges. At least I wasn't leading a secret life.

I found clerical work at the community warehouse for the prison industries (CORCAN). This helped, not just as regards employment and earning a wage, but also because it was a safe place emotionally. Everyone knew where I had recently been, and because of the outstanding staff, most of the former prisoners could feel a sense of normalcy at work.

Eventually, I began my work with the not-for-profit LifeLine In-Reach of St Leonard's Society and spent 20 years working to assist Lifers through the four stages. I represented over 600 Lifers and even a few others at panel hearings before the parole board. The vast majority of these hearings resulted in favourable decisions.

I am a Lifer. I cannot in all honesty state that I am reintegrated. Parole itself is not onerous. I see my parole officer every three months. Due to my dual US/Canada citizenship, I have even travelled to the United States—where technically I was not on parole for the duration of the visit. About 10 years ago Canada made me surrender my passport because of new policies regarding those required to remain in the country. I am not free. I carry the prison, and all it has meant, within me. I don't let it be generally known, but every once in a while a closer friend will let the cat out of the bag, "John writes poetry." As my stomach reminds me of my place, I say to my new friends, "My first book was titled *Dead Time: Poems from Prison*." Then they ask me what was I in for . . . and my shadow lengthens.

Review Questions

1. What is meant by "total institutions"?
2. What is the definition of prisonization?
3. What are the two main "classic" theories of prison adjustment?
4. What are the five "pains of imprisonment"?
5. What theory do we now know best describes prison adjustment?

Critical Thinking Questions

1. What aspects of Lifer John Rives's description of doing time seem to fit with the classic prison theories and studies?
2. How do you think a Lifer's experience would differ from that of other prisoners?
3. What aspect of doing time would be hardest for you?
4. What do you think we could be doing to help prisoners deal with the pains of imprisonment and prison adjustment?

Multimedia Suggestions

State of Incarceration
CBC documentary on the state of incarceration: https://www.youtube.com/watch?v=ihMTueI1lag

Inside Canada's Prisons
CBC News Big Picture Special taking a look inside Canada's prisons: https://www.youtube.com/watch?v=1GbMsNap0_0

"What It's Really Like to Spend Time in a Canadian Prison," Karim Martin
This VICE article provides a first-person account of life inside Canada's prisons: https://www.vice.com/en_ca/article/bn3bdw/what-its-really-like-to-spend-time-in-a-canadian-prison

Note

1. Life imprisonment in Canada is given upon conviction of certain offences (such as murder) that have an indeterminate length and a parole ineligibility period of between 7 and 25 years depending on the crime. It should be noted that though a Lifer may be paroled, they remain under the control and supervision of Correctional Service Canada for the rest of their lives.

References

Clemmer, D. (1940). *The prison community*. New York, NY: Holt, Rinehart & Winston.

Cooley, D. (1992). *Victimization behind the walls: Social control in male federal prisons*. Ottawa, ON: Research and Statistics Branch, Correctional Service of Canada.

Correctional Service Canada. (1998). *Implementing the LifeLine concept: Report of the task force on long-term offenders*. Ottawa, ON: Government of Canada.

Crewe, B. (2007). The sociology of imprisonment. In Y. Jewkes (Ed.), *Handbook on prisons* (pp. 123–51). Portland, OR: Willan Publishing.

Goffman, E. (1961). *Asylums: Essays on the social situation of mental patients and other inmates*. New York, NY: Anchor Books.

Irwin, J., & Cressey, D.R. (1962). Thieves, convicts and the inmate culture. *Social Problems, 10*(2), 142–55.

Johnson, R. (2002). *Hard time: Understanding and reforming the prison*. Belmont, CA: Wadsworth Cengage Learning.

Rives, J. (1989). *Dead time: Poems from prison*. Hamilton, ON: Mini Macho Press.

Simon, J. (2000). The "society of captives" in the age of hyper-incarceration. *Theoretical Criminology, 4*(3), 285–308.

Sykes, G.M. (1958). *The society of captives: A study of a maximum security prison*. Princeton, NJ: Princeton University Press.

Correctional Work

Negotiating Vulnerabilities While Providing Control and "Care"

5

Rosemary Ricciardelli and James Gacek

Learning Objectives

After reading this chapter, you should be able to:

- Define the term "correctional officer" and explain how it is different from other concepts, such as "guard" or "keeper."
- Outline the major considerations of the correctional officer role in provincial/territorial and federal prisons.
- Speak to the nuances of working as a self-identifying male in an institution housing adult male prisoners.
- Explain the diverse challenges faced by self-identifying women working in corrections with adult prisoner populations of any gender.
- Provide insight into the realities shaping the mental health and well-being of correctional staff in Canada.
- Explain the diverse challenges and vulnerabilities correctional officers experience in their occupational role.

Chapter Overview

Internationally, as well as in Canada, contemporary prisons are located on low-value properties, often geographically and socially isolated spaces, far removed from urban centres and accessible public transportation (Pratt, 2013a; Ricciardelli, 2014a). In response, prison work and living conditions are only notionally acknowledged or recognized by citizens. Moreover, with prisons being in isolated locations, the needs of both prisoners and staff remain unnoticed by citizens—citizens who "have come to expect such institutions, and all the connotations and symbols they carry with them, to be hidden away out of sight" (Pratt, 2013a, p. 90, 2013b; Ricciardelli, 2014a, 2014b). Although scholars have considered the implications of such practices for prisoners and, in some cases, their families, the implications for staff are largely ignored, despite the necessary role that correctional officers hold within prisons. Departing from the necessary and valuable focus on prisoners and releases, in this chapter we turn our attention to the institutional prison staff, specifically correctional officers, and what it means to engage in correctional work.

Introduction

The work of correctional officers, as put forth by **Correctional Service Canada** (CSC), is to "contribute in diverse and significant ways to *Changing Lives and Protecting Canadians*" (CSC, 2012; emphasis in original). Although correctional officers working in federal prisons have in their custody individuals sentenced to a minimum of two years, officers working in the provincial and territorial systems work with those either sentenced to a maximum of two years less a day or persons detained or remanded into custody. In essence, nearly every prisoner who goes to federal custody starts in provincial or territorial custody. Moreover, in any province or territory without federal prison facilities, including Newfoundland and Labrador, Prince Edward Island, Nunavut, Northwest Territories, and Yukon, federally sentenced prisoners may be granted permission to serve their sentence in a provincial or territorial facility (Department of Justice and Public Safety, 2014). Thus, provincial and territorial correctional officers have experience working with many different prisoners who have diverse charges, convictions, and security classifications.

In this chapter, we draw on international scholarship yet maintain a focus on correctional officers in Canada. After unpacking the nuances of the **correctional officer role**, we reflect on the orientations of correctional staff, first more generally and then those explicitly of correctional officers. We introduce the research from which the words of the correctional officers that lace the chapter are derived, and then turn to the occupational experiences of those working within provincial as well as some territorial prisons. We show how correctional officers must learn to negotiate competing mandates of "care," "control," and self-preservation while operating in contexts marked by perpetual uncertainty. We explore the differences in working in adult male versus adult female environments and suggest that correctional work, particularly in prisons housing self-identifying women, entails a considerable amount of emotional labour that is riddled with physical, personal, and legal vulnerabilities. Overall, our purpose in this chapter is to provide the reader with insight into the complex nature of the correctional officer role and the multifaceted experiences that inform officers' work experiences, and to direct attention to the well-being and needs of correctional staff.

However, first, Ricciardelli (Rose) would like to thank the over 150 men and women who have shared their stories with her over time. In addition, she is grateful and indebted to the hundreds of correctional service employees, provincial and federal, who continue to share their stories and shed light on what it means to engage in correctional work—the occupation involves care and consequences, pain,

hurt, and, more than anything, hope. She reiterates that it remains an honour and privilege to listen to and work alongside the many people she has met and learned from along the way.

The qualitative data presented in this chapter draw from the first 100 interviews Ricciardelli conducted with correctional officers between 2011 and 2014; the total sample was over 150 correctional officers with experience working in different prisons across most provinces and territories. Recruitment of officers for participation varied depending on whether the provincial department overseeing correctional services was able to provide support for the project. When departments were supportive, an email informing officers about the study was circulated through the employee listserv that notified officers about when Ricciardelli would be onsite to meet with interested officers. Once she was onsite, word-of-mouth recruitment prevailed; participants spoke of their experience with colleagues who also came forward to participate. In essence, the sample was purposive, including processes consistent with both convenience and snowball sampling. Moreover, the ability to do interviews and pass time in the institutions also provided an ethnographic experience, allowing familiarity with the different prisons, processes, people, and correctional work. In essence, Ricciardelli was able to experience how conditions of confinement are reflected in conditions of employment.

The interviews were semi-structured in nature. Although an open-ended guide was available during interviews, it was used only to check that all topics of interest were discussed. Interviews always followed the conversational paths put forth by the interviewees and ensured ample opportunity existed for the interviewee to be heard as they talked about their own experiences within the correctional officer role. On average, interviews lasted an hour; however, some were upwards of three hours in length.

As reported elsewhere (see Ricciardelli, 2016b, 2019), 60 per cent of the participants self-identified as male and 40 per cent as female, and their ages ranged from 20 to 61. Almost all the participants self-identified as white, with one participant self-identifying as white and Indigenous. Of course, this does not mean that all provincial and territorial correctional officers are white, but with some empirical support it can be reported that white officers are overrepresented in correctional work. The implications of over-representation should be an area of future inquiry, although this could also be a limitation of the study tied to the provinces in which the sample was drawn (although we do not feel this is likely, we must not discount the possibility). Participants' self-identified ethnic or racial backgrounds, as well as their education profile, are outlined in Table 5.1.

The participants had experience working with adult prisoner populations, including in correctional centres (with remanded prisoners, see Chapter 2), in jails, and in prisons that hold only prisoners sentenced to a maximum of two years less a day. Years of experience working in prison ranged from 6 months to over 25 years. Female officers had worked with women (*n*=26), men (*n*=35), and with male and female youth prisoners (*n*=33). Of the male officers, conversely, 11 had worked with adult women, 24 with youth females, 56 with adult males, and 27 with youth males.

All participation in the study was voluntary, and ethics approvals were awarded from diverse university ethics boards as well as ministries. Informed consent was confirmed before each interview, and the transcribed interviews were coded in NVivo and analyzed using an emergent theme, a semi-grounded approach that included both "a priori coding" and grounded processes (Charmaz, 2006). When doing research in a prison with staff, it is near impossible to guarantee anonymity, despite best efforts and intentions (see the box for details). We have taken the appropriate steps to ensure confidentiality here. It should be noted that the words of participants in the included narratives are edited for grammar and readability, although edits are minimal.

The Correctional Officer

When discussing the correctional officer occupational position, terminology, which can vary internationally, must be respected. For instance, in Canada and the United States, those working on the front line in prisons are referred to as "correctional officers," which as an occupation falls within the broader category of **peace officers**. In the past, correctional officers in Canada were referred to as "keepers"; however, such terminology is no longer used either officially or unofficially. In the United Kingdom, the term "prison officer" rather than "correctional officer" is standard. Although there is contention around the term "correctional" in the job title, since officers are not necessarily "correcting" a person or behaviour in their daily activities, it cannot be substituted with the even more inaccurate term "guard." "Guard" is deficient and inappropriate, and may even be interpreted as offensive. Correctional officers have explained that they are not "guards"—they do not stand guard over a person, place, or object. They are trained individuals who provide a service to Canadians. Indeed, employment positions including "correctional service officer, prison guard, prison officer, and correctional officer" fall within the Canadian National Occupational Classification (NOC) 4422, meaning they are in the category of "sales and service" occupations.

As peace officers, correctional officers' occupational responsibilities include working to "ensure the safe, secure and humane custody and control of offenders" (CSC, 1992). To this end, they are tasked with "problem solving . . . admitting, supervising, and discharging offenders—along with regular inspections and maintaining overall security" (Correctional

Table 5.1   Distribution of Participants' Self-Identified Ethnic/Racial Identities, Educational Profiles, and Institutional Work History

Variable	*n*
Self-identified ethnic/racial identity	
Black	0
White	99
White/Indigenous	1
*Educational profile	
High school	3
Some college	1
College diploma	77
Some university	22
University degree	25
Post-graduate degree	1
**Institutional Histories	
Maximum security	55
Medium security	58

* Some participants had both a diploma and some university education or were working toward completing their degree.
** Some participants had worked in multiple prisons with diverse or consistent security classifications.

Conducting Research with Correctional Staff and in Institutions

Doing research with correctional staff can be challenging for many different reasons. For example, the prison environment itself is riddled with notions of being surveilled for staff (as well as prisoners) given the constant public scrutiny as well as institutional cameras that track one's every move. So when conducting research in a prison with staff, it remains difficult to guarantee anonymity for participants. While confidentiality can always be secured and maintained in the data and each interview can be anonymized (in other words, pseudonyms are used in place of real correctional officer names, places, and institutions), when interviewing onsite, it may not be possible to ensure participant anonymity for a few different reasons. Most obviously, even if the interview is conducted in a room off camera, the pathway to that room will ensure the interviewee and

interviewer are recorded on camera entering and exiting the space, and often a swipe card or an officer posted at control will open and close the doorways (thus controlling movement), which has the latent function of documenting the onsite locations of each person in the facility. In addition, to interview an officer on shift, another officer will have to replace them in their duties (for example, on a unit), so supervisors and management likely have a role in coordinating the shift coverage for participants. Thus, ethically, when doing such work it is invaluable to be honest and explain that although confidentiality is ensured, anonymity simply is not; being clear in this regard is a central part of the informed consent process and necessary to manage expectations. Nonetheless, in Ricciardelli's experience, this has never been a deterrent to staff participation.

Services Nova Scotia, 2014, p. 4). In an ideal sense, the correctional officer would be tasked with ensuring the prison environment is open to prisoner "**rehabilitation**," although what this means is largely ambiguous and near impossible to actualize (see Maruna, 2012, for insight on the contentions around the concept of prisoner rehabilitation). Nonetheless, correctional officers are prisoners' line of contact with people both within and outside the institution, from service providers to legal representation to family and friends (Ricciardelli, 2014b; Ricciardelli & Gazso, 2013; Robinson, Porporino, & Simourd, 1993). Officers also provide basic and legally entitled material necessities to prisoners in some institutions, such a toilet paper, a change of clothes, and so on. They facilitate prisoner access to health and dental care when requested, phone calls, and visits; record reports on prisoner actions (or inactions); monitor progress; and investigate security concerns or possible institutional infractions.

Officers are obligated to provide lifesaving interventions and do so when required. In their occupational role of care, custody, and control, officers must navigate the complexities of the mental and physical states of prisoners while also navigating their own occupational

stressors and those of their colleagues. Throughout their work, officers must also remain professional and treat all those in their custody consistently, humanely, and with respect, despite their personal ethics, morals, or knowledge of the reasons for which a person is in custody. The practice of disassociating a prisoner from their crime is something that is learned over time, as most officers develop little interest in and even avoid, to the best of their ability, learning about the criminal activities leading to a person's incarceration (see Ricciardelli, 2019).

Undeniably, the officer role is complex insofar as each officer follows all federal laws pertaining to officers of the peace but also must abide by provincial or territorial laws and institutional policies (which can sometimes be a bit contradictory):

[Although] given extensive powers, peace officers are compelled to exercise such powers lawfully. They must act on reasonable grounds, without abuse of their powers; furthermore, the power to act is in some instances coupled with an obligation to act, and peace officers can be held criminally responsible for a failure to intervene in certain situations. (CSC, 1992)

To provide some additional context here, officers engage regularly in behaviours that would never be performed legally in society (for instance, routine strip searches of prisoners). Thus, such behaviours are performed with strict regulation and adherence to policy. In the case of use of force, an officer can and at times must use force, but if the use of force is found to be excessive (see s. 26 of the Criminal Code), the incumbent can be investigated, charged, and found criminally liable. Another example is that an officer, without a reasonable justification, who fails to suppress a riot can face up to two years in prison (see s. 69 of the Criminal Code), while someone who wilfully helps a prisoner escape can be sentenced to a maximum of five years (see s. 147 of the Criminal Code). Thus, officers are accountable for every action or inaction in which they engage.

No differently than the prisoners in their custody, correctional officers' actions are subject to scrutiny and monitoring. In a confined space with 20, 30, or even 60 prisoners, one or two officers, despite best efforts, would not be able to stop a riot or negate collective and organized misconduct. Thus, the goodwill of prisoners is key to correctional officers' ability to perform their occupational responsibilities without conflict, turmoil, or repercussions of any sort.

Jake, a 37-year-old self-identifying male correctional officer, had worked in secure-custody facilities for 14 years when interviewed. He shares how working with incarcerated men, women, and youth has shaped him and his views of society. Married with children, Jake's career trajectory started with a position in an open-custody youth facility and later moved into provincial correctional centres. He reflects on what he values in his co-workers and on the mundane and unusual realities of his job:

This job, there is stress, shift work, the clientele, the fact that you're going to have to redirect people that don't want to be redirected; you have to take orders from supervisors. It's pretty flexible, you can start a shift in the morning and you can be in [another city] at noon, and [another city] by two . . . The hours can be long, the hours can be short. I come to work every day, now I'm a supervisor, so basically I don't deal 100 per cent with the clientele all the time, I deal mostly with staff issues . . . [and clients'] misbehaving. Other than that I do rounds, I do all the roster work, I look after the day-to-day operations and whatever else needs to be done. And I look after public safety . . .

I started when I was quite young, I was like 21 or 22, so the whole time I was lucky. I didn't want to be a police officer, I just didn't . . . Within a month I had to basically become a good actor; I'm still a good actor, I can flip a switch and become a completely different person and turn it off. They didn't have to know that though, so I had to toughen up and grow a sack, which I did very quickly. You had to or you couldn't work here . . . [Prisoners] want to feel safe. They want to have someone firm, fair . . . I had that advantage. They respect it 100 per cent, which makes my job a lot easier.

Ricciardelli then asked, "Do you feel you've changed since you've started working in corrections?"

Yes. My compassion level, I say that yes and no it has, but I find I have to remind myself . . . You almost have to remember to be empathetic, or "okay, this is the point where I have to feel bad." So when I tell people stories, they're like "that's crazy," but that's what we do . . . Just with what we have to deal with every day; it's all negative. In order to remain positive, we have to do a lot of things. Like I said, I come to work I demand positive; if someone says something negative to me I come back with something positive. Therefore, it washes their negative. "Don't be negative around me; I don't want to hear it." I don't complain much and you can ask my wife how often I go home and complain. I did once or twice, and once was a staff-related issue, absolutely nothing to do with our clientele . . . [I do worry about] a staff member being assaulted and hurt. I don't think I was ever too much of a target. I'm not an aresehole, no one's trying to get past me to get out, or something like that. I'm pretty easy, firm, fair, and easy to get along with. I don't think I would be that arrogant guy, "I want to stab that!"

Correctional Officer Orientations: Values Shaping Occupational Practices and Interactions

In any prison and on every unit, prisoners and correctional officers (as well as management and policies of governance) shape the environment (Crewe, 2009; Liebling, 2004; Sparks, Bottoms, & Hay, 1996); officers enact and enforce informal and formal behavioural guidelines for prisoners and for staff. It is the occupational orientation of officers, which range from **liberal–humanitarian** to punitive, each informed by individual values and moral positioning, that underpin how officers' actions are interpreted. The latter, punitive orientations include officers who engage in strict monitoring and feel that consequences (even punishment) are necessary to change behaviour (see Pratt, 2008a, 2008b for more details), while the former, liberal–humanitarian orientations are based on interest in humane conditions of confinement and the positive treatment of those in custody (for example, rehabilitative ideals).

International scholars have empirically and theoretically unpacked the role orientations found across correctional officers and managers, which appear to fall somewhere on a continuum between care and control (Crawley, 2004; Farkas, 2000; Klofas & Toch, 1982; Rutherford, 1994). For instance, in state prisons in the United States, Farkas's (2000) research revealed that the orientations of the officers interviewed were forced negotiations with prisoners, enforcing rules, and keeping colleagues safe. In the United Kingdom, Crawley (2004) developed a typology that organized correctional officers into either "black-and-whiters" (rule-abiders), "give-and-takers" (rule-benders), and "care-bears" (those oriented toward helping prisoners). Almost a decade prior to Crawley's scholarship, Rutherford (1994) put forth a typology of correctional officer orientations that included three "working credos": (1) punishment, (2) humanity, and (3) efficiency. Each credo in his typology was focused on how officers effectively managed those in custody, despite if their persuasion was harmonious or punitive. More recently, and in what we consider seminal work in the area, Crewe and Liebling (2012) put forth their empirically and theoretically founded typology for conceptualizing the orientations of correctional managers. They described typologies that included, but are not limited to, those who were "alienated," "managerialist," "dualist," and "idealist." Their typology served to present "an identifiable 'liberal' and/ or 'humanitarian' position in contemporary practice" (p. 2) and is adapted in the work of Valerie Braithwaite (1998b).

Braithwaite (1998b) looked at how perceptions of the "other" in society shapes value orientations to propose that security and harmony values underpinned the political values (that is, voting behaviours) of citizens in the United Kingdom (see Crewe & Liebling, 2012). Explicitly, Braithwaite argues that harmony-based orientations are directed toward living in consensus with "others," while security-based values are more individualistic and directed toward protecting oneself. Yet she also noted that some people, who she referred to as "dualists," can and do take on both harmony and security orientations simultaneously as they strive to find a balance between both positions. Different from "dualists" for Braithwaite were "moral relativists," who she found had a weaker commitment to both harmony and security—they were more prone to follow their individualistic interests (Braithwaite, 1994, 1998a).

Crewe and Liebling (2012) applied Braithwaite's work, specifically her concept of the "dualist," to prison managers whose "approaches to the task of governing . . . are linked to personal and biographical characteristics, as well as formative experiences during careers. Underlying them are distinctive visions of the moral status of offenders, and different conceptions of the means and ends of prison work" (p. 4), the idea being that punitive and liberal–humanitarian values both exist, often simultaneously, among prison staff. Crewe and Liebling (2012) argue that prison managers with a harmony orientation to their work employ a social-justice professional practice rooted in consensus with prisoners, which they contrasted with prison managers whose approach is security oriented, which is rooted in strict and authoritative professional practices toward prisoners and always "prioritise[ing] internal order" (p. 4). Overall, prison staff orientations of whatever persuasion shape their occupational behaviours and thus interactions with the prisoners under their supervision.

Although Crewe and Liebling's (2012) typology was focused on the orientation of prison managers, their findings present an orientation that can apply to the working orientations of correctional officers as well. Consistent with their central findings, Ricciardelli (2016a) found that correctional officers, in light of the occupational mandate, cannot be either exclusively harmonious or exclusively security-focused in their orientation in Canada— they are responsible for providing care, custody, and control. Thus, correctional officers are largely dualists; however, where they fall as dualists is flexible, albeit favouring harmony or security. In addition, she also incorporated a "punisher" orientation, adapted from Rutherford's (1994) "punishment credo." The punisher orientation, although rare, requires acknowledgement because in select cases officers have expressed a disdain, even loathing, toward prisoners that will negatively impact their interactions with those in their custody. Overall, officers will be dualists who lean more toward either harmony or security, moral relativists, or, rarely, punishers. See Table 5.2 to view the full adapted typology.

Among correctional officers, harmony and security orientations coexist; they complement each other as well as support the growth of the other (that is, security creates harmony, while harmony creates security). Of course, the punisher orientation, although exceptionally rare, promotes neither harmony nor security; it pushes boundaries and encourages unpredictability and uncertainty for prisoners and staff. Officer orientations can change over time with personal experience and occupational tenure, but orientations will always shape experiences on the job, including those of prisoners and of their colleagues. Although orientations may change, an officer must always navigate competing occupational demands (Dignam & Fagan, 1996; Hayes, 1985; Sorensen, Cunningham, Vigen, & Woods, 2011).

Table 5.2 Typologies of Prisoner Interpretations of Correctional Officer Orientations

Category	Subcategory: Description
Secure dualist: "security" oriented	Operators: Strong and experienced managers who are highly skilled in operational terms with forceful personalities (often found in poorly performing prisons, where they are tasked with challenging difficult staff cultures).
	Managerial-Entrepreneurs:[a] Those of a younger generation who either tend to simplify the management task or are energetic, confident, and even effective "ideas men" focused on smoothly appeasing senior staff. Some are "technicists," who are particularly focused on and adept at the technical details of the job. They can also be "risk-takers" (impulsive) and sometimes overly optimistic. Managerial-entrepreneurs are driven by "performance" and committed to due process and decency.
Harmonious dualist: "harmony" oriented	Moral dualists: Highly competent, intelligent, and operationally astute, they seek to balance their value priorities and their management means. Their focus is on performance more broadly, and they grasp the wider purpose of performance targets (e.g., these are not simply to impress senior staff, but also to aid prisoners). They have a clear moral direction that is not "one-sided" such that they are sensitive to the dynamics of power and the plight of the individual prisoner. They see order and targets as being for other things; thus, institutional security and prisoner–officer relationships become mutually reinforcing rather than being in conflict.
	Idealists: Less pragmatic than their colleagues (of any orientation), they are thinker-speakers or value intellectuals. Some are even uncomfortable exercising or wielding power as well as with their own position of authority, where they can impose punishment or consequences.
Moral relativists	Moral relativists:[b] They are ambivalent dualists, without a strong harmony or security persuasion. The moral relativist is approaching retirement and/or has lost interest in the job. Some constitute a more toxic "traditional-resistant" subgroup who are indifferent or disparaging toward prisoners. Others are disillusioned and more liberal in their orientation. They feel alienated and are leaving the profession because they feel out of sympathy with the current organizational culture.
Punishers	Punishers: They are inspired by their own disregard and intolerance for prisoners, rather than by security. Marked by a general hatred and/or loathing for prisoners, they are perhaps newer to the field or can be more experienced. Nonetheless, set apart from others by their intolerance for prisoners and their needs, they have a disregard for the humanity of those in their custody, and their displays of revulsion, animosity, impatience, and detestation toward prisoners can lead to challenges with their colleagues. The end goal of the punisher is to simply punish prisoners for their lived experiences and any pains they may have inflicted on others. Indeed, they may themselves seek vengeance or be persuaded by such desires.

[a] Crewe and Liebling's (2012) categories of Managerialists and Entrepreneurs are collapsed into Managerial-Entrepreneur.
[b] Crewe and Liebling's (2012) category of the "alienated" is renamed as the "moral relativist."
Source: Adapted from Ricciardelli, 2016a, p. 330. Originally adapted from Crewe & Liebling, 2012, p. 4.

Correctional Officers and Prisoners: A Complex Relationship

While on duty, officers' attitudes and their behaviours can be interpreted as entering into a complex game of tug-of-war. Officers may experience job-related stresses that include violence, harassment, and assault within the prison setting (Dignam & Fagan, 1996; Ditchfield & Harries, 1996; Hayes, 1985; Lambert, Hogan, & Tucker, 2009; Lambert, Altheimer, & Hogan, 2010; Sorensen et al., 2011). Prison researchers have suggested that diverse organizational factors (such as working conditions and policies) have the potential to influence how officers view prisoners and their interpretations of the daily routine that is imposed on those in custody (e.g., Jurik, 1985; Lariviere & Robinson, 1996; Guenther & Guenther, 1974; Jackson & Ammen, 1996; Simourd, 1997). As a result, more research is always necessary regarding the factors shaping and outcomes of officers' attitudes toward prisoners. The prisoner–staff/staff–prisoner relationship can inform officer stresses (Seidman & Williams, 1999), which too often oscillate between those tied to colleagues and those of prisoners. In consequence, we would be remiss if we did not recognize that although correctional officers have a profound role in the lives of prisoners, as they govern and structure prisoners' penal experience (Guenther & Guenther, 1974; Jackson & Ammen, 1996; Simourd, 1997), they also may be victims of physical, verbal, or other forms of violence, or the threat of violence (Boyd, 2011; Seidman & Williams, 1999). Another complexity in the officer–prisoner relationship is tied to the fact that although an officer may not be aware of each prisoner's exact crime, there is a base knowledge required about prisoner criminality that is evidenced in where they are placed within the prison. Thus, as noted prior regarding **professionalism**, an officer has to manage their morals and ethics and try to treat all prisoners consistently and without prejudice (Kropp, Cox, Roesch, & Eaves, 1989; Lavoie, Connolly, & Roesch, 2006; Ricciardelli & Spencer, 2018; Scrivens & Ricciardelli, 2019).

In sum, physical prison structures, as well as **informal and formal norms** governing prison living and correctional work at all levels of the institution, play a role in shaping the quality of the relationship that develops between prisoners and staff (Kruttschnitt & Gartner, 2005; Pollack, 2009; Ricciardelli, Perry, & Carleton, 2017). Relationships at all levels will inform the working environment for officers and the living environment for prisoners, helping or hindering the quality of interactions and essence of communication. Regarding helping, Trammell (2009) found in her study in the United States that prison isolation can encourage more intimate relationships to develop between female prisoners. Turning to hindering of interactions, Bosworth and Carrabine (2001) theorized that prisoner social interactions can constitute an enactment of resistance against the pains of prison living. All relationships in their diverse positions respond to some need, either of a prisoner or an officer, and in response can and often do perform some sort of rehabilitative function; even though how may not always be clear, this fact must never be discounted.

Working in a somewhat rural prison, John was 31 years old when Ricciardelli first spoke with him. He has four years of experience as a correctional officer, and was married with a family, college educated, vibrant, and clearly well-liked by his peers.

[Among correctional officers] there are good communicators and there are really bad communicators. And there's people who have short fuses and there's people who have short fuses that can't speak to people and . . . for me I think its communication [that] breaks down a lot of times and guys don't understand what the other one's saying. And what happens when two people argue. If one person gets defensive they just keep moving farther apart and before you know it, well you're not going to drag the officer to the hole.

[Originally] I thought [prisoners] were a lot more dangerous. But I realize now that a lot of the crimes that they commit or did commit were because they were high. Or they were looking for money for drugs or [it] had something to do with drugs. Or they couldn't get a job somewhere else because they didn't have any education. [My views] changed actually pretty much the first month that I was there and I realized that, as weird as a lot of them are, they're still people. I don't think that everyone can be rehabbed—I absolutely know everyone can't be rehabilitated—but I know there's a lot of them that could be if stuff was right, but it's pretty much a dying cause. Sometimes you can get bitter over stuff like that.

Gendered Spaces: Working within a Binary Sex Environment

In light of changes in policy, practice, and advancements in technology, the role of the officer is continually shaped by evolving interpretations of a sense of being vulnerable. Each change demands officers be innovative yet consistent in their care and control of prisoners. Officers' workspaces require, for the sake of mitigating risk, that they experience and respond to each vulnerability as it arises in the prison setting. Yet how an officer overcomes or tries to mitigate their sense of vulnerabilities entails a self-regulatory process that can either confirm or even reaffirm their gender identity and ability to perform their masculinities (see Ricciardelli, 2016b). In prison, saving face and appearing stoic are valued traits for all working in the institution; these are qualities tied to traditional understandings of masculinities, such as appearing confident, with authority, and in control, which do serve officers when they have to de-escalate situations and in their communications with prisoners. Indeed, male prison environments are recognized as hyper-masculine spaces that encourage, even promote, normative understandings of masculinities that try to diminish vulnerabilities and, instead, exacerbate qualities that could align with a hegemonic ideal (see Ricciardelli, 2016a; Ricciardelli, Maier, & Hannah-Moffat, 2015; see also Connell, 1995; Connell & Messerschmidt, 2005).

In the subsequent sections we continue to examine the role of the correctional officer but with a gendered focus, given that prisons are largely **gender binary spaces** (with few exceptions), to unpack how the gender of staff and prisoners shapes correctional work. We first direct attention toward the experiences of male officers working with adult men and then to the experiences of female officers working with adult female prisoners.

Men Working with Adult Male Prisoners

It should be noted that most male correctional officers working in provincial or territorial institutions are not allowed, by their occupational mandates and policies, to work on units housing female prisoners as primary workers. Thus, they will not have experience working with incarcerated women directly. This is ironic, given that female correctional officers have worked on male units without objective for nearly half a century, yet male correctional officers continue to be unwelcome in female units and institutions. This fact represents a historic and noteworthy change, because men were able to be primary workers in the federal system in 1989, but after a series of exceptional grave events at the now closed Prison for Women in Kingston, Ontario (see CSC, 2013; see also Chapter 8), concerns remain about whether male primary workers in female units can ever be appropriate (CSC, 2013). The Cross Gender Monitoring Project undertaken by Correctional Service Canada (2013) puts forth that male officers should not work as **primary care** providers in women's institutions and should not perform any possibly invasive procedures on women (such as strip searches or bed checks).

Accounts of prison life continually indicate a combination of various experiences and struggles, some centred on fear, violence, and general mistrust and, less commonly, some starting to recognize that there can be hope in prison (Liebling et al., 2019). Policymakers and researchers have acknowledged that how prisoners "do time" is shaped by prison structures, and these formal and informal structures take different forms in men's versus women's institutions or units. For instance, incarcerated adult males engage in doing informal structures, such as participating in the "prisoner code," which plays a role in shaping what is acceptable versus unacceptable contact between staff and prisoners (or among prisoners more generally; see Adams, 1992; Bandyopadhyay, 2006; Clemmer, 1940; Einat & Einat, 2000; Irwin, 1980, 2005; Irwin & Cressey, 1962; Newton, 1994; Sykes, 1958; Trammell, 2012). When adapting to prison living, prisoners typically must learn to emotionally manage themselves to deter the aggression of other prisoners or to hide their vulnerabilities. Failing to do so may perpetuate a prisoner being physically, verbally, or socially victimized or even falsely accused of being too close to staff and thus labelled an informant—a label that can only hinder officer–prisoner relationship development. Given prison living for incarcerated men is structured under the principle that prisoners need not get "friendly" with staff (see Ricciardelli, 2014a, 2014b; Sykes, 1958), this barrier to communication plays an undeniable role in shaping the prison workspace.

Women Working with Adult Female Prisoners

Various researchers studying imprisonment have documented that incarcerated women (and sometimes staff) experience **discrimination** and **prejudice** or have been victim to stereotyping (Fox, 1984; Schram, 1997). For instance, in the United States, the Office of Justice Programs (1999) found that incarcerated women are **stereotyped**—although not exclusively—as passive, childlike, and emotional (Fox, 1984; Schram, 1997). Arguably, this has led to prison management imposing more control and limited interpretations of the needs of female prisoners. Schram, Koons-Witt, and Morash (2004) responded to the Office of Justice Programs' report by stating that "in this vein, there is a related history of paternalism towards women, and paternalism has often been the basis for limiting women's behaviors and activities 'for their own good,' that is, in order to take care of them" (p. 26). Ultimately, restrictive understanding of women's needs creates difficulties for correctional staff and added layers of work as they try to disambiguate what the women in their custody need versus what they are thought to need (see Ricciardelli, 2019; Ricciardelli & McKendy, 2020).

What becomes clear in this regard is that patriarchy continues to (re)shape women's experiences of incarceration and their conditions of confinement. For instance, incarcerated women are often in states of precarity (Jurik, 1988). For example, Pollock (1984) looked at how officers perceive the emotional states of incarcerated women, finding that incarcerated women were thought to be "prone to irrational emotion[al] outbursts" and to have a "shorter fuse than men." Officers in her study also reported feeling obliged to "watch what they said to female inmates and be more sensitive to how women might react to them" (p. 84). Furthermore, while male prisoners tend to be viewed more as individuals—with some being more emotional, aggressive, or weaker than others—incarcerated women were interpreted in a rather uniform fashion, particularly regarding their **emotionality**, further supporting that women prisoners are stereotyped and seen through a very specific (and reductionist) gendered lens (see Wolf, 1991).

The participants in our sample did, at times, categorize female prisoners as catty and competitive. The latter attribute was viewed as a potential trigger for altercations among female prisoners and thus problematized displays of authority by women and

"bragging" about criminal acts and experiences as a way to gain credibility. Unlike men, who may "brag" about their crimes to secure status on the prisoner social hierarchy (see Ricciardelli, 2014a, 2014b), women doing so were more negatively construed, suggesting some women prisoners were "power hungry" while others were "suffering" and subordinated. Correctional officers, in their occupational role, seek to keep the peace and prevent predation among prisoners, a task that requires much **emotional labour** given the more intensive communication that prevails on women's units. In addition, incarcerated women, like men, often have physical, mental, and emotional needs that can leave them increasingly vulnerable within the institution. Officers did agree that female prisoners appear more "needy" than males, but this is also a derivative of the greater communication and rapport building that defines working on women's units; unlike the emotional suppression and avoidance of dialogue with staff directed by the informal code that overlies male prisoner units (see Sykes, 1958), women's units are informed by emotionality, and interactions and communication between officers and prisoners are encouraged. In response, the occupational work requires officers to care and imposes emotion-oriented labour.

Female prisoners are more likely to disclose their feelings to staff, including loneliness, and their concerns or worries, and they are more likely to speak honestly about their well-being, needs, and concerns. The greater openness among women also makes it easier for staff to understand when a female prisoner is undergoing hardship; participants explained that discerning how female prisoners were feeling by watching their actions is an invaluable tool for building casual relationships with female prisoners more freely. In consequence, correctional officers know more about those in their custody and are able to offer more focused support, to listen and provide comfort, and in some situations to defuse poor temperament before incidents arise. Again, "emotional labour" (Hochschild, 1983, 1998) clearly laces the experiences of officers working on women's units. Officers on women's units can and do pass hours positioned as pseudo-counsellors, although they have no training or institutional guidance for taking on such roles. Thus, even staff who "loved" their jobs often reported feeling drained, physically and emotionally, after a day of listening to incarcerated women (see Pearlman & Saakvitne, 1995; Saakvitne

& Pearlman, 1996; and Stamm, 1995 for discussions on compassion fatigue and the impacts of emotional trauma). It is perhaps not surprising, then, that most female correctional officers prefer to work on male units, although some do love and prefer working with women (for example, "everybody will ask me, 'Well, who would you rather work with?' I say, 'I would take one hundred guys over five females' . . . I've worked with [females] a lot, and I've dealt with them a lot. And I respect females a lot and they respect me, but . . . '"; see Ricciardelli, 2019). Such findings are consistent with those of Pollock (1986)—72 per cent of the female officers she interviewed stated a preference for working with incarcerated men rather than women—and Britton (1999).

When interviewed by Ricciardelli, Jessica was 28 years old, a self-identifying female with nearly a decade of experience working as a correctional officer. She had experience working with both female and male prisoners. She spoke to her experiences as a woman working both in prison and on units housing adult females:

> Consistency is huge with the inmates. They want consistency. I worked in a female unit [where] I was really, really sick of all maximum inmates picking on the minimum security inmates. It just frustrated me so much to see the bullying going on cause I don't do well with bullying in life in general. Let alone inmates doing it, or offenders doing it. It was frustrating me so much . . . I didn't think it was fair that females were allowed to wear their clothes and the male offenders weren't. And they were allowed to have an abundance of make-up. And the guys weren't even allowed to have chapstick. Like it was just very frustrating for me but I know that there's a lot of E. Fry societies and John Howard societies. E. Fry societies are very strong about females, and keeping their femininity in the justice system or the jails. I found that it wasn't making them behave, [Elizabeth Fry representatives] were like, "Well they should be able to keep their own clothes" and "it makes them feel like a female." And I said, "How would you feel if you came in a size 2, and of course when you come in you get off the drugs. You constantly eat and fill your body with bad nutrition. You gain a lot of weight, because there was a very minimum exercise." They didn't have very much exercise. They didn't want to; it was offered to them but they didn't go. And they left as a size 10. And they couldn't fit into those size 2 pants they had in their cell. That didn't make them feel good . . .

Stressors, Vulnerabilities, Well-Being, and Occupational Challenges

Prisons are undeniably spaces that are laced with the omnipresent threat of violence, unpredictability, and risk potential. Not surprisingly, correctional officers experience much occupational stress (Dowden & Tellier, 2004; Finn, 1996; Ricciardelli & Power, 2019). The occupational stress includes both **operational stress** (referring to the content of the job, for example, de-escalating situations and fulfilling operational responsibilities) and **organizational stress** (which refers to job context, including the dynamics between management and staff and the implementation of policy directives; Shane, 2010, p. 815; see also Symonds, 1970; Hepburn 1987; and Huckabee, 1992; in regard to policing, see Kop, Euwema, & Schaufeli, 1999; Collins & Gibbs, 2003; Shane, 2010). In prisons, the operational stressors are often rooted in the need to work with more trying prisoners, who can be unpredictable. Unlike for police or members of the armed forces, what is unique to correctional work regarding such stressors is that these stressors are omnipresent. Correctional officers work within the environment of deployment (that is, other public safety personnel are deployed to incidents or calls for service but have a "base" environment free from risk potentiality). Thus, for correctional officers, operational stressors are constant and pronounced, although expected. In addition, officers cannot become complacent without increasing the risk potential for themselves, their colleagues, and those in custody.

Organizational stressors are rooted in the structures that both inform and limit the abilities of officers to do their jobs to the extent to which they desire or in ways they feel are optimal. Additional examples of such stressors include overcrowding and understaffing, excessive overtime or a lack of overtime, the challenges of shift work, competing demands made by supervisors and management, feelings of occupational alienation, being unheard, and powerlessness while on duty or being without agency. Organizational stressors can result in feelings of frustration, irritation, and anger among officers, which compromise their well-being (Crawley, 2013; Ricciardelli & Power, 2019).

As Ricciardelli (2019) contends, organizational stressors can amplify or mitigate (more often the former) operational stressors; however, both have vast implications for and are experienced by correctional officers. To explain, in a meta-analysis looking at predictors of occupational stress among correctional officers employed in Canada, Dowden and Tellier (2004) found that both organizational stressors and operational stressors strongly predicted occupational stress. Their findings are particularly noteworthy given that in most paramilitary organizations, such as policing, organizational stressors tend to be stronger predictors of occupational stress in comparison to operational stressors. Such stressors are also found to negatively affect public safety personnel, who may feel helpless, undervalued, unappreciated, and voiceless in their organization (Brough & Williams, 2007; Triplett, Mullings, & Scarborough, 1996).

Perhaps it is for these reasons, among others, that correctional staff screen positive for mental disorders at rates significantly higher than those in the general Canadian population (Carleton et al., 2018a; 2018b). Indeed, 54.6 per cent of correctional service employees who participated in an online survey looking at experiences of mental disorders screen positive for at least one major mental disorder (Carleton et al., 2018a). In addition, 29.1 percent screened positive for major depressive disorder and 31.1 percent for post-traumatic stress disorder. These findings were consistent with or even worse than those of other public safety personnel (like paramedics, firefighters, or police officers). This is not surprising, given that the work of correctional officers parallels that of first responders: Correctional officers police persons within confined spaces, respond to crises—including riots, fires, death, and other incidents—and are first on scene for many situations with trauma potentiality. They save lives, although this fact is often overlooked, and they are constantly the subject of media and public scrutiny. Indeed, what is often omitted from such discussions of the nuances of correctional officer occupational responsibilities is that, unlike for paramedics, when officers are providing CPR or responding to a life-threatening situation, they must continue working on the body until the paramedics or other uniformed services arrive—they cannot call time of death. Thus, correctional staff can be left to perform CPR on a corpse for prolonged periods of time (e.g., longer than an hour). Such experiences can and do impact officer mental health; nevertheless, the literature on correctional officer mental health remains limited.

The few researchers in the area have noted there are high rates of post-traumatic stress symptoms among correctional officers (Austin-Ketch et al., 2012) and the fact that **mental health** needs contribute to correctional employee absenteeism from work (Lambert et al., 2010; Lambert et al., 2009). In a recent Canadian study, Ricciardelli and colleagues (2019) found that correctional service employees (persons working in institutional, community, and administrative corrections) report symptoms consistent with mental disorders at rates of 54.6 per cent for any mental disorder, 34.3 per cent for post-traumatic stress disorder, 31.1 per cent for major depressive disorder, and 23.6 per cent for generalized anxiety disorder (see also Carleton et al., 2018a, 2018b). While it is beyond the scope of this chapter to comprehensively focus on correctional staff mental health and substance misuse, nevertheless it remains significant to briefly note here. Furthermore, others have suggested that workplace violence, including experiencing or witnessing physical, verbal, or other forms of assault, negatively affects officer mental health (Ricciardelli, Power, & Simas-Medieros, 2018; Ricciardelli, 2019). As mentioned previously, organizational stressors such as employment conditions create job strain, which can also result in compromised officer well-being (Bourbonnais, Jauvin, Dussault, & Vezina, 2007; see also Boyd, 2011).

Operational Stressors: Risk, Violence, and Vulnerabilities

Despite the image of correctional work as being based on use of force, authority, and aggressive tactics, a foundational component of working in prisons remains relationship building through communication and techniques of **de-escalation**. Prior to any **use of force**, including in crisis management situations, negotiation should be used—a reality that often counters perceptions of correctional work. Having officers with **communication skills** on staff is essential in correctional work, since officers are consistently required to respond to or intervene in challenges on a unit or within the greater prisoner population. It is only when prisoners are not able to be "talked down" from a situation or state of aggression (for example, when a prisoner is in a state of drug-induced psychosis) that officers must turn to alternative means of de-escalating a situation;

such alternatives may involve use of force, physical restraint, or assertions of authority. However, officers consistently report that prior to resorting to any force, communication is required ("go over and talk to them") in hopes of preventing unnecessary violence.

Officers also respond to incidents tied to prisoners inflicting self-harm or striving for death by suicide. Although officers do undergo training (to various degrees and of various quality) about responding to such incidents, the experiences are always potential sources of trauma (and the trauma can be compounded by the vast lack of appreciation by the victim toward the correctional officer who saved their life). Too many officers have recounted the frustration and anger put forth by individuals engaging in **self-harm** or whom they saved from death by suicide. As previously mentioned, full-fledged inquiries into deaths in custody are common, but media attention or positive acknowledgement tied to lives saved is null.

Challenges can also arise during the routine tasks correctional officers perform throughout each day. Specifically, officers will oversee the delivery of meals and drinks, mail, laundry, canteen, and all materials oriented toward meeting basic needs (such as tooth brushes, toothpaste, and deodorant). In consequence, officers may spend time retrieving materials for prisoners and looking into whether a certain request is possible to accommodate. Officers, under all circumstances, must adhere to regulation and policy or they can face disciplinary responses, but policies can also be the root of conflict—particularly if they are ambiguous or not consistently enforced. For instance, when a prisoner constantly requests a certain item that they are not allowed to have, particularly if some officers give in to the request and others do not, escalation can follow, resulting in a possible incident. This is also the case when supervising food distribution, such as if prisoners attempt to secure larger portions of food. The result may be an incident, either when the officer takes note and stops the attempt or when the prisoner is successful in their attempt but as a consequence someone else on the unit is without food. Thus, outcomes, even in the most mundane and routine of tasks, can escalate into incidents, particularly if officers lack complete awareness of their surroundings.

Laced through these examples of vulnerabilities officers face at work is the notion, either real or perceived, that they are not supported by the institution (management or the government), which can create additional layers of vulnerabilities for officers. For example, there are times when correctional officers adhere to institutional policy in instances that require the use of discretion. Here, officers can feel vulnerable because they are uncertain if management will support their decision making—a concern often mentioned in cases tied to use of force. Officers reported being concerned that an independent third-party assessment would not be in agreement with their view of the situation, causing them to start questioning their own actions and thus the degree of force used. Moreover, negative assessments can have repercussions, which range from unpaid leave to poor performance reviews to termination.

In addition, the idea among participants that prisoners hold more power, were given more respect, and had more aggressive advocacy than officers was rather commonplace. Yet, despite this fact, officers were still forceful about the insufficient programming and resources available for prisoners and the impact this had on officers' conditions of work and prisoners' conditions of confinement. While data on wellness initiatives are currently limited outside of Correctional Service Canada staff, participants spoke of the disheartening reality that many institutions did not have sufficient counselling services for mental health and addiction, violence prevention, pre-employment, or really any needed programs (including educational). They explained that placing high-need persons in facilities where their needs remain unmet, or are even exacerbated, serves no one; such a decision has the potential to harm the prisoner in particular, but also the staff and other individuals in custody. The responsibility to help prisoners cope with their ailments too often falls on officers, who lack the appropriate knowledge or training; as one stated, "I wasn't trained in psychology."

Additional challenges and vulnerabilities that must be noted include the physical threats imposed on correctional officers, often by the physical institution itself—where air quality may be compromised and potential exposure to narcotics becomes a genuine concern. In addition, correctional officers work in conditions where body fluids are used as weapons; beyond being disgusting, this also means that infectious diseases such as hepatitis C and HIV can be transmitted. Searches of cells or units can accidently result in pricked fingers by needles and the transmission of blood-borne infections. The consequence of such exposure does not just remain with the victim; the danger exists that this exposure can be passed on to their entire family. Officers who are exposed are placed on medical cocktails for upwards of six months to try to rid the body of the infectious agent. The psychological as well as physical and social toll such experiences place on officers is indisputably concerning (see Ricciardelli, 2019, Ricciardelli & Power, 2019).

Summary

In this chapter we focused on correctional work, specifically that of correctional officers employed in Canadian provincial and territorial correctional institutions. The perspectives of correctional officers, as they see themselves and in relation to the work they do with prisoners, is central to their work experiences and the lived experiences of those in their custody. As they fulfill their duties of care, custody, and control, officers encounter a number of challenges from a variety of sources: prisoners, colleagues, management, and government, to name a few. Although the ways in which officers perceive and approach their work may vary, they are professionally obligated to balance care and control in an environment that deals with a wide range of risks and vulnerabilities.

In presenting the nuances of the correctional officer role and how it varies depending on the institution and prisoner population, we unpacked how officers' relationships with each other and with prisoners shape their occupational work. The emotional labour involved in correctional work, especially in terms of navigating the physical, personal, and legal vulnerabilities witnessed in the prison, was discussed, because it is important to recognize that correctional work includes emotional labour—it is no longer an occupational role rooted in punishment and control. Communication skills are the crux of the officer skill set and are prioritized over use of force in the majority of instances, a process that will continue to gain traction and shape correctional work in the future.

Regardless of the gender of the correctional officer or the prison setting in which the officer works, the role of the officer occupies a particular position of power and authority—a position always influenced by gender dynamics and identity. To some extent, officers' as well as prisoners' gender can influence both formal and informal prison structures, communication styles, the complex relationships between individuals (staff, administrators, government, and prisoners), and how interactions are interpreted overall. In this chapter, our aim remains to inform the reader of the complicated yet comprehensive role of the correctional officer and how this role aligns with or contracts from correctional work. The well-being and needs of correctional staff remain a pressing concern; despite the challenges, correctional officers play a key part in managing prisoner populations in the Canadian correctional system.

Review Questions

1. How do you define "correctional officer"? Does this definition differ from other concepts like "guard" or "keeper"? Please explain.
2. Taking into consideration the differences between provincial and territorial and federal correctional work, what are the major considerations of the correctional officer role?
3. In terms of institutions housing adult male prisoners, what are the challenges of correctional work faced by male versus female correctional officers?
4. What are the unique complexities that female correctional officers must navigate when working with female adult prisoner populations?
5. Discuss the mental health and well-being of correctional officers in Canada. What factors play into occupational stress experienced by correctional officers?

Critical Thinking Questions

1. Is there a particular role orientation that you find significant to correctional work? How does this relate to cultural/media (television, film) depictions of correctional work?

2. How can professionalism be promoted in correctional work? Will the promotion of professionalism have an impact in the future supervision of adult prisoners?

3. Given prison is largely a sex binary space, in what ways does a correctional officer's gender identity shape their work, assisting or increasing the challenges? Do you think the recognition of gender identity can positively impact correctional work and prisoners' lives?

4. How can a positive impact be made on the mental health and well-being of correctional officers in Canada?

Multimedia Suggestions

Working at CSC—Why People Love It
CSC recruitment video: https://www.csc-scc.gc.ca/careers/003001-7001-eng.shtml

Guide to Applying for a Job at CSC
This webpage provides advice on how to apply for CSC positions: https://www.csc-scc.gc.ca/careers/003001-4000-eng.shtml

Employment Equity and Diversity
This CSC video outlines the CSC's commitment to a strong and diverse workforce: https://www.csc-scc.gc.ca/careers/003001-7000-eng.shtml

References

Adams, K. (1992). Adjusting to prison life. *Crime and Justice, 16,* 275–359.

Austin-Ketch, T.L., Violanti, J., Fekedulegn, D., Andrew, M.E., Burchfield, C.M., & Hartley, T.A. (2012). Addictions and the criminal justice system: What happens on the other side? Post-traumatic stress symptoms and cortisol measures in a police cohort. *Journal of Addictions Nursing, 23*(1), 22–9.

Bandyopadhyay, M. (2006). Competing masculinities in a prison. *Men and Masculinities, 9*(2), 186–203. doi:10.1177/1097184x06287765

Bosworth, M., & Carrabine, E. (2001). Reassessing resistance: Race, gender, and sexuality in prison. *Punishment & Society, 3,* 501–15.

Bourbonnais, R., Jauvin, N., Dussault, J., & Vezina, M. (2007). Psychosocial work environment, interpersonal violence at work and mental health among correctional officers. *International Journal of Law and Psychiatry, 30*(4–5), 355–68.

Boyd, N. (2011). *Correctional officers in British Columbia, 2011: Abnormal working conditions.* Burnaby, BC: BCGEU.

Braithwaite, V. (1994). Beyond Rokeach's equality-freedom model: Two-dimensional values in a one-dimensional world. *Journal of Social Issues, 50*(4), 67–94.

Braithwaite, V. (1998a). Communal and exchange trust norms: Their value base and relevance to institutional trust. In V. Braithwaite & M. Levi (Eds), *Trust and governance.* New York, NY: Russell Sage Foundation.

Braithwaite, V. (1998b). The value balance of political evaluations. *British Journal of Psychology, 89,* 223–47.

Britton, D.M. (1999). Cat fights and gang fights: Preference for work in a male-dominated organization. *Sociological Quarterly, 40,* 455–74.

Brough, P., & Williams, J. (2007). Managing occupational stress in a high-risk industry. *Criminal Justice and Behaviour, 34*(4), 555–67.

Carleton, R.N., Afifi, T.O., Turner, S., Taillieu, T., Duranceau, S., LeBouthillier, D.M., . . . Asmundson, G.G. (2018a). Mental disorder symptoms among public safety personnel in Canada. *Canadian Journal of Psychiatry, 63*(1), 54–64. doi:10.1177/0706743717723825

Carleton, R.N., Afifi, T.O., Turner, S., Taillieu, T., LeBouthillier, D.M., Duranceau, S., . . . Groll, D. (2018b). Suicidal ideation, plans, and attempts among public safety personnel in Canada. *Canadian Psychology, 59*(3), 220–31.

Charmaz, K. (2006). *Constructing grounded theory.* London, UK: SAGE Publications Ltd.

Clemmer, D. (1940). *The prison community.* Boston, MA: Christopher Publishing.

Collins, P., & Gibbs, A. (2003). Stress in police officers: A study of the origins, prevalence and severity of stress-related symptoms within a county police force. *Occupational Medicine, 53*(4), 256–64.

Connell, R.W. (1995). *Masculinities.* Berkeley, CA: University of California Press.

Connell, R.W. & Messerschmidt, J.W. (2005). Hegemonic masculinity: Rethinking the concept. *Gender & Society, 19*(6), 829–59.

Correctional Service Canada. (1992). Commissioner's directives: Peace officer designations (003). Retrieved from www.csc-scc.gc.ca/policy-and-legislation/003-cde-eng.shtml

Correctional Service Canada. (2012). About us. Retrieved from www.csc-scc.gc.ca/about-us/index-eng.shtml

Correctional Service Canada. (2013). The cross gender monitoring project: 3rd and final annual report. Retrieved from www.csc-scc.gc.ca/publications/fsw/gender3/cg-02-eng.shtml

Correctional Services Nova Scotia. (2014). Careers in correctional services: One industry. Three exciting paths. Nova Scotia: Department of Justice.

Crawley, E. (2004). Emotion and performance. *Punishment & Society*, 6(4), 411–27.

Crawley, E. (2013). *Doing prison work: The public and private lives of prison officers*. London, UK: Routledge.

Crewe, B. (2009). *The prisoner society: Power, adaptation and social life in an English prison*. Oxford, UK: Oxford University Press.

Crewe, B., & Liebling, A. (2012). Are liberal humanitarian penal values and practices exceptional? In T. Ugelvik & J. Dullum (Eds), *Penal exceptionalism? Nordic prison policy and practice* (pp. 175–98). Abingdon, UK: Routledge.

Department of Justice and Public Safety. (2014). Corrections: Institutional services. Retrieved from www.justice.gov.nl.ca/just/corrections/institutional_services.html

Dignam, J., & Fagan, T.J. (1996). Workplace violence in correctional settings: A comprehensive approach to critical incident stress management. In G.R. VandenBos & E.Q. Bulatao (Eds), *Violence on the job: Identifying risks and developing solutions* (pp. 367–84). Washington, DC: American Psychological Association.

Ditchfield, J., & Harries, R. (1996). Assaults on staff in male local prisons and remand centres. *Home Office Research and Statistics Directorate Research Bulletin*, 38, 15–20.

Dowden, C., & Tellier, C. (2004). Predicting work-related stress in correctional officers: A meta-analysis. *Journal of Criminal Justice*, 32(1), 31–47.

Einat, T., & Einat, H. (2000). Inmate argot as an expression of prison subculture: The Israeli case. *The Prison Journal*, 80(3), 309–25.

Farkas, M. (2000). A typology of correctional officers. *International Journal of Offender Therapy and Comparative Criminology*, 44(4), 431–49.

Finn, P. (1996). No-frills prisons and jails: A movement in flux. *Federal Probation*, 6, 35–44.

Fox, J.P. (1984). Women's prison policy, prisoner activism, and the impact of the contemporary feminist movement: A case study. *The Prison Journal*, 63, 12–26.

Guenther, A.L., & Guenther, M. (1974). Screws vs. thugs. *Society*, 11(5), 42–50.

Hayes, W.S. (1985). *Assault, battery & injury of correctional officers by inmates: An occupational health study*. Doctoral dissertation, John Hopkins University.

Hepburn, J.R. (1987). The prison control structure and its effects on work attitudes: The perceptions and attitudes of prison guards. *Journal of Criminal Justice*, 15(1), 49–64. doi:http://dx.doi.org/10.1016/0047-2352(87)90077-8

Hochschild, A. (1983). *The managed heart*. Berkeley, CA: University of California Press.

Hochschild, A. (1998). The sociology of emotion as a way of seeing. In G. Bendelow & S.J. Williams (Eds), *Emotions in social life* (pp. 28–52). London, UK: Routledge.

Huckabee, R.G. (1992). Stress in corrections: An overview of the issues. *Journal of Criminal Justice*, 20(5), 479–86. doi:http://dx.doi.org/10.1016/0047-2352(92)90081-J

Irwin, J. (1980). *Prisons in turmoil*. Boston, MA: Little, Brown.

Irwin, J. (2005). *The warehouse prison: Disposal of the new dangerous class*. Los Angeles, CA: Roxbury Publishing Company.

Irwin, J., & Cressey, D.R. (1962). Thieves, convicts, and the inmate subculture. *Social Problems*, 10(2), 142–55.

Jackson, J.E., & Ammen, S. (1996). Race and correctional officers' punitive attitudes toward treatment programs for inmates. *Journal of Criminal Justice*, 24, 153–66.

Jurik, N.C. (1985). Individual and organizational determinants of correctional officer attitudes toward inmates. *Criminology*, 23(3), 523–40.

Jurik, N.C. (1988). Striking a balance: Female correctional officers, gender role stereotypes, and male prisons. *Sociological Inquiry*, 58, 291–305.

Klofas, J., & Toch, H. (1982). The guard subculture. *Journal of Research in Crime and Delinquency*, 19, 238–54.

Kop, N., Euwema, M., & Schaufeli, W. (1999). Burnout, job stress and violent behaviour among Dutch police officers. *Work & Stress*, 13(4), 326–40.

Kropp, P., Cox, D., Roesch, R., & Eaves, D. (1989). The perceptions of correctional officers toward mentally disordered offenders. *International Journal of Law and Psychiatry*, 12, 181–8.

Kruttschnitt, C., & Gartner, R. (2005). *Marking time in the golden state: Women's imprisonment in California*. Cambridge, UK: Cambridge University Press.

Lambert, E.G., Altheimer, I., & Hogan, N.L. (2010). Exploring the relationship between social support and job burnout among correctional staff. *Criminal Justice and Behavior*, 37, 1217–36.

Lambert, E.G., Hogan, N.L., & Tucker, K.A. (2009). Problems at work: Exploring the correlates of role stress among correctional staff. *The Prison Journal*, 89, 460–81.

Lariviere, M.A., & Robinson, D. (1996). *Attitudes of federal correctional officers towards offenders*. Ottawa, ON: Correctional Service Canada.

Lavoie, J.A., Connolly, D.A., & Roesch, R. (2006). Correctional officers' perceptions of inmates with mental illness: The role of training and burnout syndrome. *International Journal of Forensic Mental Health*, 5(2), 151–66.

Liebling, A. (2004). *Prisons and their moral performance*. Oxford, UK: Oxford University Press.

Liebling, A., Laws, B., Lieber, E., Auty, K., Schmidt, B.E., Crewe, B., . . . Morey, M. (2019). Are hope and possibility achievable in prison? *The Howard Journal*, 58(1), 104–26.

Maruna, S. (2012). A signaling perspective on employment-based re-entry: Elements of successful desistance signaling. *Criminology & Public Policy*, 11(1), 73–86. doi:10.1111/i/1745-9133.2012.00789

Newton, C. (1994). Gender theory and prison sociology: Using theories of masculinities to interpret the sociology of prisons for men. *The Howard Journal*, 33(3), 193–202.

Office of Justice Programs. (1999). Conference proceedings. Paper presented at the National Symposium on Women Offenders, Washington, DC.

Pearlman, L.A., & Saakvitne, K.W. (1995). *Trauma and the therapist*. New York, NY: W. W. Norton & Company.

Pollock, J. (1984). Women will be women: Correctional officers' perceptions of the emotionality of women inmates. *The Prison Journal*, 64, 84–91.

Pollock, J. (1986). *Sex and supervision: Guarding male and female inmates*. Westport, CT: Greenwood Publishing Group.

Pollack, S. (2009). "You can't have it both ways": Punishment and treatment of imprisoned women. *Journal of Progressive Human Services, 20*, 112–28.

Pratt, J. (2008a). Scandinavian exceptionalism in an era of penal excess: Part I: The nature and roots of Scandinavian exceptionalism. *British Journal of Criminology, 48*(2), 275–92.

Pratt, J. (2008b). Scandinavian exceptionalism in an era of penal excess: Part II: Does Scandinavian exceptionalism have a future? *British Journal of Criminology, 48*(3), 275–92.

Pratt, J. (2013a). Punishment and the civilizing process. In J. Simon & R. Sparks (Eds), *The Sage handbook of punishment and society*. London, UK: SAGE Publications.

Pratt, J. (2013b). *A punitive society: Falling crime and rising imprisonment in New Zealand*. Wellington, NZ: Bridget Williams Books.

Ricciardelli, R. (2014a). An examination of the inmate code in Canadian penitentiaries. *Journal of Crime and Justice, 37*(2), 234–55. doi:10.1080/0735648X.2012.746012

Ricciardelli, R. (2014b). *Surviving incarceration: Inside Canadian prisons*. Brantford, ON: Wilfrid Laurier University Press.

Ricciardelli, R. (2016a). Canadian prisoners' perceptions of correctional officer orientations to their occupational responsibilities. *Journal of Crime and Justice, 39*(2), 324–43. doi:10.1080/0735648X.2014.972430

Ricciardelli, R. (2016b). Canadian provincial correctional officers: Gendered strategies of achieving and affirming masculinities. *Journal of Men's Studies, 25*(1), 3–24. doi:10.1177/1060826515624389

Ricciardelli, R. (2019). Also serving time: The prison officer experience in Canadian provincial and territorial correctional facilities. Toronto, ON: University of Toronto Press.

Ricciardelli, R., Bahji, A., Mitchell, M.M., Barnim, N., Carleton, R.N., & Groll, D. (2019). Correctional work, wellbeing and mental health disorders. *Advancing Corrections Journal, 8*.

Ricciardelli, R., & Gazso, A. (2013). Investigating risk perception among Canadian corrections officers with experience handling inmates in Canadian provincial jails. *Qualitative Sociological Review, 4*(3), 96–120.

Ricciardelli, R., Maier, K., & Hannah-Moffat, K. (2015). Strategic masculinities: Vulnerabilities, risk and the production of prison masculinities. *Theoretical Criminology, 19*(4), 491–513.

Ricciardelli, R. & McKendy, L. (2020). Gender and prison work: The experience of female provincial correctional officers in Canada. *The Prison Journal*.

Ricciardelli, R., Perry, K.H., & Carleton, R.N. (2017). Prison officer orientations and the implications for responsivity with incarcerated youth. In J. Ireland, C. Ireland, M. Fisher, & N. Gredecki (Eds), *The Routledge international handbook on forensic psychology in prison and secure settings* (pp. 313–30). Abingdon, UK: Routledge.

Ricciardelli, R., & Power, N. (2019). How "conditions of confinement" impact "conditions of employment": The work-related wellbeing of provincial correctional officers in Atlantic Canada. *Violence and Victims, 35*, 88–107.

Ricciardelli, R., Power, N., & Medeiros, D.S. (2018). Correctional officers in Canada: Interpreting workplace violence. *Criminal Justice Review 43*(4), 458–76.

Ricciardelli, R., & Spencer, D.C. (2018). *Violence, sex offenders, and corrections*. Abingdon, UK: Taylor & Francis.

Robinson, D., Porporino, F., & Simourd, L. (1993). The influence of career orientation on support for rehabilitation of correctional staff. *The Prison Journal, 73*(2), 162–77.

Rutherford, A. (1994). *Criminal justice and the pursuit of decency*. Winchester, UK: Waterside Press.

Saakvitne, K.W., & Pearlman, L.A. (1996). *Transforming the pain: A workbook on vicarious traumatization for helping professionals who work with traumatized clients*. New York, NY: W. W. Norton & Company Inc.

Scrivens, R., & Ricciardelli, R. (2019). "Scum of the earth": Animus and violence against sex offenders in Canadian penitentiaries. In N. Blagden, B. Winder, R. Lievesley, K. Hocken, P. Banyard, & H. Elliot (Eds), *Sexual crime and the experience of imprisonment* (pp. 61–84). London, UK: Palgrave.

Schram, P.J. (1997). *The link between stereotype attitudes and behavioral intentions among female inmates, correctional officers, and program staff*. Doctoral dissertation, Michigan State University.

Schram, P.J., Koons-Witt, B.A., & Morash, M. (2004). Management strategies when working with female prisoners. *Women & Criminal Justice, 15*(2), 25–50. doi:10.1300/J012v15n02_02

Seidman, B.T., & Williams, S.M. (1999). The impact of violent acts on prison staff. *Forum on Corrections Research, 11*(1), 30–34.

Shane, J.M. (2010). Organizational stressors and police performance. *Journal of Criminal Justice, 38*(4), 807–18.

Simourd, L. (1997). *Staff attitudes toward inmates and correctional work*. Doctoral dissertation, Carleton University.

Sorensen, J., Cunningham, M., Vigen, M.P., & Woods, S.O. (2011). Serious assaults on prison staff: A descriptive analysis. *Journal of Criminal Justice, 39*(2), 143–50.

Sparks, R., Bottoms, A., & Hay, W. (1996). *Prisons and the problem of order*. Oxford, UK: Clarendon.

Stamm, H.B. (1995). *Secondary traumatic stress: Self-care issues for clinicians, researchers, & educators*. Lutherville, MD: Sidran Press.

Sykes, G.M. (1958). *The society of captives*. Princeton, NJ: Princeton University Press.

Symonds, M. (1970). Emotional hazards of police work. *American Journal of Psychoanalysis, 30*(2), 155–60.

Trammell, R. (2009). Values, rules and keeping the peace: How men describe order and the inmate code in California prisons. *Deviant Behavior, 30*(8), 746–71. doi:10.1080/01639620902854662

Trammell, R. (2012). *Enforcing the convict code: Violence and prison culture*. Boulder, CO: Lynne Rienner Publishers Inc.

Triplett, R.A., Mullings, J.L., & Scarborough, K.E. (1996). Work-related stress and coping among correctional officers: Implications for organizational literature. *Journal of Criminal Justice, 24*(4), 291–308.

Wolf, N. (1991). *The beauty myth*. London, UK: Chatto and Windus.

Re-entry, Reintegration, and the Notion of "Rehabilitation"

6

Katharina Maier and Rosemary Ricciardelli

Learning Objectives

After reading this chapter, you should be able to:

- Define the term "prisoner re-entry" and explain how it is different from and similar to related concepts, such as reintegration and desistance from crime.
- Outline the major personal and socio-economic barriers tied to prison release.
- Discuss the different sources of stigma ex-prisoners must navigate after custody.
- Describe the different forms of post-prison supervision that exist in Canada.
- Discuss the role of non-governmental organizations in the context of prisoner re-entry.

Chapter Overview

This chapter offers an overview of the field of prisoner re-entry, drawing from existing studies as well as the authors' own research on people's experiences of re-entry and reintegration. To contextualize the experiential realities of ex-prisoners' trajectories of re-entry and reintegration, which are heavily based on the rather contentious notion of "rehabilitation," this chapter begins by defining and unpacking the concept of prisoner re-entry itself and explaining how it is different from and similar to other concepts. The multitude of barriers tied to prison release will then be discussed; those range from finding and retaining employment to reuniting with families and friends to adhering to conditions of release. Particular attention is paid throughout this chapter to the variations and consistencies in re-entry expectations, particularly in light of socio-demographic and ethnocultural factors, such as gender and race, as well as release status, criminal history, and associated stigma. The chapter concludes with an overview of the work of re-entry organizations in the context of prisoner reintegration.

Introduction

> I love life. Since I got out of jail this time, after doing so long, you just love the little things. I don't know, you don't really appreciate, you lose touch, when you go to jail, [what] it's like to be able to get up and go outside and not be monitored; its quite liberating. (Jack)

Each year in Canada, over 100,000 people are released from prisons, jails, and detention facilities. Some have been in closed custody for a few days; others for months, years, or even decades. The gap in time, however long, leaves many incarcerated individuals in an odd position—sort of in limbo—where life on the outside may feel like a distant memory. Indeed, how much and how quickly life changes on the outside can be shocking for those imprisoned, particularly given that when in custody, life may feel like it is temporarily on hold. Balancing and coming to terms with the time lost during incarceration is an underacknowledged challenge faced by many former prisoners. Recognizing this, this chapter examines the following question: What is life like for individuals who have been incarcerated and are returning to the community?

To understand how re-entry unfolds in the lives of former prisoners, we need to listen to how ex-prisoners themselves narrate their trajectories of returning to the community after a period of incarceration. Jack's narrative above is taken from a larger qualitative study with former federal prisoners who shared their stories about re-entry and whose experiences inform this chapter. Thus, before we turn to the definition of re-entry, we provide an overview of the research and methods guiding this chapter.

A Note about Methods

The narratives presented in this chapter are drawn from a three-year longitudinal study of 25 former federal prisoners in the province of Ontario. All 25 participants in this study were on conditional release. Conditional release refers to individuals who have been released into the community but are under the supervision of a correctional agency (in this case, Correctional Service Canada [CSC]) and, to remain in the community, must adhere to their conditions of release (curfews, geographic restrictions, and so on). The participants in this study were released either on parole or statutory release (both of these concepts are described later in this chapter). Participants were recruited from an employment re-entry program in the community.

Of the 25 participants, 23 self-identified as male and two as female. Their ages ranged from 22 to 53. At intervals throughout the study, these men and women were given various opportunities to describe their experiences, concerns, and opportunities during their transition from institutional to community living, including their employment-oriented experiences. Specifically, interviews were completed, with some flexibility, at entry to the pre-employment program (that is, where participants received help with things like résumé construction and job interviews); then between three and six months post-program completion (during the job placement, if possible); again between 12 and 18 months post-program completion; and then at the end of the study (which varied for different participants, but we tried to follow up with all participants prior to the study closing, which was around the three-year mark). A short demographic survey was also completed orally by each participant during the interview process, which included questions about their criminal and institutional histories.

Conducting Research with Former Prisoners

Ex-prisoners are considered a "hard-to-reach" population (see Western, 2018). Gaining access to and building rapport with criminalized populations can be challenging. Former prisoners in particular may feel reluctant or uncomfortable to share their stories with researchers, especially if they have had negative experiences with parole officers, prison staff, or other authority figures who regularly engage in questioning about their lives, plans for the future, and rehabilitative progress. Doing qualitative research with formerly incarcerated populations requires that researchers earn participants' trust.

Ricciardelli, who conducted the interviews for this study, sought to build trust between study participants and herself by listening to those who willingly expressed interest in sharing their stories. She respected the people she spoke with and sought to listen carefully to their stories, without making any promises or increasing expectations about the outcomes of participating in the research. The method of recruitment used in this study obviously meant that former prisoners who did not have access to this particular employment re-entry program were not included in this study. While this was not a point of concern for Ricciardelli, given the overall goals of her study, it is important to recognize that ex-prisoners who lack access to employment programs or other formal support services may experience different or additional challenges after incarceration. In this context, we encourage researchers in Canada to look further into the differences between federal and provincially released people's trajectories of re-entry, including the challenges of release, given that provincial ex-prisoners tend to be provided with fewer supports after their release, especially in areas such as employment and housing.

Participants' criminal sentences ranged from two years to life. The time participants had served inside federal institutions varied significantly, between 16 months and 22 years. Of our 25 participants, two were designated as long-term statutory offenders (LTSOs). As reported elsewhere (see Ricciardelli & Mooney, 2019), there were also variations among participants in terms of personal identity markers and criminal and institutional histories. Participants' self-identified ethnic or racial backgrounds as well as their education profile are outlined in Table 6.1. Some basic information regarding participants' institutional histories, such as how many participants served time in youth and/or adult correctional facilities prior to their most recent incarceration, is also provided in Table 6.1. Participants' convictions also varied tremendously, from violent to non-violent crimes and sex offences, some involving drugs, death, cybercrime, property offences, firearms, forcible confinement, and domestic violence.

All 25 participants had served time in what is referred to as "reception," a maximum security facility where prisoners are assessed based on their needs, risks, and anticipated institutional adjustment before they are transferred to their "home institution," which can be a maximum, medium, or minimum security institution. Post-reception, nine participants had experiences in a maximum security facility, 20 in a medium security, and 12 in a minimum security prison. Female participants had served time in a mixed security institution, as there are fewer women's facilities in comparison to those that house men (for more information about women's prisons, see Chapter 8).

Study participation was voluntary, and interviews were conducted in person when possible. (Due to geography and work schedules, some interviews were completed by phone.) Although we did have an interview guide, the interviews themselves were semi-structured and followed the conversational paths as led by the individual participant. Each interview was about an hour long (on average), voice recorded, and later transcribed.

Defining Prisoner Re-entry

Jack (see above) was 36 at the time of his interview. He was also designated as LTSO. He had been incarcerated as a youth and multiple times as an adult. He was fortunate to have multiple supports in his life—a family and a drive to desist from crime—but he still had to navigate the complex and complicated realities of re-entry. As you continue to read more about Jack's experiences, consider the different dimensions of prisoner re-entry that come to the fore in this interview excerpt:

> I tried to plead guilty when I got arrested right away . . . [now, post-release] I feel like I'm trapped, like basically they have me between a rock and a hard place cause if I screw up or I break one of my conditions I can go to jail for up to 10 years for each breach. Well I was fortunate that I only got 11 and a half months for my breach; they wanted three years. I met a few guys that have got breaches and they got 3–5, which is crazy for a breach . . . [Jack's breach, he explained, was going to see his child unsupervised after a severe health scare, which he explained "even the judge said that any father or mother would have done that. He gave my parole officer at the time shit"] . . .
>
> I'm fortunate enough [that] I have children that love me unconditionally and I have a partner that I've been with for 15 years. And so, I'm fortunate enough that I have that love, but it sucked losing my job . . . I felt my life was getting on track. I hate the word normal but it was, I was being a prominent member of society and going back to jail, I felt like I failed.

Table 6.1 Distribution of Participants' Self-Identified Ethnic/Racial Identities, Educational Profiles, and Criminal Histories

Variable	n
Self-identified ethnic/racial identity	
Black	13
White	7
East Indian	1
Hispanic	2
Hispanic/Black/Indigenous	1
Educational profile	
GED	18
Less than high school	1
Some college	1
Some university	2
University degree	2
Institutional histories	
Prior provincial/territorial sentence(s)	11
Prior youth sentence	10
Prior federal sentence	2

[Going back to jail] You have lots of anxiety, you have so many questions, you're unsure of how long you're gonna be there...A lot of guys I meet, they lose everything. They have to start over; I've had that experience but fortunately that time I didn't have to go through that but the fact that you lose everything is really hard on you. Guys basically go to jail and get out of jail with their pants and the shirt on their back...

Originally I got out in [month and year removed], and then I was only out for 28 days, I breached my conditions and I just got out in [11 months later], so I've been out since...It's the first months, it's hard but you get back into a routine and the only hard part for me is not being able to go right now. The plan is to try to go home in [month] next year. But I've never lived in a halfway house. I lived in a group home cause when I was a kid you know, [I was a] ward of the court...I'm 36 years [old]; I feel like I shouldn't have to answer to those people you know since I'm not in prison.

Jack's narrative demonstrates the different facets of re-entry: Re-entry denotes an event signalling a person's return to community living, as well as the informed continuous process of navigating the complexities of social life following incarceration. As this excerpt shows, ex-prisoners may also have to deal with the threat of re-incarceration or the cycle of release, re-incarceration and subsequent re-entry, as in Jack's case. The following section provides a definition of the term "prisoner re-entry" and explains how this term is different from and similar to other more "traditional" concepts, such as reintegration or rehabilitation.

Prisoner Re-entry: An Event, Process, and Cycle

Scholars tend to agree that **prisoner re-entry** refers to a process as well as a singular event (the day of release from prison)—two interconnected and overlapping realities. Visher and Travis (2003) argue that re-entry denotes "the process of leaving prison and returning to free society" (p. 89). This process, they specify, consists of a "post-release transition" (that is, time immediately after prison) and a "post-release integration" stage (the weeks and months after prison). This conceptualization emphasizes that re-entry is a long-term process or endeavour, not a short-term stint. It is a process typically laced with various challenges and barriers (see below). Durnescu (2018) has recently added to this conceptualization of re-entry as a process. According

to Durnescu, re-entry can be understood as a process consisting of multiple steps that are shaped by ex-prisoners' priorities and immediate needs. Based on ethnographic research with 58 Roma and Romanian prison releasees, Durnescu explains that re-entry is essentially "a set of sequences ordered logically on a timescale" (p. 2211): (1) a pre-release anticipation stage (the time leading up to release and the day of release); (2) the first two weeks of release, during which recovery and reunion with family are typically prioritized by returning prisoners; and (3) an "activation" phase (weeks three and four of the re-entry process), when economic activity (that is, looking for and securing work) becomes important. Following week four of the re-entry process, Durnescu finds that former prisoners tend to settle in their new roles and routines (that is, they manage to adjust to life on the outside), while others, for example those who are less successful in re-accustoming themselves to life on the outside, may start to feel frustrated and hopeless, which, at least in part, can lead to reoffending.

While a long-term process, re-entry can also be understood as an event. Durnescu's (2018) research, for example, and that of others (see Maruna, Immarigeon, & LeBel, 2004) reminds readers that re-entry includes the critical event of leaving the prison. Re-entry takes place the day a person is released from prison. It is a matter of fact—every person released from custody re-enters the community (regardless of the amount of time spent in prison) and whether they remain under penal supervision following release (on parole). To date, few scholars have studied the day of release from prison in more depth. Richards and Jones (2004) interviewed male prisoners in Iowa directly after their release from custody and accompanied them from prison to their designated community correctional facility (most often a halfway house or work release centre). Their research draws attention to some of the immediate challenges of prison release, such as the lack of clothing and financial supports faced by releasees.

Maruna (2011) has also started to problematize the day of release from prison by contemplating how a prisoner's release from custody and return to the community could be marked by what he refers to as "rituals of reintegration." He argues that in comparison to incarceration—a practice saturated with rituals—a prisoners' return to the community is left relatively unacknowledged by the wider community. "Rituals of reintegration," he suggests, should focus on affirming the prisoner's return to and reacceptance by the larger community; one such ritual could be a welcome ceremony organized by the state or local community marking a prisoner's release from prison and transition from the status of prisoner to citizen, while also celebrating their future.

Indeed, the day of release from prison is a moment of transition for both the returning prisoner and the people around them. Perhaps similar to other major life events (such as marriage or the birth of a child), it is a day that prisoners and their families associate with many expectations, fears, and hopes for the future (see Kuhlmann & Kury, 2011; Travis & Waul, 2003). Despite this significance, relatively little is known about how the day of release from prison is perceived and experienced by former prisoners. Especially in the Canadian context, pursuing this line of inquiry could be particularly fruitful, given the vast differences in release planning, context, and supports between provincial/territorial and federal prisoners (see below).

Some scholars have criticized the conceptualization of prisoner re-entry as a process for implying that a clear separation exists between the prison and the outside world when, in reality, many prisoners move between these two spheres. Wacquant (2010), for example, argues that to speak of re-entry is inaccurate "insofar as the vast majority of former convicts experience *not re-entry but ongoing circulation between the two poles of a continuum of forced confinement*" (p. 611; emphasis added; see also Blumstein & Beck, 2005; Clear, Rose, & Rider, 2001; Wacquant 2000). Bumiller (2013) too explains that the term "re-entry" is misplaced since the majority of ex-prisoners were not integrated into "mainstream" society prior to going to prison. For them, "re-entry into society would be more accurately described as prelude to another entry into the prison" (p. 611). The interpretation of re-entry as a cycle is anchored in the evidence that a large number of prisoners continue to be rearrested and returned to prison (either on a new charge or technical violation) and remain entangled in different systems of penal control even when they are not incarcerated. As Richards and Jones (2004) candidly stated: "The system is a revolving door that shuffles prisoners from one level of custody to another, from probation to prison, from prison to work release and parole and from parole back to prison" (p. 220). We explore these dynamics between re-entry and re-incarceration further below.

How Is Prisoner Re-entry Different from Other Concepts?

Although there is clearly some overlap, it is important to distinguish prisoner re-entry from related concepts and explain how the overall research goals of scholars interested in prisoner re-entry differ from those studying reintegration or criminal desistance. We also highlight that this chapter does not discuss research on *recidivism*. Recidivism refers to rates of reoffending, usually measured by re-arrest, re-conviction, or re-incarceration. This is clearly different from prisoner re-entry research, which focuses on understanding people's individual trajectories of re-entry and the processes involved in the commission or cessation of crime (Travis & Visher, 2005). Let's take a closer look at what is meant by reintegration and desistance:

- *Reintegration:* Reintegration is different from re-entry insofar as it refers not just to the process of prison release, but also to specific goals tied to release, such as to live as a law-abiding citizen and to re-establish ties within the community (Petersilia, 2003). Put differently, every prisoner released from custody *re-enters* the community as a matter of fact, but not every releasee (re) integrates "successfully." Of course, it is important to note that just like with prisoner re-entry, there is no standard definition of reintegration or, even more contentious, "successful" reintegration (see Maidment, 2006), which further complicates conceptual distinctions between these different concepts. As Goodman (2012) has stated, **rehabilitation** is "variegated and pixelated, and considerably messier than many contemporary scholarly accounts allow" (p. 439). We suggest that the term "prisoner re-entry" is broader than rehabilitation or reintegration; however, in line with Goodman's understanding, we would highlight that what matters most is how returning prisoners themselves define, experience, and give meaning to the process and goals of re-entry, rehabilitation, and reintegration.
- *Desistance:* Prisoner re-entry is also distinct from yet related to the concept of desistance. Researchers looking at criminal desistance examine why and, importantly, how people stop offending. Some researchers look at why and in

what ways social institutions (such as marriage) or experiences (such as the birth of a child) facilitate the termination of criminal behaviour. They refer to structural changes in one's life as "life transitions" (McIvor, Murray, & Jamieson, 2004), "turning points" (Laub & Sampson, 2001; Sampson & Laub, 2005), or "hooks for change" (Giordano, Cernkovich, & Rudolph, 2002). It is often noted that "turning points" alone are not sufficient to initiate behavioural change, as ex-prisoners must also be determined to stop offending—in other words, both internal and external changes are necessary to initiate desistance. Albeit different, re-entry and desistance are seen as interlinked in that understanding prisoners' experiences of re-entry may facilitate a better understanding of why some offenders are able to stop offending whereas others are not (see also Maruna et al., 2004).

Overall, then, we understand and conceptualize prisoner re-entry as a dynamic process that is influenced by various factors, including personal characteristics, community context, and structural factors, and that unfolds over time and space. Trajectories of re-entry are personal but also, as this chapter shows, significantly shaped by criminal justice professionals and other front-line workers who are tasked to act on ex-prisoners' lives in empowered ways and whose own conceptions of rehabilitation and reintegration influence ex-prisoners' experiences of re-entry.

Understanding Barriers to Re-entry

Marcus was released on his "stat" (statutory release date). Although he had served prior sentences, in this instance he was released after serving five years of his seven-year sentence. He described having a "normal" life but "dabbling" in some illegal ventures that did not work out favourably for him. After he described not only criminal involvement but also being betrayed by his co-accused, a former "friend," he provided insight into his early re-entry experiences. Although he was initially hopeful and positive, his positive views were soon tempered by his ongoing challenges with employment, reconnecting with his children, and his position within the community. As you read the narrative from

Marcus' first interview below, make note of the various challenges and barriers that may shape people's lives following incarceration:

Ricciardelli: Do you feel ready for reintegration?

Marcus: Yeah for sure, I think I was ready from day one, I just had to get the jitters out, like a squirrel in traffic at first.

Ricciardelli: What are your concerns now?

Marcus: . . . Um for me, not much worries, just to get a stable job, to get a job to obtain the money that I need to show my parole officer or these people [so that I can] get out of the halfway house. Have a nice place where I could go, that's the main thing that could most worry me; that you want to get started . . . Yeah, once you get the process going then, for me at least I know I'll be on the right up. I'll be ok.

Ricciardelli: And how do you feel about prospects for employment and stuff?

Marcus: I had an important job where experience played a factor. Experience [now] would be a factor. If I could drive [equipment] better I'd probably still be at that job. I wouldn't be talking to you today cause I'd be working. It was a nice job, a night job, night shift. It was really good and the pay was really good. $18 an hour, it was really good. But with experience; I can't just tell them I learned to drive [equipment] in four days in the penitentiary.

. . .

My plan was to be living in a condo that I shared with [family member removed], but it was leased out while I was incarcerated. And the lease is taking some time to be up so they said I would have to go to a hotel, that was the plan I made with my PO [parole officer], so I said 'it doesn't sound good' . . . it'd be good not to pay rent, good to save some money . . .

[It was] the revolving doors [of prison] and I guess, when you look back now, sometimes you tend to do the same habitual things. You have to break habits . . . If you're in a certain activity then you're more liable of getting caught up in that activity. At the end of the day at any given time if you're in criminal activity your life is at risk . . .

Currently, I'm waiting to get a job, so I can live and earn . . . I'm looking to obtain a job where I could get a pension and get these things that are obtainable . . .

[To stay out of prison and stay away from crime] it's good to be financially stable, like for me that is one of the main things that fuels my crime. My wants got to be a little bit watered down . . . Be financially stable, having a place and [it] being furnished or whatever and taking care of liabilities or whatever, responsibilities. Doing things like that, which takes time. Getting myself situated and, I think, by working full time . . . I'm ready, willing, and able, and I wanna be a hard worker, and I want the opportunity to prove to others and myself that I'm capable.

Securing Employment

Upon release from prison, most ex-prisoners are immediately confronted with the task of finding employment. The financial pressure to find work can be exacerbated by prisoners' own lack of savings or financial support from families. Many prisoners are under pressure to secure work so they can financially support their families (Braman & Wood, 2003) or, like Marcus, they may have to secure employment to satisfy release expectations. Securing formal employment is one of the key goals prisoners themselves express while still incarcerated and awaiting their release (Kuhlmann & Kury, 2011). Finding employment, however, presents an immense barrier for the majority of individuals released from prison (see Petersilia, 2003; Ricciardelli & Peters, 2017; Richards & Jones, 2004; Western, Kling, & Weiman, 2001). Moreover, if ex-prisoners are able to enter or re-enter the labour market, they are most often limited to low-paying and low-skilled jobs (Western, 2018; Western et al., 2001). As Sugie (2018) explains, ex-prisoners often remain in a state of sporadic and temporary work; they engage in "foraging" behaviour for low-skill work in which different jobs are obtained frequently.

Scholars explain that ex-prisoners face immense barriers in re-establishing employment, primarily because of the **stigma** attached to having a criminal record. The criminal record is a permanent marker of criminality and the status of offender—a form of "invisible punishment" (Travis, 2000)—carries well beyond prison walls. One of the most widely cited studies regarding the stigmatizing effect of the criminal record is research conducted by Devah Pager (2003). Using an experimental audit approach, Pager investigated the consequences of imprisonment for the employment outcomes of Black and white job seekers in Milwaukee, Wisconsin. Pager found that a criminal record presented a major barrier to employment, particularly for Black people. Having

a criminal record reduced the likelihood of a callback from an employer by 50 percent or more, and Black applicants were more disadvantaged in this regard than whites. In fact, Pager found that white applicants with criminal records received more favourable treatment than Black applicants without criminal records. Thus, Pager argued that "criminal records close doors in employment situations. Many employers seem to use the information as a screening mechanism, without attempting to probe deeper into the possible context or complexities of the situation" (p. 956). Having a criminal record can be an immediate disqualifier because in the eyes of the employer, because it labels the ex-prisoners as untrustworthy and prone to crime; the specific offence appears to be less important (Winnick & Bodkin, 2008).

In addition to the criminal record, the fact that many ex-prisoners were dealing with un- or underemployment prior to their imprisonment is another aggravating factor. As Western (2018) points out in his recent study with over 100 former prisoners in Boston, the criminal record intersects with realities of addictions, physical disabilities, and mental health issues that shape people's lives. As he notes, "a criminal record may have been an obstacle, but their job opportunities would have been very poor without the added challenge of incarceration" (p. 81). Writing within the Canadian context, Ricciardelli and Mooney (2019) note that most prisoners in their sample are not *re*-entering the labour market; instead, they are seeking gainful and legal employment for the first time. Not only does their lack of experience and (in some cases) age work against a former prisoner in such a position, but the lack of a résumé (not just a gap in their résumé) is rather difficult to explain.

Despite these various challenges, ex-prisoners do succeed in re-establishing ties within the formal labour market. To date, relatively little attention has been given to how ex-prisoners navigate the challenges associated with employment—that is, how some ex-prisoners are able to secure employment in light of the stigma and structural barriers they face. Scholars have suggested that common strategies of navigating employment barriers include drawing on personal contacts or choosing job settings in which the criminal record is not a big detriment, or may even be considered an asset (O'Brien, 2001; Petersilia, 2003). Scholars who have sought to unpack these challenges of navigating employment more extensively focus on how ex-prisoners deal specifically with having a criminal record when applying for work. Researchers consistently report that in an effort to secure work, some ex-prisoners may avoid disclosing their criminal record to a potential employer (Harding, 2003). Other strategies include "full disclosure" and "conditional disclosure" (see Harding, 2003; Ricciardelli & Mooney, 2019). The former means that ex-prisoners disclose their criminal history as early as possible in the hope that this will secure them long-term employment and the ability to be promoted once they have proven their skills and work ethic; the latter, on the other hand, refers to ex-prisoners waiting to disclose their criminal history until they have worked long enough to demonstrate their workplace skills. According to Harding (2003), conditional disclosure is "the most strategic manager of identity information" (p. 548); it improved a person's initial chances of securing work while keeping doors open for long-term employment. Ricciardelli and Mooney (2019) found that as the ex-prisoners in their sample became more embedded in the community (that is, spent more time in the community post-release and, thus, were closer to their warrant expiration date), they were more likely to feel distant from their criminal history. In consequence, parolees were less likely to feel a seeming obligation to disclose. Thus, over time, ex-prisoners moved increasingly away from practising full disclosure and even in many cases conditional disclosure. Indeed, some parolees who reported practising full disclosure eventually felt that non-disclosure was a better option for assisting in securing work, noting that many employers will not do a record check. These participants reported feeling increasingly distanced from their former prisoner identity.

Some research has also looked at the effectiveness of campaigns such as "ban the box," a social movement that seeks to encourage employers not to ask criminal history questions on initial job applications. Today, "ban-the-box laws" are in effect in various US states and cities. By erasing criminal history questions from job applications, ban-the-box laws seek to level the playing field by providing fairer chances for criminalized people, although it is important to highlight that employers may ask such questions later in the hiring process. There are also social enterprises, such as Klink Coffee in Canada and Dave's Killer Bread in the United States, which focus on providing former prisoners with employment opportunities and training after incarceration. Finally, it is important to note that ex-prisoners can eventually apply to have their record suspended, which may facilitate the process of securing work.

To conclude this section, it is important to note that the effects and stigma tied to the criminal record have only intensified in the digital era, as the Internet and other forms of digitization have resulted in new forms of "digital punishment" that serve to make criminal histories, including charges and convictions, more accessible to employers and those with interest. Indeed, the Internet makes it possible to search up people and potentially find information about their history, including any criminal charges, even after official records have been set aside (see Chapter 15 for further discussion about the ways technology is reshaping carceral spaces and penal practices). Lageson and Maruna (2018) thus argue that the criminal stigma is now an even stickier, more enduring attribute of ex-prisoners' re-entry. Criminal records "are now much more than official, state-sanctioned 'criminal records.' Criminal justice agencies have moved toward digital record-keeping, making widespread dissemination easier and cheaper across platforms as these data practices have eliminated the need to physically obtain criminal record information" (p. 117). As a result, inclined community

Record Suspension in Canada

In Canada, record suspensions (formerly called **pardons**) are regulated by the Criminal Records Act. Record suspension means that a person's criminal record is removed from the Canadian Police Information Centre database. Record suspension is different from expungement, which means that all (federal) records related to the offence in question are destroyed, not just set aside, as is the case with record suspensions. The Parole Board of Canada decides on all issues related to record suspensions. Individuals must wait for a certain amount of time before they are eligible to apply for a record suspension (five years for summary offences and ten years for indictable offences). There is also a processing fee associated with this application ($631 as of 2019).

members, employers, and others with a vested interest or curiosity are increasingly able to access information about any person's history; despite how recent, accurate, or reliable this information is, this can have dire consequences on re-entry potentiality and ex-prisoners' lived experiences in the community. (See Spencer & Ricciardelli, 2017 for a discussion of the latent consequences of online information for sex offenders.)

Rebuilding Family Relationships

Existing studies focused on prisoner re-entry and family life emphasize the gendered nature of the challenges surrounding ex-prisoners' efforts to reconnect with family and friends post-release (Braman & Wood, 2003; Haney, 2010; Leverentz, 2010, 2011; O'Brien, 2001). Specifically, scholars tend to centre their attention on the experiences of female ex-prisoners in relation to their children and romantic partners, while there is less research regarding the experiences of partnered and fathering prisoners. Existing research highlights the importance of family support for successful re-entry and reintegration following incarceration (Dodge & Pogrebin, 2001; O'Brien, 2001). For example, Travis and Waul (2003) explain that families can act as a "buffering agent" against the many difficulties returning prisoners encounter, such as being able to offer a place to live or moral support to "go straight" (that is, desist from crime). To act as a buffering agent, however, family and other social relationships must be respectful, mutual, and supportive. As Bui and Morash (2010) explain, positive relationships are linked to positive reintegration, yet negative relationships (such as abusive relationships) can lead to reoffending and inhibit successful reintegration. The apparent correlation applies particularly to female ex-prisoners, many of whom share histories of emotional, physical, or sexual abuse or involvement with romantic partners who introduced them to criminality.

To explain the turbulence caused by incarceration and re-entry on relationships with partners, we turn for a second to look at the changes in relationship status among those in our sample. Table 6.2 provides some information on participants' family situations. As this table shows, more than half of our participants reported having children, of whom 12 explained that their children were biologically theirs. One releasee had stepchildren. Only a small number (*n*=4) were married or in common law relationships prior to their most recent federal incarceration. Of those four people,

three were still in the same committed marriage/partnership post-incarceration (the other relationship had ended). In addition to those four individuals, another participant got engaged during the study period, and two had become involved in serious relationships post-imprisonment. In total then, six individuals were in committed partnerships during the study period, while 19 explained that they were single. A theme here is that, while incarcerated, relationships may end but are very unlikely to start.

Not surprisingly, given our sample is largely composed of men with transitioning relationships and children, male ex-prisoners also experience significant difficulties in trying to re-adjust to family life, although their challenges tend to differ from those of female offenders. Scholars, for example, explain that male ex-prisoners face more pressure to provide for their families, often feeling torn between accepting low-skilled work to secure their family's financial needs and making longer-term investments in their personal or career trajectories (Braman & Wood, 2003). Long-term investments such as drug treatment or job programs, for example, may benefit the ex-prisoner and his family in the long run; however, families of prisoners tend to face immediate financial needs (coupled with the pressures of traditional masculinities and the notion of "men as breadwinners"), making it necessary for the returning prisoner to accept the first job available (Braman & Wood, 2003; Travis & Waul, 2003).

As mentioned above, scholars have centred on the role of marriage, romantic relationships, and children in the re-entry and desistance process. Other kinds of relationships have received less attention; for example, the role of families of origin (O'Brien, 2001; Leverentz, 2011) or ex-prisoners' changing relationships with authorities (Farrall & Calverley, 2005) have yet to be researched in more depth.

Table 6.2 Children and Participants' Family Situations Pre- and Post-Incarceration

Variable	*n*
Children	13
Married or common law pre-incarceration	4
Single pre-incarceration	19
Married or common law post-incarceration	6
Single post-incarceration	19

Community Context

Existing research presenting the relationship between incarceration, re-entry, and community is focused on the situation in the United States. Scholars there highlight that prisoners are mostly drawn from and later return to largely impoverished, relegated, and racialized communities (Lynch & Sabol, 2001; Wacquant, 2010). Geographically, prisoner re-entry is concentrated to a limited number of neighbourhoods within a city, meaning that relatively few neighbourhoods are affected by the imprisonment and later return of offenders (Lynch & Sabol, 2001). These communities exhibit high rates of residents moving in and out of prison, a process that Clear, Waring, and Scully (2005) describe as concentrated "reentry cycling."

Scholars have pointed out that ex-prisoners are limited in their choice of residence; many would like to settle in a new neighbourhood but are often unable to because of financial constraints (see Maidment, 2006). It has also been argued that moving to a new community can present a form of "knifing off" from one's old life and facilitate desistance (Maruna & Roy, 2007). However, given that releasees tend to return to their previous neighbourhoods (Leverentz, 2010; Western, 2018), researchers argue that ex-prisoners must renegotiate how they associate with their community. Such practices allow releasees to experience their old neighbourhoods and communities differently, as a more positive force in their desistance. For individuals who return to the same neighbourhood and possibly the same associates, proving to the correctional authorities (for example, their parole officer) that they have "reformed" may be particularly difficult, especially if their former environments and social networks were deemed to be linked to their offending. In lieu of external change, these people may feel particular pressure to show to authorities that they have engaged in "internal" change, as demonstrated, for example, by perceived changes in attitudes, long-term goals, and reflection on their past life.

Although research suggests that former prisoners tend to return to their home communities, research on why and how some people manage to settle in a different place may offer insights into the processes involved in rebuilding one's post-prison life in a new setting, including the different challenges that may arise. It should also be noted that many ex-prisoners may not immediately return to their communities, as is the case, for example, for those paroled to a halfway house or work release centre outside of their home communities. In such a situation they may be required to "reintegrate" into a new setting, which may present either an opportunity or another challenge to successful reintegration (Maier, 2018). Paying attention to the situational context in which re-entry and re-integration take place can offer additional insights into reintegration as a concept, whose meaning may change depending on the environment one re-enters.

Parole, Post-Prison Supervision, and Re-entry Support

Another interviewee, Ben, participated in the longitudinal study for three full years; he was interviewed four times over that period. In his final interview he described some of his experiences in the community. Ben was able to not return to prison while on conditional release, despite his conditions of **parole** and the challenges of breaching them. Ben works full time but experiences a lot of rejection in the community, and he is in school and trying to make ends meet. He truly values the support of his family and tries not to get too down when he experiences social exclusion.

[The restrictions of parole were difficult]; it was to a point. But I was able to work around some things because I was working full time for a moving company. Pretty much my travel restrictions and my curfew normally would've been an issue but if I contacted the national reporting centre when my curfew was due and let them know I was still working, it wasn't an issue. And my travel as long as I let my PO know where I was going it was ok. As long as I let them know ahead of time then it wasn't a problem. I'm still working there now and again [but not full time because of school].

. . .

[I live at] my mother's. They wouldn't allow me into a halfway house. It's been ok, a little rocky the last few months because I haven't been working as much and the compensation doesn't really give enough for living. Well, for a single male [OSAP doesn't] give anything for living. A single male that can work they won't give a dime for living . . . I have certifications now [list removed]. I have one prospective employer . . . I have applied to a lot, and they've said that while I'm more than qualified for the job they can't take me because I have a record. I've gotten so used to it now. Like I've been to more than 20 interviews where they've said that.

It actually still is [discouraging], but I have a lot of support at school and they know my background and my charge.

. . .

[Having family support is helpful]. They're just around when I need them. My last interview I did on Tuesday I got a call back that same day to say sorry but due to our policies we can't hire you. So I got down in the dumps there cause that was the sixth one in two weeks. I was at school and I had to leave cause I couldn't deal with the rest of the day. I went home and my mom said to just take it easy and try not to think about it because she knows the first thing that happens when I keep going over something. I just go into a depression and I don't want to do anything so just take it easy, do what you have to do, do some of your homework at least.

As evinced in Ben's narrative, people's experiences of re-entry, including their employment experiences, are shaped by the broader institutional and penal context. The following section thus provides an overview of the different forms of conditional release and supervision following incarceration. In line with the data presented so far, we focus on the realities of federally sentenced prisoners.

Forms of Conditional Release in Canada

Post-prison supervision plays an essential role in prisoner re-entry and is framed by the Canadian government as an important step in the pursuit of public safety. According to the Parole Board of Canada (PBC, 2011), the goal of post-prison supervision is to "contribute to public safety by helping offenders reintegrate into society as law-abiding citizens through a gradual, controlled, and supported release with conditions." The forms of **conditional release** that exist in Canada for federal offenders are as follows:

- *Temporary absences:* Temporary absence means that a prisoner is temporarily released from a prison institution for a short time, either escorted (that is, supervised by a prison staff member or approved escort) or unescorted. Escorted temporary absences may be granted at any time (for exceptions, see s. 130(5) of the Corrections and Conditional Release Act), and workers or volunteers from various organizations (see discussion below)

are often involved in escorting prisoners for the duration of their absence from the prison. A prisoner is eligible for unescorted temporary absences at one-sixth or six months of their sentence, whichever is later.
- *Full parole:* Individuals are usually eligible for **full parole** after serving one-third of their sentence in custody or seven years (whichever is less). These people can establish their own residency in the community, but remain under the supervision of a parole officer and must abide by their conditions of release (for example, curfews).
- *Day parole:* Individuals are usually eligible for **day parole** six months prior to their full parole eligibility date. Day parolees are permitted to spend their day in the community (for purposes of work, training, or programming) but have to return nightly to a supervised residence, most often a **halfway house** or community correctional centre. In addition to these NGO-run halfway houses, there remain a small number of government-run facilities referred to as community correctional centres. These centres, which also house individuals on supervised/ conditional release, have been described as more security focused than NGO-run facilities (Bell & Trevethan 2004).
- *Statutory release:* Finally, **statutory release** is a release by law; as such, offenders are almost always released after serving two-thirds of their sentence unless there is a substantial risk of serious reoffending, as decided by the PBC. It should also be noted that individuals serving life sentences are exempt from statutory release. Although a release by law, statutory release is considered a form of conditional release and, as a result, these individuals also have conditions attached to their release, are supervised by a parole officer, and are subject to the same revocation regime as parolees.

While an in-depth discussion of the nature and process of, but also problems associated with, risk assessment goes beyond the purview of this chapter (for an overview, see Andrews, Bonta, & Wormith, 2006), we do want to mention briefly that release decisions are heavily based on assessment of offender risk and needs. Parole officers working both inside prison institutions (institutional parole officers) and the community (community parole officers) complete actuarial risk assessments, the goal of which is to assess and predict an offender's risk of reoffending. Such assessments include accounting for both static risk factors that cannot be addressed through treatment, such as a person's criminal history and offence severity, as well as dynamic risk factors that can be addressed and ideally mitigated through treatment and intervention; those include employment, drug use, family relationships, and other personal circumstances. The particular parole conditions imposed on a person (for example, curfews, residency conditions) should be targeted toward a person's specific risks of reoffending as well as a parolee's specific needs (such as for employment or housing); in other words, parole conditions must respond to people's assessed risks as well as be tailored to their specific needs (for a more in-depth discussion, see Turnbull & Hannah-Moffat, 2009).

Former prisoners on conditional release remain under penal supervision until their **warrant expiry date** (that is, the end of their sentence). Parole is earned for good behaviour and requires dedication and a commitment from prisoners to demonstrate their interest in ceasing to engage in antisocial or criminal acts early in their sentence. Statutory release, on the other hand, is awarded (not earned); it serves as a safeguard in society because it ensures that releasees pass time in the community under the supervision of the CSC, rather than being released at the end of their sentence without supervision and supports. Thus, the criteria for being deemed eligible for release after serving two-thirds of a sentence is neither as delicate nor as ingrained in prisoner lifestyles as that tied to being paroled. In either case, the PBC decides on the timing and nature of conditional release, whereas the CSC is responsible for carrying out the actual supervision regime.

Halfway Houses in Canada

Courtesy of St Leonard's Place

Halfway houses, such as St Leonard's Place Peel, located in Brampton, Ontario, are one of the ways conditional release is managed in Canada. St Leonard's Place services men over 16 years of age, and has grown from a 21-bed facility to a maximum capacity of 115.

CSC, "work on a system of gradual, supervised release" and provide "a bridge between the institution and the community" (CSC, 2014). As criminological researchers have shown, "conditional release is more effective in promoting a prisoner's successful reintegration into society as a law-abiding citizen than would be his/her sudden freedom—at sentence expiry—without any assistance or supervision" (Doob, Webster, & Manson, 2014, p. 305). Halfway houses in contemporary Canada range in capacity from 4 to 80 beds and tend to be located in urban centres, often around low-income residential neighbourhoods (Allspach, 2010; Bell & Trevethan,

Halfway houses, also referred to as community-based residential facilities, play an important role in prisoner re-entry. These houses, according to the

2004). Most are female- or male-only facilities, although there are some mixed-gender houses.

Halfway houses are run by a number of non-governmental organizations, like the Elizabeth Fry or John Howard Societies. Halfway house residents are typically required to be physically present at the halfway house overnight (for at least six consecutive hours). In addition, they must report to the halfway house, in person or over the phone, at certain times during the day. If a resident fails to comply, halfway house workers are required, as per their contracts with the Canadian government, to report such lack of compliance either to the parole officer of the resident or to what is called the National Monitoring Centre—a centralized operational centre, located in Ottawa, that oversees all halfway house and other community operations across Canada. While halfway house workers advise parole officers regarding residents' progress (in terms of employment, treatment, and general behaviour at the halfway house), the ultimate supervision authority lies with the Canadian government. Halfway house workers, as such, cannot revoke a person's parole and return them to prison. Recent research indicates that this limited power can be experienced by halfway house workers as a form of tension and conflict, given that these workers tend to conceive of themselves as supporters (rather than control agents) of former prisoners (Maier, 2018).

Statistics by Public Safety Canada show that ex-prisoners on conditional release mostly complete their conditional release successfully—that is, they complete it without a return to prison for a breach of conditions (also referred to as a "technical violation") or for a new offence. Specifically, in 2016–17, the successful completion rate of federal day parole was 92.7 per cent; for federal full parole it was 89.7 per cent, and 67.4 per cent for statutory release. Successful completion rates for all forms of conditional release have increased over the years (Public Safety Canada, 2017). As these figures show, day and full parole correlate positively with non-offending. As other researchers have noted, however, it is difficult to say if this correlation can be attributed to the more supervised regime offered by day and full parole or because "parolees who already have the best chances of success tend to apply for and receive day parole more often than higher risk offenders" (Cyca & Williams, 2020, p. 259).

Experiences of Parole and Post-Prison Supervision

As explained above, individuals on conditional release must abide by a variety of conditions and rules, such as curfews, residency conditions, or having to report intimate relationships to one's parole officer. Securing conditional release and then dealing with the specific conditions of release can be challenging (see Chapter 11 for the particular challenges faced by aging prisoners). Some scholars have pointed out that such rules have the primary effect of controlling people's geographic mobility, sexuality, and other aspects of everyday life, while keeping former prisoners under the constant threat of re-incarceration. Parole, they argue, essentially widens the carceral tent, keeping individuals entangled in a system of **transcarceral control** (Maidment, 2006). As Allspach (2010) notes, "parole stipulations symbolize a continuity of imprisonment outside the literal prison institution" (p. 719).

To date, only a select number of scholars have provided insight into how releasees experience conditional release governance (Johnson, 2015; Opsal, 2015; Werth, 2012). Their research has focused on how individuals respond to parole rules as well as how parole rules impact people's everyday lives, such as their ability to find employment or reconnect with family and friends. Opsal's (2015) research with female parolees found that parole conditions often complicate re-entry for returning prisoners and conflict with the demands of everyday life as well as parolees' own conceptions of what it means to "go straight," referring to desisting from any criminal activity (Maruna, 2011). Adding to these findings, in his research with 24 releasees in California, Werth (2012) has suggested that parolees frequently disobey those parole rules that they find unhelpful or hindering: "[P]articipants complied with those rules that they perceived essential, observing only those that were part of their own construction of parole" (p. 340). In an effort to negotiate the tension between adhering to one's parole conditions and violating them in an effort to serve one's own immediate needs,

Werth has argued that parolees "engage selectively" with their parole conditions. Specifically, individuals in his study complied with those rules they believed were necessary to avoid re-incarceration, but violated those experiences as impeding their effort to rebuild their lives. Werth's research shows that while parole presents a largely repressive force in people's lives, parolees are also agents insofar as they "construct parole in a way that allowed the rules to become open to interpretation, alteration, and restructuring" (p. 341).

Ben, whom we heard from earlier in this chapter, was able to navigate his conditions of release quite successfully. Post-prison supervision, as study participants' narratives showed and as demonstrated by others (Werth, 2012) can be conflicting. On the one hand, post-prison supervision can provide ex-prisoners with structure and (albeit temporary) sources of material support (through halfway houses, for example); on the other hand, they keep people entangled in systems of control, regulation, and surveillance. Ex-prisoners' experiences of parole and post-prison supervision thus show how punishment/control and rehabilitation/treatment can braid or blend together in a single penal practice.

Re-entry Support through Non-governmental Organizations

In addition to state-run support and supervision services, non-governmental organizations (NGOs) play an important part in facilitating the process of re-entry for former prisoners. In recent years, various scholars have called attention to what Mijs (2016) has referred to as the "organizational reality of re-entry" (p. 292). Earlier in this chapter we defined prisoner re-entry as an individual process. Departing from this conceptualization, Miller (2014, p. 307) has suggested that prisoner

re-entry should be understood as a "social institution." Re-entry, in his words, denotes "a welfare-state criminal justice hybrid institution that activates the universe of human service actors, criminal justice agencies, and policy and program planners to assist former prisoners make the transition from prison to their home communities" (p. 307). This conceptualization of prisoner re-entry draws attention to the fact that various actors of the criminal justice and social service field seek to govern and act on ex-prisoners as they return to the community. As a result, former prisoners may be confronted with different expectations of what it means to reintegrate "successfully."

Over the last few years, there has been an influx of studies examining the work of community **prisoner re-entry organizations** and their approach to and conceptions of former prisoners (Halushka, 2016; Kaufman, 2015; Miller, 2014; Mijs, 2016). These organizations have taken on an essential role in providing re-entry services while often maintaining control over ex-prisoners' lives on behalf of the state. American-based scholar Nicole Kaufman (2015), for example, has looked at how re-entry organizations seek to "incorporate" ex-prisoners in the community. She distinguishes between two broad groups of prisoner re-entry organizations. The first group, which she refers to as "classic re-entry organizations," are those specializing in the state's preferred policy areas, "namely treatment and economic incorporation" (p. 11). She finds that these organizations subscribe to the philosophy that ex-prisoners have "the potential to be citizens" (p. 12) provided they are willing to receive state-prescribed treatment and, ultimately, change into "productive," law-abiding citizens, meaning individuals who are gainfully employed and refrain from criminalized behaviour. The second group is referred to as "broader

The "Pains" of Community Supervision

It is well known that imprisonment is associated with a variety of material and emotional "pains" for incarcerated individuals (Sykes, 1958). In recent years, scholars have started to highlight that incarceration is not the only painful sanction; community supervision, such as parole, can be painful, too (see McNeill, 2019). The research outlined above, for example, points to the ways post-prison supervision can penetrate ex-prisoners'

daily lives and routines and exert a "tight" grip on their thoughts and emotions (see Crewe, 2011). Individuals on parole must also deal with the threat of re-incarceration, which can lead to added stress and anxiety. Recognizing and studying post-prison supervision as a form of punishment (rather than merely a rehabilitative practice) is important because it highlights that punishment extends beyond the boundaries of the prison.

incorporation re-entry organizations," and they differ from the first insofar as they "engage in a variety of activities and issues beyond those described in state policy." Specifically, these organizations, Kaufman says, focus more on political and religious incorporation and see ex-prisoners as deserving of citizenship and inclusion. Kaufman's (2015) research, while focused on the US context, is important for understanding the work of Canadian-based re-entry organizations because it draws attention to the fact that the work of NGO-run re-entry organizations is not uniform but rather is "institutionally patterned, and includes quite varied assumptions among NGOs about the nature of community and formerly incarcerated people's relationship to citizenship" (p. 548).

In Canada, there exist a variety of organizations that provide various services and rehabilitative programs to former prisoners. Here are some examples, although there are many more organizations and programs not listed here:

- *Elizabeth Fry Societies*: Elizabeth Fry Societies across Canada advocate on behalf of criminalized women and provide a variety of services, material and emotional supports, and rehabilitative programs. These may include clothing depots, employment and housing programs, and a variety of other rehabilitative programs focused on things such as relationship building or anger management. (www.caefs.ca)
- *John Howard Society*: The John Howard Society also has offices across Canada. Their mission is to provide "effective, just and humane responses to the causes and consequences of crime" by working with people who have been in conflict with the law and promoting community and social development activities, among other things. Local offices provide a variety of services and programs. (http://johnhoward.ca)
- *Circles of Support and Accountability (CoSA)*: CoSA is a national program that focuses on providing "a supportive space to those integrating into the community after incarceration." CoSA's focus is on formerly incarcerated people "who are at high risk of harming themselves and others." CoSA's approach is based heavily on principles of restorative justice, a "holistic" approach to helping criminalized populations, and offender accountability. (www.initiativesjc.org/wpblog/cosa)
- *M2/W2*: Some services and programs are also provided by religious organizations. One example is M2/W2 Association—Restorative Christian Ministries—a program for people involved with the criminal justice system whose goal is to "foster healthier communities." Mentoring, help with employment, and "circle base support" are some of services provided through M2/W2. (www.canadahelps.org/en/charities/m2w2-association-restorative-christian-ministries)

Research on the work of NGO-run re-entry organizations in Canada, to date, is fairly scant. Emerging research from the United States suggests that re-entry organizations emphasize remoralization and the reconstitution of ex-prisoners' selves and ways of thinking when working with former prisoners. In line with neoliberalist ideas, former prisoners are encouraged to see themselves as active subjects responsible for managing their own risks and making prudent choices that ensure a self-sufficient future. For example, Halushka (2016), in his ethnographic study of a workforce development program run by a re-entry organization in a northeastern US city, for example, explains that clients of the re-entry organization he observed received lessons in what he calls "work wisdom," which involved teaching participants a number of soft skills and cultural scripts that were believed to help them establish contacts with employers. Such lessons included teaching clients how to tailor their style of dress or how to disclose discrediting information like having a criminal record. Expanding this research to the Canadian context would be interesting and enable further insight into the work of re-entry organizations and their specific strategies of "rehabilitating" former prisoners.

Summary

Re-entry is a difficult process; it is emotionally, financially, physically, and legally taxing. As Table 6.3 shows, by the end of the three-year study, 4 of the 25 participants had returned to prison on a new charge, while another participant had temporarily returned to prison because their parole was suspended (we have since learned that others in our sample have also returned to prison).

More positively, various participants were gainfully employed by the end of this longitudinal study, as Table 6.4 outlines. Of the seven participants who had acquired and remained in full-time employment positions by the

Table 6.3   Participants' Legal Status by Year 3 of the Study

Variable	n
No re-incarceration	20
Re-incarceration	5
On a new offence	4
For a technical violation	1

Table 6.4   Participants' Employment Status by Year 3 of the Study

Variable	n
Full-time employment	7
Part-time employment	1
Unemployed	14
In school	2

end of the study, two were able to secure "management" positions. Two participants who were previously employed decided to pursue further education and were in school full time by the end of the study.

This chapter introduced readers to some of the major challenges of re-entry and provided some insight into how ex-prisoners seek to navigate those challenges. The chapter also provided information on Canada's system of conditional release and outlined the important role of various organizations in shaping ex-prisoners' trajectories of re-entry. The narratives of the men and women that lace this chapter draw attention to some of the pressures former prisoners face as they make their return from prison to community living. During their incarceration, prisoners are regularly exposed to different correctional and rehabilitative programs. Upon release, they must show to the penal authorities that they have internalized the notion of change. Specifically, they must demonstrate "good" behaviour and "pro-social" attitudes, or they may risk re-incarceration. They must show that they have "rehabilitated" and reformed, despite the various structural and socio-economic barriers and challenges that await them following incarceration. As our data and other research have shown (see Durnescu, 2018), this can create feelings of pressure, frustration, and hopelessness. Creating policy and programs that are informed by ex-prisoners' own experiences and definitions of "successful" re-entry is an essential step in mediating such feelings and facilitating the process of prisoner re-entry in positive and viable ways.

Review Questions

1. Define the term "prisoner re-entry" and explain how it differs from reintegration and criminal desistance.
2. Identify some of the major challenges returning prisoners commonly face.
3. Identify and explain the different forms of conditional release in Canada.
4. Explain the purpose of halfway houses in the context of prisoner re-entry.
5. Describe some of the existing research on the role of prisoner re-entry organizations.

Critical Thinking Questions

1. Does the term "prisoner re-entry" offer any conceptual advantage over other terms like "recidivism," "reintegration," or "rehabilitation"?
2. In what ways have digitization processes made re-entry for ex-prisoners more challenging? Do you think digitization can positively impact ex-prisoners' lives in any way? Where do you see the future of "digital punishment" going?
3. What do you believe is more important in facilitating re-entry: providing ex-prisoners with material help, or improving people's soft skills?
4. Are halfway houses about punishment/control or reintegration/treatment?
5. How important are rules and conditions to helping individuals desist from crime and re-enter the community after prison?

Multimedia Suggestions

The Road from Crime
A documentary about criminal desistance and re-entering the community after a period of incarceration: https://vimeo.com/43658591

Prisoner Re-entry Institute and StoryCorps Justice Project podcasts
Podcasts about mass incarceration, prisoner re-entry, and education, featuring the narratives of people directly impacted by the criminal justice system: http://johnjaypri.org/category/podcasts

Professor Bruce Western on Life in the Year after Prison
An interview by US scholar Bruce Western about re-entry and his new book *Homeward: Life in*

***the Year after Prison*: https://www.youtube.com/watch?v=o-PywYaGbsw**

Virtual Tour of a Hearing Room
Tour of a hearing room where parole meetings in Canada take place: https://www.canada.ca/en/parole-board/services/parole/virtual-tour-of-a-hearing-room.html

Journal of Prisoners on Prisons
A Canadian-based, prisoner written, academically oriented journal that includes accounts of both imprisonment and prisoner re-entry: http://www.jpp.org

References

Allspach, A. (2010). Landscapes of (neo-)liberal control: The transcarceral spaces of federally sentenced women in Canada. *Gender, Place and Culture, 17*(6), 705–23.

Andrews, D.A., Bonta, J., & Wormith, J.S. (2006). The recent past and near future of risk and/or need assessment. *Crime & Delinquency, 52*, 7–27.

Bell, A., & Trevethan, S. (2004). Community residential facilities in Canada: A descriptive profile of residents and facilities. Research Branch, Correctional Service of Canada (NR-157).

Blumstein, A., & Beck, A. (2005). Reentry as a transient state between liberty and recommitment. In J. Travis & C. Visher (Eds), *Prisoner reentry and crime in America* (pp. 50–79). New York, NY: Cambridge University Press.

Braman, D., & Wood, J. (2003). From one generation to the next: How criminal sanctions are reshaping family life in urban America. In J. Travis & M. Waul (Eds), *Prisoners once removed: The impact of incarceration and reentry on children, families, and communities* (pp. 157–88). Washington, DC: Urban Institute Press.

Bui, H., & Morash, M. (2010). The impact of network relationships, prison experiences, and internal transformation of women's success after prison release. *Journal of Offender Rehabilitation, 49*, 1–22.

Bumiller, K. (2013). Incarceration, welfare state and labour market nexus: The increasing significance of gender in the prison system. In B. Carlton & M. Segrave (Eds), *Women exiting prison: Critical essays on gender, post-release support and survival* (pp. 52–93). New York, NY: Routledge.

Clear, T., Rose, D., & Ryder, J. (2001). Incarceration and the community: The problem of removing and returning offenders. *Crime and Delinquency, 47*(3), 335–51.

Clear, T., Waring, E., & Scully, K. (2005). Communities and reentry: Concentrated reentry cycling. In J. Travis & C. Visher (Eds), *Prisoner reentry and crime in America* (pp. 179–208). New York, NY: Cambridge University Press.

Correctional Service Canada. (2014). Community-based residential facilities (CBRFs). Retrieved from http://www.csc-scc.gc.ca/facilities-and-security/001-0001-eng.shtml

Crewe, V. (2011). Depth, weight, tightness: Revisiting the pains of imprisonment. *Punishment & Society, 13*(5), 509–29.

Cyca, T., & Williams, T. (2020). Conditional release in Canada. In M. Weinrath & J. Winterdyk (Eds), *Adult corrections in Canada* (pp. 239–64). Whitby, ON: de Sitter Publications.

Dodge, M., & Pogrebin, M.R. (2001). Collateral costs of imprisonment for women: Complications of reintegration. *The Prison Journal, 81*, 42–54.

Doob, A., Webster, C., & Manson, A. (2014). Zombie parole: The withering conditional release in Canada. *Criminal Law Quarterly, 61*(3), 301–28.

Durnescu, I. (2018). The five stages of prisoner reentry: Toward a process theory. *International Journal of Offender Therapy and Comparative Criminology, 62*(8), 2195–215.

Farrall, S., & Calverley, A. (2005). *Understanding desistance from crime*. Maidenhead, UK: Open University Press.

Giordano, P., Cernkovich, S., & Rudolph, J.L. (2002). Gender, crime and desistance: Toward a theory of cognitive transformation. *American Journal of Sociology, 107*, 990–1064.

Goodman, P. (2012). "Another second chance": Rethinking rehabilitation through the lens of California's prison fire camps. *Social Problems, 59*(4), 437–58.

Halushka, J. (2016). Work wisdom: Teaching former prisoners how to negotiate workplace interactions and perform a rehabilitated self. *Ethnography, 17*(1), 72–91.

Haney, L. (2010). *Offending women: Power, punishment, and the regulation of desire.* Berkeley, CA: University of California Press.

Harding, D.J. (2003). Jean Valjean's dilemma: The management of ex-convict identity in the search for employment. *Deviant Behavior, 24,* 571–95.

Johnson, I. (2015). Women parolees' perceptions of parole experiences and parole officers. *American Journal of Criminal Justice, 40*(4), 785–810.

Kaufman, N. (2015). Prisoner incorporation: The work of the state and non-governmental organizations. *Theoretical Criminology, 19*(4), 534–53.

Kuhlmann, A., & Kury, H. (2011). Hopes v. re-entry realities for incarcerated women in Germany. In I. Ekunwe & R. Jones (Eds), *Global perspectives on reentry* (pp. 257–77). Tampere, Finland: Tampere University Press.

Lageson, S., & Maruna, S. (2018). Digital degradation: Stigma management in the internet age. *Punishment & Society, 20*(1), 113–33.

Laub, J.H., & Sampson, R.J. (2001). Understanding desistance from crime. *Crime and Justice: A Review of Research, 23,* 1–69.

Leverentz, A. (2010). People, places, and things: How female ex-prisoners negotiate their neighbourhood context. *Journal of Contemporary Ethnography, 39*(6), 646–81.

Leverentz, A. (2011). Neighborhood context of attitudes toward crime and reentry. *Punishment & Society, 13*(1), 64–92.

Lynch, J., & Sabol, W. (2001). Prisoner reentry in perspective. *Crime Policy Report, 3.* Urban Institute Justice Policy Centre.

Maidment, M. (2006). *Doing time on the outside: Deconstructing the benevolent community.* Toronto, ON: University of Toronto Press.

Maier, K. (2018). *Halfway to freedom: The role of halfway houses in Canada's penal landscape.* Doctoral dissertation, University of Toronto.

Maruna, S. (2011). Re-entry as a rite of passage. *Punishment & Society, 13,* 3–28.

Maruna, S., Immarigeon, R., & LeBel, T. (2004). Ex-offender reintegration: Theory and practice. In S. Maruna & R. Immariegon (Eds), *After crime and punishment: Pathways to offender reintegration* (pp. 3–26). London, UK: Willan Publishing.

Maruna, S., & Roy, K. (2007). Amputation or reconstruction? Notes on the concept of "knifing off" and desistance from crime. *Journal of Contemporary Criminal Justice, 23*(1), 104–24.

McIvor, G., Murray, C., & Jamieson, J. (2004). Desistance from crime: Is it different for women and girls? In S. Maruna & R. Immarigeon (Eds), *After crime and punishment: Pathways to offender reintegration* (pp. 181–200). London, UK: Willan Publishing.

McNeill, F. (2019). *Pervasive punishment: Making sense of mass supervision.* Bingley, UK: Emerald Publishing.

Miller, R. (2014). Devolving the carceral state: Race, prisoner reentry, and the micro politics of urban poverty management. *Punishment & Society, 16*(3), 305–35.

Mijs, J. (2016). The missing organizational dimension of prisoner reentry: An Ethnography of the road to reentry at a nonprofit service provider. *Sociological Forum, 31*(2), 291–309.

O'Brien, P. (2001). *Making it in the "free world": Women in transition from prison.* Albany, NY: State University of New York Press.

Opsal, T. (2015). It's their world, so you've just got to get through: Women's experiences of parole governance. *Feminist Criminology, 10*(2), 188–207.

Pager, D. (2003). The mark of a criminal record. *American Journal of Sociology, 108*(5), 937–75.

Parole Board of Canada. (2011). Parole Board of Canada: Contributing to public safety. Retrieved from https://www.canada.ca/content/dam/canada/parole-board/migration/001/093/001-3000_en.pdf

Public Safety Canada. (2017). 2017 corrections and conditional release statistical overview. Retrieved from https://www.publicsafety.gc.ca/cnt/rsrcs/pblctns/ccrso-2017/index-en.aspx#sectiond8

Petersilia, J. (2003). *When prisoners come home: Parole and prisoner reentry.* New York, NY: Oxford University Press.

Ricciardelli, R., & Mooney, T. (2019). The decision to disclose: Employment after prison. *Journal of Offender Rehabilitation, 57*(6), 343–66.

Ricciardelli, R., & Peters, A. (2017). *After prison: Navigating employment and reintegration.* Waterloo, ON: Wilfrid Laurier Press.

Richards, S.C., & Jones, R.S. (2004). Beating the perpetual incarceration machine: Overcoming structural impediments to re-entry. In S. Maruna & R. Immarigeon (Eds), *After crime and punishment: Pathways to offender reintegration* (pp. 201–32). London, UK: Willan Publishing.

Sampson, R.J., & Laub, J.H. (2005). A life-course view of the development of crime. *Annals of the American Academy of Political and Social Science, 602,* 12–45.

Sykes G.M. (1985). *The society of captives: A study of a maximum security prison.* Princeton, NJ: Princeton University Press.

Spencer, D., & Ricciardelli, R. (2017). "They're a very sick group of individuals": Correctional officers, emotions, and sex offenders. *Theoretical Criminology, 21*(3), 380–94.

Sugie, N.F. (2018). Work as foraging: A smartphone study of job search and employment after prison. *American Journal of Sociology, 123*(5), 1453–91.

Travis, J. (2000). But they all come back: Rethinking prisoner reentry. In *Sentencing and Corrections, No. 7* (pp. 2–11). Washington, DC: National Institute of Justice.

Travis, J., & Visher, C. (2005). Introduction: Viewing public safety through the reentry lens. In J. Travis & C. Visher (Eds), *Prisoner reentry and crime in America* (pp. 1–14). New York, NY: Cambridge University Press.

Travis, J., & Waul, M. (2003). Prisoners once removed: The children and families of prisoners. In J. Travis & M. Waul (Eds), *Prisoners once removed: The impact of incarceration and reentry on children, families, and communities* (pp. 1–29). Washington, DC: Urban Institute Press.

Turnbull, S., & Hannah-Moffat, K. (2009). Under these conditions: Gender, parole and the governance of reintegration. *British Journal of Criminology, 49*, 532–51.

Visher, C., & Travis, J. (2003). Transitions from prison to community: Understanding individual pathways. *Annual Review of Sociology, 29*, 89–113.

Wacquant, L. (2000). Deadly symbiosis: When ghetto and prison meet and mesh. *Punishment & Society, 3*(1), 95–133.

Wacquant, L. (2010). Prisoner reentry as myth and ceremony. *Dialectic Anthropology, 34*(4), 505–620.

Werth, R. (2012). I do what I'm told to, sort of: Reformed subjects, unruly citizens, and parole. *Theoretical Criminology, 16*(3), 329–46.

Western, B. (2018). *Homeward: Life in the year after prison.* New York, NY: Russell Sage Foundation.

Western, B., Kling, J., & Weiman, D. (2001). The labor market consequences of incarceration. *Crime and Delinquency, 47*(3), 410–27.

Winnick, T.A., & Bodkin, M. (2008). Anticipated status and stigma management among those labelled "ex-con." *Deviant Behaviour, 29*(4), 295–333.

Supporting Mental Health and Well-Being in Canadian Corrections

An Expectation Too High?

Adrienne M.F. Peters and Raymond R. Corrado

7

Learning Objectives

After reading this chapter, you should be able to:

- Summarize commonly accepted explanations for high rates of mental health needs among individuals involved in the correctional system in Canada.
- Explain the delivery of correctional mental health services in Canada through various forms of government.
- Identify the mental health needs of Canadian correctional populations, including unique populations, such as females, Indigenous peoples, and youth.
- Recognize additional conditions that are common among Canadian correctional populations and that may occur comorbidly with mental illness.
- Identify the range of challenges that individuals with mental health needs encounter in the community and during incarceration.
- Understand theories that are used to inform correctional mental health practices.
- Outline treatment and intervention programs that are offered to individuals with mental health needs in community and institutional correctional settings.
- Specify the continued challenges and goals moving forward for the correctional system in Canada in supporting individuals with mental health needs.

Chapter Overview

There has been growing emphasis on the mental health and well-being of correctional populations in both community and institutional settings in Canada. This chapter presents the mental health needs of individuals involved in the Canadian correctional system, exploring how political, economic, social, and cultural forces impact these needs. Despite repeated reviews of the provision of mental health supports for correctional populations—by both federal and provincial bodies—governments, correctional agencies, and community-based organizations are confronted with ongoing challenges of how to best respond to the health concerns being raised and, very basically, who is responsible for providing the necessary financial and human resources to address these issues.

Introduction

Since mental health and physical well-being generally have become a connected common theme in public discourse in recent years, there has also been increased public and government policy focus on the criminalization of people with **mental illness** and mental health needs (Chaimowitz, 2012; Teplin, 1984). Although having a mental illness does not lead to criminal conduct or contact with the criminal justice system, there are high rates of mental illness in correctional populations. Individuals involved in the correctional system are particularly vulnerable to life histories that contain both mental health issues and difficulties in obtaining family, community, and government support to address those needs. This is frequently because of early traumatic life experiences and frequent exposure to harmful events within government-provided service programs (such as child care; Corrado & Freedman, 2011). Different levels of governments (mainly provincial/territorial) and non-government institutions throughout Canada have therefore implemented a series of mental health policies and procedures throughout criminal justice systems. However, government financial constraints have limited the scope of the care delivered. There has been a long-standing consensus within governments and even the general public for improvements at all service levels and procedural stages.

This chapter begins with a review of the deinstitutionalization movement before examining the government systems that oversee the administration of mental health services. Then we look at the systematically punitive discrimination that exists within Canadian corrections involving the most vulnerable groups with major mental health needs. As will be evident, a disproportionate concentration of major correctional facilities and their programs are in major metropolitan centres, and there is limited availability of intervention programs in the community.

The identification of the specific mental health needs of correctional populations is critical to individual case planning and intervention decision making. Because of substantial differences in the mental health needs of youth populations (ages 12–17) and adult populations, these two groups will be discussed separately (see Chapter 10 for a broader discussion of youth corrections). Another critical theme is how gender, ethnicity, and culture impact mental health–related experiences, considering, for example, the distinctive needs of women and Indigenous/ethnic minority populations within corrections (see also Chapters 8 and 9).

There are numerous processes to identify and manage mental health issues throughout various levels of the correctional system, including at local police-operated jails, provincial pre-trial detention facilities, provincial criminal courts responsible for important decision making (such as assessments), and subsequent decisions regarding where an individual is placed institutionally. More recently, innovative mental health courts in several large Canadian cities provide an optional non-punitive and treatment-focused approach. With few exceptions, both standard mental health screening and assessments and certain recognized rehabilitative intervention programs are routinely available. These model programs will be presented, along with evidence on their effectiveness in supporting individuals with mental health needs. It is also important to gain knowledge concerning the availability of appropriate treatments for correctional populations. A final theme is the experience of individuals in Canadian corrections as they transition between correctional and community settings.

Canada's History of Imprisoning the Mentally Ill

The practice of institutionalizing or segregating individuals with serious mental illness has a long history in Canada. In the mid- to late nineteenth century, mental health hospitals emerged to provide care for individuals who would arguably have otherwise been ignored. Psychiatric hospitals or **asylums** were created as a "more humane" alternative to the traditional use of prisons and workhouses (Sussman, 1998). Although these policies were intended for mental health needs, their development historically occurred in an ad hoc or haphazard manner with insufficient resources. This resulted in systematic and damaging problems for both the institutionalized and the service providers.

By the 1970s, a major philosophical shift in how individuals with mental illness should receive services led to the **deinstitutionalization** movement. The primary concerns were overcrowding and non-therapeutic environments, as well as disruptive political and economic factors (such as more public awareness through mass media, smaller families) following World War II (Sussman, 1998). Currently, the care of individuals with mental health problems is primarily the responsibility of community-based services and standard hospital-based settings. This shift, however, was not well planned or executed initially, which resulted in inadequate services and systematic harm.

Much of the accepted explanation for the high prevalence of mental health issues in correctional settings today is deinstitutionalization. Originally, however, Penrose (1939) asserted that institutions of control always existed, despite changes in the specific institutional setting. For example, as the use of psychiatric hospitals decreased, arrests of those with mental health issues and admissions to jails and prisons increased. Teplin's early (1984) landmark research in Chicago demonstrated the extensive criminalization of mental disorder typically initiated by the police who lacked other suitable options.

Not only did deinstitutionalization reveal inadequate community mental health resources, there was little discussion of secondary and critical services support, including housing, education, and employment. These issues, as well as discrimination, stigma, and disorder-focused policing strategies, have been raised as additional contributors to the increase of individuals with mental health needs in the correctional system (Frederick, O'Connor, & Koziarski, 2018). A subsequent debate surrounding institutionalization, deinstitutionalization, and now re-institutionalization involves ethical questions, such as the right of individuals to choose treatment versus government-mandated treatment, especially in correctional environments (Morrow, Dagg, & Pederson, 2008.) A related theme is identifying the appropriate role structures to provide the effective and thoughtful administration and oversight of these comprehensive services.

Mental Health in Canadian Corrections: Where Does Responsibility Lie?

Mental health care in Canadian corrections occurs at multiple government levels, with the federal and provincial/territorial governments assuming much of the responsibility. Importantly, individuals incarcerated or under the supervision of federal corrections are not included in the Canada Health Act (1984); therefore, Health Canada is not responsible for covering their care. Nonetheless, the federal government's 2017 budget provided a five-year, $57.8-million investment to expand federal prisoners' mental health care, with a commitment of $13.6 million annually afterward (Government of Canada, 2017). The 2018 budget reconfirmed the government's commitment to the mental health of federally incarcerated individuals with $20.4 million over five years and $5.6 million per subsequent year (Government of Canada, 2018). This funding emphasizes improving supports for females in federal facilities.

Correctional Service Canada (CSC) is responsible for the health of individuals in the federal correctional system. The overall practices of the CSC are governed by the **Corrections and Conditional Release Act (CCRA)**. Section 85 defines health care to include medical, dental, and mental health services provided by registered health-care professionals. Every prisoner is mandated to receive "(a) essential health care; and (b) reasonable access to non-essential mental health care that will contribute to the inmate's rehabilitation and successful reintegration into the community" and that this care "shall conform to professionally accepted standards" (s. 86). According to definitions in section 85, "essential health care" includes mental health care. Prisoners' health is addressed again in section 87, where it is stipulated that health and health-care needs be considered during any decision making related to the individual (for example, placement, transfer, segregation, and release and supervision planning).

Canada's Efforts to Address Mental Health in Corrections

In 2012, Canada unveiled its first mental health strategy titled *Changing Directions, Changing Lives: The Mental Health Strategy for Canada*. There was particular emphasis on the disproportionate rates of mental illness in the justice system. A strategic priority was to "Reduce the over-representation of people living with mental health problems and illnesses in the criminal justice system, and provide appropriate services, treatment and supports to those who are in the system" (Mental Health Commission of Canada [MHCC], 2012, p. 46). The MHCC subsequently released *Advancing the Mental Health Strategy for Canada: A Framework for Action (2017–2022)* to further facilitate the *Changing Directions* goals and reinforce the commitment to improving the Canadian mental health system (MHCC, 2016). This report reiterates the need for interdisciplinary, evidence-based approaches and partnerships between health care, addictions, education, justice, and corrections. A review of the strategy found that collaborative initiatives had begun between the MHCC and new stakeholders, such as, importantly, corrections and Indigenous organizations (MHCC, 2016).

The CSC also has a mental health strategy based on initiatives within federal corrections. *The 2002 Mental Health Strategy for Women Offenders* (CSC, 2002) facilitated the CSC's overall mental health strategy, which was approved in 2004. In addition, in 2005 the Community Mental Health Initiative received $29.1 million for five years followed by an additional $21.5 million over two years in 2007. This funding supported the Institutional Mental Health Initiative (IMHI), which included electronic mental health screening (through the Computerized Mental Health Intake Screening System [CoMHISS]) and primary care (CSC, 2012). Also in 2007, correctional staff began receiving mental health awareness training. The IMHI has received permanent funding (as of 2008) that has been fully implemented since 2010.

The CSC's most recent iteration of its mental health strategy includes five main focus areas (condensed from seven previously [CSC, 2012]). The first is mental health intake screening and follow-up assessments to identify mental health issues and related needs (CSC, 2019). The CoMHISS typically takes place within three to fourteen days from institutional admission with further assessments within three months. Cases are prioritized by immediacy of needs. The second component is primary care, which includes the provision of treatment and services, with a primary focus on mental health services that are holistic and coordinated. The multiple needs of individuals with mental illness and mental health issues are explicitly recognized (for example, physical, education/employment, and substance-use needs). Intermediate mental health care is the third area and encompasses mental health-care units and complex needs units. The latter includes care and services for individuals engaging in persistent self-harm. Such units provide an intermediary stage for individuals requiring more specialized support, but not the level of supports provided in psychiatric hospitals or **Regional Treatment Centres (RTCs)**. These settings represent the fourth component of the CSC's mental health strategy and are located in CSC institutions. The CSC's suicide and self-injury prevention and intervention/management plan are also in line with the CSC's mental health strategy.

Transitional care for individuals released to the community is the final component of the mental health strategy presented by the CSC. Clinical discharge planning begins before the prisoner is released. This includes continuous services to the individual once they re-enter the community through collaborative planning between institutional staff and community mental health specialists. Access to various agencies and services, ranging from crisis intervention and counselling to assistance completing paperwork and attending appointments, are routinely part of the plan. Additional components include staff education, training, and support, as well as community support and partnerships. In effect, a continuum of care at each stage of system contact from the time of intake and incarceration to the transitional stages (release, sentence/supervision completion; CSC, 2012) is provided. In the community, service provision is the responsibility of provincial/territorial health services.

Preliminary research on the CSC's mental health strategy indicated fewer conditional release revocations or suspensions for former prisoners who received special mental health services than those who did not (Allergi et al., 2008). A longer release study (at 24 and 48 months after release) demonstrated that of three treatment groups (a group with clinical discharge planning, a group with community mental health specialist services, and a group that participated in both), males who received mental health specialist support had the lowest rates of recidivism, and males who received both types of supports were readmitted to custody at lower rates compared to males who received discharge planning only and who were in the non-treatment group (MacDonald, Stewart, & Feely, 2014). In this study, females had lower rates of recidivism for the community mental health specialist and participation in both services, compared to women who did not receive these services. However, the small female subsample illustrates the need for further research on women prisoners.

A more comprehensive evaluation of the CSC's mental health strategy revealed that the development of increased partnerships could enhance prisoner mental health services while certain reforms of the governance structure of health services provided more streamlined, integrated, and standardized services (Delveaux et al., 2017). For example, the CSC's intake processes successfully identified prisoners' needs, but the duplication of health information led to redundancies. Despite the provision of timely mental health services, there was insufficient electronic tracking of the services received. This inhibited information collection about prisoners' needs and participation in interventions (Delveaux et al., 2017). The CSC also adopted new policies to respond to populations with distinctive needs, such as females, Indigenous prisoners, and former prisoners (Delveaux et al., 2017). At the community level, access to mental health specialists frequently involved both service delays and no systematic tracking of specialist referrals. Another crucial issue was information sharing across service providers, especially involving prisoners' transfers, leading to a disruption in the continuity of care. Regarding health education, improved health awareness and positive behavioural modifications were indicated, though access to these initiatives was limited. Mental health-care outcomes following institutional intervention/treatment revealed that receiving supports led to fewer institutional incidents, serious charges, and segregation (Delveaux et al., 2017). However, because discharge planning is province/territory dependent, obtaining necessary health cards was variable and, therefore, problematic and concerning. Although the CSC's policy includes medical expense coverage for former prisoners without access to a provincial/territorial health plan, the provision of this financial assistance is not consistent.

Where former prisoners were able to access specialized community mental health services, reductions in recidivism occurred. In contrast, no significant positive outcomes were associated with clinical discharge planning services. These services are difficult to provide generally, particularly where community mental health resources are restricted and obviously when they are non-existent. Delveaux and colleagues' (2017) comprehensive study included recommendations for each of the above policy concerns. Importantly, an electronic medical records management system was introduced in 2016 as part of the national Offender Health Information System to enable real-time access to medical records for individual case planning. Chapter 15 of this text reviews the use of technology in managing the health/mental health of correctional populations, including suicide warning systems.

Despite collaborative national efforts, including the CSC's impressive research evaluation studies and its related revision of its mental health strategy, the Office of the Correctional Investigator of Canada (OCI) has periodically investigated tragic cases where unmet mental health needs resulted in major harm, including unintended yet avoidable prisoner deaths. The correctional investigator's role involves investigating and addressing offender complaints, reviewing CSC policies and procedures, and recommending policy improvements. The most recent annual report from the OCI (2017–18) identified, yet again, the immediate and priority need to reform health care in federal correctional institutions. In particular, there is insufficient oversight of cases involving complex mental health needs, especially those involving self-injurious behaviour, including suicidal concerns, as well as staff use of excessive force to subdue or control prisoners. A related concern is the use of isolation or solitary confinement cells to control mentally ill prisoners. The medical issue for the latter is the exacerbation of the existing mental health issues and the resulting trauma and increased likelihood of self-harm (OCI, 2018). The OCI focused its recommendations on prison health-care governance. These included strengthening health care by using accountability and assurance measures, such as separating health care and prison administration budgets; providing collaborative primary care with close monitoring and follow-up; offering more judgment-based and ethical training for correctional health professionals; introducing more oversight during transitional experiences; and finally conducting ongoing, national reviews and audits of medical staff and charts (OCI, 2018). The 2017–18 report highlighted the CSC's National Medical Advisory Committee, which

THE CANADIAN PRESS/Andrew Vaughan

Nova Scotia's East Coast Forensic Hospital is the first instance of a co-located hospital and correctional facility in Canada.

has assembled senior administrative personnel and could facilitate higher-quality health-care services that are delivered in an appropriate timeframe (OCI, 2018).

The delivery of mental health-care services across multiple government levels and multiple institutions has resulted in a relatively progressive set of policies and procedures (especially compared to the United States). However, the inherently complex Canadian structure of federal, provincial/territorial, and community institutions responsible for these policies continue to constitute an enormous reform challenge. Despite systematic research and oversight institutions such as the OCI, the mental health systems in Canada, particularly the criminal justice institutions, remain controversial. As we discuss in detail below, since deinstitutionalization the fundamental issue is the overuse of the criminal justice system to implement Canada's mental health strategy for the most vulnerable groups. An alternative mental health service delivery model for individuals in the justice system is transferring responsibilities to "civil" mental health systems—that is, provinces/territories' respective health departments/ministries. Several Canadian provinces (Nova Scotia, Alberta, British Columbia, and soon Newfoundland and Labrador) have restructured the administration of correctional health by transferring the responsibility from their justice departments to their health departments. The World Health Organization's 2003 declaration advocated this model based on research indicating it reduced recidivism, improved file sharing, and improved treatments for specific illnesses (World Health Organization, 2003). Arguably, the provincial civil model orientation is immediately more oriented to the health, mental health, and related socio-economic needs of vulnerable individuals across their life course, including the crucial child and adolescent developmental stages (when most mental health issues present, at least partially), as opposed to the federal adult-only jurisdiction. Again, the latter government level in Canada constitutionally has the broadest taxation mandate and responsibility for processing adult offenders with mental illness.

Emergence and Growth of Mental Health Issues in Corrections

Even currently, nearly a half century since the deinstitutionalization of traditional facilities began, the criminal justice system has been referred to as the default mental health system—that is, a last resort after many previous intervening mental health systems (hospitals [especially emergency units] and community-based programs) have been unsuccessful in stabilizing major mental health needs of individuals, particularly those who also engage in crime, typically property and drug offences. While only a minority of individuals with major mental health needs become involved in the justice system, they are more likely to be criminally victimized (Boyce, Rotenberg, & Karam, 2015). Nonetheless, individuals with mental health issues are disproportionally involved at every criminal justice stage, from street-level interactions with the police to correctional settings. The following section presents the data on this theme and examines the main events that contributed to these trends.

Rates of Mental Illness in the Criminal Justice System

Individuals with a mental health issue have higher rates of police contact than those who do not (Coleman & Cotton, 2014a). The Canadian Community Health Survey in 2012 estimated that of the approximately 5 million Canadians who reported coming into contact with police within the past year, almost one-fifth had met the diagnostic criteria for a mental or substance-use disorder (Boyce et al., 2015). The most common reason for police contact involved emotions, mental health, or substance-use issues (18.7 per cent) compared to less than 2 per cent of interactions for those without a disorder. More specifically, more police interactions among individuals who were experiencing a mental health crisis occurred independently of other police contact risk factors, including gender, age, ethnicity, education, and income.

Police agencies throughout Canada are receiving increased training in strategies for identifying and responding to mental health needs (see Hoffman, Hirdes, Brown, Dubin, & Barbaree, 2016), including diversion and multidisciplinary team program options (such as Mobile Crisis Intervention Teams; Coleman & Cotton, 2014b). Yet Boyce and colleagues (2015) still found that individuals with a mental health or substance-use disorder who interacted with the police still had a much higher ratio (12.5 per cent) of being arrested than those who did not have a disorder (2.8 per cent). Arrest typically involves several initial involvements with the criminal justice system, such as access to defence council, bail hearings (being released on bail or remanded into custody), and plea hearings (frequently leading to competency to stand trial assessments).

The lifetime prevalence of serious mental illness of 15 to 20 per cent in correctional samples in Canada was comparable across provinces. These mental illnesses included psychosis, bipolar disorder, and major depressive disorders, but not substance use disorders or antisocial personality disorder [APD]) (Simpson, McMaster, & Cohen, 2013). However, more broadly diagnostically, a recent national CSC study of male prisoners (*n*=1,110) reported that most prisoners met the diagnostic criteria for at least one mental health disorder, both over their lifetime (81 per cent) and within the past month (approximately 73 per cent; Beaudette & Stewart, 2016). The most common current (within the past month) and lifetime diagnoses were alcohol and substance-use or dependence disorders (50 per cent). Importantly, lifetime APD diagnoses also approached the majority level (44 per cent). APD typically involves the more specified psychopathy personality associated with persistent, lifetime, serious, and violent offending trajectories (McCuish, Corrado, Hart, & DeLisi, 2015). Approximately one-third had anxiety disorders (near 30 per cent, current; 34 per cent, lifetime). An earlier and smaller Canadian study found comparable lifetime rates for mood disorders, psychotic disorders, and substance-use disorders among recently admitted federal prisoners (Brink, Doherty, & Boer, 2001).

At the community level, individuals supervised on probation and parole had a high prevalence of mental illness. Based on a large sample (*n*=3,268) of adult probationers and parolees in Ontario, Wormith and McKeague (1996) reported that approximately one-fifth (19 per cent) were classified as "mentally disordered." Again, the most common disorder was a substance-related (alcohol/drugs) disorder (approximately 5 per cent), followed by depression/bipolar disorder (2.9 per cent), sexual/personality disorder (2.7 per cent), anxiety/adjustment disorder (1.8 per cent), schizophrenia/psychotic disorder (1.7 per cent), developmental disorder (1 per cent), and mental retardation/other disorder (0.4 per cent). A larger recent review of research on mental illness in probation populations primarily from the United States and the United Kingdom found varying but still high rates of mental health needs (Sirdifield, 2012).

Mental health issues are a persistent concern among parolees, too. Abracen and colleagues' (2014) study of a sample of "high-risk" parolees living in a CSC halfway house in Toronto, Ontario, identified that over half the sample (approximately 57 per cent) had a recent diagnosis of personality disorder, with 34 per cent having

APD specifically. Consistent with other institutional and community correctional samples, the next most common diagnoses were drug (39 per cent) and alcohol (38 per cent) use issues and depression (25 percent). Borderline personality disorder (BPD) and attention deficit hyperactivity disorder (ADHD) diagnoses were associated with increased parole suspensions (BPD was also associated with a triple increase in the likelihood of recidivating and a six-fold increase in the likelihood of recidivating violently). ADHD doubled the likelihood of recidivism. Importantly this study found substantial presence of co-occurring diagnoses. The study authors cautioned that their reported prevalence rates likely were underestimates because of several validity limitations of their study. Abracen and colleagues (2014) further stated that comorbid (that is, co-occurring) mental health issues were particularly challenging for correctional staff regarding control, safety, self-harm, victimization, and provision of services.

Comorbidity

Comorbid, or concurrent, disorders involving co-occurrence of multiple mental disorders or substance-use disorders among correctional populations have typically negatively impacted everyday functioning and behaviour of these multi-needs individuals with other prisoners and staff. Again, the rates of comorbid mental health disorders were almost as high as the rates of single mental health diagnoses, especially when substance-use disorders were included.

Community-located correctional samples also had high rates of single and comorbid mental health issues. In a study of individuals awaiting trial in the community under a bail supervision program in Ontario, 40 per cent of clients reported a current mental illness and 70 per cent reported issues with substances (alcohol and/or drugs), while approximately one-third (31 per cent) had co-occurring mental health and substance-use issues (John Howard Society of Ontario, 2013). In Wormith and McKeague's (1996) study of a sample of adult probationers in Canada, approximately 30 per cent identified a mental illness and a second diagnosis. Again, among a sample of federally sentenced males, Beaudette and Stewart (2016) stated that 38 per cent of the sample had a mental health disorder concurrent with an alcohol/substance-use disorder.

Comorbidity has also been evident among a preponderance of young people involved in the youth justice system (Gretton & Clift, 2011). Co-occurring mental illness/substance use as well was characteristic in youth samples with fetal alcohol spectrum disorder (Fryer, McGee, Matt, Riley, & Mattson, 2007). Cognitive deficit disorders, including the not uncommon ADHD, were more generally associated with mental illness/substance-use issues (Stewart, Wilton, & Sapers, 2016). Despite the absence of routine intellectual deficit screening, CSC program facilitators have had access to information on recommended accommodations for intellectual problems. This proactive response has resulted in successful responses to prisoners with mental health needs through specialized educational interventions. However, certain neurological developmental disorders, particularly fetal alcohol spectrum disorder and autism spectrum disorder, present unique challenges in correctional settings.

Fetal Alcohol Spectrum Disorder

Individuals with fetal alcohol spectrum disorder (FASD) have increased contact with the justice system. FASD is caused by substantial fetal or prenatal exposure to alcohol. FASD deficits include difficulties in memory, attention, judgment, regulating emotions, and understanding consequences (Streissguth, Barr, Kogan, & Bookstein, 1997). FASD itself is not included in the *Diagnostic and Statistical Manual of Mental Disorders*, Fifth Edition (DSM-5). Instead, the DSM-5 contains neurobehavioural disorder associated with prenatal alcohol exposure–related diagnosis (ND-PAE), which is categorized as a "condition for further study." The symptoms of FASD, however, can cause severe impairments for an individual and are often conflated with symptoms of mental illness, while other mental health issues often co-occur with FASD.

A study of Canadian youth with FASD reported these youth had contact with the justice system from an early age (McLachlan, Roesch, Viljoen, & Douglas, 2014). Most importantly, FASD youth exhibited significant competency challenges in navigating the criminal justice system, such as a minimum understanding of the processes necessary to proceed, including the crucial initial stage involving advisory exchanges with defence counsel. Because youth with FASD display significantly varied levels of impairment, the authors of this study recommended individualized assessment be carried out and information/education services regarding legal criteria for competency be arranged.

Canadian FASD researchers Pei, Leung, Jampolsky, and Alsbury (2016) qualitatively examined the experiences of justice-involved adults with FASD and reported how biological deficits, psychological deficits, and social factors associated with FASD negatively impacted criminal justice system experiences. However, positive factors for individuals included hope for the future, a willingness to change, and resilience. This positive perspective supports the need to target more valid assessment and diagnostic tools to enhance individualized and comprehensive strengths-based approaches for FASD case management. In effect, this includes more FASD awareness, education, and training for justice professionals. This is particularly important given that FASD is a leading factor in assessing responsibility and recidivism risk, and FASD can be viewed as a mitigating factor for some judges yet an aggravating factor for others (Chandler, 2015).

Valid prevalence estimates of FASD in the correctional system are not available. Substitute estimates include using the estimated rate of FASD in the general population and applying it to the number of youth in custody (which is likely to be an underestimate). This procedure suggests that youth with FASD were 19 times more likely to be incarcerated in Canada. Popova and colleagues applied lower and upper FASD prevalence estimates to the number of incarcerated youth in Canada in 2011–12; they estimated that 17 per cent of youth in custody had FASD (Popova, Lange, Burd, & Rehm, 2015). The study's authors applied the same approach to incarcerated adults in 2011–12; they estimated there were approximately 3,870 cases (or 10 per cent) of FASD among incarcerated adults. According to more recently updated estimates the prevalence of FASD among justice-involved youth ranges from 11 to 23 per cent and among justice-involved adults, from 10 to 18 per cent (Flannigan, Pei, Stewart, & Johnson, 2018). Popova and colleagues (2015) asserted that that their prevalence estimates suggested enormous financial resources occurred in incarcerating individuals diagnosed with FASD. Again, all the above studies underscore the need for FASD-specific screening and interventions at the beginning criminal justice stages. However, there are few validated evidence-based methods for such routine and cost-reasonable FASD screening even within custody facilities, let alone during the pre-trial stages (Flannigan et al., 2018).

Psychopathy

As mentioned above, antisocial personality disorder was prevalent within custody samples for both youth and adults. More controversially, the related psychopathy personality disorder, while not formally recognized in the DSM-5, is routinely used in CSC assessments and arguably is a critical mental health theme in Canadian corrections. There is considerable diagnostic overlap between APD and psychopathy, especially regarding aggressive, violent, and manipulative behaviours that can lead to serious justice system involvement (American Psychiatric Association [APA], 2013). Research has found that APD rates in correctional settings are as high as 80 per cent (APA, 2013); psychopathy rates (assessed using the Psychopathy Checklist-Revised [PCL-R]) have been lower, with rates ranging from approximately 15 to 30 per cent (Cale, Lussier, McCuish, & Corrado, 2015; Hare, 2003). Individuals diagnosed with psychopathy exhibit several traits and behaviours (like having a shallow affect, being callous, and displaying an absence of empathy) conducive to the persistent violation of social norms. More critically concerning policy reactions is the link between APD/psychopathy and violence risk among adults (Douglas, Ogloff, Nicholls, & Grant, 1999) and youth (Cale et al., 2015), yet there is limited research and professional consensus on how to treat psychopathy and a dearth of programs that specifically target key psychopathic domain traits, particularly "the affective and interpersonal features of the disorder" (Ribeiro da Silva, Rijo, & Salekin, 2013, p. 76).

There is ongoing debate about the construction of psychiatric illness, particularly in correctional/prison contexts. Some experts argue that the concentration on mental health issues in these environments is often a means to maintain safety and security in the institution rather than providing appropriate assessments and treatments for prisoners (Galanek, 2013). Behaviours that are viewed as "bad" are commonly conflated with symptoms of a personality disorder, and "psychopathy" is a highly debated construct viewed by some as a label that problematizes individuals in forensic mental health settings (McGhee & Castro, 2018). Among subpopulations within prisons, such as female and Indigenous prisoners, the often early and repeated traumatic experiences of these groups, which can contribute to certain attitudes and behaviours, are often overlooked. A thorough examination of this theme is beyond the scope of this chapter, but it is important to recognize this controversy.

Mental Health Needs of Special Correctional Populations

The high incidence of mental health needs among individuals in the correctional system raises several important issues related to strategies to prevent and respond to these concerns. Before this is possible, however, it is vital to have a more in-depth understanding of some of the more nuanced differences in the expression of mental health needs among the more vulnerable groups.

Females

Female populations in prison have been increasing substantially (OCI, 2018). Advocates have asserted that this trend reflects limited community program resources, especially mental health care. In addition, incarcerated females typically have distinctive health/mental health needs that are exacerbated by the criminal justice system, such as added emotional stressors and a persistent lack of social and economic supports. A greater proportion of female prisoners than male report a history of experiencing abuse, sexual abuse, and trauma (Barrett, Allenby, & Taylor, 2010). For example, in a small study of 88 federally sentenced women in Canada, the women had elevated rates of many diagnoses, with alcohol dependence being even further elevated among Indigenous females. These trends were also evident among community/probation samples of female offenders in Canada (Wormith & McKeague, 1996). Table 7.1 provides a comparison of mental health prevalence between female and male incarcerated samples. Although data were collected across two time points and there is an underrepresentation of females, the rates of mental disorders are consistently higher for women.

Research involving small focus groups of incarcerated women in Canada demonstrated that, despite their significant health problems, females' mental health needs were not being met. Embarrassment and fear due to a lack of knowledge of the services available and the elaborate and confusing bureaucratic processes needed to access health care were common barriers. A lack of consistent health and mental care services as prisoners transitioned between correctional facilities and the community were too frequently inadequate, as was support related to housing, social assistance, and employment. Paradoxically, when the latter support

Ellen Dennett (left) meets with behaviour counsellor Laura Wood at the Fraser Valley Institution for Women.

THE CANADIA68N PRESS/Darryl Dyck

Table 7.1   Prevalence Rates for a Current Diagnosis of Major Mental Disorders among Incarcerated Offenders

Current DSM Disorder	Incarcerated Female Sample February to October 2016 (n =154) %	Incoming Incarcerated Male Sample March 2012 to September 2014 (n =1,110) %
Any disorder	79.2	64.5
Alcohol/substance-use disorders (lifetime)	76.0	49.6
Anxiety disorders	54.2	29.5
Antisocial personality disorder (APD)	49.4	44.1
Borderline personality disorder (BPD)	33.3	15.9
Mood disorders	22.1	16.9
Eating disorders	11.0	0.8
Psychotic disorders	4.6	3.3

Based on Correctional Service Canada data obtained for females from Derkzen, Barker, McMillan, & Stewart (2017) and for males from Beaudette & Stewart (2016).

was provided, it was often prioritized over health needs (Ahmed, Angel, Martel, Pyne, & Keenan, 2016). Chapter 8 explores the mental health of female correctional populations in further detail, including the tragic Ashley Smith case.

Indigenous Peoples

The well-documented, devastating consequences of colonization of Indigenous peoples in Canada are most evident in the correctional system. Intergenerational trauma from residential schools and all forms of abuse associated with government policies and practices have resulted in persistently higher rates of Indigenous alcohol/substance-use disorders and personality disorders (Beaudette & Stewart, 2016). Even though some studies revealed comparable rates of mood and psychotic disorders between federally incarcerated Indigenous and non-Indigenous samples, Indigenous prisoners with mental health needs necessitated services that addressed their unique cultural identities and the above traumatic histories. However, Nelson and Wilson (2017) cautioned that this overemphasis on "problematic substance use" among Indigenous persons raised the spectre of further negative stereotyping given the broad diversity of Indigenous groups/communities, which includes Inupiat, Yupik, Alutiit, and Inuit peoples in northern regions. In addition, Indigenous peoples currently inhabit an equally broad range of lifestyles from urban and suburban to towns and rural communities both on and off reserve.

The Supreme Court of Canada has established case law that requires mitigation of sentences because of Indigenousness, and the Youth Criminal Justice Act mandates a similar special consideration to reduce their disproportionality generally in adult and youth criminal justice, especially regarding the use of custody. Yet, while these case and statutory laws have reduced the number of Indigenous individuals in the criminal justice systems, especially youth justice, the ratio of Indigenous to non-Indigenous prisoners has remained the same or increased in most provinces and territories. In addition, an array of culturally sensitive programs have been introduced into Canadian criminal justice, from police diversion to in-custody mentoring and healing involving culture authority figures such as Elders. Again, despite such concerted policy innovations, Nelson and Wilson (2017) assert that the mental health needs of Indigenous individuals in criminal justice systems have not been mitigated substantially. These researchers theorize that these limited policy impacts are most likely explained by the intrinsically complex and negative historical polices.

Brown, Hirdes, and Fries (2015) conducted a prisoner sample study using mental health scale cut-off scores and identified that nearly half (41 per cent) of Indigenous prisoners had severe symptoms of a problem. Comorbidity was evident too; 13 per cent of all prisoners in the sample displayed two or more current, severe symptoms, with depression (65 per cent) and negative symptoms (that is, negative psychotic symptoms; approximately 72 per cent) being the most common. Regarding gender and ethnicity, approximately half (48 per cent) of Indigenous females had significantly higher scores for severe mental health symptoms as well as two or more current, severe symptoms (approximately 35 per cent) compared to approximately one-tenth (12 per cent) of Indigenous males. Individuals who identified as Indigenous had significantly higher scores for current severe symptoms (approximately 75 per cent) compared with prisoners who did not identify as Indigenous (approximately 38 per cent). The former also had a higher prevalence of two or more current, severe symptoms (approximately 19 per cent); the non-Indigenous prisoners had 13 per cent of these symptoms.

This study corroborated previous studies (some discussed above) concerning the capacity for correctional settings to adequately support the specialized mental health needs of so many prisoners, in particular female and Indigenous prisoners (Brown et al., 2015). In addition, these vulnerable groups face multiple barriers when accessing services upon their return to their communities.

Youth

It is important to reiterate the policy theme concerning differences in the mental health needs of youth populations and adult populations. It was mentioned in the above comorbidity section that mental health issues were pronounced in Canadian youth correctional samples (Penner, Roesch, & Viljoen, 2011). Under the Youth Criminal Justice Act, young offenders are only sentenced to a period of incarceration for the most serious/violent offences as well as repeat offences, and these individuals have multiple service needs, including mental health. For the latter, section 34(1) of the Youth Criminal Justice Act mandates mental health diagnosis, which involves formal psychiatric assessments and appropriate programming and treatment recommendations.

Gretton and Clift (2011) studied a sample of incarcerated youth in British Columbia from 2006 to 2009 ($n=205$). Astonishingly, all the girls and nearly all the boys (approximately 92 per cent) met the criteria for at least one mental health disorder. As stated above, comorbid conditions were common. Substance-use/dependence disorders were the most common conditions (100 per cent of girls and approximately 86 per cent of boys). Conduct disorder too had high prevalence levels—84 per cent and 73 per cent, respectively. A majority of youth in the BC sample (approximately 54 per cent of females and 61 per cent of males) had been exposed to physical abuse, and a large proportion had experienced sexual abuse (42 per cent of females and 21 per cent of males). Youth also experience high levels of stress while incarcerated, which can increase feelings of anxiousness, depression, and being withdrawn (Cesaroni & Peterson-Badali, 2010).

Beyond the populations examined in this section, scholars and practitioners have also raised the issue of the mental health needs among aging populations in correctional settings. Chapter 11 reviews the literature and data on mental illness in aging prison populations, with a focus on conditions that are exclusive to older individuals, including dementia.

Main Concerns Associated with the Mental Health of People Involved in the Correctional System

Several challenges routinely occur regarding access to and the provision of mental health services in the correctional system. They include lengthy waitlists and wait times; blocked access to services because of insufficient resources (including a lack of psychologists/psychiatrists and counselling programs, both individual and group); the presence of dual/comorbid stigmas; addressing social determinants of health; and changes to pharmacological treatment regimes or mental health-care providers during transitional periods (for example, when entering institutional facilities, being transferred between institutions, or reintegrating into the community). This section examines several of these challenges in greater detail.

Stigmatization

Individuals with mental health issues in general endure various forms of stigma, both from external and internal sources. In correctional contexts, these individuals can experience dual stigmas. Research has indicated that the increased attention to and investment in specialized services to address mental health needs among correctional samples can inadvertently reinforce negative stereotypic attitudes toward prisoners in need of these services. These negative attitudes in turn are reinforced by the social (for example, physical intimidation and dominance of "weaker" prisoners) and structural (for example, health/justice system policy or design) stigmatization of mental illness that is inherent in correctional environments. This stigmatization, when internalized, can carry over into problematic behaviours in the community, such as social isolation, self-injurious drug abuse. An individualized community reintegration transition plan developed by criminal justice professionals and program coordinators to reduce the likelihood of these harmful stigmatization experiences is an important policy response (Livingston, Rossiter, & Verdun-Jones, 2011).

Social Determinants of Health

A significant challenge in addressing the mental health needs of individuals in the correctional system involves **social determinants of health**. This literature focuses on the relationships between (mental) health and various social factors, including gender, culture, early childhood experiences, home setting, education, employment, income, and social status. These factors, individually and collectively, affect mental health/health-related behaviours and access to health care (see Kouyoumdjian, Schuler, Matheson, & Hwang, 2016). In Canada, many communities and populations are more vulnerable to mental health issues as a result of these factors. Low socio-economic status individuals, for example, frequently do not have ready access to health-care professionals or treatment options for several reasons, such as a lack of transportation and the concentration of programs in large metropolitan centres.

As discussed above, certain populations are particularly vulnerable. Individuals with major mental health needs in Indigenous communities, for example, have experienced intergenerational family trauma, which has compounded other mental health issues. Disproportionate numbers of incarcerated individuals in Canada have histories of psychological or sexual abuse or witnessing abuse/violence; high residential mobility; low educational achievement; high unemployment levels or insecurity; and low-income status (Kouyoumdjian et al., 2016). Again, these factors can affect the onset and persistence of mental health issues, exacerbate existing mental health issues, and necessitate multidisciplinary, holistic interventions and persistent services. Social isolation, low educational attainment, employment obstacles, and lower income in particular interact in a causal reinforcement cycle of mental illness that has been associated with the high prevalence of mental health issues and needs in correctional populations (Burczycka, 2018).

Solitary Confinement

The use of segregation, or solitary confinement, is an extremely controversial policy generally and specifically for prisoners with mental health needs because of the too-frequent tragedies involving either suicide or staff using unnecessary or inappropriate force, resulting in the death of a prisoner. Correctional research has indicated that prisoners with mental illness have an increased likelihood to engage in routine rule violations, which result in segregation (Houser, Belenko, & Brennan, 2012). A review of administrative segregation in federal corrections found that a greater proportion of individuals with mental "disability" were segregated than those without these issues (OCI, 2015). The OCI's 2017–18 report indicated that clinical staff to psychiatric bed ratios in Regional Treatment Centres were below established standards, which was associated with the overreliance on segregation and clinical seclusion (OCI, 2018).

The overreliance on these seclusion-based practices includes the long-term confinement of prisoners. Segregating individuals for extended periods of time has serious ramifications for mental well-being, particularly in the case of individuals who have mental health needs and who are among the most likely populations to be placed in long-term solitary confinement. Not only does (long-term) segregation reduce healthy interaction with others, but it also interrupts prisoners' access to treatment and opportunities to participate in intervention programs. Furthermore, it violates prisoners' rights against cruel and unusual punishment; Ontario's Superior Court recently ruled that placement in solitary confinement for more than 15 days represents this form of punishment (White, 2019), which is consistent with the United Nations' guidelines (UN General Assembly, 2016). The federal government has also proposed Bill C-83 to replace segregation with a more rehabilitative model that would include access to treatment and services (see Chapter 14 for further discussion of solitary confinement).

Generally, there has been a reduced reliance on traditional solitary confinement practices because of mental health concerns and related high-profile cases. However, there has been a shift to secluding prisoners in their cells. Some prisoners, though, have reported a preference to be transferred to the special handling unit

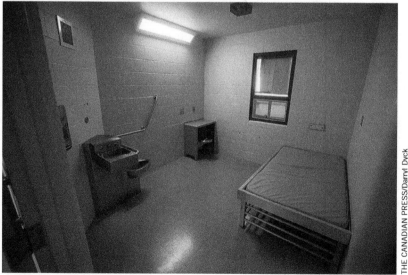

THE CANADIAN PRESS/Darryl Dyck

A cell in the segregation unit of the Fraser Valley Institution for Women in Abbotsford, British Columbia.

because they had greater access to institutional rights in segregation (OCI, 2018).

The CSC allocated greater resources to federal institutions for mental health training and services but, arguably, gaps in these services remain (Simpson et al., 2013). Encouragingly, in the CSC's recent health services evaluation, researchers found that after mental health treatment prisoners had fewer incidents, received fewer serious charges, and were transferred to involuntary segregation less (Delveaux et al., 2017).

Self-Harm

In addition to the overuse of solitary confinement, another concern related to mental health issues among correctional populations are **self-injurious behaviour (SIB)** and self-harm; these are both common in correctional settings and are particularly concerning among females and other vulnerable groups (such as Indigenous prisoners; Gordon, 2010). SIB includes "deliberate direct bodily harm . . . where suicidal intent is not known or is indeterminable," while self-harm includes SIBs as well as behaviours such as "culturally sanctioned body modifications, health neglect, risk taking, eating disorders, and when harm is not immediate but a result of cumulative effects of certain behaviours (i.e., substance abuse)" (Corabian, Appell, & Wormith, 2013, p. 3). While men have been shown to engage in their first SIB in an institution, the majority of women's onset for this behaviour is in the community; incarcerated women and men who engage in SIB indicate doing so primarily as a form of coping[1] (Power, 2014).

The use of Regional Treatment Centres (RTCs) for individuals who engage in self-harm has been a central criticism of the CSC's practices. Federally incarcerated individuals who engage in self-harm are often transferred to one of the five RTCs in Canada—the CSC's accredited psychiatric institutions, which are intended for individuals with serious mental health needs. In comparison to other types of institutions (maximum/multi, medium, minimum, and female), RTCs report a higher incidence of self-harm and a higher number of prisoners who have self-harmed at least two times (Gordon, 2010). The 2017–18 annual report from the OCI cited an external evaluation of RTCs, known as the Bradford Report, which revealed several staff-related concerns including insufficient/unrelated training, staff who were poorly matched to the needs of the populations,

and low staffing ratios to patient needs (OCI, 2018). This latter concern has been associated with increased use and overuse of clinical seclusion and solitary confinement, which can incite self-injurious behaviours (Power & Beaudette, 2013). Further findings revealed that screening and assessment tools were not adequate in identifying mental health conditions and guiding the appropriate placement of patients. The investigator's recommendation was thus for the CSC to recruit, select, and specially train staff based specifically on the needs of the individuals admitted to RTCs. There is a need as well for more training for all correctional staff employed by the CSC to improve communication and understanding between staff and prisoners to invite reporting of self-harm/self-injurious thinking, prevent cases of self-harm, and support individuals who have engaged in these behaviours (Corabian et al., 2013). The OCI's report also briefly discussed the replacement of RTCs with more therapeutic inpatient facilities or, alternatively, the increased use of existing external forensic hospitals, which is likely a more feasible option. One point of consensus is that addressing and reducing self-harm behaviours should be a priority of the CSC.

Recidivism

Mental health issues and comorbidity are a major policy concern for correctional staff and justice system policymakers because this combination has been strongly associated with both institutional misconduct and re-offending (Stewart & Wilton, 2014a). In a large national study of recently admitted male prisoners in Canada, prisoners with an Axis I diagnosis under the former DSM-IV-TR—such as anxiety and mood disorders as defined in the current DSM-5—comorbid with a substance-use disorder and/or a personality disorder had the highest parole revocation rates (Stewart, Gamwell, & Wilton, 2018). Individuals with comorbid mental health issues often have lengthy criminal histories and high rates of reconviction. Related to institutional behaviour, those with comorbid mental health issues also incur more institutional charges and transfers to segregation (Wilton & Stewart, 2017). Not only were individuals with severe mental illness more likely to reoffend, but the time they spent "successfully" residing in the community before reoffending was also briefer. In other words, the mean time to re-incarceration was lower as individuals' symptoms of serious mental illness increased (Brown, unpublished data, as cited in

Simpson et al., 2013). The policy response to this dynamic requires increased staff training and programs focused on the mental illness comorbidity profile, including community release planning.

Victimization

According to the General Social Survey, a majority (51 per cent) of individuals with a mental health–related disability (for example, anxiety, depression, bipolar disorder, anorexia, substance use) had histories of childhood physical or sexual abuse. They also experienced recent violence at much higher rates (more than double) than individuals without a mental illness (Burczycka, 2018). Women with a mental health issue were particularly vulnerable not only to violent victimization compared to men and women without a mental health–related disability, but also to sexual victimization specifically. Experiencing victimization can also lead to or exacerbate existing mental health issues. Relatedly, individuals with a mental health issue were more likely to report experiencing post-traumatic stress disorder following victimization (Burczycka, 2018). And while individuals with mental health issues sought mental health support following these incidents at higher rates than those without mental health issues, they were less likely to report their victimization to the police. This pattern again exemplifies the lack of services received for this group, despite higher levels of vulnerability and specialized mental health and social determinant needs.

Individuals involved in the justice system with some of the most severe mental illness and mental health needs also encounter unnecessarily high rates and levels of use of force while in the care of correctional services (OCI, 2019).

Addressing Mental Health in Corrections

It is evident from the above review that addressing the enormously complex mental health needs of many of the individuals in Canadian correctional facilities as well as those who are back in the community involves equally complex policies that require challenging multi-ministry and multi-agency collaborations in both the community and institutional settings. A review of the availability and access to treatments for correctional populations, including access to psychiatrists, psychologists/counsellors, substance-use counsellors, and other health-care specialists, is the main theme of the next section.

Theory and General Practices

In Canada in particular, therapeutic interventions for individuals involved in the criminal justice system with mental health issues are often based on the **risk-need-responsivity** (RNR) model developed by Andrews, Bonta, and Hoge (1990). This model consists of three key principles in offender rehabilitation *to guide screening and assessment* tools. The *risk* principle identifies an individual's likelihood to reoffend. The *need* principle identifies the factors that may hinder or help an individual's rehabilitation, such as substance use, antisocial peers, and employment. The *responsivity* principle involves evaluating an individual's learning style, especially their strengths, to assess their amenability to specific treatment protocols. Although concerns have been raised concerning RNR-based biased approaches (for example, the Western-based definitions of normative behaviour, their application to females and other cultures, an overemphasis on the individual rather than social factors), this model nonetheless, remains the most widely used one in offender rehabilitation.

The social learning model (SLM) is another guiding perspective to several mental health interventions. SLM was derived from learning theories and is based on the axiomatic assertion that deviant conduct develops through the learning process (Akers, 2011; Sutherland, 1974). It also incorporates a complex interaction of sociological and relational factors, including parenting practices, adult supervision, and peer groups in contexts typically involving a low socio-economic status family/neighbourhood, individual historical experiences of abuse and trauma, substance-use behaviours, and other factors associated with mental health.

These two broad perspectives, in turn, are related to specific treatment approaches to mental health issues and substance-use disorders, most importantly **cognitive-behavioural therapy** (CBT), motivational interviewing (MI), and various forms of behaviour modification, skills training, as well as family therapy. Both CBT and MI rely on strategies based on the individual's responsivity and mental health symptoms/disorders by focusing on replacing negative or distorted/irrational thinking and harmful self-identities with positive or pro-social thinking in response to daily challenges and to foster healthy self-identities. Mental health and criminal justice personnel use MI by communicating with clients using open-ended and non-threatening questions, often using standardized and research-validated instruments. The intention is to be client-centred and assist the individual in openly discussing and understanding the impact of their hurtful behaviours to initiate the process of alternative thought and behavioural approaches to relationships. CBT- and MI-based interventions are delivered in community or institutional settings, including correctional settings. Specific programs based on these models have been demonstrated to be effective in varying degrees for comorbid mental health and substance-use disorders and can decrease criminal justice involvement (Andrews & Bonta, 2010; Prendergast, Pearson, Podus, Hamilton, & Greenwell, 2013).

Trauma-Informed Care

In recent years, attention has been focused on the adverse and traumatic events experienced by adult and youth criminal justice populations, including exposure to stress, violence, and abuse (physical, sexual, or emotional). These experiences often commence early in childhood and persist throughout adolescence and adulthood and can result in concerning behavioural outcomes (Martin, Viau-Deschênes, & Yogarajah, 2017) and institutional placement (Espinosa, Sorensen, & Lopez, 2013). In some cases, adverse and traumatic events can lead to the development of post-traumatic stress disorder (PTSD). Even in cases that do not result in a diagnosis of PTSD, the lasting effects of these experiences can have several negative consequences, from difficulty coping with daily stressors to coping by means of offending. Exposure to trauma and rates of PTSD have been found to be higher among female (Derkzen et al., 2017) and Indigenous populations (Bellamy & Hardy, 2015), and even higher among these populations who are incarcerated (Grella, Lovinger, & Warda, 2013). Individuals who have experienced high levels of early traumatic events (often referred to as "adverse childhood experiences") and are involved in the justice system are more likely to be re-arrested and at a faster rate than those who have experienced lower levels of trauma (Wolff, Baglivio, & Piquero, 2017). They are also more likely to be involved in violent incidents while incarcerated (Martin, Eljdupovic, McKenzie & Colman, 2015).

Correctional policies and practices have thus begun to implement **trauma-informed care** (TIC). One of the leading challenges in providing this form of care is the lack of consensus surrounding the appropriate terminology; nevertheless, there appears to be a consistent theme that trauma-informed care incorporates practices that inhibit any re-triggering of trauma and support individuals' daily coping and ultimate recovery by reducing their symptoms of trauma (see Martin et al., 2017). More specifically, this includes trauma awareness and related training for staff; policies intended to reduce re-traumatization (such as avoiding the use of solitary confinement and seclusion, physical restraints, or strip searches); standardized screening and assessment; strength-based, non-stigmatizing language; and programming that is individualized and designed to address the unique and multiple needs of individuals who are involved in the correctional system (Wallace, Conner, & Dass-Brailsford, 2011).

Although the empirical research assessing the effectiveness of TIC is limited and it can be difficult to isolate the precise factors that contribute to improved outcomes, there have been studies that provide preliminary support for the effective implementation of trauma-informed programs (for example, Seeking Safety) and in assisting with trauma symptoms, mental health, and substance use (Barrett et al., 2015). Trauma-focused CBT has also been developed and is demonstrated to reduce the symptoms of trauma in adolescents who are provided with tools to manage the feelings and responses associated with traumatic memories (Cary & McMillen, 2012). Another study from the United States found fewer incidents of misconduct and use of restraints and isolation in a female youth facility using a trauma-informed organizational change intervention known as the Sanctuary Model (Elwyn, Esaki, & Smith, 2015). The staff in this setting are educated on trauma and the behavioural effects of stress, and trained in approaches that promote positive changes in behaviour (Esaki et al., 2013). Trauma-informed interventions that also incorporate gender-responsive approaches with justice-involved populations have been shown to reduce not only trauma symptoms but also depression and substance use (Covington, Burke, Keaton, & Norcott, 2008). Given women's unique and trauma-specific needs (Matheson, Brazil, Doherty,

& Forrester, 2015), the CSC (2017) developed a gender-responsive strategy for women that comprises evidence-based, gender-responsive, and trauma-informed services and programs as a means to support women's supervision and rehabilitation. These services focus on gender and culturally relevant approaches, account for past exposure to trauma, support women in coping, and include alternative activities, such as art contests through which incarcerated women can express and address their feelings. Future research should be conducted to assess the impact of these interventions on reducing trauma symptoms and supporting individuals' recovery.

Community-Based Services

While there is no consensus on research concerning institutional-based therapies, it has been asserted that correctional settings, for example, are inherently criminogenic, so connecting individuals to community-based supports should be a primary objective in addressing mental health needs. There are several models of services situated in the community that respond to the needs of individuals with mental health issues generally and for individuals who are also involved in the criminal justice system.

Diversion

Generally, diversion programs direct people who will potentially become involved with the criminal justice system away from the system and toward other treatment interventions, such as hospital psychiatric inpatient and outpatient services. Diversion occurs at various stages of the justice system, from initial contact with the police to the court sentencing stage, and even following remand to custody (McInerney et al., 2013). Diversion programs for individuals with major mental illness typically include teams of health workers that engage in case planning, often with collaboration from criminal justice personnel, both to identify the individual's needs as well as the level of protection needed for the public. These services include appointments with medical professionals who will monitor compliance with a medication regime and/or attending counselling and abstaining from other substances (such as alcohol or illicit drugs). Diversion eligibility is based on distinctive criteria for each program and criminal justice personnel (police, probation officers, and judges)

determinations. Usually, programs require that individuals accept responsibility for criminal acts and be motivated to participate. However, both the availability of and access to mental health diversion programs varies substantially across and within regional boundaries (Davidson, Heffernan, Greenberg, Waterworth, & Burgess, 2017). Nevertheless, these programs decrease justice system involvement (including arrest and incarceration) and increase community treatment access (Steadman & Naples, 2005).

Mental Health Courts

Mental health courts are present in many Canadian metropolitan centres and are an integral diversion option for the more serious offences involving individuals with mental health issues (Slinger & Roesch, 2010). However, there are major concerns that there might be inadequate planning and resource implementation with this option (Kaiser, 2010), diminished procedural rights for individuals, net-widening (that is, judicial processing for individuals who otherwise have would have been diverted by the police), potentially more restrictive outcomes and lengthier institutionalizations, and the continued criminalization of an already marginalized group (Quirouette, Hannah-Moffat, & Maurutto, 2016). However, research has demonstrated that mental health courts are a more holistic (that is, they provide more comprehensive treatments, including an assessment of social determinants needs), less stigmatizing, and less criminogenic approach for individuals with mental health needs. The **therapeutic jurisprudence** concept has been applied to mental health court models (Marinos & Whittingham, 2018) based on the idea that an individual's mental (and physical) well-being is the foremost objective, and judicial decision making should be focused on this priority. When mental health courts were well implemented, they increased access to appropriate mental health treatment(s) and other rehabilitative programs and reduced future justice system involvement (Edgely, 2014).

Canadian researchers have taken the policy position that these programs should focus more on the vulnerable minority groups discussed above (Watts & Weinrath, 2017). For example, specialized youth mental health courts are now operating in certain jurisdictions such as Ontario, and these specialized courts process cases more efficiently, connecting young people to various treatment programs (Davis, Peterson-Badali, Weagant, & Skilling, 2015).

Fitness to Stand Trail and NCRMD

In severe cases of mental illness, the Criminal Code mandates that the accused be assessed by the criminal courts to determine whether they are capable of understanding and participating in the court process and whether their mental illness at the time of the commission of the offence affected their actions. Adults and youth are rarely assessed as **unfit to stand trial (UST)** or **not criminally responsible on account of mental disorder (NCRMD)**. An individual may be found UST if it is determined they are not fully capable of instructing counsel or understanding the nature and consequences of their trial. The defence of NCRMD may be raised in cases in which the accused is determined to have been suffering from a mental disorder during the commission of an offence; it is not a finding of guilt or an acquittal. When found UST, the judge can adjourn the case to allow for a follow-up psychological assessment. More commonly, the Crown prosecutor can request a treatment order to access supports for the accused to facilitate a subsequent fitness hearing. In the cases where the defence of NCRMD is successful, an individual may be released, either without any conditions or with conditions, or admitted to a forensic psychiatric hospital. There are strict procedural practices to ensure individuals found NCRMD are not institutionalized for indefinite periods of time. Review boards assess each case on a regular basis to ensure appropriate accommodations and treatments are being provided and to determine when the individual may return to the community or if they should stay in the psychiatric facility. These types of cases are potentially appropriate for referral to the specialized mental health courts.

Mobile Crisis Teams

Mobile crisis teams provide services for individuals with mental health needs, and they often focus on diversion. In Canada, models of mobile crisis intervention teams (MCITs) are based on a multi-agency collaborative approach involving police agencies, forensic health staff, and hospitals. The MCIT typically includes a mental health nurse and a specially trained police officer to respond to calls involving a person experiencing a mental health crisis. The nurse conducts an immediate assessment of the individual and offers onsite support or a referral to the appropriate mental health services. The police officer has a secondary role of ensuring there is no immediate danger to anyone and, if needed, apprehending the individual under the province/territory's Mental Health Act (or similar legislation). The MCIT can then transport the individual to the hospital or psychiatric facility where further care is provided. An evaluation of the Toronto MCIT revealed that teams successfully connected individuals to community-based services, provided faster access to emergency department resources, and resulted in low charge rates for individuals requiring services (Lamanna et al., 2015).

Assertive Community Treatment and Assertive Outreach Teams

Assertive community treatment (ACT) teams have been implemented in large jurisdictions throughout Canada to deliver community-based treatment to individuals with severe and chronic mental health needs, with psychoses prioritized. ACT teams are multidisciplinary units that often (though teams vary in composition) include clinical staff (psychiatrists, psychologists, and registered nurses) as well as addiction counsellors, social workers, peer specialists, housing supports, and, less frequently, police officers. Given its low staff-to-client ratio and 24-hour availability, ACT teams provide intensive **wraparound services**. The client-centred care includes individualized assessment and treatment/service planning that is continually assessed. A secondary benefit of ACT teams is diversion; by addressing mental health needs immediately, the likelihood of an incident requiring more formal police/legal intervention is reduced.

Several BC-based ACT teams employ police officers who provide assistance when a potential concern for aggressive or violent behaviour arises. The officers can enhance feelings of safety not only for ACT staff but also for clients. Since their full implementation in 2012, Vancouver ACT teams have increased service access for hundreds of individuals in the community (Cohen, Plecas, McCormick, & Peters, 2014) and have facilitated the decline in apprehensions of individuals with mental health needs under the Mental Health Act (Lupick, 2017). Interviews conducted with clients and staff from a Victoria, British Columbia, ACT team found that the inclusion of police enhanced clients' perceptions of safety and relationships with the police, resulted in clients reporting feeling that officers appreciated the need to provide a range of supports in addition to health-related services (such as housing), and facilitated connections to community-based legal supports (Costigan & Woodin, 2018). ACT staff were appreciative of the specialized legal knowledge officers contributed, as well as their capacity to de-escalate conflict situations. Despite the challenges of integrating police officers (due to reasons like re-triggering previous negative police interactions, stigma, or officer availability), these ACT partnerships achieved improved information sharing among regional health agencies and police departments, often through informal agreements.

The 2014 initiated Assertive Outreach Teams (AOTs) in Vancouver, British Columbia, is another community-based initiative that involves the Vancouver Police in collaboration with psychiatric nurses. These teams provide closer monitoring of psychiatric patients who are transitioning from a hospital behavioural stabilization unit back into the community (Cohen et al., 2014). AOTs proactively supervise individuals who are decompensating in the community to ensure treatment plan compliance and to take medication non-compliant individuals to a doctor, if necessary. The psychiatric nurse can administer certain medications as well. Vancouver's ACT teams and AOTs reduced, and in some cases eliminated, clients' stays in mental health beds and decreased hospital visits (Seethapathy, n.d.). ACT and AOT clients also had improved access to primary care and overall improvements in mental and physical health. In addition, they had fewer contacts with the police, decreased substance use, and some obtained stable housing and employment.

Institutional Services

Screening

The implementation and use of standardized, evidence-based **screening tools** have become a regular practice in correctional environments, both in the community and in institutions. Numerous studies have demonstrated the validity of these instruments in identifying mental illness (Ford, Trestman, Wiesbrock, & Zhang, 2009) and their capacity to reduce delays in access to treatment and guide intervention decision making (Martin et al., 2018). Still, screening tool use is not associated with the consistent provision of

long-term treatment implementations for the most vulnerable individuals.

There is limited consensus concerning the effectiveness of various screening tools. One review found that over 20 different screening tools were in use in the United States, the United Kingdom, Canada, Australia, New Zealand, and Denmark (Martin, Colman, Simpson, & McKenzie, 2013). This study reported inconsistencies in the predictive validity of the instruments in screening males and females as well as across different ethnicities/cultures, including among Indigenous individuals. Martin and colleagues (2013) suggest that further research is needed to better understand how screening outcomes are potentially influenced by gender, race/ethnicity/culture, correctional setting, and staff. Subsequent CSC-based research on three of its screening tools revealed differences in each tool's capacity to validly identify those individuals with mental health needs and, importantly, follow-up needs (Wilton, Stewart, & Power, 2015). However, no significant differences in referral patterns for Indigenous offenders were found.

A related policy concern is that mental health screening practices have been associated with too many false positives (that is, indicating the presence of mental illness or the likelihood of violence/future criminality that is not subsequently substantiated). Similarly, certain instruments that focused on static risk factors were inadequate in considering dynamic risk and protective factors, especially in correctional settings. The latter are typically high-stress contexts, especially at intake, and over time, with "normal" adjustment experiences, prognoses change favourably (Taylor et al., 2010). There are serious institutional implications of incorrectly assessing individuals' mental health issues, including the inefficient allocation of resources, the inappropriate administration of medication/treatments, and the unnecessary labelling of individuals and behaviours. Screening may also identify new cases of mental illness among individuals whose needs are relatively low, which will then take resources away from the treatment available for those with higher/more complex needs (Martin et al., 2018). These instruments are likely more accurately employed in settings where higher rates of mental illness are normative, but this still does not fully mitigate the above concerns of instruments' validity limitations. In cases where individuals were accurately screened, successful responses included consistent follow-up with mental health professionals, although this was typically a lengthy process because delays and insufficient resources were not uncommon (Martin, Potter, Crocker, Wells, & Colman, 2016).

An associated concern is the overrating of females as high risk because of a conflating of risk and need. Women involved in the correctional system often have multiple needs, from mental health, substance use, and trauma to housing and family-related needs. This has resulted in persistent practices of rating females in the correctional system as "high risk" and placing them in maximum security institutions. Yet research has consistently demonstrated that, overall, they are less likely to reoffend than men who are low, moderate, or high risk (Nolan & Stewart, 2017). The consequences of this, however, can be detrimental to females' mental health and well-being as well as their recovery and rehabilitation, as they may not receive appropriate services/supports or they may be oversupervised and have excessive controls imposed on them. These concerns are discussed in greater detail in Chapter 8.

Counselling—Individual and Group

As part of the CSC's delivery of primary mental health services, their facilities provide early assessment and individualized interventions, including group and individual interventions that promote mental health as well as prevent the exacerbation of mental health issues or the development of new ones. Mental health teams collaborate routinely, and other program resources in the institution exist to provide a holistic, evidence-based treatment plan. The CSC's mental health services typically consider the diversity of the needs of participating individuals from the most vulnerable groups, such as females and Indigenous persons. These services comprise the CSC's continuity of care model, which endeavours to connect incarcerated individuals with treatment centres and community-based mental health services for when individuals return to the community.

Gender and Culturally Based Programming

As suggested previously, an undisputed policy position in Canada is the need for institutional programs that are gender and culturally responsive, meaningfully account for varied life experiences, focus on greater exposure to abuse/violence and trauma by women, and are considerate of the high prevalence of intergenerational abuse and trauma in certain vulnerable groups,

such as Indigenous and migrant groups. At all three main levels of government in Canada, programs that address mental health and substance-use needs have simultaneously attempted to mitigate underlying distal causes of these conditions while being sensitive to more proximate risk factors associated with life experiences and social determinants. Again, female offenders and other marginalized groups experienced considerable barriers to accessing mental health services both in the community (as a result of prioritizing their other needs, such as housing, child care, and financial support) and institutionally. The primary explanation for these programs' limitations is inadequate or absent gender-specific services (Besney et al., 2018). Other programs' service delivery obstacles include the historical distrust between vulnerable members of the community and the correctional system and service providers, and the disjointed planning and provision of services in institutional and community contexts.

Research has demonstrated success in programs designed specifically for women, which resulted in a lower likelihood of experiencing depression as well as a decrease in the number of substances used among females who completed gender-responsive treatment, compared to females with substance-use issues but who did not participate in these treatments (Saxena, Messina, & Grella, 2014). The next chapter on women and corrections presents a more thorough review of gender-responsive programming.

Culturally relevant programs have been recommended among many experts and scholars. The CSC has offered a range of programs to support the needs of Indigenous prisoners, including the Aboriginal Offender Substance Abuse Program, which has since been replaced by the Integrated Correctional Program Model. The Aboriginal Integrated Correctional Program Model (AICPM), which offered a more holistic, culturally informed program model, was introduced following consultations with Elders and Indigenous groups. Research on AICPM's effectiveness showed lower rates of re-incarceration compared to the previously delivered programs for Indigenous participants (Stewart & Wilton, 2014b). A recent meta-analysis examining programs tailored for Indigenous populations revealed that participating in these programs led to reduced likelihoods of reoffending (Gutierrez, Chadwick, & Wanamaker, 2018). Several culturally relevant components characterize the programs, such as the inclusion of therapeutic approaches delivered by

Elders and Chiefs and the integration of the respective Indigenous group's values, languages, and ceremonial traditions.

Another potentially beneficial approach to addressing the mental health needs of minority correctional populations is when therapeutic jurisprudence principles are incorporated by the courts. An evaluation of this model occurred in three criminal courts in Arctic regions of Nunavut (in which the majority of the population is Inuit) to assess whether therapeutic jurisprudence was effective in facilitating a non-adversarial and rehabilitative approach in mental health cases (Ferrazzi & Krupa, 2016). Key findings were that mental illness had a distinctive meaning in Inuit culture, primarily explained by the above-discussed distal historical experiences. Again, persistent and chronic social problems (involving alcohol and drugs) and criminality followed from traumatic colonial experiences. Furthermore, the Western medicalized model of explaining mental illness and criminality as an individual biological condition that can be explained by "free will" or rational choice was invalid. For example, Inuit culture was less likely to label, let alone criminalize, deviant behaviours and institutionally isolate these individuals away from their communities and culture. Study participants explicitly stated the importance of accounting for social and historical events (such as colonialism and residential schools) in interventions and further integrating cultural practices (for example, opportunities to be on the land) and Elders in treatment strategies. These approaches could be offered in combination with traditional Western interventions in more serious cases of mental health needs and major violent criminality (Ferrazzi & Krupa, 2016).

Even when programs are apparently sensitive to cultural differences, the formal practices that provide mental health treatments in correctional systems are themselves rooted in a colonial system that does not sufficiently account for Indigenous perspectives (Nelson & Wilson, 2017). Possible culturally sensitive policies include avoiding paternalistic and authoritarian-delivered practices. The officials involved with these service programs, along with the criminal justice system, were perceived among many Inuit prisoners as punitive agents of formal behavioural and cultural controls (Ferrazzi & Krupa, 2016). Nelson and Wilson (2017) assert that health-care professionals and practitioners working with Indigenous populations should have education and training that incorporates Indigenous perspectives on mental health and well-being and be provided with tools and strategies to integrate these teachings into the mental health services and programs offered.

Alternative Programs

In addition to the traditional counselling and pharmacological interventions, mental health-care providers and experts have begun to rely on alternative approaches to enhance mental health and well-being. These practices have been introduced varyingly and usually in an ad hoc manner into certain correctional settings. Meditation and yoga, for example, appear to be cost-effective interventions that reduce stress and aggression and mitigated depression, PTSD, and even schizophrenia (see Kerekes, Fielding, & Apelqvist, 2017 for a review). Yoga classes were also offered in combination with traditional prisoners' and releasees' ongoing treatment plans. Studies have examined the benefits of mindfulness for mental health and well-being programs, which incorporated CBT principles (Howells, Tennant, Day, & Elmer, 2010). A recent meta-analysis of 13 studies of yoga/meditation programs in male, female, and youth prisons (and substance-use treatment centres) demonstrated that prisoners who participated in a yoga/meditation program reported a moderate increase in psychological well-being, and the longer they participated in the program, the greater the positive effect (although the latter was not significant; Auty, Cope, & Liebling, 2017). As well, prison art programs and therapeutic animal-based programs using dogs and horses have also been implemented in correctional settings with improved outcomes related to mental health, general feelings of well-being, and reduced reoffending (see Donato, n.d.; Lai, 1998).

Continued Challenges

Although there is a substantial body of policy literature that emphasizes the importance of continuity in mental health-care services for individuals with these needs throughout all stages of the criminal justice system, common obstacles to achieving this policy objective include limited or no discharge or transition planning, issues with program eligibility, long wait lists, a shortage of adequate mental health programs in the community, loss of insurance while incarcerated, limited means to pay program/service costs, and the continued stigma

Best Practice Example

Ken Gigliotti/Winnipeg Free Press

The Stony Mountain Institution Peer Offender Prevention Service has been offered since 2009.

In the OCI's 2017–18 annual report, the office high-lighted the Peer Offender Prevention Service (POPS) that has been delivered at the Stony Mountain Institution outside of Winnipeg, Manitoba, since 2009 (OCI, 2018). POPS is a peer-based program that provides 24/7 access to crisis intervention for individuals with serious mental illnesses. This service is available to all prisoners regardless of security level or placement in segregation. The program is delivered primarily by individuals vernacularly labelled "Lifers" because they are serving life sentences. These program deliverers received training from community-based agencies on a range of topics associated with mental health, from knowledge of specific conditions (such as anxiety and depression) to suicide prevention and trauma. Since its inception, POPS has resulted in fewer self-harm incidents and

has prevented the segregation of individuals identified as vulnerable.

The use of peer-based program models has been assessed as beneficial to individuals who have mental illness and are in the criminal justice system. Prisoners can relate to the individuals supporting them, and it can alleviate some of the resource pressures felt by clinicians and staff working in the institutions. Peer-based programs also received attention in 2018 from Canada's then-minister of Public Safety and Emergency Preparedness, Ralph Goodale, who in his mandate letter to the new commissioner of Correctional Service Canada, Anne Kelly, emphasized the importance of delivering a variety of programs in correctional settings, which also included those that incorporate the arts, animals, and in this case peer mentoring (CSC, 2018).

toward mental illness and the dual stigma of being a former prisoner. Some programs also had strict policies on the types of individuals/offence histories they admitted and acceptable behaviours of clients once enrolled in the programs. For example, not infrequently, program eligibility specified a particular mental health condition but excluded a co-occurring category, such as substance-use disorders (or the reversal of these two often comorbid disorders). As reviewed in this chapter, comorbidities are prevalent in corrections populations, so the potentially critical service needs of these prisoners are unmet, which could negatively affect their quality of life in the community and increase the likelihood of recidivism. In addition, other released individuals were either not aware of the full extent of their mental health needs or they wilfully avoided accessing services. A study by Begun, Early, and Hodge (2016) found that soon-to-be former prisoners encountered an average of 5.6 barriers to mental health services and 4.5 barriers to substance-use treatment upon their community re-entry.

With few exceptions, the literature suggests that many jurisdictions in Canada have insufficient resources for individuals with major mental health needs transitioning back to their communities. A related policy concern is inadequate discharge plans involving multiple service needs. A potentially promising policy change in response to these challenges in several jurisdictions has been the shift of correctional mental health care and services from provincial/territorial justice departments to health departments.

Conclusion

Arguably, Canada has a reputation of being progressive in its provision of mental health services for adults and youth in the criminal justice system. Part of this positive perception is that, relative to other advanced industrial and liberal-democratic countries, particularly the United States, Canadian laws and policies during the last approximately 40 years regarding both federal and provincial/territorial criminal justice systems, especially corrections, have relied extensively on research studies. This Canadian research has highlighted the continued multi-policy challenges in responding to the complex assessment and treatment needs of its varied correctional populations. While mental health services' resources have persistently been limited because of politically driven budget decisions, another fundamental political consideration has been the constitutional division between the health-care responsibilities of provincial/territorial institutions and their federal counterparts (Simpson et al., 2013). Since a federal health service entity that would be responsible for correctional institutions' mental health care simply has not been politically feasible in Canada, the traditional policy focus will continue to require innovative collaborative service delivery policies among the CSC, regional health departments, and external agencies on the one hand and the provincial/territorial counterparts on the other hand. It has been asserted in this chapter that this integrated policy delivery approach is critical since the continuum of care model is consistently shown to be the most promising approach. The same policy themes are evident at the provincial/territorial level, and the same model is recommended there as well—the transferring of correctional mental/health service responsibilities from justice authorities to health authorities. This shift is particularly essential to facilitate access to care, improved standards of care, and smoother transitions and reintegration into the community (Simpson et al., 2013).

Review Questions

1. Compare the objectives of Canada's mental health strategy and the CSC's mental health strategy.
2. What are the strengths and weaknesses of the CSC's mental health strategy?
3. What are the greatest challenges in addressing the needs of individuals with mental health issues in the Canadian correctional system?
4. What makes British Columbia unique compared to other Canadian provinces/territories in its administration of justice-based mental health services?

5. Outline the most effective mental health interventions/treatment for Indigenous and female correctional populations. What are the critiques and persistent challenges, and what are possible solutions to these issues?

6. How does comorbidity factor into correctional services and outcomes?

7. What are social determinants of health? What are their implications for mental illness and health care in correctional contexts?

8. Identify the key principles of trauma-informed care and the special populations that benefit from this approach. Why are trauma-informed practices so important in correctional settings?

9. What specialized court-based supports are offered for individuals with mental health issues?

10. Differentiate among mobile crisis teams, assertive community treatment teams, and Assertive Outreach Teams.

11. What are the most common barriers to accessing mental health services for both the general correctional population as well as special populations within the correctional system?

Critical Thinking Questions

1. In addition to deinstitutionalization, what are alternative explanations for the rise in mental illness in correctional populations?

2. Consider the potential ramifications for both prisoners and staff of removing solitary confinement from Canadian correctional institutions (as proposed by Bill C-83). Do the positive outcomes outweigh the potentially negative consequences of eliminating this practice? What factors should the CSC take into account in addressing this issue?

3. Devise a governance structure for delivering stronger mental health services for both the general community and institutional correctional settings. What factors should be considered in the process, and what do you anticipate will be the greatest obstacles to overcome?

4. Should screening tools play a role in the mental health decision making that occurs in Canadian correctional facilities? What alternative or supplementary strategies could be created and implemented?

5. If the federal and provincial/territorial governments decide to encourage more peer support programs, how should they invest greater resources in this? What additional considerations should be made?

Multimedia Suggestions

Navigating the Adult Criminal Justice and Mental Health Systems

This annotated illustration provides information on how the criminal justice system and mental health systems in Ontario interact: https://ontario.cmha.ca/wp-content/uploads/2016/08/Adult-Criminal-Justice-Mental-Health-Systems-Map-April-24-2015-FINAL.pdf

Jail Death: What Happened to Soleiman Faqiri?

This *Fifth Estate* documentary explores the death in custody of Soleiman Faqiri: https://www.youtube.com/watch?v=VgcmP3PU1Sg

"Deadly Restraint," Shanifa Nasser

This CBC *News* article provides another discussion of the death of Soleiman Faqiri: https://newsinteractives.cbc.ca/longform/soleiman-faqiri-jail-death

Ashley Smith Case and Mental Health in Canadian Prisons

This CBC Radio broadcast discusses the death in custody of Ashley Smith: https://www.cbc.ca/player/play/2303226716

Ashley Smith: Out of Control

This *Fifth Estate* documentary explores the death of Ashley Smith: https://www.cbc.ca/fifth/episodes/2009-2010/out-of-control

"Prison Watchdog Calls for End to Solitary for Mentally Ill Inmates," Kristy Kirkup

This *Ottawa Citizen* article discusses the push to end solitary confinement: https://ottawacitizen.com/news/national/prison-watchdog-calls-for-end-to-solitary-for-mentally-ill-inmates

Transforming the Criminal Justice System: Mental Health and Addictions

This video from the Department of Justice discusses initiatives aimed at helping people with mental health and addiction needs: https://www.justice.gc.ca/eng/news-nouv/photo/video9.html

Canada's Mental Health Courts: How They Work and Why They Exist

This "In Depth" *CBC News* video showcases Canada's mental health courts: https://www.cbc.ca/player/play/1329374275795

NCR: Not Criminally Responsible

This CBC documentary explores what happens when someone is found not criminally responsible on account of mental disorder: https://www.cbc.ca/firsthand/m/episodes/ncr-not-criminally-responsible

Pathway to Wellness

This video from the Vancouver Police Department discusses how the department is working with health-care providers to help people living with mental illness: https://vancouver.ca/police/organization/investigation/investigative-support-services/youth-services/mental-health.html

Inside Canada's Corrections System

Steve Paikin from *The Agenda* explores the recommendation to remove solitary confinement from Ontario's prisons: https://www.youtube.com/watch?v=L8aKRcUlOyI

Note

1. This was the same leading motivation for male prisoners' engagement in self-injurious behaviour.

References

Abracen, J., Langton, C.M., Looman, J., Gallo, A., Ferguson, M., Axford, M., & Dickey, R. (2014). Mental health diagnoses and recidivism in paroled offenders. *International Journal of Offender Therapy and Comparative Criminology, 58*(7), 765–79. doi:10.1177/0306624X13485930

Ahmed, R., Angel, C., Martel, R., Pyne, D., & Keenan, L. (2016). Access to healthcare services during incarceration among female inmates. *International Journal of Prisoner Health, 12*(4), 204–15. doi:10.1108/IJPH-04-2016-0009

Akers, R.L. (2011). *Social learning and social structure: A general theory of crime and deviance.* New Brunswick, NJ: Transaction Publishers.

Allergi, N., Deleveus, K., Loung, D., Li, H., Jensen, T., Batten, D., . . . Henighan, M. (2008). *Evaluation report: Community mental health initiative.* Ottawa, ON: Correctional Service Canada.

American Psychiatric Association. (2013). *Diagnostic and statistical manual of mental disorders* (5th edn). Arlington, VA: Author.

Andrews, D.A., & Bonta, J. (2010). Rehabilitating criminal justice policy and practice. *Psychology, Public Policy, and Law, 16*, 39–55.

Andrews, D.A., Bonta, J., & Hoge, R.D. (1990). Classification for effective rehabilitation: Rediscovering psychology. *Criminal Justice and Behavior, 17*, 19–52.

Auty, K.M., Cope, A., & Liebling, A. (2017). A systematic review and meta-analysis of yoga and mindfulness meditation in prison: Effects on psychological well-being and behavioural functioning. *International Journal of Offender Therapy and Comparative Criminology, 61*, 689–710. doi:10.1177/0306624X15602514

Barrett, M., Allenby, K., & Taylor, K. (2010). *Twenty years later: Revisiting the task force on federally sentenced women.* Ottawa, ON, Canada: Correctional Service Canada.

Barrett, E.L., Indig, D., Sunjic, S., Sannibale, C., Sindicich, N., Rosenfeld, J., . . . Mills, K. (2015). Treating comorbid substance use and traumatic stress among male prisoners: A pilot study of the acceptability, feasibility, and preliminary efficacy of Seeking Safety. *International Journal of Forensic Mental Health, 14,* 45–55. doi:http://doi.org/http://dx.doi.org/10.1080/14999013.2015.1014527

Beaudette, J.N., & Stewart, L.A. (2016). National prevalence of mental disorders among incoming federally-sentenced men offenders. *Canadian Journal of Psychiatry, 61,* 624–32. doi:10.1177/0706743716639929

Begun, A.L., Early, T.J., & Hodge, A. (2016). Mental health and substance abuse service engagement by men and women during community reentry following incarceration. *Administration and Policy in Mental Health and Mental Health Services, 43,* 207–18. doi:10.1007/s10488-015-0632-2

Bellamy, S., & Hardy, C. (2015). Post-traumatic stress disorder in Aboriginal people in Canada: Review of the risk factors, the current state of knowledge and directions for future research. National Collaborating Centre for Aboriginal Health. Retrieved from https://www.ccnsa-nccah.ca/docs/emerging/RPT-Post-TraumaticStressDisorder-Bellamy-Hardy-EN.pdf

Besney, J.D., Angel, C., Pyne, D., Martell, R., Keenan, L., & Ahmed, R. (2018). Addressing women's unmet health care needs in a Canadian remand center: Catalyst for improved health? *Journal of Correctional Health Care, 24*(3), 276–94. doi:10.1177/1078345818780731

Boyce, J., Rotenberg, C., & Karam, M. (2015). Mental health and contact with police in Canada, 2012. *Juristat.* Retrieved from https://www150.statcan.gc.ca/n1/pub/85-002-x/2015001/article/14176-eng.htm

Brink, J.H., Doherty, D., & Boer, A. (2001). Mental disorder in federal offenders: A Canadian prevalence study. *International Journal of Law & Psychiatry, 24,* 339–56.

Brown, G.P., Hirdes, J.P., & Fries, B.E. (2015). Measuring the prevalence of current, severe symptoms of mental health problems in a Canadian correctional population: Implications for delivery of mental health services for inmates. *International Journal of Offender Therapy and Comparative Criminology, 59,* 27–50. doi:10.1177/0306624X13507040

Burczycka, M. (2018). Violent victimization of Canadians with mental health-related disabilities, 2014. Catalogue no. 85-002-X. Ottawa, ON: Statistics Canada.

Cale, J., Lussier, P., McCuish, E., & Corrado, R. (2015). The prevalence of psychopathic personality disturbances among incarcerated youth: Comparing serious, chronic, violent and sex offenders. *Journal of Criminal Justice, 43,* 337–44.

Cary, C.E., & McMillen, J.C. (2012). The data behind the dissemination: A systematic review of trauma-focused cognitive behavioural therapy for use with children and youth. *Child and Youth Services Review, 34,* 748–57. doi:10.1016/j.childyouth.2012.01.003

Cesaroni, C., & Peterson-Badali, M. (2010). Understanding the adjustment of incarcerated young offenders: A Canadian example. *Youth Justice, 10*(2), 107–25.

Chaimowitz, G. (2012). The criminalization of people with mental illness. *Canadian Journal of Psychiatry, 57*(2), 1–6.

Chandler, J.A. (2015). The use of neuroscientific evidence in Canadian criminal proceedings. *Journal of Law and the Biosciences, 2,* 550–79.

Cohen, I., Plecas, D., McCormick, A., & Peters, A. (2014). *Eliminating crime: The 7 essential principles of police-based crime reduction.* Abbotsford, BC: Len Garis, Centre for Public Safety and Criminal Justice Research.

Coleman, T., & Cotton, D. (2014a). TEMPO: A contemporary model for police education and training about mental illness. *International Journal of Law and Psychiatry, 37,* 325–33.

Coleman, T., & Cotton, D. (2014b). TEMPO: Police interactions. A report towards improving interactions between police and people living with mental health problems. Retrieved from http://www.mentalhealthcommission.ca

Corabian, G., Appell, R., & Wormith, J.S. (2013). *Female offenders and self-harm: An overview of prevalence and evidence-based approaches.* Centre for Forensic Behavioural Science and Justice Studies, University of Saskatchewan. Retrieved from https://www.usask.ca/cfbsjs/research/pdf/research_reports/ReviewOfSelfHarmInWomenOffenders.pdf

Corrado, R.R., & Freedman, L. (2011). Risk profiles, trajectories and intervention points for serious and chronic young offenders. *International Journal of Child, Youth & Family Studies, 2,* 197–232.

Correctional Service Canada. (2002). *The 2002 mental health strategy for women offenders.* Retrieved from https://www.csc-scc.gc.ca/publications/fsw/mhealth/toc-eng.shtml

Correctional Service Canada. (2012). *Towards a continuum of care: Correctional Service Canada mental health strategy.* Retrieved from https://www.csc-scc.gc.ca/health/002006-2000-eng.shtml

Correctional Service Canada. (2017). Gender responsive corrections for women in Canada: The road to successful reintegration. Retrieved from https://www.csc-scc.gc.ca/women/002002-0005-en.shtml

Correctional Service Canada. (2018). Commissioner's mandate letter. Retrieved from https://www.csc-scc.gc.ca/about-us/006-0006-en.shtml

Correctional Service Canada. (2019). Quick facts: Mental health strategy. Retrieved from https://www.csc-scc.gc.ca/publications/005007-3043-en.shtml

Costigan, C., & Woodin, E. (2018). Integrating police officers onto assertive community treatment (ACT) teams: The views of clients and staff. Victoria, BC: University of Victoria. Retrieved from https://onlineacademiccommunity.uvic.ca/actpolice/wp-content/uploads/sites/3359/2018/02/ACT-police-integration-report-final.pdf

Covington, S., Burke, C., Keaton, S., & Norcott C. (2008). Evaluation of a trauma-informed and gender-responsive intervention for women in drug treatment. *Journal of Psychoactive Drugs, Suppl 5*, 387–98.

Davidson, F., Heffernan, E., Greenberg, D., Waterworth, R., & Burgess, P. (2017). Mental health and criminal charges: Variation in diversion pathways in Australia. *Psychiatry, Psychology and Law, 24*, 888–98. doi:https://doi.org/10.1080/13218719.2017.1327305

Davis, K., Peterson-Badali, M., Weagant, B., & Skilling, T. (2015). A process evaluation of Toronto's first youth mental health court. *Canadian Journal of Criminology and Criminal Justice, 57*, 159–87.

Delveaux, K., MacDonald, C., McConnell, A., Bradley, S., Crawford, A., & Tse, F. (2017). Evaluation of CSC's health services (File #394-2-96). Evaluation Division, Correctional Service Canada. Retrieved from https://www.csc-scc.gc.ca/publications/005007-2017-eng.shtml

Derkzen, D., Barker, J., McMillan, K, & Stewart, L. (2017). Rates of current mental disorders among women offenders in custody in CSC. Correctional Service Canada.

Donato, A. (n.d.). From puppies to farming: Canada's most innovative prison rehab programs [Weblog post]. *Keeping Canada safe*. Retrieved from https://www.cbc.ca/keepingcanadasafe/blog/from-puppies-to-farming-an-in-depth-look-at-innovative-prisoner-rehab-progr

Douglas, K.S., Ogloff, J.R., Nicholls, T.L., & Grant, I. (1999). Assessing risk for violence among psychiatric patients: The HCR-20 violence risk assessment scheme and the Psychopathy Checklist: Screening version. *Journal of Consulting and Clinical Psychology, 67*, 917–30.

Edgely, M. (2014). Why do mental health courts work? A confluence of treatment, support and adroit judicial supervision. *International Journal of Law and Psychiatry, 37*, 572–80.

Elwyn, L.J., Esaki, N., & Smith, C.A. (2015). Safety at a girls' secure juvenile justice facility. *Therapeutic Communities, 36*(4), 209–18. doi:http://doi.org/10.1108/TC-11-2014-0038

Esaki, N., Benamati, J., Yanosy, S., Middleton, J.S., Hopson, L.M., Hummer, V.L., & Bloom, S.L. (2013). The Sanctuary Model: Theoretical framework. *Families in Society: The Journal of Contemporary Social Services, 94*(2), 87–95. doi:10.1606/1044-3894.4287

Espinosa, E.M., Sorensen, J.R., & Lopez, M.A. (2013). Youth pathways to placement: The influence of gender, mental health need and trauma on confinement in the juvenile justice system. *Journal of Youth and Adolescence, 42*, 1824–36. doi:10.1007/s10964-013-9981-x

Ferrazzi, P., & Krupa, T. (2016). "Symptoms of something all around us": Mental health, Inuit culture, and criminal justice in Arctic communities in Nunavut, Canada. *Social Science & Medicine, 165*, 159–67.

Flannigan, K., Pei, J., Stewart, M., & Johnson, A. (2018). Fetal alcohol spectrum disorder and the criminal justice system: A systematic literature review. *International Journal of Law and Psychiatry, 57*, 42–52.

Ford, J.D., Trestman, R.L., Wiesbrock, V.H., & Zhang, W. (2009). Validation of a brief screening instrument for identifying psychiatric disorders among newly incarcerated adults. Psychiatric Services, 60, 842–6.

Frederick, T., O'Connor, C., & Koziarski, J. (2018). Police interactions with people perceived to have a mental health problem: A critical review of frames, terminology, and definitions. *Victims & Offenders, 13*, 1037–54. doi:10.1080/15564886.2018.1512024

Fryer, S.L., McGee, C.L., Matt, G.E., Riley, E.P., & Mattson, S.N. (2007). Evaluation of psychopathological conditions in children with heavy prenatal alcohol exposure. *Pediatrics, 119*, e733–e741.

Galanek, J.D. (2013). The cultural construction of mental illness in prison: A perfect storm of pathology. *Culture, Medicine, and Psychiatry, 37*(1), 195–225. doi:10.1007/s11013-012-9295-6

Gordon, A. (2010). Self-injury incidents in CSC institutions over a thirty-month period. Correctional Service Canada. Retrieved from https://www.csc-scc.gc.ca/005/008/092/005008-0233-01-eng.pdf

Government of Canada. (2017). *Budget 2017: Building a strong middle class*. Retrieved from https://www.budget.gc.ca/2017/docs/plan/budget-2017-en.pdf

Government of Canada. (2018). *Budget 2018: Equality and growth: A strong middle class*. Retrieved from https://www.budget.gc.ca/2018/docs/plan/budget-2018-en.pdf

Grella, C.E., Lovinger, K., & Warda, U.S. (2013). Relationships among trauma exposure, familial characteristics, and PTSD: A case-control study of women in prison and in the general population. *Women & Criminal Justice, 23*, 63–79. doi:10.1080/08974454.2013.743376

Gretton, H.M., & Clift, R.J.W. (2011). The mental health needs of incarcerated youth in British Columbia, Canada. *International Journal of Law and Psychiatry, 34*, 109–15. doi:10.1016/j.ijlp.2011.02.004

Gutierrez, L., Chadwick, N., & Wanamaker, K.A. (2018). Culturally relevant programming versus the status quo: A meta-analytic review of the effectiveness of treatment of Indigenous offenders. *Canadian Journal of Criminology and Criminal Justice, 60*, 321–53. doi:10.3138/cjccj.2017-0020.r2

Hare, R.D. (2003). *Manual for the Hare Psychopathy Checklist-Revised* (2nd edn.). Toronto, ON: Multi-Health Systems.

Hoffman, R., Hirdes, J., Brown, G.P., Dubin, J.A., & Barbaree, H. (2016). The use of a brief mental health screener to enhance the ability of police officers to identify persons with serious mental disorders. *International Journal of Law and Psychiatry, 47*, 28–35.

Houser, K.A., Belenko, S., & Brennan, P.K. (2012). The effects of mental health and substance abuse disorders on institutional misconduct among female inmates. *Justice Quarterly, 29*, 799–828.

Howells, K., Tennant, A., Day, A., & Elmer, R. (2010). Mindfulness in forensic mental health: Does it have a role? *Mindfulness, 1*, 4–9.

John Howard Society of Ontario. (2013). *Reasonable bail?* Centre of Research, Policy & Program Development, John Howard Society of Ontario. Retrieved from https://johnhoward.on.ca/wp-content/uploads/2014/07/JHSO-Reasonable-Bail-report-final.pdf

Kaiser, H.A. (2010). Commentary: Too good to be true: Second thoughts on the proliferation of mental health courts. *Canadian Journal of Community Mental Health, 29*, 19–25.

Kerekes, N., Fielding, C., & Apelqvist, S. (2017). Yoga in correctional settings: A randomized controlled study. *Frontiers in Psychiatry, 8*, 204. doi: 10.3389/fpsyt.2017.00204

Kouyoumdjian, F., Schuler, A., Matheson, F.I., & Hwang, S.W. (2016). Health status of prisoners in Canada: Narrative review. *Canadian Family Physician, 62*, 215–22.

Lai, J. (1998). Pet facilitated therapy in correctional institutions: Women offender programs and issues. Office of the Deputy Commissioner for Women, Correctional Service Canada. Retrieved from http://www.csc-scc.gc.ca/publications/fsw/pet/pet-eng.shtml

Lamanna, D., Kirst, M., Shapiro, G., Matheson, F., Nakhost, A., & Stergiopoulos, V. (2015). Toronto mobile crisis intervention team: Outcome evaluation report. Centre for Research on Inner City Health, St. Michael's Hospital. Retrieved from http://stmichaelshospitalresearch.ca/research-programs/urban-health-solutions/resources-and-reports/toronto-mobile-crisis-intervention-team-outcome-evaluation-report

Livingston, J.D., Rossiter, K.R., & Verdun-Jones, S.N. (2011). "Forensic" labelling: An empirical assessment of its effects on self-stigma for people with severe mental illness. *Psychiatry Research, 188*, 115–22.

Lupick, T. (2017, September 20). Vancouver police apprehensions under the Mental Health Act fall sharply after a long climb. *Georgia Straight*. Retrieved from https://www.straight.com/news/969536/vpd-apprehensions-under-mental-health-act-fall-sharply-after-long-climb

MacDonald, S.F., Stewart, L.A., & Feely, S. (2014). *Research report: The impact of the Community Mental Health Initiative (CMHI)* (Report No. R-337). Ottawa, ON: Correctional Service Canada.

Marinos, V., & Whittingham, L. (2018). The role of therapeutic jurisprudence to support persons with intellectual and developmental disabilities in the courtroom: Reflections from Ontario, Canada. *International Journal of Law and Psychiatry, 63*, 18–25. doi:10.1016/j.ijlp.2018.07.004

Martin, M.S., Colman, I., Simpson, A.F., & McKenzie, K. (2013). Mental health screening tools in correctional institutions: A systematic review. BMC *Psychiatry, 13*, 275–84.

Martin, M.S., Eljdupovic, G., McKenzie, K., & Colman, I. (2015). Risk of violence by inmates with childhood trauma and mental health needs. *Law and Human Behavior, 39*(6), 614–23. http://doi.org/10.1037/lhb0000149

Martin, M.S., Potter, B.K., Crocker, A.G., Wells, G.A., & Colman, I. (2016). Yield and efficiency of mental health screening: A comparison of screening protocols at intake to prison. *PLoS ONE, 11*(5), e0154106. doi:10.1371/journal.pone.0154106

Martin, M.S., Potter, B.K., Crocker, A.G., Wells, G.A., Grace, R.M., & Colman, I. (2018). Mental health treatment patterns following screening at intake to prison. *Journal of Consulting and Clinical Psychology, 86*, 15–23.

Martin, M.S., Viau-Deschênes, C., & Yogarajah, T. (2017). Trauma-informed care for incarcerated offenders who engage in chronic self-injurious behaviour: A rapid evidence assessment. Correctional Service of Canada. Retrieved from http://publications.gc.ca/collections/collection_2018/scc-csc/PS83-3-388-eng.pdf

Matheson, F.I., Brazil, A., Doherty, S., & Forrester, P. (2015). A call for help: Women offenders' reflections on trauma care. *Women & Criminal Justice, 25*(4), 241–55. http://doi.org/10.1080/08974454.2014.909760

McCuish, E.C., Corrado, R.R., Hart, S.D., & DeLisi, M. (2015). The role of symptoms of psychopathy in persistent violence over the criminal career into full adulthood. *Journal of Criminal Justice, 43*(4), 345–56.

McGhee, K., & Castro, M. (2018). Constructing "the psychopath": A discourse analysis of psychologists' understandings of psychopathy. *Asian Journal of Human Services. 14*, 38–52.

McInerney, C., Davoren, M., Flynn, G., Mullins, D., Fitzpatrick, M., . . . O'Neill, C. (2013). Implementing a court diversion and liaison scheme in a remand prison by systematic screening of new receptions: A 6-year participatory action research study of 20,084 consecutive male remands. *International Journal of Mental Health Systems, 7*, 18–29.

McLachlan, K., Roesch, R., Viljoen, J.L., & Douglas, K.S. (2014). Evaluating the psycholegal abilities of young offenders with fetal alcohol spectrum disorder. *Law and Human Behavior, 38*(1), 10–22.

Mental Health Commission of Canada. (2012). *Changing directions, changing lives: The mental health strategy for Canada.* Retrieved from https://www.mentalhealthcommission.ca/sites/default/files/MHStrategyStrategyENG.pdf

Mental Health Commission of Canada. (2016). *Advancing the mental health strategy for Canada: A framework for action (2017–2022)*. Retrieved from https://www.mentalhealthcommission.ca/sites/default/files/2016-08/advancingthementalhealthstrategyforcanadaaframeworkforaction.pdf

Morrow, M., Dagg, P.D., & Pederson, A. (2008). Is deinstitutionalization a "failed experiment"? The ethics of re-institutionalization. *Journal of Ethics in Mental Health, 3*(2), 1–7.

Nelson, S.E., & Wilson, K. (2017). The mental health of Indigenous peoples in Canada: A critical review of research. *Social Science & Medicine, 176*, 93–112.

Nolan, A., & Stewart, L. (2017). Low risk offenders: What does the research tell us? Correctional Service Canada. Retrieved from http://publications.gc.ca/collections/collection_2017/scc-csc/PS83-3-383-eng.pdf

Office of the Correctional Investigator. (2015). Administrative segregation in federal corrections: 10-year trends. Ottawa, ON: Author.

Office of the Correctional Investigator. (2018). *Annual Report, 2017–2018*. Ottawa, ON: Author.

Office of the Correctional Investigator. (2019). *Annual Report, 2018–2019*. Ottawa, ON: Author.

Pei, J., Leung, W.W., Jampolsky, F., & Alsbury, B. (2016). Experiences in the Canadian criminal justice system for individuals with fetal alcohol spectrum disorders: Double jeopardy? *Canadian Journal of Criminology and Criminal Justice, 58*, 56–86.

Penrose, L.S. (1939). Mental disease and crime: Outline of a comparative study of European statistics. *British Journal of Medical Psychology, 18*, 1–15.

Popova, S., Lange, S., Burd, L., & Rehm, J. (2015). Cost attributable to fetal alcohol spectrum disorder in the Canadian correctional system. *International Journal of Law and Psychiatry, 41*, 76–81.

Power, J. (2014). Self-injurious behaviour in Canadian corrections: The offenders, the behaviour, and perceptions of what works from the frontline. Correctional Service Canada and Carleton University. Retrieved from https://www.usask.ca/cfbsjs/va_symposia/VA2014/Presentations/Power%20VA%202014%20no%20notes%202014.05.pdf

Power, J., & Beaudette, J. (2013). A qualitative study of self-injurious behaviour in treatment centres. Correctional Service Canada. Retrieved from http://publications.gc.ca/collections/collection_2015/scc-csc/PS83-3-294-eng.pdf

Prendergast, M.L., Pearson, F.S., Podus, D., Hamilton, Z.K., & Greenwell, L. (2013). The Andrews' principles of risk, needs, and responsivity as applied in drug treatment programs: Meta-analysis of crime and drug use outcomes. *Journal of Experimental Criminology, 9*, 275–300.

Quirouette, M., Hannah-Moffat, K., & Maurutto, P. (2016). "A precarious place": Housing and clients of specialized courts. *British Journal of Criminology, 56*, 370–88. doi:10.1093/bjc/azv050

Ribeiro da Silva, D., Rijo, D., & Salekin, R.T. (2013). Child and adolescent psychopathy: Assessment and treatment needs. *Aggression and Violent Behavior, 18*, 71–8.

Saxena, P., Messina, N.P., & Grella, C.E. (2014). Who benefits from gender-responsive treatment? Accounting for abuse history on longitudinal outcomes for women in prison. *Criminal Justice & Behaviour, 41*, 417–32. doi:10.1177/0093854813514405

Seethapathy, V. (n.d.). Assertive community treatment (ACT) assertive outreach team (AOT). Canadian College of Health Leaders. Retrieved from http://cchl-ccls.ca/document/1125/BCLMSlidesJan302015Seethapathy.pdf

Simpson, A.F., McMaster, J.J., & Cohen, S.N. (2013). Challenges for Canada in meeting the needs of persons with serious mental illness in prison. *Journal of the American Academy of Psychiatry and the Law, 41*, 501–9.

Sirdifield, C. (2012). The prevalence of mental health disorders amongst offenders on probation: A literature review. *Journal of Mental Health, 21*, 485–98. doi:10.3109/09638237.2012.664305

Slinger, E., & Roesch, R. (2010). Problem-solving courts in Canada: A review and a call for empirically-based evaluation methods. *International Journal of Law and Psychiatry, 33*, 258–64.

Steadman, H.J., & Naples, M. (2005). Assessing the effectiveness of jail diversion programs for persons with serious mental illness and co-occurring substance use disorders. *Behavioral Sciences and the Law, 23*, 163–70.

Stewart, L.A., Gamwell, L., & Wilton, G. (2018). Comorbid mental disorders: Prevalence and impact on community outcomes. (R-404). Correctional Service Canada. Retrieved from http://publications.gc.ca/collections/collection_2017/scc-csc/PS83-3-379-eng.pdf

Stewart, L.A., & Wilton, G. (2014a). Correctional outcomes of offenders with mental disorders. *Criminal Justice Studies, 27*, 63–81.

Stewart, L.A., & Wilton, G. (2014b). Outcomes of federal Aboriginal offenders in correctional programs: Follow-up from the ICPM evaluation (Research Report R-328). Ottawa, ON: Correctional Service Canada.

Stewart, L.A., Wilton, G., & Sapers, J. (2016). Offenders with cognitive deficits in a Canadian prison population: Prevalence, profile, and outcomes. *International Journal of Law and Psychiatry, 44*, 7–14.

Streissguth, A.P., Barr, H., Kogan, J., & Bookstein, F. (1997). Primary and secondary disabilities in fetal alcohol syndrome. In A.P. Streissguth & J. Kanter (Eds), *The challenge of fetal alcohol syndrome: Overcoming secondary disabilities*. Seattle, WA: University of Washington.

Sussman, S. (1998). The first asylums in Canada: A response to neglectful community care and current trends. *Canadian Journal of Psychiatry, 43*, 260–64.

Sutherland, E.H. (1974). *Criminology* (9th edn.). Philadelphia, PA: Lippincott.

Taylor, P.J., Walker, J., Dunn, E., Kissell, A., Williams, A., & Amos, T. (2010). Improving mental state in early imprisonment. *Criminal Behavior and Mental Health, 20*, 215–31. doi:10.1002/cbm.774

Teplin, L.A. (1984). Criminalizing mental disorder: The comparative arrest rate of the mentally ill. *American Psychologist, 39*, 794–803.

UN General Assembly. (2016). *United Nations standard minimum rules for the treatment of prisoners (the Nelson Mandela Rules)*. A/RES/70/175. Retrieved from https://www.unodc.org/documents/justice-and-prison-reform/GA-RESOLUTION/E_ebook.pdf

Wallace, B.C., Conner, L.C., & Dass-Brailsford, P. (2011). Integrated trauma treatment in correctional health care and community-based treatment upon reentry. *Journal of Correctional Health Care, 17*(4), 329–43. doi:http://doi.org/10.1177/1078345811413091

Watts, J., & Weinrath, M. (2017). The Winnipeg Mental Health Court: Preliminary findings on program implementation and criminal justice outcomes. *Canadian Journal of Community Mental Health, 36*, 67–82.

White, P. (2019, April 10). Landmark ruling in Ontario caps solitary confinement at 15 days. *Globe and Mail.* Retrieved from https://www.theglobeandmail.com/canada/article-solitary-confinement-for-more-than-15-days-constitutes-cruel-and

Wilton, G., & Stewart, L.A. (2017). Outcomes of offenders with co-occurring substance use disorders and mental disorders. *Psychiatric Services, 68*, 704–09.

Wilton, G., Stewart, L., & Power, J. (2015). *Agreement among three mental health screening measures (Research Brief B-58).* Ottawa, ON: Correctional Service Canada

Wolff, K.T., Baglivio, M.T., & Piquero, A.R. (2017). The relationship between adverse childhood experiences and recidivism in a sample of juvenile offenders in community-based treatment. *International Journal of Offender Therapy and Comparative Criminology, 61*, 1210–42. doi:10.1177/0306624X15613992

World Health Organization. (2003). *Declaration on prison health as part of public health (Moscow Declaration).* Retrieved from http://www.euro.who.int/__data/assets/pdf_file/0007/98971/E94242.pdf

Wormith, J.S., & McKeague, F. (1996). A mental health survey of community correctional clients in Canada. *Criminal Behaviour and Mental Health, 6*, 49–72.

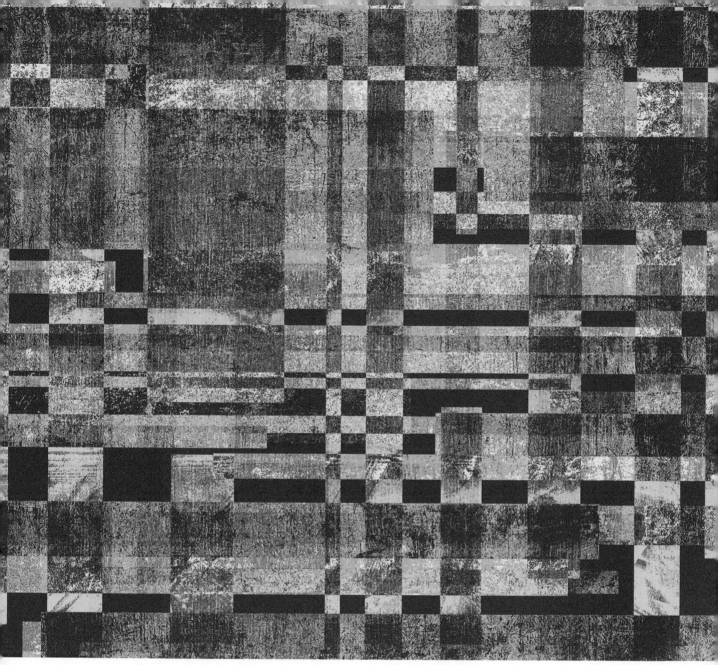

PART III

Special Populations

Women, Crime, and Criminalization in Canada

8

Understanding the Canadian Correctional Landscape for Incarcerated Women

Jennifer M. Kilty and Rebecca Jaremko Bromwich

Learning Objectives

After reading this chapter, you should be able to:

- Describe the general demographic trends in women's criminality.
- Enumerate women's pathways into crime.
- Define the construction and evolution of women-specific carceral spaces.
- Understand the importance and explain the lasting impacts of the Task Force on Federally Sentenced Women and the *Creating Choices* document, the 1994 "incident" at the Kingston Prison for Women and Justice Arbour's Commission of Inquiry into those events, and the Ashley Smith case.
- Critically analyze the use of risk/need assessment as the governing correctional logic.
- Understand and critique gender-responsive programming.
- Consider the value of adopting an abolitionist perspective for the future.

Chapter Overview

This chapter critically explores the criminalization and federal incarceration of women in Canada in both historical and social contexts. It begins with a demographic portrait of federally incarcerated women (noting differences according to race, Indigeneity, marginalization, and victimization) and an outline of how assumptions and constructions of harm and fault under Canadian criminal law intersect with women's main "pathways" into crime. The chapter then moves on to provide an historic overview of the evolution of federal corrections for women in Canada, discussing the birth of the first federal penitentiary for women, the Kingston Prison for Women (P4W) (1934–2000), noting in particular the long-standing critiques and condemnation of P4W by of a series

of federal government reports and inquiries. We outline how these critiques shaped the modern reforms done to corrections for federally sentenced women, crystallizing the conditions and practices (including risk/need assessment and gender-responsive programming) they continue to endorse to the present day, as well as how the Correctional Service Canada failed to implement key reform features that were proposed by feminist scholars, advocates, and prisoners. The chapter also reviews two significant cases, the disturbing events that happened at the P4W in April 1994 and the haunting parallels seen in the events that led to Ashley Smith's preventable death in 2007, to help problematize the commonly accepted progress narrative pertaining to the evolution of federal corrections for women in Canada. The chapter concludes with an intersectional discussion of how women, while by no means a uniform group, experience the pains of imprisonment, including their experiences of segregation, psychiatrization, and self-harm.

Demographic Portrait

Statistics Canada data from 2017 (the most recent year available) indicate that women make up 25 per cent of the criminally accused across the country (Savage, 2019). Women have historically (and continue to) comprised a small percentage of the individuals held in federal custody and make up a smaller portion of criminal accuseds than do men, although the percentage of women accuseds has been gradually increasing for several years. While federally sentenced women constitute only about 3 per cent of the individuals held in federal custody in Canada, they are the fastest growing segment of the prison population and the rate is exponentially worse for Indigenous women. Between 2007 and 2016, the number of female prisoners increased by 29.7 per cent, while the number of Indigenous women increased by 60 per cent (Office of the Correctional Investigator [OCI], 2017).

Those women who do become criminalized and federally incarcerated tend to have serious physical and mental health challenges; women in federal custody are more likely to have serious physical and mental health issues than women in the general population. For instance, the rates of sexually transmitted infections, including HIV and hepatitis, were greater for women in federal custody than the rates in the general Canadian population and were again highest amongst Indigenous women in custody (Thompson, Zakaria, & Grant, 2011). Further, and illustrating the common connection between women's substance use and their criminality, approximately 10 per cent of women in federal custody are participating in methadone maintenance programs (MacSwain, Cheverie, MacDonald & Johnson, 2014).

Women in federal **incarceration** tend to hail from **marginalized** circumstances of poverty, have racial or ethnic minority heritage, and have histories of being victimized by violence. Perhaps most significantly, women in federal custody are disproportionately Indigenous. In fact, the regions with the highest per capita number of women accused of crimes were also regions with larger Indigenous populations, such as the territories and the prairie provinces of Manitoba and Saskatchewan (Savage, 2019).

Women's Pathways into Crime

Too often, rigid distinctions between what is expected of women and men or what is normal for men and women submerge differences between members of the same gender. Additionally, contemporary debates and advocacy around transgender prisoner issues highlight that it is important not to make overly simplistic black-and-white assumptions about what "women" and "men" want, think, or do. Having said that, there remain distinct patterns, on the whole, in which pathways into **criminalization** diverge based on the gender of the individual accused (Chesney-Lind & Pasko, 2004). These divergent patterns relate to the fact that women are more likely to be victims of violent crime and are far less likely to be convicted for perpetrating crimes of violence.

Overwhelmingly, criminalized women have experienced victimization from physical and sexual abuse, childhood neglect, and other **traumas** (Adelberg & Currie, 1987; Chesney-Lind & Pasko, 2004; Hannah-Moffat, 2001; Hayman, 2006; Pollack, 2009; Task Force on Federally Sentenced Women [TFFSW], 1990). In fact, feminist scholars largely consider women's trauma histories as informing their offending patterns and influencing their pathways into criminality. Many researchers have found a clear link between victimization by early abuse and trauma and women's criminalization (Salisbury & Van Voorhis, 2009), which has been characterized as a "gender-specific pathway" into criminalization for women (Topitzes, Mersky & Reynolds, 2011).

Notably, when women are criminally charged, it is often for different types of crimes than men; women are frequently criminalized as parties to the crimes of others, for example, acting in subordinate roles of **aiders or abettors** where violent men with whom they are associated are the primary "ringleaders" of the offending behaviour. Further, charge rates against women for simple assault have been greatly increasing in recent years, which feminist activists have noted is due to the fact that women are incurring charges in the context of abusive relationships where they are generally the victim of the abuse (Johnson & Dawson, 2011). This is problematically caused by police practices of charging both partners in cases of partner assault where both parties claim to have been victimized, commonly referred to as "mandatory" or "dual-charging" policies. Relatedly, charges in relation to violent crime are more likely to be stayed or withdrawn against women accused in comparison to men (Savage, 2019). These facts speak to the context of women's violent crime, which tends to be situated in larger conditions of marginality and within their experiences of victimization. Indigenous women are more likely than other women in Canada to be criminally charged and were 27 times more likely than non-Indigenous women to be charged with homicide (Savage, 2019). Women are more likely to commit or be accused of homicide against their spouse or conjugal partner (Savage, 2019), who often has a history of committing violence against her (Johnson & Dawson, 2011).

Historically, and still today, it is not just differences in women's material behaviour that produce different pathways into criminalization relative to gender, but also different cultural expectations of gender-appropriate behaviours (Sprott & Doob, 2009). Because women are culturally expected to be passive, nurturing, and more rule-abiding, criminalized women are constructed as "acting out" and are often treated more harshly in response (Dell, Kilty, & Fillmore, 2009). Unruliness or rebellion have historically been understood in Western cultures as to be expected, or at least not an unusual part of coming of age for young men, while women are expected not to disobey rules, engage in offending behaviour, or rebel. In consequence, girls are disproportionately criminalized for status offences such as "incorrigibility" or "promiscuity" relative to boys and are more likely to face harsh penalties for disobedient acts that form the basis of administration of justice offences (Sprott & Doob, 2009).

Women in federal custody, on average, serve briefer periods of incarceration than men (Lutfy & Forrester, 2014). As of 2014, approximately one-third of recently admitted women offenders were serving sentences of 25 months or less. However, women in federal custody are more likely to be held in maximum security custody while serving sentences—even for minor crimes—because they are classified by Correctional Service Canada (CSC) as having greater needs and posing higher risks to the safety and security of the institution (Lutfy & Forrester, 2014). Similarly, while those held in maximum security custody constitute 11 per cent of the overall federally sentenced women population, Indigenous women make up 50 per cent of the maximum security population (OCI, 2017). While widely held ideas about feminine passivity are changing

to some extent, stereotypical ideas about what is "naturally" feminine persist.

The Birth of the Kingston Prison for Women (1835–1934)

Prior to the construction of the Kingston Prison for Women[1] (P4W), federally sentenced women served their sentences at Kingston Penitentiary,[2] a maximum security prison for men located across the street from the site where P4W would eventually be built. Kingston Penitentiary, also known as Kingston Pen or the abbreviated KP, was constructed over the course of two years in 1833–4 and opened on 1 June 1835. Originally designated as the Provincial Penitentiary of the Province of Upper Canada, it was one of the oldest **penitentiaries** in continuous use in the world at the time of its closure on September 30, 2013. The first women to serve time in KP arrived in 1835. Reflecting the historical and continued correctional practice of segregating prisoners on the basis of gender, Susan Turner, Hannah Downes, and Hannah Baglen, who were all serving one to two years for larceny, were initially housed in the hospital wing of KP until a separate facility could be found. It took four years, but in 1839 they were moved to the North Wing of the facility, which was at the time designated as the first prison for women in Canada (CSC, 2000).

Foreshadowing the mother–child program[3] that the CSC would eventually implement in 2001 (Brennan, 2014), some women who gave birth while incarcerated in KP were permitted to keep their babies in their cells, "only as long as was necessary to wean them, after which the child would be sent to an orphanage or to family members" (CSC, 2000). Unfortunately, the conditions of confinement for women were no better than they were for men:

> Their quarters were cold, damp and crawling with bugs. Punishment for infractions of rules included floggings and placement in the "box": a coffin-like container with air holes, in which a woman was forced to stand, hunched over, for hours at a time. Women, like men offenders, could also be chained, submerged in ice water, put in a dark cell or fed only bread and water. And so it went for years. In 1881, Matron Mary Leahy reported for the year that various members of the inmate population of 15 had spent a total of 14 days in solitary confinement on a diet of bread and water. (CSC, 2000)

Mirroring the contemporary rates of incarceration, historically there were far fewer women than men housed in KP. Typically seen as "too few to count" (Adelberg & Currie, 1987), meaning that because of their small number not only did correctional administrators fail to consider women's unique needs and pathways into crime and use the norms and standards designed to govern men to manage incarcerated women, but women were also relegated to smaller, overcrowded spaces, even being forced to sleep on the floor in prison corridors (CSC, 2000). In 1867, the prison inspector made the first official call to build a standalone women's prison outside the grounds of the Kingston Penitentiary in his annual report; however, it would take until 1909 for construction to begin on a separate building, and it remained within KP's walls (CSC, 2000). Constructed by male prisoners, the new Northwest Cell Block opened in early 1913 and housed 32 single-occupancy cells and two double sick-bay cells. While broadly considered a progressive step forward, the year after it opened the Royal Commission on Penitentiaries declared "that the interests of all concerned would be best served if those few inmates were transferred to an institution for women" (CSC, 2000). The document also suggested that transfer agreements be made so that federally sentenced women could be housed in provincial institutions for women.

Over the years, many reports would recommend building a separate prison for women. Again signalling the small number of female prisoners in comparison to men, it took significant advocacy to mount the political pressure needed for the government to eventually commit to the construction project, and the male prisoner labour gangs would only commence construction on P4W in 1925. In 1934, after 99 years, women finally had a designated federal prison space of their own.

Costing approximately $374,000 to build (CSC, 2000), the new 108-cell maximum security facility would create harmful geographic dislocation for all criminalized women hailing from outside southern and central Ontario whose friends and families could not afford to visit them (TFFSW, 1990). In fact, between 1934 and 1990 no fewer than 15 government reports would outline serious limitations and problems with the Kingston Prison for Women, such as the fact that regardless of their security classification all women were housed in maximum security conditions, with many of the reports recommending that P4W be closed (TFFSW, 1990). Perhaps the most infamous condemnation of P4W's conditions of confinement was brought forth by Mark McGuigan, who in his 1977 *Report to Parliament* wrote that the prison was "unfit for bears, much less women" (p. 135).

Thomas Szlukovenyi / The Globe and Mail

Kingston Prison for Women had notoriously poor conditions, but it was the only federal prison for women in Canada.

Creating Choices

Canada's **criminal justice system** and **correctional** system were designed, organized, and until the late twentieth century operated based on standards set for managing a predominantly male population (Hannah-Moffat, 2001). More attention started to be paid institutionally and governmentally to the needs of federally incarcerated women in the late twentieth century. In response to the lobbying of advocacy groups like the Canadian Association of Elizabeth Fry Societies (a national **abolitionist** organization that advocates for criminalized women), the Native Women's Association of Canada, the Aboriginal Women's Caucus, and the National Organization of Immigrant and Visible Minority Women of Canada, among others, as well as the buildup of government reports decrying the poor conditions of confinement at P4W, in 1989 the governor in council created a task force to review the CSC's approach to the management of federally incarcerated women from a feminist and woman-centred perspective (TFFSW, 1990). As part of this review, research was initiated to survey women and examine their lives, needs, and experiences before, during, and after incarceration (Shaw, 1991). The resulting *Creating Choices* report critically examines the correctional management of federally sentenced women from the moment a woman's sentence begins to the date she is released. It was intended to be useful in developing a plan to holistically guide and direct the process of correctional management in a manner that is responsive to the particular needs of women. The report takes and advocates for a "woman-centred" approach—an orientation that focuses on the voices of women prisoners. The report concludes by articulating a set of principles intended to guide and focus institutional change. These principles included empowerment of prisoners, facilitating women prisoners to make meaningful and responsible choices, fostering respect and dignity, cultivating a supportive environment, and acknowledging shared responsibility (TFFSW, 1990).

While activists and academics initially expressed some optimism about the *Creating Choices* project, the final report was met with criticism by feminist activists and scholars. Criticisms were raised that the choice-based framework fails to acknowledge the systemic and structural forces that shape women's circumstances—including their victimization—and the researchers displayed an "us" versus "them" mentality by focusing on their own selfish need for affirmation rather than the material needs or interests of the federally sentenced women for whom the report was supposed to be written. Consequently, a number of feminists withdrew their support for the *Creating Choices* report.

Even laying aside these flaws with the vision of *Creating Choices*, critics contend that the CSC failed to meaningfully implement the vision as it was articulated in the principles set forth in the report, noting in particular that the government merely adopted feminist discourses and the language of women's empowerment but did not actually change their practices (Dell et al., 2009; Faith, 2000; Hannah-Moffat, 2001; Hayman, 2006). These scholars contend that the woman-centred empowerment model of punishment "feminizes" the discourses and practices of imprisonment without fundamentally challenging or restructuring the disciplinary relations of power in prison. For example, while the notion of "empowerment" originated as an ideal result of feminist consciousness-raising, feminist scholars contend that the CSC's choice-based framework of empowerment in correctional programming decontextualizes women's structural pathways into crime by aiming to make women assume full responsibility for their offending and rehabilitation (Kendall & Pollack, 2005; Pollack, 2009). Moreover, the very fact that the CSC cites "fostering respect and dignity" and "cultivating a supportive environment" as guiding principles yet they rejected the recommendation to forgo the use of maximum security and segregation units (see more on this below), both of which actively strip prisoners of respect and dignity or the opportunity to live in a supportive environment, boldly illustrates the semantic shift in correctional governance without the substantive reforms required to implement real change for women.

The 1994 "Incident" at P4W and the Arbour Inquiry

In 1990, following the federal government's acceptance of the task force's recommendations that the Kingston Prison for Women be closed and that regional institutions and an Aboriginal healing lodge be constructed where female prisoners would be able to access women-centred programming, and that a community strategy be implemented as an alternative to confinement, tensions began to emerge at the prison. The employee turnover was high over the next four years as staff sought permanent employment in other Kingston-based institutions, meaning there were often new and less experienced staff members working with high-needs prisoners. Moreover, prisoners, many of whom had lengthy sentences, became anxious about where in the country they would be transferred, and they continued to endure horrendous conditions of confinement. Pressure came to a head on 22 April 1994, when a brief but violent physical confrontation took place between six women and correctional staff. The women were immediately placed in segregation and criminally charged. Two days later, three women in segregation who were not involved in the earlier violent incident engaged in self-injurious behaviour, took a hostage, and attempted suicide (Arbour, 1996, p. 23). Escalating the tension inside the prison, on 26 April 1994 correctional staff demonstrated outside demanding the transfer of the women that were involved in the 22 April incident.

That night, although it is illegal for male staff to strip search women, Warden Thérèse Leblanc called in a male institutional emergency response team (IERT) from Kingston Penitentiary to conduct a cell extraction and strip search of eight women in segregation, including the six involved in the 22 April incident. Following correctional policy, the cell extractions and strip searches, which lasted nearly eight hours, were videotaped. At the end of the lengthy procedure, the women were left in empty segregation cells wearing paper gowns, restraints, and leg irons. The next day, seven of the eight women were subject to body cavity searches, which took place on the concrete floors of their segregation cells rather than in a clinical setting as required by law (Arbour, 1996). The six women involved in the 22 April incident were kept in segregation for between eight and nine months, again in violation of the Corrections and Conditional Release Act, the legislation that structures correctional policy and management (see Chapter 2). Some were transferred and segregated in protective custody units in men's prisons, where they were among sex offenders that taunted them (Arbour, 1996).

On 14 February 1995, the correctional investigator of Canada sent a special report to the solicitor general that was expressly critical of the CSC's internal investigation of the 1994 events, which failed to address the illegality of the warden calling in a male IERT, the conditions of segregation, or the length of time the women spent isolated. One week later, on 21 February 1995, the solicitor general tabled the correctional investigator's special report in the House of Commons and called for an independent inquiry. Ironically, the CBC investigative journalism program, *The Fifth Estate*,[4] aired an episode showing substantial extracts of the IERT video the same day.

Select Recommendations from the Arbour Inquiry

(4) The management of women's corrections

- The creation of a deputy commissioner of women's corrections
- Designating the new regional facilities as minimum rather than maximum security
- The creation of gender-responsive programming and making vocational training available

(5) Cross-gender staffing

- Restrictions on cross-gender staffing
- That CSC's sexual harassment policy be extended to apply to prisoners
- The appointment of an external agent to monitor and report annually for three years on the implementation of the cross-gender staffing policy and the extension of the sexual harassment policy to prisoners
- That appropriate measures be put in place to ensure that men do not observe on camera the private activities that women may be engaged in in their cells

(6) The use of force and use of IERTs

- Formal prohibition of male IERTs being deployed in prisons for women

- That men be prohibited from strip searching women, unless a delay in the search poses a danger to human life
- That prisoners have the right to counsel before expressing their consent to a body cavity search
- That body cavity searches only be performed in surroundings that are appropriate for consensual, non-emergency medical examination or intervention and that they be performed with consent and conducted by a female physician

(7) Aboriginal women and the healing lodge

- Access to the healing lodge be available to all Indigenous women, regardless of their security classification
- Access to Elders be formalized
- Culturally sensitive programming be made available to all staff and Indigenous prisoners

(8) Broader correctional issues

- That the Department of Justice and solicitor general examine legislative ways to create sanctions for inference with the integrity of a sentence

The videotaped evidence clearly shows the stark trauma of this form of intervention; visible is a group of men in riot gear with full facial masks and plexiglass shields who proceed to handcuff the women in waist-hand restraints and leg irons and who, in at least one case, forcefully remove a woman's clothing by cutting it off of her body with scissors. Given criminalized women's common histories of trauma and sexual, physical, and emotional victimization (Adelberg & Currie, 1987; Arbour, 1996; Chesney-Lind & Pasko, 2004; Johnson & Dawson, 2011; Salisbury & Van Voorhis, 2009; TFFSW, 1990), these scenes of state-sanctioned violence are particularly disturbing to watch (Kilty, 2018). On 10 April 1995, the governor general in council appointed Justice Louise Arbour to head the Commission of Inquiry into Certain Events at the Kingston Prison for Women.

Following a year-long investigation, Justice Arbour's report was published in 1996. At the crux of the 300-page report was the importance of following the rule of law, which she concluded CSC officials violated repeatedly in a number of different ways. At the end of the report, Arbour (1996, pp. 132–7) made an exhaustive list of over 100 recommendations across 14 major areas. The first three areas were outlined so as to ensure and protect public transparency and public availability of the information pertaining to the case, namely the preservation and archiving of both the report and the IERT videotape. In the box below, we outline some of the suggested recommendations made by Justice Arbour across the remaining key substantive areas for reform.

As the six new regional facilities for women were constructed and the closure of the Kingston Prison for Women neared, the CSC attempted to implement a number of the recommendations made by Justice Arbour, which not only outlined a host of significant policy changes but also those to correctional culture

- That all staff be educated about prisoner rights and that the CSC commit to ensuring these rights are respected

(9) The use of segregation

- Restrictions on the possible duration and use of segregation and the abolition of segregation for those suffering from mental illness
- That segregation decisions be made at an institutional level subject to confirmation within five days by an independent adjudicator, who should be a lawyer

(10) Accountability in correctional operations

- That all National Boards of Investigation include a member from outside the Correctional Service
- That boards of investigation monitor the CSC's compliance with the law, especially with respect to prisoners' rights

(11) Complaints and grievances

- That the deputy commissioner for women be mandated to explore and experiment with alternative dispute resolution techniques for complaints and grievances

(12) Outside agencies

- That citizens advisory committees (CAC) play a central role in oversight and that the CSC refrain from taking or permitting action to chastise CAC members

(13) CSC's interaction with other participants in the administration of criminal justice

- Recruit staff with experience in other branches of the criminal justice system (for example, police, lawyers)
- That the legal profession increases its awareness of correctional issues
- That judges be sensitized to women's correctional needs through programs developed by the National Judicial Institute

(14) Miscellaneous issues arising from the facts of this case

- That the women who were the subject of the cell extractions conducted by the male IERT on 26/27 April 1994 and who were kept in prolonged segregation afterwards be properly compensated by Correctional Service Canada for the infringement of all their legal rights as found in the report

and practice. While the CSC successfully created the position of deputy commissioner of women's corrections, many of the important recommendations made by both Justice Arbour and the TFFSW were either rejected or problematically executed differently than were proposed. For example, and as we discuss in greater detail below, the CSC has continued to support the problematic use of segregation, including for those with mental health concerns; use-of-force incidents remain unduly elevated (OCI, 2017); the grievance process has not improved (Sapers, 2008; Kilty, 2014); and outside agencies are faced with significant challenges entering carceral sites to do programming (Dell et al., 2009; Kendall & Pollack, 2005) or other forms of education support work (Duguid, 2000; Fayter, 2016).

The End of an Era and the Dawn of a New Age in Women's Corrections: The Closure of the P4W and Construction of Regional Facilities

After 64 years as the only federal prison for women in the country, P4W closed its doors in 2000. In its place, six regional correctional facilities were constructed. The Nova Institution for Women in Truro, Nova Scotia, the Okimaw Ohci Healing Lodge in Maple Creek, Saskatchewan, and the Edmonton Institution for Women in Edmonton, Alberta, opened in 1995, merely six months before the release of the Arbour Report. Notably, the Okimaw Ohci Healing Lodge was the first institution of its kind and was developed with First Nations communities so that its design and operational philosophy was based on Indigenous teachings, spirituality, and traditions; it accepts only women classified as minimum or medium security. Joliette Institution for Women in Joliette, Quebec, and Grand Valley Institution for Women in Kitchener, Ontario, opened in 1997. The sixth regional women's institution, Fraser Valley Institution for Women in Fraser Valley, British Columbia, opened in 2004 following the closure of Burnaby Correctional Centre for Women, a provincial institution that held federally sentenced women from the Pacific region by way of an exchange of services agreement with the province. Finally, the CSC maintained the Isabel MacNeill House[5] (IMH), which housed up to 10 women, in Kingston, Ontario, as a pre-release transitional residence between 1990 and 2009. As the only standalone minimum security facility for federally sentenced women, the closure of IMH meant that all minimum security women are housed in multi-level security institutions. Not only was this standalone minimum security facility closed, the recommendation to implement a community strategy as an alternative to confinement never materialized.

While the new regional facilities did help to alleviate some of the women's geographical distance from their families, friends, and communities, a number of concerns about the way the institutions were managed remained. For example, the new facilities were designated as multi-level security sites rather than minimum security as proposed by both Justice Arbour (1996) and the TFFSW (1990), although minimum security cottage-style living quarters do reflect the design of the community-living environment[6] proposed in *Creating Choices*. And when a number of serious incidents occurred in late 1995 and early 1996 at the Edmonton Institution for Women, the CSC responded by housing maximum security women in separate, isolated units at men's institutions, notably

Courtesy of Correctional Service Canada

The Okimaw Ohci Healing Lodge in Maple Creek, Saskatchewan.

in Saskatchewan Penitentiary, Springhill Institution in Nova Scotia, and at the Regional Reception Centre in Quebec, until security could be enhanced at the regional women's institutions (CSC, 2006). To avoid critique of their failure to follow the recommendations made by the TFFSW (1990) and Justice Arbour (1996), the CSC initially adopted the term "enhanced units" to describe the maximum security segregation units they constructed, which reflects a shift in semantics rather than actual conditions of confinement (Hayman, 2006). Notably, Indigenous women were disproportionately isolated in this form of holding due to the CSC's use of the now defunct "management protocol" that placed women deemed "high risk" in segregation for indefinite periods of time (Acoby, 2011), paralleling their continued overrepresentation in segregation today (OCI, 2017). Notably, high-profile cases, such as that of Karla Homolka or Terri-Lynne McClintic, often generate political discussion about the creation of "enhanced security cottages" for women who are interpreted as high risk for escape or whose perceived risk of violent behaviour may be overemphasized based on single (albeit serious) index events. These high-profile cases are often mobilized by politicians to rouse community fear and subsequent support for more punitive methods of correctional governance (McAleese & Kilty, 2019).

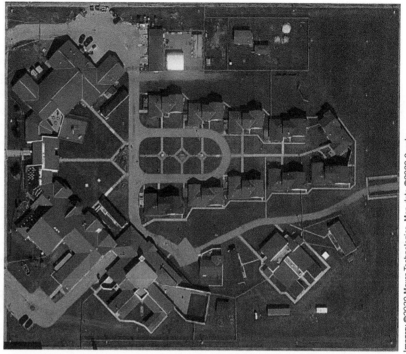

The new regional facilities for women, such as the Edmonton Institution for Women, shown here, were designed as cottage-style separate living quarters, which came with their own difficulties.

Imagery ©2020 Maxar Technologies. Map data ©2020 Google.

Women's Corrections in the New Millennium

Gender-Responsive Programming

Prior to the construction of the regional prisons, the CSC offered very little programming for women in prison, and the programs that were on offer were limited to stereotypically "female" roles, such as clothes manufacturing, needlework, and hairdressing (CSC, 2000; Hannah-Moffat, 2001; Hayman, 2006). Without programs that attended to women's material needs, no programs or services that were specific to francophone women, and no programs and very few services to meet the specific cultural needs of Indigenous women (CSC, 2006), CSC staff were tasked with completely revamping not only the operational management of women's corrections but also their overall approach to intervention and rehabilitation. To do this, they adopted a "gender-responsive" approach to programming, which originated in the field of addiction treatment—traditionally a core area for correctional intervention (Bloom, Owen & Covington, 2003; Covington, 2001; Covington & Bloom, 2006).

Put simply, gender-responsive programming acknowledges that men and women[7] have different experiences and pathways into crime, which means that interventions should be tailored to meet the specific needs of each group. Problematically, due to the small number of federally sentenced women in comparison to men (Adelberg & Currie, 1987), correctional programs were historically designed based on research conducted with incarcerated men, thereby creating a "generalizability problem" when used with women (Daly & Chesney-Lind, 1988). While the premise of gender responsivity challenges the use of programs based on male norms, it also produces "a set of new gender-informed norms" that have "underlying as-sumptions about women" and that do not always con-sider cultural, racial, or classed differences, so "it is important to question the normative femininities upon which [gender-responsive] penality is based" (Hannah-Moffat, 2011, p. 200).

Leading scholars in the field identified six key prin-ciples of gender-responsive programming for correc-tional settings:

1. Acknowledge that gender makes a difference;
2. Create an environment based on safety, respect, and dignity;
3. Develop policies, practices, and programs that are relational and that promote healthy connec-tions to children, family, significant others, and the community;
4. Address substance abuse, trauma, and mental health issues through comprehensive, inte-grated, and culturally relevant services and ap-propriate supervision;
5. Provide women with opportunities to improve their socio-economic conditions;
6. Establish a system of community supervision and re-entry with comprehensive, collabora-tive services (Bloom, Owen & Covington, 2003; Covington & Bloom, 2006, pp. 12–14).

To implement these principles effectively, correc-tional programming must take care to consider the content of the programs (which should be based on contemporary theoretical understandings of women's pathways into the criminal justice system), the context and environment in which they are offered, and the staff who will facilitate them (Covington & Bloom, 2006). Feminist scholars and advocates have long argued that it would be best to offer correctional program-ming for women in the community with various social service providers, rather than in and through correc-tions (Faith, 2000). Doing so would create the much-needed distance between the agents responsible for incarceration and punishment and those responsible for intervention and treatment, which for many can be essential to foster trust in the therapeutic relation-ship (Pollack, 2009; Kendall & Pollack, 2005; TFFSW, 1990). Community-based treatment would also help to develop the supportive network that is essential to suc-cessful reintegration post-incarceration (Shantz, Kilty, & Frigon, 2009). Moreover, feminist scholars have

critiqued how the CSC mobilizes contemporary ex-planations of women's involvement in criminality (for example, relational theory and trauma theory) so as to primarily focus on addressing women's psychological needs, akin to assigning all responsibility for crimin-ality to poor individual decision making, with little attention paid to the socio-structural and political con-texts that give rise to the very issues (such as poverty) that are linked to women's criminality. As Kendall and Pollack (2005) contend,

> In practice the treatment models used by CSC bear little resemblance to the holistic empowering para-digm advocated in *Creating Choices*. Instead, cor-rectional treatment regimes utilize pathological and medical constructions of women offenders that typ-ically ignore the psycho-social realities of women of-fenders. This appears to be at least in part because of the CSC's reliance on cognitive-behavioral treatment approaches . . . If program facilitators acknowledge external factors, such as violence or poverty, they are thought to be feeding in to the offenders' denial and rationalizations of their offense. (pp. 74–5)

Challenging the choice-based framework, research suggests that correctional programming and interven-tion focus should instead shift to trauma-informed care (Gido & Dalley, 2009; Pollack, 2009). Current cor-rectional interventions too often ignore the context in which women's psychological needs arise and fail to ac-knowledge the outcomes of trauma as crucially contrib-uting to mental health issues, including post-traumatic stress disorder, which is one of the most common disorders women are diagnosed with (Gido & Dalley, 2009; OCI, 2017). Not to mention that the effectiveness of gender-responsive programming is detrimentally affected by the risk/need assessment process that has become the foundation of correctional management.

Risk/Need Assessment

The CSC has become a world leader in corrections for their development of the risk-need-responsivity (RNR) model, which comprises a series of actuarial assessment tools used to determine (1) the level of service required to meet and manage each prisoner's level of risk; (2) the individual's criminogenic needs[8] for targeted treat-ment intervention; in order to (3) maximize the indi-vidual's responsivity to different cognitive-behavioural treatment opportunities (Bonta & Andrews, 2007). There are two aspects—general and specific—of the responsivity principle; general responsivity uses cognitive social learning methods to influence behaviour (for example, pro-social modelling, the use of positive reinforcement and disapproval, and problem solving), while specific responsivity is supposed to refine the intervention to take into account the individual's strengths, learning style, personality, motivation, and bio-social (gender, race) characteristics (Bonta & Andrews, 2007). Now on its fourth generation of assessment tools, the RNR model is the foundation of CSC's approach to correctional management.

While touted by correctional officials as "better at predicting criminal behaviour than professional judgement" (Bonta & Andrews, 2007, p. 11), critical scholars have identified a number of problems that arise from the use of these actuarial tools. Notably, while the RNR model distinguishes between criminogenic needs (dynamic individual attributes that with targeted intervention are linked to a lower probability of recidivism) and non-criminogenic needs (dynamic and changeable variables that are not necessarily linked to reoffending behaviour and thus occupy a lower priority in terms of intervention—such as poverty, health, or experiences of abuse), "because the criminogenic factors included in generic risk tools are derived from statistical analyses of aggregate male correctional population data and are based on male-derived theories of crime, a gender problem is built into them" (Hannah-Moffat, 2009, p. 211). As internationally renowned Canadian criminologist and risk theorist Kelly Hannah-Moffat (2005) argued, the RNR model overestimates women's risk and creates a kind of "hybridization of risk/need." By joining the term "risk/need," Hannah-Moffat demonstrates how correctional assessment models see women's treatment needs (that is, their histories of trauma and victimization) as the very characteristics that put them at risk for reoffending (Hannah-Moffat, 2000). For example, and as we discuss below, self-injurious behaviours are interpreted as risks not just to the individual but to the safety and security of the institution (Kilty, 2006, 2014, 2018).

One of the more serious implications of the RNR model for women in prison is the categorization of the simultaneously high-risk, high-need woman. Perhaps it is an unanticipated outcome of the new woman-centred regime, but the creation of this new category of prisoner in effect constitutes a dichotomy between those women who are assessed as being "empowerable" and those who are not (Hannah-Moffat, 2000, 2001, 2009, 2011).

Because gendered risk-need classification and related program strategies explain women's criminality in terms of normative femininities, non-normative "masculine" conduct and resistance to institutional authority can only be explained as anomalies. These behaviours are positioned as risky, rare and abnormal; the [gender-responsive] template is not sufficiently equipped to plan for "non-standard" cases and women who do not fit these new normative criteria remain unexplained or "difficult to manage." In Canada, for example, women with substantial mental health needs, as well as women with tendencies to self-injure (many of whom have extensive histories of victimization and trauma) or "act out" are often classified as "high risk-need," separated from the general population, and housed in secure segregated units and/or placed on behavioural contracts . . . This framing of concerns in terms of risk typically results in a security-based response to behaviour. (Hannah-Moffat, 2011, p. 203)

"Unempowerable" women are especially demonized and pathologized in part because they resist correctional interventions. This group of women disproportionately includes Indigenous women (Acoby, 2011) and those deemed mentally ill, both of whom are portrayed as risky and even dangerous to the security of the prison, the public, and themselves (Hannah-Moffat, 2011; Kilty, 2006). With the construction of "problem prisoners" we see how the new benevolent "empowering" women's correctional regime has actually doubled enhanced security cells in new regional facilities for these women (Acoby, 2011; Dell et al., 2009; Hayman, 2006; OCI, 2013, 2017). Not only do elevated assessments of risk and need tend to result in higher-than-necessary security classifications and segregation use, and despite the fact that the most recent generations of the RNR model are more fluid and dynamic than the earlier generations (Hannah-Moffat, 2005), the fact that women's needs are reconstituted as potential risk factors suggests that the model and the actuarial assessment tools it has contributed to generating actually "contradict[s] the trend toward gender-responsive policy and programming" (Hannah-Moffat, 2009, pp. 209–10).

The Preventable Death of Ashley Smith (2007)

Growing up in Moncton, New Brunswick, Ashley Smith started to get into trouble with various authorities during her early adolescence, and questions were raised about her mental health. By age 15 she had been before juvenile court 14 times for various minor offences, such as trespassing and causing a disturbance. In March 2003, after a series of court appearances, Ashley was admitted to the Pierre Caissie Centre, a mental health centre, for assessment. She was diagnosed with various conditions, including "ADHD, learning disorder, borderline personality disorder and narcissistic personality traits." Ashley was discharged early from the centre for unruly and disruptive behaviour (Bromwich & Kilty, 2017). Later that year, Ashley was sentenced to a one-month period of incarceration as a youth for the single offence of throwing crab apples at a postal carrier. While she had been in trouble for minor things before, like disobeying teachers and stealing a CD, she had never spent time in custody. She was quickly isolated in solitary confinement—misleadingly labelled by youth corrections as "therapeutic quiet time"—for what correctional officers determined to be disruptive behaviour on her first day in custody. While Ashley's original sentence was short, she accumulated hundreds of institutional convictions for disciplinary incidents, including for self-harming, which resulted in her remaining in youth custody for three years; she spent the majority of this time in segregation (Bromwich & Kilty, 2017).

In January 2006, Ashley Smith turned 18. On the same day, a motion was made under the Youth Criminal Justice Act by the Crown to transfer her to an adult women's federal penitentiary; the transfer occurred on October 5. While incarcerated in the adult federal prison system, Ashley was transferred 17 times between eight institutions over a period of 11 months, which was done to keep her in segregation past the legally prescribed limits (Sapers, 2008). While in segregation, she was subject to repeated body cavity and strip searches, and she was frequently pepper-sprayed and mechanically restrained (Sapers, 2008). She was under the care of a series of psychiatrists, several of whom prescribed her a number of different psychotropic medications; she was sometimes given these drugs by force via involuntary chemical injections. Ashley was periodically given an opportunity to speak with a series of psychologists, but only through the food slot in her cell door. It was widely reported that Ashley Smith suffered from very serious mental health issues that were never properly assessed and thus went untreated (Sapers, 2008).

Mirroring her experience in youth custody, while in federal custody Ashley was involved in hundreds of reported "incidents" that figured prominently in daily SITREPS, or situation reports, that circulate to CSC management, including regional authorities and bureaucrats at national headquarters in Ottawa. Correctional officers documented that Ashley self-injured and/or tied a ligature around her neck on at least 150 separate occasions, many of which were treated as disciplinary infractions (Sapers, 2008). As her sentence lengthened because of these institutional infractions, Ashley was never released from segregation. For long periods of time while in solitary confinement, she was not given soap, deodorant, adequate sanitary and menstrual supplies, or clean underwear; she was also prohibited from having writing utensils or paper, which prevented her ability to file formal grievances about her mistreatment (Sapers, 2008). To avoid physical confrontations with Ashley, front-line staff were instructed not to enter her cell to remove the ligatures that she frequently tied around her neck until she had passed out, which was dubbed the "wait and see" approach. Subsequently, on 19 October 2007, Ashley Smith, then 19, died in a hospital gown on the concrete floor of a Grand Valley Institution segregation cell from self-strangulation. This occurred while a group of prison guards watched and videotaped her last moments from a few feet away in the hall outside her cell, not intervening or performing CPR for 45 minutes as she lay dying before their eyes.

Ultimately, while the CSC adopted the woman-centred language of *Creating Choices*, they failed to implement the new gender-responsive programs or to attend to women's risks and needs in ways that reflect the progressive and more humane spirit of the document, instead absorbing the new strategies into their existing risk governance logic (Chartrand & Kilty, 2017; Hannah-Moffat, 2001, 2011; Hayman, 2006; Pollack, 2009; Kendall & Pollack, 2005). The result is that women are often held in higher-than-necessary security levels, spend undue lengths of time in segregation, and are subject to excessive psychotropic medication use with limited discharge and reintegration planning, the results of which can lead to tragic outcomes, as demonstrated by Ashley Smith's carceral death. The box above describes Smith's journey from being incarcerated in the youth system through her transfer to the adult federal correctional system and the events surrounding her death.

In 2011, four years after her death, Ashley Smith's family filed a wrongful death lawsuit against the Correctional Service of Canada for $11 million. The suit was settled confidentially in May 2011 for an undisclosed amount, and the acting warden, deputy warden, and several correctional officers from Grand Valley Institution for Women were fired, although many were later rehired by the CSC in other capacities. Ashley Smith's death has been the subject of two coroner's inquests in the province of Ontario. The first was complex and involved many legal challenges as well as a change of coroner before it finally ended as a mistrial in September 2011. A new inquest into Ashley's death began in September 2012 and concluded in December 2013, making history as the first time the death of a federally incarcerated person was deemed to be a homicide where the perpetrator was not a fellow prisoner (Coroner for Ontario, 2013). Indeed, the party implicated in her homicide was not one individual, but rather the broader criminal justice and correctional systems themselves (Bromwich, 2015). Also notable is the fact that this decision was made by an all-female inquest jury.

In response to the homicide verdict, government actors and social reformers have been examining how the mentally ill—and mentally ill women in particular—can be better served by the prison system and how to limit the use of segregation in Canadian prisons. The CSC released a report in December 2014 in which they claim to have already addressed the concerns raised by the 104 recommendations of the coroner's inquest (CSC, 2014). In this report, the CSC rejects the recommendations to place limits on the use of segregation and that correctional management be independently overseen. In his 2015 mandate letter to the new minister of Justice, Prime Minister Justin Trudeau tasked the attorney general with addressing the problems revealed by the Smith case.

Ongoing examinations of Ashley Smith's case by academics, advocates, and the government position her life and death as important and as opening up new ways of understanding citizenship and inciting conversations about carceral abuses of power, especially in relation to the use of segregation. Conversations about and advocacy emanating from her case continue to spur social movement around the unique needs of women and girls that persist in inspiring reform efforts to improve Canada's federal correctional system as well as its criminal justice and correctional systems. Despite the attention it has received, the Ashley Smith case remains unresolved in that a homicide verdict was entered while no individuals or institutions were officially blamed or held accountable for her death, and no significant changes to carceral segregation practices as recommended by the coroner's inquest have been legally mandated.

Gendered Pains of Imprisonment: Psychiatrization, Segregation, Pregnancy, and Motherhood

The majority of federally sentenced women have been found to display symptoms "consistent with a psychiatric disorder," and upwards of half are prescribed psychotropic medications (OCI, 2017). In fact, a CSC research report documents that "overall, 30.4 per cent of offenders had an active psychotropic medication prescription. Differences were seen by gender, with considerably more women than men having an active psychotropic medication prescription (45.7 per cent and 29.6 per cent, respectively)" (Farrell MacDonald et al., 2015). Using psychotropic medications as a mechanism of carceral control illustrates how therapeutic interventions contribute to the generation of a "**psy-carceral complex**" (Kilty, 2014). Another part of this complex involves the correctional interpretation of self-injurious behaviour simultaneously as a security risk and as a symptom of mental distress; it is an unfortunately common practice for some incarcerated women, especially for those who are isolated in austere forms of holding such as the maximum security units and segregation (Kilty, 2014; OCI, 2013). While most women suffering from mental illness or who self-injure are estranged from their families (including their children), spent their childhood in group homes or foster care, have histories of violent physical and sexual victimization, and have very little external social support (OCI, 2013), the correctional response to isolate them when they "act out" or are "difficult to manage" illustrates the use of punishment rather than therapy as the primary intervention response (Dell et al., 2009; Gido & Dalley, 2009).

Women suffering from mental distress, including those who self-injure, are typically placed in segregation so that they can be monitored through 24-hour closed-circuit television surveillance. Left with no cell effects (personal items), strip searched, left in a hospital-style gown called a "baby-doll," and having no access to programming and only one hour of yard time a day, women in segregation report that this isolation is experienced as a form of punishment that aggravates the severity and frequency of their self-injurious

Office of the Correctional Investigator of Canada

Photo of a segregation cell with a plexiglass covering.

behaviour (OCI, 2013). To try to prevent women from self-harming, the CSC uses Pinel restraints, which involves strapping an individual on their back to a board in five-point restraints (hands, feet, head, chest, hips, and legs) to cease bodily movement. The CSC does not consider this to be a use of force but rather part of the woman's "treatment plan," despite the fact that it is not a medical or approved clinical intervention procedure (OCI, 2013). This is another example of how the primary governing logic in prison administration—risk management—has nothing to do with treating the underlying causes of mental illness or distress.

While the CSC differentiates disciplinary segregation (isolation as a form of punishment, typically for committing or threatening acts of violence against staff or other prisoners and for more serious forms of institutional rule-breaking and destruction of property) from administrative segregation (isolation for "safety reasons," typically to facilitate direct monitoring of individuals who are considered to be suicidal, engaging in self-injurious behaviour, or who are in emotional distress), there is no difference in the actual cell space used, nor in the conditions of confinement. In his most recent report (2017), the correctional investigator noted that he witnessed segregation "yards" that were no more than cages similar to a dog kennel, segregation and isolation units without a source of natural light or ventilation, that in at least one institution women were provided with earplugs to help drown out the screaming from other women in segregation, and the door to one segregation cell "inexplicably covered over in plastic safety glass":

> When I asked why, staff could not form a cogent defense or reason that did not default to some undefined but ubiquitous "security" concern of one kind or another. As is so often seen in corrections, the extraordinary case becomes the response upon which all other future actions are mediated. Once implemented it is rare for a "temporary" security measure to be removed or lowered: it simply becomes the new standard. (OCI, 2017)

This is a particularly telling statement that reveals an especially harmful outcome of governing through risk logic, namely that extraordinary security measures quickly become adopted as the new norm. It is also indicative of the historical continuity of mobilizing punitive carceral practices to manage vulnerable women in prison, which feminist scholars have long critiqued and documented (Arbour, 1996; Chartrand & Kilty, 2017; Dell et al., 2009; Hannah-Moffat, 2001, 2005, 2009, 2011; Kilty, 2014, 2018; Maurutto & Hannah-Moffat, 2006; Hayman, 2006; Pollack, 2009; Kendall & Pollack, 2005; TFFSW, 1990).

Given the CSC's refusal to make significant changes to their segregation practices, two provincial legal challenges have been raised regarding the use of indefinite segregation, the segregation of mentally ill prisoners, and the use of segregation as a response to self-injurious behaviour. The decisions rendered in these two legal challenges are poised to significantly change segregation practices in federal prisons in Canada. In January 2015, the British Columbia Civil Liberties Association and the John Howard Society of Canada filed a joint lawsuit against the attorney general of Canada to challenge the use of administrative segregation in Canadian prisons. One week later, the Canadian Civil Liberties Association filed a similar petition in Ontario Superior Court. In December 2017, Associate Chief Justice Frank Marrocco of the Ontario Superior Court struck down Canada's laws on segregation as unconstitutional, citing the lack of independent review and the harms caused by isolation. While the Canadian Civil Liberties Association applauded the decision, they are now launching an appeal to prohibit segregation beyond 15 days and for certain vulnerable groups (the mentally distressed, young people, and those seeking safety). In January 2018, just one month after the Ontario decision, the British Columbia Supreme Court went even further by declaring that segregation laws violate sections 7 and 15 of the Charter of Rights and Freedoms because they permit prolonged indefinite isolation, fail to provide an independent review of segregation placements, deprive prisoners of the right to counsel at segregation review hearings, authorize administrative segregation for the mentally distressed, and because the regime discriminates against Indigenous prisoners.

Having failed to meet the one-year deadline, in December 2018 the government of Canada received a four-month extension to make its segregation oversight process compliant with the Charter of Rights and Freedoms. The government has proposed Bill C-83,[9] which would create "Structured Intervention Units" in each prison where prisoners could access better health care and programming than exists in segregation, as well as four hours a day outside their cells (up from two hours) and two hours a day of "meaningful human contact" (up from one hour). With no hard cap on the number of days someone can spend in a structured intervention unit and no provision for the meaningful independent review prescribed by Justice Marrocco, the proposal appears to be segregation by a different name that will fail to substantively alter the experience of isolation (Mendelsohn Aviv, 2019).

Conclusion: Innovation, Reforms, and Abolitionist Visions for the Future

Despite the feminist, woman-centred, and gender-responsive innovations and reforms in women's corrections that have been proposed or implemented over the past three decades, the carceral logic of risk assessment and management remains the primary method of interpreting and governing criminalized women in Canada. The historical continuity of harmful penal discourses that situate criminality as a poor choice of individual women and that fail to adequately consider the role of structural disadvantages in criminal behaviour result in even more harmful penal practices, such as prolonged periods of isolation in segregation cells, lack of access to community-based rehabilitative and reintegrative programming, and excessive psychotropic medication use, among others (Kilty, 2018). This demonstrates how fiscal and human resources continue to be routinely diverted to maintain enhanced security institutions rather than to address women's needs in a more comprehensive and compassionate manner as has been outlined by feminist scholars and advocates. Moreover, while we have concentrated our discussion in this chapter on the evolution of federal corrections for women in Canada, which receives not only greater funding but also more research attention, it is important to note that the majority of criminalized women are actually sentenced to time in provincial institutions where programs are sorely needed. Problematically, provincial correctional systems do not maintain the same degree of publicly available information about their institutions, programs, or the demographics of the populations they imprison and manage—making analysis of these systems much more difficult.

Mothers and Mothers-to-Be in Incarceration

As aforementioned, the federal correctional system maintains a program for mothers to keep children under the age of four with them while they are incarcerated. To be eligible for this residency program, the mother must not have been convicted of an offence against a child or for an offence that "could reasonably be seen as endangering a child" (CSC, 2016). Only those mothers who are classified as either minimum or medium security and who do not reside in the structured living environment, "except if she has a child who is eligible for participation in the part-time residency program using the private family visiting unit location" (CSC, 2016), may participate. Children up to the age of four are eligible for full-time residency, and children up to the age of six are eligible for part-time residency. The institutional head (warden) has the power to approve, suspend, or terminate the residency program, and this power has resulted in the program being rarely used. Subsequently, since there are no special facilities for incarcerated mothers, women who give birth while in either a federal or provincial prison must give custody of the baby to a relative who is willing and able to care for the child or to the Children's Aid Society. Should the child be removed, the mother's future visitation opportunities with the child commonly take place through glass, although this practice is more common in the provincial correctional system.

While women in prison are legally entitled to the same level of health care as free women, there are numerous reports from criminalized women who contend that their health or the health of their fetus was compromised by inadequate access to care. Once again illustrating the harm of prioritizing risk and security assessments over more empathic considerations of a prisoner's needs and rights, like any other prisoner incarcerated pregnant women are shackled while in transfer and are subject to standard transfer procedures, such as being seated in the back of correctional vans rather than being moved in a safer way, such as via ambulance (Malone, 2017). A notable case in the Ontario provincial correctional system exemplifies the dangers of these punitive health-care practices well. In 2012, Julie Bilotta was incarcerated at the Ottawa-Carleton Detention Centre. Bilotta was eight months pregnant at the time and had yet to be found guilty of a crime when she was placed in **remand custody** to await trial. When she began bleeding heavily and experiencing regular intervals of pain and cramping, she called for assistance from correctional staff, believing she was going into labour. Despite her screams, staff did not believe her until her amniotic sac broke and the child's feet (the baby was in breech position) were visibly protruding from Bilotta's body, which resulted in Bilotta giving birth in her segregation cell. Bilotta reported that the amniotic fluid colour was greenish-yellow, which indicates the presence of meconium and signals that the unborn child passed its first bowel movement in utero. When ingested, meconium can block or inflame the unborn child's lungs, causing respiratory distress; when left untreated, "infants may experience significantly increased risk of long-term complications and even death" (Fiander, 2016, p. 42). Bilotta's son, Gionni, died shortly after his first birthday due to respiratory complications, which she attributes to the conditions surrounding his birth. In 2014, Bilotta filed a civil lawsuit seeking $1.3 million in damages for failing to provide adequate medical care. The lawsuit was settled, although the terms remain confidential.

In conclusion, we advocate taking a more critical and abolitionist perspective that requires we learn from the past to do things differently in the future. Every day in Canada there are women in prison receiving "institutional misconduct" charges for unfeminine behaviour, just as there were women a century ago experiencing some form of regulation or imprisonment for "status offences." Twelve years have passed since Ashley Smith died in a segregation cell in the Grand Valley Institution for Women, yet women who suffer from mental distress continue to be housed in segregation cells, despite the fact that isolation only increases their suffering. When external bodies investigate and review penal policies and practices, such as occurred during the Arbour Inquiry, the coroner's inquiry into Ashley Smith's death, and even the annual reports produced by the correctional investigator, there are always a series of recommendations made for improving and reforming the correctional environment. Calls for external accountability and oversight of institutional management, specialized staff training, thorough mental health assessments and care, the abolition of indefinite segregation, and specialized facilities for high-risk/high-need women are common suggestions.

Yet these ideas for reform "continue to see some form of carceral response as the appropriate solution. Nowhere is this more evident and problematic than in the CSC's refusal to abolish the use of segregation for criminalized women and prisoners with mental health concerns" (Chartrand & Kilty, 2017, p. 126). Taking an abolitionist view requires that we see the prison system by and large as a failed socio-political experiment that primarily functions to inflict pain on imprisoned people, their friends and families, and thus on our communities as a whole. Instead of improving the conditions of confinement, which only further solidifies the place and role of carceral institutions in our communities, abolitionists challenge carceral logics and seek alternatives to confinement that will strengthen our community bonds rather than weaken them. In that sense, it is time to invest in ourselves rather than the political whims of every new government that is elected based on a factually inaccurate "get tough on crime" agenda. Since we know empirically that harsher punishments do not make us safer and do not work to deter criminality, we must derive more inclusive and proactive community-based alternatives to incarceration that will serve those functions.

Review Questions

1. Statistically speaking, what are some of the more common characteristics of women accused of crimes in Canada?
2. What is the historical timeline for the construction of women-specific carceral spaces for federally sentenced women in Canada?
3. What does it mean to conceptualize criminalized women as "too few to count"?
4. Describe the main recommendations for reform as outlined by Justice Arbour.
5. Discuss ways in which experiencing trauma is connected to the psychological treatment needs commonly experienced by federally incarcerated women, and critically examine the extent to which trauma-informed care is available.
6. What are the six key principles of gender-responsive programming for criminalized women?

Critical Thinking Questions

1. Problematize the use of prison labour to construct carceral institutions, such as occurred for the Kingston Penitentiary and the Kingston Prison for Women.
2. Why did some feminist organizations remove their support for the 1990 task force report *Creating Choices*?
3. Describe the historical continuity in how women in prison are governed by noting the similarities between how the women involved in the 1994 "incident" at P4W and Ashley Smith were managed and treated by correctional staff.
4. How does gender-responsive programming further entrench gendered norms of behaviour? How does this come to disproportionately affect Indigenous and other women of colour in harmful ways?

5. Think like a Crown attorney. How might you use your discretion to reduce the rates of incarceration for marginalized women?
6. Analyze and outline the harmful impacts of segregation on women in prison. Consider the role that isolation plays in aggravating self-harming behaviour and mental distress.
7. Think like a penal abolitionist. How can we better respond to women's lawbreaking in ways that would not only address their needs, but would also strengthen community-based resources, bonds, and support systems?

Multimedia Suggestions

Missing and Murdered: Finding Cleo
CBC podcast episode: https://www.cbc.ca/radio/findingcleo

Behind the Wall
This documentary from CBC's *The Fifth Estate* discusses the tragic death of Ashley Smith: http://www.cbc.ca/fifth/episodes/2010-2011/behind-the-wall

Out of Control
Another episode from CBC's *The Fifth Estate* discussing the Ashley Smith case: http://www.cbc.ca/fifth/episodes/2009-2010/out-of-control

The Ultimate Response
This documentary from CBC's *The Fifth Estate* discusses the 1994 "incident" at P4W: https://curio.ca/en/video/the-ultimate-response-4162

Lannan Podcasts: Ruth Wilson Gilmore with Rachel Kushner
An interview with abolitionist Ruth Wilson Gilmore:
• Audio: https://podcast.lannan.org/2019/04/21/ruth-wilson-gilmore-with-rachel-kushner-17-april-2019-audio
• Video of talk: https://podcast.lannan.org/2019/04/21/ruth-wilson-gilmore-with-rachel-kushner-talk-17-april-2019-video

Notes

1. Notable female prisoners to have served time in the Kingston Prison for Women include Karla Homolka, Marlene Moore, Anne Hansen, and Joey Twins.
2. Two notable female prisoners to have served time in Kingston Penitentiary include Marie-Anne Houde, who was convicted for participating in the murder of her young stepdaughter, Aurore Gagnon, and Grace Marks, the main character of famed Canadian author Margaret Atwood's best-selling historical fiction novel *Alias Grace*. Marks was an Irish-Canadian maid who was convicted of the 1843 murder of her Richmond Hill, Ontario, employer Thomas Kinnear, a farmer, and his housekeeper with whom he was having an affair, Nancy Montgomery. The trial and Marks's conviction for Kinnear's murder was controversial because it was unclear whether she was instrumental in the murder or an unwitting accessory after the fact. Marks served nearly 30 years in the Kingston Penitentiary, less the year and a half between 1852–3 that she spent incarcerated in an asylum; she was released in 1872, later pardoned, and eventually moved to New York State.
3. The mother–child program permits mothers with children up to the age of four to live together, as long as the woman has not been convicted of a crime against a child and is designated as either minimum or medium security. To the detriment of criminalized women and their children, this program is rarely used (CSC, 2016).
4. In an obvious attempt to thwart transparency regarding what occurs inside Canadian prisons, the CSC went to court to try to prevent the CBC from airing footage from the IERT video. They would later engage the same approach when the show was developing two episodes dedicated to investigating Ashley Smith's 2007 death in a segregation cell in Grand Valley Institution for Women. These episodes can be viewed online on the show's website: www.cbc.ca/fifth/episodes. Kilty (2018) examined the historical continuity of these two cases, documenting how the visual images presented in the three episodes of *The Fifth Estate* not only generated national attention, public outrage, and greater awareness of the harms of carceral segregation, but also created a deepened public conscience regarding the importance of humane treatment of incarcerated women in Canada.
5. The Isabel MacNeill House was constructed in 1910 as the residence for the warden of the Kingston Penitentiary.

6. The minimum security units consist of standalone houses that are clustered behind the main buildings that contain the staff offices, program spaces, health-care unit, and a visiting area. Each house has a communal living space, kitchen and dining area, bathrooms, a laundry room, and access to the grounds with up to 10 women living in each house. These houses accommodate women designated as minimum or medium security and include a "structured living environment"; these living units do not contain cells or pods like those found in the secure units and segregation units.

7. To date, there has been no substantive efforts to research and design programming specifically to address the needs of transgendered men or women.

8. The authors identify seven major risk/needs factors (antisocial personality pattern; pro-criminal attitude; social supports for crime; substance abuse; family/marital relationships; school/work; and pro-social recreational activities) and four non-criminogenic minor needs factors (self-esteem; vague feelings of personal distress; major mental disorder; and physical health) (Bonta & Andrews, 2007, p. 14).

9. It is worth noting that Bill C-83 references the Ashley Smith case and the recommendations made by the coroner's jury.

References

Acoby, R. (2011). On segregation. *Journal of Prisoners on Prisons, 20*(1), 89–93.

Adelberg, E., & Currie, C. (1987). *Too few to count: Canadian women in conflict with the law.* Vancouver, BC: Press Gang Publishers.

Arbour, L. (1996). *Commission of inquiry into certain events at the Prison for Women in Kingston.* Retrieved from http://www.caefs.ca/wp-content/uploads/2013/05/Arbour_Report.pdf

Bloom, B., Owen, B.A., & Covington, S. (2003). *Gender-responsive strategies: Research, practice, and guiding principles for women offenders.* Washington, DC: National Institute of Corrections.

Bonta, J., & Andrews, D.A. (2007). *Risk-need-responsivity model for offender assessment and rehabilitation.* Ottawa, ON: Public Safety Canada.

Brennan, S. (2014). Canada's mother–child program: Examining its emergence, usage, and current state. *Canadian Graduate Journal of Sociology and Criminology, 3*(1), 11–33.

Bromwich, R.J. (2015). *Looking for Ashley: Re-reading what the Smith case reveals about the governance of girls, mothers, and families in Canada.* Bradford, ON: Demeter Press.

Bromwich, R., & Kilty, J.M. (2017). Introduction: Law, vulnerability, and segregation: What have we learned from Ashley Smith's carceral death? *Canadian Journal of Law and Society/Revue Canadienne Droit et Société, 32*(2), 157–64. doi:10.1017/cls.2017.10

Chartrand, V., & Kilty, J.M. (2017). Corston principles in Canada: Creating the carceral other and moving beyond women in prison. In L. Moore, P. Scraton, & A. Wahidin (Eds), *Women's imprisonment and the case for abolition: Critical reflections on Corston ten years on* (pp. 109–28). London, UK: Routledge.

Chesney-Lind, M., & Pasko, L. (2004). *The female offender: Girls, women, and crime.* Thousand Oaks, CA: SAGE Publications.

Coroner for Ontario. (2013). *Coroner's inquest touching the death of Ashley Smith: Verdict of coroner's jury.* Retrieved from: https://www.csc-scc.gc.ca//publications/005007-9009-eng.shtml

Correctional Service Canada. (2000). The closing of the prison for women in Kingston, July 6, 2000. Retrieved from http://www.csc-scc.gc.ca/text/pblct/brochurep4w/index-eng.shtml

Correctional Service Canada. (2006). Ten-year status report on women's corrections 1996–2006. Retrieved from http://www.csc-scc.gc.ca/publications/fsw/wos24/tenyearstatusreport_e.pdf

Correctional Service Canada. (2014). *Response to the coroner's inquest touching the death of Ashley Smith.* Retrieved from http://www.csc-scc.gc.ca/publications/005007-9011-eng.shtml

Correctional Service Canada. (2016). *Institutional mother–child program, commissioner's directive 768.* Retrieved from http://www.csc-scc.gc.ca/politiques-et-lois/768-cd-eng.shtml

Covington, S. (2001). Creating gender-responsive programs. *Corrections Today, 63*(1), 85–7.

Covington, S., & Bloom, B.E. (2006). Gender responsive treatment and services in correctional settings. *Women & Therapy, 29*(3/4), 9–33.

Daly, K., & Chesney-Lind, M. (1988). Feminism and criminology. *Justice Quarterly, 5*(4), 497–538.

Dell, C.A., Kilty, J.M., & Fillmore, C. (2009). Looking back 10 years after the Arbour Inquiry: Ideology, practice and the misbehaved federal female prisoner. *The Prison Journal, 89*(3), 286–308.

Duguid, S. (2000). *Can prisons work? The prisoner as object and subject in modern corrections.* Toronto, ON: University of Toronto Press.

Faith, K. (2000). Reflections on inside/out organizing. *Social Justice, 27*(3), 158–67.

Farrell MacDonald, S., Keown, L.-A., Boudreau, H., Gobeil, R., & Wardrop, K. (2015). Prevalence of psychotropic medication prescription among federal offenders. (Research Report R-373). Correctional Service Canada. Retrieved from https://www.csc-scc.gc.ca/research/005008-r373-eng.shtml

Fayter, R. (2016). Social justice praxis within the walls to bridges program: Pedagogy of oppressed federally sentenced women. *Journal of Prisoners on Prisons*, 25(2), 56–71.

Fiander, S. (2016). *Pregnancy, birth, and mothering behind bars: A case study of one woman's journey through the Ontario criminal justice and jail systems*. Master's thesis, Wilfrid Laurier University. Retrieved from https://scholars.wlu.ca/cgi/viewcontent.cgi?article=2980&context=etd

Gido, R.L., & Dalley, L. (2009). *Women's mental health issues across the criminal justice system*. Upper Saddle River, NJ: Pearson Education Inc.

Hannah-Moffat, K. (2000). Reforming the prison—rethinking our ideals. In K. Hannah-Moffat & M. Shaw (Eds), *An ideal prison? Critical essays on women's imprisonment in Canada* (pp. 30–40). Halifax, NS: Fernwood Publishing.

Hannah-Moffat, K. (2001). *Punishment in disguise: Penal governance and federal imprisonment of women in Canada*. Toronto, ON: University of Toronto Press.

Hannah-Moffat, K. (2005). Criminogenic needs and the transformative risk subject: Hybridizations of risk/need in penality. *Punishment & Society*, 7(1), 29–51.

Hannah-Moffat, K. (2009). Gridlock or mutability: Reconsidering "gender" and risk assessment. *Criminology & Public Policy*, 8(1), 209–19.

Hannah-Moffat, K. (2011). Sacrosanct or flawed: Risk, accountability and gender-responsive penal politics. *Current Issues in Criminal Justice*, 22(3), 193–215.

Hayman, S. (2006). *Imprisoning our sisters: The new federal women's prisons in Canada*. Montreal, QC: McGill-Queen's University Press.

Johnson, H.L., & Dawson, M. (2011). *Violence against women in Canada: Research and policy perspectives*. Toronto, ON: Oxford University Press.

Kendall, K., & Pollack, S. (2005). Taming the shrew: Regulating prisoners through women-centred mental health programming. *Critical Criminology*, 13(1), 71–87.

Kilty, J.M. (2006). Under the barred umbrella: Is there room for a women-centred self-injury policy in Canadian corrections? *Criminology and Public Policy*, 5(1), 161–82.

Kilty, J.M. (2014). Examining the "psy-carceral complex" in the death of Ashley Smith. In G. Balfour & E. Comack (Eds), *Criminalizing women: Gender and (in)justice in neoliberal times* (2nd edn., pp. 236–54). Winnipeg, MB: Fernwood Press.

Kilty, J.M. (2018). Carceral optics and the crucible of segregation: Revisiting scenes of state-sanctioned violence against incarcerated women. In J.M. Kilty & E. Dej (Eds), *Containing madness: Gender & "psy" in institutional contexts* (pp. 119–44). New York, NY: Palgrave MacMillan.

Lutfy, M., & Forrester, T. (2014). Shorter sentences among federally sentenced women offenders (Report No. RS 14-11). Ottawa, ON: Correctional Service Canada.

MacGuigan, M. (1977). *Report to parliament: Second session of the thirtieth parliament, 1976–77*. Ottawa, ON: Supply and Services Canada.

MacSwain, M.-A., Cheverie, M., MacDonald, S.F., & Johnson, S. (2014). Characteristics of women participants in the Methadone Maintenance Treatment Program (MMTP) (Report No. R-307). Ottawa, ON: Correctional Service Canada.

Malone, K. (2017, December 3). "They have a lot to teach us": Inmates call for Canadian justice reform in journal. *CBC News*. Retrieved from https://www.cbc.ca/news/canada/manitoba/prisoners-on-prisons-justice-reform-1.4430769

Maurutto, P., & Hannah-Moffat, K. (2006). Assembling risk and the restructuring of penal control. *British Journal of Criminology*, 46(3), 438–54.

McAleese, S., & Kilty, J.M. (2019). Stories matter: Reaffirming the value of qualitative research. *The Qualitative Report*, 24(4), 822–45.

Mendelsohn Aviv, N. (2019, January 21). Rebranding solitary confinement doesn't change what it is. *Globe and Mail*. Retrieved from https://www.theglobeandmail.com/opinion/article-rebranding-solitary-confinement-doesnt-change-what-it-is

Office of the Correctional Investigator. (2013). *Risky business: An investigation of the treatment and management of chronic self-injury among federally sentenced women*. Retrieved from http://www.oci-bec.gc.ca/cnt/rpt/oth-aut/oth-aut20130930-eng.aspx

Office of the Correctional Investigator. (2017). *Annual report of the Office of the Correctional Investigator 2016–2017*. Retrieved from http://www.oci-bec.gc.ca/cnt/rpt/annrpt/annrpt20162017-eng.aspx

Pollack, S. (2009). "You can't have it both ways": Punishment and treatment of imprisoned women. *Journal of Progressive Human Sciences*, 20(2), 112–28.

Salisbury, E.J., & Van Voorhis, P. (2009). Gendered pathways: A quantitative investigation of women probationers' paths to incarceration. *Criminal Justice and Behaviour*, 36(6), 541–66.

Sapers, H. (2008). *A preventable death*. Office of the Correctional Investigator. Retrieved from http://www.oci-bec.gc.ca/cnt/rpt/pdf/oth-aut/oth-aut20080620-eng.pdf

Savage, L. (2019). Female offenders in Canada. *Juristat*, 39(1). Ottawa, ON: Statistics Canada.

Shantz, L., Kilty, J.M., & Frigon, S. (2009). Echoes of imprisonment: Women's experiences of "successful (re) integration." *Canadian Journal of Law & Society/La Revue Canadienne Droit et Société*, 24(1), 85–106.

Shaw, M. (1991). *The federal female offender: Report on a preliminary study*. Ottawa, ON: Ministry of the Solicitor General.

Sprott, J.B., & Doob, A.N. (2009). *Justice for girls? Stability and change in the youth justice systems of the US and Canada.* Chicago, IL: University of Chicago Press.

Task Force on Federally Sentenced Women. (1990). *Creating choices: Report of the task force on federally sentenced women.* Correctional Service Canada. Retrieved from https://www.csc-scc.gc.ca/002/002/toce-eng.shtml

Thompson, J., Zakaria, D., & Grant, B. (2011). Summary of the 2007 National Inmate Infectious Diseases and Risk-Behaviours Survey for women (Report No. R-238). Ottawa, ON: Correctional Service Canada.

Topitzes, J., Mersky, J.P., & Reynolds, A.J. (2011). Child maltreatment and offending behaviour: Gender-specific effects and pathways. *Criminal Justice and Behaviour, 38*(5), 492–511.

Colonialism and Cultural Disruption

9

Intergenerational Pathways to Incarceration for Indigenous Peoples

Christopher Mushquash, Jessie Lund, Elaine Toombs, and Chris Grol

Learning Objectives

After reading this chapter, you should be able to:

- Describe current prevalence rates of incarcerated Indigenous peoples in Canada.

- Identify and validate contributing pathways to higher prevalence rates of Indigenous peoples within federal and provincial criminal justice systems through an evidence-based explanatory model of individual-difference variables as related to psychological functioning.

- Specifically examine how individual-difference variables, including neurobiology, can contribute to the development of criminal behaviour.

- Provide evidence of promising culturally and contextually relevant interventions and practices that can prevent incarceration or reduce recidivism rates for Indigenous peoples.

- Recommend future research areas of need and potential approaches to generate preventative and tertiary intervention best practices for Indigenous incarceration.

Chapter Overview

Indigenous peoples are disproportionately represented in the Canadian criminal justice system, and rates of Indigenous incarceration continue to rise. While it is often understood that these disproportionate rates have their roots in the intergenerational effects of colonization, the specific mechanisms by which colonization is associated with increased risk for incarceration in recent generations is often disregarded. This chapter provides an overview of the pathways that put many Indigenous peoples at increased risk for engaging in illegal activity through a neurodevelopmental lens. Intergenerational trauma is explored as it relates to prenatal and postnatal adversity and subsequent cognitive, affective, and behavioural impairments, such as fetal alcohol spectrum disorder and deficits in executive functioning. Gang membership, addiction, and recidivism are discussed as they relate to early life adversity and associated developmental impairments. The latter half of this chapter will provide an overview of promising primary interventions for early adversity and tertiary interventions needed in corrections facilities to better support Indigenous offenders with cognitive impairments through culturally relevant interventions. This includes best practices to support reintegration into society to decrease the risk of reoffending in those presenting with executive function difficulties. Ultimately, to intervene against the long-standing intergenerational effects of colonization, first understanding the neurodevelopmental relationship between early life adversity and increased risk for incarceration and recidivism is required.

Introduction

Indigenous populations remain disproportionally represented in the criminal justice system in Canada. From 2017 to 2018, 30 per cent of those incarcerated identified as Indigenous (Malakieh, 2019), despite Indigenous peoples comprising only 5 per cent of the general Canadian population (Statistics Canada, 2017). The number of Indigenous peoples in the Canadian criminal system has increased by approximately 9 per cent in the past 10 years. Increases to incarceration between the years 2007–8 and 2017–18 indicated that rates of federal incarceration of Indigenous women increased by 51 per cent, youth increased 17 per cent, and men increased 18 per cent (Malakieh, 2019). Rates of police-reported crime, as measured by the Crime Severity Index (CSI), within Indigenous communities are higher on average than in non-Indigenous communities, particularly for incidences of violent crime. In addition, more Indigenous people report victimization by crime (28 per cent) compared to non-Indigenous people (18 per cent). For violent offences, rates of victimization were higher across offence types for Indigenous people when compared to non-Indigenous people (Boyce, 2016).

Indigenous incarceration is an oft-cited concern within Canadian criminal justice regulatory systems and has been described as a national crisis (Hopkins, 2015; Roberts & Reid, 2017). In 2016, a *Maclean's* article described this disproportional representation as "Canada's new residential schools" (MacDonald, 2016), stating that despite reducing rates of overall criminal charges, rates of Indigenous incarceration continue to increase. Many community leaders, service providers, and scholars have attempted to understand why Indigenous people are more likely to be involved with the criminal justice system than non-Indigenous people in Canada. What is it about the developmental trajectories of some Indigenous people that result in an increased likelihood of incarcerated? What pathways lead to criminal behaviour, subsequent apprehension, and eventual incarceration?

In 2015, recommendations were provided by the Truth and Reconciliation Commission's (TRC) *Calls to Action* to ameliorate the legal system for Indigenous peoples. Recommendations have included specialized legal training pertaining to Indigenous histories for all law students in Canada (recommendation 28), governmental commitment to eliminating Indigenous offender overrepresentation (recommendation 30), increased funding for alternative sentencing for Indigenous offenders (recommendation 31), and reforms targeted to address the needs of offenders with fetal alcohol spectrum disorder (recommendation 34). Such recommendations are designed to address the historical disruption of cultural practices that occurred through the implementation of residential schools in Canada from 1842 to 1996 (TRC, 2015). It is recognized that because Indigenous peoples in Canada have unique histories, in addition to differing contextual and cultural factors, strategies to address overrepresentation must be those that are tailored to meet the needs of these populations.

Literature examining Indigenous peoples in the justice system offers few comprehensive models that explain the specific mechanisms that cause their disproportional representation. Rather, the emphasis in the literature often includes broader determinants of potential pathways that, although relevant to understanding social or institutional contributions to the problem, may not explain specific pathways to incarceration at the individual level—an important level for intervention. Specifically, if measures that assess

**Truth and Reconciliation
Commission of Canada:
Calls to Action**

The Truth and Reconciliation Commission produced several reports, including this list of *Calls to Action,* which includes ways to improve the legal system for Indigenous peoples.

the risk of reoffending conceptualize Indigenous and non-Indigenous levels of risk in different ways, it is likely that each group will have different experiences within the criminal justice system overall. For example, if Indigenous people are assessed as being more likely to have a higher risk of reoffending by a measure, regardless if they actually would be more likely to commit another crime, they may serve more time in jail, be less likely to receive parole, receive longer parole sentences, or have more punitive sentencing. Often, the actuarial risk assessment measures that are used were developed using population-level data for Canadians in general, so they may not accurately capture unique Indigenous experiences.

Canadian legislation addressed this concern through a landmark case, *R.v. Gladue* (1999), which has resulted in new legislation that attempts to address disparities between Indigenous and non-Indigenous offenders within Canadian correctional facilities. A *Gladue* analysis is an optional approach courts can use to examine cultural and personal circumstances of an individual prior to sentencing. For this to occur, the individual must self-identify as Indigenous and express they would engage in **restorative justice** practices. A *Gladue* analysis identifies specific factors such as childhood adversity, discrimination, cultural assimilation, and other personal experiences that could influence an individual's pathway to initial criminal activity but also predict successful rehabilitation. Such information is obtained through interviews with the individual, family members, Elders, and additional community members.

In 2018, a Supreme Court of Canada justice ordered Correctional Service Canada (CSC) to cease using common risk assessment measures to assess inmate risk and eligibility for parole (these include the Hare Psychopathy Checklist-Revised, Violence Risk Appraisal Guide, Sex Offender Risk Appraisal Guide, Static 99, and the Violence Risk Scale—Sex Offender). These measures were deemed unreliable for measuring Indigenous inmates' levels of risk because they have not been statistically validated for use with Indigenous inmates and are measures that may be susceptible to cultural bias (*Ewert v. Canada*, 2018). Similarly, the Custody Rating Scale (CRS), a measure used across federal and provincial justice systems to calculate the security risk of an inmate, was criticized for how it may overclassify Indigenous offenders as higher security risks. One explanation in support of this critique is that the original scale was developed 25 years ago using

data from non-Indigenous offenders, so it may not be reliable for Indigenous offenders. Despite these claims, a study assessing the empirical validity (otherwise known as the accuracy and usefulness) of this scale found that there was *no bias* of a higher classification of risk for both Indigenous female (Barnun & Gobeil, 2012) and Indigenous male offenders (Gobeil, 2011). The variance (or bias) within Indigenous scores when compared to non-Indigenous scores on the measure did not significantly contribute to overclassification of Indigenous people as higher-risk offenders.

The CRS has since been replaced by the Criminal Risk Index to assess static risk and guide intervention decisions. The CRS may be used in conjunction with other related factors, such as Aboriginal social history, when assessing risk. "Aboriginal social history" refers to many different circumstances that have affected the lives of the majority of Indigenous people. Alternate interventions can be determined by considering these circumstances. The CSC includes the following as circumstances to be considered (though this list is not exhaustive): effects of the residential school system; the Sixties Scoop into the adoption system; effects of the dislocation and dispossession of Inuit people; family or community history of suicide; family or community history of victimization; level or lack of formal education; level of connectivity with family/community; experience in the child welfare system; experience with poverty; and loss of or struggle with cultural/spiritual identity.

In psychology, complex relationships are theorized through the use of quantitative research methods. Quantitative methods are used to describe how explanatory (**independent**) variables influence specific outcomes (**dependent variables**). For example, researchers might examine how cigarette smoking (independent variable) influences risk for lung cancer (dependent variable). The relationship between how specific independent variables contribute to increased rates of Indigenous incarceration (the dependent variable) remain poorly understood. A thorough understanding of how these constructs relate to one another allows for the development of interventions that can ultimately reduce rates of Indigenous incarceration by targeting the most robust indicators of change. Unfortunately, there appear to be many factors that contribute to high rates of Indigenous peoples being incarcerated, which makes understanding these relationships quite complex. **Mediators** (alternative variables that partially or fully explain the relationship between

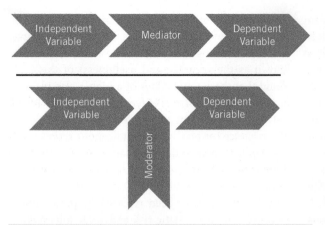

Figure 9.1 How Mediators and Moderators Work to Complicate the Independent/Dependent Variable Relationship

independent and dependent variables) and moderators (alternative variables that influence the direction or strength of the relationship between independent and dependent variables) can further complicate these understandings (see Figure 9.1).

Understanding Pathways to Indigenous Incarceration

In order to begin to conceptualize pathways to incarceration for Indigenous peoples, attention must be given to both individual and environmental-level factors that influence behaviour and contribute to increased risk

(see Figure 9.2). In relation to incarceration, proximal factors are those that represent an immediate risk for a particular event to occur. These proximal factors can accumulate and increase the prediction of future behaviours (at least at a population level). For example, the greater the frequency of a behaviour, the more likely that behaviour is to occur again in the future. These are factors that are perceived to be generally related to individual-level decision making and tend to be more immediately causal. These are contrasted with intermediate and distal factors, which are factors that are more broadly associated with increased risk through increasing the likelihood of generating vulnerability. Intermediate and distal factors are predictive at the population level (that is, they increase risk) but are more difficult to incorporate in planning at the individual level. For example, while childhood adversity increases risk of criminal behaviour at the population level, only a small proportion of individuals who have experienced childhood adversity engage in criminal behaviour.

Acknowledgement of factors that range from proximal to distal allows for consideration of a range of variables that may come together to explain higher rates of incarceration among Indigenous peoples and can also demonstrate the cumulative effect of each of these components. The more risk factors an individual has, the higher the likelihood that they might become incarcerated; however, the strength of the effect of

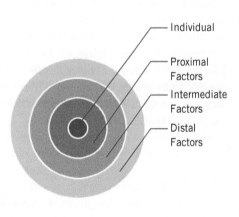

Examples of Risk Indicators	
Proximal	Nutrition Sleep Regulation Substance Use Experiencing Abuse Chronic Life Stress
Intermediate	Parent Incarceration Employment Educational Attainment Presence of Gangs in Community
Distal	Poverty Colonization Discrimination

Figure 9.2 The Range of Factors That Can Influence the Likelihood of an Individual's Incarceration

each variable at the individual level may be different across individuals. That is, exposure to violence at a young age might increase the likelihood of one individual committing violence, while that same exposure might decrease the likelihood of violence in another individual. It is important to make the distinction between population-level and individual-level risk and prediction clear because failing to do so could result in stereotyping that collects across time and population and manifests as systemic bias. Therefore, exploring all variables of relevance and understanding the effect of these variables on incarceration rates, particularly in conjunction with other variables through more advanced modelling techniques, allows researchers to uncover those variables that contribute most to Indigenous incarceration rates.

Choosing what type of risk indicators to analyze becomes particularly important, as some indicators may be more likely to explain high rates of Indigenous incarceration than others, and these relationships can determine how rates of offending are understood. Focusing on distal determinants can explain how broad characteristics influence outcomes for Indigenous offenders. For example, socio-economic status (SES), specifically having an income below the poverty line (between $10,000 and $15,000), has been used as an explanatory variable as to why Indigenous offending rates are higher than the general population. For those with lower SES, they may be more motivated to generate income illegally as a way to make ends meet, pay rent, feed their families, or obtain substances. Living in poverty is considered a distal indicator of a higher risk for criminal activity. Given that Indigenous populations experience poverty at higher rates than non-Indigenous Canadians, and poverty is conceptualized as an indicator of risk, it is likely that more Indigenous people will be considered to be higher-risk offenders by those assessing risk. Therefore, presumably they may spend more time incarcerated and have longer or more restrictive probations as a function of a distal factor—SES.

Unfortunately, the specific pathway between poverty and incarceration is unclear. While poverty tends to be higher for many Indigenous people, not all of those living in poverty engage in criminal activity, which means that this variable may only explain a small portion of why incarceration rates are higher among Indigenous peoples and may not provide much utility in determining risk of offending or

reoffending at an individual level. Therefore, the incorporation of other variables may be more helpful when understanding these relationships, particularly ones that discriminate more effectively between a high- and low-risk offender. Let's go back to the example of biased risk assessments, specifically the use of the Custody Rating Scale. Although some have questioned the use of this measure for Indigenous populations, recent studies have found that the CRS does not arbitrarily rate Indigenous people as a higher security risk than other inmates. Despite this evidence, the systematic application of this measure is cited as being problematic since it was not initially developed for Indigenous populations. This is a valid concern with many psychological measures used with Indigenous peoples, however the mechanisms for why the measure is unhelpful could be due to the psychometric properties (that is, how well the scale can be used to measure what it is intending to measure) rather than another less empirically valid argument. If the causal mechanisms of the independent variable (in this case, the distal risk factor of poverty as measured by SES) remain poorly understood, it is likely that subsequent assessment and intervention approaches to reduce such experiences may be ill-suited or lack effectiveness.

One commonly proposed explanatory variable for higher Indigenous incarceration rates is the systematic use of discriminatory practices throughout the justice system. People who emphasize this distal risk factor would argue that the continuous use of the CRS indicates the presence of colonial procedures that result in perpetual inequality for Indigenous peoples within the criminal justice system (see Figure 9.3). **Colonialism** is broadly defined as the exploitation and control of one population group over another, historically attributed to practices that allowed one population to transfer acquired territories into colonies (TRC, 2015). Within academic literature, many authors have attributed higher rates of Indigenous incarceration to systematic practices of both oppression and assimilation experienced by Indigenous peoples in Canada (Corrado, Kuehn, & Margaritescu, 2014; Monchalin, Marques, Reasons, & Arora, 2019; Nichols, 2017).

Figure 9.3 Conceptualizing Colonialism as an Independent Variable

Such approaches attribute historical injustices experienced by Indigenous peoples, such as being forced to attend a residential school or policies and practices related to the Sixties Scoop (a time when child welfare workers removed many children from Indigenous families and placed them up for adoption or into non-Indigenous families) as being a causal variable of current incarceration rates.

Describing incarceration rates of Indigenous peoples as a result of colonial processes has been an important development that has led to a number of changes in sentencing procedures, not least of which is the incorporation of **Gladue reports**. Indeed, orienting police, lawyers, justices, probation officers, and society at large to the historic and ongoing disruptions to Indigenous peoples as a consequence of colonial assimilation processes has contributed to important processes of reconciliation. However, despite authors attributing higher rates of incarceration broadly to colonialism, operationalization and standardization of this construct into a concrete variable that can be studied and understood is challenging, which results in inconsistencies across studies.

Many authors have acknowledged that colonialism may perpetuate unique differences experienced by Indigenous peoples in Canada. Discriminatory policies across government, educational, and judicial institutions may increase the likelihood of overrepresentation in the criminal justice system. Given that the vast majority of Indigenous people in Canada have experienced some form of detrimental outcome related to historical oppression, an overemphasis on such factors, particularly those within *Gladue* reports, has been argued to perpetuate the incorrect idea that Indigenous offending is inevitable (Williams, 2007). However, contextual and cultural factors perpetuated within such reports do positively influence individual decisions by Canadian courts related to bail, sentencing, parole, and appeals.

Structural inequalities, such as decreased accessibility to health care, inconsistent funding structures for community-level programming, or structural barriers to accessing resources such as those enshrined in the Indian Act, are attributed to detrimental colonialist activities that continue to result in poorer outcomes for Indigenous peoples to date. The proposed relationship between the independent variable (colonialism) and the dependent variable (rates of offending) are shown in Figure 9.4.

If this relationship is a robust predictor of our dependent variable, reducing the impact of colonialism (thus modifying the primary explanatory variable) should result in reduced Indigenous incarceration. To date, data have demonstrated that modifying the independent variable (reducing colonial practices) has little effect on the dependent variable (reducing Indigenous incarceration rates)—in fact, incarceration rates continue to rise. Fortunately, there are no residential schools remaining in Canada, but removal of such discriminatory institutions has not resulted in a decrease in Indigenous incarceration rates, which have remained stable or increased over time. Racial sensitivity training, Indigenous-specific offending policies or justice systems, and ending historical practices that have resulted in overt discrimination have therefore been considered as best-practice interventions to reduce rates of offending. Unfortunately, research has indicated that such practices, provided with the intention to reduce discriminatory actions within the criminal justice system, have not yet empirically demonstrated utility in reducing Indigenous incarceration (Office of the Correctional Investigator [OCI], 2016). For example, although participation in Indigenous-specific cultural programming has been affiliated with lower rates of recidivism (Gutierrez, Chadwick, & Wanamaker, 2018), some cases studies suggest that those who participate in healing lodges (an intervention designed to reduce colonial influences within justice systems) show higher rates of recidivism (CSC, 2002). Numerous factors, such as potential differences between inmates participating in each intervention (including federal/provincial offence or the security risk of the inmate), inconsistent funding and application of approaches, and difficulties separating effects of generalized restorative justice rather than specific cultural treatments further complicate our understanding of these relationships. Empirical outcomes of the effects of these interventions, including specific recidivism rates and probability of escape/safety to the community during the intervention, need to be provided.

Figure 9.4 The Relationship between Colonialism and Rates of Indigenous Offending with Mediating Factors

Recent evaluation of these approaches has focused on community need, cost–benefit analysis, and comparison of types of healing lodges (CSC, 2011), which although worthwhile, does not provide new knowledge on the specific outcomes intended from these approaches.

Given the complexity of these relationships, it is highly plausible that many interventions aimed to reduce colonial influences (such as the Aboriginal Justice Strategy) have a pro-social effect on Indigenous well-being and may reduce recidivism rates (Department of Justice, 2016). It is also plausible that the mechanism of change remains tied to a mediating variable (or variables) distally related to colonialism. Therefore, to best explain high Indigenous incarceration rates and generate the most effective (rather than partially effective) interventions, careful examination of other possible hypotheses, including more proximal individual-difference variables, to explain this phenomenon is required. By narrowing assessment of these relationships to individual differences and often more objectifiable variables it is possible that these relationships can be more plausibly targeted through preventative or tertiary intervention.

Some literature has examined additional specific and proximal explanatory variables for Indigenous people when compared to non-Indigenous people in Canada, although such comparisons are limited. Acknowledgement of how developmental outcomes can perpetuate youth offending, including individual experiences with both educational and child welfare systems, have been proposed (Piquero, 2015). For example, when compared to non-Indigenous youth, Indigenous youth have demonstrated no higher rates of offending, suggesting that there are other independent factors associated with risk of offending beyond Indigenous identity itself (see Figure 9.5). It is possible to examine the influence of individual developmental differences as they relate to disproportionate incarceration rates seen in Indigenous peoples while also maintaining the influence of historical experiences of colonization and discriminatory practices against Indigenous peoples on such outcomes.

When proximal factors of reoffending have been examined, a common model used to assess risk of non-Indigenous reoffenders has been found to significantly predict rates of Indigenous reoffending as well (Guiterrez, Wilson, Rugge, & Bonta, 2013; Wilson & Gutierrez, 2014). Eight risk factors of recidivism, first described by Andrews and Bonta (2010), have demonstrated the ability to predict rates of future reoffending for Indigenous people relatively as accurately as for those who are non-Indigenous (Guiterrez et al., 2013). This type of **predictive validity** was found to be acceptable across six of the eight indicators of recidivism, including history of criminal behaviour, pro-criminal peers/associates, presence of family or marital concerns, presence of education or employment concerns, and substance use. Two factors, poor use of recreational or leisure time and pro-criminal attitudes, still predicted Indigenous offending but were not as predictive as the other variables. This suggests that proximal determinants of risk assessment may inform potential pathways to not only reoffending, but initial offending as well.

The Adverse Childhood Experience Model of Indigenous Incarceration

Adverse childhood experiences (ACEs) are experiences during childhood that have consistently been related to detrimental health outcomes across the lifespan. First conceptualized by Felitti and colleagues (1998), ACEs are categorized by abuse (physical, sexual, or emotional), neglect (physical or emotional), and environmental indicators (a family member with a substance-use problem, a household family member who was incarcerated, a family member with a mental illness, parental separation or divorce, or a mother who was treated violently in the home). Increased incidence of ACEs experienced before the age of 18 has been associated with increased risk for health concerns later in life. For all children, experiencing four or more ACEs is associated with detrimental health outcomes across the lifespan (Bellis et al., 2013). This dose-response relationship has been associated with several life-threatening medical conditions, including ischemic heart disease, lung disease, cancer, skeletal

Figure 9.5 The Relationship between Childhood Adversity and Rates of Offending, with Mediating Factors

fractures, and others (Bellis et al., 2013; Kalmakis & Chandler, 2015). It is also associated with adverse mental health outcomes, with people with four or more ACEs being three times more likely to smoke, four and a half times more likely to develop depression, 11 times more likely to use drugs intravenously, two to five times more likely to attempt suicide, and seven time more likely to have problematic alcohol use. The cumulative effect of an increased number of ACEs demonstrated that as the number of ACEs increases, so does the risk for various health concerns, in a dose-response relationship.

The adverse childhood experience model can be applied to explain specific mechanisms that underlie how incarceration rates are higher for Indigenous populations. This model uses a developmental approach that describes how early life experiences can result in fundamental neurobiological changes in brain structure and functioning. Through such changes, an individual may be more likely to experience difficulties with decision making and goal-directed behaviour. They are more likely to have interpersonal difficulties, since social functioning may be impaired. This type of impairment can be attributed to disrupted attachment from the child to their primary caregiver, but may also manifest in romantic relationships. Through the adverse childhood experience model of Indigenous incarceration (see Figure 9.6), we establish that pre- and postnatal adverse experiences disrupt normative neurodevelopment and consequently put individuals at risk for cognitive, affective, and social impairments—all of which is underpinned by colonial impositions that have disrupted the cultures, communities, and families of Indigenous peoples. Such impairments increase the likelihood that affected individuals will engage in high-risk behaviours. Engagement in high-risk behaviours can include criminal behaviour, thus increasing a person's risk for incarceration. These relationships will be explained in more detail below.

Factors that Affect Incarceration Rates

Disrupted Neurodevelopment

Neurodevelopment is described as the brain's development of neurological pathways that help individuals develop skills to function across the lifespan. Neurodevelopment begins while the fetus is in the mother's womb and continues throughout childhood and into adulthood. There are certain periods of brain development that are particularly sensitive and critical

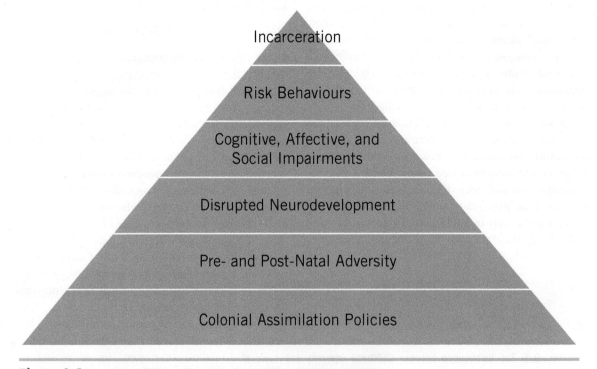

Figure 9.6 The Adverse Childhood Experience Model of Indigenous Incarceration

for healthy development. These periods are extremely vulnerable to environmental inputs, and such inputs, both positive and negative, can have a significant influence on neuronal diversity, connectivity, and the maturation of the fetal brain (Levitt & Veenstra-VanderWeele, 2015). The fetal nervous system is particularly sensitive to environmental changes because it is only in the beginning stages of development. The fetus's brain and spinal cord are the first systems to develop and often have undergone many early and important aspects of growth before the mother even knows she is pregnant. Prenatal stress (such as maternal physical stress, psychological stress, infection/illness, nutrition or hormonal disruption, and drug/alcohol intake) can have a lasting effect on the developing fetus's brain. The type of prenatal stress, the timing of the stress, and the amount of exposure to the stressor all influence the type of disruption in neurodevelopment and the implications this has on the developing fetus later in life.

Once the infant is born, the early years of life are also formative for neurodevelopment. During infancy, the child's brain is sensitive to the external experiences it is exposed to. Chronic stress at this time has the ability to disrupt major developmental pathways in the brain needed later in life. For example, the more risk factors (such as exposure to maltreatment, poverty, domestic violence, caregiver mental health problems, or caregiver substance use) children aged 0 to 36 months are exposed to, the higher the risk of experiencing lifelong developmental problems (Barth et al., 2007). Historically, Indigenous children were exposed to familial and cultural fragmentation, and many experienced various forms of maltreatment, including physical or sexual abuse through residential school attendance (TRC, 2015). These experiences likely disrupted the normative brain development of the children involved and have since had intergenerational influences on brain development, leading to increased alcohol and drug use, poverty, child abuse and neglect, and mental illness seen in subsequent generations (Blackstock, Trocmé, & Bennett, 2004).

Cognitive Impairment

Disruptions in neurodevelopment both in utero and during early life have significant implications for cognitive functioning throughout the lifespan. These effects can influence how individuals navigate making decisions, regulate their emotions, interact in social relationships (these factors are subsumed under the broad neuropsychological category of executive functions), as well as decrease the likelihood for success in academic, employment, and parenting endeavours. **Cognitive impairments** associated with prenatal and early life adversity simultaneously serve as significant risk factors for criminal behaviour and incarceration later in life.

Fetal Alcohol Spectrum Disorder

Exposure to alcohol in utero can cause significant disruptions in neurodevelopment and, as a result, the exposed infant is at risk for developing **fetal alcohol spectrum disorder (FASD)**. FASD is an umbrella term used to describe a range of outcomes (including fetal alcohol syndrome, partial fetal alcohol syndrome, alcohol-related neurodevelopmental disorder, and alcohol-related birth defects) that can occur in individuals whose mother consumed alcohol during pregnancy. FASD is the leading cause of cognitive and developmental disability in Canada, occurring in approximately 4 per cent of Canadians (Flannigan, Unsworth, & Harding, 2018). Prevalence of FASD appears to be particularly high in

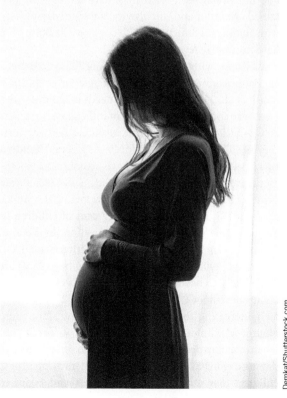

Demkat/Shutterstock.com

some Indigenous communities. While recent data are limited, findings from a remote Indigenous community in British Columbia 30 years ago showed that approximately 19 per cent of infants met the criteria for FASD (Robinson, Conry, & Conry, 1987). And 20 years ago in a Manitoban Indigenous community, the prevalence of FASD was estimated at approximately 6–10 per cent of the community (Square, 1997). Although not recent, these studies would now place those affected by FASD at 20–30 years of age—which is a highly represented demographic in corrections facilities.

FASD presents a range of possible impairments, including intellectual difficulties, poor academic performance, adaptive behaviour difficulties, and lack of social awareness and communication; deficits in receptive and expressive language, abstract thinking, and overall executive function difficulties; and specific difficulties in memory, attention, judgment, organization, prioritizing, and regulating one's emotions (Chudley et al., 2005). The type of brain injury that occurs as a result of alcohol exposure is dependent on many different factors, including genetics, nutrition, environment, timing of exposure, extent of exposure, and interaction with other drugs. As such, FASD can present itself differently from person to person (Fraser, 2008). While one individual with FASD may have issues with sustained attention and impulsivity, another may present with significant difficulties with cognitive flexibility but have normative levels of attention.

Children with FASD are also more likely to experience abuse or neglect early in life (Fuglestad et al., 2013; Smith et al., 2007). The complex needs of children with FASD also increase the number of difficulties caregivers face as well as the number of resources and supports they need to support the children. As a result, children with FASD are more likely to have unstable living situations and remain overrepresented in the foster care system (Lange, Shield, Rehm, & Popova, 2013; Smith et al., 2007). For example, 60 per cent of children in a child and family service organization in Kenora, Ontario, were expected to meet the criteria for FASD (Michaud, 2008). Children in care who have FASD are more likely to become permanent wards compared to children without FASD (Gough & Fuchs, 2006), ultimately increasing their risk for difficult transitions into adulthood. Children with FASD tend to perform better when clear expectations are provided in relation to day-to-day behaviours and in social interactions. These children may struggle more to adjust and adapt to changing environments as a result of placement within the child welfare system. Such children often engage in concrete thinking strategies and may have difficulty recovering from previously experienced abuse or neglect, as many cognitive strategies employed in psychological treatments rely on abstract reasoning. For children living with developmental disabilities, symptom presentations of trauma can differ from children with otherwise normative neurodevelopment, resulting in lower rates of identification as well.

Individuals with FASD are at risk of engaging in criminal activity because of a variety of risk factors associated with presenting symptoms. These risk factors include poorer impulse control, difficulty with connecting behaviour to consequences, difficulty planning and delaying gratification, difficulty predicting long-term consequences of behaviour, deficits in empathy and social awareness, difficulties regulating emotions (including frustration and anger), vulnerability to peer pressure, and increased susceptibility to engage in substance use. These difficulties, as well as an increased risk for unstable living conditions throughout childhood and exposure to other adverse childhood experiences, highlight the cumulative risk seen in these adolescents and young adults for engagement in criminal behaviour. Moreover, should they engage in criminal behaviour, the legal counsel representing such individuals may or may not include the FASD diagnosis as part of their defence for fear that a more severe sentence will be given because of the perception of the needs associated with the client as well as the likelihood of recidivism (Verbrugge, 2003). Indeed, there are Canadian cases of both youth and adult offenders where they arguably received more severe sentencing because of their FASD diagnosis because the court held the view that this diagnosis made the offender untreatable.

As a consequence of the aforementioned risk factors, FASD is extremely overrepresented in Canadian corrections facilities. While it is approximated that 1 per cent of Canadians have FASD, it is estimated that approximately 10–23 per cent of individuals in North American criminal justice systems have FASD (Fast, Conry, & Loock, 1999; MacPherson, Chudley, & Grant, 2014; McLachlan, 2017; Rojas & Gretton, 2007) and an estimated 10 per cent in the Canadian criminal justice system. However, there appears to be regions of Canada that have higher prevalence rates of FASD and a higher representation of FASD in corrections facilities. For example, in 2017 it was estimated that 100 per cent of offenders in a corrections facility in Kenora, Ontario, had FASD, with 90 per cent of those offenders identifying as Indigenous (Mandhane, 2017). The colonial imposition of assimilation policies, the ensuing disruptions in cultures, communities, and families, combined with the poverty and substance use associated with increased rates of mental health difficulties like trauma, depression, anxiety, and grief all converge to amplify risk. In this way, an individual-differences variable conceptual model such as the adverse childhood experience model of Indigenous incarceration acknowledges and holds accountable the colonial influence but improves specificity in causal variable identification—and subsequent intervention targets.

Executive Functions

As infants grow, they acquire skills to begin to develop their executive functions. **Executive functions** are higher-order processes that occur in the prefrontal cortex of the brain and are used to focus our attention, hold information in our minds, switch gears, and make decisions. They are analogous to the air traffic control system at an airport, managing many different planes and runways simultaneously (Shonkoff et al., 2011). Executive function skills build substantially during early childhood and continue to build as children grow into adolescents and young adults. Caregiver–infant relationships shape the early development of executive functions, allowing infants to observe, learn, and practise skills in a supportive and enriching environment— that is, neurodevelopment is mediated by early attachment relationships and continues to be nurtured through childhood and adolescence through the presence of warm, validating, stable, consistent (that is, loving) relationships characterized by clear, developmentally appropriate expectations, and reliable and valid consequences. Children then use social situations to learn and practise how to resist distractions, control emotions, and manage behaviours—thus refining their executive function skills.

Infants who experience neglect are often not given the opportunity to practise higher-order skills through interactions with a caregiver. Ultimately, early neglect puts individuals at risk for developing executive function problems that last into adulthood (Gould et al., 2012; Nikulina & Widom, 2014). Meanwhile, unpredictable and often highly stressful environments associated with drug use, domestic violence, and physical, emotional, and sexual abuse expose children to chronic fear that alters important stress responses in the brain—including the production and secretion of important biochemicals such as cortisol (the stress hormone). Such stress responses are intrinsically connected to the brain pathways associated with executive function development in the frontal lobe. As a result, exposure to early adversity puts individuals on a pathway to struggle with higher-order executive processing in adulthood, including the components necessary to carry out effective decision making.

Executive function deficits as a result of exposure to ACEs often present similarly to many impairments associated with FASD. These cognitive impairments also increase the risk for criminal behaviour and incarceration in adolescence and adulthood. In a sample of Canadian offenders, 10 per cent met the criteria for FASD, while another 45 per cent met the criteria for neuropsychological deficits unrelated to prenatal alcohol exposure (MacPherson et al., 2011). Specifically, deficits in inhibition, attention, cognitive flexibility, and working memory are all associated with criminality and incarceration (Meijers, Harte, Jonker, & Meynen, 2015). Individual executive functions do not operate in isolation, so impairments in one or two areas may have an effect on other areas of higher-order processing. For instance, an impairment in attention can have an influence on working memory. As such, executive function deficits can have widespread implications on goal-directed behaviour and the ability to learn from one's mistakes, making recidivism more likely. Indeed, individuals with executive function difficulties are also more likely to reoffend than those without (Hancock, Tapscott, & Hoaken, 2010; Langevin & Curnoe, 2011; Ross & Hoaken, 2011).

Affect and Social Impairment

Disrupted Attachment Processes

The quality and type of relationship between a child and their primary caregiver can predict outcomes seen in adulthood. **Attachment**, defined as an emotional bond between a parent and child (Bowlby, 1982), can be disrupted when children experience adversity in early development (Thomson & Jaque, 2017). Disruption of attachment processes reduce the likelihood that a child will develop positive self-regulation/self-soothing skills and self-worth, which is often defined as "insecure attachment." Being securely attached means that there is an emotional attunement between child and parent, resulting in a relationship that is perceived to be stable and safe by the child. Unfortunately, many ACEs involve parents or family members in the home of the child and can cause disrupted attachment. For example, if the primary caregivers are unavailable to a child, or if they are parenting in a way that is unhelpful to the child's positive development, the child may be more likely to have disrupted relationships later in life. Parental behaviours, such as providing high levels of both warmth and control (appropriate boundary setting), have resulted in positive child development and pro-social life outcomes. Providing consistent structure with predictable enforcement of rules gives children stability. Endorsing this stability in the context of unconditional positive regard (love) ensures relationships remain stable despite any ongoing ruptures that may result. For example, a child may have a temper tantrum because it is time to go to bed, and may be put in time out by the mother as a result, but when they have self-regulated, they still know that mom loves them and that the relationship remains unharmed. Therefore, the child goes to bed feeling relaxed, happy, and loved. Of note here, attachment in the academic literature is often defined in terms of mother–infant dyads. However, in many Indigenous communities, the attachment constellation can include grandparents, aunts, uncles, cousins, and siblings (Neckoway, Brownlee, & Castellan, 2007).

Attuned parenting results in secure attachment between the parent and child, and subsequently the child is less likely to use substances, engage in impulsive behaviours, or quit school prior to graduating. Secure attachment with a primary caregiver can influence the type of relationships sought later in life. Securely attached children are more likely to have securely attached romantic relationships as adults. Partners who are securely attached express greater trust, respect, and stability in their romantic relationships than those who are not. Conversely, children who are insecurely attached are more likely to maintain these types of attachments in their adult romantic relationships as well, although with corrective positive relationship experiences and evidence-based psychotherapeutic approaches they can maintain relationships that are more secure.

Children with an increased number of ACEs often do not experience consistent pro-social parenting. It can be challenging to parent effectively if a parent is struggling with problematic substance use, is involved in intimate partner violence, or is incarcerated. The cycle of Indigenous involvement with the criminal justice system is also perpetuated by previously having parents involved with the system. High rates of Indigenous incarceration have disrupted access to children and subsequent attachment of the child to that parent. For example, Indigenous Australian fathers have reported increased difficulty parenting their children while incarcerated, and less than half of study participants (41 per cent) stated they were not currently involved in parenting any of their children. About one-quarter of fathers (22 per cent) indicated that a child visited them at least one time while they were incarcerated, and 24 per cent indicated that they did not have direct contact with their children or their children's current caregiver at all

RyersonClark/Getty Images

Children who have formed healthy attachments to their parents can bring those positive relationship experiences into their adulthood and are more able to maintain relationships that are secure. Among parents who were not able to form healthy attachments as children, corrective positive relationship experiences and evidence-based psychotherapeutic approaches can also improve their ability to maintain secure relationships.

(Dennison et al., 2014). With reduced access, it can be challenging to maintain positive relationships between parent and child, particularly if the parent was the primary caregiver of the child prior to incarceration. Thus, the effects of colonial processes ripple intergenerationally through communities, families, and individuals in myriad ways.

Social Determinants of Health

Social determinants of health describe distal, social, and economic mechanisms that influence the overall health of an individual. This includes individual demographical traits and environmental characteristics that influence risk of disease (Mikkonen & Raphael, 2010). Social determinants of Indigenous peoples' health include proximal determinants related to health behaviours, physical environments, employment and income, education, and food security. Intermediate determinants include health-care systems, educational systems, community infrastructure, environmental stewardship, and cultural continuity. Distal determinants are colonialism, racism/social exclusion, and self-determination (Loppie Reading & Wein, 2009).

Social determinants of health can influence parenting and can result in an increased likelihood of child welfare intervention. Lower socio-economic status, unstable housing, and reduced access to health care or nutrition also influence a parent's ability to convey consistent warmth and control to a child. Such factors can increase the likelihood of unintentional neglect of a child, which can have repercussions related to a child's ability to reach appropriate developmental milestones but also increases the likelihood of involvement with the child welfare system. In Canada, Indigenous children are overrepresented in the child welfare system, with four times the number of children in care than at the height of the residential school era. Although Indigenous children aged 14 and under comprise approximately 7 per cent of the total population, they represent about 48 per cent of children in foster care (Turner, 2016). Many families are initially investigated because of suspicions of neglect, which are often caused by social determinants of health–related concerns, such as unstable housing or inaccessibility to nutrition (Ma, Fallon, & Richard, 2019). Children are also more likely to be placed in care as a result of parental incarceration (Reid, 2018), and when Indigenous and non-Indigenous inmate familial experiences were compared, children of

Indigenous inmates were significantly more likely to be placed in care, with a placement rate of 41 per cent as compared to 19 per cent for non-Indigenous children (Trevethan, Auger, & Moore, 2001).

Indigenous children involved with the child welfare system, particularly when placed in care at a younger age and having a high number of placements with non-relatives, are more likely to become incarcerated—likely mediated by disruptions in attachment. Such chronic instability increases the probability of homelessness and gang affiliation for Indigenous youth, both of which are associated with increased propensity toward criminal activity and eventual incarceration (Barker et al., 2015).

Risk Behaviours

Individuals struggling to develop a sense of hope, belonging, meaning, or purpose (Health Canada, 2015) combined with neurocognitive impairments may be more likely to engage in behaviours that meet their individual needs in the short term, but may not be healthy or helpful for them across their lifespan. Engagement in risky behaviours can increase the likelihood that an individual will eventually become incarcerated (see Figure 9.7).

Gang Membership

Gang membership can provide a sense of family or attachment that has not previously been experienced, particularly for youth attempting to build relationships and foster stability in their lives. Gangs offer organizational support by which a youth can engage in like-minded goal-directed activity, often to gain power, recognition, and control (Totten, 2009). This can provide youth with a sense of belonging, shared meaning with peers, and connection to a common goal. Gang

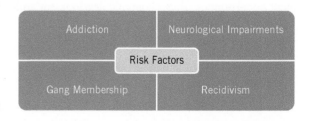

Figure 9.7 Risk Factors Influencing Likelihood of Incarceration

involvement can provide a sense of social support and safety, particularly if incarcerated, where gang affiliation may be required for protection within a correctional facility.

Unfortunately, these seemingly pro-socially motivated aspects result in many more detrimental outcomes. Consequences of gang membership range from lower educational attainment, poor reported health, greater problematic substance use, and higher rates of illegal income generation, crime, and incarceration (Gilman, Hill, & Hawkins, 2014). Youth gang members engage in criminal activity, violence, and intimidation, and many youth offences, particularly violent offences, are more likely to be completed by a gang-affiliated youth rather than a youth who is not affiliated with a gang. Additional predictors of gang involvement for Indigenous youth in North America include lower per capita family income, lower parental monitoring, increased academic difficulties, increased peer delinquency, substance use, higher impulsivity, and perceived racial discrimination (Hautala, Sittner, & Whitbeck, 2016). As a result, Indigenous people remain disproportionally represented in these organizations, with 22 per cent of all gang members in Canada identifying as Indigenous (Totten, 2010). Within some communities, children join as young as age eight, although most gang-affiliated members are over age 18. Further, if a youth has a family member affiliated with a gang, they are more likely to become involved in the future (Dunbar, 2017).

The most successful predictor of disaffiliation with gang involvement is for an individual to obtain legal employment. However, the income generated must match what was generated illegally through gang activity (Goodwill, 2009). For Indigenous people, rates of employment are lower than similarly matched non-Indigenous people, particularly within remote and rural communities where vocational and educational training opportunities are lower and there are fewer employment opportunities. Thus, economic development and workforce entry opportunities are also important intervention considerations for Indigenous peoples.

Addiction

There are high rates of problematic alcohol and substance use in many Indigenous communities in Canada, and findings suggest that Indigenous adolescents begin using substances and consuming alcohol at a younger age than non-Indigenous adolescents (Falk, Yi, & Hiller-Strumhofel, 2006; Miller, Beauvais, Burnside, & Jumper-Thurman, 2008). Among a sample of Indigenous youth in the upper Midwest of the United States and Ontario, there was a 54 per cent chance of meeting the criteria for a **substance-use disorder** by late adolescence (Hautala, Sittner, & Walls, 2018). Among the youth, alcohol-use disorder (43 per cent risk) was the most common, followed by marijuana-use disorder (35 per cent risk) and then nicotine dependence (22 per cent risk). Hautala and colleagues (2018) also found that internalizing disorders (for example, depression or anxiety) increased the risk for having multiple substance-use disorders, while externalizing disorders (for example, attention-deficit hyperactivity disorder, oppositional defiant disorder, or conduct disorder) increased the risk for alcohol-use disorder, marijuana-use disorder, as well as multiple substance-use disorders. This speaks to the importance of the availability of evidence-based treatment for mental health difficulties—an intermediate social determinant of health, of which many Indigenous communities lack access.

Substance-use disorder is reflected in the high rates of Indigenous incarceration in Canada. In general, 16–51 per cent of male and 10–30 per cent of female offenders meet the diagnosis for an alcohol-use disorder, and approximately 30 per cent of male and 51 per cent of female offenders meet the diagnosis for a drug-use disorder (Fazel, Yoon, & Hayes, 2017). In federal correctional institutions in Canada, 86 per cent of Indigenous offenders had substance-use problems compared to 56 per cent of non-Indigenous offenders. Indigenous offenders were also younger than non-Indigenous offenders with regards to their age of first use of alcohol (13 versus 15 years, respectively) and drugs (15 versus 16 years, respectively). In female offenders specifically, 94 per cent of Indigenous female offenders had substance-use problems compared to 71 per cent of non-Indigenous female offenders (CSC, 2014). Pre- and postnatal adversity, including prenatal alcohol exposure, abuse, neglect, parental substance use, and parental incarceration, all increase the likelihood for early first use of substances as well as problematic substance use later in life. Indeed, deficits in inhibition, attention, and emotional regulation increase the likelihood to engage in substance use as a means to cope with traumatic memories and distressing thoughts and emotions. Moreover, deficits in executive function processes that involve working memory and planning, making it difficult to consider long-term goals, can increase the likelihood of engaging in high-risk behaviours like chronic substance use because of an inability to consider the consequences of short-term behaviour.

Recidivism

Indigenous offenders have been shown to have higher rates of recidivism than non-Indigenous offenders (LaPrairie, 1996), potentially as a result of the high prevalence of Indigenous offenders with neurocognitive impairments. FASD and executive function difficulties increase the risk for recidivism for a number of reasons. Successfully adhering to probation involves using many different executive skills, including planning, organizing, managing time, making meetings, controlling impulses, regulating emotions, and refraining from substance use. This is difficult for individuals with cognitive impairments to do without sufficient support. Cognitive impairments also increase the risk that offenders are unable to fully understand the charges they have received as well as adequately participate in their trial and assist in their own defence. They may not be able to understand the charges against them nor the sentence and probation they have received. Service providers working with Indigenous peoples with FASD provided a case example that demonstrates the lack of understanding regarding consequences seen in a young girl with FASD:

> A young girl used to set fires to bales of hay, which she quite enjoyed. Once, she set fire to a trailer while somebody was still inside and this person died. The young girl did not understand that setting fire to a trailer could lead to the loss of life. In her mind, it was fun to set fires, regardless of the consequence or the destruction that would ensue. (Aboriginal Peoples Collection, 2010)

Interventions

We can not only use the ACE framework to understand the disproportionate rates of Indigenous offenders in Canada, but we can also reference it to inform interventions as well. The usefulness of an intervention must be directly affiliated with a specific target variable. An evidence-based, social learning approach, entitled the risk-need-responsivity (RNR) model, matches an individual's level of risk and targets specific interventions to the risks and needs of the offender. The RNR model has been found to be effective with Indigenous youth and may be more likely to identify and address unique cultural needs (Lockwood, Peterson-Badali, & Schmidt, 2018). It is likely that the interventions described below will be more successful when implemented within a generalized RNR framework. Some of these interventions address factors previously related to risk of recidivism. Of the eight factors used to assess this risk (Andrews & Bonta, 2010), the interventions provided address the four environmental factors in this model: social relationship formation, educational/employment concerns, structural recreation/leisure time, and substance-use concerns. The first three of these four environmental factors are those that have been long disrupted through colonial processes within cultures, communities, and families. When Indigenous youth have more of these needs addressed through RNR intervention approaches, they are less likely to reoffend (Lockwood et al., 2018).

Interventions aimed to decrease rates of Indigenous incarceration can be separated into two categories. First, we consider possible *primary interventions* that are aimed at preventing pre- and postnatal adversity that put children at risk for cognitive, emotional, and behavioural difficulties later in life. Second, we consider possible *tertiary interventions* that aim to decrease the impact of ongoing illnesses (such as FASD) that have lifelong effects and detrimental outcomes (for example, recidivism). See Figure 9.8.

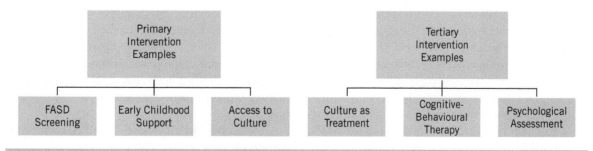

Figure 9.8 Primary and Tertiary Interventions Aimed at Decreasing Indigenous Incarceration

Primary Interventions

Decreasing exposure to pre- and postnatal adversity (FASD, abuse, neglect, child welfare involvement, and so on) that put Indigenous children at risk for psychological difficulties acts as a strong intervention for decreasing criminal behaviour later in life. For example, the Public Health Agency of Canada developed four levels of prevention to decrease the prevalence of FASD (Canada FASD Research Network, 2013). First, public awareness that support girls' and women's health was suggested as a needed preventative effort to promote the development of protective factors for women against alcohol and substance use, ultimately mitigating the risk that they drink during pregnancy. Second, girls and women of childbearing years are given a safe avenue to discuss reproductive health, contraception, pregnancy, and alcohol use by connecting them with related health and support services. Third, at-risk women who may have issues with alcohol are provided services that are culturally and contextually relevant and support women not only while they're pregnant but throughout their childrearing years as well. Fourth, support can be given to new mothers, regardless of whether they were able to make changes to their substance use during their pregnancy. To add to this, support can also be given at a young age for youth who have been identified as being exposed to alcohol in utero, while also supporting the mother to promote her well-being.

Early screening of FASD in children is necessary to provide evidence-based interventions to decrease risk of criminal activity in adolescence and early adulthood. In order for FASD to be detected, further awareness around its presentation is needed. FASD often goes undiagnosed because of its similar presentation to other behavioural and emotion-related problems and in the absence of the physical features often associated with FASD. In Dryden, a small town in northwestern Ontario, an initiative was developed to help educate caregivers and teachers regarding the neurodevelopment of FASD as it relates to supporting children both at home and at school (EBBS FASD Project, 2010). This included a five-day training workshop for service workers by an expert in the neurodevelopment and subsequent behaviour-related issues associated with FASD. Those who received the training engaged in a "train-the-trainer" model, such that they then relayed the knowledge to group home staff, caregivers, and educators, all who work with children and adolescents with FASD.

This training included possible environmental modifications to improve behaviours at home and school. Those who received the training reported that it significantly increased their level of confidence for engaging in FASD interventions as well as their confidence to support and train others to do so. Other service providers working with Indigenous community members have also highlighted that the incorporation of cultural programming is necessary for targeting FASD prevention (Aboriginal Peoples Collection, 2010). They reference cultural teachings that discuss the stages of pregnancy and the proper nutrition and care associated with such stages. Moreover, service providers noted that services needed by individuals with FASD varied across developmental stages, and thus a "one size fits all" approach would not meet each person's needs.

Tertiary Interventions

In order to provide accurate interventions to individuals incarcerated in corrections facilities who have cognitive difficulties, individual assessment is needed. Protocols to screen for FASD in all offenders who enter into prison are needed to identify those who need specific interventions. There are different methods of varying comprehensiveness to screen for FASD to ultimately increase the speed and efficiency so that FASD interventions can be provided in correctional systems (Burd, Martsolf, & Juelson, 2004). Once an inmate meets the criteria for FASD based on the initial screen, they can receive further neuropsychological assessments. Such assessments can be used to establish whether the inmate meets the formal diagnosis for FASD. Moreover, these assessments can be used to distinguish where specific areas of impairment exist to target improvement through specific interventions. Currently, few FASD assessments occur in correctional facilities. This may in part be due to the difficulty of assessing FASD and the lack of individuals who are trained and qualified to assess it. Indeed, this approach would require significant investment in the training of psychologists and neuropsychologists. However, identifying those who meet the criteria for FASD or executive function difficulties unrelated to prenatal alcohol use is needed to employ appropriate treatments to decrease the risk of reoffending upon release—thus offsetting the training and assessment costs associated with psychologists and neuropsychologists.

Corrections facilities have found success with cognitive-behavioural interventions, which aim to help individuals identify, question, and change the thoughts that cause them difficulty. However, individuals with FASD or other executive function difficulties are often not able to benefit from such treatments because they are not able to think abstractly, have difficulty learning from mistakes, and have difficulty planning ahead. Role-playing exercises and behavioural interventions may be more beneficial for those with such difficulties. Interventions that specifically target executive function skills have been found to be effective in decreasing recidivism (Lipsey & Cullen, 2007).

Cognitive difficulties substantially increase the likelihood for recidivism. Prison life is highly regimented and involves little autonomous decision making or situations that involve exerting self-regulation (Meijers et al., 2015). Inmates make very few decisions for themselves, and they are highly monitored and punished for any inadequate behaviour. Such environments do not enrich or challenge the growth of executive function skills; rather, they provide a relief of the need to use such skills to function in daily life. However, anecdotally, it has been noted that many inmates with FASD seem to benefit from such structure. Unfortunately, corrections facilities are the wrong environment to provide appropriate environmental support for those with difficulties in executive functions. Interventions to support offenders with executive function challenges can focus on adaptive skills to help them live autonomously upon exit from the regimented lifestyle they have been provided in prison. Offenders who have had minimal experience practising regulating their emotions effectively, making pro-social decisions for themselves, or engaging in goal-oriented behaviour while in prison are not likely to succeed when such demands are put on them as they re-enter the community. Comprehensive cognitive assessments provided to inmates who have an extensive history of past crime are particularly useful to identify their needs and the possible deficits that contribute to unsuccessful re-entry. For instance, should attentional capacity be identified as a difficulty for a particular individual through assessment, treatment sessions can be decreased in length to maintain attention during sessions. Should working memory be a presenting problem, extra sessions to learn, relearn, and practise functional skills may be required. Tailoring approaches toward individual-difference variables improves therapeutic outcomes.

Cultural programming may be particularly useful to help promote positive identity in Indigenous peoples in corrections facilities who have experienced significant childhood adversity. The CSC offers the Integrated Correctional Program Model (ICPM) to target multiple risk factors for offending by helping offenders learn the underlying risk factors linked to their criminal behaviour as well as learn skills needed to navigate challenging situations they experience in daily life. The Aboriginal Integrated Correctional Program Model is a stream of the ICPM that was developed through consultation with Elders and Indigenous stakeholders. It aims to address the unique needs and risks of Indigenous offenders by exploring experiences of foster care, adoption, residential schools, cultural disruption, and gang involvement, among others. The program has levels such that, depending on an individual's level of risk, they are streamlined to programming to best meet their individual needs (Statistics Canada, 2014).

Additional programming available to Indigenous offenders can vary based on individual preference but also availability within an institution. Many approaches have been used with some success, but multiple barriers exist for some cultural services related to availability and cultural specificity. For example, Elders are available to provide cultural programming for inmates in some locations, but such services are considered inaccessible in other regions (Standing Senate Committee on Human Rights, 2019). The Elders available are those that may be recognized to be knowledge keepers by criminal justice institutions but were not considered as such within the community. Consultation with the community in relation to who is an Elder and what types of services or ceremonies can be performed seems to be lacking. Availability of medicines and other cultural tools to provide ceremony can be limited within institutions as well. Further, eligibility requirements based on level of security classification can deter access to these services, with many limited to men classified at a minimum security level and women at a minimum to medium security classification (Standing Senate Committee on Human Rights, 2019).

In an attempt to address such concerns, culturally specific rehabilitation practices have been implemented in both federal and provincial/territorial correctional systems. For example, the Waseskun Healing Centre in Quebec has aimed to connected Indigenous offenders with ceremony and other cultural practices. Other examples include access to healing lodges, circle parole hearings, and First Nations–specific court. Such programs can promote healing and reduce rates of recidivism, but these types of services are still not available in all areas of the country.

Some strategies have attempted to reduce the gap of Indigenous and non-Indigenous incarcerated offenders, such as the First Nations Policing Program (FNPP). Since the launch of FNPP in 1992, the program has reduced concerns related to both underpolicing and representation of Indigenous people with local

How Do Cultural Treatments Influence Rates of Recidivism for Indigenous Offenders?

A recent meta-analysis by Gutierrez, Chadwick, and Wanamaker (2018) examined how culturally relevant programming influenced rates of reoffending for Indigenous participants when compared to Indigenous adult offenders who did not engage in cultural programming while incarcerated. By systematically reviewing five databases and additional grey literature (literature that has not been published through a peer-reviewed process or that is often excluded from large databases and other indexed sources), the authors identified seven studies relevant to their research question. Data from all studies were combined, resulting in a total of 1,731 offenders, 728 of which received cultural programming and 1,003 who were in a comparison group.

Results of this study found that culturally specific programming in treatment influenced better outcomes for Indigenous adult offenders. When the authors combined these data, they found that offenders who received cultural programming were 0.72 times less likely to reoffend than those who did not receive cultural programming. Statistically significant differences between these groups were found, as recidivism rates were 9 per cent lower for those who received cultural programming compared to those who did not. Although at first glance these differences seem small, such reductions can have increased clinical significance, as findings can be used to modify and implement future recidivism interventions. By providing effective interventions in a manner that is accessible and relevant to participants (that is, which aligns with their beliefs, values, and needs), it is possible that an intervention will be more useful and attrition rates of participation will be lower.

Future research can build on these findings and explore mechanisms that can specifically explain how culture may reduce recidivism. It is possible that such interventions may directly target RNR-model factors that influence pro-social outcomes

for these individuals. For example, engaging in an increased number of cultural activities is a positive way to spend leisure time, so by engaging in these activities more frequently it means there is less time throughout the rest of the day to engage in maladaptive behaviours. But it is clear that practising culture has so many more benefits than just the simple math of time well spent; the effects of cultural and spiritual practices on fostering greater well-being, including fostering hope, belonging, meaning, and purpose, within an individual are well known. And for many Indigenous people, engaging in culturally based programming in a custody facility may be their first exposure. Establishing a sense of identity as an Indigenous person, connecting with Elders, and learning more about oneself may help to repair the disrupted attachment experiences and trauma experienced throughout their life. Exploring these relationships can inform future models to prevent initial incarceration and intervene to reduce recidivism.

There are some contextual considerations and cautions that need to be taken into account when interpreting these data for diverse Indigenous populations. The majority of the included studies were unpublished reports from New Zealand, and only three studies included in the review were completed with Indigenous populations in Canada. This may affect the generalizability of the study results to Canadian Indigenous populations, as specific Indigenous populations may have unique cultural needs, and criminal justice systems can vary between countries. Further, many studies in this review did not describe specific practices or ways by which these programs were implemented. Although cultural practices can be specific to Indigenous identity or region, the way in which practices were implemented may be useful to understanding the relationships between Indigenous culture and recidivism.

police forces (Lithopoulos, 2009). By establishing First Nation–administered police services and community tripartite agreements with the Royal Canadian Mounted Police, reported crime, as measured in the Crime Severity Index for on-reserve criminal activity, decreased from 2007 to 2011. Residents living in these communities reported that the FNPP were more effective, professional, and accountable. Compared to non-FNPP policing, residents stated that FNPP officers tended to rely on more preventative policing strategies, such as increasing patrols (particularly for youth-related crime), and fostered better relationships within communities. Despite the evidence suggesting that such programming is beneficial within communities, the funding for such programs is not reflective of the need within communities, including population growth of on-reserve communities and overall inflation rates.

Earlier in the chapter we noted that an offender's FASD diagnosis may not be included in their legal defence because of the implications it carries with regard to recidivism and treatment resistance as well as the lack of accessibility to FASD assessments. In 2016, Bill C-235 was introduced to amend the Criminal Code and the Corrections and Conditional Release Act. This bill would require the courts to consider FASD as a mitigating factor in sentencing. This also allowed judges to order an assessment of someone they suspect may have FASD and required the courts to facilitate the development of an external support plan for those with an FASD diagnosis that ensures they receive the supports needed to reintegrate into society after incarceration. The bill, however, was defeated at its second reading. Arguments against the bill included that it would provide an opportunity for further consideration of many other disabilities and mental disorders, ultimately complicating the justice system (Morin, 2016). Clearly, there is work to be done to ensure balance in process and improved outcomes.

Conclusions

We can begin to understand the relationships between intergenerational trauma and rates of incarceration of Indigenous peoples by examining how the colonial imposition set the preconditions for pre- and postnatal adversity influences on neurodevelopment; subsequent cognitive, affective, and behavioural impairments; and risk for addiction, exposure to violence, and other high-risk behaviours. Historical experiences of cultural disruption as well as abuse and neglect have denied many Indigenous peoples the nurturing environments inherent in their cultural values. Many Indigenous communities are working hard to ameliorate the effects of colonial processes through focusing on the well-being of children. If children are gifts from the Creator and remain at the centre of the wellness circle, we can begin to improve Indigenous outcomes through understanding and addressing the proximal, intermediate, and distal factors simultaneously without ignoring important individual-differences variables in biological, neurological, and psychological constructs.

Review Questions

1. What are independent and dependent variables? Provide an example that includes both types of variable as they relate to one another.
2. What impairments are associated with pre- and postnatal adversity?
3. Provide a definition of social determinants of health and explain how they relate to Indigenous incarceration.
4. Compare and contrast rates of substance use in Indigenous versus non-Indigenous offenders.
5. What outcomes are associated with the use of culturally relevant programming for Indigenous offenders?

Critical Thinking Questions

1. Why would an Indigenous youth be at increased risk for incarceration later in life if one of their parents has been incarcerated?
2. How might Canadian corrections facilities better support Indigenous offenders with FASD?

Multimedia Suggestions

"Indigenous Incarceration Rates: Why Are Canada's Numbers so High and What Can Be Done about It?" Lenard Monkman

> This *CBC News* article discusses the high rate of Indigenous incarceration: https://www.cbc.ca/news/indigenous/indigenous-incarceration-justice-system-panel-1.4729192

"Without Screening or Supports, Offenders with FASD Face Revolving Door of Justice," Kelly Malone

> This *CBC News* article discusses the impacts of FASD on Indigenous incarceration: https://www.cbc.ca/news/indigenous/without-screening-or-supports-offenders-with-fasd-face-revolving-door-of-justice-1.4536103

"Indigenous Over-Incarceration"

> This episode of Steve Paikin's *The Agenda* discusses the prevalence of Indigenous overincarceration: https://www.tvo.org/video/indigenous-over-incarceration

Indigenous Youth Justice Toolkit

> This resource created by Level, a charitable organization that aims to level barriers to justice, is designed to help Indigenous youth navigate the justice system through traditional teachings: https://leveljustice.org/news/levels-indigenous-youth-justice-toolkit

References

Aboriginal Peoples Collection. (2010). Fetal alcohol spectrum disorder and the criminal justice system. Public Safety Canada. Retrieved from https://www.publicsafety.gc.ca/cnt/rsrcs/pblctns/ftl-lchl-spctrm/index-en.aspx

Andrews, D.A., & Bonta, J. (2010). *The psychology of criminal conduct* (5th ed.). Newark, NJ: LexisNexus/Anderson.

Barker, B., Alfred, G.T., Fleming, K., Nguyen, P., Wood, E., Kerr, T., & DeBeck, K. (2015). Aboriginal street-involved youth experience elevated risk of incarceration. *Public Health*, 129(12), 1662–8.

Barnum, G., & Gobeil, R. (2012). Revalidation of the Custody Rating Scale for Aboriginal and non-Aboriginal women offenders. Research Report R273. Ottawa, ON: Correctional Service Canada.

Barth, R.P., Scarborough, A.A., Lloyd, E.C., Losby, J.L., Casanueva, C., & Mann, T. (2007). *Developmental status and early intervention service needs of maltreated children.* Washington, DC: U Department of Health and Human Services, Office of the Assistant Secretary for Planning and Evaluation.

Blackstock, C., Trocmé, N., & Bennett, M. (2004). Child maltreatment investigations among Aboriginal and non-Aboriginal families in Canada: A comparative analysis. *Violence Against Women, 10*, 901–16. doi:10.1177/1077801204266312

Bellis, M.A., Lowey, H., Leckenby, N., Hughes, K., & Harrison, D. (2013). Adverse childhood experiences: Retrospective study to determine their impact on adult health behaviours and health outcomes in a UK population. *Journal of Public Health, 36*(1), 81–91.

Bowlby, J. (1982). Attachment and loss: Retrospect and prospect. *American Journal of Orthopsychiatry, 52*(4), 664–78.

Boyce, J. (2016). Victimization of Aboriginal people in Canada, 2014. *Juristat.* Retrieved from https://www150.statcan.gc.ca/n1/en/pub/85-002-x/2016001/article/14631-eng.pdf?st=lHrkVswd

Burd, L., Martsolf, J., & Juelson, T. (2004). Fetal alcohol spectrum disorder in the corrections system: Potential screening strategies. *Journal of FAS International, 2*, e1.

Canada FASD Research Network. (2013). Prevention of fetal alcohol spectrum disorder (FASD): A multi-level model. Retrieved from https://canfasd.ca/wp-content/uploads/sites/35/2017/02/FASD-prevention-issue-paper_linksupdated2017.pdf

Chudley, A.E., Conry, J., Cook, J.L., Loock, C., Rosales, T., & LeBlanc, N. (2005). Fetal alcohol spectrum disorder: Canadian guidelines for diagnosis. *Canadian Medical Association Journal, 172*(Suppl. 5), S1–S21.

Corrado, R.R., Kuehn, S., & Margaritescu, I. (2014). Policy issues regarding the overrepresentation of incarcerated Aboriginal young offenders in a Canadian context. *Youth Justice, 14*, 40–62. doi: 10.1177/14732254135

Correctional Service Canada. (2002). An examination of healing lodges for federal offenders in Canada. Retrieved from https://www.csc-scc.gc.ca/research/r130-eng.shtml

Correctional Service Canada. (2011). Aboriginal healing lodges. Retrieved from https://www.csc-scc.gc.ca/publications/092/005007-2005-eng.pdf

Correctional Service Canada. (2014*). Comparing substance use patterns of Aboriginal and non-Aboriginal women offenders.* Retrieved from https://www.csc-scc.gc.ca/research/005008-rs14-26-eng.shtml

Dennison, S., Smallbone, H., Stewart, A., Freiberg, K., & Teague, R. (2014). "My life is separated": An examination of the challenges and barriers to parenting for Indigenous fathers in prison. *British Journal of Criminology, 54*(6), 1089–1108.

Department of Justice. (2016). Evaluation of the Aboriginal Justice Strategy. Retrieved from https://www.justice.gc.ca/eng/rp-pr/cp-pm/eval/rep-rap/2016/ajs-sja/ajs-sja.pdf

Dunbar, L.K. (2017). *Youth gangs in Canada: A review of current topics and issues.* Public Safety Canada. Retrieved from https://www.publicsafety.gc.ca/cnt/rsrcs/pblctns/2017-r001/2017-r001-en.pdf

EBBS FASD Project. (2010). *Final evaluation report: EBBS FASD Project.* Retrieved from http://www.kpdsb.on.ca/assets/uploads/FASD/FASDFinalReport.pdf

Ewert v. Canada. [2018] 2 SCR 165. Retrieved from https://www.canlii.org/en/ca/scc/doc/2018/2018scc30/2018scc30.html?autocompleteStr=Ewert%20v.%20Canada&autocompletePos=1

Falk, D., Yi, H., & Hiller-Sturmhofel, S. (2006). An epidemiologic analysis of co-occurring alcohol and tobacco use disorders. *Alcohol Research & Health, 29*, 162–71.

Fast, D.K., Conry, J., & Loock, C.A. (1999). Identifying fetal alcohol syndrome among youth in the criminal justice system. *Journal of Developmental and Behavioral Pediatrics, 20*(5), 370–72. doi:10.1097/00004703-199910000-00012

Fazel, S., Yoon, I.A., & Hayes, A.J. (2017). Substance use disorders in prisoners: An updated systematic review and meta-regression analysis in recently incarcerated men and women. *Addiction, 112*(10), 1725–39. doi: 10.1111/add.13877

Felitti, V.J., Anda, R.F., Nordenberg, D., Williamson, D.F., Spitz, A.M., Edwards, V., & Marks, J.S. (1998). Relationship of childhood abuse and household dysfunction to many of the leading causes of death in adults: The adverse childhood experiences (ACE) study. *American Journal of Preventive Medicine, 14*(4), 245–58. doi: 10.1016/S0749-3797(98)00017-8

Flannigan, K., Unsworth, K., & Harding, K. (2018). *The prevalence of fetal alcohol spectrum disorder.* Canada FASD Research Network. Retrieved from https://canfasd.ca/wp-content/uploads/sites/35/2018/08/Prevalence-1-Issue-Paper-FINAL.pdf

Fraser, C. (2008). Victims and fetal alcohol spectrum disorder (FASD): A review of the issues. In S. McDonald (Ed.), *Victims of crime research digest, issue 1.* Ottawa, ON: Department of Justice Canada.

Fuglestad, A.J., Fink, B.A., Eckerle, J.K., Boys, C.J., Hoecker, H.L., Kroupina, M.G., … Wozniak, J.R. (2013). Inadequate intake of nutrients essential for neurodevelopment in children with fetal alcohol spectrum disorders (FASD). *Neurotoxicology and Teratology, 39*, 128–32. doi:10.1016/j.ntt.2013.06.005

Gilman, A.B., Hill, K.G., & Hawkins, J.D. (2014). Long-term consequences of adolescent gang membership for adult functioning. *American journal of public health, 104*(5), 938–45.

Gobeil, R. (2011). The Custody Rating Scale as applied to male offenders. Retrieved from https://www.publicsafety.gc.ca/lbrr/archives/cn21484-eng.pdf

Goodwill, A. (2009). In and out of Aboriginal gang life: Perspectives of Aboriginal ex-gang members. Unpublished doctoral dissertation, University of British Columbia, Vancouver.

Gough, P. and Fuchs, D. (2006) *Children with FASD-related disabilities receiving services from child welfare agencies in Manitoba.* Centre of Excellence for Child Welfare. Retrieved from http://www.cecwcepb.ca/files/file/en/CICwithFASDrelateddisabilities33E.pdf

Gould, F., Clarke, J., Heim, C., Harvey, P.D., Majer, M., & Nemeroff, C.B. (2012). The effects of child abuse and neglect on cognitive functioning in adulthood. *Journal of Psychiatric Research, 46*(4), 500–506.

Gutierrez, L., Chadwick, N., Wanamaker, K.A. (2018). Culturally relevant programming versus the status quo: A meta-analytic review of the effectiveness of treatment of indigenous offenders. *Canadian Journal of Criminology and Criminal Justice, 60*(3), 321–53. https://doi.org/10.3138/cjccj.2017-0020.r2

Gutierrez, L., Wilson, H.A., Rugge, T., & Bonta, J. (2013). The prediction of recidivism with Indigenous offenders: A theoretically informed meta-analysis. *Canadian Journal of Criminology and Criminal Justice, 55*, 55–99. doi:10.3138/cjccj.2011.E.51

Hautala, D.S., Sittner, K., & Walls, M. (2018). Onset, comorbidity, and predictors of nicotine, alcohol, and marijuana use disorders among North American Indigenous adolescents. *Journal of Abnormal Child Psychology, 47*(6), 1025–38. doi:10.1007/s10802-018-0500-0

Hautala, D.S., J. Sittner, K., & Whitbeck, L.B. (2016). Prospective childhood risk factors for gang involvement among North American Indigenous adolescents. *Youth Violence and Juvenile Justice, 14*(4), 390–410.

Hancock, M., Tapscott, J.L., & Hoaken, P.N. (2010). Role of executive dysfunction in predicting frequency and severity of violence. *Aggressive Behavior, 36*(5), 338–49.

Health Canada. (2015). First Nations mental wellness continuum framework. Health Canada Publication No. 140358.

Hopkins, A. (2015). The national crisis of indigenous incarceration: Is taking indigenous experience into account in sentencing part of the solution? *Legaldate*, *27*(2), 4.

Kalmakis, K.A., & Chandler, G.E. (2015). Health consequences of adverse childhood experiences: A systematic review. *Journal of the American Association of Nurse Practitioners*, *27*(8), 457–65.

Lange, S., Shield, K., Rehm, J., & Popova, S. (2013). Prevalence of fetal alcohol spectrum disorders in child care settings: a meta-analysis. *Pediatrics*, *132*(4), 80–95. doi:10.1542/peds.2013-0066

Langevin, R., & Curnoe, S. (2011). Psychopathy, ADHD, and brain dysfunction as predictors of lifetime recidivism among sex offenders. *International Journal of Offender Therapy and Comparative Criminology*, *55*(1), 5–26.

LaPrairie, C. (1996) Examining Aboriginal corrections in Canada. Public Safety Canada. Retrieved from https://www.publicsafety.gc.ca/cnt/rsrcs/pblctns/xmnng-brgnl-crrctns/index-en.aspx

Levitt, P., & Veenstra-VanderWeele, J. (2015). Neurodevelopment and the origins of brain disorders. *Neuropsychopharmacology*, *40*, 1–3. doi:10.1038/npp.2014.237

Lipsey, M.W. and Cullen, F.T. (2007). The effectiveness of correctional rehabilitation: A review of systematic reviews. *Annual Review of Law and Social Science*, *3*, 279–320. doi:10.1146/annurev.lawsocsci.3.081806.112833

Lithopoulos, S. (2009). *Aboriginal sovereignty and the resurgence of bottom-up policing in Canada*. Ottawa, ON: Public Safety Canada.

Lockwood, I., Peterson-Badali, M., & Schmidt, F. (2018). The relationship between risk, criminogenic need, and recidivism for Indigenous justice-involved youth. *Criminal Justice and Behavior*, *45*(11), 1688–1708.

Loppie Reading, C., & Wein, F. (2009). Health inequalities and social determinants of Aboriginal people's health. National Collaborating Centre for Aboriginal Health. Retrieved from https://www.nccah-ccnsa.ca/docs/social%20determinates/nccah-loppie-wien_report.pdf

Ma, J., Fallon, B., & Richard, K. (2019). The overrepresentation of First Nations children and families involved with child welfare: Findings from the Ontario incidence study of reported child abuse and neglect 2013. *Child Abuse & Neglect*, *90*, 52–65.

MacDonald, N. (2016, February). Canada's prisons are the "new residential schools." *Maclean's*. Retrieved from https://www.macleans.ca/news/canada/canadas-prisons-are-the-new-residential-schools

MacPherson, P.H., Chudley, A.E., & Grant, B.A. (2011). Fetal alcohol spectrum disorder (FASD) in a correctional population: Prevalence, screening and characteristics. Correctional Service Canada. Retrieved from https://www.csc-scc.gc.ca/research/005008-0247-eng.shtml

Malakieh, J. (2019). Adult and youth correctional statistics in Canada, 2017/2018. Statistics Canada. Retrieved from https://www150.statcan.gc.ca/n1/en/pub/85-002-x/2019001/article/00010-eng.pdf?st=Jc92DPxl

Mandhane, R. (2017). MCSCS corrections reform—Findings from tour of Kenora jail. Ontario Human Rights Commission. Retrieved from http://www.ohrc.on.ca/en/re-mcscs-corrections-reform-findings-tour-kenora-jail

McLachlan K. (2017). *Final report to Yukon Justice: Estimating the prevalence of FASD, mental health, and substance use problems in the justice system*. Whitehorse, YK: Yukon Department of Justice.

Meijers, J., Harte, J.M., Jonker, F.A., & Meynen, G. (2015). Prison brain? Executive dysfunction in prisoners. *Frontiers in Psychology*, *6*(43), 1–6. doi:10.3389/fpsyg.2015.00043

Michaud, D. (2008) Estimated rate of children in the care of Kenora-Patricia Child and Family Services living with an FASD. D. Michaud, Kenora-Patricia Child and Family Services, Children's Services/Sioux Lookout Agency Operated Home Supervisor, in personal communications with author, based on the proportion of children screened who have an identifying factor.

Mikkonen, J., & Raphael, D. (2010). *Social determinants of health: The Canadian facts*. Toronto, ON: York University School of Health Policy and Management.

Miller, K., Beauvais, F., Burnside, M., & Jumper-Thurman, P. (2008). A comparison of American Indian and non-Indian fourth to sixth graders rates of drug use. *Journal of Ethnicity in Substance Abuse*, *7*, 258–67. doi: 10.1080/15332640802313239

Monchalin, L., Marques, O., Reasons, C., & Arora, S. (2019). Homicide and indigenous peoples in North America: A structural analysis. *Aggression and Violent Behavior*, *46*, 212–18. doi: 10.1016/j.avb.2019.01.011

Morin, P. (2016, December 14). Parliament spikes FASD bill, Yukon MP and advocates disappointed. CBC *News*. Retrieved from https://www.cbc.ca/news/canada/north/larry-bagnell-fasd-bill-vote-parliament-1.3896513

Neckoway, R., Brownlee, K, & Castellan, B. (2007). Is attachment theory consistent with Aboriginal parenting realities? *First Peoples Child & Family Review, 3*, 65–74.

Nichols, R. (2017). The colonialism of incarceration. In J. Nichols & A. Swiffen (Eds), *Legal Violence and the Limits of the Law* (pp. 49–67). Abingdon, UK: Routledge.

Nikulina, V., & Widom, C.S. (2014). Do race, neglect, and childhood poverty predict physical health in adulthood? A multilevel prospective analysis. *Child Abuse & Neglect*, *38*(3), 414–24.

Office of the Correctional Investigator. (2016). *Annual report of the Office of the Correctional Investigator*. Retrieved from https://www.oci-bec.gc.ca/cnt/rpt/pdf/annrpt/annrpt20152016-eng.pdf

Piquero, A.R. (2015). Understanding race/ethnicity differences in offending across the life course: Gaps and opportunities. *Journal of Developmental and Life-Course Criminology*, *1*(1), 21–32.

R. v. Gladue. [1999] 1 SCR 688. Retrieved from https://www.canlii.org/en/ca/scc/doc/1999/1999canlii679/1999canlii679.html?resultIndex=1

Reid, J. (2018). The forgotten victims: Impact of parental incarceration on the psychological health of the innocent children left behind. *Under-Served: Health Determinants of Indigenous, Inner-City, and Migrant Populations in Canada,* 141.

Roberts, J.V., & Reid, A.A. (2017). Aboriginal incarceration in Canada since 1978: Every picture tells the same story. *Canadian Journal of Criminology and Criminal Justice, 59*(3), 313–45.

Robinson, G.C., Conry, J.L., & Conry, R.F. (1987). Clinical profile and prevalence of fetal alcohol syndrome in an isolated community in British Columbia. *Canadian Medical Association Journal, 137*(3), 203–7.

Rojas, E.Y., & Gretton, H.M. (2007). Background, offence characteristics, and criminal outcomes of Aboriginal youth who sexually offend: A closer look at Aboriginal youth intervention needs. *Sexual Abuse, 19*(3), 257–83. doi:10.1007/s11194-007-9048-1

Ross, E.H., & Hoaken, P.N. (2011). Executive cognitive functioning abilities of male first time and return Canadian federal inmates. *Canadian Journal of Criminology and Criminal Justice, 53*(4), 377–403. doi: 10.3138/cjccj.53.4.377

Shonkoff, J.P., Duncan, G.J., Fisher, P.A., Magnuson, K., & Raver, C. (2011). Building the brain's "air traffic control" system: How early experiences shape the development of executive function. Center of the Developing Child. Retrieved from http://www.developingchild.harvard.edu

Smith, D.K., Johnson, A.B., Pears, K.C., Fisher, P.A., & DeGarmo, D.S. (2007). Child maltreatment and foster care: Unpacking the effects of prenatal and postnatal parental substance use. *Child Maltreatment, 12*(2), 150–60. doi:10.1177/1077559507300129

Square, D. (1997). Fetal alcohol syndrome epidemic on Manitoba reserve. *Canadian Medical Association Journal, 157*(1), 59–60.

Statistics Canada. (2014). Integrated Correctional Program Model. Retrieved from https://www.csc-scc.gc.ca/correctional-process/002001-2011-eng.shtml

Statistics Canada. (2017). *Focus on geography series, 2016 Census.* Catalogue no. 98-404-X2016001.

Standing Senate Committee on Human Rights. (2019). Interim report of the Standing Senate Committee on Human Rights. Retrieved from https://sencanada.ca/content/sen/committee/421/RIDR/Reports/RIDR_Report_Prisioners_e.pdf

Thomson, P., & Jaque, S.V. (2017). Adverse childhood experiences (ACE) and adult attachment interview (AAI) in a non-clinical population. *Child Abuse and Neglect, 255.* doi: 10.1016/j.chiabu.2017.06.001

Totten, M. (2009). Aboriginal youth and violent gang involvement in Canada: Quality prevention strategies. *IPC Review, 3*(March), 135–56.

Totten, M. (2010). Investigating the linkages between FASD, gangs, sexual exploitation and woman abuse in the Canadian Aboriginal population: A preliminary study. *First Peoples Child & Family Review, 5*(2), 9–22.

Trevethan, S., Auger, S., & Moore, J.P. (2001). The effect of family disruption on Aboriginal and non-Aboriginal inmates. Correctional Service Canada. Retrieved from http://www.csc-scc.gc.ca/research/r113-eng.shtml

Truth and Reconciliation Commission. (2015). *Honouring the truth, reconciling for the future: Summary of the final report of the Truth and Reconciliation Commission of Canada.* Vancouver, BC.

Turner, A. (2016). Insights on Canadian society: Living arrangements of Aboriginal children aged 14 and under. Statistics Canada. Retrieved from http://www.statcan.gc.ca/pub/75-006-   x/2016001/article/14547-eng.htm

Verbrugge, P. (2003). Fetal alcohol spectrum disorder and the youth criminal justice system: A discussion paper. Ottawa, ON: Department of Justice.

Wilson, H.A., & Gutierrez, L. (2014). Does one size fit all? A meta-analysis examining the predictive ability of the level of service inventory (LSI) with Indigenous offenders. *Criminal Justice and Behaviour, 41,* 196–219. doi:10.1177/0093854813500958

Williams, T. (2007). Punishing women: The promise and perils of contextualized sentencing for Aboriginal women in Canada. *Cleveland State Law Review, 55,* 269.

Adolescents and Young Adults in Custody

10

Carla Cesaroni and Michele Peterson-Badali

Learning Objectives

After reading this chapter, you should be able to:

- Outline why we should study and understand the experiences of youth in custody.
- Explain the history of the legislative framework for custody dispositions.
- Explain what is meant by a developmental model of custody.
- Describe an integrated model of adjustment to custody.
- Explain reasons for considering young adults a separate subpopulation of adult corrections.

Chapter Overview

The central argument of this chapter is that understanding the experiences of young people in custody within a developmental framework provides important direction for correctional policy, practice, and research. There are empirically supported justifications for the differential treatment of adolescents (12–17 years old) and emerging adults (18–24 years old) within the legal system. This chapter reviews what we know about adolescents and young (also called emerging) adult development, the adjustment and coping of youth and young adults in custody, and how this research should be taken into account when considering legislation, policy, and best practices for incarcerated young people. It is based in large part on the research that the two authors have conducted on the experience and adjustment of incarcerated adolescents and young adults over the last two decades. The original data and analyses in this chapter is drawn from close to 800 interviews of incarcerated youth and correctional staff.

Why Study Youth in Custody?

There are several important reasons to understand the experiences of incarcerated young people. First, relative to adults, youth have special needs and are vulnerable. Indeed, separate prisons for youth began a move toward a whole separate youth justice system based on the understanding that youth are developmentally different than adults (Bala & Anand, 2012). Second, it is a serious act for the government to take a child away from their family, whether that is for child welfare purposes or to place a youth in custody. Indeed, custody is the most serious sentence that the Canadian justice system has at its disposal. Therefore, it is important to understand the consequences of such a sentence. Third, evidence-based decision making is important for those running custodial institutions: It is vital that they base their decision about the treatment of youth on research. How a young person experiences and adapts to custody has important implications for program effectiveness. It is difficult for a youth in custody to commit to programming if they are stressed, depressed, anxious, or worried about their day-to-day survival. Finally, a custody experience can have negative consequences for the long-term well-being of a young person. Thus, a developmental perspective is relevant for rights-based/justice-based rationales, research-based rationales, and practice-based rationales.

History of Youth Criminal Justice Legislation in Canada

Canada's legislative framework has a direct impact on how many youth are sentenced to custody, for what offences, and to some degree on the conditions of their confinement. The Juvenile Delinquents Act (JDA) (1908–84) was the first piece of Canadian legislation to directly impact youth who were in conflict with the law. Under the JDA, notions regarding adolescents' special needs, their vulnerabilities, and the need to avoid stigmatization were the impetus to establish separate youth custody facilities (Bala & Anand, 2012; Doob & Sprott, 2004). Concerns regarding the corruption or possible abuse of adolescents by adults (when serving time within adult correctional facilities) was also a concern of legislators. The establishment of youth custody facilities was part of a larger move toward the establishment of a separate youth criminal justice system and separate youth courts (Bala & Anand, 2012; Doob & Sprott, 2004).

The JDA proposed two different types of custodial **dispositions** (which is what sentences are called in the Canadian youth justice system): commitment to the local Children's Aid Society or commitment to an industrial school or "training school" (normally secure-custody facilities; Doob & Sprott, 2004). The JDA created a single offence of "delinquency" for children and youth from 7 to 16/18 (depending on the province) for any municipal, provincial, or federal offence (Webster, Sprott, & Doob, 2019). Sentences were indeterminate, meaning that officials could keep a youth until they determined that the young person was "cured" (Bala & Anand, 2012). Once a youth received a custodial disposition, their case was transferred to provincial authorities. The child welfare orientation of the JDA meant that the focus was on "saving" youth. It also meant that many youth spent long periods of time in custody for minor offences such as truancy (skipping school) and "sexual immorality" (particularly for young girls; Bala & Anand, 2012). With a lack of clear sentencing guidelines, there were also disparities in custodial sentences across the country (Doob & Sprott, 2004).

The Young Offenders Act (YOA) (1984–2003) moved youth justice legislation away from a child welfare orientation toward decidedly criminal justice principles. It made the youth justice system more consistent with the spirit of the recently enacted Canadian Charter of Rights and Freedoms (Bala & Anand, 2012; Doob & Sprott, 2004). This included aligning the law with adult criminal justice legislation, and narrowing federal law to only include federal offences. More importantly, it standardized the age of youth criminalization to 12 to 17 years old, provided definite lengths for all dispositions, stipulated maximum sentence lengths, provided certain legal protections that adults already enjoyed (for example, due process rights, including the right to a lawyer and provisions governing statements to police), and contained specific provisions to address young people's lack of full maturity (such as including parental involvement at various stages of the legal process; Peterson-Badali & Broeking, 2010).

Two types of custody were proposed under the YOA: open and secure custody. **Open custody** meant (1) a community residential centre, group home, child-care institution, or wilderness camp; or (2) any like place or facility. **Secure custody** is defined as any place designated by the lieutenant governor in council in a province for the secure containment or restraint of young persons. Secure-custody facilities are what most people would think of as a typical prison, except for young people. They are generally facilities where restrictions are continuously placed on young people by physical barriers, close supervision, and limited access to the community. Open custody is less stringent and generally used for young people with less serious offences. Generally, open custody consists of a several small residential facilities and a network of community homes. Youth in open-custody facilities sometimes have access to community schools, recreation in the community, local employment, and treatment. Open-custody facilities are often operated by local community not-for-profit organizations, while secure facilities are operated by the provincial ministry. Custodial sentences under the YOA were limited to two to three years (depending on the offence) (Webster et al., 2019). If a youth was 18 or older when sentenced and was sentenced to more than two years, they may have been sent to a federal penitentiary. If the youth turned 20 in a youth facility, they may have been transferred to an adult facility.

Unfortunately, under the YOA youth were placed in custody at a higher rate than in most Western nations (Bala & Anand, 2012; Bala, Carrington, & Roberts, 2009; Department of Justice Canada, 1998; Doob & Sprott, 2004), due in large part to receiving custody dispositions for minor and non-violent offences, including those for which adults might receive a fine (Doob

& Cesaroni, 2004). Lack of clarity in the sentencing principles for judges (including broad and vague language such as "whenever possible," "reasonable in the circumstance") meant that there was enormous variation in the use of custody across the country (Bala et al., 2009; Barnhorst, 2004). Additionally, Indigenous youth were overrepresented in custody (Barnhorst, 2004; Doob & Cesaroni, 2004).

Enacted in 2003, the **Youth Criminal Justice Act (YCJA)** was created to decrease the use of youth courts and reduce and restrict the use of custody. Under the YCJA, custody may only be used if at least one of four conditions is met (see the box below). Custody is now known as "custody and supervision." Under the YOA, a high number of youth served their custody sentence and then were released "cold" back into the community, without any reintegration plan (that is, there was no plan for a gradual transition back into community life, including probation or community service). To address this problem, under the YCJA two-thirds of each custodial sentence is served in custody and the remaining portion is served in the community.

There was a large drop in the rate of sentencing youth to custody immediately following—and directly attributable to—the implementation of the YCJA in 2003 (Bala et al., 2009; Webster et al., 2019), suggesting that judges have acted in the way that the YCJA intended them to. Nearly 4,000 youths were serving custody dispositions in Canada in 1997–8; by 2015–16 the number of youth in custody was 527, representing an 86 per cent reduction (Webster et al., 2019). Despite this drop in the use of custody, understanding the experiences and adjustment of incarcerated youth remains important.

Institutional Life: What Is Custody Like?

It is important to note that for some young people, a custody sentence may mark the first time away from home of some duration (Biggam & Power, 1997; Cesaroni & Bala, 2008; Goldson, 2006). A custodial sentence increases disengagement from family, prosocial peers, and familial/social values at a critical stage of the young offender's development (Roberts, 2004). In addition, custody removes youth from local schools and therefore may affect young people who already have little commitment to their school. This may place them at risk for reoffending, delinquency, and other problem behaviours (Wasserman et al., 2003). Many of the youth we interviewed still share youthful preoccupations. They talk about the importance of negotiating friendships within the institution, about missing girlfriends, about crying when they are alone, and about being homesick. The following is a typical account from a young person whose incarceration experience is the first real moment they've spent away from home (note that this youth was in an open-custody facility; see Cesaroni & Peterson-Badali, 2009):

> Having to be away from my family for a really long time—when I got here I was up in my room I wouldn't come downstairs. I stayed up in my room and cried; I could not handle it—I didn't want to associate with anyone—the police holding cell was crappy—it's not that bad (now), but I've never been away from my family for this amount of time and I am not used to it—I've never even gone camping

---

Guidelines for Judges on Using Custody (YCJA, Section 39)

According to the YCJA, custodial sentences can only be imposed by a judge if one or more of four conditions are met:

- It is a violent offence.
- The youth has failed to comply with previous non-custodial sentences.
- The youth has been found guilty of a moderately serious offence and has a history of patterns of findings of guilt (that is, more than one and possibly more than two).
- In exceptional cases where the young person has committed an offence "such that the imposition of a non-custodial offence would be inconsistent with the purpose and principles [of sentencing]" (section 39(1)).

Richard Ross/Juvenile-In-Justice

Youth placed in secure-custody facilities often feel depressed given their lack of freedom due to high levels of security and the prison-like environment. Some youth experience stressful interactions with other youth (many of whom are serious and violent offenders), and some live far away from family members, making it difficult to have visits. Despite the best efforts of the staff members, these facilities can be dangerous places for some youth.

before with or without . . . I've just been at home with my family the whole time—I can stay away for a weekend that is only two days.

Research suggests that the "pains of imprisonment" (Sykes, 1958)—such as loss of freedom and missing family and friends—may be felt even more acutely by a young person than by an adult (Cesaroni & Fredericks, 2019; Cesaroni & Peterson-Badali, 2005, 2010, 2013, 2017a; Liebling, 1999). A study of the impact of visits by

parents to incarcerated youth concluded that any parental visits, regardless of parental relationship quality, served to ameliorate difficulties in adjustment during incarceration (Monahan, Goldweber, & Cauffman, 2011). This finding has important implications for facilities charged with the care of young persons, in which parental visits are suspended as punishment for bad behaviour by youth.

Custody ranks high among traumatic lifetime stressors for young people, right behind the death or divorce of parents (Frydenberg, 1997; Vandergoot, 2006). The interpretation of this relationship is in keeping with our assertion that incarceration exposes vulnerable individuals (in this case youth) to additional risk because of the coping mechanisms that are required to adjust to the custodial environment (Cesaroni & Peterson-Badali, 2005, 2010, 2013, 2017b).

The aggression many youths display in custody may in fact be a reflection of impaired coping (Coid et al., 2003; Kolivoski & Shook, 2016; Leigey & Hodge, 2013; Mackenzie, 1987). It may also be a reflection of the social dynamic of adult guards versus youthful inmates, including the fact that, for youth, the inmate–staff power imbalance is exacerbated by the power dynamic of adult versus adolescent/young adult (Cesaroni & Peterson-Badali, 2017a). Young people differ in important ways from adults that render them more vulnerable. Younger people are less able to cope with the stress of imprisonment and experience much higher levels of anxiety as a result of having been deprived of their families and social networks (Bala & Anand, 2012; Roberts, 2004; Shulman & Cauffman, 2011).

The fact that youth have generally been found to be involved in more disciplinary infractions, prisoner–staff assaults, and conflicts with others compared to adult prisoners may also reflect their response to stress and difficulty coping (Coid et al., 2003; Gover, Perez, & Jennings, 2008; Klatt, Hagl, Bergmann, & Baier, 2016; Kolivoski & Shook, 2016; Kuanliang, Sorensen, & Cunningham, 2008; Lahm, 2008; Leigey & Hodge, 2013; McShane & Williams, 1989). At least one study suggests that fighting and violence by incarcerated youth are forms of active coping used to reduce institution stress (Shulman & Cauffman, 2011). MacKenzie (1987) provides a number of theories regarding youth and prison adjustment. She argues that a youth's violence in prison is a young person's impulsive reaction to stress and may be a sign of immature coping ability. This may also manifest not only in striking out at others but in self-harm; for example, unlike older prisoners—whose risk of self-harm or suicide risk is often related to psychiatric illnesses—young people's self-harm or suicide vulnerability can also be connected to their inability to cope with the custody environment itself (Liebling, 1999).

Adolescents and young adults have to cope with being incarcerated with the additional burden of immaturity. Sociologist Robert Johnson explored the concept of "mature coping" in relation to incarcerated individuals. He argues that mature coping is defined by the ability of an offender to learn how to be an adult with some autonomy in an environment where the individual has little "formal" power: "Mature coping means, in essence, dealing with life's problems like a responsive and responsible human being, one who seeks autonomy without violating the rights of others, security without resorting to deception or violence, and relatedness to others as the finest and fullest expression of human identity" (Johnson, 2001, p. 83).

In contrast to this description of mature coping, prisoners who report that they cannot adapt to life in prison have difficulty regulating their thoughts and emotions (Johnson, 2001). A number of the studies conclude that for as much as a quarter of young offenders and young adults, custody is an isolating experience in which youth spend their free time in the facility alone and far from family, feeling that staff cannot be trusted or relied on for support; they are fearful and never fully get over the initial stress of incarceration (Cesaroni & Fredericks, 2019; Cesaroni & Peterson-Badali, 2010; Liebling, 2003; Zamble & Porporino, 1988).

Differences in philosophy that characterize youth and adult justice systems have generally meant that youth and adult facilities have different organizational climates (Bishop & Frazier, 2005; Kolivoski & Shook, 2016; Lane, Lanza-Kaduce, Frazier, & Bishop, 2002). Adult facilities in many Western nations tend to be focused on security and order through various demonstrations of correctional power. In contrast, juvenile facilities focus more on rehabilitation, offer a kinder tone and a more supportive environment,

and have staff that care about youth, are able to provide guidance, and are skilled at modelling and teaching appropriate behaviour (Inderbitzin, 2007; Kolivoski & Shook, 2016). This delicate balance between control and flexibility that is required for successful rehabilitation or treatment in secure facilities is one of the main factors that shapes institutional climate (Van der Helm, Stams, & Van der Laan, 2011).

Youth with impulsive traits and interpersonal skills deficits may present as defiant, manipulative, and uncaring when confronted by authority figures, particularly in stressful situations. This is in part because they lack the social skills and maturity necessary to deal with confrontational situations (Vandergoot, 2006). Further, the manner in which front-line staff relate to prisoners may impact their well-being and psychological health. As noted previously, young people have more disciplinary problems than adults, and adult facilities have a different culture and climate that is more enforcement and authority oriented (rather than focusing on supportive relationships). Together, these facts suggest that young people are particularly disadvantaged in an adult-oriented, authoritarian-type facility; those features we have delineated previously come together to heighten the negative impacts of prison on young people and may only escalate acting-out behaviours (see Figure 10.1).

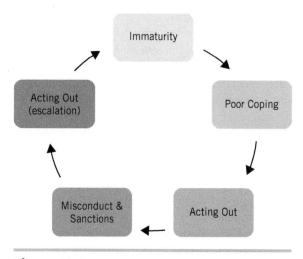

Figure 10.1 Negative Cycle of Poor Coping and Acting Out

What's It Like for Youth to Do Time?

Fear and Safety

The connection between peer support and fear is an important one. Findings from our previous work (see in particular Cesaroni & Peterson-Badali, 2010) suggest that internal support at entry into custody and a young person's current level of fear (whether at entry or later on in custody) predict adjustment as more time is spent in a facility. Previous studies of youth in custody suggest the importance of knowing that there are friends in the institution who will "watch your back" (Maitland & Sluder, 1996). Youth who are friendless within a custodial institution are at serious risk of victimization (Office of the Child and Family Service Advocacy, 2003). As McCorkle (1993) suggests, high levels of fear in prison may undermine the state's efforts to help youth. He argues that personal security is an essential requirement in any program designed to effect changes in pro-social attitudes or behaviours. At least one study suggests that there is an important connection between youths' fear in custody and later recidivism (Windzio, 2006).

Most incarcerated adolescents and young adults said they found not getting along with, or having conflicts with, other young offenders to be "hard" or "very hard" (Cesaroni & Fredericks, 2019; Cesaroni & Pelvin, 2013; Cesaroni & Peterson-Badali, 2005, 2010, 2013, 2017a). While most young people said they feel "safe" in their facility, very few endorse feeling "very safe." This tends to be common to young offender institutions, where fights between young people tend to be spontaneous and unpredictable—a feature that most of the staff we interviewed noted was different between youth and adult custody facilities (Cesaroni & Fredericks, 2019). Across all of our studies, youth reported that they always had to watch their back. They often stated that they were not worried about *starting* a fight but that it was hard to know what *other* youth might do.

It is interesting to note that while the vast majority of young people we interviewed noted that if a fight broke out staff would stop it, a non-trivial proportion (15–30 per cent across studies) said "no," "eventually," or it "depends on who the kid is." This is concerning given that correctional staff may play a role in peer-on-peer violence in youth custody facilities, and this pertains not only to direct control methods (using force

to stop them) but also in allowing youth to continue fighting with each other. It is important to note that incarcerated youth tend to differentiate between staff in terms of how they approach their job, their attitudes, and their treatment of youth (Peterson-Badali & Koegl, 2002).

Peer-on-Peer Victimization and Violence: A Key Part of Doing Time

There is well-documented literature on the use of **peer-on-peer violence** among youth in custody and young adult prisons (Beck, 1995; Connell, Farrington, & Ireland, 2016; Häufle & Wolter, 2015; Mutchnick & Fawcett, 1991; Power, Dyson, & Wozniak, 1997; Shields & Simourd, 1991). There is also some indication that bullying experiences are a salient part of doing time for most youth; 20–50 per cent of prisoners in young offender institutions report that they have been victimized during the course of their current sentence (Adler, 1994; Beck, 1995; Connell et al., 2016; Klatt et al., 2016). Age is strongly and inversely related to misconduct and fighting in prisons; as discussed previously, younger prisoners are responsible for more assaults, misconduct, and behavioural problems in institutions (Kuanliang et al., 2008; Mackenzie, 1987). It should be noted that bullying is not restricted to physical aggression but can include verbal or indirect victimization (spreading rumours about someone, talking behind someone's back, leaving someone out or isolating them, and so on). At least one study found that most young people in residential settings were verbally and indirectly victimized at least once a month (Attar-Schwartz & Khoury-Kassabri, 2015).

Four interrelated themes appear to contribute to violence among residents: (1) residential peer culture; (2) vulnerability at the beginning of institutionalization; (3) deprivation, frustration, and stigmatization; and (4) poor relationships with staff (Sekol, 2013). Contextual factors may include activities, the structure and physical size of a facility, along with a peer culture that is characterized by high levels of hierarchy and poor emotional bonds between youth and staff (Mazzone, Nocentini, & Menesini, 2018).

Despite findings suggesting that the nature of prison life breeds bullying and that violence is entrenched as normal behaviour (Howard League for Penal Reform, 1995), certain youth are at greater risk than others for victimization. Adams (1992) suggested that "predatory inmates tend to select as victims inmates who are perceived to be weak and easy targets, either because they are physically unimpressive or because they are intellectually or emotionally limited" (p. 311). Maitland and Sluder (1996) found that victims were generally less psychologically healthy, were more afraid of being victimized, and experienced the pains of imprisonment more severely than did non-victims.

Research also suggests that inmates who are afraid of being victimized tend to have more conflicts with both other inmates and guards (Mackenzie, 1987). More recent research (Connell et al., 2016) suggests that bullies tend to have extensive custody and offending histories, do drugs, and have a hard time staying in school (mostly because of conduct problems), while victims tend to be loners with mental health needs, have low school attainment, and have victimization histories in other facilities. A recent study by Connell, Farrington, and Ireland (2016) notes that more established prisoners are familiar with the prisoner code, and those who aren't are more likely to be bullied.

Findings from our research are in keeping with previous studies on peer-on-peer victimization, which is somewhat worrisome. The vast majority of the youth we interviewed said that it is important to be "tougher on the inside." Many youth suggested that making sure other youth did not see them as weak was an important key to not being victimized. The importance of being "manly," standing up for oneself, withholding emotion, and the existence of a male pecking order was clear in the vast majority of narratives and is illustrated in the following statements by three young men (see, for example, Cesaroni, 2009; Cesaroni & Alvi, 2010; Cesaroni & Fredericks, 2019):

> You're living with 85 guys, it's a show; guys are always in competition.

> There is a lot of testosterone because it's a place filled with all guys; everyone wants to be the top dog, constantly testing each other. If you don't stand up, you're called a bitch. Usually it's the biggest guy, everyone is scared of him, that is the top dog. Or the one that everyone knows from the outside has a reputation.

> It is important to stand up and show you are a man and defend yourself. If you show that you have a weakness, then you will get picked on and punked off a lot. If you show you can defend yourself, you will be ok.

Youth consistently reported the fact that they settled beefs often or sometimes by fighting, punching, and pushing. Youth also reported indirect modes of victimizing, including leaving people out/ignoring them, making fun of someone, and talking behind their back (Cesaroni & Fredericks, 2019; Cesaroni & Pelvin, 2013). We should note that in our comparative study of boys and girls, girls also reported settling beefs in a similar fashion to boys, however at a lower rate for physical violence. Additionally, they did not report the need to "be tough" and there was no hierarchy or "top dog" among them.

Within the offender population, McCorkle (1993) and Maitland and Sluder (1996) reported that inmates' fear of being victimized in prison is a strong predictor of psychophysiological well-being in young offenders. As noted previously, a consistent finding in our research is that incarcerated youth report that "you always have to watch your back" because you never know what another youth might do. This consistent theme regarding the need to be vigilant is concerning. Maitland and Sluder (1996) stated that "the inmate with a high level of fear regarding personal safety reports more problems and has prominent concerns for his overall well-being" (p. 28). Outcomes of victimization in the general adolescent population include low self-esteem, depression, loneliness, and anxiety (Boulton & Smith, 1994; Boulton, Trueman, Chau, Whitehand, & Amatya, 1999; Häufle & Wolter, 2015; Olweus, 1993). Additionally, there is some evidence to suggest that people engaging in aggressive behaviour in prison may have a harder time reintegrating back into the community (South & Wood, as cited in Häufle & Wolter, 2015).

Internal Support

Though we have discussed the difficulties of coping with peers while incarcerated, previous studies of youth in custody have highlighted the importance of peer relations in *alleviating* the psychological distress of incarceration (Biggam & Power, 1997). Gibbs (1982) argued that group formation is a common reaction to the deprivations of confinement, and research has confirmed that peers can play an important role in reducing stress in jail. With respect to the impact of peer relations on young offenders' functioning, Maitland and Sluder (1996) found that social isolation (that is, not spending free time with friends) negatively predicted general well-being, whereas the belief that friends would assist if an inmate was attacked positively predicted well-being. Therefore, friends or the lack of friends plays an important role in the psychosocial functioning of incarcerated young people (Cesaroni & Fredericks, 2019; Cesaroni & Peterson-Badali, 2005, 2010, 2013, 2017a).

Given the importance of peers to young people, it is not surprising that the support and friendships a young person can garner in custody is important. Relationships among peers in custody, however, may be volatile and include friction with fellow prisoners. Friction with fellow prisoners has been found to be an important predictor of anxiety and depression within young offender institutions (Biggam & Power, 1997). In addition, the nature of the institution itself may make it impossible for a youth to form close friendships. High population turnover within institutions limits the establishment of relationships that can promote a sense of stability (Gibbs, 1982). Many custody facilities tend to have a high turnover of youth because of the number of short sentences. Staffing within facilities may remain relatively stable, but if the inmate population is constantly changing youth are required to constantly renegotiate peer relationships.

The level of support that youth can garner from staff and other youth at entry into prison has increased importance as youth spend more time in a facility (Cesaroni & Peterson-Badali, 2010). In our studies, youth were probed about internal/institutional support and friendships. The vast majority of youth in our studies reported that they had many friends they had made in the facility. The majority of youth also felt there were staff they could talk to. However, sadly, a significant number of youth did not feel that there was another resident or staff member they could talk to about their feelings or problems. For a minority of youth, being in prison appears to have been an isolating experience in that they spent their free time in the facility alone and felt that if they were attacked, other residents would not help them out.

Relationships with Staff

As discussed previously, immaturity makes the power dynamic and interplay between adult staff and young adult prisoners particularly salient. **Legitimacy theory** suggests that there are conditions that make it more likely for prisoners to accept the authority of their custodians (Sparks & Bottoms, 1995). Sunshine and Tyler (2003) note that a major determinant of legitimacy is an individual's perception of fairness in regard to the manner in which authority figures make decisions. Individuals are more likely to accept adverse outcomes and recognize the legitimacy of a system if decisions are procedurally correct and if individuals are accorded respect in the process. In addition to the impact of fair treatment on prison order, Liebling, Durie, Stiles, and Tait (2013) argue that how prisoners are treated is a more important contributor to prisoners' functioning than the physical environment.

There is often a direct relationship between the nature of rule enforcement and the quality of life that prisoners experience in prison (Liebling & Arnold, 2004). There is likely a strong connection between correctional officers' rule enforcement and general behaviour and perceptions of fairness. Within the adult prison literature, there is evidence that prisoners often feel trapped in a maze of rules that are extensive and seem inconsistently and arbitrarily enforced, making it difficult to know how to comply (Irwin & Owen, 2005). Our research seems to suggest that perceptions of staff fairness have a direct impact on a young person's adjustment to custody, above and beyond the personal characteristics they walk in with and above and beyond a facility's staff culture or environment (Cesaroni & Peterson-Badali, 2017b).

In our studies that include data on staff fairness, findings are consistent: The majority of youth feel staff make rules and regulations clear, but there is inconsistency in how they are enforced and youth note that some staff play "favourites." In many young people's eyes this lack of consistency between staff members makes the rules harder to follow. It is troubling that our research suggests a significant number of youth agreed with the statement "Staff don't really care about you; they are only doing a job" (Cesaroni, 2009; Cesaroni & Fredericks, 2019; Cesaroni & Pelvin, 2013).

The Background of Incarcerated Youth: What Do They "Walk In" to Custody With?

Incarceration is a potentially damaging hardship in a life that may already be filled with trauma and adversity (Hochstetler, Murphy, & Simons, 2004). It is foreseeable that a custodial sentence could act as an acute stressor in the lives of vulnerable youth, with potential negative consequences. We have conducted four separate studies of incarcerated adolescents (12–17 years old) and one on incarcerated young adults (18–24 years old). In each of our studies, young people reported multiple forms of familial, socio-emotional, and academic disadvantage, including instability of living, difficulties in school, substance-use problems, delinquent friends, contact with Children's Aid Society, and being victims of and witnessing violence (Cesaroni & Fredericks, 2019; Cesaroni & Peterson-Badali, 2005, 2010, 2013, 2017b).

In addition, in our study of young adults, high rates of trauma, head injury, and bereavement were reported (Cesaroni & Fredericks, 2019). For example, the majority of respondents had experienced the death of a friend (56 per cent), and 12 per cent had lost more than one friend. Though medical (6 per cent) and natural (3 per cent) causes were reasons for their friends' deaths, the leading reasons were traumatic bereavements in that they included deaths that were drug related (10 per cent), due to an accident (19 per cent; many of them horrific), murder (19 per cent), and suicide (13 per cent; Cesaroni & Fredericks, 2019). In the two studies in which we collected data on sexual and physical abuse, abuse was overrepresented among the youth relative to prevalence in the general population (Cesaroni & Fredericks, 2019; Cesaroni & Pelvin, 2013). Given the manner in which the data on sexual and physical abuse were collected (face-to-face interviews) as well as the general underreporting of abuse, the estimates of abuse in our studies is likely conservative.

Young people in our studies came from violent and traumatic environments. Many reported witnessing violence in their communities, including fighting with or without weapons, killing and attempts at killing, and gang violence. In their homes youth were party to violent arguments between their parents, some of which became physical. Following is one example of a young man's response to whether he had ever witnessed violence in his neighbourhood (Cesaroni, 2009):

Everything—swearing, fighting, shooting, people being put on fire, people buried alive—it's like a movie—it's crazy—sometimes I think this is a movie—this shit is only in made up stories . . . I lost one of my children at 8 months old. I was carrying her in my arms and I was shot at [in a drive-by, by a rival gang] and she was shot [dead]. That's why you cannot get attached to people . . . that's life—you can't dwell on it, you have to accept it and move on.

As will be discussed below, the higher the level of vulnerabilities that a young person walks into a facility with, the greater the likelihood of their having adjustment problems within the institution.

Understanding Adjustment of Youth in Custody: An Integrated Approach

Studies of inmates' adaptation to prison have been heavily influenced by classic prison sociology/criminology, and thus the majority of research on adjustment has overwhelmingly focused on adult males (Cesaroni & Peterson-Badali, 2017a). To date there has been little systematic research into the adjustment and experiences of adolescents or young adults (Lösel, 2012; Migden, 2017; Steinberg, Grisso, Scott, & Bonnie, 2016). Until recently, consideration has not been given to the possibility that youth find certain events particularly problematic relative to adults, nor is there recognition that adolescence and emerging adulthood are characterized by unique stresses that may be relevant to a custody setting (Cesaroni & Peterson-Badali, 2017a). Though there is some recognition of the inherent vulnerability of young people because of age, youth incarceration is generally examined from an adult perspective and belief system. In many studies there is a tendency to describe age as only a small aggravating factor in terms of stress of and adjustment to prison life. For example, there is often no consideration of the fact that for a young person time does not have the same relative meaning and weight as for an adult (Cesaroni & Peterson-Badali, 2017a). For example, a year in a custody facility for a 14-year-old has a very different meaning and consequences than a year in prison for a 50-year-olds relative to the time they have spent on Earth and relative to their stage in life.

Over the past two decades we have attempted to integrate sociological/criminological theory on adult prison adjustment with developmental psychological theory on adolescent risk/vulnerability and stress. Adult models of prison adjustment—including **importation theory** and **deprivation theory** (see Chapter 4)—have been used as a basis for analysis, in conjunction with **developmental models of risk** or vulnerability to stress. Across all of our studies we have taken a developmental approach to examine the impact of pre-existing vulnerabilities (an importation model) and institutional factors (a deprivation model) on youths' **psychosocial adjustment** in custody (see Figure 10.2).

The key findings of our five studies are as follows (Cesaroni & Peterson-Badali, 2005, 2009, 2010, 2013, 2017b): First, as a young person's pre-existing vulnerabilities increase (as they walk in with a higher number of vulnerabilities, such as school problems, child welfare involvement, or substance-use issues), the likelihood that the number of psychosocial adjustment problems (such as anxiety, depression, or withdrawal) also increase during the time they are incarcerated (see Figure 10.3). This is a typical importation theory of prison adjustment. Second, institutional vulnerabilities/stressors (the custody environment, internal support, fear, and so on) also help us understand the adjustment problems of a young person. This is a typical deprivation theory of prison adjustment. However, the best way of understanding a young person's adjustment to custody is an **integrated approach**, which looks at both pre-existing vulnerabilities/stressors and prison vulnerabilities/stressors *combined* (see Figure 10.2). Therefore, young people who enter an institution with a high number of pre-existing vulnerabilities/stressors and have a high number of institutional vulnerabilities/stressors are likely to experience psychosocial adjustment problems in custody. Specifically, youth who had a high level of pre-existing vulnerabilities, who feel they have little support in the institution, and are relatively fearful are more likely to experience adjustment

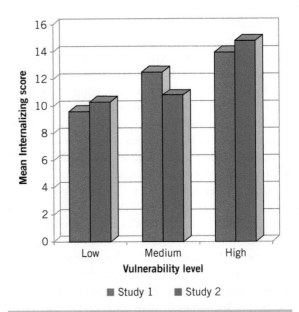

Figure 10.3 Young People's Self-Reported Internalizing Factors (Depression, Anxiety) in Custody as a Function of Pre-existing Vulnerability Levels

Source: Cesaroni & Peterson-Badali, 2009

problems than other youth. Our recent research suggests that this developmental integrated model also explains the adjustment of young adults to adult prison (Cesaroni & Fredericks, 2019).

Our research suggests that most young people find custody stressful upon entry but adapt to custody over time as they learn to cope with life within an institution. A small proportion (10–15 per cent) of incarcerated youth continue to be fearful and find custody a lonely, isolating, stressful, and difficult time. It is important to identify, assess, and intervene with these particularly vulnerable youth to support their functioning within the institution and minimize the immediate and long-term harms associated with custody.

One of our critical findings has been that as youth spend more time in an institution, pre-existing vulnerabilities remain important, but current levels of internal support and fear become more important in understanding adjustment to custody (Cesaroni & Peterson-Badali, 2010). Additionally, perceptions of staff fairness are an important predictor of adjustment above and beyond pre-existing vulnerabilities/stressors and institutional vulnerabilities/stressors (Cesaroni & Peterson-Badali, 2017b). These two findings make the critical role of staff in the adjustment of youth quite clear.

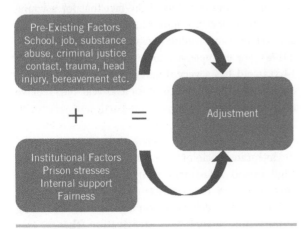

Figure 10.2 Integrated Model of Youth's Adjustment to Custody

Girls in Custody

In 2016–17, female young offenders made up 24 per cent of admissions to custody in Canada (Malakieh, 2017). Though we know how many female youths are admitted to custody, for what, and for how long, little research exists on how young women actually experience custody. For instance, we have not been able to adequately answer the following question: What factors are associated with female young offenders' adjustment while incarcerated?

Girls have perhaps been the most marginalized, the least studied, and the least understood of custodial populations (Dohrn, 2004). They comprise an addendum or footnote to the study of adult populations and even to adolescent boys in custody (Brennan, Breitenbach, Dieterich, Salisbury, & Van Voorhis, 2012; Dohrn, 2004). The small number of girls within custodial institutions has produced the same problems that have often characterized women's prison populations: Female young offenders are often overlooked in a system designed to hold young men. Perhaps even more than their adult female counterparts, they are "the forgotten few" (Chesney-Lind & Pasko, 2004). Notably absent from a record of over a century of incarcerating girls have been the voices and experiences of the girls themselves (Dohrn, 2004). A general lack of understanding regarding the experiences of female young offenders in custody perhaps explains the reluctance of staff to work with girls and, additionally, the perception among practitioners that girls in custody are complex and demanding (Cernkovich, Lanctôt, & Giordano, 2008).

Research on female young offenders in custody tends to focus on pathways to custody, the need for gender-sensitive programs, and peer-on-peer violence (see, for example, Belknap & Cody, 2008; Belknap & Holsinger, 2006, 2008; Belknap, Holsinger, & Dunn, 1997; Chesney-Lind, 1988; Dohrn, 2004; Jones, Brown, Wanamaker, & Greiner, 2014; Macdonald & Chesney-Lind, 2001). Although there has not been a focus on adjustment to custody, several studies have identified the fact that girls share many of the same pre-existing vulnerabilities as boys, such as poverty, dysfunctional families, problems with school, delinquent peers, and substance-use problems.

However, they have also identified vulnerabilities that are unique to adolescent girls, including histories of sexual abuse, sexual assault, dating violence, unplanned pregnancy, and motherhood (Chesney-Lind & Pasko, 2004; Corrado, Odgers, & Cohen, 2000; Gavazzi, Yarcheck, & Chesney-Lind, 2006; Jones et al., 2014; MacDonald & Chesney-Lind, 2001). Additionally, girls in custody have been found to have a higher incidence of self-harm, post-traumatic stress disorder, and depression (Dohrn, 2004). The impacts of social control during female adolescence may be quite different from that of boys (Jones et al., 2014; Medlicott, 2007). Institutional practices that are routine to boys' facilities, such as strip searches, may be problematic for girls with a history of victimization (Chesney-Lind & Pasko, 2004). For girls with a history of suicidal ideation or self-harm, other institutional practices like isolation or segregation is worrisome, given that this has been a problem for adult women in prison (see Office of the Correctional Investigator, 2013).

Our comparative study on incarcerated boys versus girls suggests a number of important findings (see Table 10.1). First, abuse appears to be higher among girls than boys; 32 per cent of boys we interviewed were physically or sexually abused, compared to 58 per cent of girls. Second, girl's lives appear to be more unstable, as their lives seemed more likely to include contact with the child welfare system and demonstrate multiple signs of family dysfunction. Half of the sample of girls we interviewed had moved four or more times in the past three years compared to 12 per cent of boys.

Eighty per cent of girls had involvement with the Children's Aid Society (CAS) compared to 48 per cent of boys. Of these girls, 66 per cent had been removed from their family homes and 54 per cent had lived in a group home at some point. In contrast, only 18 per cent of CAS-involved boys had been removed from their family homes, and 18 per cent had lived in a group home. Dysfunction in the family home included parents having substance-use issues or had spent time in prison, and participants had suffered neglect, lived in inadequate housing, and witnessed violence in the home. On each one of these measures, girls were more likely to report that this was true "often or always."

Boys appeared to be more likely to report over-surveillance by police. For example, 57 per cent of boys reported being stopped by the police "more times than I can count," compared to 18 per cent of girls. Additionally, boys were more likely to report that they have witnessed multiple acts of violence in their neighbourhood (54 per cent; this was often tied to gang activity) compared to girls (34 per cent). This finding

Table 10.1 Percentage of Youth Reporting Pre-existing Vulnerabilities

	Boys (n=50)	Girls (n=50)
Sexual abuse	10	22
Physical abuse	22	36
Moved 4+ times in past three years	12	50
Suspended from school (4+)	28	36
Uses drugs	92	90
Uses alcohol	77	74
Police stops (more than I can count)	57	18
Death of parent	20	17
Children's Aid involvement	48	80
Removal from family	18	66
Lived in group home	18	54
Parents with drinking problem (always/often)	14	42
Parents been to prison (4+ times)	2	20
Poor housing, unable to pay bills (always/often)	6	29
Left unfed, unwashed, unsupervised (always/often)	8	18
Witnessed domestic violence (always/often)	8	25
Witnessed violence or someone killed in neighbourhood (3+ times)	54	34

is in keeping with previous research that suggests male young offenders are more likely to report higher exposure to *community* violence. Overall, while both groups have members who report a high level of pre-existing vulnerabilities and difficulties with adjustment, girls are more likely to have *higher* levels of pre-existing vulnerabilities and *higher* levels of difficulties with adjustment.

While boys expressed feelings that stress the importance of sticking up for oneself, not being a target or weak, and not being "punked off" or taken advantage of, girls report that although you have to take care of yourself, acting tough is actually not a good strategy while inside, and that most girls seemed to get along.

Within the boys' unit, our respondents knew exactly what we were referring to when we asked them about "top dogs" on the unit and hierarchies. Boys told us that status was often related to charges, reputation on the street, what neighbourhood someone was from, whether someone was well known on the street or whether an individual was someone who took "no shit." When this question was posed to the girls, they were often perplexed, did not understand, or would tell us "there is no such thing here." Additionally, they told us

it was important to get along, smile, and have a sense of humour rather than be adversarial.

As noted previously, pre-existing vulnerabilities and institutional vulnerability both contribute to boys' and girls' psychosocial adjustment to pre-trial detention. Equally important in predicting the adjustment of boys, pre-existing vulnerability appears to have slightly more predictive power in predicting girls' adjustment to detention than institutional vulnerability.

With the exception of Shelley Brown and colleagues at Carleton University, an insufficient amount of research continues to be done on incarcerated girls in Canada. Much more work needs to be done before we can understand the unique experiences of girls who are overrepresented in custody, particularly black and Indigenous girls.

A New Population for Consideration: Young Adults

Thus far we have discussed the importance of taking a developmental approach to understanding the incarceration experiences of youth when considering criminal justice legislation, policy, and practice (Migden, 2017; Osgood, Foster, Flanagan, & Ruth, 2005;

Shust, 2014; Steinberg et al., 2016; Steinberg & Schwartz, 2000). How to deal with young adult offenders is currently one of the most important areas of youth justice reform. The criminal laws of most European countries provide for special arrangements to be made when dealing with young adults in either criminal or juvenile law (Dükel & Pruin, 2012). Offenders aged 18 to 21 are dealt with differently than older adults in 19 European countries, including Austria, Germany, and the Netherlands (Farrington, Loeber, & Howell, 2012). In many Western nations, however, where and how to draw the line between the adult and youth justice systems has been an ongoing and sometimes contentious debate. Only recently has Canada and the United States begun to consider the validity of treating young adults as a unique and special subpopulation within the adult corrections system.

The United Nations defines "youth" as spanning ages 15 to 24. The 2003 Council of Europe recommended that young adult offenders under age 21 be treated in a manner comparable with juveniles when the judge is of the opinion that they are not as mature or responsible for their actions as full adults. In 2004, the International Association of Penal Law passed a final resolution stating that the special provisions for juveniles should be extended to the age of 25. In Germany, juvenile law is applied to a young adult if, at the time of the offence, "the youth's moral and psychological development was like a juvenile" and "the offence was similar to a typical juvenile crime" (Dükel & Pruin, 2012, p. 21).

The courts have recognized that age is an imperfect proxy for diminished capacity (Shust, 2014). The age of 18 is an arbitrary, rather than evidence-based, dividing line between youth and adulthood given that cognitive functioning changes quite gradually (Farrington et al., 2012; Shust, 2014; Steinberg et al., 2016). There is strong evidence that, from a neurological perspective, the human brain is not fully developed in its capacity for cognitive functioning and emotional regulation until well into young adulthood (Justice Committee House of Commons, 2016; Kramers-Olen, 2015; Migden, 2017; Prior et al., 2011). From a psychological perspective, psychosocial capacities and moral reasoning abilities vary considerably between individuals so that some remain immature longer than others, including after the legal age of adulthood (Justice Committee House of Commons, 2016; Prior et al., 2011; Steinberg et al., 2016). As a group, young adult offenders are more similar to adolescents than to adults with respect

to features such as executive functioning, impulse control, malleability, responsibility, susceptibility to peer influence, and competence (Farrington et al., 2012). Certainly, they do not reach all the attributes associated with our conceptions of "adulthood" by age 18 (Farrington et al., 2012; Justice Committee House of Commons, 2016; Kramers-Olen, 2015; Migden, 2017; Steinberg et al., 2016). Indeed, in *Roper v. Simmons*, the case that ultimately concluded that the death penalty was unconstitutional for juveniles in the United States, the decision of the US Supreme Court recognized the psychological and neuroscientific evidence for youthfulness and noted that "the qualities that distinguish juveniles from adults do not disappear at 18" (Shust, 2014, p. 685).

In fact, developmental psychologists now recognize the age from late teens to mid-twenties as a developmental stage that is distinguishable from both adolescence and adulthood. Scholarly attention to this developmental period has increased tremendously in recent years and it is now widely referred to as "emerging adulthood," a phrase first coined by psychologist Jeffrey Arnett (2000). Arnett maintains that it is an important developmental period—biologically, socially, and legally—for the transition into adulthood.

Based on qualitative data from structured interviews with emerging adults in multiple settings, Arnett (2006) posited that there are five unique psychosocial features of this developmental period. Emerging adulthood is an age of identity exploration, as youth begin to make independent decisions and discover who they are; it is an age of instability as youth plan and change plans in various areas of their lives (living arrangements, career, romantic partners, and so on); it is the most self-focused life stage, with decreased responsibility to parents; it is an age of feeling "in between" adolescence and adulthood; and it is an age of optimism about future possibilities (Arnett, 2006).

Emerging adults struggle if they are part of especially vulnerable populations, such as those aging out of foster care, coming out of the criminal justice system, or experiencing disabilities (Osgood et al., 2005). The added stressors of transitioning to adulthood may overwhelm already-compromised coping capabilities (Schulenberg, Bryant, & O'Malley, 2004). Though the transition to adulthood cannot be separated from what has happened earlier in a young person's life, it is an important life stage with its own critical avenue of influence for young adults (Altschuler, 2005; Migden, 2017;

Shust, 2014; Steinberg et al., 2016). Gaining acceptance of emerging adulthood as a developmental concept is similar to efforts a century ago, when psychologists made the case that adolescence was a new developmental stage (Migden, 2017).

A developmental understanding of young adults is critical to understanding the differences between adults and young adults and the ways they adjust to being incarcerated. Criminologists have argued that the need to treat emerging adults differently than adults is especially important if a psychological evaluation reveals a "youthful" personality in terms of intelligence and emotional maturity (Albrecht, 2004; Justice Committee House of Commons, 2016; Prior et al., 2011; Shust, 2014). Indeed, research suggests that youthful offenders (whether adolescent or young adult) tend to be developmentally less mature than their non-offending peers (Monahan, Steinberg, Cauffman, & Mulvey, 2009; Steinberg, Chung, & Little, 2004; Vandergoot, 2006). As a result, it has been suggested that "[b]ecause transitional periods have been prolonged and entrance into the adult world more difficult, failure to respect the differences between young adults and adults risks failure of adequate justice for young adult offenders" (Albrecht, 2004, p. 474). Prior and colleagues (2011) summarize the current state of research and practice as follows:

> Overall, the research reviewed points emphatically to the inappropriateness of an arbitrary age limit as the key factor determining the kind of judicial response an offender should receive, and that in the young adult group, the level of maturity exhibited by an offender is a valid factor to be considered within the legal process. There are, moreover, indications that this conclusion is becoming accepted in a growing number of national jurisdictions, albeit to varying degrees. (p. 35)

A study of youth who had done time in both young offender and adult facilities concluded that when the youth justice system had an effect, it was positive: Youth gained skills and had hope. In contrast, when the adult system had an effect, it was negative: Youth lost the connection to family members and community, feelings of safety, and environments where they were treated with respect (Lane et al., 2002). Generally, the few studies that have compared the treatment of youth in juvenile and adult facilities have found that youth in adult facilities had fewer services and rated staff more negatively. Education was a particular area of note, where youth facilities tended to focus on educational attainment, whereas adult facilities placed more focus on vocational training. Differences in counselling, medical attention, and quality of staff were also significant (Ng et al., 2011)

In terms of differences in coping in adult versus juvenile facilities, a study comparing suicide rates noted that young people's odds of completing suicide were 36 times greater in an adult jail than in a juvenile facility (Austin, Johnson, & Gregoriou, 2000). Research also suggests that in addition to increasing the risk of suicide, incarcerating young people in adult facilities increases the risk of depression and post-traumatic stress disorder (Birckhead, 2015; Ng et al., 2011). Interviews with front-line staff and probation officers who deal with both young people and adults revealed that young people are viewed as needier and more likely to crave contact with staff (Crawley, 2006). It is critical to remember that, as Gooch (2006) suggests, "The moral, social and emotional climate of a prison has a direct bearing on prisoner well-being and levels of distress" (p. 280).

Taken together, the evidence from developmental psychology and the criminological and sociological literature suggest that young adults constitute a distinct subgroup of the adult prison population who need the kind of institutional climate that characterizes the youth system. In our most recent study of young adults in adult prisons in both Scotland and Canada, an overwhelming number of both incarcerated young adults and staff in adult prisons agreed that young adults were different from adults and that it was important that young adults have a separate, developmentally appropriate regime and programming (Cesaroni & Fredericks, 2019). Following are comments by staff regarding the challenges of working with young adults in an adult institution:

> [T]hey are more needy, they look for attention constantly, they crave attention and [if] they don't know how to find that attention they act out, be loud or aggressive, or make noise to get the attention they want . . . because they are young, immature, and [have] no life skills they are adolescents basically . . . very reactive and they will punch you and then think . . .

As noted previously, the integrated adjustment model, which helps us understand the adjustment of incarcerated adolescents, appears to also have predictive validity for young adults.

Conclusion

Our research on incarcerated adolescents and young adults have illustrated the importance of taking an integrated, developmentally appropriate approach to understanding how young people adjust to custody and prison. As we have suggested, what a young person walks into an institution with is key to adjustment. Understanding, knowing, and being sensitive to this is important. Though facilities cannot change what a young person walks into an institution with, from a management perspective they can shape the environment and the attitudes and behaviour of staff. Facilities can create an environment that is developmentally appropriate and educate staff to the reasons young people act as they do when incarcerated. They can create an internally supportive environment in which youth do not have to be fearful.

Young adults still constitute a non-trivial number of those serving time in adult facilities. Our most recent study suggests that both youth and staff feel that there should be special treatment to deal with young adults, particular developmental needs. Indeed, as the two authors testified at the coroner's inquest into the death of Ashley Smith (see Chapter 8), the federal government should make this change immediately. The coroner's jury at the Ashley Smith inquest supported our findings and assertions, and more recently the Office of the Correctional Investigator has called for a similar change. To date, no changes in legislation have happened.

Regardless of how many adolescents and young adults continue to be incarcerated in Canada, how they experience doing time will continue to be important.

Review Questions

1. What is the best model for explaining adjustment to custody for incarcerated youth?
2. What are some of incarcerated young people's pre-existing vulnerabilities/stressors?
3. What are some of the institutional stressors/vulnerabilities incarcerated youth experience?

Critical Thinking Questions

1. Do you feel it is important that we understand the experiences and adjustment of incarcerated youth? Why or why not?
2. Is a developmental view of adjustment to custody necessary?
3. Do you think that the current guidelines for using a custodial disposition under the Youth Criminal Justice Act are sufficient?
4. Do you feel that young adults (18–24 years old) should have a separate regime within the adult system?

Multimedia Suggestions

Kids in Jail
This National Film Board documentary takes an in-depth look at youth serving time in jail: https://www.nfb.ca/film/kids_in_jail

Kids Behind Bars
This documentary looks at experiences of teenagers who have been sentenced as adults in the United States: https://www.youtube.com/watch?v=xQJYEB-E4e8

"How Should Manitoba Deal with Its Worst Young Offenders?" Sarah Petz
This *CBC News* article discusses how young offenders are dealt with in Manitoba, comparing it to a progressive juvenile treatment centre in Wisconsin: https://www.cbc.ca/news/canada/manitoba/mental-health-youth-corrections-manitoba-1.5036223

References

Adams, K. (1992). Adjusting to prison life. In M. Tonry (Ed.), *Crime and justice: A review of research: Vol. 16* (pp. 275–359). Chicago, IL: University of Chicago Press.

Adler, J. (1994). The incidence of fear: A survey of prisoners. *Prison Service Journal, 96*, 34–7.

Albrecht, H.-J. (2004). Youth justice in Germany. In M. Tonry & A.N. Doob (Eds), *Youth crime and youth justice: Comparative and cross-national perspectives* (pp. 443–93). Chicago, IL: University of Chicago Press.

Altschuler, D. (2005). Policy and program perspectives on the transition to adulthood for adolescents in the juvenile justice system. In D.W. Osgood, E.M. Foster, C. Flanagan, & G.R. Ruth (Eds), *On your own without a net: The transition to adulthood for vulnerable populations* (pp. 92–113). Chicago, IL: University of Chicago Press.

Arnett, J.J. (2000). Emerging adulthood: A theory of development from the late teens through the twenties. *American Psychologist, 55*(5), 469–80. https://doi.org/10.1037/0003-066X.55.5.469

Arnett, J.J. (2006). *Emerging adulthood: The winding road from the late teens through the twenties.* New York, NY: Oxford University Press.

Attar-Schwartz, S., & Khoury-Kassabri, M. (2015). Indirect and verbal victimization by peers among at-risk youth in residential care. *Child Abuse and Neglect, 42*, 84–98. https://doi.org/10.1016/j.chiabu.2014.12.007

Austin, J., Johnson, K.D., & Gregoriou, M. (2000). *Juveniles in adult prisons and jails: A national assessment.* Washington, DC: Bureau of Justice Assistance, Institute on Crime, Justice and Corrections at the George Washington University and National Council on Crime and Delinquency.

Bala, N., & Anand, S. (2012). *Youth criminal justice law.* Toronto, ON: Irwin Law.

Bala, N., Carrington, P.J., & Roberts, J.V. (2009). Evaluating the Youth Criminal Justice Act after five years: A qualified success. *Canadian Journal of Criminology and Criminal Justice, 51*(2), 131–67. https://doi.org/10.3138/cjccj.51.2.131

Barnhorst, R. (2004). The Youth Criminal Justice Act: New directions and implementation issues. *Canadian Journal of Criminology and Criminal Justice, 46*(3), 273–99. https://doi.org/10.3138/cjccj.46.3.231

Beck, G. (1995). Bullying among young offenders in custody. *Issues in Criminological and Legal Psychology, 22*, 54–70.

Belknap, J., & Cody, B. (2008). Pre-adjudicated and adjudicated girls' reports on their lives before and during detention and incarceration. In R.T. Zaplin (Ed.), *Female offenders: Critical perspectives and effective interventions* (pp. 251–82). Burlington, MA: Jones and Bartlett Publishers, Inc.

Belknap, J., & Holsinger, K. (2006). The gendered nature of risk factors for delinquency. *Feminist Criminology, 1*, 48–71. https://doi.org/10.1177/1557085105282897

Belknap, J., & Holsinger, K. (2008). An overview of delinquent girls: How theory and practice have failed and the need for innovative change. In R. Zaplin (Ed.), *Female offenders:*

Critical perspectives and effective interventions (pp. 31–64). Gaithersburg, MD: Aspen.

Belknap, J., Holsinger, K., & Dunn, M. (1997). Understanding incarcerated girls: The results of a focus group study. *Prison Journal, 77*(4), 381–404. https://doi.org/10.1177/0032855597077004003

Biggam, F.H., & Power, K.G. (1997). Social support and psychological distress in a group of incarcerated young offenders. *International Journal of Offender Therapy and Comparative Criminology, 41*, 213–30. https://doi.org/10.1177/0306624X97413002

Birckhead, T.R. (2015). Children in isolation: The solitary confinement of youth. *Wake Forest Law Review, 50*(1), 1–67.

Bishop, D., & Frazier, C. (2005). Consequences of transfer. In J. Fagan & F.E. Zimring (Eds), *The changing borders of juvenile justice: Transfer of adolescents to the criminal court* (pp. 227–76). Chicago, IL: University of Chicago Press.

Boulton, M.J., & Smith, P.K. (1994). Bully/victim problems in middle-school children: Stability, self-perceived competence, peer perceptions and peer acceptance. *British Journal of Developmental Psychology, 12*, 315–29. https://doi.org/10.1111/j.2044-835x.1994.tb00637.x

Boulton, M.J., Trueman, M., Chau, C., Whitehand, C., & Amatya, K. (1999). Concurrent and longitudinal links between friendship and peer victimization: Implications for befriending interventions. *Journal of Adolescence, 22*, 461–6. https://doi.org/10.1006/jado.1999.0240

Brennan, T., Breitenbach, M., Dieterich, W., Salisbury, E.J., & Van Voorhis, P. (2012). Women's pathways to serious and habitual crime: A person-centered analysis incorporating gender responsive factors. *Criminal Justice and Behavior, 39*(11), 1481–1508. https://doi.org/10.1177/0093854812456777

Cernkovich, S.A., Lanctôt, N., & Giordano, P.C. (2008). Predicting adolescent and adult antisocial behavior among adjudicated delinquent females. *Crime and Delinquency, 54*(1), 3–33. https://doi.org/10.1177/0011128706294395

Cesaroni, C. (2009). The experiences of adolescent males in secure detention. Discussion paper prepared for Ministry of Children and Youth Services, Research and Outcome Measurement Branch.

Cesaroni, C., & Alvi, S. (2010). Masculinity and resistance in adolescent carceral settings. *Canadian Journal of Criminology and Criminal Justice, 52*(3), 303–20. https://doi.org/10.3138/cjccj.52.3.303

Cesaroni, C., & Bala, N. (2008). Deterrence as a principle of youth sentencing: No effect on youth but a significant effect on judges. *Queen's Law Journal, 34*, 447–81.

Cesaroni, C., & Fredericks, K. (2019). *A comparative study of incarcerated young adults in Scotland and Canada part 1: Scotland.* Edinburgh, Scotland.

Cesaroni, C., & Pelvin, H. (2013). Adolescent boys and girls in detention: A comparative study. Discussion paper prepared for the Ministry of Children and Youth Services, Research and Outcome Measurement Branch.

Cesaroni, C., & Peterson-Badali, M. (2005). Young offenders in custody: Risk and adjustment. *Criminal Justice and Behavior*, *32*(3), 251–77. https://doi.org/10.1177/0093854804274370

Cesaroni, C., & Peterson-Badali, M. (2009). Understanding the experiences of incarcerated male youth: The importance of a developmental framework. In A. Renshaw & E. Suarez (Eds), *Prisons: Populations, health conditions and recidivism* (pp. 35–61). New York, NY: Nova Science Publishers Inc.

Cesaroni, C., & Peterson-Badali, M. (2010). Understanding the adjustment of incarcerated young offenders: A Canadian example. *Youth Justice*, *10*(2), 1–19. https://doi.org/10.1177/1473225410369290

Cesaroni, C., & Peterson-Badali, M. (2013). The importance of institutional culture to the adjustment of incarcerated youth and young adults. *Canadian Journal of Criminology and Criminal Justice*, *55*(4), 563–76. https://doi.org/10.3138/cjccj.2012.ES04

Cesaroni, C., & Peterson-Badali, M. (2017a). Ashley Smith and incarcerated young women: Marginalized at any age. *Canadian Journal of Law and Society*, *32*(2), 249–67. https://doi.org/10.1017/cls.2017.11

Cesaroni, C., & Peterson-Badali, M. (2017b). Incarcerated youth. In R.J. Levesque (Ed.), *Encyclopaedia of adolescence* (2nd ed). New York, NY: Springer Publishing.

Chesney-Lind, M. (1988). Girls in jail. *Crime & Delinquency*, *34*(2), 150–68. https://doi.org/10.1177/0011128788034002003

Chesney-Lind, M., & Pasko, L. (2004). *The female offender: Girls, women, and crime* (3rd ed). Thousand Oaks, CA: SAGE Publications.

Coid, J.W., Petruckevitch, A., Bebbington, P., Jenkins, R., Brugha, T., Lewis, G., . . . Singleton, N. (2003). Psychiatric morbidity in prisoners and solitary cellular confinement, I: Disciplinary segregation. *Journal of Forensic Psychiatry and Psychology*, *14*(2), 298–319. https://doi.org/10.1080/1478994031000095510

Connell, A., Farrington, D.P., & Ireland, J.L. (2016). Characteristics of bullies and victims among incarcerated male young offenders. *Journal of Aggression, Conflict and Peace Research*, *8*(2), 114–23. https://doi.org/10.1108/JACPR-12-2015-0200

Corrado, R.R., Odgers, C., & Cohen, I.M. (2000). The incarceration of female young offenders: Protection for whom? *Canadian Journal of Criminology*, *4*(2), 189–207.

Crawley, E. (2006). Doing prison work: The public and private lives of prison officers. In Y. Jewkes & H. Johnston (Eds), *Prison readings* (pp. 209–21). London, UK: Taylor & Francis.

Department of Justice Canada. (1998). *A strategy for the renewal of youth justice*. Ottawa, ON: Author.

Dohrn, B. (2004). All Ellas: Girls locked up. *Feminist Studies*, *30*(2), 302–24. https://doi.org/10.2307/20458965

Doob, A.N., & Cesaroni, C. (2004). *Responding to youth crime in Canada*. Toronto, ON: University of Toronto Press.

Doob, A.N., & Sprott, J.B. (2004). Changing models of youth justice in Canada. In M. Tonry & A. Doob (Eds), *Youth crime and youth justice: Comparative and cross-national perspectives: Vol. 31. Crime and justice: A review of research* (pp. 185–242). Chicago, IL: University of Chicago Press.

Dükel, F., & Pruin, I. (2012). Young adult offenders in juvenile and criminal justice systems in Europe. In F. Lösel, A. Bottoms, & D.P. Farrington (Eds), *Young adult offenders: Lost in transition* (pp. 11–38). New York, NY: Routledge.

Farrington, D.P., Loeber, R., & Howell, J.C. (2012). Young adult offenders: The need for more effective legislative options and justice processing young adult offenders. *Criminology and Public Policy*, *11*(4), 729–50. https://doi.org/10.1111/j.1745-9133.2012.00842.x

Frydenberg, E. (1997). *Adolescent coping: Theoretical and research perspectives*. New York, NY: Routledge.

Gavazzi, S.M., Yarcheck, C.M., & Chesney-Lind, M. (2006). Global risk indicators and the role of gender in a juvenile detention sample. *Criminal Justice and Behavior*, *33*(5), 597–612. https://doi.org/10.1177/0093854806288184

Gibbs, J.J. (1982). The first cut is the deepest: Psychological breakdown and survival in the detention setting. In R. Johnson & H. Toch (Eds), *The pains of imprisonment* (pp. 97–114). Beverly Hills, CA: Sage.

Goldson, B. (2006). Damage, harm and death in child prisons in England and Wales: Questions of abuse and accountability. *The Howard Journal of Criminal Justice*, *45*(5), 449–67. https://doi.org/10.1111/j.1468-2311.2006.00437.x

Gooch, K. (2016). A childhood cut short: Child deaths in penal custody and the pains of child imprisonment. *Howard Journal of Crime and Justice*, *55*(3), 278–94. https://doi.org/10.1111/hojo.12170

Gover, A.R., Perez, D.M., & Jennings, W.G. (2008). Gender differences in factors contributing to institutional misconduct. *The Prison Journal*, *88*(3), 378–403. https://doi.org/10.1177/0032885508322453

Häufle, J., & Wolter, D. (2015). The interrelation between victimization and bullying inside young offender institutions. *Aggressive Behavior*, *41*, 333–45. https://doi.org/10.1002/ab.21545

Hochstetler, A., Murphy, D.S., & Simons, R.L. (2004). Damaged goods: Exploring predictors of distress in prison inmates. *Crime and Delinquency*, *50*(3), 436–57. https://doi.org/10.1177/0011128703257198

Howard League for Penal Reform. (1995). *Banged up, beaten up, cutting up: Report of the Howard League Commission of Inquiry into Violence in Penal Institutions for Teenagers Under Eighteen*. London, UK: Author.

Inderbitzin, M. (2007). A look from the inside: Balancing custody and treatment in a juvenile maximum-security facility. *International Journal of Offender Therapy and Comparative Criminology*, *51*(3), 348–62. https://doi.org/10.1177/0306624X06291462

Irwin, J., & Owen, B. (2005). Harm and contemporary prison. In A Liebling & S. Maruna (Eds), *The effects of imprisonment* (pp. 94–117). Portland, OR: Willan Publishing.

Johnson, R. (2001). *Hard time: Understanding and reforming the prison*. Belmont, CA: Wadsworth Publishing Company.

Jones, N.J., Brown, S.L., Wanamaker, K. & Greiner, L.E. (2014). A quantitative exploration of gendered pathways to crime in a sample of male and female juvenile offenders. *Feminist Criminology, 9*(2), 113–36. https://doi.org/10.1177/1557085113501850

Justice Committee House of Commons. (2016). *The treatment of young adults in the criminal justice system.* London, UK: House of Parliament.

Klatt, T., Hagl, S., Bergmann, M.C., & Baier, D. (2016). Violence in youth custody: Risk factors of violent misconduct among inmates of German young offender institutions. *European Journal of Criminology, 13*(6), 727–43. https://doi.org/10.1177/1477370816643733

Kolivoski, K.M., & Shook, J.J. (2016). Incarcerating juveniles in adult prisons: Examining the relationship between age and prison behavior in transferred juveniles. *Criminal Justice and Behavior, 43*(9), 1242–59. https://doi.org/10.1177/0093854816631793

Kramers-Olen, A.L. (2015). Neuroscience, moral develop-ment, criminal capacity, and the Child Justice Act: Justice or injustice? *South African Journal of Psychology, 45*(4), 466–79. https://doi.org/10.1177/0081246315603633

Kuanliang, A., Sorensen, J.R., & Cunningham, M.D. (2008). Juvenile inmates in an adult prison system: Rates of disciplinary misconduct and violence. *Criminal Justice and Behavior, 35*(9), 1186–1201. https://doi.org/10.1177/0093854808322744

Lahm, K.F. (2008). Inmate-on-inmate assault: A multilevel examination of prison violence. *Criminal Justice and Behavior, 35*(120), 120–37. https://doi.org/10.1177/0093854807308730

Lane, J., Lanza-Kaduce, L., Frazier, C.E., & Bishop, D.M. (2002). Adult versus juvenile sanctions: Voices of incarcerated youths. *Crime and Delinquency, 48*(3), 431–55. https://doi.org/10.1177/0011128702048003004

Leigey, M.E., & Hodge, J.P. (2013). And then they behaved: Examining the institutional misconduct of adult inmates who were incarcerated as juveniles. *The Prison Journal, 93*(3), 272–90. https://doi.org/10.1177/0032885513490270

Liebling, A. (1999). Prison suicide and prison coping. In M. Tonry & J. Petersilia (Eds), *Prisons: Crime and justice: A review of research* (pp. 283–359). Chicago, IL: University of Chicago Press.

Liebling, A. (2003). *Legitimacy, prison suicide and the moral performance of prisons.* Paper presented at the Annual Meeting of the American Society of Criminology, Chicago, IL.

Liebling, A, & Arnold, H. (2004). *Prisons and their moral performance: A study of values, quality, and prison life.* Oxford, UK: Oxford University Press.

Liebling, A., Durie, L., Stiles, A., & Tait, S. (2013). Revisiting prison suicide: The role of fairness and distress. In A. Liebling & S. Maruna (Eds), *The effects of imprisonment.* London, UK: Taylor & Francis. https://doi.org/10.4324/9781843926030

Lösel, F. (2012). What works in correctional treatment and rehabilitation for young adults? In F. Lösel, A. Bottoms, & D.

Farrington (Eds), *Young adult offenders: Lost in transition?* (pp. 74–112). https://doi.org/10.4324/9780203128510

MacDonald, J.M., & Chesney-Lind, M. (2001). Geneder bias and juvenile justice revisited: A multiyear analysis. *Crime & Delinquency, 47*(2), 173–95.

Mackenzie, D.L. (1987). Age and adjustment to prison: Interactions with attitudes and anxiety. *Criminal Justice and Behavior, 14*(4), 427–47. https://doi.org/10.1177/0093854887014004002

Maitland, A.S., & Sluder, E.D. (1996). Victimization in prisons: A study of factors related to the general well-being of youthful inmates. *Federal Probation, 60*, 24–31.

Malakieh, J. (2017). Youth correctional statistics in Canada, 2015/2016. *Juristat, 85*, 27. Retrieved from http://www.statcan.gc.ca/pub/85-002-x/2016001/article/14318-eng.htm

Mazzone, A., Nocentini, A., & Menesini, E. (2018). Bullying and peer violence among children and adolescents in residential care settings: A review of the literature. *Aggression and Violent Behavior, 38*, 101–12. https://doi.org/10.1016/j.avb.2017.12.004

McCorkle, R.C. (1993). Living on the edge: Fear in a maximum-security prison. *Journal of Offender Rehabilitation, 20*(1/2), 73–91. https://doi.org/10.1300/J076v20n01_06

McShane, M.D., & Williams III, F.P. (1989). The prison adjustment of juvenile offenders. *Crime and Delinquency, 35*(2), 254–69.

Medlicott, D. (2007). Women in prison. In Y. Jewkes (Ed.), *Handbook on prisons* (pp. 245–68). Portland, OR: Willan Publishing.

Migden, S.E. (2017). The injustice of a felony conviction for offenders under age twenty-one: A new option for the courts to save our youths' futures. *Family Court Review, 55*(2), 292–306. https://doi.org/10.1111/fcre.12278

Monahan, K.C., Goldweber, A., & Cauffman, E. (2011). The effects of visitation on incarcerated juvenile offenders: How contact with the outside impacts adjustment on the inside. *Law and Human Behavior, 35*(2), 143–51. https://doi.org/10.1007/s10979-010-9220-x

Monahan, K.C., Steinberg, L., Cauffman, E., & Mulvey, E.P. (2009). Trajectories of antisocial behavior and psychosocial maturity from adolescence to young adulthood. *Developmental Psychology, 45*(6), 1654–68. https://doi.org/10.1037/a0015862

Mutchnick, R.J., & Fawcett, M. (1991). Group home environments and victimization of resident juveniles. *International Journal of Offender Therapy and Comparative Criminology, 25*, 126–42. https://doi.org/10.1177/0306624X9103500205

Ng, I.H., Shen, X., Sim, H., Sarri, R.C., Stoffregen, E., & Shook, J.J. (2011). Incarcerating juveniles in adult prisons as a factor in depression. *Criminal Behaviour and Mental Health, 21*(1), 21–34. https://doi.org/10.1002/cbm.783

Office of the Child and Family Service Advocacy. (2003). Review of Toronto Youth Assessment Centre (TYAC). Toronto, ON: Author.

Office of the Correctional Investigator. (2013). Correctional Service Canada data: Federal inmates under 25. Ottawa, ON: Author.

Olweus, D. (1993). *Bullying at school: What we know and what we can do*. Oxford, UK: Blackwell.

Osgood, D.W., Foster, E.M., Flanagan, C., & Ruth, G. . (2005). *Programs and policy goals for helping vulnerable youth as they move into adulthood*. Philadelphia, PA: University of Pennsylvania Press.

Peterson-Badali, M., & Broeking, J. (2010). Parents' involvement in the youth justice system: Rhetoric and reality. *Canadian Journal of Criminology and Criminal Justice, 52*, 1–27. https://doi.org/10.3138/cjccj.52.1.1

Peterson-Badali, M., & Koegl, C.J. (2002). Juveniles' experiences of incarceration: The role of correctional staff in peer violence. *Journal of Criminal Justice, 29*, 1–9. https://doi.org/10.1016/S0047-2352(01)00121-0

Power, K.G., Dyson, G.P., & Wozniak, E. (1997). Bullying among Scottish young offenders: Inmates' self-reported attitudes and behaviour. *Journal of Community & Applied Social Psychology, 7*, 209–18.

Prior, D., Farrow, K., Hughes, N., Kelly, G., Manders, G., White, S., & Wilkinson, B. (2011). *Maturity, young adults and criminal justice: A literature review*. Birmingham, UK: University of Birmingham.

Roberts, J.V. (2004). Public opinion and the evolution of juvenile justice policy in western nations. In M. Tonry & A. Doob (Eds), *Youth crime and youth justice: Comparative and cross-national perspectives: Vol. 31. Crime and justice: A review of research*. Chicago, IL: University of Chicago Press.

Schulenberg, J.E., Bryant, A.L., & O'Malley, P.M. (2004). Taking hold of some kind of life: How developmental tasks relate to trajectories of well-being during the transition to adulthood. *Development and Psychopathology, 16*(4), 1119–40. https://doi.org/10.1017/S0954579404040167

Sekol, I. (2013). Peer violence in adolescent residential care: A qualitative examination of contextual and peer factors. *Children and Youth Services Review, 35*(12), 1901–12. https://doi.org/10.1016/j.childyouth.2013.09.006

Shields, I.W., & Simourd, D.J. (1991). Predicting predatory behavior in a population of incarcerated young offenders. *Criminal Justice and Behavior, 18*, 180–94. https://doi.org/10.1177/0093854891018002006

Shulman, E.P., & Cauffman, E. (2011). Coping while incarcerated: A study of male juvenile offenders. *Journal of Research on Adolescence, 21*(4), 818–26. https://doi.org/10.1111/j.1532-7795.2011.00740.x

Shust, K.B. (2014). Extending sentencing mitigation for deserving young adults. *Journal of Criminal Law and Criminology, 104*(3), 668–704.

Sparks, J.R., & Bottoms, A.E. (1995). Legitimacy and order in prisons. *British Journal of Sociology, 46*(1), 45–62. https://doi.org/10.2307/591622

Steinberg, L., Chung, J.R., & Little, M. (2004). Reentry of young offenders from the justice system: A developmental perspective. *Youth Violence and Juvenile Justice, 2*(1), 21–38. https://doi.org/10.1177/1541204003260045

Steinberg, L., Grisso, T., Scott, E.S., & Bonnie, R.J. (2016, April 29). Don't treat young adults as teenagers. *New York Times*. Retrieved from https://www.nytimes.com/2016/05/01/opinion/sunday/dont-treat-young-adults-as-teenagers.html

Steinberg, L., & Schwartz, R.G. (2000). Developmental psychology goes to court. In T. Grisso & R.G. Schwartz (Eds), *Youth on trial: A developmental perspective on juvenile justice* (pp. 9–31). Chicago, IL: University of Chicago Press.

Sunshine, J., & Tyler, T.R. (2003). The role of procedural justice and legitimacy in shaping public support for policing. *Law and Society Review, 37*(3), 514–48. https://doi.org/10.1111/1540-5893.3703002

Sykes, G.M. (1958). *The society of captives: A study of a maximum security prison*. Princeton, NJ: Princeton University Press.

Van der Helm, P., Stams, G.J., & Van der Laan, P. (2011). Measuring group climate in prison. *The Prison Journal, 91*(2), 158–76.

Vandergoot, M.E. (2006). *Justice for young offenders: Their needs, our response*. Saskatoon, SK: Purich Publishing Ltd.

Wasserman, G.A., Keenan, K., Tremblay, R.E., Coie, J.D., Herrenkohl, T.I., Loeber, R., . . . Petechuk, D. (2003). Risk and protective factors of child delinquency. In *Child Delinquency Bulletin Series*. Washington, DC: Office of Juvenile Justice and Delinquency Prevention. https://doi.org/10.1037/e501772006-001

Webster, C., Sprott, J.B., & Doob, A.N. (2019). The will to change: Lessons from Canada's successful decarceration of youth. *Law and Society Review 53*(4), 1092–1131.

Windzio, M. (2006). Is there a deterrent effect of pains of imprisonment? The impact of "social costs" of first incarceration on the hazard rate of recidivism. *Punishment and Society, 8*(3), 341–64. https://doi.org/10.1177/1462474506064701

Zamble, E., & Porporino, F. (1988). *Coping, behaviour and adjustment in prison inmates*. New York, NY: Springer-Verlag.

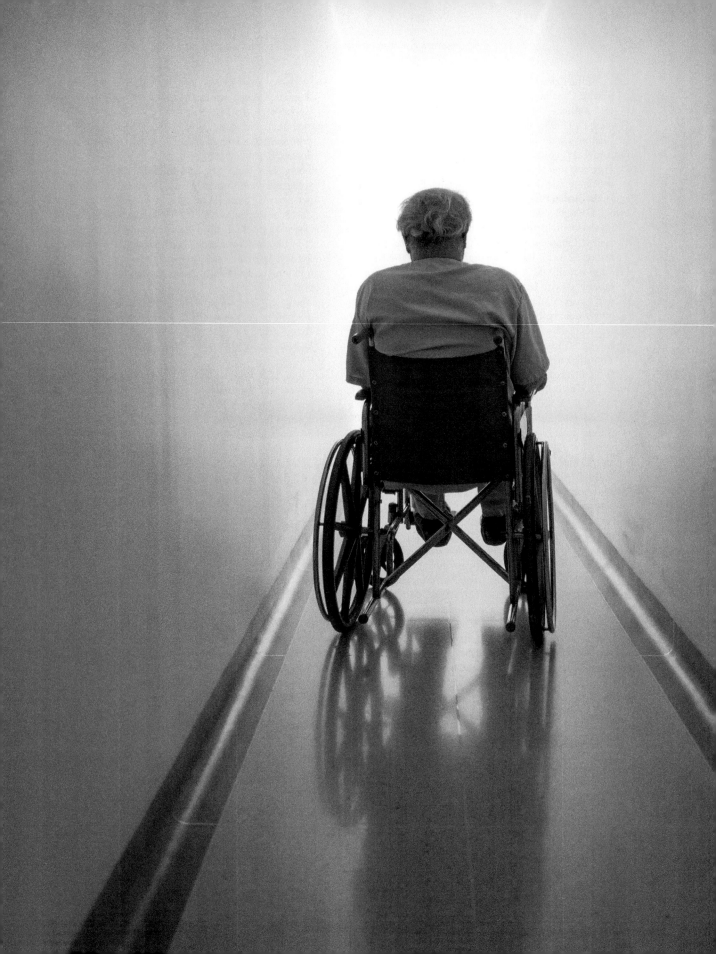

Aging Prisoners in the Canadian Federal Correctional System

11

Adelina Iftene

Learning Objectives

After reading this chapter, you should be able to:

- Understand the demographic shifts taking place in the federal correctional system, its causes, and its impacts.
- Understand the intersecting needs of individuals aging in prisons.
- Describe the challenges institutions face in meeting the needs of older prisoners.
- Describe the challenges older prisoners face in obtaining early release.
- Critically assess the impact of aging of the prison population on correctional facilities, prisoners, and the ability of administrators to uphold their legal obligations.
- Critically reflect on the changes needed within the correctional system and beyond to adequately respond to the shift in the prison demographic, and what such adequate responses might be.

Chapter Overview

Drawing on original statistical and quantitative data as well as governmental reports, this chapter provides an overview of the health-care, ethical, and legal challenges brought about by a shift in the federal prison demographic in Canada and the drastic increase in the number of incarcerated people considered "older." First, the chapter reviews the demographic and criminogenic data of incarcerated individuals over the age of 50, with a specific focus on the health profiles of these individuals. Second, the chapter provides a description of the legal obligations Correctional Service Canada has toward those in its custody and raises concerns regarding how these obligations are discharged in relation to aging prisoners. The lack of medication, medical personnel, and other health resources; the inadequacy of prison infrastructure; and institutions' inappropriate disciplinary responses to prisoners' health

needs are also highlighted to demonstrate the need for reform. Third, the chapter describes the difficulties older prisoners face in accessing release, despite the well-documented inverse relation between reoffending and aging, with the aim of encouraging the reader to think critically about the current functioning of correctional mechanisms.

Introduction

The last couple of decades have seen a significant increase in the aging of prison populations worldwide (Aday, 2003; Colsher, Wallace, Loebffelholz, & Sales, 1992; Fazel, Hope, O'Donnell, Piper, & Jacoby, 2001; Hayes, 2017; Lemieux, Dyeson, & Castiglione, 2002). This phenomenon has not escaped the correctional landscape in Canada, and in particular the **federal**

correctional system, where the number of people considered "older" has doubled over the last decade. Literature is inconsistent in defining "older prisoners," with the lower limit of seniority placed between 45 and 65 years of age. There is, however, some agreement that individuals who experience incarceration tend to age faster because they have significantly more health problems than their community counterparts. This often leads to them exhibiting health problems present in individuals at least 10 years older than them who have never experienced incarceration (Office of the Correctional Investigator [OCI] & Canadian Human Rights Commission [CHRC], 2019). In Canada, 50 is often used as the lower limit of seniority for prisoners (OCI & CHRC, 2019).

Until recently, the aging of the prison population has received little attention, and older prisoners are not formally recognized, in legislation or policies, as a category of **vulnerable individuals** with different or enhanced needs (OCI & CHRC, 2019). In the last few years however, some new research (see Iftene, 2017b, 2017c, 2019) as well as reports from the Office of the Correctional Investigator (see, for example, Sapers, 2010, 2012a, 2016; Zinger, 2018; OCI & CHRC, 2019) have emerged showing that older prisoners present intersecting physical and mental health problems (including physical disabilities, chronic pain, terminal illnesses, and dementia); are more vulnerable to abuse; and have difficulties engaging in programs designed for younger prisoners but which are, nonetheless, mandatory to them for successful early release applications. **Aging/older prisoners** are the most expensive cohort to incarcerate (see Sapers, 2015; OCI & CHRC, 2019), feel both the lack of adequate prison health care and the overall negative consequences of incarceration most intensely, while being at the lowest risk of disciplinary incidents or of reoffending once released (see Sapers, 2011). Correctional Service Canada (CSC) appears ill prepared, in terms of infrastructure, expertise, and resources, to address these unique needs.

The goal of this chapter is twofold. First, this chapter helps the reader understand the unique challenges older prisoners face, as a vulnerable group, in federal penitentiaries. Second, it highlights the disconnect that sometimes exists between the legal obligations administrators have toward vulnerable prisoners and the way they discharge those obligations. To achieve these goals, I will draw on a quantitative and qualitative study I conducted with 197 men over 50 years of age in seven federal penitentiaries (all levels of security).[1] Additionally,

I will draw from data obtained from different governmental agencies, including the CSC, the **Parole Board of Canada (PBC)** and the OCI, either from published reports or through Access to Information requests.

Later in the chapter, I will offer an overview of the demographic shift that has occurred in federal prisons over the last decade. This shift has led to a higher number of older, higher-needs, and lower-risk individuals being incarcerated for longer periods. This population demands significant health care and accommodation—each of which I will address in turn—and, arguably, these demands make incarceration more difficult for members of this population. I will then discuss the legal obligations prison administrators owe to vulnerable individuals and how those obligations are being discharged in relation to the needs of older prisoners. The chapter also covers an important aspect of anyone's sentence: re-entry to the community. This issue is more broadly discussed in Chapter 6, along with reintegration and rehabilitation; here I will focus on some of the release options and the challenges older prisoners face in accessing these mechanisms. I conclude by inviting the reader to contemplate some of the potential legal and ethical implications of the current status quo of older prisoners and how best to address their needs in the future.

Facing Old Age in a Federal Prison: Demographics and Needs

Demographics

In 2017, the percentage of people over the age of 50 serving time in a federal prison reached nearly 25 per cent, a twofold increase in the last decade (Public Safety Canada, 2017). This increase can be explained by a multitude of factors that include "tough on crime" agendas (which take away the sentencing judge's discretion to show leniency toward individuals who were old or sick), which have resulted in more mandatory minimum sentences, longer sentences, tougher criteria for release,[2] and an increase in the prosecution of **historic crimes** (that is, more individuals are being convicted for crimes, especially sexual abuse, committed many decades ago). These realities are partially reflected in the fact that the number of people admitted to prison over the age of 50 has increased over the last decade by 44 per cent, despite the fact that the overall number of admissions to prison has decreased slightly (Public Safety Canada, 2017).

The growing number of older individuals can also be attributed to an increase in individuals who are serving life or **indeterminate sentences** (Public Safety Canada, 2017), which are the most common types of sentences served by older prisoners (OCI & CHRC, 2019).

Among the incarcerated individuals over age 50, three groups can be identified (see Figure 11.1). First, individuals who serve long sentences (10 years or more) and have been in prison prior to turning 50, form 24 per cent of older prisoner population. Second, 28 per cent are individuals who have been sentenced later in life. Finally, 45 per cent are recidivists (individuals who have been in and out of prison throughout their lives; OCI & CHRC, 2019).

The increasing frequency of life and indeterminate sentences coupled with growing admissions of prisoners aged 50 and older suggests that the number of incarcerated people over 50 will continue to grow (OCI & CHRC, 2019). This, in turn, presents a myriad of medical, ethical, and legal challenges that prison administrators must grapple with.

Intersecting Health Needs in Older Age

Across age groups, there is a much higher prevalence of blood-borne diseases (such as hepatitis C and HIV) in incarcerated populations than in community populations. Some evidence suggests that the prevalence of cardiovascular diseases, diabetes, asthma, and other respiratory diseases is also higher in incarcerated people (Kouyoumdjian, Schuler, Matheson, & Hwang, 2016).

Rates of illness appear to be particularly high in older individuals. Individuals admitted to federal custody over the age of 50 tend to have, at admission, more chronic problems (such as cardiovascular disease, diabetes, prostate issues, arthritis, cancer history, and so on) and physical disabilities than any other age group (Stewart et al., 2015).

Of the 197 individuals interviewed for the aging prisoner study, 99 per cent reported suffering from at least one medical condition, 37 per cent suffered from four to seven different medical conditions, and 28 per cent suffered from eight to sixteen medical conditions (Iftene, 2019; see Figure 11.2). Commonly reported diseases included arthritis, asthma, cancer, digestive problems, severe heart problems, diabetes, back problems, and circulation problems. Issues such as incontinence, reported by 14 per cent of the sample, were particularly challenging in the prison environment:

> The officers find it [wetting myself] hilarious. Once, I was struggling to change my soiled clothes. This officer asked me if he should call an ambulance (XX, 81, in prison for 22 years). (Iftene, 2019, p. 39).

In terms of physical disabilities, 54 per cent of the participants reported having mobility problems that interfered with their daily activities. Walking, getting on and off the bed, and climbing stairs were particularly challenging. Disability was often associated with chronic pain. Pain was reported as one of the most debilitating aspects of life in prison and was reported by 62 per cent of the participants (Iftene, 2019).

When compared to their physical health, older prisoners' mental health shows similar trends: Rates of mental illness are higher in prison than in the community, and this is true for all age groups (for more on this see Chapter 7). The international literature indicates that rates of mental illness in older incarcerated individuals is higher in comparison to both a younger cohort of incarcerated individuals and older people in the community (Aday, 2003). In the aging prisoner study, 39 per cent of the individuals interviewed reported being diagnosed with at least one chronic mental health condition, including depression, anxiety, dementia, memory loss, and suicidal ideation (Iftene, 2017c). The 5 per cent rate of dementia was particularly surprising, especially because those reporting it tended to be prisoners in maximum security and, more generally, people serving life sentences. Similar or higher rates of dementia among incarcerated individuals have been identified in the literature (Aday, 2003; Williams, Goodwin, Baillargeon, Ahalt, & Walter, 2012).[3]

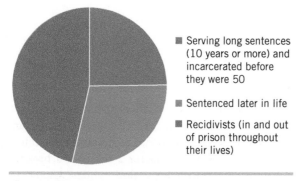

Figure 11.1 Incarcerated Individuals over Age 50

Source: Based on data from OCI & CHRC (2019, p. 12).

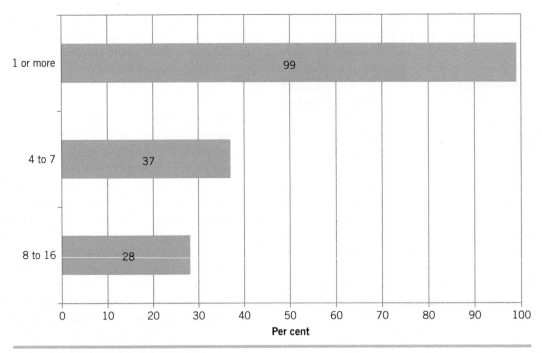

Figure 11.2 Number of Medical Conditions
Source: Iftene (2019, p. 42).

Given this trend, there is consensus that the prison environment is not only ill-suited for supporting individuals suffering from these conditions, but likely exacerbates their symptoms (Fazel, McMillan, & O'Donnell, 2002; Maschi, Kwak, Ko, & Morrissey, 2012).

One individual interviewed described the struggles of living with dementia:

> I have been here [maximum security] for a while. Last year I was diagnosed with Stage 1 dementia. I don't think anything worse can happen. I am serving life and no one will release me directly from here. However, by the time I will be transferred to a lower level of security I will not even remember my name. That's scary. That's very scary (LL, maximum security, in prison for seven years). (Iftene, 2019, p. 56).

Finally, with an increase in aging prisoners comes an increase in the number of people dying inside following a long-fought battle with an illness. In the aging prisoner study, 4 per cent of individuals over 50 were **terminally ill** (Iftene, 2017a). This helps explain the increase in natural **deaths in custody** over the last decade. The CSC noted that over a 16-year period, from 2000–01 to 2015–16, 66 per cent (857) of all deaths in custody were "**natural deaths**" (CSC, 2017). The leading

causes of death, overlapping with the most prevalent diseases among older prisoners more broadly, were cancer, cardiovascular illness, respiratory diseases, liver issues and infections. During the same period of time, the average age at death was 55. More recently, the OCI reported that over a seven-year period, the average age at death was 60 (Zinger, 2018). Both numbers are significantly lower in prison than the average age of death in the community (which is around 82; Statistics Canada, 2018). It is also worth noting that the most common sentence among those dying of natural causes was the indeterminate sentence (which, as described, is common among older individuals and on the rise overall; CSC, 2017).

Responses to Needs

Legal Obligations

In Canada, incarcerated individuals do not exist in a legal vacuum. Rather, their rights are stated and guaranteed by the constitution, national statutes, and international instruments. Chapter 2 provides a broader review of the prison legislation, while Chapter 14 deals specifically with some of these rights and their sources.

I will only mention a few of these rights here to provide context for the realities described below. First, the CSC has certain duties arising from Canada's international commitments. For instance, Canada is signatory to the United Nation's (1990) *Basic Principles for Treatment of Prisoners* and the United Nations (2015) *Standard Minimum Rules for the Treatment of Prisoners* (known as the Mandela Rules), both of which recommend that prisoners have access to the same health-care services as available in the community (see Chapter 2). Furthermore, the Mandela Rules require that prisons protect and promote the rights of people with special needs (Rule 2.2) and that people with physical or mental disabilities are adequately accommodated (Rule 5.2) so that the suffering brought about by the deprivation of liberty is not heightened by other prison practices (Rule 3). In addition, individuals with mental or physical disabilities should not be placed in solitary confinement (United Nations, 2015, Rule 45).

Second, the CSC is bound by a legal duty of care owed to those in its custody (Criminal Code, s. 197(1)(i); Iftene, Hanson, & Manson, 2014; see also *Levasseur v. R.,* 2004; *Lipcsei v. Central Saanich (District),* 1994; *Steele v. Ontario,* 1993; *Sutherland v. R.,* 2003; *Swayze v. Dafoe,* 2002). This duty of care dictates that the services available to prisoners must be adequate at all times, even where community services are not (OCI, 2013, p. 17).

Third, legislative provisions in Canada's Correctional and Conditional Release Act (CCRA) set out legal obligations for prison administrators. Specifically, section 86 states that an individual must have access to essential health care, including mental health care, and reasonable access to non-essential health care, both of which are to be provided at "professionally accepted standards." In light of this, section 121 of the CCRA has been interpreted, in correlation with section 748 of the Criminal Code, as bestowing a responsibility on the CSC to seek alternatives to incarceration for "palliative or terminally ill offenders" (OCI, 2013, p. 23). This means that the CSC must support palliative or terminally ill prisoners who apply for release on grounds related to health and ensure their safe transition to the community or to community institutions (OCI, 2013).

Finally, the CCRA also includes legislative provisions targeted at bettering vulnerable populations' experiences in prison. These provisions require that the CSC's practices and policies respond to "the special needs of women, aboriginal peoples, persons requiring mental health care and other groups" (s. 4(g)).

Accommodation based on health and age is also required under the Canadian Human Rights Act (s. 3) and is constitutionally protected by the equality guarantee entrenched in the Canadian Charter of Rights and Freedoms (s. 15).

Institutional Realities

Inadequate Access to Health Care

The inadequacies of prison health-care systems have been discussed in the literature (see Iftene, 2017b; Kouyoumdjian et al., 2016; Miller, 2013a, 2013b). One of the most striking deficiencies is the lack of medical professionals, which leads to long wait times, even for urgent matters.[4] For example, most institutions do not have a 24/7 nurse on site (Iftene, 2017b). The aging prisoner study showed that in most institutions the wait time to see a nurse, regardless of the problem, was between three days and a week. The availability of specialized care varied from institutions to institution. Most institutions had reasonable access to a dentist (with a wait time of about two months for non-emergencies), but the maximum security facility also had a similar wait time for dental emergencies. The optometrist was generally available within three months. The psychiatrist was in very high demand, and in some places the wait time to see one was years if the prisoner was not deemed to be a suicide risk. For other specialists, like oncologists, cardiologists, surgeons, and urologists, prisoners had to be sent to a community hospital, and the wait time was generally over a year. There were also reports of individuals being denied access to specialized treatment due to lack of resources, including a psychologist (14 per cent), optometrist (5 per cent), and cardiologist (14 per cent; 43 per cent were waiting to see a cardiologist at the time of their interview; Iftene, 2019).

Further, the provision of medication is regularly interrupted (Kouyoumdjian et al., 2016). This is because physicians' autonomy to prescribe a course of treatment appears to be restricted because of ill-defined reasons (Sapers, 2015). For example, certain medications are of limited availability according to the CSC **National Drug Formulary**.[5] These facts help explain why health care leads in the number of complaints the OCI receives every year (see Sapers, 2016; Zinger, 2018).

Health-care inadequacies tend to have more devastating effects on groups of people that have heightened needs, such as older individuals. First, pain medication availability presents some of the most serious restrictions, since it is crucial for a group where the incidence of pain is high. The only prescription pain-killers available in penitentiaries are Tylenol 3 and, in special cases, methadone or morphine. The National Drug Formulary also mentions that all community pre-scriptions for painkillers will be changed to Tylenol 3, since it is the cheapest compound (CSC, 2016).

This reality was confirmed in the aging prisoner study: Out of 62 per cent of participants who reported regular pain, nearly all were treated with Tylenol 3. The consequences to the prisoners are dire: 43 per cent of participants who received pain treatment reported that it is ineffective in alleviating their suffering (Iftene, 2017b; see also OCI & CHRC, 2019):

> When I came in after my accident they put me on morphine for my headaches [the individual suffered from a brain injury as a result of a car accident]. I was on it for a couple weeks and it was not working. After two weeks they went back to my chart and realized I was a heroin addict and that's why it didn't work. So now I am back on Tylenol 3. Doesn't do any good (RR, 53, in prison for eight years). (Iftene, 2019, p. 49)

Restrictions on the availability of medication is not the only rule that limits prisons' ability to address symptoms such as pain. In all prisons, direct observa-tion therapy is applied. This means that, for security reasons, medication intake is supervised. Medication distribution takes place once or twice daily: Dosages are adjusted to accommodate this process. Thus, cer-tain classes or dosages of medication are automatically barred, regardless of how sick the individual is or how inefficient the alternative treatment is (Sapers, 2012b). The medication pickup model itself also hinders access, especially for individuals who are significantly sick or disabled. In most institutions, medication needs to be picked up in person by standing in line, sometimes for an hour or two. In some institutions, lines form outside, regardless of the weather (Iftene, 2017b). This can prove insurmountable to the sickest prisoner, who would benefit the most from accessing their medication:

> My gall bladder has been removed and I have diabetes and circulation problems. It's difficult to stand out-doors daily, for hours, with a diaper on, to pick up my pills (FF, 52, in prison for six years). (Iftene, 2019, p. 50)

The chronic shortage of medical staff and the absence of specialists is problematic not only because it creates

long wait times, but also because it decreases the qual-ity of treatment and care people receive. Due to over-lapping health problems, older prisoners take a number of different medications daily. All of these interact with each other and may have different effects in older age, beyond what a primary health-care provider is able to identify and address. Prisoners will have their medi-cations, including psychiatric medication, renewed or unchanged for decades without being seen by a doctor. In certain federal prisons, for instance, one psychiatrist and one psychologist serve up to 600 people. This only allows for five-minute visits per person every two years (Iftene, 2019). It is thus not surprising that certain age-specific conditions, such as dementia, are often mis-diagnosed as alcohol withdrawal or behaviour issues and go unaddressed for years.

The lack of specialists means that federal prisons are often reliant on community doctors. In addition to the wait times to see a specialist, visits to community doctors are dependent on the availability of officers to escort pris-oners to their community appointments. For instance, in one of the minimum security facilities visited for the aging prisoner study, where 70 per cent of the population was over the age of 50 and significantly burdened by dis-ease, including terminal illnesses, there were two officers available per day to escort prisoners into the commun-ity. This means that sometimes, even if they had been granted an escorted **temporary absence**, prisoners could find that their hospital visit to see a doctor (for which they would have waited months) or their chemother-apy or dialysis session was cancelled because of a lack of available escorting officers that day (Iftene, 2019).

Finally, with the increase of people spending the end of their lives in prisons, the demands for palliative care are increasing. There is little doubt that a prison cell or a prison infirmary is an ill-suited place for provid-ing end-of-life care, even in the best of circumstances (Zinger, 2017; OCI & CHRC, 2019). The CSC states that it provides palliative care to dying prisoners on a regular basis (CSC, 2013). However, the health-care inadequa-cies presented above call this assertion into question. Furthermore, it is unclear how claims insinuating that palliative care is provided in prisons are supported, be-cause there are no palliative-care specialists working in the prison system, there is a shortage of mental health specialists, many institutions do not have 24/7 med-ical personnel, and adequate pain management is not available. All of these aspects are inherent requirements for effective palliative care (National Cancer Institute, 2014).

Challenging Infrastructure

With a 54 per cent physical disability rate, older individuals often face ambulatory difficulties, may not be able to live independently, and may need assistance with their daily living routines. The OCI has pointed out that the older, inaccessible institutions that currently form the majority of federal prisons present a challenge for an increasing number of people (Sapers, 2011). For example, double bunking is still a reality in many institutions. Six out of the seven institutions visited for the aging prisoner study were double bunking individuals, including older individuals. This poses a variety of challenges for older people, among which include climbing onto the top bunk (especially when some bunks do not have a ladder); being bunked with a younger prisoner who listens to loud music, leaves windows open after working out, or who goes to bed late; the humiliation of sharing a room when one is incontinent; and the degrading situation where one has to crawl into the room after leaving the wheelchair outside because it could not be manoeuvred inside (Iftene, 2019). The long distances between buildings make it difficult for prisoners living with a physical disability or using a walker to get to different activities by the required time. This is particularly challenging in winter, where the pathways are often not properly cleared and de-iced:

> He yelled and screamed and hit the first couple times I pissed myself at night. He was sleeping in the bed underneath. The diapers help but it depends . . . Then he gave me the lower bunk. He wasn't reasonable but didn't like being pissed on either. I guess in the end, regardless of the reasons, he was more reasonable than the CSC, who refused to assign me a different cell (FF, 52, in prison for six years). (Iftene, 2019)

Furthermore, some of the institutions lack basic accessibility infrastructure, such as bathroom handrails or accessible toilets. In one minimum security facility, all rooms were upstairs and no elevators connected the upper level to the kitchen and programming area downstairs. In another minimum security facility, individuals lived in separate houses spread across the perimeters of the institution but did not have any emergency buttons in the bathrooms (Iftene, 2019). The fear of slipping and falling was apparent throughout the interviews carried out there. In fact, 35 per cent of individuals across institutions reported having slipped and fallen at least once within the previous 12 months

(Iftene, 2019). The leading causes were slipping on inadequately cleaned yards or pathways in winter, falling from top bunks, slipping in the shower, and falling down the stairs. This situation was compellingly summarized by one elderly participant:

> I fall mostly on the stairs because I can't avoid them [the rooms were upstairs; everything else was downstairs]. I need to eat and I need my pills. I also can't avoid the shower. I wet myself and I need to clean up. Otherwise I wouldn't ever wash. Not since I know I may bash my head every time I come out of the shower (XX, 81, in prison for 22 years). (Iftene, 2019, p. 46)

The OCI has also, in its report on "Aging and Death in Prison," described the significant challenges infrastructure poses for aging prisoners (OCI & CHRC, 2019).

Increased Isolation and Vulnerability

Increased health needs and older age are determinants for increased isolation and vulnerability. The OCI has raised concerns regarding the fact that, compared to younger prisoners, older individuals spend most of their time locked up, with little stimulation (Sapers, 2011). The reasons for this are multiple.

First, older individuals engage less with their peers, avoid group activities, and spend more time in their cells reading or watching TV. This behaviour pattern is due to unaddressed pain, health conditions such as incontinence, and physical infrastructure that ignores mobility issues.

Second, most prison programs are not targeted toward older individuals. In many institutions, the only programs available are either classes for GED (high school) completion or vocational programs that prepare people for getting a job upon release. These have limited value for a retired and sick 70-year-old. However, in some institutions there is a chronic lack of space for programming of any kind (Iftene, 2019). It appears that where space is limited, younger people with shorter sentences will always have priority, and this leaves many of the older prisoners serving life completely idle. By the same token, because half of the older adult population is serving a life sentence (and often have spent decades in prison), many would partake in relevant and irrelevant programs alike just to pass the time. Indeed, some of the participants in the aging prisoner study declared that they have been attending AA and NA meetings for years, even though they never had a substance-use issue, only because those were the programs they had access to.

Third, older individuals may choose to interact less with others as a safety precaution. As reported by the OCI, older individuals enjoy a lesser social status within prison. In combination with reduced physical strength, they tend to be victims of bullying, harassment, manipulation, extortion, and ridicule more often (see Sapers, 2011). The perceived loss of masculinity in the prison environment as individuals age has been documented outside of Canada as well (Mann, 2012, 2016).

> I keep to myself because really . . . if I fear something is that I will piss myself in front of them when I don't have a diaper on. And then there is no hiding that I am really weak (PZ, 65, in prison for 26 years). (Iftene, 2019, p. 39)

In the aging prisoner study, over half of the individuals interviewed reported having suffered regular abuse by their peers, and 48 per cent reported suffering abuse at the hands of staff. The latter tended to take the form of ridicule (particularly name calling, like "old fart" or "grandpa"), humiliation, and pranks (such as tying their wheelchair to a table when the individual is sleeping, or hiding their walking aids; Iftene, 2019). Peer abuse was more diverse. In addition to the various types of abuse listed in Figure 11.3, 42 per cent of participants also reported having property stolen, in particular food and medication:

> I keep asking for new peer caregivers. They are useless. The one I have now is not bad. He fails to show up, like this morning I had to wheel myself here, and it's hard. But he is better than the last one. The last one I had was stealing my pills to sell them. I had him for a few months. It was hard time. I really need my pills (QQ, 63, in prison for eight years). (Iftene, 2019, p. 43)

In light of these trends, safety concerns were commonly reported. Over a quarter (29 per cent) said they were afraid for their safety at the moment of the interview, with 48 per cent reporting having felt in danger in prison at one point after turning 50. Thirteen per cent identified violations of safety as their greatest fear in prison (Iftene, 2017c). Safety concerns manifest in avoidance: Many of the participants in the study reported avoiding the gym or the

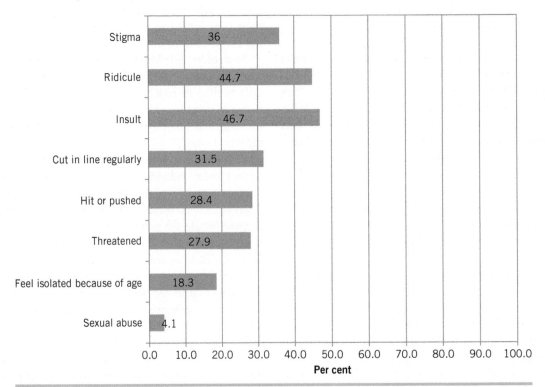

Figure 11.3 Types of Abuse Suffered by Older Prisoners
Source: Based on data from Iftene (2019, p. 75).

exercise yard in particular, "because [that] is where things go down" (Iftene, 2019, p. 52). The gym and the weight pit are the places mostly associated with masculinity and strength. Numerous individuals claimed they were bullied or pushed aside from the gym for being too weak or too slow. A significant number of individuals stopped using the gym altogether in an attempt to hide their weakness and protect themselves. This is likely problematic, as the individuals who kept active and still exercised reported less mental problems (34 per cent) than those who did not (49 per cent; Iftene, 2019).

Anxiety tied to increased vulnerability, isolation due to lack of stimulation or motivation and mobility issues, and the lack of exercise because of safety concerns may have devastating effects on mental well-being. The outlook for mental well-being is not much better when one turns to the protective measures in place to address these concerns. As described below, the older and sicker the individual is, the more likely it is that they will be placed in segregation, either for protection or to manage unwanted behaviour. Regardless of the reason, segregation is punitive in nature and only exacerbates isolation and mental decay.

Punitive Responses

Use of segregation was not commonly reported by this age group (for the use of segregation generally, see Chapter 14). Similarly, the rate of disciplinary incidents was relatively low. About 23 per cent had spent time in segregation since turning 50, while 31 per cent had been charged with disciplinary offences since turning 50 (Iftene, 2019). However, both the number of physical conditions or the number of mental illness diagnoses seemed to influence or be influenced by the time individuals spent in segregation (see Table 11.1).[6] While some individuals were placed in solitary confinement for protection, health also seemed to influence placement in disciplinary segregation.

Individuals with mental illnesses were more often sent to segregation (including disciplinary segregation) than their healthier counterparts (36 per cent as opposed to 15 per cent). Similarly, of the people who requested segregation for their own safety, the majority reported suffering from a psychiatric condition (73 per cent; Iftene, 2019). Further, other forms of disciplinary action aside from segregation were more common among individuals who reported suffering from some

Case Study: Mark, 60, Medium Security

Mark is an Indigenous prisoner serving a life sentence without possibility of parole for 25 years for first-degree murder. At the time of the interview, Mark had already served 18 years in prison.

In the months prior to the interview, Mark was diagnosed with stage 1 dementia. For three years his erratic behaviour had been misconstrued as rowdy behaviour. Even though he was classified as a minimum security prisoner, he was moved back to medium security so he could be placed in solitary confinement, where his behaviour was easier to manage.

While in segregation, Mark's mental state declined sharply, probably in no small part due to the lack of stimulation. He was eventually diagnosed with dementia and moved to a quieter unit. He is nonetheless constantly at the tail end of assaults, having food stolen and being verbally abused—for example, being called "pops" or "old fart." As a result, he returns to segregation at regular intervals.

In addition to dementia, Mark lives with eight other chronic conditions, including multiple sclerosis, and

takes 12 different pills daily. He also uses a walker to move around. The combination of dementia, mobility limitations, chronic pain, and fear of abuse leads him to spend almost the entire day in his room.

Mark's daughter and her family are willing to look after him in the community; however, there are few options for Mark to be released at this stage in his sentence. As he is serving life without possibility of parole for 25 years, he is not yet eligible to apply for parole. With his mental health continuing to decline, it is not clear if he will be able to apply by the time he has served 25 years. In addition, parole by exception, Canada's version of compassionate release, does not allow for the release of people serving life unless they are terminally ill. As serious as dementia and multiple sclerosis are, they are not considered "terminal" (in the sense that death is likely to occur within a few months). While Mark could apply for the Royal Prerogative of Mercy, he had not at the time of the interview and it was unclear if there was anyone willing to help him with the application. In addition, Royal Prerogatives of Mercy are rarely granted.

Table 11.1 Time Spent in Segregation per Number of Physical Conditions

Time spent in segregation for disciplinary reasons	Number of Conditions			Total
	1–4	5–7	8–16	
No	38.1% (61)	37.5% (60)	24.4% (39)	100% (160)
Yes	21.6% (8)	32.4% (12)	45.9% (17)	100% (37)

Chi-square = 7.467, df = 2, p = .024
Source: Based on data from Iftene (2019, p. 51).

sort of mental illness. Importantly, this reinforces the likelihood that disease-related behaviour may be misconstrued as disobedience (see Table 11.2).

The disciplinary responses of institutions to mental health conditions, as well as the increased use of segregation for people with both physical and mental health problems, reflect the larger issue of institutional inability to respond to the medical needs of older prisoners in a meaningful way. This inability also reflects the need for better training for first responders, so they can differentiate between medical and behavioural issues. Addressing the issue of institutional inability is important, especially because punitive responses further isolate and stigmatize individuals from a cohort that already tends to be withdrawn. More physical isolation means less stimulation and has negative impacts on the mental and physical well-being of a group that already presents high rates of illnesses. Furthermore, punitive responses may negatively impact the individual's record and thus reduce their chance of obtaining early release or enjoying privileges. As discussed below, all of this may unduly raise hurdles that prevent the return of some older prisoners to the community.

Release

Regular Parole

As a cohort, older individuals have some of the most difficult medical needs, are highly vulnerable, spend most of their time in isolation with little stimulation, and rank the lowest in terms of risk compared to other prison groups. This ranking is reflected in the overall low number of disciplinary incidents. Yet there is no evidence that these individuals receive **early release** in higher numbers than other prisoners. They appear to be subjected to the same rigid parole processes, and their vulnerabilities often prevent them from obtaining release as opposed to leading to it.

Early release processes have been described as bureaucratic, inefficient, and underutilized. Doob, Webster, and Manson (2014) analyzed the use of conditional release in the federal and provincial systems and concluded that it is used so little that if it were abolished altogether it would make little numeric difference (for example, the federally incarcerated population would increase by only 4.5 per cent). This is surprising, especially since the rate of reoffending for parolees is very low.[7] In the words of Doob and colleagues (2014), "if the purpose of parole is to facilitate the safe and peaceful reintegration of prisoners into society, it is failing" (p. 317).

Underutilization of parole is not the only problem. The parole process is also poorly regulated. Aside from the eligibility dates for different types of sentences, the CCRA and its regulations do not provide any other operational criteria that should be considered by parole board members in their conditional release decision making. It is, however, clear that the criteria used focus on risk posed and on reintegration into the community (s. 100). More criteria are provided by the Decision-Making Policy Manual for Board Members. The manual elaborates on certain factors, including criminal history, family relationships, employment,

Table 11.2 Disciplinary Charges per Mental Health Rates

Disciplinary Charges Since Turning 50	Does Prisoner Mention Mental Illness?		Total
	No	Yes (one or more)	
No	66.2% (90)	33.8% (46)	100% (136)
Yes	49.2% (30)	50.8% (31)	100% (61)

Chi-square = 5.109, df = 1, p = .024
Source: Based on data from Iftene (2019, p. 62).

substance use, the gravity of current offences, breaches of previous conditional releases, history of reoffending, history of violent behaviour, attempts to escape, recommendations of the sentencing judge, and victim impact statements. Other factors relate to the prisoner's involvement in correctional programs, diagnosis of a mental disorder, behaviour during incarceration, and whether the individual has a release plan. Signs of change in behaviour, revealed by the manner in which the prisoner completed their correctional plan, and by professional report assessments[8] (that is, a psychological report) are also important (Parole Board of Canada, 2018).

Similarly, a commissioner's directive mentions institutional behaviour and the completion of correctional plans (as well as attitude during completion) as information to be collected and presented to the parole board by the parole officer in each case (CSC, 2018). These factors are considered because the parole process is centred on not creating an undue risk to society (PBC, 2018). Nonetheless, many of the release criteria are geared toward rewarding "good behaviour" (which is not a stated purpose of early release) and are sometimes out of the prisoner's control. These include "motivation," fulfillment of the correctional plan, attitude and statements made by the offender, early engagement in the parole process, and securing employment upon release (Jackson & Stewart, 2009). At the same time, factors like health status, disability, the physical capacity of committing further crime, and age are not listed at all, even though they might more accurately predict the capacity of an individual to reoffend.

In 2010, Sapers (2012b), the former federal correctional investigator, identified four practical barriers to release: lack of efficiency in moving prisoners down security levels; program access and availability; case management and case preparation; and restricted access to discretionary and conditional release. Sapers (2012b) stated that in 2009, one in four prisoners had to waive, postpone, or withdraw their parole application because they were "waitlisted" and had not yet completed their programs. In addition, every day, only one in four individuals participate in a required program, generally because most prisoners are waitlisted. People who serve long periods of time (like half of the older prisoners) do not have access to these programs until well into their sentences and often past their parole dates (Sapers, 2012b).

In the aging prisoner study, only 33 per cent of the participants had not yet reached their first parole eligibility date. The rest had passed it and either did

not apply or had been rejected, sometimes repeatedly (Iftene, 2019). The reasons reported for rejection were similar to the reasons people gave for not applying and aligned with Sapers' (2012b) findings. For example, the inability to fulfill the requirements of their correctional plans was a big problem. More than half of the people serving life mentioned that they had not completed their correctional plan by their first parole eligibility date, generally because there were no spots available in the mandated program (Iftene, 2019). As well, the lack of post-release plans (including housing or jobs in the community) was a major reason participants reported both for not applying for parole and for being rejected for parole. In particular, the issue of having a job lined up upon release raises problems. Almost 45 per cent of the participants were over the age of 60, and some mentioned being already retired when they entered prison (Sapers, 2012b). Others just grew old in prison. While most participants were working in prison, they mentioned that at their age and level of disability, finding work on the outside would be exceedingly difficult. Finding housing without significant case management support was also challenging: Halfway houses may not be willing to take in sick individuals, while nursing or retirement homes may not take individuals coming out of prisons.

The success of parole applications seems at times to be random and unpredictable, and this impacts all prison groups. However, circumstances that may lower an individual's risk (disease, age, and so on) do not appear to be systematically considered, a fact that disproportionately impacts older people. In addition, older people are less likely to find jobs, housing, or, due to having to serve long sentences, to still have community support. The reasons for parole application rejections point out key institutional shortcomings, such as inadequate release plans (for example, a lack of support for individuals in finding housing and employment in the community) or lack of availability of required programs. Among other things, such shortcomings may lead to older prisoners spending longer periods in prison than needed from a public safety perspective.

Special Forms of Release

Canada does not have an adequate compassionate release process. Section 121 of the CCRA mandates that individuals who are (1) terminally ill, (2) whose physical or mental health is likely to suffer serious damage if the offender continues to be held in confinement, or (3) for whom continued confinement would constitute excessive hardship that was not reasonably foreseeable at the time the offender was sentenced may be considered for release even if they have not served the period of time mandated by law for regular parole. It is thus an exceptional form of release, known as **parole by exception**. However, this provision is significantly underused. In the study conducted, none of the participants, including the terminally ill ones, had heard of this option.

From data received through an Access to Information Act request, between 2007 and 2017 the Parole Board of Canada has received 28 requests under section 121 of the CCRA and granted 21 of these (75 per cent). All requests were based on serious medical conditions: brain injury, cancer, end-stage liver failure, ALS (amyotrophic lateral sclerosis, or Lou Gehrig's disease) mental health, and some unspecified terminal illnesses. The requests granted were based on the individual's condition being terminal for all but two situations in which the PBC determined that the condition was not terminal but continued incarceration would amount to excessive hardship under section 121(1)(c). The denied requests included a case of end-stage liver failure with a poor prognosis requiring palliative care, a case of stage 4 cancer with a prognosis of weeks to a few months, and a case of severe mental illness with suicidal ideation.[9] The low number of requests is surprising given that during a similar period of time (2005–15) there were 350 natural deaths in custody, the majority of which were expected (CSC, 2017).

There are a multitude of reasons why compassionate release is not being used (Iftene, 2017a). First, individuals serving life are excluded from the application of this provision unless they have proof that their condition is terminal. Second, this form of parole must be supported by the CSC, in particular the parole officer, otherwise the case will not make it before the parole board (thus, unlike for regular parole, there is no automatic right to file an application at some point). This is not a task that many case workers appear willing to stand behind (Sapers, 2015). Third, the medical evidence is onerous. Proof of "terminal illness" or "excessive hardship" due to illness are required, but these terms are not defined anywhere in the legislation or policy. Fourth, the parole board retains discretion and it continues to use ill-defined criteria in granting this form of parole, such as "attitude during incarceration," "completion of correctional programs," and the nature of the crime committed.[10] Arguably, these criteria are irrelevant if release is to be granted on health grounds for individuals who pose a low risk to society by disease itself.

Under section 748 of the Criminal Code, individuals may have their sentence commutated through the Royal Prerogative of Mercy and will spend the remainder of their sentence in the community under supervision. While Commissioner's Directive 712-1 (a policy document regulating the application of parole provisions) states that non-terminally ill prisoners serving a life sentence are eligible to apply for the Royal Prerogative of Mercy (CSC, 2018), such a release has not been granted to anyone in decades (Sapers, 2011, 2016).

It is problematic that Canada does not have a form of compassionate or medical-based release and that old and sick individuals are left at the mercy of the regular parole system. With its focus on community reintegration and post-release productivity, long waiting times and bureaucratic requirements, statutory retributivist demands that every single individual spend a one-size-fits-all, pre-established proportion of time in custody before even being eligible to apply, the Canadian parole system is at odds with a growing population whose needs cannot be met behind bars and who may present a reduced risk to society.

Conclusion

Prison systems are under strict international, constitutional, and statutory obligations to protect the people in their custody, to uphold their rights, and to meet their needs. Shifts in prison demographics, especially increasing numbers of vulnerable individuals with intersecting needs, like aging prisoners, challenge Canada's commitment to the rule of law behind bars. Faced with overwhelming and complex issues such as dementia, terminal illness, and overlapping chronic and acute mental and physical conditions, the CSC is having a difficult time upholding its duty of care and other statutory health-care obligations. Security concerns limit the ability of an already-strained prison health-care system to prioritize the physical and mental integrity of high-needs prisoners. In addition, failure to provide appropriate programming and accommodation to the disabled and the sick raises both human rights and constitutional concerns under the Charter. The use of segregation and disciplinary measures to respond to what may be health-driven behaviour disproportionately impacts high-needs individuals and may increase their suffering. It also directly contradicts international recommendations like the Mandela Rules.

The CSC appears to be failing in its duties to seek alternatives to incarceration for those who are very sick or terminally ill. At the same time, the early release processes themselves are antiquated. This means that they often fail to account for the realities of the increasing number of people who may present a low risk to society due to age, health, or disability. Furthermore, the lack of a true compassionate release mechanism is a significant legislative and policy failure.

The only prison cohorts that are increasing in number are vulnerable sectors (Public Safety Canada, 2017), which includes aging prisoners. These trends suggest that the experiences described in this chapter will continue to replicate over the next decades, and the challenges they bring will not subside. The CSC would be well advised to develop a robust, evidence-based strategy, grounded in Canada's international commitments and legislative duties, that would result in adequate health care, accommodation, and programming for this cohort. More than that, this strategy should aim to create community relations and plan for systemic decarceration. However, when it comes to decarceration strategies for the old and the sick, the CSC is not the only one that fails to meet its duties and who needs to bear responsibility. Indeed, the PBC must develop policies and provide training to their members on how to assess applications coming from special-needs individuals. As well, the creation of better compassionate release mechanisms should be a legislative priority. Finally, investing in community resources and partners that could take over the responsibility of caring for the elderly and sick who get released and do not have family support is a governmental responsibility.

Review Questions

1. Why has the last decade brought about a significant shift in the age of the prison demographic?
2. What defining features may render older prisoners a "vulnerable population" even if not specifically listed as such in the legislation?
3. What are some of the ethical, medical, and legal concerns raised by the increasing number of people aging in prisons?
4. What kind of steps should the CSC take to adjust to the prison demographic shift?

Critical Thinking Questions

1. Why are older prisoners facing challenges in obtaining early release? Why is this problematic?
2. The chapter mentions that prisoners normally present with the health problems of someone at least 10 years older than them in the community. Can you think of potential reasons for that?
3. What features should a working compassionate release system contain?

Multimedia Suggestions

Aging in Prison
   This Instagram account (@aginginprison) records the lives of aging Americans in prison: https://www.instagram.com/aginginprison

Prison Terminal: The Last Days of Private Jack Hall
   This Academy Award–nominated documentary tells the story of the final months of a terminally ill prisoner in Iowa State Penitentiary: https://www.prisonterminal.com

"Getting Out Gray"
   This podcast episode features José Saldana, who was released from prison at the age of 66 after serving 38 years behind bars: https://www.grayareapodcast.nyc/reentry

Prisoners of Age
   This series of photographs and interviews features elderly inmates from prisons in both Canada and the United States since 1996: http://www.prisonersofage.com/project_project

"'There Isn't Anywhere to Go': Ontario Halfway House for Aging Inmates Addressing Gap in Prison System"
   This *CBC Radio* episode features Cliff Strong, a 75-year-old ex-prisoner who is staying in Haley House, a unique halfway house that houses mostly senior or

palliative federal offenders on parole: https://www.cbc.ca/radio/outintheopen/there-isn-t-anywhere- to-go-ontario-halfway-house-for-aging-inmates-addressing-gap-in-prison-system-1.4838918

Notes

1. For the description of the methodology employed for this study, see Iftene 2017c.
2. See the Safe Streets and Community Act, which brought about changes that are discussed more fully in Iftene and Manson (2012). See also the Protecting Canadians by Ending Sentence Discounts for Multiple Murders Act, which allows for periods of incarceration without possibility of parole of up to 75 years.
3. A large range is reported for dementia and cognitive impairment rates among prisoners—between 1 to 30 per cent. See Cipriani, Danti, Carlesi, and Di Fiorino (2017).
4. Information obtained from Document A 2017-0302 (2018), sent from Correctional Service Canada in response to an Access to Information Act request.
5. See CSC (2016), a document sent from Correctional Service Canada in response to an Access to Information Act request.
6. For an overview of the influence of solitary confinement on the physical health of older prisoners, see Williams (2016).
7. In the fiscal year of 2012–13, only three people on parole for violent offences had their parole revoked, compared to 1,190 who successfully completed their full parole. See Doob, Webster, and Manson (2014), and Zinger (2012).
8. The content of the case managers' report is regulated by Commissioner's Directive CD 710-1: Progress against the Correctional Plan. It stipulates that the report will document the institutional adjustment and attitude of the prisoner, the programs he participated in, and his institutional employment history, as well as the professional counselling he received. For more details, see Correctional Service Canada (2018).
9. Information obtained from "Parole by Exception 2007–2017," a document received in response to an Access to Information Act request.
10. Information obtained from "Parole by Exception 2007–2017," a document received in response to an Access to Information Act request.

References

Aday, R.H. (2003) *Aging prisoners*. Westport, CT: Greenwood Publishing Group.

Cipriani, G., Danti, S., Carlesi, C., & Di Fiorino, M. (2017). Old and dangerous: Prison and dementia. *Journal of Forensic and Legal Medicine, 51*, 40–44.

Colsher, P.L., Wallace, R.B., Loebffelholz, P.L., & Sales, M. (1992). Health status of older male prisoners: A comprehensive survey. *American Journal of Public Health, 82*(6), 881–84.

Correctional Service Canada (2013). *Mortality review for deaths by natural causes*. Ottawa, ON: Author.

Correctional Service Canada. (2016). National Drug Formulary. Obtained through an Access to Information Act request.

Correctional Service Canada. (2017). *Annual report on deaths in custody 2015/2016*. No. SR-17-02. Retrieved from: http://www.csc-scc.gc.ca/research/092/005008-3010-en.pdf

Correctional Service Canada. (2018). Progress against the correctional plan. Commissioner's Directive 710-1. Retrieved from http://www.csc-scc.gc.ca/politiques-et-lois/710-1-cd-eng.shtml

Doob A., Webster C.M., & Manson A. (2014). Zombie parole: The withering of conditional release in Canada. *Criminal Law Quarterly, 61*(3), 301–28.

Fazel, S., Hope, T., O'Donnell, I., Piper, M., & Jacoby, R. (2001). Health of elderly male prisoners: Worse than the general population, worse than the younger prisoners. *Age and Ageing, 30*, 403–7.

Fazel, S., McMillan, J., & O'Donnell, I. (2002). Dementia in prison: Ethical and legal implications. *Journal of Medical Ethics, 28*, 156–9.

Hayes, A. (2017). Aging inside: Older adults in prison. In B.S. Elger, C. Ritter, & H. Stover (Eds), *Emerging issues in prison health* (pp. 1–12). Dordrecht, Netherlands: Springer.

Iftene, A. (2017a). The case for a new compassionate release statutory provision. *Alberta Law Review, 54*(4), 929–54.

Iftene, A. (2017b). The pains of incarceration: Aging, rights and policy in federal penitentiaries. *Canadian Journal of Criminology and Criminal Justice, 59*(1), 63–93.

Iftene, A. (2017c). Unlocking the doors to Canadian older inmate mental health data: Rates and potential legal responses. *International Journal of Law and Psychiatry, 47*, 36–44.

Iftene, A. (2019). *Punished for aging: Vulnerability, rights and access to justice in Canadian federal penitentiaries*. Toronto, ON: University of Toronto Press.

Iftene, A., Hanson, L., & Manson, A. (2014). Tort claims and Canadian prisoners. *Queen's Law Journal, 39*(2), 655.

Iftene, A., & Manson, A. (2012). Recent crime legislation: The challenge for prison health care. *Canadian Medical Association Journal, 185*(10), 886–9.

Jackson, M., & Stewart, G. (2009). A flawed compass: A human rights analysis of the roadmap to strengthening public safety. Retrieved from http://www.justicebehindthewalls.net/resources/news/flawed_Compass.pdf

Kouyoumdjian, F., Schuler, A., Matheson, F.I., & Hwang, S.W. (2016). Health status of prisoners in Canada: Narrative review. *Canadian Family Physician 62*(3), 215–22.

Lemieux, C.M., Dyeson, T.B., & Castiglione, B. (2002). Revisiting the literature on prisoners who are older: Are we wiser? *The Prison Journal, 82*, 440–58.

Levasseur v. R. (2004). FC 976.

Lipcsei v. Central Saanich (District). (1994). 8 BCLR (3d) 325. Retrieved from https://www.canlii.org/en/bc/bcsc/doc/1994/1994canlii16701/1994canlii16701.html?resultIndex=1

Mann, N. (2012). *Doing harder time? The experiences of an ageing male prison population in England and Wales.* Farnham, UK: Ashgate.

Mann, N. (2016). Older age, harder time: Ageing and imprisonment. In Y. Jewkes, B. Crewe, & J. Bennett (Eds), *Handbook on prisons.* London, UK: Routledge.

Maschi, T., Kwak, J., Ko, E., & Morrissey, M.B. (2012). Forget me not: Dementia in prison. *The Gerontologist, 1*, 4–5.

Miller, A. (2013a). Health and hard time. *Canadian Medical Association Journal 185*(3), e139–e40.

Miller, A. (2013b). Prison health care inequality. *Canadian Medical Association Journal 185*(6), e249–e50.

National Cancer Institute. (2014). Support for people with cancer: Pain control. NIH Publication Number 19-6287. Retrieved from https://www.cancer.gov/publications/patient-education/paincontrol.pdf

Office of the Correctional Investigator. (2013). *An investigation of the Correctional Service of Canada's mortality review process.* Catalogue number: PS104-9/2014E-PDF. Retrieved from http://www.oci-bec.gc.ca/cnt/rpt/oth-aut/oth-aut20131218-eng.aspx

Office of the Correctional Investigator & Canadian Human Rights Commission (2019). *Aging and dying in prison: An investigation into the experiences of older individuals in federal custody.* Catalogue Number: PS104-17/2019E-PDF. Retrieved from: http://www.oci-bec.gc.ca/cnt/rpt/pdf/oth-aut/oth-aut20190228-eng.pdf

Parole Board of Canada. (2018). *Decision-making policy manual for board members* (2nd edn). Retrieved from https://www.canada.ca/content/dam/pbc-clcc/documents/manual-manuel/Decision-Making_Policy_Manual_2nd_Ed_No_13.pdf

Public Safety Canada. (2017). *Corrections and conditional release statistical overview 2017 annual report.* Catalogue number: PS1-3E-PDF. Retrieved from https://www.publicsafety.gc.ca/cnt/rsrcs/pblctns/ccrso-2017/ccrso-2017-en.pdf

Sapers, H. (2010). *Annual report of the Office of the Correctional Investigator 2009–2010.* Catalogue number: PS100-2010E-PDF. Retrieved from http://www.oci-bec.gc.ca/cnt/rpt/pdf/annrpt/annrpt20092010-eng.pdf

Sapers, H. (2011). *Annual report of the Office of the Correctional Investigator 2010–2011.* Catalogue number: PS100-2011E-PDF. Retrieved from http://www.oci-bec.gc.ca/cnt/rpt/pdf/annrpt/annrpt20102011-eng.pdf

Sapers, H. (2012a). *Annual report of the Office of the Correctional Investigator 2011–2012.* Catalogue number: PS100-2012E-PDF. Retrieved from http://www.oci-bec.gc.ca/cnt/rpt/pdf/annrpt/annrpt20112012-eng.pdf

Sapers, H. (2012b). Barriers to conditional release. In P. Healey & P.A. Molinari (Eds), *Sentencing and corrections: Sentencing theory meets practice.* Montreal, QC: Canadian Institute for the Administration of Justice.

Sapers, H. (2015). *Annual report of the Office of the Correctional Investigator 2014–2015.* Catalogue number: PS100E-PDF. Retrieved from http://www.oci-bec.gc.ca/cnt/rpt/pdf/annrpt/annrpt20142015-eng.pdf

Sapers, H. (2016). *Annual report of the Office of the Correctional Investigator 2015–2016.* Catalogue number: PS100E-PDF. Retrieved from http://www.oci-bec.gc.ca/cnt/rpt/pdf/annrpt/annrpt20152016-eng.pdf

Statistics Canada. (2018). Life expectancy and other elements of the life table, Canada and provinces. Table 39-10-0007-01. Retrieved from https://www150.statcan.gc.ca/t1/tbl1/en/tv.action?pid=3910000701

Steele v. Ontario. (1993). 42 ACWS (3d) 562.

Stewart, L., Nolan, A., Sapers, J., Power, J., Panaro, L., & Smith, J. (2015). Chronic health conditions reported by male inmates newly admitted to Canadian federal penitentiaries. *Canadian Medical Association Journal 3*(1), 97–102.

Sutherland v. Canada. (2003). FC 1516. Retrieved from https://www.canlii.org/en/ca/fct/doc/2003/2003fc1516/2003fc1516.html?resultIndex=7

Swayze v. Dafoe. (2002). 116 ACWS (3d) 781.

United Nations. (1990). *Basic principles for the treatment of prisoners.* Resolution number A/RES/45/111. Retrieved from: http://www.un.org/documents/ga/res/45/a45r111.htm

United Nations. (2015). United Nations standard minimum rules for the treatment of prisoners (the Nelson Mandela Rules). Resolution number A/RES/70/175. Retrieved from: https://undocs.org/A/RES/70/175

Williams, B.A. (2016). Older prisoners and the physical health effects of solitary confinement. *American Journal of Public Health 106*(12), 2126–7.

Williams, B.A., Goodwin, J.S., Baillargeon, J., Ahalt, C., & Walter, L.C. (2012). Addressing the aging crisis in U.S. criminal justice healthcare. *American Geriatrics Society 60*(6), 1150–56.

Zinger, I. (2012). Conditional release and human rights in Canada: A commentary. *Canadian Journal of Criminology and Criminal Justice 54*(1), 117–35.

Zinger, I. (2017). *Annual report of the Office of the Correctional Investigator 2016–2017.* Catalogue number: PS100. Retrieved from http://www.oci-bec.gc.ca/cnt/rpt/pdf/annrpt/annrpt20162017-eng.pdf

Zinger, I. (2018). *Office of the Correctional Investigator annual report 2017–2018.* Catalogue number: PS100. Retrieved from http://www.oci-bec.gc.ca/cnt/rpt/pdf/annrpt/annrpt20172018-eng.pdf

Sex Offenders

A Special Correctional Population

Eric Beauregard and Kylie Reale

12

Chapter Overview

This chapter presents an overview of some of the key issues related to inmates who have committed sexual crimes—the so-called "sex offender." The chapter starts by discussing the "specialization" debate about individuals convicted of sexual crimes and how they are labelled once incarcerated. The chapter then describes the experience of life in prison for sex offenders and some of the challenges they face in their daily routine inside the walls. Then, the issue of risk assessment for sex offenders is reviewed. The chapter also covers treatment for sex offenders as well as whether these interventions are effective. Finally, various measures that have been put in place specifically for sex offenders, such as the registry, community notification, and residence restrictions, will be reviewed as well as the issue of recidivism.

Introduction

Inmates admitted to the correctional system who have committed a sexual offence are automatically designated as **sex offenders**. Even when presenting an extensive list of previous convictions for non-sexual crimes, these inmates are flagged by correctional authorities,

and their journey through the correctional system—from admission to supervision in the community—will be largely influenced by a conviction for a sexual crime. In the majority of cases, these inmates will be directed to a special unit of the institution for their own protection. In addition, these inmates will go through a psychological assessment with a specific focus on their risk of recidivism and their level of dangerousness. Following the initial assessment, most of these inmates will be transferred to an institution adapted to house offenders with such a **criminal career**. Moreover, they will be offered (indeed, encouraged) to take part in various treatment programs, some of which specialize in sexual violence. Finally, after being released, many of these offenders will remain under supervision and will have various conditions and measures to reduce their risk of **recidivism** imposed.

Sex Offenders as a Special Inmate Population?

Criminal career information is used by clinicians and the different actors of the criminal justice system involved in the monitoring of sex offenders. Criminologists and psychologists often must assess the risk level of an offender, and the criminal career is often the starting point of this assessment. One strange fact related to the criminal career is that once an inmate presents a conviction for a sexual offence—whether a sexual assault or another crime of sexual nature—this inmate will be designated as a sex offender, despite presenting a variety of other non-sexual convictions. This practice originates from the **specialization** hypothesis. According to this hypothesis, sex offenders are a special case of offender, having a specific propensity to commit sexual crimes. Thus, it is suggested that if the criminal activity of a sex offender persists, it would be primarily in sexual crimes (Lussier, 2005). According to this hypothesis, we should expect inmates convicted for sexual crimes to present a majority—if not all—of their prior convictions for similar crimes. We should also expect them to recidivate in the same type of crime. Recidivism studies, however, have shown otherwise. In line with the *generalist* hypothesis, several studies have shown that the criminal activity of sex offenders is **versatile**—that is, they do not tend to restrict themselves to one particular type of crime. According to this hypothesis, sexual crime should occur in a random fashion in the criminal activity of offenders, something that can be described as "cafeteria-style" offending (Lussier, 2005).

The research on criminal careers has generally revealed some evidence of specialization couched within a broader behavioural pattern of versatile antisocial behaviours in sex offenders (Blokland & Lussier, 2015; Cale, Lussier, McCuish, & Corrado, 2015; Harris, Smallbone, Dennison, & Knight, 2009). For instance, Lussier (2005) has shown that the criminal activity of sex offenders was not restricted to sexual crimes, with rapists participating more in non-sexual crimes than child molesters, who in turn participate more in sexual crimes. Similarly, studies have demonstrated that the criminal activity of rapists was similar to that of the violent offender (DeLisi, 2001), whereas child molesters tended to show a less diversified criminal repertoire with more sexual crimes (Simon, 2000).

Despite the research on the criminal career of individuals having committed sexual crimes, the corrections system continues to label these inmates as "sex offenders." This label designates a special population in corrections that carries a negative perception not only in the community but also inside the prison.

These inmates present specific issues for correctional management, from their initial admission to their supervision when released back into the community. One of the challenges associated with these offenders is their daily functioning within the correctional institution.

Doing Time as a Sex Offender

Because you were convicted of a sex crime, you will not be winning any popularity contests with your fellow prisoners. At first, the other prisoners may mark you to be victimized and harassed. If you don't stand tall and fight back, you'll be victimized your entire prison term. You must stand up for yourself when you are tested by some idiot who thinks you're a rape-o, "Chester," "tree jumper," or "freak." (Anderson, 1997)

Individuals entering the prison system with sexual crimes convictions are considered at the bottom of the prisoner hierarchy (Crewe, 2009; Winfree, Newbold, & Tubb, 2002; Waldram, 2007). Furthermore, there seems to be a hierarchy among sex offenders themselves, where those who have assaulted adult women have a higher status than those who have targeted children (Vaughn & Sapp, 1989). As illustrated by the quote above, these inmates live in constant fear of being a victim of violence from other inmates and sometimes even correctional officers (Hogue, 1993; O'Donnell & Edgar, 1999; Sim, 1994; Sparks, Bottom, & Hay, 1996; Thurston, 1996). They are considered the most vulnerable population—both inside and outside of prison (Petrunik & Weisman, 2005)—and they are openly targeted for victimization (Ricciardelli & Moir, 2013). Due to the nature of their convictions, sex offenders are rejected not only by other inmates but also by some staff.

One of the first objectives of sex offenders entering a correctional institution is to make sure that their convictions remain unknown to the general inmate population. Research has shown that sex offenders are particularly vulnerable in prison once other inmates become aware of the nature of their convictions (Blagden & Pemberton, 2010). Some sex offenders have even been murdered in prison as a result of their convictions (Groth, 1983; Knopp, 1984). In order to avoid having their convictions known, some sex offenders will use various strategies to remain undiscovered. For example, some sex offenders will minimize the risk by requesting to be put in **protective custody** right after being admitted to prison. This is especially likely to happen if the crimes of the offender have been featured in the media and are well known publicly. Other offenders may opt for the creation of a cover story where they present an elaborate and complicated story about their crime to save face among inmates (Ricciardelli & Spencer, 2017). For instance, some sex offenders may prepare a story where they were caught committing much elaborated acts of fraud, which could be confusing for most inmates. Finally, as mentioned by Ricciardelli and Spencer (2017), some sex offenders will also try to change their appearance to look more like gangsters as opposed to the typical sex offender—described by inmates as a middle-aged, tattoo-free, white man wearing glasses.

> I can remember when I was at the Joliet prison in Illinois when a baby raper came onto the tier below me. First attack was someone tossing a coffee can of crap and piss into his cell, which was followed later that day when he was stabbed multiple times. He survived that attack but spent his remaining time in protective custody. (Norton, 2018)

According to Ricciardelli and Spencer (2017), the fear of being exposed—because of the potential consequences—can be used as a means of informal social control by inmates and even correctional officers. In addition to the risk of being a victim of violence, if a sex offender's status is exposed it may trigger a move to protective custody or even a transfer to a different institution. As these offenders are no longer part of the general inmate population, they see their opportunity of movement reduced as well as their opportunities to work.

Although the risk of victimization is often cited as the greatest consequence associated with being a sex offender behind bars, it is important not to overlook social isolation. Some sex offenders will even serve part or all of their sentence in isolation or solitary confinement for their own safety, leading them to become socially withdrawn (Blagden & Pemberton, 2010). As mentioned by Van den Berg and colleagues (2018), the support provided by staff and other inmates represents one key component of the prison climate (see also Blagden, Winder, & Hames, 2014). As mentioned earlier, sex offenders often experience stigmatization, not only by other inmates but also from correctional staff, which results in being treated negatively (Ireland, 2000; Schwaebe, 2005; Spencer, 2009). Several studies have shown that correctional staff in general hold negative attitudes toward sex offenders and are likely to treat them less favourably (Ricciardelli & Spencer, 2017). For instance, studies have shown that correctional officers presented a more negative attitude toward sex offenders than psychologists and probation officers (Hogue, 1993). Higgins and Ireland (2009) found that correctional officers held the most negative attitudes toward sex offenders compared to forensic staff and even the general public.

Recidivism

Despite the perception of the general public, not all sex offenders will recidivate. In probably one of the most widely cited studies on the topic, Hanson and Bussière (1998) have indicated that the recidivism rate for sex offenders was 13 per cent. However, another study that attracted a lot of attention was published by Langevin and colleagues (2004). In their study, the authors found

Correctional Staff and Their Attitudes toward Sex Offenders

In a study on 82 federal correctional officers in Canada, Weekes and colleagues (1995) compared their attitudes toward three groups of inmates: sex offenders against adult women, sex offenders against children, and non-sex offenders. Their findings showed that sex offenders were generally perceived as dangerous, harmful, violent, bad, unpredictable, and unchangeable, and the most negative attitudes were toward those offenders who targeted children, who were described as immoral and mentally ill (Weekes, Pelletier, & Beaudette, 1995). For their own safety, it is not unusual to see many sex offenders serving their sentence with other prison "outcasts" (such as informants, also known as "rats") in protective custody or even in solitary confinement, which can cause social isolation in an already socially isolated environment (Blagden & Pemberton, 2010).

that the recidivism rate for sex offenders was 88.3 per cent. In a subsequent study, Webster, Gartner, and Doob (2006) explained how such findings were not representative of all sex offenders and how sampling biases and measures of recidivism were important to provide the full picture of this problem. Here are some of the factors that could influence recidivism rates reported in various studies:

- *Definition of recidivism:* The definition of what constitutes as "recidivism" may vary from study to study. Some studies will only consider a new conviction, whereas other studies will consider a new charge to constitute a new sexual offence, even if the offender has not been convicted of that crime. Some studies will use the re-arrests as evidence of recidivism.
- *Data source:* When reviewing the literature of sex offender recidivism, it is important to examine the data source. Some studies will only consider the official recidivism—that is, recidivism observed in official data, such as police files, court convictions, and so on. However, other studies will also consider self-reported recidivism to have a more complete picture of the criminal career of the offender. Both sources of data present advantages and disadvantages. For instance, although it can be expected that sex offenders are not likely to report crimes for which they have not been convicted, official data are likely to underestimate the number of sexual offences committed as only a minority of victims report their victimization and only a fraction of these cases will end up with a conviction.
- *Sample characteristics:* Research has shown that certain groups of sex offenders present a greater likelihood of sexual recidivism (for example, homosexual pedophiles). Moreover, certain groups may present different characteristics that may influence the recidivism rates (persons receiving treatment in the community, persons released from prison, those released from mental hospitals, and so on). Therefore, it is important to consider the characteristic of the sample when assessing the results of recidivism studies.
- *Follow-up period:* This may seem obvious, but the longer the **follow-up period**, the more opportunities the offender has to recidivate.

For instance, when looking at a study with a follow-up period of five years—that is, the offenders were followed for a period of five years after being released—compared to a study with a follow-up period of 20 years, you can expect to find different recidivism rates. This is a factor to consider when explaining some of the disparities in recidivism rate studies.

Several studies have examined recidivism in sex offenders. Alexander (1999) found that the recidivism rate was 13 per cent for treated offenders compared to 18 per cent for untreated offenders. Similarly, the **meta-analysis** by Hanson and colleagues (2002) included 38 studies and showed that the recidivism rate was 12 per cent for treated offenders compared to 17 per cent for a comparison group (which included dropouts, treatment refusers, and untreated offenders) over an average follow-up period of 46 months. When looking at within-group studies, Quinsey and colleagues (1995) have broken down the recidivism rate for various subgroups of sex offenders:

- 23 per cent for rapists
- 18 per cent for heterosexual child molesters
- 35 per cent for homosexual child molesters
- 8 per cent for incest offenders

In the study by Alexander (1999), it was found that the recidivism rate for various groups of treated and untreated sex offenders were as follows:

- 20 and 24 per cent for treated and untreated rapists, respectively
- 16 per cent for treated and untreated heterosexual child molesters
- 18 and 34 per cent for treated and untreated homosexual child molesters, respectively
- 4 and 12 per cent for treated and untreated incest offenders

These studies have also shown that some factors were influencing the probability of committing a new sexual crime. For instance, the likelihood of committing another sexual crime increased the longer the follow-up period. Moreover, these studies showed that the recidivism rates varied according to the group of sex offenders. Thus, the recidivism rate of rapists dropped gradually with age, whereas for child molesters it remained steady until the late forties. Finally, the studies showed that the most important factors related to recidivism were different for rapists and child molesters. Although previous sexual charges were predictive of sexual recidivism for child molesters, it was the presence of previous violent charges that was the most important factor for rapists (see Lussier, 2005).

In line with the generality hypothesis, it is also interesting to look at the general recidivism of sex offenders. In the study by Hanson and colleagues (2002), they showed that the general recidivism rate was 28 and 39 per cent for treated and untreated sex offenders, respectively, whereas the sexual recidivism was 12 and 17 per cent for treated and untreated sex offenders, respectively. In the Hanson and Bussière (1998) study, findings showed that the reoffending rate was 36 per cent for general, 12 per cent for violent, and 13 per cent for sexual crime recidivism. What these findings are suggesting is that following a sexual offence, the general reoffending rate tends to be lower than for non-sexual offenders. Moreover, compared to child molesters, rapists show a precocious age of onset for general and sexual offending and they commit more crime in general, both property crimes as well as more violent crimes. Their criminal activity is more diversified, whereas child molesters' criminal careers include more sexual crimes (Lussier, 2005).

Two studies that examine recidivism, both for sex and non-sex offenders, are particularly interesting because of their large sample sizes. Langan, Schmitt, and Durose (2003) compared the recidivism rate for sex offences following the release of sexual ($n=9,691$) and non-sexual ($n=262,420$) offenders across 15 states in the United States. Non-sexual offenders showed a recidivism rate for sex crimes of 1 per cent, compared with 5 per cent for sex offenders. When looking at re-arrest rates for any type of crime (not just sex crimes), the study found that 43 per cent of the released sex offenders were re-arrested, compared to 68 per cent of the non-sex offenders. The re-arrest offence was a felony for 75 per cent of the re-arrested sex offenders, compared to 84 per cent for the non-sex offenders. The second study, by Sample and Bray (2003), looked at the recidivism rates of individuals arrested between 1990 and 1997 ($n=146,918$). After a follow-up period of five years, the sexual recidivism rate was about 6 per cent for sexual offenders, compared with 0 to 3 per cent for non-sexual offenders. As a comparison, when considering other crimes, findings showed that 17.9 per cent of robbers were re-arrested for robbery and 23.1 per cent of burglars were re-arrested for burglary. However, there are problems related to the use of official statistics: They are limited to those persons who come to official attention; they sometimes more accurately reflect police procedures than actual criminal occurrences; and finally, many sexual assaults are not reported to police (Sample & Bray, 2003).

Beyond the recidivism rate studies, it is crucial to understand what some of the factors associated with sexual recidivism are. It is possible to classify risk factors as either **static factors** or **dynamic factors**. Table 12.1 presents a list of static and dynamic risk factors associated with sexual recidivism. All these factors are associated with a higher likelihood of recidivism.

There is some indication that dynamic factors are more important in predicting risk than historical items, as the former better describe the individual's current life situation. However, according to Hanson

Table 12.1 Examples of Static and Dynamic Risk Factors of Sexual Recidivism

Static	Dynamic
Early age of onset	Current age is younger than 40
Low education level	Low current education level
Never married	Current marital status is single
Current offence of robbery, burglary, or theft	High-security prison level
Prior supervision violation	Poor record of prisoner conduct
Poor past employment record	Currently unemployed
Prior substance-use problem	Currently no financial assistance
Past gang affiliation	Currently associated with offenders
Prior mental health problem	Unstable residency situation
Prior alcohol-use problems	Not participating in treatment (if needed)

(2005), dynamic risk factors are best used to identify *when* offenders are at risk for reoffending, rather than *who* will reoffend. This is because dynamic factors fluctuate over time and are contingent upon the offender's release environment. For example, assessing an offender's self-regulation capacities, level of hostility, or sexual preoccupation is less relevant when they are in an institutionalized setting compared to when they are out on community release (Campbell, 2014).

Risk Assessment

As these studies reveal, the common perception that all or most sex offenders reoffend is not supported by the research; within the population of sex offenders, however, some subpopulations pose a high risk of reoffending. To that end, **risk assessment instruments** have been developed to estimate the likelihood of reoffending (Doren, 2004).

Risk prediction has been an element of criminal justice decision making for several decades (Monahan, 1981; Morris & Miller, 1985). Professional clinical judgment has been one of the most common methods in corrections to assess an inmate's risk—not only in terms of recidivism, but also for parole, placement in protective custody, and so on. Moreover, such assessment may be undertaken right after an offender's admission into prison but also at various stages of their prison sentence. For instance, it is not unusual that risk assessment will be performed as part of mandated treatment and when preparing for release. This type of risk assessment has been widely used, mainly due to the fact that it was simple—all that is necessary is a professional expert, who has the skill and experience to do the assessment. However, such methodology has also been shown to be the least accurate risk assessment method, relying too much on intuition from the experts with varying skills. In the seminal work of Meehl (1954), he determined that the **predictive validity** of unstructured clinical judgment was not much better than "pure luck."

Accordingly, critics in the 1980s assailed the first generation of instruments designed to assess risk as vastly inaccurate; they argued that the best one can hope for "is one true prediction of danger for two false positives" (Morris, 1982, p. 519). Since that time, however, technological innovations have allowed researchers to create a second generation of what are known as **actuarial prediction instruments**. These instruments are exceptionally stable when subject to cross-validation (see Bonta, Harman, Hann, & Cormier, 1996; Rice & Harris, 1997) and have been shown to be highly superior to clinical prediction. For adult sex offenders, the most commonly used risk prediction instruments are the STATIC 99 (Hanson & Thornton, 1999), the SORAG (Quinsey, Harris, Rice, & Cormier, 1998), and the MnSOST-R (Epperson, Kaul, & Hesselton, 1998).

One of the questions related to the use of actuarial instruments is whether these specialized instruments for sex offenders work better than those instruments used

The STATIC-99

Probably the most commonly used actuarial instrument for the assessment of risk of sexual recidivism is the STATIC-99 (Hanson & Thornton, 1999). The STATIC-99 is used to evaluate the likelihood of a convicted sexual offender committing subsequent sexual offences. It was developed by Hanson and Thornton, who combined two previously existing risk assessment instruments, the Rapid Risk Assessment for Sexual Offense Recidivism (RRASOR; Hanson, 1997a) and the Structured Anchored Clinical Judgment—Minimum (SACJ-Min; Grubin 1998). Both the RRASOR and the SACJ-Min were intended to be brief screening instruments for risk of sexual offence recidivism that use only case file data and do not require a face-to-face interview by the screener. These two instruments, however, have different emphases, and they assess related but different constructs. The RRASOR focuses almost exclusively on factors related to sexual deviance, whereas the SACJ-Min also incorporates non-sexual criminal history factors. The STATIC-99 is a 10-item prediction scale that is scored by combining both types of data and using information collected solely from individual case file information (see Table 12.1). These 10 items are (1) any male victims, (2) never married, (3) any non-contact sex offences, (4) any unrelated victims, (5) any stranger victims, (6) any prior sexual offences, (7) any current non-sexual violence, (8) prior non-sexual violence, (9) four or more prior sentencing occasions, (10) age less than 25 years.

These 10 risk factors are scored and summated, producing a single numeric score (maximum total of 12). The summated score is then categorized into one of four risk groups: low (0–1), moderate-low (2–3), moderate-high (4–5), and high (6+). Doren (2004)

identified at least 22 studies testing the STATIC-99's predictive validity concerning sexual recidivism across different countries (see Barbaree, Seto, Langton, & Peacock, 2001; Beech, Friendship, Erikson, & Hanson, 2002; McGrath, Cumming, Livingston, & Hoke, 2003; Nunes, Firestone, Bradford, Greenberg, & Broom, 2002). Of the 22 studies, 20 support the instrument's predictive validity, whereas two were less clear in that regard (Doren, 2004).

Question number	Risk Factor	Codes		Score
1	Age at release	Aged 18 to 34.9		1
		Aged 35 to 39.9		0
		Aged 40 to 59.9		−1
		Aged 60 or older		−3
2	Ever lived with	Ever lived with a lover for at least two years?		
		Yes		0
		No		1
3	Index non-sexual violence – any convictions	No		0
		Yes		1
4	Prior non-sexual violence – any convictions	No		0
		Yes		1
5	Prior sex offences	Charges	Convictions	
		0	0	0
		1, 2	1	1
		3–5	2, 3	2
		6+	4+	3
6	Prior sentencing dates (excluding index)	3 or less		0
		4 or more		1
7	Any convictions for non-contact sex offences	No		0
		Yes		1
8	Any unrelated victims	No		0
		Yes		1
9	Any stranger victims	No		0
		Yes		1
10	Any male victims	No		0
		Yes		1
	Total Score	Add up scores from individual risk factors		

Translating STATIC-99R scores into risk categories	Score	Label for Risk Category
	−3 through 1	Low
	2, 3	Low-Moderate
	4, 5	Moderate-High
	6+	High

STATIC-99r form

Source: From Static-99R Coding Rules, Revised – 2016 Public Safety Canada, RESEARCH REPORT: 2017–R012. © Her Majesty the Queen in Right of Canada, 2017.

for regular offenders, such as the LSI-R (Level of Service Inventory-Revised). The research that is currently available does not provide an answer to this question. However, one study compared risk classifications made

using the STATIC-99 and the LSI-R. Interestingly, findings revealed significant differences between the two instruments, with the STATIC-99 identifying higher risk classifications than the LSI-R (Gentry, Dulmus,

& Theriot, 2005). Such discrepancy between a specialized instrument for sex offenders and instruments used for general offenders might be explained by the fact that specialized instruments are designed to assess those factors empirically associated to sexual recidivism, whereas the more general instruments, such as the LSI-R, look at general recidivism and do not assess certain risk factors associated to sexual reoffending (for example, prior male victims, prior sexual offence).

Although the actuarial methods present a higher level of reliability and validity than the clinical judgment, and the level of skills required to score these instruments is reasonable, some have stated that this type of risk assessment might not be flexible enough to consider the professional judgment of the person responsible for the assessment. Therefore, a new risk assessment tool has been developed: the adjusted actuarial assessment (AAA). This tool now allows for the modification and addition of additional information not included in the actual scoring system, where a clinician assesses risk by the initial employment of one or more actuarial instruments followed by potential adjustments based on clinical, contextual, or dispositional considerations (Beech & Ward, 2004). For example, when relying on AAA, evaluators may consider anger problems, substance abuse, depression, anxiety, denial, motivation for treatment, length of treatment, and empathy for victims. However, there are generally no standardized manuals or practice guidelines detailing how to use AAA. As a result, AAA typically involves considerable variations in the clinical judgments for different evaluators (Campbell, 2014).

Physiological Assessment Tools

When reviewing some of the assessment methods specific to sex offenders, it is impossible not to mention **phallometry**. In the meta-analysis conducted by Hanson and Bussière (1998), which included 61 studies and 28,972 sex offenders, findings revealed that a sexual preference for a child assessed phallometrically is one the best predictors of sexual recidivism. Phallometry is known under different names, such as PPG, penile plethysmography, sexophysiological assessment, or assessment of sexual preferences. It was first developed to identify the sexual orientation of soldiers. However, it was Freund who used it with sex offenders for the first time in 1957.

Phallometry measures male sexual arousal by assessing the magnitude of blood accumulation in the penis (that is, erection). It measures penile erectile responses to various sexual and non-sexual stimuli in a laboratory setting. Phallometry involves the use of a small circumferential-type transducer, a mercury-in-rubber strain gauge, placed upon the penis in order to assess erectile responses. Electrical conductance changes in the gauge, resulting from changes in penile circumference, are recorded with the plethysmograph and digitized using a customized software. This tool may not be used to prove or disprove sexual crime; it measures only sexual arousal and identifies sexual preferences. Phallometry has been used in different settings (clinics, penitentiaries, and psychiatric hospitals). This tool may also involve various types of stimuli, such as films, slides, or audiotape recordings. For example, if audiotape recordings are used, they will generally vary in the age of the victim depicted in the scenario, the gender, as well as the level of violence used.

Although some issues concerning its validity need further examination, phallometry has several advantages over other methods. For example, it is less likely to be falsified by the offenders compared to self-reports about their sexual arousal. Despite being the best method to measure sexual preferences, this tool presents several limitations. First, there is a lack of standardization. For instance, there exists a variability in the measures, the stimuli (that is, the content, duration, and number of), and the scoring methods across settings. Second, some offenders will try to control their sexual arousal during the assessment. The use of this "**faking**" technique is reduced by the use of a semantic tracking task (for example, the inmate has to press a button every time he hears sexual or violent content). Finally, there is also an issue with low responders—that is, inmates who were unable to achieve a minimal sexual arousal during the assessment. This can be due to the age of the inmate (older offenders may experience sexual dysfunctions), the context of the evaluation (it may trigger stress), or the use of certain medications that could influence sexual arousal.

In addition to the phallometric assessment, other physiological methods have been used with sex offenders. These methods have focused on measuring galvanic skin response, cardiovascular responses, changes in respiration, as well as pupil dilatation. Although these methods have proven useful as indicators of general arousal, they present difficulties in differentiating erotic arousal from general arousal.

The polygraph may also be used in the risk assessment of sex offenders. Studies have shown that when it was used, it elicited significantly more information regarding sexually deviant behaviour and lifetime sexual offending. Also, more than three times the number of incidents of sexually deviant behaviour had been reported after polygraph testing, and the number of paraphilias reported was doubled after such testing. However, polygraph results are highly dependent on the examiner's expertise, and results are generally not admissible in court (Coric, Feuerstein, Fortunati, et al., 2005). Similar to other psychophysiological measures, the use of polygraph testing has been criticized for its lack of standardization and generalizability of research findings.

Finally, another risk assessment tool measuring sexual interest is based on **viewing time**. Visual reaction time is generally considered to be a non-intrusive method to measure sexual interest (Coric et al., 2005). Research has shown that visual attention discriminated between high and low sexual interest, and increased visual attention was associated with preferred versus non-preferred sexual objects in normal adults. The Abel Assessment (Abel et al., 1994) is a tool based on viewing time. It includes 160 slides of models photographed fully clothed and not in sexually explicit poses, with unlimited viewing time. The computer measures in milliseconds how long each image is projected on the screen. The reliability and validity of the Abel Assessment has been debated in the literature; however, when it is used as part of a more comprehensive psychiatric evaluation, it may be a useful tool to assess sexual interest.

Specific Legislation

Despite the general trend of a decline in crime in the mid-1990s and early 2000s, public concern over sexual crimes has risen. Response to this growing concern took various forms in the United States, such as increases in sentence length (for example, mandatory minimum prison terms of 25 years for first-time felony sex offenders against children; National Conference of State Legislators, 2008), indefinite civil commitment of highly dangerous sex offenders (Gookin, 2005), as well as the creation of special provisions for sex offenders after their release from incarceration. These post-release provisions are aimed at decreasing the anonymity of sex offenders and restricting their access to victims.

Registration ordinances were first introduced in the United States in the 1930s, and they originally focused on habitual violators of criminal laws (Logan, 2009).

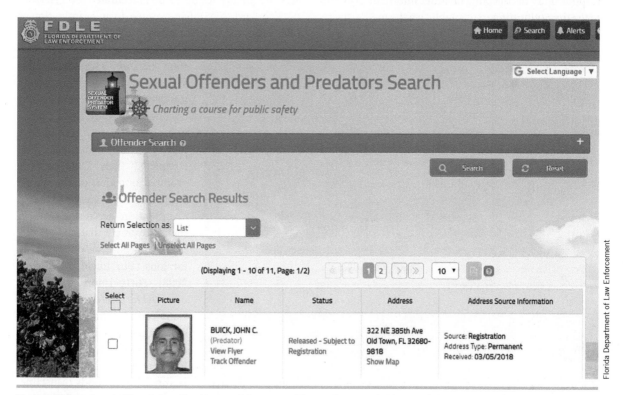

The Florida Department of Law Enforcement is one of the states with an online, searchable sex offender registry that allows anyone to see details on any registered sex offender by location.

These ordinances had modest use until the 1990s, when they were resurrected as a means of decreasing sex crimes. Starting in 1990 in Washington state, authorities required convicted sex offenders, upon release from custody or after sentencing, to register with local law enforcement. The 1990 law also authorized officials to notify the public when dangerous sex offenders were released into the community. These measures were intended to "restrict the access of known sex offenders to vulnerable populations, and also to improve law enforcement's ability to identify convicted offenders" (Task Force on Community Protection, 1989). Following Washington state, numerous states passed similar legislation through the mid-1990s. The federal government entered this field with the 1994 Jacob Wetterling Act, which required states to implement a sex offender registry or face a financial penalty.

Community notification is a measure put in place to allow the distribution of information regarding released sex offenders to citizens and community organizations. Although notification protocols vary between the United States and Canada, some basic principles remain constant, such as it only applies to potentially dangerous sex offenders and local police have the responsibility of collecting offender information and to make the notification to the public via the media, flyers, newspapers, or telephone.

Several studies have demonstrated that citizens are supportive of these laws (Lieb & Nunlist, 2008; Levenson, Brannon, Fortney, & Baker, 2007; Proctor, Badzinski, & Johnson, 2002). In fact, a 2005 Gallup poll found that 94 per cent of Americans were in favour of the laws; interestingly, only one-quarter reported that they checked the available registries (Saad, 2005). A 1997 public opinion survey in Washington found that 80 per cent of 400 residents were familiar with Megan's Law and believed community notifications would help prevent sexual abuse because they believed it would increase awareness and surveillance by neighbours (Phillips, 1998).

However, these laws could provide a false sense of security by enabling the community to believe that the majority of at-risk sex offenders are known to the police, when this is not the case. In fact, most victims know their abuser, yet notification laws tend to mislead the public into fearing stranger sexual violence (Brannon, Levenson, Fortney, & Baker, 2007). Moreover, the police tend to lack the necessary resources to maintain the registries, verify the accuracy of the information, and inform the public (Houston, 1994). Because registration laws require the compliance of sex offenders, they have been frequently found to be inaccurate (see Peterson, 1995; Ballard, 2005). For example, in an examination of a Kentucky registry, Tewksbury (2002) found almost 25 per cent of registrants' addresses were invalid. Some have also suggested that such measures imposed additional punishment on offenders (difficulties reintegrating into society or finding a job), especially when they had completed their sentence. For example, offenders on the sex offender registry who are on parole or probation face restrictions on their movement that make it difficult to even seek out or apply for jobs (Burchfield & Mingus, 2008). Furthermore, registrants often have limited housing options and difficulty attaining a legitimate source of income, leading many to live in low-income and socially disorganized neighbourhoods (Mustaine, Tewksbury, & Stengel, 2006).

THE CANADIAN PRESS/Sue Bailey

Winnipeg Police Service posts community notifications of known sex offenders on social media, including their Facebook and Twitter pages.

Studies on the effectiveness of these measures in reducing recidivism have produced mixed findings. Two studies have analyzed multiple states and relied on aggregate-level data to determine whether registration and notification laws have changed crime rates. Prescott and Rockoff (2008) analyzed National Incident-Based Reporting System data to examine the effects in 15 states, taking account of the timing and scope of state laws. For registration laws, the authors found evidence that registration reduces the frequency of sex offences because law enforcement is knowledgeable about the location of registered offenders. Notification laws were found to deter first-time sex offenders but to increase the recidivism rates of registered sex offenders. The overall net effect is a 10 per cent reduction because registration has a greater effect than notification. Shao and Li (2006) used Uniform Crime Report panel data for all 50 states from 1970 to 2002 and estimated that registration led to a 2 per cent reduction in rapes reported to police.

Other studies did not find such positive effects of these laws. Schram and Milloy (1995) compared a group of sex offenders who were subject to notification laws with a similar group of sex offenders who were released prior to the implementation of such laws. Although the notification group had a lower rate of recidivism than the comparison group, the difference was not significant. In another study, Tewksbury and Jennings (2010) compared the recidivism trajectories of 759 pre-SORN (Sex Offender Registration and Notification) releasees and 823 post-SORN releasees in Iowa. What they found was that SORN did not reduce the rate of sex offender recidivism for sex offences. Tewksbury, Jennings, and Zgoba (2012) examined the recidivism rates of two samples of sex offenders released pre- and post-SORN in New Jersey. Similar to prior studies, they found that there was an overall low rate of sex offence recidivism, and that SORN status failed to predict which sex offenders would reoffend sexually. Finally, studies in both New Jersey (Zgoba, Witt, Dalessandro, & Veysey, 2008) and New York (Sandler, Freedman, & Socia, 2008) concluded that Megan's Law had no significant impact on rates of recidivism or sexual violence, suggesting that the cost of implementing these laws may outweigh the perceived benefits.

Furthermore, the registry can lead to concerning collateral consequences, such as vigilantism. Vigilantes are private citizens who take the law into their own hands to harass, assault, or physically harm another individual. In some states, the registries provide full access to the offender's current address; the make, model, and licence plate of their vehicle; and their physical characteristics, thereby enabling members of the public to identify these individuals in the community. While this identification is intended to empower the public to protect themselves from high-risk offenders, there are some citizens who have used this information to proactively locate and harm registered sex offenders. For sex offenders that are out on community release, the risk of vigilantism tends to be even worse for those who have offences against children. For example, Cubellis, Evans, and Fera (2018) found that of 279 incidents of vigilantism against sex offenders in the United States, 65 per cent were against those who had a sexual offence against a child. This indicates the general disdain the public feels toward individuals who sexually victimize children. The majority of those attacked had also been identified through the registry, leading to concern about the role the registry plays in facilitating acts of vigilantism by private citizens.

Moreover, vigilante acts can lead to collateral victims. As one Illinois legislator put it, "we have documented cases of vigilantism with people going to the wrong house or beating up the wrong guy" (Sample & Kadleck, 2008, p. 56). In their study, Cubellis and colleagues (2018) found that 10 per cent of victims of vigilantes were either mistakenly identified as a sex offender or were family members or friends of sex offenders who were with the sex offender at the time of the attack. There have also been several documented cases of extreme acts of violence against registered sex offenders as a result of information provided through the registry. For example, in April 2006, a man travelled from Canada to Maine intending to kill 34 registered sex offenders whose names he had collected from the Maine Sex Offender Registry. He murdered two before he was caught (Bonnar-Kidd, 2010).

In addition to registration and notification laws, electronic monitoring has been used in 34 states with sex offenders released into the community (Interstate Commission for Adult Offender Supervision, 2007). One form of these devices relies on global positioning system (GPS) technology, which allows real-time monitoring of the geographical locations of individuals. A majority of the jurisdictions that use GPS technology for this purpose apply it to high-risk, violent, or aggressive sex offenders (Nieto & Jung, 2006). In terms of GPS systems and their use with high-risk sex offenders, the most rigorous study to date did not find any re-cidivism reduction in a preliminary report (Turner & Janetta, 2007). In 2009, a woman kidnapped 18 years earlier was found living in the backyard of a registered sex offender who was on electronic monitoring and subject to monthly visits; this discovery led to debates about the value of registries and electronic monitoring (Davey, 2009). In past decades, decisions about where sex offenders could live when they were released from custody were either made by individual offenders or, if the person was under the authority of a parole of-ficer, in conjunction with the paroling authority. This decision-making apparatus continues but is signifi-cantly restricted by the recent proliferation of state and municipal laws restricting where sex offenders can live (Meloy, Miller, & Curtis, 2008). These laws are intended to restrict the access of sex offenders to victims and force them to live outside populated areas and away from children. Two types of laws have been passed: "child safety zones," where offenders are not allowed to loiter, and "distance marker" laws that give specific space re-strictions where offenders cannot live—typically 1,000 to 2,500 feet from schools, playgrounds, and other areas where children congregate (Nieto & Jung, 2006). Some communities have passed ordinances restricting regis-tered sex offenders from living there (Fonce-Olivas, 2006); some developers are building "sex offender–free subdivisions" (Axtman, 2006).

The first residence restriction policy was passed in Florida in 1995 and aimed to prevent sex offenders on probation from living within 1,000 feet of a school, park, playground, daycare centre, or other place where children congregate. Following the sexual homicide of Jessica Lunsford by a convicted sex offender in Florida in 2005, these residence restrictions gained enormous popularity. However, it is unclear whether residency restrictions are effective in reducing sex offences. A Minnesota study examined new offences commit-ted by released sex offenders and identified residential locations for these offenders and victims. The authors concluded that "none of the 224 incidents of sex of-fender recidivism fit the criteria of a known offender making contact with a child victim at a location within the distances typically covered by residential restriction laws" (Duwe, Donnay, & Tewksbury 2008, p. 498).

In addition to the absence of evidence that such measures are effective in reducing sexual crimes, studies have identified several collateral damages of residence restrictions. Although there are no studies linking increased homelessness among sex offenders with higher rates of recidivism, the criminological literature links stability and support with successful community re-entry for offenders (Petersilia, 2003). Levenson and Cotter (2005) conducted a survey involv-ing 135 sex offenders on probation in Tampa and Fort Lauderdale and found that approximately one-quarter of the offenders reported having to relocate as a result of the state's 1,000-foot buffer zone, and almost half said they were unable to live with family members, which increased their isolation and stress. In a similar study of 109 sex offenders in Broward, Florida, Levenson and colleagues (2007) found that 22 per cent of the offend-ers had to relocate two or more times and that 13 per cent spent time in jail due to a residence violation. In a study by Levenson and Hern (2007) in Indiana, the authors found that more than a quarter of sex offend-ers were unable to return to their homes after being re-leased from prison.

Not surprisingly, one of the main consequences of the residence restrictions have been the reduction of housing availability. For instance, when mapping the locations of dwellings located within 2,500 feet of schools in Orange County, Florida, Zandbergen and Hart (2006) found that no less than 64 per cent of the properties zoned for residential use were located within that area. In some cities, the distance used for residence restrictions has been based on the absence of available housing for these offenders, similar to a banishment of sex offenders from certain cities. This incapacity to find housing leads to some offenders becoming home-less and transient, which has an impact on the reli-ability and validity of the sex offender registry (Rood, 2006). Finally, it is important to keep in mind that these specific laws for sex offenders may potentially increase the stress for these offenders who are trying to reinte-grate into the community, which in some cases may trigger their offence cycle and lead them to recidivate—causing the opposite of what the public actually wants.

Treatment of Sex Offenders

In spite of controversy about its effectiveness, treatment for sex offenders continues to be a relatively common component of the criminal justice system response. A key rationale for the treatment focus with sex offend-ers, particularly for cases with child victims, has been to encourage victim reporting and co-operation with the criminal justice system. The other argument is that sex offender recidivism can be reduced with specialized treatment (Berliner et al. 1995).

The debate in the scientific literature on the effectiveness of sex offender treatment has been extensive. Depending on which studies are given weight and the methods of analysis, researchers have concluded that treatment reduces recidivism (Hall, 1995; Hanson, Bourgon, Helmus, & Hodgson, 2009; Lösel & Schmucker, 2005; MacKenzie, 2006), whereas others have determined that the research evidence is still insufficient to draw a firm conclusion (Furby, Weinrott, & Blackshaw, 1989; Harris, Rice, & Quinsey, 1998; Kenworthy, Adams, Bilby, Brooks-Gordon, & Fenton, 2004; Rice & Harris, 2003).

As highlighted by Harkins and Beech (2007), several criticisms can be made about the various methodologies used in treatment effectiveness studies looking strictly at recidivism. For some, only looking at the outcome of recidivism is limited, not considering other progress or changes that could have been made while participating in a treatment program. Thus, some have suggested that proximate outcomes need to be examined (that is, changes made during treatment; see, for instance, Hanson, 1997b) as well as within-treatment changes for a more complete picture of effectiveness (Friendship, Falshaw, & Beech, 2003). In doing so, it allows a more individualized approach, permitting researchers to identify a subset of the group that could have been successfully treated while the group as a whole was not (Harkins & Beech, 2007). According to Harkins and Beech (2007), pairing short-term (within-treatment changes) with long-term outcomes (recidivism) leads to a more accurate assessment of the effectiveness of the treatment program.

In reviewing sex offender programming along with the prior assessments and the meta-analyses, sex offender treatment programs using cognitive-behavioural therapy and chemical castration/psychotherapy were generally found to be the most effective in reducing recidivism (see Kim, Benekos, & Merlo. 2015; Lösel & Schmuker, 2005; MacKenzie, 2006). Furthermore, a systematic review of meta-analyses on the effects of sex offender treatment by Kim, Benekos, and Merlo (2015) revealed that chemical and surgical treatments were more effective than psychosocial treatments. However, chemical and surgical treatment methods are not without controversy. Surgical procedures refer to mechanical castration, and chemical castration refers to hormonal drugs such as antiandrogen, which are used to reduce sexual arousal. There are also clear legal and ethical issues for sex offenders referred to these forms of treatment. For example, long-term effects of chemical castration on health, sexual behaviour, and sexual recidivism are key concerns for researchers, clinicians, and health-care professionals. Nonetheless, there are several states in the United States, including California and Florida, that require repeat sex offenders to undergo chemical castration. The use of surgical castration is even more controversial, and although it is performed less frequently, it has been used in both Western Europe and the United States. Despite some empirical support, the dearth of studies on these treatment approaches and the lack of control groups have caused reluctance among researchers and clinicians to embrace surgical and chemical castration as viable primary treatment options (Kim, Benekos, & Merlo, 2015). Finally, several meta-analytic studies have revealed that sex offender treatment programs involving the community rather than institutional treatment appear to be more effective at reducing recidivism (Hanson et al., 2009; Lösel & Schmuker, 2005; Mackenzie, 2006). These findings run counter to the more traditional punitive approaches to treatment and instead highlight the need for legislative reform and support that would authorize more sex offender treatment programs in the community rather than in institutions, where they appear to be less effective.

However, that is not to say that institutionalized treatment cannot be successful. A study by Nicholaichuk and colleagues (2000) evaluated an in-patient sex offender treatment program in a Canadian maximum security correctional facility and found that comparisons between treatment and control groups revealed significant differences at 2-, 3-, 5-, and 10-year follow-up periods. Across all follow-up periods, the treatment group had significantly lower prevalence of reconvictions for a new sex offence.

Circles of Support and Accountability (CoSA) is a correctional program based on restorative justice principles. This program was created in Ontario, when the first Circle was put together in 1994 to help a high-risk sex offender who was trying to reintegrate into the community. Due to the success of that first Circle, a partnership was formed with Correctional Service Canada to implement it to the whole country. Since its creation, more than 350 Canadian sex offenders have participated in CoSA (Duwe, 2018). This program offers support to offenders and requires that all offenders take responsibility for their actions. The goal is to facilitate a successful reintegration to the community with no more victims (Hannem & Petrunik, 2007). The Circle is composed of core members (that is, community volunteers) as well as the members of the "Bouter Circle," who are generally community-based professionals (psychologists, police officers, parole officers, and so on). They generally meet on a weekly basis, and the Circles usually last between 6 and 12 months (Duwe, 2018). A recent study by Duwe (2018) has shown that CoSAs significantly reduced sexual recidivism, reducing the risk of re-arrest for a new sexual offence by 88 per cent. Moreover, the program is associated with reductions in various measures of general recidivism, ranging between 49 and 57 per cent. Finally, the study by Duwe (2018) showed that the program avoided approximately $2 million in costs to the state of Minnesota. In fact, results suggest that for every dollar spent on CoSA, the program yielded a benefit of $3.73.

Summary

Sex offenders are treated as a special population in the criminal justice system. Extensive media coverage of violent sexual crimes committed by convicted sex offenders has intensified community outrage and fuelled the public's desire for immediate solutions to a complex public policy issue (LaFond, 2005). However, findings on the criminal career of these offenders have shown that most of the so-called "sex offenders" are in fact generalist offenders. Despite their relatively low recidivism rate for sexual crimes, correctional systems continue to isolate these offenders from the general population to prevent institutional violence. Moreover, risk assessment tools have been developed specifically to predict the risk of recidivism and the dangerousness of these sex offenders. After being assessed with various methods—some more intrusive than others (for example, phallometry), these inmates are generally directed to a treatment program specialized in sexual violence. The focus on the sexual nature of their crimes will also extend beyond incarceration, where offenders will be subjected to specific measures in the community, such as registration, community notification, and even residence restriction. Despite a clear lack of evidence showing either the effectiveness or ineffectiveness of these measures, they continue to be used to prevent future sexual offending by limiting opportunities for these offenders.

When looking at recidivism rates, certain types of sex offenders (such as homosexual child molesters) represent a high risk to the community. However, as we have seen, the recidivism risk for sex offenders varies by the type of offence and offender characteristics. Recent policy changes for sex offenders typically target all sex offenders indiscriminately, which leads to the diffusion of scarce resources to a large pool of offenders and unintended collateral consequences. Knowledge about sex offenders can be used to focus application of these restrictive measures to the most dangerous offenders.

Review Questions

1. Are sex offenders better described as generalists or specialists, and does this vary by the type of sexual offender?
2. How do registries and residence restrictions lead to unintended consequences for sex offenders reintegrating back into the community?
3. What are some of the unique challenges sex offenders face in prison?
4. A popular belief among the general public is that sex offenders are at a "high risk" of reoffending. How do recidivism studies counter this view?
5. What treatment methods have been found to be most effective for offenders who have committed sexual offences?

Critical Thinking Questions

1. Do you think the STATIC-99 is an instrument that should be used to assess the risk of an offender prior to being released from prison?

2. What are some of the factors that could influence the negative attitude of correctional staff toward sex offenders?

Multimedia Suggestions

Sex Offender

This National Geographic video discusses the hierarchy among sex offenders in prisons: https://www.youtube.com/watch?v=nkz87lS0jjY

Sex Offender Village

This Op-Doc from the *New York Times* highlights a small community in Florida where more than 100 registered sex offenders have settled since 2009: https://www.youtube.com/watch?v=YTm9efzHaTk

The Ontario Provincial Sex Offence Registry

This video talks to experts about the Ontario Sex Offence Registry, including why it was created and how it affects the lives of everyone in the province: https://www.youtube.com/watch?v=aFKkEcLu0nY

References

Abel G.G., Lawry, S.S., Karlstrom E., Osborn, C.A., & Gillespie, C.F. (1994). Screening tests for pedophillia. *Criminal Justice Behaviour, 21*(1), 115–31. doi:10.1177/0093854894021001008

Alexander, M.A. (1999). Sexual offender treatment efficacy revisited. *Sexual Abuse, 11*(2), 101–16.

Anderson, J.D. (1997). How to survive in prison as an innocent man convicted of a sex crime. *Institute for Psychological Therapies, 9.* Retrieved from http://www.ipt-forensics.com/journal/volume9/j9_3_6.htm

Axtman, K. (2006, July 28). Efforts grow to keep tabs on sex offenders. *The Christian Science Monitor.* Retrieved from http://www.csmonitor.com/2006/0728/p01s02-ussc.html

Ballard, P. (2005, October 4). State officials grapple with problems in tracking sex offenders. *The Herald-Mail.* Retrieved from http://www.herald-mail.com/?module¼displaystory&story_id¼121167&format¼html

Barbaree, H.E., Seto, M.C., Langton, C.M., & Peacock, E.J. (2001) Evaluating the predictive accuracy of six risk assessment instruments for adult sex offenders. *Criminal Justice and Behavior, 28,* 490–521.

Beech, A., Friendship, C., Erikson, M., & Hanson, R.K. (2002). The relationship between static and dynamic risk factors and reconviction in a sample of UK child abusers. *Sexual Abuse: A Journal of Research and Treatment, 14,* 155–67.

Beech, A.R., & Ward, T. (2004). The integration of etiology and risk in sexual offenders: A theoretical framework. *Aggression and Violent Behavior, 10*(1), 31–63. http://dx.doi.org/10.1016/j.avb.2003.08.002

Berliner, L., Schram, D., Miller, L., & Milloy, D.C. (1995). Sentencing alternative for sex offenders. *Journal of Interpersonal Violence, 10,* 487–502.

Blagden, N., & Pemberton, S. (2010). The challenge in conducting qualitative research with convicted sex offenders. *The Howard Journal of Criminal Justice, 49*(3), 269–81. https://doi.org/10.1111/j.1468-2311.2010.00615.x

Blagden, N., Winder, B., & Hames, C. (2014). "They treat us like human beings": Experiencing a therapeutic sex offender's prison impact on prisoners and staff and implications for treatment. *International Journal of Offender Therapy and Comparative Criminology, 60*(4), 371–96. https://doi.org/10.1177/0306624X14553227

Blokland, A., & Lussier, P. (Eds). (2015). *Sex offenders: A criminal career approach.* Malden, MA: Wiley-Blackwell.

Bonnar-Kidd, K.K. (2010). Sexual offender laws and prevention of sexual violence or recidivism. *American Journal of Public Health, 100*(3), 412–19. doi:10.2015/AJPH.2008.153254

Bonta, J., Harman, W.G., Hann, R.G., & Cormier, R.B. (1996). The prediction of recidivism among federally sentenced offenders: A re-validation of the SIR scale. *Canadian Journal of Criminology, 38*(1), 61–79.

Brannon, N.Y., Levenson, J.S., Fortney, T., & Baker, J.N. (2007). Attitudes about community notification: A comparison of sexual offenders and the non-offending public. *Sexual Abuse, 19*(4), 369–79. https://doi.org/10.1177/107906320701900403

Burchfield, K.B., & Mingus, W. (2008). Not in my neighborhood: Assessing registered sex offenders' experiences with local social capital and social control. *Criminal Justice and Behavior, 35*(3), 356–74. https://doi.org/10.1177/0093854807311375

Cale, J., Lussier, P., McCuish, E., & Corrado, R. (2015). The prevalence of psychopathic personality disturbances among incarcerated youth: Comparing serious, chronic, violent and sex offenders. *Journal of Criminal Justice, 43*(4), 337–44. http://doi.org/10.1016/j.jcrimjus.2015.04.005

Campbell, T.W. (2014). *Assessing sex offenders: Problems and pitfalls.* Springfield, IL: Charles C. Thomas Publisher.

Coric, V., Feuerstein, S., Fortunati, F., Southwick, S., Temporini, H.D., & Morgan, C.A. (2005). Assessing sex offenders. *Psychiatry, 2*(11), 26–9.

Crewe, B. (2009). *The prisoner society: Power, adaptation, and social life in an English prison.* Oxford, UK: Oxford University Press.

Cubellis, M.A., Evans, D.N., & Fera, A.G. (2018). Sex offender stigma: An exploration of vigilantism against sex offenders. *Deviante Behavior, 40*(2), 225–39.

Davey, M. (2009, September 1). Case shows limits of sex offender alert programs. *New York Times.* Retrieved from http://www.nytimes.com/2009/09/02/us/02offenders.html

DeLisi, M. (2001). Extreme career criminals. *American Journal of Criminal Justice, 25*(2), 239–52. http://dx.doi.org/10.1007/BF02886848

Doren, D.M. (2004). Toward a multidimensional model for sexual recidivism risk. *Journal of Interpersonal Violence, 19*(8), 835–56.

Duwe, G. (2018). Can Circle of Support and Accountability (CoSA) significantly reduce sexual recidivism? Results from a randomized controlled trial in Minnesota. *Journal of Experimental Criminology, 14,* 463–84.

Duwe, G., Donnay, W., & Tewksbury, R. (2008). Does residential proximity matter? A geographic analysis of sex offense recidivism. *Criminal Justice and Behavior, 35*(4), 484–504. http://dx.doi.org/10.1177/0093854807313690

Epperson, D.L., Kaul, J.D., & Hesselton, D. (1998, October). Final report of the development of the Minnesota Sex Offender Screening Tool-Revised (MnSOST-R). Presentation at the 17th Annual Research and Treatment Conference of the Association for the Treatment of Sexual Abusers, Vancouver, British Columbia.

Fonce-Olivas, T. (2006, February 24). Proposal to ban sex offenders from border may not be legal. *El Paso Times,* 1A.

Friendship, C., Falshaw, L., & Beech, A.R. (2003). Measuring the real impact of accredited offending behaviour programmes. *Legal and Criminological Psychology, 8*(1), 115–27. https://doi.org/10.1348/135532503762871282

Furby, L., Weinrott, M.R., & Blackshaw, L. (1989). Sex offender recidivism: A review. *Psychological Bulletin, 105*(1), 3–30.

Gentry, A.L., Dulmus, C.N., & Theriot, M.T. (2005). Comparing sex offender risk classification using the Static-99 and LSI-R assessment instruments. *Research on Social Work Practice, 15*(6), 557–63.

Gookin, K. (2005). *Involuntary commitment of sexually violent predators: Comparing state laws.* Document No. 05-03-1101. Olympia, WA: Washington State Institute for Public Policy.

Groth, A.N. (1983). Treatment of the sexual offender in a correctional institution. In J.G. Greer & I.R. Stuart (Eds), *The sexual aggressor: Current perspectives on treatment.* New York, NY: Van Nostrand Reinhold Company.

Grubin, D. (1998). Sex offending against children: Understanding the risk. Police Research Series, Paper 99. London, UK: Home Office, Policing and Reducing Crime Unit, Research, Development and Statistics Directorate.

Hall, G.C. (1995). Sexual offender recidivism revisited: A meta-analysis of recent treatment studies. *Journal of Consulting and Clinical Psychology, 63,* 802–9.

Hannem, S., & Petrunik, M. (2007). Circles of support and accountability: A community justice initiative for the reintegration of high-risk sex offenders. *Contemporary Justice Review, 10,* 153–71.

Hanson, R.K. (1997a). The development of a brief actuarial risk scale for sexual offense recidivism. User Report No. 1997-04. Ottawa, ON: Department of the Solicitor General of Canada.

Hanson, R.K. (1997b). How to know what works with sexual offenders. *Sexual Abuse: A Journal of Research and Treatment, 9,* 129–45.

Hanson, R. (2005). Twenty years of progress in violence risk assessment. *Journal of Interpersonal Violence, 20*(2), 212–17. https://doi.org/10.1177/0886260504267740

Hanson, R.K., Bourgon, G., Helmus, L., & Hodgson, S. (2009). The principles of effective correctional treatment also apply to sexual offenders. *Criminal Justice and Behavior, 36*(9), 863–91. https://doi.org/10.1177/0093854809338545

Hanson, R.K., & Bussière, M.T. (1998). Predicting relapse: A meta-analysis of sexual offender recidivism studies. *Journal of Consulting and Clinical Psychology, 66*(2), 348–62.

Hanson, R.K., Gordon, A., Harris, A.R., Marques, J.K., Murphy, W., Quinsey, V.L., & Seto, M.C. (2002). First report of the Collaborative Outcome Data Project.

Hanson, R.K., & Thornton, D. (1999). Static 99: Improving actuarial risk assessments for sex offenders. Retrieved from https://www.publicsafety.gc.ca/cnt/rsrcs/pblctns/sttc-mprvng-actrl/sttc-mprvng-actrl-eng.pdf

Harkins, L., & Beech, A. (2007). Measurement of the effectiveness of sex offender treatment. *Aggression and Violent Behavior, 12*(1), 36–44. http://dx.doi.org/10.1016/j.avb.2006.03.002

Harris, G.T., Rice, M.E., & Quinsey, V.L. (1998). Appraisal and management of risk in sexual aggressors: Implications for criminal justice policy. *Psychology, Public Policy, and Law, 4*(1–2), 73–115.

Harris, D.A., Smallbone, S., Dennison, S., & Knight, R.A. (2009). Specialization and versatility in sexual offenders referred for civil commitment. *Journal of Criminal Justice, 37*(1), 37–44. http://doi.org/10.1016/j.jcrimjus.2008.12.002

Higgins, C., & Ireland, C. (2009). Attitudes towards male and female sex offenders: A comparison of forensic staff, prison officers and the general public in Northern Ireland. *British Journal of Forensic Practice, 11*(1), 14–19. doi:10.1108/14636646200900004

Hogue, T.E. (1993) Attitudes towards prisoners and sexual offenders. In N.K. Clark & G.M. Stephenson (Eds), *Sexual offenders: Context, assessment and treatment* (pp. 27–32). Leicester, UK: The British Psychological Society for the Division of Criminological and Legal Psychology.

Houston, J.A. (1994). Sex offender registration acts: An added dimension to the war on crime. *Georgia Law Review, 28,* 729–67.

Interstate Commission for Adult Offender Supervision. (2007). ICAOS GPS update survey April 2007. Retrieved from http://www.interstatecompact.org/LinkClick .aspx?fileticket¼1U6GvRmuPwM%3D&tabid¼105& mid¼431

Ireland, J.L. (2000). "Bullying" among prisoners: A review of research. *Aggression and Violent Behavior, 5*(2), 201–15. http://dx.doi.org/10.1016/S1359-1789(98)00031-7

Kenworthy, T., Adams, C.E., Bilby, C., Brooks-Gordon, B., & Fenton, M. (2004). Psychological interventions for those who have sexually offended or are at risk of offending. *Cochrane Database Systems Review, 3,* CD004858.

Kim, B., Benekos, P.J., & Merlo, A.V. (2015). Sex offender recidivism revisited: Review of recent meta-analyses on the effects of sex offender treatment. *Trauma, Violence, & Abuse, 17*(1), 105–17. https://doi .org/10.1177/1524838014566719

Knopp, F.H. (1984). *Retraining adult sex offenders: Methods and models* (rev. ed.). Syracuse, NY: Safer Society Program of the New York State Council of Churches.

LaFond, J.Q. (2005). *Preventing sexual violence: How society should cope with sex offenders.* Washington, DC: American Psychological Association.

Langan, P.A., Schmitt, E.L., & Durose, M.R. (2003). *Recidivism of sex offenders released from prison in 1994.* Washington, DC: Bureau of Justice Statistics.

Langevin, R., Curnoe, S., Fedoroff, P., Bennett, R., Langevin, M., Peever, C., Pettica, R., & Sandhu, S. (2004). Lifetime sex offender recidivism: A 25-year follow-up study. *Canadian Journal of Criminology and Criminal Justice, 46*(5), 531–52.

Levenson, J.S., Brannon, Y.N., Fortney, T., & Baker, J. (2007). Public perceptions about sex offenders and community protection policies. *Analyses of Social Issues and Public Policy, 7*(1), 1–25. https://doi. org/10.1111/j.1530-2415.2007.00119.x

Levenson, J., & Cotter, L. (2005). The effect of Megan's Law on sex offender reintegration. *Journal of Contemporary Criminal Justice, 21*(1), 49–66. https://doi .org/10.1177/1043986204271676

Levenson, J.S., & Harn, A.L. (2007). Sex offender residence restrictions: Unintended consequences and community re-entry. *Justice Research and Policy, 9,* 59–73.

Lieb, R., & C. Nunlist. (2008). *Community notification as viewed by Washington's citizens: A 10-year follow-up.* Document No. 08-03-1101. Olympia, WA: Washington State Institute for Public Policy.

Logan, W.A. (2009). *Knowledge as power: Criminal registration and community notification laws in America.* Stanford, CA: Stanford University Press.

Lösel, F., & Schmucker, M. (2005). The effectiveness of treatment for sexual offenders: A comprehensive meta-analysis. *Journal of Experimental Criminology, 1*(1), 117–46.

http://dx.doi.org/10.1007/s11292-004-6466-7

Lussier, P. (2005). The criminal activity of sexual offenders in adulthood: Revisiting the specialization debate. *Sexual Abuse: A Journal of Research and Treatment, 17*(3), 269–92. https://doi.org/10.1177/107906320501700303

MacKenzie, D.L. (2006). *What works in corrections: Reducing the criminal activities of offenders and delinquents.* Cambridge, UK: Cambridge University Press.

McGrath, R.J., Cumming, G., Livingston, J.A., & Hoke, S.E. (2003). Outcome of a treatment program for adult sex offenders: From prison to community. *Journal of Interpersonal Violence, 18,* 3–17.

Meehl, P.E. (1954). *Clinical versus statistical prediction: A theoretical analysis and review of the evidence.* Minneapolis, MN: University of Minnesota.

Meloy, M.L., Miller, S.L., & Curtis, K.M. (2008). Making sense out of nonsense: The deconstruction of state-level sex offender residence restrictions. *American Journal of Criminal Justice, 33(2), 209–22.* http://dx.doi.org/10.1007/ s12103-008-9042-2

Monahan, J. (1981). The clinical prediction of violent behavior. *Crime & Delinquency Issues: A Monograph Series, ADM* 81-921, 134.

Morris, N. (1982). *Madness and the criminal law.* Chicago, IL: University of Chicago Press.

Morris, N., & Miller, M. (1985). Predictions of dangerousness. In M. Tonry & N. Morris (Eds), *Crime and justice: An annual review of research* (pp. 1–50). Chicago, IL: University of Chicago Press.

Mustaine, E.E., Tewksbury, R., & Stengel, K.M. (2006). Social disorganization and residential locations of registered sex offenders: Is this a collateral consequence? *Deviant Behavior, 27*(3), 329–50.

National Conference of State Legislatures. (2008). State statutes related to Jessica's Law: Criminal justice report. Retrieved from: http://www.ncsl.org/print/cj/2006crime.pdf

Nicholaichuk, T., Gordon, A., Gu, D., Wong, S. (2000). Outcome of an institutional sexual offender treatment program: A comparison between treated and matched untreated offenders. *Sexual Abuse: A Journal of Research and Treatment, 12,* 139–53.

Nieto, M., & Jung, D. (2006). The impact of residency restrictions on sex offenders and correctional management practices: A literature review. Sacramento, CA: California Research Bureau. Retrieved from http://digitalcommons .law.ggu.edu/caldocs_agencies/303

Norton, K. (2018, January 27). What's it like being in prison as a known sex offender? [Weblog post]. Retrieved from https://www.quora.com/Whats-it-like-being-in-prison-as-a-known-sex-offender

Nunes, K.L., Firestone, P., Bradford, J.M., Greenberg, D.M., Broom, I. (2002). A comparison of modified versions of the Static-99 and the Sex Offender Risk Appraisal Guide. *Sexual Abuse: A Journal of Research and Treatment, 14,* 253–69.

O'Donnell, I. & Edgar, K. (1999). Fear in prison. *The Prison Journal, 79*(1), 90–9.

https://doi.org/10.1177/0032885599079001006

Petersilia, J. (2003). *When prisoners come home: Parole and prisoner reentry.* New York, NY: Oxford University Press.

Peterson, I. (2005, January 12). Mix-ups and worse arising from sex offender notification. *New York Times.* Retrieved from https://www.nytimes.com/1995/01/12/nyregion/mix-ups-and-worse-arising-from-sex-offender-notification.html

Petrunik, M., & Weisman, R. (2005). Constructing Joseph Fredericks: Competing narratives of a child sex murderer. *International Journal of Law and Psychiatry, 28*(1), 75–96.

Phillips, D.M. (1998). *Community notification as viewed by Washington citizens.* Olympia, WA: Washington State Institute for Public Policy.

Prescott, J.J., & Rockoff, J.A. (2008). Do sex offender registration and notification laws affect criminal behavior? NBER Working Paper No. 13803. 3rd Annual Conference on Empirical Legal Studies Papers, University of Michigan Law and Economics. Retrieved from http://ssrn.com/abstract=1100663

Proctor, J.L., Badzinski, D., & Johnson, M. (2002). The impact of media on knowledge and perceptions of Megan's Law. *Criminal Justice Policy Review, 13*(4), 356–79. https://doi.org/10.1177/088740302237804

Quinsey, V.L. Harris, G.T. Rice, M.E. & Cormier, C.A. (1998). *The law and public policy: Psychology and the social sciences series. Violent offenders: Appraising and managing risk.* Washington, DC: American Psychological Association.

Quinsey, V.L., Lalumière, M.L., Rice, M.E., & Harris, G.T. (1995). Predicting sexual offenses. In J.C. Campbell (Ed), *Assessing dangerousness: Violence by sexual offenders, batterers, and child abusers* (pp. 114–37). Thousand Oaks, CA: Sage.

Ricciardelli, R., & Spencer, D. (2017). *Violence, sex offenders, and corrections.* London, UK: Routledge.

Rice, M.E. & Harris, G.T. (1997). Cross-validation and extension of the Violence Risk Appraisal Guide for child molesters and rapists. *Law and Human Behavior, 21*(2), 231–41.

Rice, M.E. & Harris, G.T. (2003). The size and sign of treatment effects in sex offender therapy. *Annals of the New York Academy of Sciences, 989,* 428–40.

Rood, L. (2006), January 23). New data shows twice as many sex offenders missing. *Des Moines Register.*

Saad, L. (2005, June 9). Sex offender registries are underutilized by the public. *Gallup News Service.* Retrieved from http://www.gallup.com/poll/16705/sex-offender-registries-underutilized-public.aspx

Sample, L.L., & Bray, T.M. (2003). Are sex offenders dangerous? *Criminology and Public Policy, 3,* 59–82.

Sample, L., & Kadleck, C. (2008). Sex offender laws: Legislators' accounts of the need for policy. *Criminal Justice Policy, 19*(1), 40–62. https://doi.org/10.1177/0887403407308292

Sandler, J., Freeman, N., & Socia, K. (2008). Does a watched pot boil? A time-series analysis of New York state's sex offender registration and notification law. *Psychology, Public Policy, and Law, 14*(4), 284–302. doi: 10.1037/a0013881

Schram, D.D., & Miloy, C.D. (1995). Community notification: A study of offender characteristics and recidivism. Olympia, WA: Washington State Institute for Public Policy. Retrieved from http://www.wsipp.wa.gov/ReportFile/1208/Wsipp_Community-Notification-A-Study-of-Offender-Characteristics-and-Recidivism_Full-Report.pdf

Schwaebe, C. (2005). Learning to pass: Sex offenders' strategies for establishing a viable identity in the prison general population. *Interpersonal Journal of Offender Therapy and Comparative Criminology, 49*(6), 614–24. doi:10.1177/0306624X05275829

Shao, L., & Li, J. (2006). *The effect of sex offender registration laws on rape victimization.* Unpublished manuscript, University of Alabama.

Simon, L.J. (2000). An examination of the assumptions of specialization, mental disorder, and dangerousness in sex offenders. *Behavioral Sciences and the Law, 18,* 275–308.

Sim, J. (1994) Tougher than the rest? Men in prison. In T. Newburn & E.A. Stanko (Eds), *Just boys doing business? Men, masculinities and crime* (pp. 100–117). London, UK: Routledge.

Sparks, R., Bottoms, A.E., & Hay, W. (1996) *Prisons and the problem of order.* Oxford, UK: Clarendon Press.

Spencer, D. (2009). Sex offender as homo sacer. *Punishment & Society, 11* (2), 219–40. https://doi.org/10.1177/1462474508101493

Task Force on Community Protection. (1989). *Task Force on Community Protection: Final report to booth Gardner, governor, state of Washington.* Olympia, WA: Author.

Tewksbury, R. (2002). Validity and reliability of the Kentucky sex offender registry. *Federal Probation, 66*(1), 21–6.

Tewksbury, R., & Jennings, W.G. (2010). Assessing the impact of sex offender registration and community notification on sex-offending trajectories. *Criminal Justice and Behavior, 37*(5), 570–82.

Tewksbury, R., Jennings, W.G., & Zgoba, K.M. (2012). A longitudinal examination of sex offender recidivism prior to and following the implementation of SORN. *Behavioral Sciences and the Law, 30*(3), 308–28.

Thurston, R. (1996). Are you sitting comfortably? Men's storytelling, masculinities, prison culture and violence. In M. Mac an Ghaill (Ed.), *Understanding masculinities: Social relations and cultural arenas* (pp. 139–52). Buckingham, UK: Open University Press.

Turner, S., & Janetta, J. (2006). Evaluating the effectiveness of global positioning devices for high risk sex offenders in San Diego, California. The Annual Meeting of the American Society of Criminology, Los Angeles, California.

Van den Berg, C., Beijersbergen, K., Nieuwbeerta, P., & Dirkzwager, A. (2018). Sex offenders in prison: Are they socially isolated? *Sexual Abuse, 30*(7), 828–45. https://doi .org/10.1177/1079063217700884

Vaughn, M.S. & Sapp, A.D. (1989). Less than utopian: Sex offender treatment in a milieu of power struggles, status positioning, and inmate manipulation in state correctional institutions. *The Prison Journal, 69*(2), 73–89.

Waldram, J.B. (2007). Everybody has a story: Listening to imprisoned sexual offenders. *Qualitative Health Research, 17*(7), 963–70. doi: 10.1177/1049732307306014

Webster, C., Gartner, R., & Doob, A. (2006). Results by design: The artefactual construction of high recidivism rates for sex offenders. *Canadian Journal of Criminology and Criminal Justice, 48*, 79–93.

Weekes, J.R., Pelletier, G., & Beaudette, D. (1995). Correctional officers: How do they perceive sex offenders? *International Journal of Offender Therapy and Comparative Criminology, 39*, 55–61.

Winfree, L., Newbold, G., & Tubb, S. (2002). Prisoner perspectives on inmate culture in New Mexico and New Zealand: A descriptive case study. *The Prison Journal, 82*(2), 213–33. https://doi.org/10.1177/003288550208200204

Zandbergen, P.A., Hart, T.C. (2006). Reducing housing options for convicted sex offenders: Investigating the impact of residency restriction laws using GIS. *Justice Research and Policy, 8*(2), 1–24.

Zgoba, K., Witt, P., Dalessandro, M., and Veysey, B. (2008). *Megan's Law: Assessing the practical and monetary efficacy.* Washington, DC: U.S. Department of Justice, Office of Justice Programs, National Institute of Justice. Retrieved from www.ncjrs.gov/pdffiles1/nij/grants/225370.pdf

PART IV

Current/Emerging Issues

The "Prison [Tourism] Fix"

Carceral Habitus and Retasking in Kingston, Ontario

Jarrod Shook, Justin Piché, and Kevin Walby

13

Learning Objectives

After reading this chapter, you should be able to:

- Describe how Kingston Penitentiary went from being a notorious federal penitentiary to a prominent tourism destination.
- Describe how operational and decommissioned sites of human caging are normalized, and how a carceral habitus shapes and is shaped by particular contexts.
- Explain and apply key concepts in the sociology of punishment to the growing cultural phenomenon of prison tourism.
- Outline an abolitionist critique of prison tourism as a form of carceral retasking.

Chapter Overview

With several federal penitentiaries near the municipality, Kingston, Ontario, is Canada's most prominent pen-city. Kingston Penitentiary (KP), in particular, has been central to the region's identity since it opened in 1835, decades before the founding of Canada. This chapter explores how multiple actors participated in the reimagining of KP following the April 2012 announcement of its closure. Applying Gilmore's (2007) notion of the "prison fix," we explain how the dormant land and buildings at KP were reactivated by initiating tours of the site informed and reinforced by what Schept (2015) calls "carceral habitus," which naturalizes imprisonment to the point that its material and symbolic roles go unquestioned. In so doing, we reveal local dynamics contributing to the stability of Canada's culture of punishment that serves as a barrier to efforts to further reduce the use and pains of imprisonment.

Introduction

Constructed in 1835 by a captive labour force who would later be confined there (Taylor Hazell Architects, 2017), Kingston Penitentiary became a fixture in the Kingston region and central to its identity as it developed into the prison capital of Canada post-Confederation.[1] Before it was closed by Correctional Service Canada (CSC) on 30 September 2013, KP held the distinction of being the country's longest running site of confinement (Ferguson, Lay, Piché, & Walby, 2014).

Given the penitentiary's significance to Kingston's residents, many of whom are CSC employees or retirees, the April 2012 decision to decommission KP (Public Safety Canada, 2012) was met with criticism from dozens of stakeholders who benefited from the operation of this carceral space (Piché, Ferguson, & Walby, 2019). Aware that the "465 staff that are currently employed at the prison contribute to Kingston's local economy and to city tax revenues," Kingston City Council

(KCC) passed a motion in October 2012 requesting the federal government "detail the true net savings of the closure to Canadian taxpayers" and that it "transfer as many jobs as it can to the other local penitentiaries in the region" (KCC, 2012a, p. 702).

While efforts were made to keep CSC employees working, ideas about what could be done with KP began to circulate (Ferguson et al., 2014), ranging from erecting recreation facilities (such as a sailing centre) or tourism destinations (a casino) to housing (condos on Lake Ontario). While KP's future was debated, many proposals for its reuse remained rooted in its carceral past, with many suggesting that the site become a prominent **prison tourism** destination. In the first six years since human captivity ceased at KP, the site has often been used as a dark tourism destination, attracting thousands of "penal spectators" (Brown, 2009, p. 8) from Canada and across the world who seek to experience being inside penitentiary walls (Ferguson, Piché, & Walby, 2015). Dark tourism involves visitation to sites associated with death and suffering (Stone, 2013) "for education or entertainment purposes" (Ferguson et al., 2014, p. 84). Forms of dark tourism, such as prison tourism, derive their popularity, in part, through visitors' fascination with human horror stories (Wilson, Hodgkinson, Piché, & Walby, 2017).

Following our research on KP's first tours in October and November 2013, where imprisonment was presented as necessary in the past and at present, we began to use the term **carceral retasking**. The concept refers to instances when decommissioned penitentiaries, prisons, jails, lock-ups, and other sites of confinement are transformed into enterprises, like prison tourism destinations, which "continue to reproduce imprisonment as a dominant idea and/or material practice" (Ferguson et al., 2014, pp. 83–4). We have since examined the role CSC played in this process as a means of neutralizing the criticism they faced from staff members, Kingston-area residents, as well as local and national news media when KP's closure was announced (Piché et al., 2019).

This chapter explores how actors in business, news media, and municipal and federal politics participated in the reimagining of KP. Drawing from scholarship on state efforts to open new carceral sites, we examine the inverse process at KP. Applying Gilmore's (2007) notion of the "prison fix," we explain how the dormant land and buildings at KP were reactivated by initiating tours of the site informed and reinforced by what Schept

(2015) calls carceral habitus, which naturalizes imprisonment to the point that its material and symbolic roles go unquestioned. We reveal local dynamics contributing to the stability of Canada's culture of punishment that serves as a barrier to efforts to further reduce the use and pains of imprisonment.

Theorizing the Role of Penal Infrastructure Development and Its Relationship to Prison Tourism in Neoliberal Times

While people living in the United States are incarcerated at a rate nearly six times greater per capita than in Canada (Wagner & Sawyer, 2018), insights can be drawn from scholars who study US developments that are pertinent to understanding penality in the Canadian context. Under neoliberalism, which gained acceptance in mainstream US politics beginning in the 1970s, state restructuring is characterized by decreases to government revenue capacity via tax cuts, divestment from welfare, as well as greater investment in war-making capacity at home (via the "criminal justice" system and "security" establishment) and abroad (via the military; Gilmore, 2007). Technological change and the liberalization of trade has also translated into disruptions in long-standing sectors of the economy on Turtle Island (known now as North America) during this period. Many Canadian (Piché, Kleuskens, & Walby, 2017) and US (Schept, 2015) jurisdictions have sold the construction of new, bigger sites of confinement as a means of putting "back to work" the surpluses generated by the waste that neoliberal politics and economics leave behind (Gilmore, 2007, p. 88).

Gilmore's book *Golden Gulag: Prisons, Surplus, Crisis, and Opposition in Globalizing California* is instructive in this regard. With the idea of the **prison fix**, Gilmore focuses on how governments turn to imprisonment as a way of addressing fiscal, social, and political crises. Her study begins with the 1973–5 global recession. Facing massive unemployment in "inner cities and in rural counties most reliant on resource extraction and agriculture" (Gilmore, 2007, p. 41), California, then headed by Governor Ronald Reagan (a future US president), began to lower taxes while also rolling back social safety-net programs such as education and employment retraining. As the state became less involved in the redistribution of wealth, attention was directed toward "capital's needs—particularly on how to minimize impediments, and maximize opportunities for capital recruitment and retention" (Gilmore, 2007, p. 53). What ensued was a crisis that required state intervention to restore stability to California's capitalist economy. The situation left many "workers at the extreme edges, or completely outside, of restructured labor markets, stranded in urban and rural communities" (Gilmore, 2007, p. 70).

Facing a legitimacy crisis, California needed to mobilize its unused surplus state capacity to resolve the crises of multiple surpluses (Gilmore, 2007, p. 84). What emerged was a new state that "built itself in part by building prisons" using the "ideological and material means at hand to do so, renovating its welfare-warfare capacities into something different by molding surplus finance capital, land, and labor into the workfare-warfare state" (Gilmore, 2007, p. 85). A "law and order" agenda was central to paving the way for surplus finances to be dis-accumulated through private loans to the state to build massive new prisons on vacant land no longer being used for capitalist production. The push to build more human cages was intended to put surplus labour to work through the confinement of the urban poor in facilities located in areas that would employ the rural poor.

New penal infrastructure has arisen in Canada related to crises in capitalism, too. A notable example of this is when Prime Minister Brian Mulroney ordered a halt to a penitentiary under construction in Quebec City in the mid-1980s. The project was relocated to his riding of Port-Cartier, Quebec, to provide employment to some of his rural constituents who had lost work in the preceding decade following the closure of local paper mills, mines, and factories (Rosner, 2008).

In communities where imprisonment has become a taken-for-granted part of life (Davis, 2003), and building more human cages is presented as a road toward economic salvation in the face of crushing poverty and meagre job prospects (Christie, 2000), a **carceral habitus** can be observed (Schept, 2015). Drawing on Bourdieu (1990, p. 56), Schept (2013) describes this as a form of "embodied history, internalized as second nature and so forgotten as history" (p. 76). Carceral habitus is not simply an individual routine, but an entrenched way of thinking and acting that permeates economic, political, cultural, and social relations (Schept, 2015). As a result, imprisonment is normalized

in dealing with conflict, rather than a violent human experiment. The carceral habitus is embodied by local officials and residents whose decisions and actions reproduce existing relations and institutions (Schept, 2015).

Capital reactivation through a "prison fix" and informed by a carceral habitus is not just at work when governments engage in campaigns to erect new sites of confinement. These processes are also present when different actors scramble to sustain the carcerality that has been built up in their communities over time (Walby & Piché, 2015) when sites of confinement are closed, even when they are replaced by new, bigger human warehouses locally (Piché, 2014). Sometimes these efforts result in carceral retasking through the establishment of prison tourism, which is true of sites like KP, which we focus on below.

"They Shouldn't Level It or Blast It to Hell"

Following the announcement that KP would be closing, there were many public interventions from stakeholders who referred to the role of imprisonment in the region in a way that highlights the depth of carceral habitus in the Kingston region. The *Kingston Whig-Standard* (*The Whig*) is one prominent site where such sentiments are captured. Like KP, the newspaper shares a long history with the city. Founded in 1834, one year before KP opened, *The Whig* is "Canada's oldest continuously published daily newspaper" (Murphy, 2013).

One of the first interventions in *The Whig* following KP's closure seemed to challenge this carceral habitus as historian and author of *Canada's Big House: The Dark History of Kingston Penitentiary*, Peter Hennessy, remarked "It's a blessing that it's finally going to be closed . . . It ceased to have any practical utility as long ago as the 1971 Riot" (Norris, 2012). Yet when asked what might become of the facility, he suggested, "It will be an interesting experience in ingenuity and planning to put the old institution to use. They shouldn't level it or blast it to hell. That would be a terrible mistake" (Norris, 2012). Hennessy saw the prison as a cultural product and wished "to see the prison converted into a museum or some sort of tourist attraction, perhaps a bed and breakfast," citing "the infamous Alcatraz" and the "boon to tourism" for San Francisco because they "left it the way it was" (Norris, 2012). Steven Maynard,

Reflections on the Closure of KP and RTC by a Former Indigenous Prisoner

In 1987, I was placed in Millhaven Maximum Institution. During the two years that I served there I went into a really dark place after being locked up all the time. I couldn't see the light at the end of the tunnel. A mixture of depression and anger overtook me, and I decided to "string up" [die by suicide]. I tied bed sheets together and did the deed only to be cut down by a correctional officer (CO) who happened to be doing rounds. I was sent to the local hospital, where I went into a coma and suffered brain damage. After one week in the hospital, I was transferred to the Regional Treatment Centre (RTC) on the grounds of Kingston Penitentiary (KP).

Upon my arrival, I experienced zero compassion. It was like being held in a dungeon. I was at RTC for one month and underwent analysis by a psychiatrist. Much of the time I spent at RTC I was forced to wear a baby doll [a type of medical dress one would be put into for an examination or operation] and only had a mattress in my cell. The psychologist would visit me with his chair placed out front of the cell. I was careful about being too open with him for fear of the consequences of being honest. Each day I received one shower. I was led to and from the shower in handcuffs. There was no fresh air on the range and constant screaming. It wasn't a treatment setting, despite its name.

I was finally sent back to Millhaven and received a transfer to Joyceville where I ended up applying for parole, which was denied because of my suicide attempt. I'm an Indigenous man and, while at RTC, I requested to see an Elder and was refused. Treatment at RTC didn't exist. After my time at RTC, I was stigmatized and marginalized. Years later, I studied criminology at Carleton University where I came across numerous articles about assimilation and found out that the penitentiary sat on a "federal reserve." KP and RTC was simply another federal reserve where First Nations' peoples and others were displaced. While I was incarcerated I knew why I was so angry, but I didn't understand what was happening. I now know what I was experiencing was systemic racism.

The hellhole that KP and RTC represented were due for closure. KP needed to close because it maimed the incarcerated, their loved ones, the community, and even those who worked there. When I think of KP and RTC, all I think about are the deaths by suicide. The tours that they give there now only offer a one-sided narrative, involving ex-CO's giving the tour and glorifying punishment. No one ever talks about the 19-year-old kid who sat in that shit hole and took his own life. We don't hear those stories. Some people refer to Canadian prisons as the "new residential schools." There's nothing new about this. It's been going on for quite some time. Just like the early days when they cut your hair, took your name, and assigned you a number. It's all the same.

I think they ought to tear the fucking thing down. It's just like any other colonial structure, statue, or building to me. If they do anything with it, they ought to honour the prisoners who lost their lives there, not make it into a prison tourism site. How about in the spirit of reconciliation they make it a memorial site for Indigenous people and others who lost their lives?

---

from the Department of History at Queen's University, opined that "the real story here is less about infamous inmates and more about the central place KP has occupied in the everyday life of Kingston for almost 180 years . . . KP is so intertwined with Kingston's identity that its closure will tear a big hole in both the historical and present-day fabric of Kingston life" (Norris, 2012).

One of the ways in which KP has managed to become intertwined with Kingston's identity is through the cultural work of its staff, performed using rituals that elevate their status and profile. A recent ceremony organized by a group of CSC staff to commemorate a past colleague killed by a prisoner[2] while performing his job at KP in 1936 stands out as one such example (VandenBrink, 2012). The "newly unveiled gravestone in remembrance of the fallen officer," which reminds others of "the sacrifices correctional officers make" (VandenBrink, 2012), also stands as a symbol of and vehicle for the embodiment of carceral habitus. Valorization of state captors is the product of deliberate cultural work engaged in by carceral stakeholders like Dave St. Onge, who was until recently a CSC employee and curator of the Federal Penitentiary Museum across the street from KP. For St. Onge, it is necessary to "create a record of each officer to pass on to future generations," because "if we don't record it . . . it's just an inexcusable loss" (VandenBrink, 2012).

Members of the community lacking official affiliations with KP also engaged in advocacy that fed into the local carceral habitus. The Kingston Municipal Heritage Committee, a working group of KCC, "voted unanimously" in fall 2012 to have the "Historic Properties Research Working Group study the maximum security prison" to see if it could be designated as a "heritage property so that the city would have some control over the fate of the 177-year-old institution should the federal government sell the property someday" (Hendra, 2012). Having KP designated as a "heritage property" was important because, as city councillor Bill Glover argued, its designation as a national historic site granted by the federal government in 1990 would "not protect the property should it be sold to a private buyer" and conceivably "they could level the whole site," which "would be absolutely atrocious, grievous, scandalous" (Hendra, 2012). With a "provincial or municipal designation" there would be "a very clear process" concerning the changes that could be made to the property, which "not only protects the buildings themselves, but the property as a whole" (Hendra, 2012). If it succeeded, KCC would have "control over the prison's fate" (Hendra, 2012) and could preserve its carceral roots.

Preserving KP or Planning Its Future Commodification?

While a carceral habitus permeates daily life in Kingston, it is also contested. One year after the decommissioning was announced a "group of 50 people gathered" across from KP at the Prison for Women—another decommissioned federal penitentiary—for an "Idle No More demonstration as part of the national day of action for Indigenous prisoners in the Canadian justice system" (Boudreau, 2013). Rally co-organizer James Sayeau, a member of the Algonquin and Mohawk nations, indicated the protest location was chosen because "Kingston penitentiary is significant in its historical value and how long it's been a part of Canadian society generally," and "many groups of people have walked through those doors at one time or another" (Boudreau, 2013). They used the occasion to "raise awareness of the disproportionate number of Aboriginal [people] in Canadian prisons and jails"

(Boudreau, 2013). Such events, however, are fleeting in a region consumed by punishment.

As the fall 2013 closure of KP neared, several actors went public with their development proposals. These interventions highlighted tension between those who envisaged the property as a commodity ripe for economic development, sometimes without an explicit interest in memorialization, versus those who wished to conserve it, and others who wanted to preserve elements of KP but commodify it through operations beyond prison tourism.

One of the first groups to go public with their plans for KP included George Hood, George Jackson, Michael de La Roche, and John Curtis, four locals operating under the Hatter's Bay banner. They wanted to turn KP into a "top-flight sailing training centre" that would make "Kingston an international sailing capital that is unprecedented in the world" (Hendra, 2013). Challenging the local carceral habitus, this group declared "there are some things that shouldn't be saved—this is one of them" (Hendra, 2013). Viewing the property as a commercial opportunity, they envisioned a site with "restaurants, some of which would overlook the water, and stores, some of which would sell sailing-specific merchandise" (Hendra, 2013). For funds, the group intended to rely on the "sale of the 500 or so planned high-end condominiums" (Hendra, 2013).

In response to this proposal, the chief executive officer of the Kingston Economic Development Corporation (KEDCO), Jeff Garrah, weighed in, noting their preference for a "hybrid model" or a "public-private development opportunity" similar to the "revamped distillery District in Toronto" (Hendra, 2013). Touting the potential of tours, Garrah's position was that "you have to respect the heritage" of KP (Hendra, 2013). While KEDCO emphasized the economic opportunities that could be harnessed by transforming the site through "mixed development," it insisted that development at KP should tap into its carceral legacy. When referencing the annual tourist draw of 25,000 to 30,000 to the Federal Penitentiary Museum (Walby & Piché, 2011), Garrah remarked, "If that's what we're getting for the little warden's house, what will we be getting for Kingston Penitentiary?" (Hendra, 2013).

As discussions continued about KP's future, one retired CSC employee could not imagine a post-carceral future for the site, but also could not envisage making "a museum out of it" (Lea, 2013). Others, such as former KP warden Monty Bourke, envisioned a carceral future that could show off KP's legacy to the world. Bourke thought the site would serve well as a "tourist attraction" similar to the "old Melbourne Gaol in Australia," where experiential tours of the facility, including actors, could provide a "learning experience for anyone wanting to learn about the justice system" and "a different era of the prison" during each stop on the tour (Schliesmann, 2013). Tapping into an ingrained carceral habitus, Bourke stated that his mission to preserve the site "has taken on a personal significance" as "the thing about KP is, if you worked there, there is something in the limestone—some osmosis—that seeps into you" (Schliesmann, 2013). Bourke noted that he was involved in two proposals to operate the site as a heritage destination to showcase "the good, the bad and the ugly" at KP (Schliesmann, 2013).

While the future of KP was being deliberated, a first wave of tours was offered by former KP staff as a fundraiser for the local United Way after KP closed in September 2013. With former KP staff serving as guides, the tours positioned imprisonment as rehabilitative and

Photo inside Kingston Penitentiary, taken during a tour offered in October 2013.

necessary to community safety, while also focusing on prisoner violence and escapes (Ferguson et al., 2014), which underscores cultural tropes concerning dangerous and cunning "criminals" (Piché et al., 2019). The voices of prisoners themselves, who could have provided alternative ways of fathoming life at KP, were excluded from the tours. Yet despite this glaring deficiency, the tours were popular. In just a few weeks the tours generated $188,000 through the sale of 9,400 tickets at $20 each (Ferguson, 2013). Throughout this period, local and national media put more wind in the sails of a carceral future for the site, touting KP tours as an "opportunity to look felony in the face" in a "historic complex" that "is a memory-bank of murderous and fiendish reality" where you can pay "to sense severe punishment" of a "remorseless enemy of the community" (Patterson, 2013). In a typical dichotomy between *us* and *them* that justifies confinement (Brown, 2009), journalists and commentators positioned the tours as a chance to "improve the public's understanding of a correctional officer's job, of its dangers" and their "commitment to the disinterested enforcement of rules" against "cutthroats and deceivers" (Patterson, 2013).

The October 2013 United Way tours were followed by KP tours benefiting Habitat for Humanity the following month. Once again, the dormant capital of KP was tapped into as a means of serving both the CSC and the not-for-profit sector (Piché et al., 2019) through a "prison [tourism] fix" (Gilmore, 2007), this time with 9,000 tickets sold and more than $180,000 raised to build houses using the labour of federal prisoners.

From a "Contaminated" Penitentiary to Expanding Access to "This Natural Treasure of Ours"

After an initial run of tours, discussions concerning KP's future continued in spring 2014. At this time, officials from the City of Kingston became aware that portions of the property were contaminated along the western wall, requiring the site be closed off to the public due to "hazardous substances such as arsenic, lead and benzene in concentration above acceptable levels" (*Kingston Whig-Standard*, 2014). In fact, "in one area lead was 93 times the acceptable level and copper was 840 times over. In another spot arsenic was recorded 68 times over" (*Kingston Whig-Standard*, 2014). A member of city council noted, "we're not surprised when we discover contaminated soil. I mean we're an old industrial town so we're used to it . . . I am still concerned because we still have to . . . assist Corrections in dealing with the situation to get the site cleaned up so that it can properly be turned over to the next user" (*Kingston Whig-Standard*, 2014). While it was "believe[d] some of the contamination is due to the storage and use of coal during the prison's 179-year history," with KP's future being the central concern there was no mention made about the potential poisoning of those who worked or were confined there in the past (*Kingston Whig-Standard*, 2014).

Following this, KCC received better news as KP was designated a national historic site, giving the city control over its retasking or commodification through future development. In a letter in *The Whig*, then Liberal MP for Kingston and the Islands Ted Hsu indicated that "The Federal Heritage Building Review Office had also issued Classified and Recognized Heritage Designations to certain parts of the property" and "we are now presented with a wonderful opportunity to open up the doors of KP and let Canadians see, first-hand, one of the most famous prisons in our country" (Hsu, 2014). Directing his intervention at the then-Conservative government, it was Hsu's position that the site should continue to operate as an attraction providing tours, as such an endeavour would be "fiscally responsible," and it "would be a shame" to miss an "important opportunity to capitalize on KP tours." This sentiment was shared by incoming Mayor Bryan Paterson, who in his inaugural mayoral address emphasized "the importance of a new future for Kingston Penitentiary" while committing to "push this vision forward to expand access and beautify this natural treasure of ours" (KCC, 2014, pp. 3–5). In so doing, he tapped into the local carceral habitus in which imprisonment is understood as a natural and permanent fixture of Kingston's landscape.

The day following Ted Hsu's appeal, CSC indicated they had "no plans for the time-being to turn the now closed penitentiary into a tourist attraction" and that its "sole function is as a storage facility for the Library and Archives of Canada" for the time being (MacAlpine, 2014). Despite the success of KP tours in 2013, no such excursions were offered to the paying public in 2014 and 2015 as the site functioned as a document, instead of a human, warehouse.

Dis-accumulating Surplus (Carceral) Capital at KP

As campaigning for the federal election got underway in fall 2015, candidates from all parties in the Kingston and the Islands constituency engaged in debates regarding KP's future, which were moulded by the region's carceral habitus. When candidates were asked what they would do to "further the priorities of city council" in terms of rejuvenating the Kingston Penitentiary site, NDP candidate Daniel Beals stated that he would "work to represent the wishes and priorities of all people" and "not just a select few . . . so that everyone gets a voice in it" (Schliesmann, 2015). Former mayor of Kingston and eventual winner of the seat, Liberal Mark Gerritsen, stated "that most of the city's priorities dovetail with the platform of the Liberal Party" (Schliesmann, 2015). He added "the federal conservatives only gave him, as mayor, half an hour's notice before they publicly announced the closure of Kingston Penitentiary" (Schliesmann, 2015).

With the Liberals having gained power in Ottawa, the KCC announced in December 2015 that it had "partnered up with three federal government agencies, Correctional Service Canada, the Department of Fisheries and Oceans, and Canada Lands Company, to begin a visioning process" for KP (*Kingston Whig-Standard*, 2015). New Kingston Mayor Bryan Paterson promised that "the visioning process will give all Kingston residents a voice in what the future of KP will look like" while advancing his preferred outcome of the process by noting that the redevelopment of the site represents "an enormous opportunity to create an incredible tourist destination" (*Kingston Whig-Standard*, 2015; see also KCC, 2015a, p. 20).

By spring 2016, KCC tabled a supplemental information report to "provide council with information on short-listed consultants", as well as to request an "additional budget for the Kingston Penitentiary and Portsmouth Olympic Harbour visioning exercise" (KCC, 2016a, p. 1). The KCC documents reveal that the Canada Lands Company had completed their selection process and chose Taylor Hazell Architect to deliver the "master planning and community engagement process" services, as well as "heritage expertise on the project" (KCC, 2016a, p. 1).

While planning was happening behind closed doors, it was announced that tours of KP would occur during summer 2016 through a partnership between the City of Kingston, Correctional Service Canada, and the St. Lawrence Parks Commission. Mayor Paterson also enrolled local tourism agencies who began pushing the tours to see his vision through. On this occasion, the funds raised from KP tours were to benefit "tourism initiatives and youth programming from the United Way" (Ferguson, 2016a). Local politicians at the provincial level were celebrating the plan, with then–Kingston and the Islands MPP Sophie Kiwala stating KP tours were a "massive tourism opportunity for Kingston" (Ferguson, 2016a). Other stakeholders who celebrated the announcement included Darren Dalgleish, general manager and chief executive of the St. Lawrence Parks Commission, who stated "I think people would come from all over the world to see this Alcatraz of the North" (Ferguson, 2016a). Framing the initiative as an economic opportunity, Dalgleish said "the tours will create 30 summer student jobs and are expected to boost Kingston's tourism economy by at least $6 million" (Ferguson, 2016a). At this stage, the nexus between the carceral retasking and commodification of KP began to intensify. Then CSC Commissioner Don Head weighed in to support the plan to continue KP tours, noting "one of the advantages of opening the doors to a place like Kingston Pen is not only to tell the story of the history itself and its relationship to Kingston, but also to give people an insight as to kinds of conditions people had to live in as well as work in" (Ferguson, 2016a).

Even as the costs for the KP visioning exercise climbed to "about $350K" (KCC, 2016b, p. 2), news media continued to promote prison tourism. KP continued to be described as "Canada's most notorious prison" that "held serial killers, rapists and bank robbers" (Canadian Press, 2016). Constructing a narrative around "Canada's Alcatraz," these stories included repeated references to the fact that KP "has been home to an ongoing roster of the country's worst criminals," including Paul Bernardo, who raped and killed two school-aged girls (Canadian Press, 2016).

Documents from a May 2016 KCC meeting recorded a unanimous vote in favour of an "agreement with Correctional Service Canada for the city of Kingston to have access to the Kingston Penitentiary property to provide public tours" (KCC, 2016c, p. 349). This was followed by a request from the KCC for "the creation of a community working group for the Kingston Penitentiary and Portsmouth Olympic Harbour visioning exercise" (KCC, 2016d, p. 21). The working group was to be "comprised of representatives from city council, interested community members and representatives from relevant agencies/interest groups" (KCC, 2016d, p. 21).

As efforts to develop KP ramped up, the local media continued to report on the future of KP and tours at the site, privileging the views of former staff members. While most sung the praises of KP tours, one former guard—who spent 38 years in uniform and was at KP from 1982 until it closed—challenged the idea that the public tours of KP would offer an authentic account of life behind the wall (Lea, 2016). He remarked that although former CSC staffers, "including two ex-wardens," had been brought in to add a more personal dimension to the tours, "the nastier side of KP, the horrific happenings that scarred inmates and correctional officers alike, will go unspoken . . . none of those stories are going to come out" (Lea, 2016). On this point, he noted that "we all have a script and we are allowed to talk outside the script," but only to a certain degree (Lea, 2016). With the absence of prisoners' voices and a sanitized version of events offered by former CSC staff tour guides at KP who abided by the credo that "people don't really need to know all the gory details about the unpleasant things that happened in the prison" (Lea, 2016), penal spectators flocking to the site were unlikely to be "confronted with the violence that has and continues to be perpetrated" through incarceration (Ferguson et al., 2014, p. 97).

With 2016 summer tourism underway, businesses in the city, from hotels to cruise lines, got into the action through Tourism Kingston, which encouraged those coming to town to take tours of KP or to attend the "Tragically Hip at the Rogers K-Rock Centre" finale concert to visit their local establishments and participate in other events (Balakrishnan, 2016). KP also became a destination to host major events, like the North American Police Equestrian Championships (Crosier, 2016). With "700 and some odd people going through every day at the pen," Murray Matheson, executive director of Kingston Accommodation Partners, celebrated the contribution of prison tourism to the local economy (Gibson, 2016). While the afterlife of KP had not yet been finalized, the "prison [tourism] fix" (Gilmore, 2007) appeared to be in, shaping a carceral future for the site.

The (Carceral) Visioning Exercise

As the visioning exercise officially began in fall 2016, Floyd Patterson, who presided over the Kingston Municipal Heritage Committee (Hendra, 2012) and successfully pushed for the designation of KP as a heritage property, penned an article in *The Whig*. In it, he problematized the "joint city/correctional service visioning project," stating he was worried the initiative was "missing Kingston Penitentiary's overriding historical and social/economic importance to the Kingston region, how it has been a cultural anchor for decades" (Patterson, 2016). Reflecting on how KP is part of Kingston's identity, he argued that "this must not fade to black but be commemorated in the redevelopment of the site" as "seven generations of breadwinners—builders, architects, prison guards, health-care trained staff, warden's staff"—had driven the Kingston economy, minimizing "evil and danger lurking among the law abiding for 177 years" (Patterson, 2016). Tapping into the local carceral habitus, he noted "before Kingston was incorporated as a town in 1836, KP has been part of Kingston's DNA" and that its "impressive incarceration story has been respected as part of our culture" (Patterson, 2016).

In late November 2016, KEDCO released its "Tourism Kingston" report, outlining the importance of the tourism sector to the local economy and its priorities with respect to the retasking and commodification of KP. The report noted that tourism is an essential part of the Kingston economy, accounting "for close to 7,500 jobs and an estimated $840 million in annual visitor economic impact" (KEDCO, 2016, p. 122). The document concluded that "the future of the former Kingston Penitentiary is of utmost interest to Tourism Kingston and represents the largest potential tourism opportunity in the province" (p. 124).

The importance of the carceral retasking of KP to Kingston was also underscored during a 5 December 2016 press conference where Mayor Bryan Paterson remarked "[t]his year's tours from June to October drew approximately 60,000 visitors, with about 70 per cent coming from outside Kingston" (Ferguson, 2016b). It was noted that the "tours generated about $5 million for the regional economy and employed 40 students and about 20 retired correctional service staff" while contributing "revenue of more than $644,000, with half of that amount going to the United Way of Kingston, Frontenac, Lennox, and Addington" (Ferguson, 2016b). Darren Dalgleish of the St. Lawrence Parks Commission stated that "not only did it create funds for the United Way, but it allowed our marketing colleagues from Tourism Kingston and the Kingston Accommodation Partners to do some destination marketing" (Ferguson, 2016b).

Benefiting from this carceral windfall, Mayor Paterson announced that "tours of Kingston Penitentiary will return for another season in 2017" (Ferguson, 2016b). Signalling plans for future development of the KP site, Mayor Paterson stated that "2016 was a banner year for tourism in Kingston" and that "tourism will likely be a part of the future development" (Ferguson, 2016b).

At the same time as Mayor Paterson was celebrating the success of the KP tours, the president of the Frontenac Heritage Foundation, Shirley Bailey (2016), lamented that the mandate of the city's municipal heritage committee had been "pitifully reduced in what appears to be a continuing effort to eliminate their voice at council." This criticism illustrates the tension between those such as Heritage Kingston, who were interested in preservation and against plans for medium- to high-density residential development, versus Mayor Paterson, KEDCO, and the working group who saw the KP property as a form of untapped, dormant capital that could be reactivated for its economic potential and commercial value (Bailey, 2016).

As the KCC (2016e) moved in partnership with CSC and the St. Lawrence Parks Commission to deliver KP tours in 2017, they continued to celebrate the economic benefit to the city. They underscored that demand for the tours "far exceeded capacity" and that interest "originates far beyond Kingston" and is "proven to be an international attraction" (KCC, 2016f, p. 10). Given the cost to the city, which had been renting portions of Kingston Penitentiary from the CSC for $1 (KCC, 2016f, p. 12), is it any wonder that the content of the KP tours continued to paint the federal penitentiary system in a positive light (Piché et al., 2019)?

With prison tourism having become a fixture at KP before the visioning process had concluded, the Hatter's Bay group, who had proposed the development of a sailing centre, along with other commercial enterprises and residential development came forward to "meet with federal and municipal officials" regarding their vision. Having "been working together behind the scenes for more than four years to turn a vision for the property into a reality," the group envisioned a "prime site for Canada's first sailing centre of excellence as well as a wind research facility, prison museum, condominium development" and "a hotel similar to the Liberty Hotel in Boston, which was built from a former prison, along with shops and lots of outdoor space" (MacAlpine, 2016a). The group had secured $300 million in financing from the Bank of Nova Scotia for the project and claimed that no member of the group would be profiting from the development. The vision they tabled backed away from their original vision to re-develop KP in a way that would depart from its penitentiary past. Although their objective remained erecting a "world class sailing centre" while "turning the property into something of which the entire community can be proud of" (MacAlpine, 2016a), they abandoned their resistance to the "prison [tourism] fix" (Gilmore, 2007) and embraced the local carceral habitus.

Following the Hatter's Bay announcement, it was reported that "their vision may not jibe with a consultant's report, which is currently being prepared for the city" (MacAlpine, 2016b). Mayor Paterson distanced himself from any endorsement of the group's plans, stating "[w]e're looking forward to . . . a concept that will come to city council for approval, and once that concept has been approved, certainly we look forward to interested parties coming forward with proposals that would align with that final vision" (MacAlpine, 2016b). The distancing is unsurprising given that the vision called for from Canada Lands included "a continuous water's-edge promenade accommodating walking cycling, seating, landscaping and public art," with KP buildings accommodating "a range of uses, including tourism, culture, studios and performance areas as well as commercial, including small startup businesses, learning space, retail, a restaurant, a market, medical offices, residential apartments, seniors housing, a hotel and possibly a convention space, and harbour and marina support facilities" (MacAlpine, 2016b). It became clear that the Hatter's Bay and Canada Lands' visions were not oriented toward conserving the history of KP as preservationists had hoped, but rather to commodify the past as a means of securing capital and carceral futures.

Will the Walls Come Down?

As KCC proceeded ahead, there were rare moments when some community members voiced concerns. In January 2017, "a petition bearing approximately 130 names was presented" (KCC, 2017a, p. 104). This petition claimed that the "closures and potential re-development" of KP and other institutions "has our neighbourhoods under assault" and that "we need by-law amendments that consider the community costs of intensification and related infrastructure demands and their impact on existing, stable family neighbourhoods" (KCC, 2017a, p. 105). The petition went on to argue, "we must have a City Plan that preserves the

integrity of our community neighbourhood" and that their group "be a part of the discussions regarding City planning and by-law amendments that will have a direct impact on our lives, homes and families" to "stop the destruction of these wonderful historic neighbourhoods" (KCC, 2017a, p. 105).

Despite some opposition, later in 2017 KCC made amendments to their *City of Kingston Official Plan* to advance their preferred vision for KP in a way that could appease heritage preservationists. They added a section entitled "Museums and Collections," affirming that "some of Kingston's many stories are told through museums . . . and historic sites that collect, interpret and display objects that communicate a segment of Kingston's tangible cultural heritage in a historical and/or contemporary context" (KCC, 2017b, p. 153). KCC now recognized that "museums are cultural symbols" and "contributors to community enterprise," including the penitentiary museum (KCC, 2017b, p. 153).

While the municipal government moved to ensure prison tourism had a more prominent role in KP's future, in early February 2017 Hatter's Bay ramped up their efforts to promote their vision for KP by releasing some conceptual drawings of portions of the project, which included "people attending a community event inside the penitentiary property while watching a large screen of a sailing competition," as well as an "outside shopping area complete with a large fountain and people sitting at bistro tables sipping white wine" (MacAlpine, 2017a). The Hatter's Bay group, who envisioned the centrepiece of the site being a sailing centre, had a prominent architect from Boston, Norris Strawbridge, involved in the design. They also retained the services of an architectural firm based in Toronto, whose recent projects included the conversion of the Don Jail into a hospital campus. The project had received "favourable reviews from the public" and they felt confident they had a decent shot to "take a building that has inherent negativity attached to it and convert it to a different kind of use" (MacAlpine, 2017a).

Carceral culture preservationists, like the Friends of the Penitentiary Museum, continued to push their vision of "maintaining the former Kingston Penitentiary as a historic site" with "much of the property to remain as is" (MacAlpine, 2017b). Then president Simonne Ferguson—a retired regional vice-chair with the Parole Board of Canada—stated "the focus of the site should remain as a prison, and any renovations done to the property should not include tearing down the walls of the institution" (MacAlpine, 2017b). As noted elsewhere (Piché et al., 2019), those in proximity to the penitentiary, especially officials from CSC and other organizations involved in carceral control, typically express the greatest interest in preserving its historical memory in ways that reinforce imprisonment.

As the municipality prepared to unveil its vision for KP's future, actors like Simonne Ferguson became critical of city officials' motives. Ferguson charged that the public are "getting the version of what should happen from the folks who have a lot of influence and a lot of money" and that "it's important that they hear there's another vision of what might happen over there" (MacAlpine, 2017b). Illustrating the embeddedness of the carceral habitus of Kingstonians who "grew up around Kingston Pen . . . and generations of people [who] have worked there," Ferguson went on to state that "our concern as the friends of the museum is the huge potential of that place over there as a tourism attraction, as a historical attraction" and as "part of the social fabric of what happened in Kingston" (MacAlpine, 2017b). Ferguson then turned her attention to both KCC and the Hatter's Bay group, arguing that "bringing down the walls of the penitentiary, turning its focus to a sailing centre and putting up condominiums, would be a mistake" (MacAlpine, 2017b).

In February 2017, it was reported that citizens and stakeholders would get one more chance to have their opinions known on what the Kingston Penitentiary might look like in the future as the City of Kingston held its last two public workshops. The Hatter's Bay project and the Friends of the Penitentiary Museum continued to push their own agendas, with the former "in favour of tearing down some of the outer walls of the prison" and "building on-site condominiums to help pay for the project" (MacAlpine, 2017c). The Friends of the Penitentiary Museum sought to keep "the walls up to preserve the feel of a prison" and "scale back the sailing aspect of the development, and not allow condos on the property" (MacAlpine, 2017c). Both groups were in support of carceral retasking through penitentiary tours and putting the prison museum on the site.

During a February 2017 meeting of Kingston residents and members of the Kingston Penitentiary–Portsmouth Olympic Harbour Visioning group, plans for development of the site continued to be framed in terms of capital windfalls. During the meeting, it was announced that "the north portion of the penitentiary site will essentially remain as is, with the walls around

that portion staying up," which could also include "adaptive reuse of the guard towers" with an emphasis on memorializing "the Kingston Penitentiary and its influence on Kingston over time" (MacAlpine, 2017d). Plans for demolishing other wall portions were framed in terms of "mixed residential and commercial development" to help pay for the site and make it financially viable (MacAlpine, 2017d).

Several letters to the editor appeared in *The Whig* following the announcement. In one letter, entitled "Retain penal history in redevelopment," the author stated that plans for future development will "have erased irreplaceable Canadian history" (Hartley, 2017). In another, a participant in the city's consultations who is part of Haunted Walks, which runs tours in Toronto, Kingston, and Ottawa, referred to KP as a "tourism gem" and claimed that "irreversible mistakes will be made in underestimating the value and importance of this site as a historic and tourism attraction" as its "dark history must be commemorated appropriately" (Shackleton, 2017). The author went on to state that "you cannot erase the dark history of the site" and "are far better off to embrace the penitentiary for what it is: a unique opportunity to create our own Alcatraz of the North" (Shackleton, 2017). He also made reference to tours of the old Ottawa Jail, which his company runs (Walby & Piché, 2011), as beneficial to sustained growth, asserting that "jail tourism is one of the fastest growing sectors of the tourism industry worldwide" and that "San Francisco faced the same economic pressures and chose to preserve and invest in Alcatraz as a historic site," which "draws in a multi-billion-dollar tourism industry for that city" (Shackleton, 2017). In the most critical intervention, another letter to the editor stated that "inmates and staff have lived and died inside the walls" and "both have had to deal with the pain and trauma of solitary confinement, possible physical and psychological trauma, and the fear of release into a hostile community where failure is not an option but an expectation" (Korderas, 2017). This author suggested that the prison grounds should include both the past and the future, hoping that each could enrich the other.

In a final letter to the editor of *The Whig*, entitled "Kingston Pen is a heritage site worth saving," the author criticized plans for condo development as selling out the history of the site. Sticking to the cultural preservation narrative, this author saw KP as "an anchor for the city of Kingston" and stated "if we tear it down or remove sections or deface it in any way . . . the city would snap off the shore and float out into the lake" (Baird, 2017). This author called for readers to "plant your flag of heritage on the mountain top that is Kingston Penitentiary and its future uses and stand strong and proud, greet the tourists that come in droves . . . and keep taking that endless supply of tourism money that the entire community will enjoy" (Baird, 2017). Beyond the passion for heritage, these excerpts reveal how the emotions entrenched in "criminal justice" debates (De Hann & Loader, 2002) transfer to debates about the retasking of carceral sites following their decommissioning.

As tours of KP resumed in spring 2017, it was announced that they had been "updated and modified" to include "reauthentication of the Indigenous grounds with the aid of Indigenous offenders on work releases." An enhanced "premium tour," which was meant to "bring historic, architectural and criminological components to the tours to create an overall more in-depth and immersive experience," was also launched (*Kingston Whig-Standard*, 2017).

By June 2017, consultants from the Canada Lands Company held an open house to promote their "preferred design" for developing KP. At the unveiling, the preferred design was promoted as a "balance between protecting the site's heritage and open space and incorporating new development and residential building" (Ferguson, 2017a). The plan, which included a 25-storey residential building, prompted architectural historian Jennifer McKendry to state that if the proposal moved ahead it would "make a joke out of the tourism value of the prison" (Ferguson, 2017a). Similar criticism was made from the Frontenac Heritage Foundation, who argued that the planning process had "ignored key input from experts in architectural history and is being rushed through in the middle of the summer" (Ferguson, 2017a). Nevertheless, KCC moved to "endorse the recommended vision, developed with Canada Lands Company" for KP (KCC, 2017c, p. 473), "but only with the assurances that local heritage experts would get a say in how the sites are preserved" (Ferguson, 2017b). With the federal government spending about $1.5 million a year to maintain the prison property, the Canada Lands Company was eager to have the visioning process concluded (Ferguson, 2017b).

As our analysis shows, the "prison [tourism] fix" (Gilmore, 2007) was in long before KP was decommissioned as an operational penitentiary given that the identity of Kingston and many of its residents are so tied to this carceral space (Norris, 2012).

The pro-prison mindset, which we have described as "carceral habitus" (Schept, 2015), is embedded to the point that it seemed unnatural to not include prison tours as part of KP's future. The final plans for development at KP were solidified in a visioning report produced during the summer of 2017 by the Planning Partnership and Taylor Hazell Architects (Planning Partnership, 2017). Under the plan, KP will continue to operate as a "key destination for tourism and other cultural purposes" with "continued public tours and potential museum use," ensuring that many of the "existing walls and structures" of confinement will remain to deliver "an authentic tourism experience" (KCC, 2017d, pp. 159–60). This monument of suffering (Mayhew, 1988) will also become one of Kingston's community gathering places and a community park space (p. 165) as well as a prop to be exploited in accommodating "local and international film requests" (p. 167). Plans also include "residential, commercial, and office space" (pp. 167–8). While KP will serve as one of the city's "tourism products" (p. 167), it will also become a place where the city's residents can live, work, and play, while downplaying the suffering endured by prisoners that made it all possible. While the federal government prepares for the eventual sale of the site to new owners who will implement the vision for KP, the site will be leased to the City of Kingston for $1 million per year. Under the agreement, the municipality can run tours and other for-profit activities 110 days annually (Mussell, Piché, & Walby, 2020).

Forging a Non-carceral Path

Although our chapter focuses on the "prison [tourism] fix" and "carceral habitus" of the Kingston region, there are many pen-cities and prison towns across Canada that materially and symbolically rely on their carceral past and present to propel their communities into the future. While it would take another paper to unpack the costs and pitfalls associated with this (Piché, 2014), as well as alternatives to human caging (Knopp, Boward, Morris, & Morris, 1976) such as restorative justice (Elliott, 2011) and transformative justice (Morris, 2000), it is clear that the underlying culture of punishment that exists in the Canadian context is one that makes locking people up seem natural and justifiable. The tours at KP reflect a carceral habitus with a cozy relationship to commodified suffering that views imprisonment-based suffering as necessary and normal. Revealing trends in the Kingston case adds to literature

Critical Punishment Memorialization and Abolitionist Alternatives to Prison Tourism

Based on fieldwork conducted in dozens of prison tourism sites across Canada and observations of how these entities tend to communicate through tours, exhibits, and cultural depictions that dehumanize prisoners while honouring staff, we have illustrated how social distance between authors (that is, "law-abiding citizens") and recipients of punishment (prisoners) is produced in ways that justify the deprivation of liberty and pains of imprisonment. Having problematized the meanings of penality circulating in these settings (Walby & Piché, 2015), we have often been asked how prison tourism could be done differently or whether it should exist at all.

So long as there is a demand for prison tourism, there is an urgent need to humanize people who have been caged—both in the past and present. This can be accomplished by creating opportunities for visitors to engage with those with lived experience of incarceration in ways that bridge social distance. This could be accomplished in several ways: (1) having former prisoners as tour guides (such as is done at the Old Prison in Trois-Rivières, Quebec); (2) providing detailed testimonials of the pains of imprisonment (for example, the solitary confinement exhibit at the Peel Art Gallery, Museum and Archives in Brampton, Ontario); and (3) locating the criminalization and punishment of individuals within larger structures of oppression, such as colonialism (for example, the story of Almighty Voice explored at the Duck Lake Interpretation Centre in Duck Lake, Saskatchewan). These are exceptional practices that should become the norm at prison tourism destinations (Fiander, Chen, Piché, & Walby, 2016).

It would be important for these sites to raise questions about the place of confinement in society, including costs to prisoners, those working in the penal

system, as well as the loved ones and communities of both. Eastern State Penitentiary in Philadelphia is beginning to do this work through its "Prisons Today: Questions in the Age of Mass Incarceration" exhibits that, among other things, explore the social implications of putting young people behind bars instead of offering them more educational opportunities as a means of affecting positive changes in their lives. However, Eastern State also hosts its annual "Terror Behind the Walls" haunted house every Halloween as a means of generating revenue for the heritage site (Bruggerman, 2012) in ways that tap into problematic cultural tropes about prisoners as dangerous, even following their deaths (see also Luscombe, Walby & Piché, 2017).

Since many penal heritage sites turn to entertainment as a means of generating revenue or, in the case of businesses, to turn a profit, injecting and sustaining critical punishment memorialization into prison tourism sites will require funding through sources that are committed to the humanization—rather than demonization—of incarcerated people.

Given the limits of prison tourism, there are other ways that abolitionists have sought to transform decommissioned sites of confinement and other spaces that memorialize penal history in manners that contest human caging. For instance, as the former maximum

The last prisoner was transferred out of Kingston Prison for Women in 2000. The building was sold to an investment company in 2018.

security Prison for Women (P4W)—which operated as the only federal penitentiary for women in Canada from 1934 to 2000, when it was replaced by several multi-level penitentiaries for women across the country—remained vacant following its closure despite being purchased by Queen's University, a group of former prisoners and their supporters established the P4W Memorial Collective with the goal of building a memorial garden at the site (Mussell, 2019). As Queen's University moved to sell the property they had purchased from the federal government years earlier to a private developer who is planning a mixed-use development site (Nease, 2018), the P4W Memorial Collective (2018a) advanced its own vision for the future:

> The current silence of P4W's abandoned architectural carcass is a betrayal of the histories it housed. The age and emptiness of the buildings can easily mislead passers by to think that the painful facts of women's incarceration in Canada and the painful facts of colonization are things of the past. Indigenous people are the most marginalized, least secure, and the most incarcerated in Canada. The links between these facts were made clear in the Truth and Reconciliation Report. Recommendation 30 of the TRC's 94 Calls to Action says: "We call on federal, provincial, and territorial governments to commit to eliminating the overrepresentation of Aboriginal people in custody over the next decade, and to issue detailed annual reports that monitor and evaluate progress in doing so." This overrepresentation is especially acute for Indigenous women. Since P4W closed, more Indigenous women have been imprisoned than any other segment of the population (increasing by 109% between 2001 and 2012). A memorial garden with art and educational panels acknowledging the connections between colonization, residential schools, violence against Indigenous women, and the lives and deaths of women incarcerated at P4W represents a unique opportunity for community engagement and public education. Moreover, it would contribute to Queen's efforts to uphold its commitment to new nation-wide Principles on Indigenous Education.

Despite these efforts, Queen's University finalized the sale of P4W to ABNA Investments. Since that time, the collective has engaged the new owner of the property and has submitted a package outlining their proposed memorial garden to Kingston City Council in late 2018 (P4W Memorial Collective, 2018b). Time will tell if P4W's future will be marked by abolitionist engagement or the erasure of the pains of human captivity in the name of capital gain, as is the case at neighbouring Kingston Penitentiary.

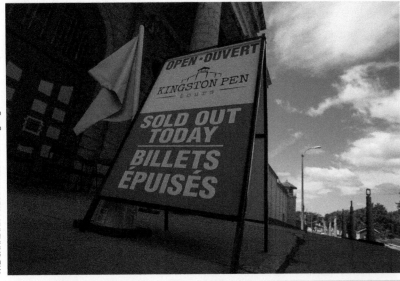

THE CANADIAN PRESS IMAGES Lars Hagberg

The St. Lawrence Parks Commission runs Kingston Pen Tours, which take the public through many areas of the formerly active prison. Photos and historical information about the prison are available at www.kingstonpentour.com.

on prison politics and support for the building and siting of carceral institutions (see Gilmore, 2007) by extending these debates and applying them to decommissioned penal sites. We have suggested elsewhere that when sites like KP operate as prison tourism destinations, part of the work social researchers should focus on—whether they are reformists who are working toward less and more humane imprisonment or abolitionists that are seeking an end to imprisonment—is to reveal the damage of confinement through the accounts of prisoners and its intersections with overlapping forms of oppression (Piché & Walby, 2018). Without engaging in "critical punishment memorialization" (Fiander et al., 2016), which commemorates and admonishes the suffering caused by imprisonment, it is unlikely that Canada's use of imprisonment can be significantly ratcheted downward in a sustained way. Scholars who seek to disrupt the status quo must not only study cultural representations of penality, but also create them to effect social change and work toward justice.

Review Questions

1. What is meant by the term "prison fix," and how does it apply to future development at KP?
2. What is meant by the term "carceral habitus," and how does it apply to future development at KP?
3. What is meant by the term "carceral retasking," and how does it apply to future development at KP?
4. What are the key issues identified by critics of prison tourism at KP?
5. What does the process of determining the future of KP following its decommissioning as a federal penitentiary reveal about the factors shaping municipal development?

Critical Thinking Questions

1. How could decommissioned sites of confinement be transformed to serve non-carceral purposes or challenge the necessity of punishment?
2. How could the voices of prisoners become part of the conversation about how to transform or reuse former sites of imprisonment like KP?

Multimedia Suggestions

Beyond the Fence: A Virtual Tour of a Canadian Penitentiary

This tour from Correctional Service Canada provides an inside look at Canada's federal institutions: https://www.csc-scc.gc.ca/csc-virtual-tour

Canada's Penitentiary Museum

Canada's Penitentiary Museum is housed in the warden's house at Kingston Penitentiary: https://www.penitentiarymuseum.ca

Carceral Cultures Research Initiative

The Carceral Cultures Research Initiative aims to generate knowledge about Canada's culture of punishment and includes links to completed and ongoing studies that are part of the initiative: http://www.carceralcultures.ca

Journal of Prisoners on Prisons

The *Journal of Prisoners on Prisons* is a prisoner-written, academically oriented, and peer-reviewed journal that brings the voices of prisoners together with academic arguments to discuss the current state of carceral institutions: http://www.jpp.org

Kingston Penitentiary & Portsmouth Olympic Harbour—Public Engagement

This website provides a historical account of the public consultations that took place in deciding the fate of Kingston Penitentiary after it was decommissioned: https://www.cityofkingston.ca/city-hall/projects-construction/archived-projects/kingston-pen/consultation

Kingston Penitentiary Tours

The website for tours offered at Kingston Penitentiary: www.kingstonpentour.com

Notes

1. When Millhaven Institution opened in 1971, there were a total of nine federal penitentiaries in the Kingston area. That number dropped to eight when the Prison for Women (P4W) closed in 2000 and was replaced by regional penitentiaries across Canada (Hayman, 2007). Millhaven remains in operation, along with three multi-level penitentiaries owing to administrative mergers of Collins Bay and Frontenac institutions (now known as Collins Bay Institution), Joyceville and Pittsburgh institutions (now known as Joyceville Institution), as well as Bath Institution where the Regional Intermediate Mental Health Unit was established to assume the functions of the regional treatment centre that closed on the grounds of the KP reserve in 2013.

2. The prisoner was sentenced to be executed; however, months later he was found "dead of unknown causes in his cell" (CSC, 2018).

References

Bailey, S. (2016, December 6). City's heritage situation sad. *Kingston Whig-Standard*. Retrieved from https://www.thewhig.com/2016/12/06/citys-heritage-situation-sad/wcm/442edd59-d1d0-873d-08ee-d33e95b36596

Baird, M. (2017, March 28). Kingston Pen a heritage site worth saving. *Kingston Whig-Standard*. Retrieved from https://www.thewhig.com/2017/03/28/letters-to-the-editor-march-29/wcm/f63b0700-33e3-aa82-adb4-9e8eb4f51dc3

Balakrishnan, J. (2016, August 19). Prize winner "honoured" to see Hip concert. *Kingston Whig-Standard*. Retrieved from https://www.thewhig.com/2016/08/19/prize-winner-honoured-to-see-hip-concert/wcm/75512d28-e377-1944-2595-710990bddb22

Boudreau, L. (2013, April 5). Protestors slam number of natives in prison system. *Kingston Whig-Standard*. Retrieved from https://www.thewhig.com/2013/04/05/protestors-slam-number-of-natives-in-prison-system/wcm/893fcfa0-b58d-7297-4d11-856d814cc824

Bourdieu, P. (1990). *The logic of practice*. New York, NY: Polity Press.

Brown, M. (2009). *The culture of punishment: Prison, society, and spectacle*. New York, NY: New York University Press.

Bruggeman, S. (2012). Reforming the carceral past: Eastern State Penitentiary and the challenge of the twenty-first-century prison museum. *Radical History Review, 113*, 171–86.

Canadian Press. (2016, May 13). Kingston Penitentiary opens its doors to the public again this summer. *Toronto Sun*. Retrieved from https://torontosun.com/2016/05/13/kingston-penitentiary-opens-its-doors-to-the-public-again-this-summer/wcm/ff5ddf8c-1c74-4ff6-8a9f-61fa969ecc57

Christie, N. (2000). *Crime control as industry: Towards gulags, western style* (3rd edn). New York, NY: Routledge.

Correctional Service Canada. (2018). Honouring our fallen officers. Retrieved from https://www.csc-scc.gc.ca/about-us/006-0011-en.shtml

Crosier, S. (2016, September 14). Smaller horse defends big title. *Kingston Whig-Standard*. Retrieved from https://www.thewhig.com/2016/09/14/smaller-horse-defends-big-title/wcm/6c2c031c-1fc2-0327-b258-85da593bde47

Davis, A.Y. (2003). *Are prisons obsolete?* New York, NY: Seven Stories Press.

De Haan, W., & Loader, I. (2002). On the emotions of crime, punishment and social control. *Theoretical Criminology, 6*(3), 243–53.

Elliott, E.M. (2011). *Security with care: Restorative justice & healthy societies*. Winnipeg, MB: Fernwood.

Ferguson, E. (2013, October 2). Inside the walls of Kingston Penitentiary. *Kingston Whig-Standard*. Retrieved from https://www.thewhig.com/2013/10/02/inside-the-walls-of-kingston-penitentiary/wcm/4a22f902-c64b-c480-1315-ac623965187f

Ferguson, E. (2016a, May 13). Kingston Pen tours to begin again. *Kingston Whig-Standard*. Retrieved from https://www.thewhig.com/2016/05/13/kingston-pen-tours-to-begin-again/wcm/263919ea-d28a-fe6c-acda-fa527b7522e7

Ferguson, E. (2016b, December 5). Penitentiary tours continue. *Kingston Whig-Standard*. Retrieved from https://www.thewhig.com/2016/12/05/penitentiary-tours-continue/wcm/0b280a80-d295-7de0-3a80-ed4c69f3a953

Ferguson, E. (2017a, July 11). Groups present cases to council. *Kingston Whig-Standard*. Retrieved from https://www.thewhig.com/2017/07/11/groups-present-cases-to-council/wcm/93d0c844-7305-7f47-12d2-9dfa7c42e092

Ferguson, E. (2017b, July 12). Council approves plan for Kingston Pen, Portsmouth Harbour properties. *Kingston Whig-Standard*. Retrieved from https://www.thewhig.com/2017/07/12/council-approves-plan-for-kingston-pen-portsmouth-harbour-properties/wcm/4939ccba-e8de-191e-b4f2-a74d38abd876

Ferguson, M., Lay, E., Piché, J., & Walby, K. (2014). The cultural work of decommissioned carceral sites: Representations of confinement and punishment at Kingston Penitentiary. *Scapegoat: Landscape, Architecture, Political Economy, 7*, 83–98.

Ferguson, M., Piché, J., & Walby, K. (2015). Bridging or fostering social distance? An analysis of penal spectator comments on Canadian penal history museums. *Crime, Media, Culture, 11*(3), 357–74.

Fiander, S., Chen, A., Piché, J., & Walby, K. (2016). Critical punishment memorialization. *Critical Criminology, 24*(1), 1–18.

Gibson, V. (2016, August 26). Tourism uptick more than Hip phenomenon. *Kingston Whig-Standard*. Retrieved from https://www.thewhig.com/2016/08/26/tourism-uptick-more-than-hip-phenomenon/wcm/1ac4b5a6-ef5d-7f45-ac76-1ed27eeb87c3

Gilmore, R.W. (2007). *Golden gulag: Prisons, surplus, crisis, and opposition in globalizing California*. Los Angeles, CA: University of California Press.

Hartley, L. (2017, March 1). Retain penal history in redevelopment—Re: "Support good development in city." *Kingston Whig-Standard*.

Hayman, S. (2007). *Imprisoning our sisters: The new federal women's prisons in Canada*. Montreal, QC: McGill-Queen's University Press.

Hendra, P. (2012, September 11). Kingston Penitentiary: Hoping to have a say on Kingston Penitentiary. *Kingston Whig-Standard*.

Hendra, P. (2013, September 23). Kingston Penitentiary: Group floats sailing centre for Kingston Penitentiary. *Kingston Whig-Standard*. Retrieved from https://www.thewhig.com/2013/09/23/group-floats-sailing-centre-for-kingston-penitentiary/wcm/e3c35796-b251-fe01-e9bb-0da67511f8df

Hsu, T. (2014, July 15). Make Kingston Penitentiary a tourist attraction. *Kingston Whig-Standard*. Retrieved from https://www.thewhig.com/2014/07/15/make-kingston-penitentiary-a-tourist-attraction/wcm/e33b2716-1a84-5198-46c0-80b93e29b769

Kingston City Council. (2012a, October 16). City council meeting no. 2012-25. *Meeting Archive 2012*. Retrieved from https://www.cityofkingston.ca/documents/10180/89570/CO_Minutes_2512.pdf/669d01d6-f948-45d3-bf72-5464cb0cdc58

Kingston City Council. (2014, December 2). City council meeting no. 2015-01. *Meeting Archive 2014*. Retrieved from https://thirdcrossing.cityofkingston.ca/documents/10180/7762529/COU_Minutes-0115.pdf/217881ac-f01a-4cea-80be-f9055f943378

Kingston City Council. (2015a, December 15). Report to council report number 16-035. *Meeting Archive 2015*. Retrieved from https://www.cityofkingston.ca/documents/10180/12015737/COU_A0216-16035.pdf/fa93db0e-bf2e-4be1-9880-0dfb6a3b17a6

Kingston City Council. (2016a, May 3). Council meeting number 2016-14 added. *Meeting Archive 2016*. Retrieved from https://www.cityofkingston.ca/documents/10180/12118161/COU_Minutes-1416.pdf/64d8fbb7-772a-4094-a975-661254fc99f7

Kingston City Council. (2016b, May 3). Report to council report number 16-159. *Meeting Archive 2016*. Retrieved from https://www.cityofkingston.ca/documents/10180/13859205/COU_A1416-16159.pdf/40fab3f0-f0b2-415e-b8b4-4ef7cef8405a

Kingston City Council. (2016c, May 17). City council meeting number 2016-15. *Meeting Archive 2016*. Retrieved from https://www.cityofkingston.ca/documents/10180/12118161/COU_Minutes-1516.pdf/5f0813a6-020b-4a48-8aa4-60d745755443

Kingston City Council. (2016d, June 7). Report to council report number 16-173. *Meeting Archive 2016*. Retrieved from https://www.cityofkingston.ca/documents/10180/14331847/COU_A1616-16173.pdf/b2012177-7f92-4535-bff0-96cef21a1285

Kingston City Council. (2016e, December 6). City council meeting number 2017-01. *Meeting Archive*. Retrieved from https://www.cityofkingston.ca/documents/10180/16841074/COU_A0117-17003.pdf/f3206d21-e58d-41a5-8f62-234cd63fec09

Kingston City Council. (2016f, December 6). Report to council report number 17-017. *Meeting Archive*. Retrieved from https://www.cityofkingston.ca/documents/10180/16841074/COU_Agenda-0117AD.pdf/08b8a33a-0845-4698-bcdd-f47ec187d3e1

Kingston City Council. (2017a, January 24). City council meeting number 2017-04. *Meeting Archive*. Retrieved from https://www.cityofkingston.ca/documents/10180/17104261/COU_Minutes-0417.pdf/d3a5a925-63dd-422e-b650-2463d0c74ff9

Kingston City Council. (2017b, March 11). Amendment number 50 to the City of Kingston Official Plan. *Meeting Archive*. Retrieved from https://www.cityofkingston.ca/documents/10180/15083595/Official+Plan+Amendment+No.+50.pdf/a97309ec-04f9-4ec9-9bf4-342489cd6aa8

Kingston City Council. (2017c, July 11). City council meeting number 2017-18. *Meeting Archive*. Retrieved from https://www.cityofkingston.ca/documents/10180/17104261/COU_Minutes-1817.pdf

Kingston City Council. (2017d, July 11). Report to council report number 17-206. *Meeting Archive*. Retrieved from https://www.cityofkingston.ca/documents/10180/19984298/COU_A1817-17206.pdf/74a809bf-fa9b-41b3-9a8e-bcb7982d10ea

Kingston Economic Development Corporation. (2016). 2016 operating and sales plan. Retrieved from http://business.kingstoncanada.com/en/about-us/resources/KEDCO_Operating_and_Sales_Plans_2016.pdf

Kingston Whig-Standard. (2014, April 25). More details on Kingston Penitentiary contamination. Retrieved from https://www.thewhig.com/2014/04/25/more-details-on-kingston-penitentiary-contamination/wcm/79dd453c-f4cf-76fd-0fc8-bd16b1b98be8

Kingston Whig-Standard. (2015, December 10). Pen, harbour subject of visioning process. Retrieved from https://www.thewhig.com/2015/12/10/pen-harbour-subject-of-visioning-process/wcm/5ff3c6e8-99e7-48a4-794d-67b961716806

Kingston Whig-Standard. (2017, April 24). Prison tour tickets go on sale Monday. Retrieved from https://www.thewhig.com/2017/04/23/prison-tour-tickets-go-on-sale-monday/wcm/db8a7e36-ac16-05ac-db1d-620d113eb452

Knopp, F.H., Boward, B., Morris, M., & and Morris, B.S. (1976). *Instead of prisons: A handbook for abolitionists.* Syracuse, NY: Prison Research Education Action Project.

Korderas, C. (2017, March 26). Prison grounds should include past, future. *Kingston Whig-Standard.*

Lea, M. (2013, September 23). An insider's look at Kingston Penitentiary history. *Kingston Whig-Standard.* Retrieved from https://www.thewhig.com/2013/09/23/an-insiders-look-at-kingston-penitentiary-history/wcm/bf17e7c5-c114-6efb-fa9d-79d06cc534bd

Lea, M. (2016, June 14). There is so much history here. *Kingston Whig-Standard.* Retrieved from https://www.thewhig.com/2016/06/14/there-is-so-much-history-here/wcm/957e5c2f-350a-de70-a50c-0133a4d6a90d

Luscombe, A., Walby, K., & Piché, J. (2017). Haunting encounters at Canadian penal history museums. In J.Z. Wilson, S. Hodgkinson, J. Piché, & K.Walby (Eds), *Handbook of prison tourism (pp. 541–57).* London, UK: Palgrave.

MacAlpine, I. (2014, July 16). KP as a tourism destination not in the short-term plans. *Kingston Whig-Standard.* Retrieved from https://www.thewhig.com/2014/07/16/kp-as-a-tourism-destination-not-in-the-short-term-plans/wcm/a62a5cb1-3fec-3fdc-b913-cf78f0469639

MacAlpine, I. (2016a, December 13). Group details development plan. *Kingston Whig-Standard.* Retrieved from https://www.thewhig.com/2016/12/13/group-details-development-plan/wcm/07ea6783-a213-6400-3dd1-1cf4be2a81dd

MacAlpine, I. (2016b, December 14). City keeps "door open for other" KP plans. *Kingston Whig-Standard.* Retrieved from https://www.thewhig.com/2016/12/14/city-keeps-door-open-for-other-kp-plans/wcm/13081c80-f365-4972-c951-ed9839a12e58

MacAlpine, I. (2017a, February 9). Group shares its vision for former KP property. *Kingston Whig-Standard.* Retrieved from https://www.thewhig.com/2017/02/08/group-shares-its-vision-for-former-kp-property/wcm/f5b87186-67df-f9d5-3672-86909f7908e8

MacAlpine, I. (2017b, February 17). Historical thing should take precedence. *Kingston Whig-Standard.* Retrieved from https://www.thewhig.com/2017/02/16/historical-thing-should-take-precedence/wcm/0a1db88e-cc33-e174-5cda-07b0197a92eb

MacAlpine, I. (2017c, February 24). Last ideas exchange for future of Kingston Penitentiary. *Kingston Whig-Standard.* Retrieved from https://www.thewhig.com/2017/02/24/last-ideas-exchange-for-future-of-kingston-penitentiary-property/wcm/8802e785-0c51-314a-2fbd-a23a990ba1e6

MacAlpine, I. (2017d, February 28). KP visions inching closer to reality. *Kingston Whig-Standard.* Retrieved from https://www.thewhig.com/2017/02/28/kp-visions-inching-closer-to-reality/wcm/eb109fef-56aa-ade1-2fc4-692b9c77a20e

Mayhew, J. (1988). Untitled. *Journal of Prisoners on Prisons, 1*(1), i.

Morris, R. (2000). *Stories of transformative justice.* Toronto, ON: Canadian Scholars' Press.

Murphy, J. (2013, August 27). Davies immortalized with stamp. *Kingston Whig-Standard.* Retrieved from https://www.thewhig.com/2013/08/27/davies-to-be-immortalized-in-stamp/wcm/e5328035-5e03-5bc9-1e51-c7602f288703

Mussell, L. (2019). After the prison closes: Seeking healing, memory and awareness at P4W. *Journal of Prisoners on Prisons, 28*(1), 66–73.

Mussell, L., Piché, J., & Walby, K. (2020, March 19). Public consultation needed on multi-year use of KP. *Kingstonist.* Retrieved from https://www.kingstonist.com/culture/opinion/letter-public-consultation-needed-on-multi-year-use-of-kp

Nease, K. (2018, July 6). Memorial garden at former women's prison takes root. *CBC News.* Retrieved from https://www.cbc.ca/news/canada/ottawa/kingston-womens-prison-memorial-garden-proposal-1.4734826

Norris, M. (2012, April 20). Kingston Penitentiary's cell blocks were "schools for crime." *Kingston Whig-Standard.*

P4W Memorial Collective. (2018a, March 21). P4W memorial garden—Solidarity letter. Retrieved from https://docs.google.com/forms/d/e/1FAIpQLSclj8cx7N6m--taPupmQ6xY_eFlgl2fiujcoTHf0DA-9xoxoA/viewform?fbclid=IwAR2wWVnDZfeE9eyDmhB05OFYZQBKqSjiOQm4vKfHiN6yRRGnmSlkhZpqv1U

P4W Memorial Collective. (2018b, November 19). Untitled. Retrieved from https://www.facebook.com/P4W-Memorial-Collective-2001214023489977

Patterson, F. (2013, October 21). Macabre memories, talented keepers and elegant architecture. *Kingston Whig-Standard.* Retrieved from https://www.thewhig.com/2013/10/21/macabre-memories-talented-keepers-and-elegant-architecture/wcm/218b2d56-d60d-a8ce-0778-7ddffd8005a9

Patterson, F. (2016, November 2). Kingston Penitentiary's next life. *Kingston Whig-Standard.* Retrieved from https://www.thewhig.com/2016/11/02/kingston-penitentiarys-next-life/wcm/faece138-539f-3083-f364-600712b50d6e

Piché, J. (2014). A contradictory and finishing state: Explaining recent prison capacity expansion in Canada's provinces and territories. *Champ pénal/Penal Field, 11.* Retrieved from https://journals.openedition.org/champpenal/8797

Piché, J., Ferguson, M., & Walby, K. (2019). A "win-win for everyone involved . . ." except prisoners: Kingston Penitentiary tours as a staff, media and public relations campaign. *Annual Review of Interdisciplinary Justice Research, 8,* 91–119.

Piché, J., Kleuskens, S., & Walby, K. (2017). The front and back stages of carceral expansion marketing in Canada. *Contemporary Justice Review, 20*(1), 26–50.

Piché, J., & Walby, K. (2018). Les musées de prison au Canada: Une réflexion abolitionniste. *Déviance et Société, 42*(4), 643–62.

Planning Partnership. (2017, June). Portsmouth visioning: Former Kingston Penitentiary & Portsmouth Olympic Harbour draft executive summary of the recommendations report. Retrieved from https://www.cityofkingston.ca/documents/10180/14979570/Projects_KPPOH_DraftExecutiveSummary.pdf/34804ed7-8ae4-4ace-9ce4-3383ccc5c0d5

Public Safety Canada. (2012, April 19). Harper government announces the closure of two federal prisons. Retrieved from https://www.canada.ca/en/news/archive/2012/04/harper-government-announces-closure-two-federal-prisons.html

Rosner, C. (2008). *Behind the headlines: A history of investigative journalism in Canada*. Toronto, ON: Oxford University Press.

Schept, J. (2013). "A lockdown facility . . . with the feel of a small, private college": Liberal politics, jail expansion, and the carceral habitus. *Theoretical Criminology, 17*(1), 71–88.

Schept, J. (2015). *Progressive punishment: Job loss, jail growth, and the neoliberal logic of carceral expansion*. New York, NY: New York University Press.

Schliesmann, P. (2013, September 27). Former warden sees bright future for Kingston Penitentiary. *Kingston Whig-Standard*. Retrieved from https://www.thewhig.com/2013/09/27/former-warden-sees-bright-future-for-kingston-penitentiary/wcm/852dbf61-49f4-144a-44a4-e640d2a3e77e

Schliesmann, P. (2015, September 23). Election debate: A closer look. *Kingston Whig-Standard*. Retrieved from https://www.thewhig.com/2015/09/23/election-debate-a-closer-look/wcm/9776e130-7415-faf5-0abd-e3e628015ec0

Shackleton, G. (2017, March 13). Kingston Pen a tourism gem. *Kingston Whig-Standard*. Retrieved from https://www.thewhig.com/2017/03/13/letters-to-the-editor-march-14/wcm/339c1326-c423-7011-0ca9-9377c4e75fb2

Stone, P. (2013). Dark tourism scholarship: A critical review. *International Journal of Culture, Tourism and Hospitality Research, 7*(3), 307–18.

Taylor Hazell Architects. (2017, June). Kingston Penitentiary & Portsmouth Olympic Harbour opportunities & constraints report. Retrieved from https://www.cityofkingston.ca/documents/10180/14979570/Projects_KPPOH_OpportunitiesConstraintsReport.pdf/6a6f4cbf-eccb-4840-b78c-bff6a699f305

VandenBrink, D. (2012, July 13). Kingston Penitentiary—fallen corrections officer finally recognized. *Kingston Whig-Standard*.

Wagner, P., & Sawyer, W. (2018). States of incarceration: The global context 2018. Prison Policy Initiative. Retrieved from https://www.prisonpolicy.org/global/2018.html

Walby, K., & Piché, J. (2011). The polysemy of punishment memorialization: Dark tourism and Ontario's penal history museums. *Punishment & Society, 13*(4), 451–72.

Walby, K., & Piché, J. (2015). Making meaning out of punishment: Penitentiary, prison, jail and lock-up museums in Canada. *Canadian Journal of Criminology and Criminal Justice, 57*(4), 475–502.

Wilson, J.Z., Hodgkinson, S., Piché, J., & Walby, K. (Eds). (2017). *The handbook of prisons tourism*. London, UK: Palgrave-Macmillan.

The Use of Solitary Confinement and Prisoner Rights

14

Kelly Struthers Montford, Jihyun Kwon, and Kelly Hannah-Moffat

Learning Objectives

After reading this chapter, you should be able to:

- Understand the historical context of solitary confinement.
- Describe the psychological, physical, and emotional harms associated with solitary confinement.
- Understand various ways in which vulnerable populations are affected by the discriminatory use of segregation in Canadian prisons.
- Examine various constitutional, legislative, and human rights frameworks that apply to segregation practices in Canada.
- Describe the challenges associated with monitoring, overseeing, and regulating segregation practices.

Chapter Overview

Various high-profile cases have documented the damaging effects of segregation and its routine use in Canadian prisons. Provincial and federal correctional policies state that correctional services need to use the principle of "least restrictive measures" and to consider alternatives prior to the segregation of a prisoner. Prisoners' rights continue to be violated despite the establishment of various accountability and oversight measures to ensure policy and procedural compliance. This chapter provides an overview of international literature on segregation. In doing so, we place recent Canadian legal cases that have challenged the use of segregation on human rights grounds, including gender and disability, in a wider context. We also examine changes to legislation and policy, as well as the implementation of oversight and accountability mechanisms that emerged from these decisions. Finally, we review the limitations of these measures in protecting the rights of prisoners kept in conditions of isolation.

Historical Background

Solitary confinement emerged as part of the humane prison reform movement. During the late eighteenth and early nineteenth century, the spectacle of public punishment, shaming, physical torture, and execution fell out of favour with reformers in Europe, the United States, and Canada, who saw these practices as inconsistent with modernity, beliefs about humanity, and the concepts of reform and rehabilitation. Rather than punishment being crudely applied to the body, reformers argued that opening penitentiaries would provide the conditions and discipline necessary for prisoners to reflect on their wrongdoing and become productive members of society (Foucault, 1977; Guenther, 2013; Hannah-Moffat, 2001; McCoy, 2012). Solitary confinement is rooted in ideas about moral reform, penance, and, later, **incapacitation** and **deterrence**—namely, that imposed solitude would provide the conditions in which prisoners could reflect on their offending, receive vocational training, and commit to becoming law-abiding members of society.

Opened in 1829, the Eastern State Penitentiary in Philadelphia was the first purpose-built prison for solitary confinement. Prisoners were to be locked in their cells for 23 hours a day, where they would labour, eat, and sleep. When outside of their cells, they were still meant to be isolated. Prisoners were required to wear hoods when moving about the prison and during recreation; they were forbidden from talking to each other or otherwise interacting. This approach to prison management was named the "separate system" and came to dominate prison regimes in Europe by the latter half of the nineteenth century. The Auburn system—named after the Auburn Prison in New York—also ascended to popularity at this time. Similarly premised on the redemptive potential of isolation, this system mandated total silence (the "silent system"), but unlike the separate system, it allowed prisoners to work side-by-side during the day (Guenther, 2013; Jackson, 1983; Smith, 2006). While practices of isolation are rooted in reformist and seemingly progressive approaches to correction, from its inception isolation has also been used as an explicitly punitive response for those who violate prison rules.

Canada's first and arguably most notorious penitentiary—Kingston Penitentiary—opened in 1835. The regime subscribed to the silent prison system, where prisoners worked and ate together but were not permitted to engage in any form of communication with each other, including looking at one another, nodding, or gesturing (Jackson, 1983, p. 28). In addition to a regime of silence, isolation was available to penitentiary management to deal with "incorrigible" criminals (McCoy, 2012, p. 226). The Penitentiary Act of 1834 provided for the solitary confinement of individuals found guilty of institutional misconduct, a provision that has remained in effect throughout various legislative reforms. In 1894 a new cell block, the "Prison of Isolation," opened at Kingston to house those deemed vicious, who routinely broke prison rules, and who were considered to be bad influences who would inhibit the reformation of fellow prisoners. Referred to as Canada's first super-maximum institution, the Prison of Isolation remained in operation until 1920 (Jackson, 2001).

Negative psychological effects were evident soon after the implementation of solitary confinement. From the mid-nineteenth century, those in American and European prisons reported that prisoners in solitary confinement experienced substantial psychological deterioration (Smith, 2006). There now exists a considerable amount of academic literature detailing the adverse psychological and physical effects of solitary confinement. Isolation often leaves prisoners "deeply traumatized" and "socially disabled" (Lowen & Isaacs, 2012), with many experiencing anger, depression, impaired concentration, loss of the sense of reality, suicidal thoughts, trouble sleeping, confusion, paranoia, hallucinations, and delusions (Grassian, 1983; Haney, 2003, 2005; Korn, 1988; Kupers, 2006; Martel, 1999; Rhodes, 2004). The harms of segregation can also be experienced more severely by women and potentially more so by Indigenous peoples and those with disabilities. Because women have unique pathways into segregation as well as experience and react to isolation differently than men, they are more likely to experience isolation as invisibilizing, rejection, abandonment, and a denial of their existence (Canadian Human Rights Commission, 2003, Vera Institute of Justice, 2018). The operational realities of segregation units often entail the more frequent use of strip searching and cell searches, practices that are retraumatizing and triggering for those with lived experiences of trauma and abuse and few if any cell effects (e.g., books, writing materials, radio, and toiletries).

Although mentally ill prisoners are more likely than other prisoners to be sent to solitary confinement, long-term segregation has also been linked to the development of previously undetected psychiatric symptoms (Arrigo & Bullock, 2008; Haney, 2009; Metzner & Fellner, 2010). These damaging effects do not appear to be mitigated by antipsychotic medication, as it has been reported to lose some effectiveness for those in segregation. Furthermore, segregation can produce a vicious cycle where a prisoner's extreme behaviour and "acting out" leads to an increase in physical altercations with prison staff, which ultimately increases the level of frustration and violence engaged in by both parties (Kupers, 2006). Recent studies have likewise suggested that psychological stressors such as isolation are comparable to physical torture (Metzner & Fellner, 2010; Reiter, 2016). Because Indigenous people are more likely to have lived experiences of trauma, victimization, and mental health conditions, experts have suggested that solitary confinement can be both culturally inappropriate and more detrimental to Indigenous people than their non-Indigenous counterparts (Cheung et al., 2013, Shalev, 2017; OCI, 2015b). Thus, solitary confinement (whether in supermax prisons or in segregation units in regular prisons) can actually increase or lead to the behaviours it purports to control and can severely hinder a prisoner's reintegration into the general prison population and community. This is especially pronounced if the prisoner is released directly from segregation into the community (see Mears & Bales, 2009).

International and Domestic Provisions

The practice of solitary confinement continues to be integral to prison operations and has been the source of ongoing human rights–based litigation in Canada. Until June 2019, Canadian regulations and policies broadly use the terminology of **administrative segregation** or **disciplinary segregation** to refer to the practice of removing a prisoner from the general population and confining them in a cell for a minimum of 22 hours a day. Psychiatric holds/statuses and the conditions of confinement in federal women's maximum security units are often akin to segregation. Solitary confinement in Canada is meant to be guided by international provisions, with federal and provincial regulations governing its use in federal and provincial institutions.

Although there is no formal international legal definition of solitary confinement, the practice is widely accepted as entailing social and physical isolation for 22 hours per day or more (UN General Assembly, 2015). There is also a general consensus that the threshold marking prolonged segregation is 15 days. For example, the United Nations (UN) special rapporteur on torture and other cruel, inhuman, or degrading

Solitary Confinement and Segregation

Correctional Service Canada (CSC) has repeatedly argued that its practice of administrative segregation does not amount to solitary confinement. In its response to the Coroner's Inquest Touching the Death of Ashley Smith, for example, the CSC wrote, "To be clear, the term solitary confinement is not accurate or applicable within the Canadian federal correctional system. Canadian law and correctional policy allows for the use of administrative segregation for the shortest period of time necessary, in limited circumstances, and only when there are no reasonable, safe alternatives" (2014). It has also stated that "the term 'solitary confinement' (as defined by the [UN]) is not applicable in the Canadian penitentiary context" (CSC, 2017b) on the basis that contact with guards counts as "meaningful contact" and that, under the revised Commissioner's Directive 709, segregated prisoners are permitted a minimum of two hours outside their cell per day in addition to a shower (see *CCLA v. The Queen*, 2017).

Judges have dismissed these claims in recent decisions. In *CCLA v. The Queen*, Justice Marrocco found that administrative segregation as practised by the CSC constitutes solitary confinement as per the international framework noted above. Justice Marrocco also stated, "I recognize that an inmate in segregation will have perfunctory contact with [CSC] staff. I am not persuaded by the evidence that this type of contact is 'meaningful'" (*CCLA v. The Queen*, 2017, para. 44). Justice Leask, for his part, concluded that "The time spent taking a shower is a de minimis increase in the two hours per day that segregated inmates are allowed out of their cells. More importantly, the time spent locked down in a cell only partly describes the nature of segregation" (para. 41). In *BCCLA v. Canada* (2018), Justice Leask concluded "I am satisfied that administrative segregation as currently practiced in Canada conforms to the definition of solitary confinement found in the Mandela Rules. In particular, I find as a fact that inmates in administrative segregation are confined without meaningful human contact" (para. 137).

These findings point to the fact that solitary confinement entails more than confinement in a cell for a number of hours as stipulated in legal frameworks. Instead, "meaningful human contact" is both subjective to the person experiencing it and is undermined by the very nature of being imprisoned, the operational realities of the prison, and the psychological harms associated with solitary confinement.

treatment or punishment identified this threshold based on medical literature showing that after 15 days, some of the physiological harms associated with solitary confinement are potentially irreversible (Méndez, 2011; UN General Assembly, 2015).[1] Because solitary confinement causes extreme hardship for prisoners, its use not only relates to international legal principles on the treatment of prisoners, but also to those on cruel, inhuman, or degrading treatment as well as torture.

The Convention against Torture and Other Cruel, Inhuman, or Degrading Treatment or Punishment (CAT) and the International Covenant on Civil and Political Rights (ICCPR) are the two main international treaties governing the treatment of prisoners. The CAT was adopted in 1984 by the UN General Assembly and came into effect in 1987. Canada ratified the CAT in June 1987 and is legally bound by its terms. The ICCPR was adopted by the UN General Assembly in 1966 and came into effect in 1979. Canada ratified the ICCPR in May 1976 and is legally bound by its terms (UN 1976, 1987). While Canada has ratified and is bound by the CAT, it has not yet ratified the Optional Protocol to the Convention against Torture and Other Cruel, Inhuman, or Degrading Treatment or Punishment (OPCAT; UN 2006b), despite a commitment by the federal government to do so. The Office of the Correctional Investigator (OCI 2016, 2017) and the Canadian Human Rights Commission (2012) have recommended that Canada ratify the OPCAT. If ratified, the OPCAT would require that places of detention be inspected using national and international independent monitoring schemes.

Solitary Confinement and Torture Thresholds

The special rapporteur was univocal that when used as a method of *punishment*, solitary confinement "cannot be justified for any reason, precisely because it imposes severe mental pain and suffering beyond any reasonable retribution for criminal behaviour" (Méndez, 2011, p. 20). Various bodies of the UN have found that prolonged solitary confinement constitutes torture as defined and prohibited in the CAT and ICCPR (*BCCLA v. Canada*, 2018; Méndez, 2011). According to the special rapporteur, solitary confinement can amount to cruel, inhuman, or degrading treatment or torture given the intent in which it is imposed, the material conditions of confinement, its indefinite or prolonged nature, and its

use on persons with mental disabilities for any amount of time. For those not yet convicted, such as pre-trial detainees, the use of solitary confinement can function as "a de facto situation of psychological pressure" that can be used to extract a confession or other information, regardless of whether it was used explicitly for this purpose (Méndez, 2011, p. 20).

Conditions of Confinement

The UN *Standard Minimum Rules for the Treatment of Prisoners* (commonly known as the **Mandela Rules**) set out how international norms are to be interpreted and applied in operational contexts (UN General Assembly, 2015). Minimum standards outlined in the Mandela Rules include, but are not limited to, the following:

- Cell conditions (including lighting and ventilation)
- Hygiene, bedding, and cleanliness of the institution
- Time out of cell, including time outdoors, and adequate space for exercise
- Meaningful contact with others and mental stimulation (including access to current events and media)
- Access to education, cultural practices, and other programs
- Access to medical care delivered by staff who do not have decision-making powers regarding segregation placement or disciplinary measures

These rules are widely known and meant to guide legal decision making and the treatment of prisoners, but they are not legally binding.

Cell conditions and the regime of solitary confinement are important when determining whether an individual in solitary confinement is being subjected to conditions that constitute cruel, inhuman, or degrading treatment or torture. This determination can relate to the duration of placement, the strictness of the prison regime, and the quality of the living conditions (Méndez, 2011, p. 20). An indefinite placement in solitary confinement can cause uncertainty and hopelessness. Consequently, the special rapporteur, relying on the CAT and ICCPR, has determined that indefinite segregation can amount to cruelty and torture (Méndez, 2011, p. 20). Indefinite or prolonged solitary confinement also impedes the delivery of programming and services to the point where rehabilitation and treatment—guiding principles of corrections as per the ICCPR—are undermined. Given medical and psychological findings, in addition to its detrimental impact on rehabilitation, the special rapporteur has called on "the international community . . . to impose an absolute prohibition on solitary confinement exceeding 15 consecutive days" (Méndez, 2011, p. 21).

In light of international human rights law, Canada is obliged to prevent and disallow cruel, inhuman, or degrading treatment and torture. The assessment of whether solitary confinement meets these thresholds according to international law requires a case-by-case analysis of the following:

> The daily length, overall duration and predictability of solitary confinement. In addition, attention must be paid to: access to natural light, and to darkness for sleep; ability to take exercise; access to fresh air; human contact, especially with family members; cleanliness of the facilities, ability to ensure personal hygiene and access to clean bedding; and access to medical care that is not connected to the determination of liability to the punishment of solitary confinement. Finally, strong authority exists for the proposition that anyone suffering from mental illness should not be subjected to solitary confinement. (Toope, 2017, p. 18)

Some conditions of confinement, including the provision of reading materials, access to family and current events, programming, and time outdoors, can be considered mitigating factors against the detrimental effects of solitary confinement. As such, the quality and extent to which these are provided or denied will influence whether the prisoner in question is subjected to conditions amounting to cruelty or torture.

Disability

Individuals with mental disabilities are hypervulnerable in prison settings. Knowing that isolation can exacerbate pre-existing mental health conditions, the special rapporteur found that for those with a mental disability, placement in segregation for *any* duration constituted cruel, inhuman, or degrading treatment as per Article 7 of the CAT and Article 16 of the ICCPR. The Convention on the Rights of Persons with Disabilities (CRPD) applies in situations where prisoners experience mental illness or disability (UN 2006a). It was adopted by the UN General Assembly in 2006, and came into effect in 2008. Canada ratified the CRPD

in March 2010 and is legally bound by its provisions, including the reasonable accommodation of incarcerated individuals with disabilities. Furthermore, the CRPD explicitly prohibits the deprivation of liberty *because* someone is disabled. Put another way, under the CRPD, prison services cannot place those with mental health disabilities in segregation or other conditions of increased confinement because they are unable to accommodate their needs in the general population. To do so would cause a further deprivation of liberty and fail to provide reasonable accommodation under Article 14 of the CRPD.

Gender

The 2010 UN Rules for the Treatment of Women Prisoners and Non-custodial Measures for Women Offenders, otherwise known as the **Bangkok Rules** (UN, 2011) contains various provisions against isolation for women, which are reiterated in the Mandela Rules. Specifically, Rule 22 stipulates that solitary confinement shall not be used for women who are pregnant or breastfeeding, or whose infants live with them in prison. Rule 23 also prohibits the use of restraints for women during labour, birth, and immediately following delivery. Furthermore, gender can influence how individuals experience and react to isolation. To this end, the UN has outlined that "prison administrators should demonstrate sensitivity to the distress caused by isolation on female prisoners, the particular risk of self-harm and suicide among women, and use this measure only in exceptional circumstances" (UN, 2011, p. 41).

Legal Provisions for Federal Prisons in Canada

Segregation in Canadian federal penitentiaries is governed by the Corrections and Conditional Release Act (CCRA) and its regulations (CCRR) and is operationalized in specific commissioner's directives (CDs).[2] The CCRA and the CCRR provide the legislative basis for the operations of the CSC. To meet the legislative standards set out in the CCRA and CCRR, the CSC develops and implements CDs. CDs operationalize legislation and are meant to guide daily institutional practices. CD 709 pertains to administrative segregation, CD 580 includes provisions for disciplinary segregation, and CD 843 permits the isolation of individuals who are self-harming or suicidal. Sections 31–37 of the CCRA pertain to segregation and outline the purpose, rationale for admission, review processes, release, schedule and requirements for meetings between the institutional head and segregated prisoner, and the rights of segregated prisoners. Sections 38–44 of the CCRA outline disciplinary measures, of which segregation is included as a sanction permissible to a maximum of 30 days.

Administrative Segregation

The CCRA stipulates that the official purpose of administrative segregation is for the safety and security of the penitentiary or the individual being segregated. While prisoners are to be released from segregation "at the earliest appropriate time," the legislation does not limit the amount of time a prisoner can spend in segregation (s. 31(2)). Authority to place an individual in administrative segregation rests with the head of each institution. While segregation placements are reviewed by the institutional head or their designate, the decision ultimately lies with the head as to maintain or release the person in question. As per section 22 of the CCRR, the head of the region or their designate must review the placement of each individual segregated for 60 days and at each 60-day interval thereafter. Though the CCRA and CCRR distinguish between "voluntary" and "involuntary" administrative segregation, the CSC has removed this distinction in their operational and data collection processes (CSC, 2015a) because it acknowledges that "voluntary" segregation requires context and is not a choice freely entered into by prisoners. The OCI (2015b) has also noted that the former "legal distinction between voluntary and involuntary administrative segregation [was] largely illusory" (p. 31), and that voluntarily requesting segregation is often symptomatic of unsafe prison conditions in the general population. These positions highlight the important distinction between asking to be removed from unsafe conditions versus asking to be placed in segregation—a placement that carries the potential for physical and psychological harm, especially for women, Indigenous peoples, those with pre-existing mental health concerns, and those with histories of trauma.

According to the CSC (2017a), prisoners in administrative segregation retain the "same rights and conditions of confinement as other inmates, except those that must be limited due to security requirements." This includes access to programming, education, visits, correspondence, personal effects, reading materials, current events, health care, mental health services, and spiritual services.

Despite this provision, the realities and routines of segregation units often make this operationally unfeasible. The built environment of segregation units, coupled with blanket concerns about security, impede the delivery of services or contact. For example, visits, psychological services, health assessments, and cell studies/educational programs are often conducted through the food slot, and visits with family and friends are dependent on the level of risk assigned to the prisoner. The OCI has condemned such practices (2015a, 2016). Despite these general observations, it is difficult to know the extent to which segregated prisoners retain the same conditions of confinement as those in general population, because the CSC often refers to their policies—rather than their practices—in response to such questions (Hannah-Moffat, 2016).

Disciplinary Segregation

Disciplinary segregation is one penalty available to institutions in response to offences and misconduct committed by prisoners. As per sections 38–44 of the CCRA, disciplinary segregation can be imposed to a maximum of 30 days for those found guilty of serious disciplinary offences. However, if the individual is alleged to have committed an offence of a serious nature, they are entitled to a hearing adjudicated by an independent chairperson within 10 days following the charge; the disclosure of offence reports and evidence against them; the right to call witnesses; and the right to legal representation. As such, the placement of an individual in disciplinary segregation requires a guilty finding, is independently adjudicated, and is for a predetermined amount of time—provisions that do not exist in the context of administrative segregation. Included as part of their sanction, prisoners in disciplinary segregation might have their visits with family, friends, and others restricted for a maximum of 30 days (CD 580).

Bill C-83 and the End of Segregation?

Bill C-83 received Royal Assent on 21 June 2019 and has been lauded by public safety officials as the elimination of both administrative and disciplinary segregation in federal penitentiaries, as well as creating positions for independent external reviewers. Under Bill C-83, segregation will be replaced with "structured intervention units" (SIUs). While the SIUs are meant to afford prisoners four hours of out-of-cell time per day, one example of when external oversight will be triggered is when someone in the SIU does not meet the four-hour minimum for five consecutive days or for 15 out of 30 days. As such, Bill C-83 still permits the use of solitary confinement *without* external oversight for these specified amounts of time (Public Safety Canada, 2019). At the time of writing, Bill C-83 has not yet been implemented or operationalized, meaning that the regimes of administrative and disciplinary segregation remain. Some sections of Bill C-83 came into force on 30 November 2019, but other dates have not been announced (Parliament of Canada, 2019). In the meantime, the CSC has already established Voluntary Limited Association Ranges, which will likely fall outside the limited protections afforded in the SIUs. With several other population management practices, such as lockdowns and observation ranges, that continue to produce conditions that constitute segregation, whether Bill C-83 will meaningfully "eliminate" solitary confinement remains to be seen.

Canada's Use of Segregation: Racialization, Self-Harm, and Mental Illness

Historically, the most comprehensive information on segregation in Canadian federal institutions comes from the OCI and publicly available CSC policy documents and reports. For instance, recent data on segregation trends are documented in the OCI special report titled "Administrative Segregation in Federal Corrections: 10 Year Trends" (OCI, 2015a). According to this report, the federal correctional population increased by 13.6 per cent (from 12,623 to 14,335) between March 2005 and March 2015. The number of incarcerated women has increased by 77.4 per cent (from 368 to 653), as has the number of Black (by 77.5 per cent, from 792 to 1,406) and Indigenous (by 52.4 per cent, from 2,296 to 3,500) prisoners (OCI, 2015a, p. 2).

The segregation rate is increasing at a slower rate than the general prison population, with the exception of the rate for black prisoners, which is growing at a faster rate than the black prison population (OCI, 2015a, p. 2). This does not, however, mean that segregation is being used less often, just that *who* is being segregated proportionate to population growth is changing. Average lengths of stay in administrative segregation have decreased over time: from 2005 to 2015, the average length of stay decreased from 40 days to 27 days. Indigenous prisoners consistently have the longest average stays in segregation (OCI, 2015a, p. 2). The 2018 report of the OCI revealed that while segregation placements have declined overall, this is not true for Indigenous prisoners, who represented 36 per cent of segregation admissions despite representing 28 per cent of the federal prison population and 4.3 per cent of the Canadian population (OCI, 2018). See Table 14.1 and Figure 14.1 for a summary of these statistics.

A disproportionate number of individuals placed in administrative segregation have histories of self-injury (86.6 per cent of the prisoners with a history of self-injury have been segregated). The 2018 OCI report continues to reveal that segregation is used as a response to self-injurious behaviour. In their investigation into the 2016 death of Terry Baker, the OCI found that over her 10-and-a-half years in federal custody, Baker had 300 documented incidences of self-harm, 56 documented use-of-force interventions, and 20 segregation placements, 11 of which were for self-injurious behaviour. She was also placed on clinical observation status for periods ranging from two to four-and-a-half-months in cells on the segregation unit.

Women and Indigenous peoples were also segregated and have histories of self-injury at disproportionately higher rates of segregation than their white, male counterparts (OCI, 2015a, p. 2). Cheung and colleagues (2013) argued that a security-based response to

Table 14.1 Population Snapshots of the CSC Incarcerated Population Compared to Growth in Segregation Admissions between 2005–6 and 2014–15

	Male	Female	Total Population	Indigenous	Non-Indigenous	Black	White
% Incarcerated Population Growth	11.60	77.40	13.60	52.40	4.90	77.50	−6.80
% Segregation Growth	8.10	35.00	9.20	31.10	1.90	100.40	−12.30

Source: Adapted from OCI (2015a, p. 7).

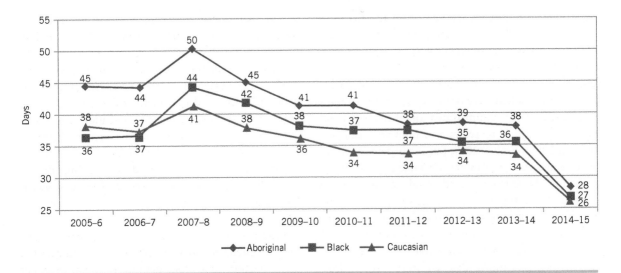

Figure 14.1 Average Length of Stay in Segregation—Indigenous, Black, and White Offenders
Source: Adapted from OCI (2015a, p. 8).

self-harm has resulted in the disproportionate place-ment of Indigenous women in administrative segrega-tion. This has placed Indigenous women at increased risk of self-harm, given that most self-injury is known to occur in settings of isolation (OCI, 2012; Cheung et al., 2013). Cheung and colleagues also noted that ad-ministrative segregation has the effect of exacerbating colonial legacies, given that it can cause the onset of mental illness, be experienced more harshly by indi-viduals with histories of abuse, and have lasting effects following release and reintegration. Because the condi-tions of confinement in segregation or clinical isolation include the application of restraints and forms of force, these practices have been characterized as "a means of manipulating and controlling the bodies of Indigenous women" (Cheung et al., 2013). Such practices should be understood as systemic rather than as individual "management" strategies.

The disproportionate use of administrative segregation for Indigenous women also leads to discriminatory treatment in terms of institutional lib-erties and access to services, including psychological treatment, vocational training, correctional program-ming, and cultural services. Likewise, the segregation of Indigenous women has negative effects on their future life chances. Because services and treatment are more limited in segregation, coupled with the possi-bility of psychological harm and lowered emotional regulation, segregation often increases one's risk and reduces the likelihood of being granted conditional release. The negative effects from segregation also create challenges when reintegrating into the com-munity (Native Women's Association of Canada, 2017). These limitations—combined with high rates of past abuse, violence, and trauma flowing from the historical legacy of colonialism—make it possible that segregation will have harsher effects on Indigenous persons than it might for non-Indigenous people.

The CSC's use of segregation and the isolation of self-harming individuals as allowed under CD 843 has been widely criticized. For instance, a 2013 OCI report, "Risky Business: An Investigation of the Treatment and Management of Chronic Self-Injury among Federally Sentenced Women," found that self-injury was foremost considered an issue of non-compliance and security rather than symp-tomatic of complex mental health issues or a coping mechanism. Overall, it concluded that despite policy directives, the seclusion of self-injuring women was "a significant management strategy" (OCI, 2013, p. 20). While the CSC has committed to moving away from security-based responses to self-harm, including their "zero tolerance" for self-injury approach that includes placement in segregation, the OCI remains skeptical. Over the past decade there have been ongoing rec-ommendations and calls for change to the CSC's ap-proach to managing self-harm and injury. While in response the CSC has committed to some changes and best practices, meaningful implementation has not occurred (OCI, 2018).

Under the CCRA, the CSC is required to provide essential health care that is consistent with professionally accepted standards of practice (s. 86). Furthermore, a prisoner's health status must be considered in all correctional decisions (s. 87) and the informed and voluntary consent of prisoners is required for all health-care interventions (s. 88). Upon review of the files of chronically self-injuring women, the OCI found the CSC's approach to be inconsistent with these provisions. In addition, until August 2018, prisoners engaging in self-harming behaviour could and often were placed in administrative segregation. CD 709 now stipulates that "inmates actively engaging in self-injury which is deemed likely to result in serious bodily harm or at an elevated or imminent risk for suicide" are inadmissible to segregation (CSC, 2017a, CD 709.19(b)).[3] This, however, does not prohibit the placement of individuals who are self-harming in administrative segregation, nor does it require that a prisoner who begins to engage in self-harming behaviour or whose self-harming escalates in severity be immediately removed.

The use of segregation in provincial and territorial institutions varies according to the legislation governing each jurisdiction. Most provincial and territorial policies and operating documents are not available to the public because of unspecified "safety and security" concerns. This lack of transparency prevents meaningful public dialogue and maintains the translation of legislation into operational requirements behind prison walls. As well, because of limited data available to the public and non-standardized data collection methods, it is not possible to meaningfully compare the use of solitary confinement across these institutions. However, we suggest that the use of segregation across the grounds of race, gender, mental health, and disability in provincial and territorial facilities is similar to the use of segregation in facilities in the federal system.

Based on data from the Ontario provincial system, it is evident that Indigenous peoples are overrepresented in admissions to institutions, segregation placements, mental health conditions, and length of stay. In 2016, Indigenous peoples represented 2.4 per cent of the general population in Ontario but made up 12 per cent of admissions to provincial jails. At the same time, Indigenous males represented 13 per cent of total admissions to administrative segregation (Sapers, 2017b, p. 117). Of the Indigenous males in administrative segregation during this period, 51.73 per cent (1,354) had a suicide risk alert attached to their file, whereas for non-Indigenous prisoners this rate was 33 per cent

(Sapers, 2017b, p. 117). Furthermore, Indigenous men were kept in administrative segregation longer than the provincial average, with the mean segregation placement length for Indigenous men in 2016 being 14.8 days compared to 12.8 days for non-Indigenous men. Further, in 2016 the median of the placement lengths was five and four days for Indigenous and non-Indigenous men in segregation, respectively (Sapers, 2017b, p. 124).

Howard Sapers, the former correctional investigator of Canada and then independent reviewer of Ontario corrections wrote:

> Corrections is often an end point on a long journey of injustices for Indigenous peoples. For many, it is a journey that involves the inter-generational trauma of Indian Residential Schools, forced relocation, community displacement, loss of identity, loss of language, loss of culture, involvement with the child welfare system, extreme poverty, racism, systemic discrimination, gender discrimination, violence, physical abuse, sexual abuse, emotional abuse, depression, and death. (2017a, pp. 168–9).

In September 2017, as part of their efforts to develop a "culturally relevant and responsive justice system," the Government of Ontario (2017) formally acknowledged that correctional settings are "alienating environments" for Indigenous peoples. Subsequent data released by the province of Ontario continue to show that segregation remains a common management technique for vulnerable populations, including racial minorities and those with mental health concerns. For instance, data pertaining to human rights factors show that in 2018, Indigenous prisoners were segregated at a disproportionate rate when compared to the overall proportion of Indigenous prisoners in many institutions (Rankin, 2018). A snapshot study of six institutions over a one-day period in June 2018 also showed that 88 per cent of those who were segregated had a mental health or suicide alert on file (Ontario, 2018). Like the federal context, Ontario's provincial prison system shows a racialized pattern of segregation use, and it continues to use isolation to manage those with mental illness. Given various international prohibitions on the use of solitary confinement as a disciplinary technique, including for vulnerable populations, those remanded to custody, and those with physical and mental disabilities, these patterns remain troubling.

Long-Term Segregation, Violation of Rights, and Litigation

In the 1975 case of *McCann v. The Queen*, conditions of administrative confinement in the "Penthouse" (the solitary confinement unit) of the British Columbia Penitentiary were found to contravene the provision in the Canadian Bill of Rights against cruel and unusual treatment or punishment. Justice Louise Arbour's 1996 report of the Commission of Inquiry into Certain Events at the Prison for Women in Kingston followed events on 26 April 1994, in which an incident between staff and eight prisoners resulted in a male institutional emergency response team (IERT) being called in to remove the women from their cells and perform strip searches. Following this, the women were placed in segregation wearing only paper security gowns and were restrained using body belts, shackles, and leg irons. The windows were left open, and they were not provided cell effects, including mattresses, blankets, or towels, until the afternoon of the following day, when they were provided with security blankets. They were subjected to further body cavity searches. Some women were transferred to mental health units within the men's penitentiary, and six women remained in administrative segregation for approximately seven to eight months.

Overall, Arbour observed that the CSC exhibited a defensive corporate culture that lacked an appreciation for human rights and respect for the rule of law. The use of an all-male IERT faced heavy scrutiny, with women prisoners reporting that they experienced these events as re-victimizing, traumatic, and humiliating. The Arbour Commission catalyzed various changes, including the following:

1. The resignation of the then-commissioner of corrections, John Edwards
2. A phased and planned closure of the Prison for Women
3. Development of policy documents and policies, including the management protocol (CSC, 2010) and intensive intervention strategy (CSC, 2011), crossgender staffing (Lajeunesse & Jefferson, 1999; Lajeunesse, Jefferson, Nuffield, & Majury, 2000), a review of security classification (CSC, 2014), a new mental health strategy (CSC, 2014,

CSC, 2015b; Laishes, 2002), and new program strategies (Fortin, 2004)
4. Establishment of the Task Force on Administrative Segregation (1997)
5. Establishment of a Working Group on Human Rights (1997)
6. The appointment of a deputy commissioner for women

Many of the recommendations contained in the Arbour Report remain unimplemented (Hannah-Moffat, 2016; Pate & Parkes, 2006), and ongoing issues surrounding the treatment of those in segregation continue (Canadian Human Rights Commission, 2003; Jackson, 2016).

On 19 October 2007, Ashley Smith, a 19-year-old self-injuring prisoner, died at Grand Valley Institution for Women in Kitchener, Ontario, after being held in segregation for more than 1,000 days. A **coroner's inquest** was called to examine the death: after six years of deliberation, it ruled Ashley's death a homicide in December 2013. The inquest revealed that the problems identified by Arbour about a lack of alternatives to segregation, the heavy reliance on segregation rather than crisis de-escalation, the systemic use of prolonged segregation, and a lack of independent, judicial oversight for segregation continue. The coroner's jury made many recommendations, some of which the CSC dismissed, including: that indefinite solitary confinement be abolished; that longterm segregation not exceed 15 days; and, that restrictions should be imposed on the length and number of times prisoners can spend in segregation, including a requirement of no more than a cumulative total of 60 days in a calendar year (Carlisle, 2013; CSC, 2014).

Prisoners have continued to die in Canadian segregation cells. Edward Snowshoe committed suicide in 2010; he had spent 162 consecutive days in segregation. Terry Baker died in July 2016 after being found unresponsive in a segregation cell at Grand Valley Institution for Women. Baker had been on suicide watch in the weeks preceding her death. Soleiman Faqiri died in the Central East Correctional Centre in Lindsay, Ontario, in December 2016. In a lawsuit recently brought against the Ministry of Community Safety and Correctional Services, Faqiri's family alleges that he died following the excessive use of force by guards. Faqiri, who had been diagnosed with schizophrenia and who was held in segregation over a period of days, was awaiting transfer to a mental health facility. These cases show that while official reasons for placement in segregation include threats to the safety of the institution or oneself, such a placement does not necessarily protect individuals or prevent self-harm or suicide. Empirical evidence from jurisdictions that have eliminated solitary confinement or significantly reduced its use show that rates of institutional violence have remained stable or have decreased. As well, guard workplace compensation claims have decreased concurrent with moves away from solitary confinement (see, for example, American Civil Liberties Union of Maine, 2013; Chammah, 2016). Thus, while the link between institutional safety and solitary confinement is a deeply held belief, it is not supported by evidence.

Despite Canada's obligation to uphold human rights in the prison context as outlined by international and domestic provisions, recent legal cases pertaining to federal and provincial institutions have revealed that segregation continues to be used in a manner that contravenes Charter protections and human rights.

In the *Jahn v. MCSCS* (2013a) case, the Ontario Human Rights Commission (OHRC) and the province of Ontario reached a wide-reaching settlement specific to segregation and mental illness that emerged from a human rights application filed by Christina Jahn in 2012. Jahn—who suffered from mental health disability, addictions, and cancer—had been held in prolonged segregation for approximately 210 days at the Ottawa-Carleton Detention Centre. In response to the allegation of discriminatory treatment on the basis of gender and disability, Ontario and the OHRC agreed to a series of **public interest remedies** pertaining to **gender-responsive corrections** and evidenced-based mental health screening for all prisoners, a prohibition on the use of segregation for those with identified mental illness to the point of undue hardship, and the accommodation and management of those with major mental illness.

In 2017, the OHRC filed a contravention of settlement application, alleging that Ontario had failed to comply with the 2013 settlement. The Human Rights Tribunal of Ontario issued the consent order in January 2018 in response. Included in the order is the requirement for Ontario to define segregation as *any* condition of confinement in which a prisoner is physically isolated for 22 or more hours per day (with the exception of a lockdown). It is also required to identify and track those in conditions of restrictive confinement, thus recognizing the potential for prisoners to be held in **seg-like/lite** conditions, and to release annual human rights–based data. As per the order, Ontario must develop a systematic method for identifying and responding to prisoners with mental health conditions, with an overall view to eliminating the segregation of individuals with identified mental health concerns. The implementation of the order is ongoing.

In *CCLA v. The Queen* (2017), Associate Chief Justice of the Ontario Superior Court, Frank Marrocco, presented reasons for his judgment that the laws governing administrative segregation in federal penitentiaries are unconstitutional. For example, a lack of independent oversight in administrative segregation decision-making processes was found to impede protections outlined in section 7 of the Canadian Charter of Rights and Freedoms, namely "the right to life, liberty and security of the person and the right not to be deprived thereof except in accordance with the principles of fundamental justice":

> I am satisfied that the statutory review of the decision to segregate is procedurally unfair under the *Baker* test and contrary to the principles of fundamental justice because the procedure chosen provides that the Institutional Head is the final decision maker for admission, maintenance and release from administrative segregation and is the final institutional decision-maker of required reviews and hearings which occur immediately after an inmate is segregated (para. 155).

The CCLA also argued that administrative segregation, as practised by the CSC, violates section 12 of the Charter, which states that "everyone has the right not to be subjected to any cruel and unusual treatment or punishment." Justice Marrocco concluded that while administrative segregation can produce irreversible effects within 48 hours of placement, it did not violate section 12 protections because the CSC has mechanisms in place that monitor deterioration. However, the effectiveness of these mechanisms has been disputed by formerly segregated individuals. While Justice Marrocco found that sections 31–37 of the CCRA "do not authorize administrative segregation after the fifth working day as it does not have sufficient procedural protections to ensure that continued administrative segregation does not deprive inmates of liberty or

Segregation and Alternative Housing

With solitary confinement facing increased scrutiny and various judicial rulings about the unconstitutionality of administrative segregation practices, some correctional systems have indicated that they would reduce their use of segregation, including prohibitions on the segregation of vulnerable populations. However, despite their pledges to explore "alternatives" and concerted efforts to demonstrate reduced segregation counts, the default *conditions* of confinement that many vulnerable groups continue to face in correctional settings constitute de facto segregation and are alternatives in name only.

In the federal context, Zinger (2013) referred to units used for unofficial segregation as "segregation lite," noting that these are variously known as "alternative housing arrangements, secure living environments, special needs units, mental health units, intensive support units or gang ranges." He also noted that these units lack appropriate procedural safeguards and oversight since they operate "outside the boundaries of the administrative segregation law, yet have many segregation-like conditions of confinement" (Zinger, 2013). In the 2017 annual report of the OCI, Zinger further noted his concern that the CSC could be using legal loopholes to unofficially manage prisoners in conditions of confinement equivalent to segregation:

[I]t is not at all clear where those who would otherwise have been placed in administrative segregation are ending up . . . in the absence of other alternatives, specialized units (dubbed "segregation lite") may be used to manage groups of offenders (subpopulations) with behavioural, emotional or cognitive issues. These units often have restricted routines, including limited out-of-cell and association time. Known by various names, such as structured or enhanced supervision, they may approximate (but not quite reach) the international definition of solitary confinement as "22 hours or more a day without meaningful human contact." Technically not solitary confinement, in the CSC context it may just be segregation by any other name—or means (OCI, 2017, p. 42).

This remains a significant concern given the current prohibitions outlined in CD 709 and the likelihood that prisoners with complex mental health needs will instead be managed under CD 843—a measure that is not subject to the same oversight procedures or scrutiny because of its categorization as a clinical intervention.

security of the person in a manner inconsistent with the principles of fundamental justice" (para. 273), he suspended his ruling of invalidity of these provisions for 12 months to allow Parliament to reform legislation so that administrative segregation could be administered in a manner consistent with constitutional protections.

In the January 2018 decision in *BCCLA v. Canada (Attorney General)*, the Supreme Court of British Columbia ruled that administrative segregation, as practised by the CSC, both constitutes solitary confinement as outlined in international legal principles and violates sections of the Charter. Specifically, Justice Leask had issue with the sections of the CCRA that allow for prolonged or indefinite solitary confinement, a lack of external oversight and independent decision makers regarding segregation placement, and the fact that prisoners could not have legal counsel at **segregation reviews**. Altogether,

these practices violated of section 7 of the Charter. Justice Leask also found that administrative segregation, as practised by the CSC (and as permitted under the CCRA), constituted a violation of section 15 of the Charter because it allows the segregation of people with disabilities, including mental illness. Furthermore, Justice Leask argued that the operation of administrative segregation was discriminatory against Indigenous peoples on the basis that "the impugned laws fail to respond to the needs of Aboriginal inmates and instead impose burdens or deny benefits in a manner that has the effect of perpetuating their disadvantage and thus violating s. 15" (para. 489).

The ubiquity of human rights legislation on solitary confinement has resulted in judges now taking "judicial notice" of the harms of segregation. Put otherwise, the detrimental psychological effects associated with segregation are now approached as a matter of general

Photo by David Jackson for The Globe and Mail.

Adam Capay (right), a 27-year-old member of the Lac Seul First Nation, spent 1,647 days in solitary confinement as a remanded prisoner at the Thunder Bay and Kenora jails. Capay was placed in segregation to await trial following the alleged murder of fellow prisoner Sherman Quisses. Capay's conditions of segregation entailed being held behind plexiglass in a windowless cell. Capay quickly deteriorated, suffering memory loss and impaired speech. With the help of the OHRC, his case received media and public attention in 2016, and he was moved to a forensic psychiatric centre. His murder charge was stayed in February 2019, with the Superior Court confirming that Ontario had violated multiple sections of his Charter rights (see *R. v. Capay*, 2019).

knowledge rather than a claim that must be proven and defended. In *R. v. Roberts* (2018), Justice Morgan stated,

> There is ample evidence from Mr. Roberts that the long-term confining of him in segregation had serious psychological consequences for him. But even if he had not deposed to that fact, it could today be taken as a matter of judicial notice. One does not need an affidavit to say that a gunshot to the arm hurts the arm; likewise, one does not need an affidavit to say that over a year in segregation, with almost no yard or other recreational time and simply sitting alone in a small cell for up to 23 hours a day, will turn a person into himself and create anxiety in dealing with others. Of course, Mr. Roberts was adversely impacted by spending 426 days in segregation. (para. 34).

Despite practices of segregation being the ongoing target of scrutiny and legislation, Canada has appealed the *BCCLA* and *CCLA* decisions. In so doing, they have continued to position solitary confinement as central to the administration of prisons. This reaction is historically consistent with other calls for change and subsequent reform measures following various legal cases and inquests.

Regulatory Capture and the Status Quo

Across correctional jurisdictions, various external administrative oversight mechanisms have emerged since the late twentieth century. Meant to ensure that prison administrations comply with the rule of law, procedural justice, and basic principles of civil and human rights, such mechanisms have replaced traditional, court-based oversight processes. Over time, the judiciary came to be seen as inefficient and ill-equipped to order remedies appropriate to the context of imprisonment. Unless cases before the courts were extreme or contained irrefutable evidence, the judiciary was often reluctant to interfere with prison management, administration, and operations. This hands-off approach often meant that prisoners and their advocates were unable to seek justice through legal action (Carrabine et al., 2009; Deitch, 2012; Feeley & Rubin, 1999; Van Zyl Smit, 2007).

An increased emphasis on the rights of prisoners, coupled with a proliferation of legal professionals and an increased number of lawsuits brought by prisoners, their advocates, and interest groups against prison services provided the conditions for a change in oversight. To address gaps created by *vertical* oversight, such as the court-led procedures, many instead called for the establishment of independent administrative oversight mechanisms that are structurally *horizontal* to the prison administrations. Many jurisdictions around the world have now established what is known as "the tripartite model," which includes multilayered oversight measures for monitoring, inspecting, and handling prisoner complaints (Behan & Kirkham, 2016; Ellis, 2013).

In Canada, likewise, there currently exists a variety of oversight mechanisms that seek to address rights violations that occur behind prison walls. For example, federal prisons across Canada are frequently monitored and inspected by the OCI, which has a regular presence in federal corrections. As an external, administrative oversight body, the primary function of the OCI is to receive, investigate, and resolve prisoners' complaints. Each province has a similar ombudsperson service that operates externally to the prison administration. For instance, the Investigations and Standards Office in British Columbia and the Office of Ombudsman in Ontario independently receive, investigate, and bring resolution to prisoner complaints. These bodies liaise with prison and government units and are responsible for making various recommendations to address systemic concerns. To ensure there is a public presence in prisons, the CSC has also established citizen advisory committees, and Ontario has established community advisory boards for some of its institutions. This allows volunteer community members to monitor and provide advice regarding correctional facilities. In addition, federal and provincial prisons are subject to respective human rights systems, which receive and adjudicate complaints regarding violations on human rights grounds.

Many oversight bodies also play an essential role in producing research that provides insight into prison realities. Given that the relationship of these bodies is characterized as horizontal to prison services rather than vertical to it, it was anticipated that such mechanisms would allow for early resolution and intervention, coupled with better co-operation from prison staff. If achieved, such measures can lead to more effective oversight.

Over the past few decades, research has shown that horizontal mechanisms—in contrast to the vertical or hierarchical processes of the courts—substantially increases information flow, transparency, and communication between external bodies and the closed prison system. However, horizontal accountability measures do not have the same enforcement authority of the courts and therefore cannot require that their recommendations are compiled with (Schillemans, 2010, 2012). Consequently, the ability of horizontal oversight bodies to effect large-scale prison reform is often thwarted. Research shows that independent prison watchdogs are often structurally or ideologically influenced by the correctional regime they are meant to oversee (Vagg, 1994; Wood, 2009, 2012). This phenomenon is called **regulatory capture** and refers to under-resourced oversight bodies over time aligning and working toward achieving the values and goals of the overseen rather than those of their mandate (Gautier & Agrell, 2011; Laffont & Tirole, 1993; Makkai & Braithwaite, 1992; Prenzler, 2000; Tirole, 1986; Vagg, 1994).

In particular, the system for seeking remedies for human rights violations in Ontario has been criticized for its structural and financial dependence on the government of Ontario. This system also entails lengthy and legalized complaints resolution processes, making it inaccessible for many individuals, including prisoners (OHRC, 2005). Because the OHRC has insufficient funding and personnel, it cannot independently investigate and resolve countless rights violations—many of which are highly complex. Furthermore, external complaints mechanisms "strongly" encourage prisoners to first exhaust internal grievance procedures before lodging complaints to their offices (Swearingen, 2008). During the investigation phase, prison watchdogs are required to rely on information provided by the prison administration, meaning they work with a limited availability of documents that can confirm prisoners' accounts (Agrell & Gautier, 2012).

Evidence suggests that non-state actors who seek to contribute to more transparent and accountable correctional practices are similarly susceptible to capture. For example, CD 009 that details the requirements for external researchers appears to be apolitical. In practice, however, access to prison contexts is resolutely political. Interviews with various senior administrators and front-line correctional staff as well as external stakeholders have confirmed that the CSC deliberately makes research overly cumbersome (Watson, 2015). Such strategies include maintaining "stringent control over research," shaping the type of data collected and its use, controlling findings that are reported, and having ownership over all materials and data produced through these "partnerships" (Watson, 2015, p. 342). Some have observed that those who are not ideologically aligned with the CSC are blocked from accessing the institutions for research purposes as they "challenge the assumptions underpinning hegemonic correctional approaches [and that their] research may bring the system into disrepute" (Hannah-Moffat, 2011, p. 446).

Additionally, various rights violations identified by state oversight agencies and non-governmental agencies, such as the OCI and the Canadian Association of Elizabeth Fry Societies, are often hastily rejected by prison services on the basis of "security and safety concerns." Such a position maintains the systems and practices that are causing the violation of rights (Parkes & Pate, 2006). In the context of Ontario provincial corrections, multiple lawsuits and independent reviews have called for *substantive* change in how Ontario manages prisoners, especially for those who are vulnerable and segregated (Dubé, 2017; *Jahn v. MCSCS*, 2013b; *OHRC v. Ontario*, 2018; Sapers, 2017a, 2017b). Despite Ontario's public commitment to reform, little has changed in how segregation is used. The restrained enforcement capacity of multiple oversight bodies contributes, in part, to the continued and routine segregation of vulnerable prisoners. In short, correctional settings remain concealed, penal cultures that embody substantial power differentials between captors and captives are left unchallenged, and prison managers continue to have wide-sweeping discretion and authority that undermine the ideal operation of oversight.

Summary

This chapter has provided an overview of the historical context in which solitary confinement emerged, its psychological effects, and its ongoing use in Canadian prison settings. The chapter also described recent Charter challenges and human rights–based legal challenges brought by prisoners, civil liberties organizations, and advocacy groups. In a variety of manners, the judges in these cases found solitary confinement to not only be occurring in Canadian prisons, despite being labelled "segregation" or "enhanced observation status," but that it is administered in such a manner that it constitutes a violation of Charter protections and human rights grounds. The CSC and various provincial systems have committed to reforming their use of segregation, but we caution that this might signal a shift in labelling rather than in the conditions of confinement for prisoners. Seg-lite/like units operate without the review and tracking processes required for segregation, which, while limited, do provide some manner of oversight.

The chapter has also shown how exceptional cases and the ensuing calls for reform are often subsumed by the broader penal culture and an inflexible understanding of safety and security. Despite the establishment of horizontal oversight bodies, prison administrations in Canada continue to exercise significant authority over its overseers. In the absence of rigorous accountability measures, the routine use of solitary confinement can and will continue in a largely unaccountable manner.

Current international best practices take seriously the fact that segregation often produces the issues it is meant to control, and that by causing or exacerbating mental illness, it can have an adverse effect on public safety. In doing so, some jurisdictions, including the state of Colorado, have eliminated segregation for women as well as their use of administrative segregation for men. Men remain subject to disciplinary segregation for a maximum of 15 days and there are stringent protocols in place to divert those with mental illness from segregation. The state has found that its rates of institutional violence have decreased, as did rates of mental illness among its prisoner population. Colorado was also able to close one of their supermax units, and wait times for accessing mental health beds no longer exist since the demand has decreased so steeply (Raemisch, 2018a, 2018b).

Review Questions

1. Describe the historical context that relates to the practice of solitary confinement. What are some key terms that relate to various modes of isolation?
2. What are some main concerns regarding the ways in which racial minorities, women, and those with mental health and self-injury concerns are segregated in Canadian institutions?

3. What are some key constitutional, legislative, and human rights frameworks that apply to the correctional regimes in Canada? Give a few examples of both international and domestic provisions and explain their significance.
4. What are some of the ways in which prison conditions can be monitored, overseen, and challenged in Canada? Give a few examples of and explain how they may differ from one another.

Critical Thinking Questions

1. A series of prison reforms have taken place over time, but tragic events and rights violations continue to occur in Canadian prisons. What are some of the challenges to meaningful reform? Suggest how these can be overcome.
2. What are some viable alternatives to segregation that can be explored by Canadian prison administrations? How could these alternatives be responsive to gendered, cultural, and mental health concerns?

Multimedia Suggestions

Ashley Smith: Out of Control
   This *Fifth Estate* documentary discusses the tragic death of Ashley Smith, who died while in a segregation unit: https://www.youtube.com/watch?v=yryXNq00_c0

The Ultimate Response
   This *Fifth Estate* documentary (which is available to certain educational institutions and subscribers) discusses the events that occurred

at P4W in April 1994: https://curio.ca/en/video/the-ultimate-response-4162

"How to Get Out of Solitary—One Step at a Time," Maurice Chammah
   This article from The Marshall Project discusses best practices and the reduction of segregation: https://www.themarshallproject.org/2016/01/07/how-to-get-out-of-solitary-one-step-at-a-time

Notes

1. The special rapporteur did note the rather arbitrary nature of this threshold.
2. The use of segregation in provincial and territorial institutions is governed by legislation and policies specific to the jurisdiction in question.

3. Given that conditions under CD 843 are structurally similar, we caution that this merely represents a change in policy to limit institutional liability rather than a change in approach. Self-harm likely remains understood as a security issue rather than a mental health issue managed using a trauma-informed treatment approach.

References

Agrell, P.J., & Gautier, A. (2012). Rethinking regulatory capture. In J.E. Harrington & Y. Katsoulacos (Eds), *Recent advances in the analysis of competition policy and regulation* (pp. 286–302). Cheltenham, UK: Edward Elgar Publishing.

American Civil Liberties Union of Maine. (2013). Change is possible: A case study of solitary confinement reform in Maine. Portland, ME: Author.

Arrigo, B.A., & Bullock, J.L. (2008). The psychological effects of solitary confinement on prisoners in supermax units: Reviewing what we know and recommending what should change. *International Journal of Offender Therapy and Comparative Criminology, 52*(6), 622–40.

Behan, C., & Kirkham, R. (2016). Monitoring, inspection and complaints adjudication in prison: The limits of prison accountability frameworks. *The Howard Journal of Crime and Justice, 55*(4), 432–54.

British Columbia Civil Liberties Association [BCCLA] v. Canada (Attorney General). 2018 BCSC 62. Retrieved from https://www.bccourts.ca/jdb-txt/sc/18/00/2018BCSC0062.htm

Canadian Human Rights Commission. (2003). Protecting their rights: A systemic review of human rights in correctional services for federally sentenced women. Retrieved from http://www.caefs.ca/wp-content/uploads/2013/05/fswen.pdf

Carlisle, J. (2013). Coroner's inquest touching the death of Ashley Smith: Verdict of coroner's jury—The Coroners

Act—province of Ontario. Retrieved from http://www.csc-scc.gc.ca/publications/005007-9009-eng.shtml

Carrabine, E., Cox, P., Fussey, P., Hobbs, D., South, N., Thiel, D., & Turton, J. (2014). *Criminology: A sociological introduction*. New York, NY: Routledge.

CCLA v. The Queen. 2017 ONSC 7491. Retrieved from https://ccla.org/cclanewsite/wp-content/uploads/2017/12/Corp-of-the-Canadian-Civil-Liberties-Association-v-HMQ-121117.pdf

Chammah, M. (2016, January 7). How to get out of solitary—One step at a time. *The Marshall Project*. Retrieved from https://www.themarshallproject.org/2016/01/07/how-to-get-out-of-solitary-one-step-at-a-time

Cheung, C., Mandhane, R., Pate, K., Edwards, T., Brayton, B., & Milne, C. (2013). Rights violations associated with Canada's treatment of federally-sentenced Indigenous women: Submission to the United Nations special rapporteur on the rights of Indigenous peoples in advance of his official visit to Canada.

Correctional Service Canada. (2010). Management of higher-risk women: Results of consultation on an alternative to management protocol (women offender sector).

Correctional Service Canada. (2011). Intensive intervention strategy for women offenders. Retrieved from http://www.csc-scc.gc.ca/publications/005007-2006-eng.shtml#2.6

Correctional Service Canada. (2014). Response to the Coroner's Inquest Touching the Death of Ashley Smith. Retrieved from http://www.csc-scc.gc.ca/publications/005007-9011-eng.shtml

Correctional Service Canada. (2015a). Policy Bulletin 512. Retrieved from http://www.csc-scc.gc.ca/politiques-et-lois/512-pb-eng.shtml

Correctional Service Canada. (2015b). Toward a continuum of care: Correctional Service Canada mental health strategy. Retrieved from http://www.csc-scc.gc.ca/002/006/002006-2000-eng.shtml

Correctional Service Canada. (2017a). CD 709: Administrative segregation. Retrieved from http://www.csc-scc.gc.ca/politiques-et-lois/709-cd-eng.shtml

Correctional Service Canada. (2017b, January 3). Quick facts: Administrative segregation. Retrieved from http://www.csc-scc.gc.ca/publications/005007-3005-eng.shtml

Deitch, M. (2012). The need for independent prison oversight in a post-PLRA world. *Federal Sentencing Reporter, 24*(4), 236–44.

Dubé, P. (2017). *Out of oversight, out of mind: Investigation into how the Ministry of Community Safety and Correctional Services tracks the admission and placement of segregated inmates, and the adequacy and effectiveness of the review process for such placements*. Toronto, ON: Ombudsman of Ontario.

Ellis, R. (2013). *Unjust by design: Canada's administrative justice system*. Vancouver, BC: University of British Columbia Press.

Feeley, M.M., & Rubin, E.L. (2000). *Judicial policy making and the modern state: How the courts reformed America's prisons*. New York, NY: Cambridge University Press.

Fortin, D. (2004). Program strategy for women offenders. Correctional Service Canada. Retrieved from http://www.csc-scc.gc.ca/publications/fsw/fsw18/fsw18_e.pdf

Foucault, M. (1977). *Discipline and punish: The birth of the prison*. New York, NY: Vintage Books.

Gautier, A., & Agrell, P.J. (2011). A theory of soft capture. No. 1107. Centre de Recherche en Economie Publique et de la Population (CREPP), HEC-Management School, University of Liège.

Government of Ontario. (2017, September 28). The journey together: Ontario's commitment to reconciliation with Indigenous peoples. Retrieved from https://www.ontario.ca/page/journey-together-ontarios-commitment-reconciliation-indigenous-peoples

Grassian, S. (1983). Psychopathological effects of solitary confinement. *American Journal of Psychiatry, 140*(11), 1450–54. https://doi.org/10.1176/ajp.140.11.1450

Guenther, L. (2013). *Solitary confinement*. Minneapolis, MN: University of Minnesota Press.

Haney, C. (2003). Mental health issues in long-term solitary and "supermax" confinement. *NCCD News, 49*(1), 124–56. https://doi.org/10.1177/0011128702239239

Haney, C. (2005). *Reforming punishment: Psychological limits to the pains of imprisonment*. Washington, DC: American Psychological Association.

Haney, C. (2009). The social psychology of isolation: Why solitary confinement is psychologically harmful. *Prison Service Journal, 181*, 12–20.

Hannah-Moffat, K. (2001). *Punishment in disguise: Penal governance and federal imprisonment of women in Canada*. Toronto, ON: University of Toronto Press.

Hannah-Moffat, K. (2011). Criminological cliques: Narrowing dialogues, institutional protectionism and the next generation. In M. Bosworth & C. Hoyle (Eds), *What is criminology?* (pp. 440–55). Oxford, UK: Oxford University Press.

Hannah-Moffat, K. (2016). Expert witness report of Dr. Kelly Hannah-Moffat in the case of *British Columbia Civil Liberties Association and the John Howard Society of Canada v. Attorney General of Canada*. Supreme Court of British Columbia, S-150415.

Jackson, M. (1983). *Prisoners of isolation: Solitary confinement in Canada*. Toronto, ON: University of Toronto Press.

Jackson, M. (2001). The psychological effects of administrative segregation commentary #3. *Canadian Journal of Criminology, 43*, 109–16.

Jackson, M. (2016). Expert report of professor Michael Jackson, Q.C. *British Columbia Civil Liberties Association and the John Howard Society of Canada v. Attorney General of Canada*. SCBC Vancouver Registry No. S-150415. Retrieved from https://bccla.org/wp-content/uploads/2017/07/Day-03-and-04_2016-09-23-Expert-Report-of-Michael-Jackson.pdf

Jahn v. Ministry of Community Safety and Correctional Services (MCSCS). (2013a). 2013 HRTO 169. Retrieved from https://www.canlii.org/en/on/onhrt/doc/2013/2013hrto169/2013hrto169.html?resultIndex=20

Jahn v. MCSCS. (2013b). Public interest remedies. Retrieved from http://www.ohrc.on.ca/sites/default/files/Jahn%20Schedule%20A_accessible.pdf

Korn, R. (1988). The effects of confinement in the high security unit at Lexington. *Social Justice, 15*(1), 8–19.

Kupers, T.A. (2006). How to create madness in prison. In D. Jones (Ed.), *Humane prisons* (pp. 47–59). Oxford, UK: Radcliffe Publishing.

Laffont, J.J., & Tirole, J. (1991). The politics of government decision-making: A theory of regulatory capture. *Quarterly Journal of Economics, 106*(4), 1089–1127.

Laishes, J. (2002). The 2002 mental health strategy for women offenders. Correctional Service Canada. Retrieved from http://www.csc-scc.gc.ca/publications/fsw/mhealth/toc-eng.shtml

Lajeunesse, T., & Jefferson, C. (1999). *Cross-gender monitoring project: Federally sentenced women's facilities second annual report*. Correctional Service Canada. Retrieved from http://www.csc-scc.gc.ca/publications/fsw/gender2/toc-eng.shtml

Lajeunesse, T., Jefferson, C., Nuffield, J., & Majury, D. (2000). *Cross-gender monitoring project: Third and final annual report*. Correctional Service Canada. Retrieved from http://www.csc-scc.gc.ca/publications/fsw/gender3/toc-eng.shtml

Lowen, M., & Isaacs, C. (2012). *Lifetime lockdown: How isolation conditions impact prisoner reentry*. Tucson, AZ: American Friends Service Committee.

Makkai, T., & Braithwaite, J. (1992). In and out of the revolving door: Making sense of regulatory capture. *Journal of Public Policy, 12*(1), 61–78.

Martel, J. (1999). *Solitude & cold storage: Women's journeys of endurance in segregation*. Edmonton, AB: Elizabeth Fry Society of Edmonton.

McCoy, T. (2012). *Hard time: Reforming the penitentiary in nineteenth-century Canada*. Edmonton, AB: Athabasca University Press.

Mears, D.P., & Bales, W.D. (2009). Supermax incarceration and recidivism. *Criminology, 47*(4), 1131–66. https://doi.org/10.1111/j.1745-9125.2009.00171.x

Méndez, J. (2011). Report of the special rapporteur on torture and other cruel, inhuman or degrading treatment or punishment. No. UN Doc A/66/268. Retrieved from http://solitaryconfinement.org/uploads/SpecRapTortureAug2011.pdf

Metzner, J.L., & Fellner, J. (2010). Solitary confinement and mental illness in U.S. prisons: A challenge for medical ethics. *Journal of the American Academy of Psychiatry and the Law Online, 38*(1), 104–8.

Native Women's Association of Canada. (2017). Indigenous women in solitary confinement: Policy backgrounder. Retrieved from https://www.nwac.ca/wp-content/uploads/2017/07/NWAC-Indigenous-Women-in-Solitary-Confinement-Aug-22.pdf

Office of the Correctional Investigator. (2012). *Annual report of the Office of the Correctional Investigator 2011–2012*. Retrieved from http://www.oci-bec.gc.ca/cnt/rpt/pdf/annrpt/annrpt20112012-eng.pdf

Office of the Correctional Investigator. (2013). Risky business: An investigation of the treatment and management of chronic self-injury among federally sentenced women. Retrieved from http://www.oci-bec.gc.ca/cnt/rpt/pdf/oth-aut/oth-aut20130930-eng.pdf

Office of the Correctional Investigator. (2015a). Administrative segregation in federal corrections: 10-year trends. Retrieved from http://www.oci-bec.gc.ca/cnt/rpt/pdf/oth-aut/oth-aut20150528-eng.pdf

Office of the Correctional Investigator. (2015b). *Annual report of the Office of the Correctional Investigator 2014–2015*. Retrieved from http://www.oci-bec.gc.ca/cnt/rpt/pdf/annrpt/annrpt20142015-eng.pdf

Office of the Correctional Investigator. (2016). *Annual report of the Office of the Correctional Investigator 2015–2016*. Retrieved from http://www.oci-bec.gc.ca/cnt/rpt/pdf/annrpt/annrpt20152016-eng.pdf

Office of the Correctional Investigator. (2017). *Annual report of the Office of the Correctional Investigator 2016–2017*. Retrieved from http://www.oci-bec.gc.ca/cnt/rpt/pdf/annrpt/annrpt20162017-eng.pdf

Office of the Correctional Investigator. (2018). *Annual report of the Office of the Correctional Investigator 2017–2018*. Retrieved from https://www.oci-bec.gc.ca/cnt/rpt/annrpt/annrpt20172018-eng.aspx

OHRC v. Ontario (Community Safety and Correctional Services). 2018 HRTO 60. Retrieved from https://www.canlii.org/en/on/onhrt/doc/2018/2018hrto60/2018hrto60.html?resultIndex=1

Ontario. (2018). 2018 data release. Ministry of the Solicitor General. Retrieved from https://www.mcscs.jus.gov.on.ca/english/Corrections/JahnSettlement/2018Datarelease.html

Ontario Human Rights Commission. (2005). Reviewing Ontario's human rights system: Discussion paper. Retrieved from http://www.ohrc.on.ca/en/consultation-report-strengthening-ontarios-human-rights-system-what-we-heard

Parkes, D., & Pate, K. (2006). Time for accountability: Effective oversight of women's prisons. *Canadian Journal of Criminology and Criminal Justice, 48*(2), 251–85.

Parliament of Canada. (2019, August 16). LEGISinfo—House Government Bill C-83 (42-1). Retrieved from https://www.parl.ca/LEGISInfo/BillDetails.aspx?Language=E&billId=10078426&View=6

Pate, K., & Parkes, D.L. (2006). Time for accountability: Effective oversight of women's prisons Social Science Research Network. Retrieved from https://papers.ssrn.com/abstract=1583191

Prenzler, T. (2000). Civilian oversight of police. *British Journal of Criminology, 40*(4), 659–74.

Public Safety Canada. (2019, June 21). Statement from Minister Goodale on the passage of Bill C-83 to strengthen federal corrections and keep communities safe. Retrieved from https://www.canada.ca/en/public-safety-canada/news/2019/06/statement-from-minister-goodale-on-the-passage-of-bill-c-83-to-strengthen-federal-corrections-and-keep-communities-safe.html

R. v. Capay. 2019 ONSC 535. Retrieved from https://www.canlii.org/en/on/onsc/doc/2019/2019onsc535/2019onsc535.html?resultIndex=1

R. v. Roberts. 2018 ONSC 4566. Retrieved from https://www.canlii.org/en/on/onsc/doc/2018/2018canlii69343/2018canlii69343.html?resultIndex=71

Raemisch, R. (2018a, January 20). Opinion: Why we ended long-term solitary confinement in Colorado. *New York Times*.

Retrieved from https://www.nytimes.com/2017/10/12/opinion/solitary-confinement-colorado-prison.html

Raemisch, R. (2018b, September). How I came to believe in restricted housing reform. Presented at the New Approaches to Restrictive Housing: A Conference for Stakeholders. Albuquerque, New Mexico. Retrieved from https://new-approaches-to-restrictive-housing-a-c.eventcreate.com

Rankin, J. (2018, November 18). Years after landmark case, some Ontario inmates with mental health issues still segregated for months at a time, ministry data dump reveals. *Toronto Star*. Retrieved from https://www.thestar.com/news/gta/2018/11/18/years-after-landmark-case-some-ontario-inmates-with-mental-health-issues-still-segregated-for-months-at-a-time-ministry-data-dump-reveals.html

Reiter, K. (2016). *23/7 Pelican Bay Prison and the rise of long-term solitary confinement*. New Haven, CT: Yale UniversityPress.

Rhodes, L.A. (2004). *Total confinement: Madness and reason in the maximum security prison*. Berkeley, CA: University of California Press.

Sapers, H. (2017a). Corrections in Ontario, directions for reform: Independent review of Ontario corrections. Retrieved from https://www.mcscs.jus.gov.on.ca/sites/default/files/content/mcscs/docs/Corrections%20in%20Ontario%2C%20Directions%20for%20Reform.pdf

Sapers, H. (2017b). Segregation in Ontario: Independent review of Ontario Corrections. Retrieved from https://www.mcscs.jus.gov.on.ca/english/Corrections/IndependentReviewOntarioCorrections/IndependentReviewOntarioCorrectionsSegregationOntario.html

Schillemans, T. (2010). Redundant accountability: The joint impact of horizontal and vertical accountability on autonomous agencies. *Public Administration Quarterly, 34*(3), 300–37.

Schillemans, T. (2011). Does horizontal accountability work? Evaluating potential remedies for the accountability deficit of agencies. *Administration & Society, 43*(4), 387–416.

Shalev, S. (2017). Thinking outside the box? A review of seclusion and restraint practices in New Zealand. Retrieved from https://papers.ssrn.com/sol3/papers.cfm?abstract_id=2961332

Smith, P.S. (2006). The effects of solitary confinement on prison inmates: A brief history and review of the literature. *Crime and Justice, 34*(1), 441–528.

Swearingen, V. (2008). Imprisoning rights: The failure of negotiated governance in the prison inmate grievance process. *California Law Review, 96*, 1353.

Task Force on Administrative Segregation. (1997). Commitment to legal compliance, fair decisions and effective results: Reviewing administrative segregation. Retrieved from https://www.publicsafety.gc.ca/lbrr/archives/hv%208395.a6%20t37%201997-eng.pdf

Tirole, J. (1986). Hierarchies and bureaucracies: On the role of collusion in organizations. *Journal of Law, Economics, and Organization, 2*(2), 181–214.

Toope, S.J. (2017). Expert report of Stephen J. Toope in the case of *The Queen v. Adam Mark Capay*. No. CR-13-0070. Superior Court of Justice (northwest region).

UN General Assembly. (2015). United Nations standard minimum rules for the treatment of prisoners (the Mandela Rules). A/C.3/70/L.3.

United Nations. (1976). International covenant on civil and political rights. Retrieved from http://www.ohchr.org/en/professionalinterest/pages/ccpr.aspx

United Nations. (1987). Convention against torture and other cruel, inhuman or degrading treatment or punishment. Retrieved from http://www.ohchr.org/EN/ProfessionalInterest/Pages/CAT.aspx

United Nations. (2006a) Convention on the rights of persons with disabilities. Retrieved from https://www.un.org/development/desa/disabilities/convention-on-the-rights-of-persons-with-disabilities/convention-on-the-rights-of-persons-with-disabilities-2.html

United Nations. (2006b). Optional protocol to the convention against torture and other cruel, inhuman or degrading treatment or punishment. Retrieved from http://www.ohchr.org/EN/ProfessionalInterest/Pages/OPCAT.aspx

United Nations. (2011). The Bangkok Rules: United Nations rules for the treatment of women prisoners and non-custodial measures for women offenders. Retrieved from https://www.unodc.org/documents/justice-and-prison-reform/Bangkok_Rules_ENG_22032015.pdf

Vagg, J. (1994). *Prison systems: A comparative study of accountability in England, France, Germany, and the Netherlands*. Oxford, UK: Clarendon Press.

Van Zyl Smit, D. (2007). Prisoners rights. In Y. Jewkes (Ed.), *Handbook on prisons*. Cullompton, UK: Willan.

Vera Institute of Justice. (2018). Women in segregation: Fact sheet. Retrieved from https://storage.googleapis.com/vera-web-assets/downloads/Publications/women-in-segregation/legacy_downloads/women-in-segregation-fact-sheet.pdf

Watson, T.M. (2015). Research access barriers as reputational risk management: A case study of censorship in corrections. *Canadian Journal of Criminology and Criminal Justice, 57*(3), 330–62.

Wood, S. (2009). "Capture" and the South African Judicial Inspectorate of Prisons: A micro-level analysis. *International Criminal Justice Review, 19*(1), 46–63.

Wood, S.R. (2012). An exploratory study of staff capture at the South African Inspectorate of Prisons. *International Journal of Comparative and Applied Criminal Justice, 36*(1), 45–59.

Working Group on Human Rights. (1997). Human rights and corrections: A strategic model. Public Safety Canada. Retrieved from https://www.publicsafety.gc.ca/lbrr/archives/jl%20103.c6%20w6%201997-eng.pdf

Zinger, I. (2013, March). Segregation in Canadian federal corrections—A prison ombudsman's perspective. Presented at Ending the Isolation: An International Conference on Human Rights and Solitary Confinement, University of Manitoba. Retrieved from http://www.oci-bec.gc.ca/cnt/comm/presentations/presentations20130322-23-eng.aspx

The Use of Technology within Correctional Institutions and Community Corrections

15

Karla Dhungana Sainju

Learning Objectives

After reading this chapter, you should be able to:

- Understand the various forms of technologies currently being used within corrections and community corrections systems.
- Identify ways in which technology contributes to increased safety and efficiency.
- Recognize how technology can also serve as serious threats to correctional institutions.
- Critically reflect on the effectiveness of various technological tools while also considering the potential limitations associated with them.
- Describe some upcoming technological tools that may be part of the criminal justice system in the near future.

Chapter Overview

The use of technology continues to proliferate and evolve all around us, and the criminal justice system is no exception. In this chapter, we introduce the various technologies currently being used within Canadian and American correctional institutions and community corrections. An overview of each technology will be provided and, if available, relevant research associated with the technology will be highlighted. When applicable, examples or comparisons between the technology's use in Canada and the United States will also be emphasized, and potential concerns with these technological uses will be discussed. Finally, the chapter will examine some upcoming technologies that may be a part of the criminal justice system in the near future.

Introduction

Technology is all around us and has revolutionized the way we live our lives. By enabling people to easily access information, resources, and tools, technology has created a more effective, efficient, and instant world. These modern technologies have transformed many areas, including the criminal justice system. In this chapter, we will delve into the various technologies that have made its way into our corrections system.

Corrections is an umbrella term for agencies that establish, maintain, operate, and monitor the punishment, treatment, and supervision of offenders. These offenders can serve their sanctions and sentences in custody or in community settings. Within Canada, offenders who receive a custody sentence of two years or more are sent to a federal penitentiary and are supervised by Correctional Service Canada (CSC). Offenders with sentences of less than two years will complete their sentence in a provincial correctional facility under provincial jurisdiction. Within the United States, if an offender violates a federal law, they will serve their sentence in a federal prison under the purview of the federal Bureau of Prisons (BOP), while offenders who violate state laws will be sentenced to state prisons and be under state jurisdiction. Most correctional facilities employ various types of technologies to ensure the safety and well-being of their staff, correctional officers, and inmates.

Community corrections refers to sanctions or supervision programs, such as diversion, probation, or parole, provided to pre-trial defendants, convicted adults, or adjudicated youth within community settings. To enhance the effectiveness of supervising defendants and post-conviction populations in the community, community correction agencies currently use multiple electronic monitoring (EM) tools, including location monitoring and activity monitoring technologies. These tools may be used as prison or jail diversion tools to help reduce overcrowding in correctional facilities by offering a less expensive option compared to incarceration. They could also be used to prevent future delinquency through appropriate monitoring, rehabilitation, and community reintegration through earned release as an intermediate sanction tool to respond to violations or as a tailored condition for specialized cases such as drunk driving, domestic violence, and so on. Let's begin by discussing technologies being used within correctional facilities.

Correctional Facilities: Current Technologies

Ion Mobility Spectrometry (IMS) Devices

The CSC admits that drug abuse is a serious concern within their facilities and that eliminating drugs from their penitentiaries is a top priority (CSC, n.d.; Hansard, 2018; McVie, 2001). Drugs are considered **contraband**, or illegal items, within correctional institutions, and yet the flow and access to drugs still occur within prison walls. Inmate responses from the CSC's 2007 National Inmate Infectious Diseases and Risk-Behaviours Survey found that while in federal custody, 34 per cent of men and 25 per cent of women engaged in non-injection drug use such as snorting, sniffing, smoking, or swallowing, while 17 per cent of men and 14 per cent of women admitted to using injected drugs (Zakaria, Thompson, Jarvis, & Borgotta, 2010). The problem isn't limited to just federal institutions. According to Alberta Health Services data, between January 2016 and October 2018, 224 suspected

overdoses were reported within Alberta provincial jails (Wakefield, 2018). Additionally, qualitative interviews with ex-offenders from Ontario revealed that drugs were readily available within prison. Participants were quoted as saying "There are more drugs in there than on the streets sometimes," and "It finds its way in. You know what I mean? Everything finds its way in there . . ." (Van Der Meulen, 2017, p. 886).

One of the CSC's detection tools for contraband drugs is the **ion mobility spectrometry (IMS) device**, also referred to as ion scanners. It is used as a drug detection system to screen visitors, staff, inmates, and incoming mail for drug residue. Ion scanners are non-intrusive trace-detecting devices that have been in use in Canada since 1995. It does not determine whether an individual has consumed or is carrying contraband; rather, it detects minute traces of residue of a variety of chemical substances and determines whether the individual or an item has potentially been in contact with an illegal substance (Johnson & Dastouri, 2011; McKay, 2018). The tool is used by correctional staff to assess the person's or item's threat level in regard to contraband introduction. Residue of substances can be absorbed by or cling to surfaces such as clothing, skin, hair, containers, paper, and so on. Correctional staff collect samples by wiping or vacuuming objects and place the filter or swipe into the ion scanner unit, with results displayed in as quickly as six seconds (Johnson & Dastouri, 2011). Table 15.1 highlights the number of positive ion scan results in 2017. Of the total 23,500 visitors to CSC facilities, 324 visitors, or 0.25 per cent, were denied entry.

Studies examining the effectiveness of ion scanners are limited. Research findings reveal that while the device reliably detected cocaine, it did not accurately detect heroin and amphetamine and had a limited capacity for detecting cannabis (Butler, 2002; Sheldon et al., 1998). The US BOP conducted a pilot project where they compared two institutions that used ion scanners to other institutions that did not use the technology during the same time period. Results indicated significant reductions in drug-related offender misconduct at the pilot sites compared to the other institutions (Hogsten, 1998). Similarly, another evaluation found that introduction of trace technology led to statistically significant reductions in positive findings within the mailroom of an institution in Arizona (National Criminal Justice Reference Service, 2008). While some of these studies suggest that ion scanners can serve as a valuable tool in controlling the issue of drugs being

Table 15.1 Number of Visitors per Site and Ion Scan Positive Results, 2017

Region	Number of Unique Visitors	Total Number of Visits	Total Number of + Results on the Ion Scanner	Out of +, Total Number of Visitors Denied Entry	Percentage of Visits Denied Entry Based on the Threat Risk Assessment (TRA) Being Completed as a Result of a + on the Ion Scanner
Atlantic	1,643	7,817	57	17	29.8 of + hits / 0.22 of total visits
Quebec	6,851	38,187	31	8	25.8 of + hits / 0.02 of total visits
Ontario	6,218	27,285	468	148	31.6 of + hits / 0.54 of total visits
Prairies	5,939	34,793	565	119	21.1 of + hits / 0.34 of total visits
Pacific	2,849	20,059	86	32	37.2 of + hits / 0.16 of total visits
Total	23,500	128,141	1,207	324	26.8 of + hits / 0.25 of total visits (average)

Source: Correctional Service Canada, Interim Report: Use of Ion Mobility Spectrometers retrieved from https://www.ourcommons.ca/content/Committee/421/SECU/Reports/RP9998633/421_SECU_Rpt25_PDF/421_SECU_Rpt25-e.pdf p. 34

brought into prison, it is also clear that additional and more recent examinations into the effectiveness of ion scanners are needed.

In addition to their limited ability to detect certain types of drugs, ion scanners have also faced criticism about being oversensitive, measuring the drug particulate down to the nano gram and thus resulting in false positives (Johnson & Dastouri, 2011). The Office of the Correctional Investigator's (OCI) 2016–17 report addressed this concern and made a recommendation that the CSC conduct a review on the use and reliability of the ion scanners (OCI, 2017). Public groups, such as Ontario-based MOMS (Mothers Offering Mutual Support), a group that has loved ones who are incarcerated, have been vocal about the impact of false positives on family visitations. They point out that false positives cannot only lead to denied visitations, but can also affect future private family visits, transfers, and parole (Harris, 2016). In 2016, a Canadian federal government e-petition opposing the ion scanner was sponsored by member of Parliament Matthew Dubé and received over 600 signatures. After being tabled in the House of Commons, the government issued a response on 29 May 2018 stating that the CSC will review the use of ion scanners in institutions with regard to its reliability issues and that "safely facilitating visits by friends and family, as an important pillar of successful inmate rehabilitation, continues to be a priority for the government" (Hansard, 2017, p. 2).

Cellphone Jamming Technology

The CSC and the US Department of Justice (DOJ) both point to illegal cellphones as being another contraband

item that poses a serious threat (Bronskill, 2014; US DOJ, 2018). They can be used to further facilitate criminal activities from within prison, including drug trafficking, money laundering, organized crime, and ordering hits on potential witnesses. The US BOP is reported to have confiscated 5,116 illegal phones in 2016, and preliminary numbers for 2017 showed a 28 per cent increase (Horwitz, 2018). The CSC has also seen the numbers of confiscated phones continue to increase, with 137 phones reported for a 10-month period in 2013–14, up from 51 phones in 2008–9 and 94 in 2009–10 (Bronskill, 2014).

Contraband cellphones have been linked to many dangerous and concerning situations. According to court records, an inmate at the Mission Institution in British Columbia who was involved in the prison's drug subculture and with ties to organized crime had a cellphone seized in 2011 (Bronskill, 2014). In August 2018, officials from Collins Bay Institution, a federal penitentiary in Ontario, seized packages containing contraband worth over $100,000. The items included illicit drugs as well as cellphones, chargers, and SIM cards (*Global News*, 2018). Former South Carolina corrections officer Robert Johnson was shot six times in the chest and stomach as a result of a hit planned by an inmate using a contraband cellphone (Thomas & Krolowitz, 2010). Additionally, numerous drug rings within prisons operated by prisoners with contraband cellphones have also been identified (Associated Press, 2012; Riley, 2017). In April 2018 a deadly seven-hour riot that left seven prisoners dead and wounded 17 others in a South Carolina prison was attributed in part to contraband cellphones (McKenzie, 2018).

To counter and address the dangers posed by contraband cellphones, some correctional facilities use cellphone jamming technology. These technologies can work in several ways; they can use radio frequency technology to block and disrupt cell signals across multiple signal bands or a particular frequency, or they can use a technique called "scan and jam" to detect and disrupt a suspicious signal (Burke & Owen, 2010; Hsu, 2009). Currently, some prisons in countries like New Zealand, Australia, France, Honduras, El Salvador, and Mexico use cellphone jammers (Figueroa, 2014; Makuch, 2014; Robbins, 2014). Correctional Services of New South Wales in Australia conducted a five-year trial at a correctional facility and reported significant reductions in contraband cellphone seizures (Correctional News, 2018). Honduras has blocked cellphone signals in all 24 of the country's prisons, and the Honduran National Anti-Extortion Force reports that this has led to a 75 per cent reduction in reported extortions (Figueroa, 2014; La Prensa, 2014). Similarly, prisons in El Salvador have also installed technology that blocks signals from cellphones (Robbins, 2014).

However, critics of this technology point to several concerns, including the risk of interfering with other nearby signals, which could pose a safety hazard during emergencies, such as 911 calls and public safety communications (Federal Communications Commission [FCC], n.d.). It could also cut out signals for legal cell users, such as residents who live in close proximity to the correctional facility (Clarke, 2009; FCC, n.d.). Under current law in the United States, cellphone jamming is illegal within correctional institutions and requires approval from the FCC. In the past, the FCC has raised concerns about the potential risks associated with using jamming technologies, however, after meeting with members of the phone industry, lawmakers, prison officials, and the FCC voted to streamline the process for jails and prisons to use jamming technology in the future (FCC, n.d.; Kinnard, 2017).

In January 2018, the BOP in collaboration with the National Telecommunications and Information Administration and the FCC conducted a test of micro-jamming technology at a federal correctional facility in Maryland (US DOJ, 2018). Results from the test indicated that it was able to successfully block commercial cell signals within the facility while having no impact on commercial airwaves 20 feet outside the facility's walls (Rockwell, 2018). The test provides promising results for the use of micro-jamming technology

and getting US correctional institutions one step closer to using this technology within their facilities. With no public records noting use of jammers in Canada, it is not clear whether Canada currently uses this technology. However, when asked about it prison officials have responded by stating that the "CSC continues to work with service providers and other criminal justice system partners to monitor advancements in the field of detection of illicit cell phone usage" (Bronskill, 2014; Makuch, 2014).

Tablets for Inmate Use

Prisons and county jails in about 30 states in the United States provide inmates with tablets, such as iPads (GTL, 2019; JPay, 2019a; Kaufman, 2018; Kruzman, 2018). Some correctional officials also see this technological tool as a possible way to combat the issue of contraband cellphones. While illicit cellphones facilitate criminal activities, they are also used to stay in touch with loved ones. By providing a legal and different technological device to communicate with loved ones outside, correctional officials hope it will reduce the attractiveness of contraband cellphones (Kinnard, 2019).

The tablets are tamper-proof and modified for correctional facilities; they have multilayered security features that restrict access to approved content only, allow email exchanges with people on an approved contacts list, restrict access to the Internet, and all messages are limited in length and screened for security (GTL, 2019; JPay, 2019a; Kruzman, 2018). The tablet can open up access to educational content, including audiobooks, instructional videos, law libraries, self-help courses, and educational curriculum such as GED prep courses. Entertainment features, like approved music, games, and movies, are also accessible. Efficiency is promoted through easy access to grievance paperwork, ordering items from the commissary, and receiving money from loved ones. Perhaps one of the most important features for inmates is the communication aspect, which comes in the form of emails, messaging, and video chats (GTL, 2019; JPay, 2019a).

Correctional facilities point to reduced violence, improved security, and a positive impact on inmate rehabilitation, stress, and behaviour with the introduction of the tablets (Kruzman, 2018; Stewart, 2017). No empirical studies have been conducted specifically on the tablet programs, but the proposed benefits are anchored in research that supports the role of educational programs while incarcerated in reducing recidivism rates after release. A meta-analysis conducted by the RAND Corporation found that, on average, participating in an educational program lowered the likelihood of recidivism upon release by 43 per cent and increased the likelihood of getting employment by 13 per cent (Davis, Bozick, Steele, Saunders, & Miles, 2013). Additionally, correctional officials and companies that provide the tablets also point to research that has established strong associations between maintaining contact with loved ones during incarceration and the increased likelihood of success after release (diZerega & Villalobos Agudelo, 2011; Shanahan & Villalobos Agudelo, 2012).

Nonetheless, the program is not without controversy. Several states, including Colorado, New York, Florida, and Georgia, provide tablets to inmates for free. However, stating that the tablets are at no cost is misleading, since there are usage fees associated with most if not all aspects of using the tablet. JPay, one of the largest providers of tablets within prisons, states that fees and availability vary by facility. A look at the cost in a prison in Florida reveals that a 15-minute video call costs $2.95, while each email can cost upwards of 39 cents. Inbound and outbound videograms cost about $1.76 each. Sending money also comes with a price tag. Want to send $20.00–$29.99? That will cost $4.95. How about $100.00–$199.99? The cost goes up to $11.95 (JPay, 2019b). GTL, another competitor in the prison technology business, similarly charges for calls and messaging based on usage. They also offer music for up to $19.99 per month and games through monthly subscriptions ranging from $5 to $15 per month (Raher, 2017). Alarmingly, these companies have the authority to change the prices at their discretion, with prices fluctuating during peak times such as holidays (Law, 2018; Raher, 2017).

The CSC pay levels for inmates allows for a maximum of $6.90 to be earned per day (CSC, 2016b). The hourly wage paid to incarcerated inmates in the United

REUTERS/Brendan McDermid

An inmate using the JPay5 Mini tablet.

States working regular prison jobs is between 14 to 63 cents an hour (Sawyer, 2017). The incarcerated population are at the lower end of the socio-economic ladder, and this applies to all gender, race, and ethnicity groups (Rabuy & Kopf, 2015). Critics argue that the program is a profit-making endeavour, targeting those who can least afford it—incarcerated individuals and their families (Law, 2018; Raher, 2017; Riley, 2018; Waters, 2018). There are also security concerns associated with the tablets. In 2018, 364 inmates in Idaho discovered a vulnerability within JPay's system and applied credits worth $225,000 to their accounts (Associated Press, 2018). In 2015, just five days into a six-month pilot program, Napa County corrections officials in California had to halt the program due to concerns that two inmates allegedly tried to bypass the security features and access the Internet (Yune, 2015). Similarly, in 2018, amid concerns over security, Colorado corrections officials took away all 15,000 tablets from its state prisons (*US News*, 2018).

The OCI's 2015–16 report made several recommendations, including exploring various technology and communications options within Canadian correctional settings (OCI, 2016). A pilot program where inmates were given free tablets was implemented in two provincial institutions in Nova Scotia in 2017. Similar to the US programs, the program was set up to have inmates pay for services and applications on a pay-per-use basis. However, amid issues of security and privacy, the program was suspended. Officials stated that some inmates attempted to access personal information of other inmates using the tablets, while another physically assaulted a prisoner with a tablet (Mulligan, 2018). The program is currently on hold while security concerns are addressed. Additional pilot programs were also being tested in provincial institutions in New Brunswick and Alberta; however, both these programs are also temporarily on hold (Mulligan, 2018). At the federal level, CSC officials reported that they were still in the exploration phase for tablet programs in 2017 (Harris, 2017).

Drone Detection Technology

Drones are pilotless, remote-controlled devices. They are an "unmanned aerial vehicle," or UAV. The device is controlled by a remote or accessed via a smartphone app and allows access to remote or unreachable locations without posing any risk to the person controlling the device. Historically, the use of UAVs has been primarily for military applications; however, use of the devices has grown exponentially in the commercial and consumer sectors. Drones are being used for surveillance, precision agriculture, surveying and mapping, traffic monitoring, search and rescue, drone-based professional photography and videography, and even delivery services (Joshi, 2017).

Some individuals are now using personal drones to illegally deliver drugs, weapons, cellphones, and other contraband items into correctional facility grounds. The CSC has acknowledged that between July 2013 and December 2016, there were 41 drone incidents at federal facilities (Egan, 2017). Staff at multiple federal correctional facilities across the country, including Stony Mountain Institution in Manitoba, Matsqui Institution in British Columbia, Collins Bay Institution in Ontario, and Cowansville Institution in Quebec, have all reported drones being used to deliver contraband into their institutions (*CBC News*, 2018; Cherry, 2017; Egan, 2017; Judd, 2018). Data from Quebec's provincial detention centres reveal that the use of drones to sneak in contraband is rising dramatically; during 2013 to 2014, four drone sightings were reported, whereas between 2016 and 2017, there were 120 reports (Cherry, 2017). The CSC has even attempted to enlist the general public's help by sending out tweets regarding drone sightings.

To combat the issue of drones being used to smuggle in contraband, correctional facilities in other countries have been testing out various drone detection technologies. In 2018, the Georgia Department of Corrections in the United States deployed the AeroDefense AirWarden within its correctional facilities (Securus Technologies, 2018). The radio frequency–based technology detects unauthorized drones, locates both the drone and pilot, and alerts authorized personnel via text, email, or command centre console so that they can deploy appropriate measures to search the facility or the drop zone area (Dormehl, 2018; *US News*, 2018). Radio frequency detection and tracking technologies are also being offered by companies such as DroneShield and Dedrone. These technologies, however, only detect the drones and do not provide any way to bring them down. Under US federal law, it is currently illegal to willfully damage or destroy an aircraft, and a drone or UAV would be considered an aircraft (US DOJ, 2019). Thus, correctional officials cannot simply shoot down a drone that illegally enters a facility. Another option would be to jam the signals of UAV devices, which could shut them down mid-flight. The US Federal Communications Commission, however, currently prohibits these types of technology, stating that "jammers" or similar devices designed to intentionally block, jam, or interfere with authorized radio communications is a violation of federal law (FCC, 2019).

In October 2018, the CSC put out a request for proposal "seeking an innovative and cost-effective technology solution to detect, track and prevent contraband items from entering the perimeter via Unmanned Aerial Vehicle (UAV), commonly known as drones" (Government of Canada, 2019). The proposal specifically noted that the CSC does not consider jamming countermeasures to be safe, and that while air and ground intrusion detection systems are available, they do not include legal, safe, or affordable measures to deploy to its institutions. In June 2019, *CBC News* reported that the CSC will be spending $6 million on a pilot project to install radar-based drone detection equipment at six facilities throughout the country (Thurton, 2019). The CSC aims to have the detection equipment running in one institution by March 2020 and the remaining locations by March 2022. While the CSC has not identified the specific

Correctional Service ✔ @CSC_SCC_en · 13 Nov 2018

We are asking for your assistance in detecting suspicious UAV activities such as late night operations, hovering over a particular location for a period of time, or carrying packages.

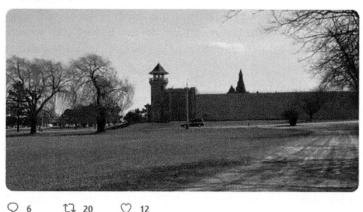

💬 6   🔁 20   ♡ 12

Correctional Service ✔
@CSC_SCC_en   (Follow) ⌄

If you believe UAVs are being used suspiciously around Collins Bay Institution, or any of the Kingston area correctional institutions, please call us immediately at 1-866-780-3784 (toll free).

11:27 AM - 13 Nov 2018

Tweets sent out by the CSC seeking the public's assistance in reporting suspicious drone activity around their Kingston, Ontario, facilities.
Courtesy of Correctional Service Canada

approach they will be taking to address the drone problem, Ghislain Sauvé, a director general with the CSC notes that they are "going to make sure we get a system that works . . . And once we're satisfied with that . . . there'll be more decisions in the future" (Thurton, 2019).

Radio Frequency Identification (RFID) Tags

Radio frequency identification (RFID) tags in the form of ankle bracelets are used in some correctional institutions to track inmates, allowing staff to conduct investigations more efficiently, keep rival gang members apart, as well as track any suspected contraband carrier by following their interactions and movement throughout the day. While still limited in its use, correctional facilities

in California, Virginia, Michigan, Illinois, Ohio, and Minnesota have deployed RFID tracking systems to help manage inmates (McKay, 2008). It is used only for security purposes and does not eliminate or limit the number of correctional staff in any way. Antennas are placed throughout the facility, and signals are captured from each RFID ankle bracelet, which allows correctional staff to determine where an individual is at any given time. It gives them the ability to efficiently manage and enhance security within a facility (McKay, 2008).

The US National Institute of Justice, in collaboration with the RAND Corporation and the District of Columbia Department of Corrections, is working on a study to examine the effectiveness of RFID bracelets within DC jails. The study hopes to determine if the system can detect potentially volatile situations and prevent incidents of violence within the facilities (Bulman, 2009). Federal and provincial facilities in Canada do not currently employ this technological tool, but as it expands in use within US facilities and results about the effectiveness of the tools emerge, it may find its way into Canadian institutions if the need arises.

Correctional Facilities: Upcoming Technologies

Suicide Warning System

Suicide is the leading cause of non-natural deaths within federal institutions and accounts for about one-in-five deaths in custody (CSC, 2017; OCI, 2014b). Several high-profile cases have brought attention and scrutiny to the issue of suicide in custody, particularly the cases of Ashley Smith and Eddie Snowshoe. Smith, a 19-year-old teenager, died by self-inflicted strangulation in 2007 while under suicide watch at the Grand Valley Institution for Women (OCI, 2014a). Snowshoe, a 24-year-old Gwich'in man, committed suicide by hanging in 2010 in the Edmonton Institution, a maximum security federal facility in Alberta (Province of Alberta, 2014). It is also worth noting that both Smith and Snowshoe's suicide came after extensive periods in solitary confinement—1,047 days and 162 days, respectively (Darrow, 2017). See Chapter 8 for additional details on the case of Ashley Smith. Suicides in custody, however, is not just a problem within Canada; a study examining prison suicide prevalence rates in 24 high-income countries across Europe, Australasia, and North America reported 3,906 suicides in custody between 2011 and 2014 (Fazel, Ramesh, & Hawton, 2018).

Suicide is a complex issue with multiple risk factors, including mental health, substance abuse, childhood experiences, trauma, and other adverse experiences (Fazel et al., 2018; Marzano, Fazel, Rivlin, & Hawton, 2011; Rivlin, Fazel, Marzano, & Hawton., 2013). The World Health Organization (WHO) states that all correctional institutions should implement a comprehensive suicide prevention plan, which should include properly trained correctional staff, appropriate intake screening procedures, and vigilant post-intake observation. Appropriate monitoring and follow-up measures should include communication, social intervention, mental health treatment, and checking the physical environment and architecture (WHO, 2007).

The US National Institute of Justice is currently funding a multi-phase program with General Electric to create a system that can serve as an unobtrusive suicide warning system (Ashe et al., 2012). The system is a Doppler radar–based sensor system placed in a room, away from an inmate's reach. The non-contact monitoring device is based on a modified version of a commercialized range-controlled radar, which was originally used as a motion detector for home security systems. The system is able to detect subtle motions of an individual's body, such as heartbeat, breathing, and limb movement, and can quickly interpret and relay any changes in vital signs associated with asphyxia through self-strangulation or hanging (See Figure 15.1). This could allow correctional officials more time to intervene in the event of a suicide attempt. Additional anticipated benefits of the system include minimized post-traumatic care, reduction in workflow issues associated with prison monitoring, and a potential decrease in liability associated with wrongful death (Ashe et al., 2012, p. 121). The system is still undergoing testing to optimize the configurations, settings, and features to meet all necessary requirements to be approved for safe use and the benefit of inmates and correctional staff. Once the system is ready for deployment, it is unclear whether the CSC will adopt this system; however, there are some potential benefits that could come from doing so.

Biometrics

Another technological advancement being piloted within prisons and jails include the use of biometric technologies. **Biometrics** use an individual's physiological data, such as fingerprints, retinal eye scan, facial features, or voice patterns, to verify and record an individual's identity. The US National Institute of Justice and the US Department of Defense conducted a three-year study evaluating the use of the Biometric Inmate Tracking System. It specifically assessed the iris, facial, retinal, finger, hand geometry, voice, and fingerprint biometric methods (Miles & Cohn, 2006). The aim of the pilot project was to examine how biometrics could be used during the initial booking process, move large number of inmates safely from one area of the prison to another, and verify the location of an inmate or to confirm whether an inmate is authorized to go to certain parts of the facility. It also allowed for increased staff efficiency to identify potential security breaches or any out-of-place inmates much more quickly (Miles & Cohn, 2006).

A review of the various methods found that the fingerprint recognition method provided the most

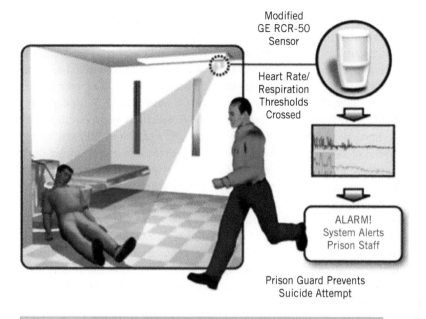

Modified
GE RCR-50
Sensor

Heart Rate/
Respiration
Thresholds
Crossed

ALARM!
System Alerts
Prison Staff

Prison Guard Prevents
Suicide Attempt

Figure 15.1 **Summary of the Suicide Warning System Currently Being Developed**
Source: Ashe (2012).

accurate and reliable matches. It cost less than the iris, facial, and retinal methods; was easier to use; and was more durable (Miles & Cohn, 2006). In June 2018, an inmate in Albuquerque, New Mexico, posed as his cellmate by switching their identification wristbands and was mistakenly released by jail officials. The inmate also groomed his facial hair to resemble his cellmate as well as memorized his personal information. The incident prompted the facility to examine their booking and release process. The chief of the institution has now taken steps to include biometric technology as part of all booking and release procedures to avoid such mistakes in the future (Boetel, 2018).

Biometric technologies have the potential to significantly change the way prisons and jails are managed, and it is expected that more facilities will begin to adopt them in the future. Similar to the suicide detection system, it has yet to be seen whether Canadian corrections will adopt biometrics systems within their facilities.

Community Corrections: Current Technologies

Community corrections agencies currently use multiple electronic monitoring (EM) tools to safely and efficiently supervise defendants and post-conviction populations within the community. These tools include location monitoring and activity monitoring technologies. Location monitoring technologies allow for data to be collected to track offenders, pinpoint their exact location at a certain time, and set up inclusion and exclusion zones. On the other hand, activity monitoring technologies are tools and communication technologies that do not track an offender, but instead allow for remote monitoring and check-ins.

Location Monitoring Technologies

One of the most commonly used location monitoring technologies are **radio frequency (RF) devices**. RF devices are static technologies that track an individual's location at a single fixed place. Most often used with individuals on house arrest or home detention, the devices are equipped with a battery-powered transmitter worn by the defendant or offender on their ankle. The technology works by sending RF signals to a receiver device installed in the person's home and connected to their landline phone (Doffing, 2012). Each person has a preapproved schedule and conditions that they need to comply with. If there is a violation (for example, if a person leaves their home during an unscheduled time), an alert will immediately be sent to the monitoring centre or the offender's supervising officer (Doffing, 2012).

There are several limiting features of the RF device, including the inability to track offenders once they leave their home location, the requirement that offenders have access to a landline, and the concerns over features such as call waiting, call forwarding, answering machines, or call blocking being used by offenders to manipulate and interfere with the RF receiver's ability to detect transmitters (Bottos, 2008; DeMichele & Payne, 2009; Hoshen & Drake, 2001). With more advanced location monitoring technologies such as GPS devices readily available, the use of RF devices has steadily declined. A 2016 national survey conducted in the United States found that between 2000 and 2015, the number of active RF devices fell by 25 per cent, from more than 50,000 to below 38,000 (Stevenson, Fahy, & Dhungana Sainju, 2017).

The decline of RF devices has led to a dramatic increase in the use of **global positioning system (GPS) devices**. In the United States, the use of GPS devices went from about 29,000 units in 2005 to about 88,000 in 2015 (Stevenson et al., 2017). GPS devices offer several advantages over the RF device. The biggest advantage is the ability for GPS devices to track defendants and offenders in real time by sending, receiving, and triangulating geographical coordinates to and from GPS satellites and cellular towers (DeMichele, Payne, & Button, 2008). GPS devices can also be configured based on the risk level and needs of the defendant or offender. Statutory requirements may necessitate that inclusion and exclusion zones be defined for each individual. **Inclusion zones** are predefined and authorized locations that the individual can have access to during approved times and dates. **Exclusion zones** are unauthorized locations where an individual is restricted from entering. When the offender enters an exclusion zone, an alert is immediately sent to the supervising officer or monitoring centre, and a warning alert may also be sent to the offender. Inclusion zones may consist of the offender's place of employment, residence, treatment programs, or educational institution. Exclusion zones could include parks, places where young children frequent, areas known for drug transactions, and if applicable the victim's home or place of employment.

Provincially, the Ontario Ministry of Community Safety and Correctional Services uses location monitoring devices as part of their Electronic Supervision Program to monitor offenders' compliance with house arrest and curfew conditions (Ontario MCSCS, 2018). The Community Corrections division of British Columbia's Ministry of Public Safety and Solicitor General primarily uses them as a condition of conditional sentence orders for the purpose of curfew monitoring (British Columbia MPSSG, 2017). Additionally, Alberta, Saskatchewan, Manitoba, Nova Scotia, and Newfoundland and Labrador also use the devices as part of their community corrections services (Sorenson, 2012; Wilson, 2013). At the federal level, the Corrections and Conditional Release Act provides the CSC with the authority to demand that an offender wear an electronic monitoring device to monitor compliance with geographical special conditions of a temporary absence, work release, parole, statutory release, or long-term supervision (CSC, 2016a).

Examining the available empirical evidence on the effectiveness of RF and GPS devices suggests that despite the rapid expansion of the technology, the research has not kept pace and the results are still not conclusive (Dhungana Sainju et al., 2016). Comparing the use of EM in three provinces, British Colombia, Saskatchewan, and Newfoundland, Bonta and his colleagues (2000) examined monitored versus unmonitored offenders and found that the use of EM had no significant impact on reducing recidivism rates. They asserted that offender treatment rather than sanctions were a more promising approach to reducing recidivism and that the use of EM may also result in a net widening effect (Bonta, Wallace-Capretta, & Rooney, 2000). In 2008, the minister of Public Safety Canada in conjunction with the CSC conducted an Electronic Monitoring Pilot Program in Ontario for federally sentenced offenders. The evaluation of the program suffered from significant limitations, and the research team concluded that the "evaluation findings were inconclusive . . . with respect to the rehabilitative impact of electronic monitoring" (Olotu, Beaupre, & Verbrugge, 2009, p. 64).

The CSC is currently conducting a second pilot study to evaluate the use, impact, and cost effectiveness of EM with federal offenders (Hanby, 2017). The Electronic Monitoring Research Pilot (EMRP) is a three-year study currently being implemented in the Atlantic, Quebec, Ontario, Prairies, and Pacific regions of the country (Hanby, 2017). The EMRP is using EM technology that combines both GPS and RF into one device. This hybrid device allows for data to be transmitted at programmable times throughout the day (Brown, McCabe, & Wellford, 2007; Steele, Brydon, & Hare, 2012). During times when the offender is allowed to be outside of their homes, the active feature of the GPS technologies can track offenders in real time and enforce exclusion and inclusion zones. When the offender returns back to their home, the device can revert back to RF, which saves the battery life and helps to eliminate GPS "drift," which can affect the accuracy of a GPS point (Brown, et al., 2007; CSC, 2015; Steele et al., 2012).

A report on the implementation of the EMRP program suggests that EM is being used by parole officers appropriately as a discretionary tool to monitor supervision conditions, yet no significant differences were found between offenders who were on EM versus those who were not (Hanby, Nelson, & MacDonald, 2018). As part of the EMRP, 171 offenders were also asked about their experience with the monitoring device (Hanby & Cociu, 2018). Most of the offenders reported that EM had no impact on their ability to comply with their supervision conditions, however, some reported it having a positive impact on their compliance. Similarly, most offenders noted that EM had neither a negative nor a positive impact on their daily lives. But some of the respondents did note that it negatively impacted the quality of the job they could get (32 per cent), their ability to find a job (30 per cent), and the relationships with their spouse/partner (29 per cent) and friends (28 per cent; Hanby & Cociu, 2018). Interestingly, when CSC staff with EM experience were asked about the impact on offenders' daily lives, a majority of them did not feel that EM had a negative impact on their daily lives such as employment or personal relationships (Hanby & Nelson, 2017).

Studies conducted on EM outside of Canada also offer mixed results (Dhungana Sainju et al., 2016). A meta-analysis conducted in 2005 concluded that the data do not support the effectiveness of EM devices in reducing crime (Renzema & Mayo-Wilson, 2005). A more recent 2017 meta-analysis found that, overall, EM still did not lead to statistically significant reductions in recidivism rates; however, it did suggest that there were some positive effects for specific offenders, such as sex offenders, when used as an alternative to a prison sentence or when used as part of specific conditions of release (Belur et al., 2017). The difficulty in answering the question of whether devices such as RF or GPS devices work is partly because of the complexities of how it is used. Jurisdictions use it for various phases of community supervision, including pre-trial, probation, and parole. It is also used on a variety of populations, including but not limited to high-risk offenders, domestic violence offenders, sex offenders, juveniles, violent offenders, and gang members.

Several studies on specific populations suggest that EM can be effective in reducing recidivism rates. Research examining the use of EM devices among high-risk offenders has found that it significantly reduces the likelihood of recidivism (Bales et al., 2010; Padgett, Bales & Blomberg, 2006). The use of GPS devices on sex offenders has also grown rapidly, and several studies examining the effectiveness of EM among sex offenders have found that it reduces the likelihood of recidivism and makes them less likely to fail to register and less likely to abscond compared to sex offenders subject to traditional supervision (Finn & Muirhead, 2002; Gies et al., 2012). Studies on the use of EM devices on those accused of domestic violence to strengthen protective orders and provide an increased sense of security for victims also show promising results. These included positive effects such as reduced violations of protective orders, such as breaching exclusion zones or contacting the victim (Dahlstedt, 2013; Erez, Ibarra, Bales, & Gur, 2012; Ibarra & Erez, 2005; Rhodes, 2012). One study examining the use of GPS devices on high-risk gang offenders found that it reduced the likelihood of being re-arrested for a violent crime by 32 per cent (Gies et al., 2013). Additionally, some recent studies examining the use of EM devices for pre-trial defendants suggest that it may increase the likelihood of showing up to court (Dhungana Sainju et al., 2018) and may also reduce the likelihood of getting arrested for a new crime (Wolff et al., 2017).

However, the evidence to suggest that EM devices reduce recidivism rates is not always consistent. Finn and Muirhead-Stevens's (2002) research found that there are no significant differences between violent male offenders on EM versus traditional community supervision. Another study found that there are no statistically significant differences between traditionally supervised sex offenders and GPS-monitored sex offenders (Turner, Chamberlain, Janetta, & Hess, 2010). As already stated earlier, the Canadian studies conducted by Bonta and colleages (2000) and the CSC evaluation of the first EM pilot study also showed similar null and inconclusive results about the effectiveness of RF and GPS devices (Olotu et al., 2009).

Activity Monitoring Technologies

This section will discuss two activity monitoring technologies: ignition interlock devices and continuous alcohol monitoring devices, both of which are related to alcohol consumption and impaired driving. Impaired driving is the leading criminal cause of death and injury in Canada (Canada Department of Justice, 2018). In 2015, police reports indicate that there were a total of 72,039 impaired driving incidents during that year (Perreault, 2016). Furthermore, Mothers Against

Invasiveness of Technology and Data Protection

The increasing use of EM monitoring tools have raised questions about the amount of data collected on individuals placed on these devices. Compared to RF devices, GPS devices tend to be far more invasive, tracking every movement of the individual with little or no oversight as to what happens to the data in most cases. Critics point to potential concerns over privacy and data protection. It has been suggested that data collection should be limited in some way—such as restricting how much data are collected or how much of the data are retained and stored (Jones, 2014).

Data protection is central to the German approach to using EM. Aware of the potential for privacy violations with GPS technology, German legislators established restrictive measures for GPS data collection. The data have to be automatically deleted after two months unless valid reasons to keep the data are identified and approved. In order for this data to be kept, the offender has to have committed a sex offence, tampered with the EM equipment, or violated EM conditions. Furthermore, only certain agencies are granted authority to view the data (Eilzer, 2014).

Drunk Driving (MADD) reports that in 2014 there were an estimated 2,297 motor vehicle fatalities on public roadways in Canada, and alcohol or drugs were involved in 55.4 per cent (1,273) of these (Solomon, Ellis, & Zheng, 2018). The data suggest that every day, on average, up to four Canadians are killed with many more injured due to alcohol- or drug-related vehicle crashes on public roads (MADD, 2019).

Canada's Criminal Code prohibits driving while impaired, and the maximum legal blood alcohol concentration (BAC) is 0.08 or 80 milligrams of alcohol in 100 millilitres of blood for fully licensed drivers (Canada Department of Justice, 2018). However, recognizing that even those under the maximum limit of 0.08 per cent can cause harm on the roads, all provinces except Quebec have established a **warn range** of BACs between 0.05 and 0.08. Additionally, for novice drivers who have a G1, G2, M1, or M2 licence or for youth under the age of 21, there is a strict 0.00 per cent BAC restriction across all provinces and territories (MADD, 2019). Penalties for impaired driving are serious and immediate. They will vary based on the province or territory, age of the individual, licence type, amount of alcohol in the system, and the number of previous convictions. As part of the penalties for impaired driving, two technological tools include the ignition interlock device and continuous alcohol monitoring devices.

Ignition Interlock Device

Ignition interlock is an in-car alcohol breath-screening device. The device is installed inside a motor vehicle and is connected to the engine's ignition system. In order to start the vehicle, offenders are required to provide a breath sample through the device. If alcohol is detected and the BAC is over the allowed limit (typically 0.02), the vehicle will not start (Robertson & Vanlaar, 2012; Willis, Lybrand & Bellamy, 2009). Ignition interlock devices often also require individuals to provide a breath sample at random pre-set times while the engine is running to ensure compliance. If a sample is not provided, the BAC exceeds the limit, or the individual attempts to tamper with the device, an alarm system may be triggered (lights flashing, horn honking) until the ignition is turned off (Ontario Ministry of Transportation, 2019a). Some ignition interlock devices are also equipped with cameras that record the offender every time they use the device to ensure that the correct person is providing the breath sample.

According to MADD Canada, there are approximately 11,000 ignition interlocks installed in vehicles across Canada. All provinces have ignition interlock programs, although every province has their own requirements concerning who is subject to having the device installed based on the circumstances of the conviction. Additionally, through the Reduced Suspension with Ignition Interlock Conduct Review Program, Ontario allows eligible drivers convicted of a first-time offence to have an early reinstatement of a suspended licence with the voluntary installation of the ignition interlock device (Ontario Ministry of Transportation, 2019b). (See Figure 15.2). In Nova Scotia, the Alcohol Ignition Interlock Program allows drivers with permanently revoked licences to have an opportunity for licence reinstatement. Applicants would follow a multistep process to apply for the program and, if accepted, must install the device in their vehicle and participate in the program for a minimum of five years (Service Nova Scotia, 2019).

Standard HTA sanctions for first-time offenders:

1 year: HTA Suspension   1 year: Ignition Interlock

Reduced Suspension with Ignition Interlock Conduct Review Program – Stream "A":

Minimum 9 months:
Ignition Interlock**

Min. 3-month
Suspension*

Reduced Suspension with Ignition Interlock Conduct Review Program – Stream "B":

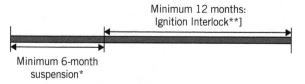

Minimum 12 months:
Ignition Interlock**]

Minimum 6-month
suspension*

Figure 15.2 **An Overview of Ontario's Reduced Suspension with Ignition Interlock Conduct Review Program and the Difference between the Standard Highway Traffic Act (HTA) Sanctions for First-Time Offenders versus Those Who Are Eligible and Participate in the Program**

Notes:
* The court may increase this period.
** The minimum ignition interlock installation period is determined in reference to the length of the driving prohibition period ordered by the court. The Criminal Code provides for a driving prohibition period of one to three years for a first-time alcohol-impaired driving conviction. The ignition interlock installation period will not end before the driving prohibition period expires.
Source: Ontario Ministry of Transportation, 2019, retrieved from http://www.mto.gov.on.ca/english/safety/ignition-interlock-conduct-review-program.shtml

Research examining the effectiveness of ignition interlock devices has found strong results that point to significant reductions in drinking and driving. An evaluation by Casanova-Powell and colleagues (2015) on the effectiveness of 300,000 ignition interlock devices across 28 states revealed that interlock devices were reliable. Offenders with ignition interlock devices installed in their motor vehicle were 50 per cent less likely to be re-arrested for DUIs than offenders who did not have ignition interlock devices in their vehicles. A 2004 meta-analysis found that when installed, an ignition interlock reduced the likelihood of impaired driving by 64 per cent (Willis et al., 2005). Similarly, Marques and Voas (2010) note that previous research suggests that while installed on the vehicle, ignition interlocks can reduce repeat offences by between 35 and 75 per cent.

Continuous Alcohol Monitoring Devices

Continuous alcohol monitoring (CAM) devices, typically designed to be worn as ankle bracelets, work by using sensor functions that detect the alcohol concentration level in the offender's body by sampling perspiration on the skin (McKnight, Fell, & Auld-Owens, 2012; Robertson, Vanlaar, & Simpson, 2007). Similar to other EM devices, it is equipped with tamper-proof features that can immediately alert supervising officials if the device has been interfered with. Depending on the type of technology, devices can be used for periodic, random, or continuous remote alcohol monitoring of the offender (McKnight et al., 2012). The most commonly used transdermal alcohol device is the Secure Continuous Remote Alcohol Monitoring (SCRAM) bracelet.

CAM devices are largely used in the United States as a sanction imposed on driving while impaired or driving under the influence (DWI or DUI) offences (McKnight et al., 2012). They may be used as a condition of release for pre-trial supervision, as part of a condition of probation, or through specialty programs such as DWI/DUI courts. The use of CAM devices such as SCRAM is still relatively limited in Canada, with its use being reported since early 2010. Pilot studies are ongoing to examine the impact of SCRAM on offenders' behaviour (SCRAM Systems, 2019).

While still limited in the number of empirical studies conducted to date, previous research suggests that CAM devices can be effective in increasing compliance with alcohol-related interventions and reductions in impaired driving offences. Flango and Cheesman's (2009) research compared the recidivism levels of offenders who wore CAM devices to those that did not and found that CAM device wearers had lower recidivism levels. Tison and her colleagues (2015) examined Wisconsin County's intensive supervision program and found that the recidivism rates were slightly higher for repeat offenders (8.3 per cent) than first-time offenders (5.1 per cent). Another study examined the compliance and non-compliance rates (defined as a confirmed drinking event or confirmed tamper attempt) of CAM bracelet wearers in six US jurisdictions and revealed compliance rates ranging from 68 to 82 per cent (McKnight et al., 2012).

There are, however, a few issues noted with the CAM devices. Environmental factors can affect the validity and reliability of the devices. For instance, an individual's skin properties (that is, cold skin) and sweat can potentially affect the device's readings (Marques, McKnight, 2007). Moreover, substances that contain alcohol, including mouthwash, perfume, and hand sanitizer, can potentially interfere with the bracelet and result in false positives and alerts being sent to supervisors (Robertson et al., 2007; Spanggaard & Davidson, 2011). As a preventative measure, offenders assigned to wear the bracelets are given a list of substances to avoid and provided with a list of common products that may interfere with the effectiveness of their device. Additionally, supervising personnel are trained to recognize alcohol curves based on the data to identify true positive alcohol responses as opposed to those generated by interferants (Robertson et al., 2007).

Community Corrections: Upcoming Technologies

Driver Alcohol Detection System for Safety

As discussed above, impaired driving is a serious problem leading to tragic consequences. Upward of four Canadians and an estimated 29 Americans die every day in a motor vehicle crash that involves an impaired driver (MADD, 2019; National Highway Traffic Safety Administration, 2017). In 2006, the Automotive Coalition for Traffic Safety, which represents the world's leading auto manufacturers, the US National Highway Traffic Safety Administration, Transport Canada, the Insurance Institute of Highway Safety, the Institute for Highway Safety, MADD Canada, and MADD USA established a blue ribbon panel for the development of a driver alcohol detection system for safety (DADSS).

The program is working to create an in-car alcohol detection system that will automatically detect a driver's blood alcohol level and prevent a vehicle from starting if the driver is intoxicated. The program began in 2008, focusing on research and creating proof-of-concept prototypes to examine various technologies that could be used for vehicle integration. The program is currently examining a breath-based and touch-based system as viable options. The breath-based system will measure the concentration of alcohol and carbon dioxide in a driver's breath as they breathe normally when seated in the driver's seat, while the touch-based system will measure blood alcohol levels under an individual's skin. Extensive research is being conducted to determine how to best install the system in vehicles; potential locations being considered include the driver's side door, the steering wheel, the start button, or having multiple sensors placed throughout the vehicle's cabin (DADSS, 2019). Pilot manufacturing, vehicle installation, and field operation tests for the technology began in 2018. Once it has met rigorous performance standards and becomes commercially ready and available, the program hopes to present a new way to prevent alcohol-impaired driving and will offer it as a voluntary safety option in new vehicles, similar to other driver-assist technologies like lane departure warning and automatic braking (DADSS, 2019).

In 2018, the state of Virginia became the first state to partner with DADDS to create the Driven to Protect partnership. The partnership will conduct in-vehicle, on-road test trials of the alcohol detection technology throughout the state. The data and feedback from the pilot testing will further prepare the technology for widespread commercial use (DADSS, 2019).

Smartphone-Based Monitoring

Several companies are now marketing smartphone-based monitoring systems, which eliminates the need for specialized equipment such as ankle bracelets and instead provides an unobtrusive means to track and supervise an offender using a smartphone with voiceprint verified check-ins. Similar to traditional ankle bracelets, smartphone-based monitoring can still set up specific schedules, identify inclusion and exclusion zones, and enforce the same conditions of supervision.

However, the technology also allows for innovative features that can encourage the offender to make more pro-social and rehabilitative choices.

One company that currently markets this technology and service is Outreach Smartphone Monitoring (OSM). They note that the OSM app is capable of sending notifications to the offender to remind them of upcoming court dates, drug testing dates, reporting dates, and other important events (OSM, 2019). The device can also send a warning directly to the phone if the offender is approaching an exclusion zone to avoid a violation. It can send automated positive reinforcement messages, and additional resources can also be uploaded to the offender's phone, such as housing, shelter locations, employment sites, and counselling services (OSM, 2019). The technology also features a built-in state of the art Bluetooth Breathalyzer that allows supervising agencies to monitor the offender's BAC. The company states "by removing the hardware of old technology and replacing it with modern technology that they already own and use every day we are changing the view offenders have and their willingness to comply with monitoring requirements" (OSM, 2019). The product is currently being used by some jurisdictions within the United States.

Summary

As discussed, technological advances have provided corrections with many benefits, but also some significant challenges. Technologies such as ion scanners, biometric technologies, RFID tags, and drone detection systems provide increased safety, security, and compliance within correctional facilities. Similarly, electronic monitoring devices such as RF and GPS devices, along with ignition interlocks and CAM devices, allow for increased accountability and supervision for community corrections. Technology can, however, also be used as tools by offenders to engage in illicit activities and pose serious threats. In addition, technology can lead to unintended consequences, as can be seen with the issue of ion scanners and false positives and the potential privacy violations posed by technologies that collect large amounts of data.

At the end of the day, we should remember that these technologies are just tools. They still require proper oversight, training, and management to ensure that they are used appropriately. As noted, there are also limited empirical explorations for most of these tools. This gap is critical and needs to be addressed to make sure we are implementing systems that not only work but work equitably for all. With the growth and constant evolution of technologies, our criminal justice system needs to be able to harness the power of technological opportunities to increase public safety and efficiency while also ensuring there is limited harm or exploitation of the very individuals that the system is mandated to supervise and rehabilitate.

Review Questions

1. What kind of problems do contraband items within prisons pose for both correctional staff and inmates?
2. Technological advances provide both benefits and challenges to correctional facilities. What are some ways that technology has helped increase safety and security within prisons? In contrast, how has technology served as a serious threat to correctional facilities?
3. How can electronic monitoring tools such as RF and GPS devices provide increased accountability and supervision for community corrections?
4. How can activity monitoring devices such as ignition interlock and continuous alcohol monitoring devices assist with reducing the number of impaired driving incidents?
5. What are some emerging technological advances currently being tested for increased efficiency and public safety within corrections and community corrections?

Critical Thinking Questions

1. With technology advancing, how do you see the criminal justice system evolving in the future? Could technology be used to create a more just and humane system? If so, how?

2. Do you think an increased dependency and reliance on technology within the criminal justice system could be a disadvantage? Explain why you think this may be a possibility.

3. Technological tools such as biometrics and location monitoring devices like RF and GPS devices collect large amounts of data about an individual. What are some concerns that may come up regarding the invasiveness of these technologies and data privacy?

4. In an age where punishment is often the key focus of corrections and community corrections, how can technology be used to promote positive and rehabilitative behaviours for those who are incarcerated or under supervision?

Multimedia Suggestions

Facing the "Dreaded" Ion Scanner
This video from CBC Radio's *The Doc Project* features family members' experiences with the ion scanner when visiting incarcerated loved ones: https://www.youtube.com/watch?v=LYhmKjNSgaU

Mothers on the Outside Looking In: The Pain of Dealing with a Child Behind Bars
This episode from CBC Radio's *The Doc Project* discusses the hardships faced by mothers whose children are in prison: https://www.cbc.ca/radio/docproject/mothers-on-the-outside-looking-in-the-pain-of-dealing-with-a-child-behind-bars-1.3683624

Calls to Jam Signals around Prisons over Unauthorized Cellphones
This report from *NBC Nightly News* discusses how the South Carolina riot and officer Robert Johnson's shooting has reignited cell phone jamming debates in the state: https://www.youtube.com/watch?v=ZpmkHyxqNco

The Battle against Drones Smuggling Drugs into Prison
This VICE News feature focuses on the Georgia Department of Corrections and their battle against drones: https://www.youtube.com/watch?v=BezZxQF2pRw

Video Success Story: Inmate Tracking with RFID + Mobile
See how the Crow Wing County Jail in Minnesota is using RFID wristbands to maximize its inmate tracking, activity logging, and security rounds: https://www.youtube.com/watch?v=J3OcwFBqsnI

MADD Canada: Who We Are—Part I
Learn more about Mothers Against Drunk Driving, a grassroots charitable organization that is committed to stopping impaired driving and supporting the victims of this violent crime: https://youtu.be/jd-VVyd5wdw

For additional multimedia content from MADD Canada, visit their YouTube channel. https://www.youtube.com/user/maddcanada

What Is an Ignition Interlock Device?
Watch this video from LifeSafer to see an ignition interlock device works: https://www.youtube.com/watch?v=w1uS3QD8Pnc

The Driver Alcohol Detection System for Safety (DADSS)—Technology Overview
This short video provides an overview of the DADSS technology and how it works: https://youtu.be/yykyT4YRw4A

References

Ashe, J.M., Ganesh, M., Yu, L., Graichen, C., Welles, K., Platt, B. & Chen, J. (2012). Unobtrusive suicide warning system: Final technical report. Report submitted to the US National Institute of Justice. Retrieved from https://www.ncjrs.gov/pdffiles1/nij/grants/243922.pdf

Associated Press. (2012, August 22). 40 people indicted in methamphetamine ring run from Indiana prison. *Fox News*. Retrieved from https://www.foxnews.com/us/40-people-indicted-in-methamphetamine-ring-run-from-indiana-prison

Associated Press. (2018, July 27). Idaho prisoners hack iPads and transfer $225,000 worth of credits to themselves. *The Guardian*. Retrieved from https://www.theguardian.com/us-news/2018/jul/26/idaho-prison-hacking-ipad-transfer-credit

Bales, W., Mann, K., Blomberg, T., Gaes, G., Barrick, K., Dhungana, K., & McManus, B. (2010). Quantitative and qualitative assessment of electronic monitoring. National Institute of Justice. Retrieved from https://www.ncjrs.gov/pdffiles1/nij/grants/230530.pdf

Belur, J., Thornton, A., Tompson, L., Manning, M., Sidebottom, A., & Bowers, K. (2017). A systematic review of the effectiveness of the electronic monitoring of offenders. UCL Department of Security and Crime Science, University College London.

Boetel, R. (2018). NM jail to scan irises to verify inmates' identities. CorrectionsOne. Retrieved from https://www.correctionsone.com/prison-technology/articles/476667187-NM-jail-to-scan-irises-to-verify-inmates-identities

Bonta, J., Wallace-Capretta, S. & Rooney, J. (2000). Can electronic monitoring make a difference? An evaluation of three Canadian programs. *Crime and Delinquency, 46*(1), 61–75.

Bottos, S. (2007). An overview of electronic monitoring in corrections: The issues and implications. Correctional Service Canada. Retrieved from http://www.csc-scc.gc.ca/research/r182-eng.shtml

British Columbia Ministry of Public Safety and Solicitor General. (2017). A profile of BC corrections: Reduce reoffending, protect communities. Retrieved from https://www2.gov.bc.ca/assets/gov/law-crime-and-justice/criminal-justice/corrections/reports-publications/bc-corrections-profile.pdf

Bronskill, J. (2014, September 15). Canadian prisons crack down on clandestine cellphone problem. *Globe and Mail*. Retrieved from https://www.theglobeandmail.com/news/national/canadian-prisons-crack-down-on-clandestine-cellphone-problem/article20598885

Brown, T., McCabe, S., & Wellford, C. (2007). Global positioning systems (GPS) technology for community supervision: Lessons learned. Center for Criminal Justice Technology. Retrieved from https://www.ncjrs.gov/pdffiles1/nij/grants/219376.pdf

Bulman, P. (2009). Using technology to make prisons and jails safer. *National Institute of Justice Journal, 262*. Retrieved from https://www.nij.gov/journals/262/pages/corrections-technology.aspx

Burke, T. & Owen, S. (2010). Cell phones as prison contraband. *FBI Law Enforcement Bulletin*. Retrieved from https://leb.fbi.gov/articles/featured-articles/cell-phones-as-prison-contraband

Butler, R.F. (2002). Mailroom scenario evaluation. Report submitted to the National Institute of Justice. Retrieved from http://www.ncjrs.gov/pdffiles1/nij/grants/199048

Canada Department of Justice. (2018). Impaired driving laws. Retrieved from https://www.justice.gc.ca/eng/cj-jp/sidl-rlcfa

Casanova-Powell, T., Hedlund, J., Leaf, W., & Tison, J. (2015). Evaluation of state ignition interlock programs: Interlock use analyses from 28 states, 2006–2011. National Highway Traffic Safety Administration. Retrieved from https://pdfs.semanticscholar.org/2a31/1507a089028755cc7e75b5945b34ca007b25.pdf

CBC News. (2018, December 6). Stony Mountain Institution inmates using drones to sneak in contraband, say staff. Retrieved from https://www.cbc.ca/news/canada/manitoba/stony-mountain-instution-drones-1.4935825

Cherry, P. (2017, September 24). Number of drone sightings near Quebec detention centres skyrockets. *Montreal Gazette*. Retrieved from https://montrealgazette.com/news/quebec/number-of-drone-sightings-near-provincial-detention-centres-has-skyrocketed

Clarke, M. (2009). Entire Texas prison system locked down to search for phones; prison cell phone problem is pandemic. *Prison Legal News*. Retrieved from https://www.prisonlegalnews.org/news/2009/mar/15/entire-texas-prison-system-locked-down-to-search-for-phones-prison-cell-phone-problem-is-pandemic

Correctional News. (2018). Kordia Solutions jams mobile phone signals in prison. Retrieved from http://correctionalnews.com/2018/04/26/kordia-solutions-jams-mobile-phone-signals-in-prisons

Correctional Service Canada. (n.d.). Keeping drugs out: A visitor's guide. Retrieved from https://www.csc-scc.gc.ca/about-us/092/trnsfrmtn-drgs-vstrsg-eng.pdf

Correctional Service Canada. (2015). Electronic monitoring. Retrieved from http://s3.documentcloud.org/documents/1681847/electric-monitors.pdf

Correctional Service Canada. (2016a). Electronic monitoring of offenders. Retrieved from https://www.csc-scc.gc.ca//politiques-et-lois/566-11-cd-eng.shtml

Correctional Service Canada. (2016b). Offender program assignments and inmate payments. Commissioner's Directive no. 730. Retrieved from http://www.csc-scc.gc.ca/acts-and-regulations/730-cd-eng.shtml#s5

Correctional Service Canada. (2017). Annual report on deaths in custody 2015/2016. Retrieved from https://www.csc-scc.gc.ca/research/092/005008-3010-en.pdf

Dahlstedt, J. (2013). Notification and risk management for victims of domestic violence. *Wisconsin Journal of Law, Gender & Society, 7*, 1–38.

Darrow, P. (2017, June 20). Solitary confinement: How four people's stories have changed hearts, minds and laws on the issue. *Globe and Mail*. Retrieved from https://www.theglobeandmail.com/news/national/solitary-confinement-canada-required-reading/article35391601

Davis, L.M., Bozick, R., Steele, J.L., Saunders, J., & Miles, J.N. V. (2013). *Evaluating the effectiveness of correctional education: A meta-analysis of programs that provide education to incarcerated adults*. Santa Monica, CA: RAND Corporation.

DeMichele, M., & Payne, B. (2009). *Offender supervision with electronic technology: Community corrections resource*. Lexington, KY: American Probation and Parole Association.

DeMichele, M., Payne, B., & Button, D. (2008). Electronic monitoring of sex offenders: Identifying unanticipated consequences and implications. *Journal of Offender Rehabilitation, 46*(3–4), 119–35.

Dhungana Sainju, K., Fahy, S., Baggaley, K., Filippelli, V., Baker, A., & Minassian, T. (2016). Electronic monitoring in the United

States: The transition and expansion of usage in offender populations. *Journal of Offender Monitoring, 29*(2), 7–19.

Dhungana Sainju, K., Fahy, S., Baggaley, K., Baker, A., Minassian, T., & Filippelli, V. (2018). Electronic monitoring for pretrial release: Assessing the impact. *Federal Probation, 82*(3), 3–10.

diZerega, M., & Villalobos Agudelo, S. (2011). Piloting a tool for reentry: A promising approach to engaging family members. Vera Institute of Justice. Retrieved from https://www.vera.org/publications/piloting-a-tool-for-reentry-a-promising-approach-to-engaging-family-members

Doffing, D. (2012). BLU+ RF Monitoring. *Journal of Offender Monitoring, 25*(2), 19–21.

Dormehl, L. (2018). Prisons are fighting back against contraband-dropping drones. Here's how. *Digitial Trends.* Retrieved from https://www.digitaltrends.com/cool-tech/airwarden-drone-survaillance

Driver Alcohol Detection System for Safety. (2019). Retrieved from https://www.dadss.org

Egan, K. (2017, August 23). Prison drop – drones caught 41 times hovering near facility yards. *Ottawa Sun.* Retrieved from https://ottawasun.com/2017/08/23/egan-prison-drop-drones-caught-41-times-hovering-near-facility-yards/wcm/ecb2597b-a24a-4107-9edc-be8720553b66

Eilzer, S. (2014). Data protection and electronic monitoring in Germany. *Criminal Justice Matters, 95*(1), 8–9.

Erez, E., Ibarra, P.R., Bales, W.D., & Gur, O. (2012). GPS monitoring technologies and domestic violence: An evaluation study. Retrieved from https://www.ncjrs.gov/pdffiles1/nij/grants/238910.pdf

Fazel, S., Ramesh, T., & Hawton, K. (2018). Suicide in prisons: An international study of prevalence and contributory factors. *Lancet Psychiatry, 4*(12), 946–52.

Federal Communications Commission. (n.d.). Putting an end to illegal cell phone use in prison. Retrieved from https://transition.fcc.gov/pshs/docs/summits/Combating-Contraband-Cell-Phones-in-Prison-Handout-v4.pdf

Federal Communications Commission (FCC). (2019). Jammer enforcement. Retrieved from https://www.fcc.gov/general/jammer-enforcement

Figueroa, J. (2014). They will verify that blocking of calls is effective in prisons in Honduras. *La Prensa.* Retrieved from https://www.laprensa.hn/migrantes/hondurenos enrestodelmundo/475809-96/verificaran-que-bloqueo-de-llamadas-sea-efectivo-en-carceles-de-honduras

Finn, M.A., & Muirhead-Stevens, S. (2002). The effectiveness of electronic monitoring with violent male parolees. *Justice Quarterly, 19*(2), 293–312.

Flango, V., & Cheesman, F. (2009). Effectiveness of the SCRAM alcohol monitoring device: A preliminary test. *Drug Court Review, 1*(2).

Gies, S.V., Gainey, R., Cohen, M.I., Healy, E., Duplantier, D., Yeide, M. . . . Hopps, M. (2012). Monitoring high- risk sex offenders with GPS technology: An evaluation of the California supervision program final report (2009-SQ-B9-K018). Retrieved from https://www.ncjrs.gov/pdffiles1/nij/grants/238481.pdf

Gies, S.V., Gainey, R., Cohen, M.I., Healy, E., Yeide, M., Bekelman, A., Bobnis, A. (2013). monitoring high-risk gang offenders with GPS technology: An evaluation of the California supervision program final report (2009-SQ-B9-K018). Retrieved from https://www.ncjrs.gov/pdffiles1/nij/grants/244164.pdf

Global News. (2018, August 29). Over $100K worth of contraband seized from Collins Bay Institution. Retrieved from https://globalnews.ca/news/4416169/contraband-seized-collins-bay-institution

Government of Canada. (2019). Request for proposal: Preventing contraband delivery via air and ground. Retrieved from https://www.ic.gc.ca/eic/site/101.nsf/eng/00042.html

GTL. (2019). GTL tablet solutions. Retrieved from http://www.gtl.net/gtl-tablet-solutions

Hanby, L. (2017). A profile of offenders in the Electronic Monitoring Research Pilot: The first year. Correctional Service Canada. Retrieved from https://www.csc-scc.gc.ca/research/err-16-08-eng.shtml

Hanby, L. & Cociu, L. (2018). Offender perspectives on electronic monitoring (ERR 18-01). Correctional Service Canada. Retrieved from https://www.csc-scc.gc.ca/research/err-18-01-en.shtml

Hanby, L. & Nelson, A. (2017). Staff perspectives on the Electronic Monitoring Research Pilot (ERR 16-25). Correctional Service Canada. Retrieved from https://www.csc-scc.gc.ca/research/err-16-25-eng.shtml

Hanby, L., Nelson, A., & MacDonald, S.F. (2018). Implementation of the Electronic Monitoring Research Pilot (research report R-419). Correctional Service Canada. Retrieved from https://www.csc-scc.gc.ca/research/r-419-en.shtml

Hansard. (2017). Response to petition no: 421-01279. House of Commons. Retrieved from http://www.ourcommons.ca/Content/ePetitions/Responses/421/e-516/421-01279_PS_E.pdf

Hansard. (2018). Testimony from superintendent Warren Coons, director general, preventive security and intelligence for Correctional Service Canada. Standing Committee on Public Safety and National Security. Retrieved from http://publications.gc.ca/collections/collection_2018/parl/xc76-1/XC76-1-2-421-100-eng.pdf

Harris, K. (2016, December 21). Inmates families say prison drug-scanning tool finds false positives at "alarming" rate. *CBC News.* Retrieved from https://www.cbc.ca/news/politics/federal-prisons-drugs-ion-scanners-1.3905662

Harris, K. (2017, July 30). Email from behind bars? Prisoner advocates push for access to laptops, tablets and internet. *CBC News.* Retrieved from https://www.cbc.ca/news/politics/prison-csc-computer-internet-1.4222230

Hogsten, K. (1998). Drug interdiction test pilot in a prison environment: Federal Bureau of Prisons. Proceedings of the 32nd Annual International Carnahan Conference on Security Technology (pp. 174–80).

Horwitz, S. (2018, January 8). Justice department scrambles to jam prison cell phones, stop drone deliveries to inmates. *Washington Post.* Retrieved from https://www

.washingtonpost.com/world/national-security/justice-dept-scrambles-to-jam-prison-cellphones-stop-drone-deliveries-to-inmates/2018/01/08/42492896-f4a0-11e7-b34a-b85626af34ef_story.html?utm_term=.46def1af8143

Hoshen, J. & Drake, G. (2001). Offender wide area continuous electronic monitoring systems. National Criminal Justice Reference Services. Retrieved from https://www.ncjrs.gov/pdffiles1/nij/grants/187102.pdf

Hsu, S. (2009). Can't make a cell phone call? You may be getting jammed. *The Bulletin*. Retrieved from https://www.bendbulletin.com/news/1444168-151/cant-make-a-cell-phone-call-you-may

Ibarra, P.R., & Erez, E. (2005). Victim-centric diversion? The electronic monitoring of domestic violence cases. *Behavioral Sciences & the Law, 23*(2), 259–76.

Johnson, S. & Dastouri, S. (2011). Use of ion scanners in correctional facilities: An international review. Correctional Service Canada. *Research Review, 11*(1). Retrieved from http://www.csc-scc.gc.ca/005/008/092/rr11-01-eng.pdf

Jones, R. (2014). The electronic monitoring of offenders: Penal moderation or penal excess? *Crime, Law and Social Change, 62*(4), 475–88.

JPay. (2019a). JP5 tablets. Retrieved from https://www.jpay.com/PMusic.aspx

JPay. (2019b). Calhoun Correctional Institution. Florida State prison system. Retrieved from https://www.jpay.com/Facility-Details/Florida-State-Prison-System/Calhoun-Correctional-Institution.aspx

Joshi, D. (2017). Exploring the latest drone technology for commercial, industrial and military drone uses. *Business Insider*. Retrieved from https://www.businessinsider.com/drone-technology-uses-2017-7

Judd, A. (2018, January 12). Someone used a drone to drop $26,500 of drugs, tobacco over B.C. prison wall. *Global News*. Retrieved from https://globalnews.ca/news/3961889/drone-drugs-b-c-prison-wall

Kaufman, E. (2018). In New York, all 51,000 state prisoners will get their own tablet computers. CNN. Retrieved from https://www.cnn.com/2018/02/01/us/new-york-inmates-tablet-trnd/index.html

Kinnard, M. (2017, March 23). FCC approves measures intended to combat prison cellphones. *US News*. Retrieved from https://www.usnews.com/news/best-states/south-carolina/articles/2017-03-23/ex-guard-shot-in-attack-via-inmates-cellphone-to-testify

Kinnard, M. (2019, January 17). SC inmates get tablets for movies, calling. Associated Press. Retrieved from https://apnews.com/be63082ecc7b44cfb5de8afbfa513f4a

Kruzman, D. (2018, July 18). In U.S. prisons, tablets open window to the outside world. Reuters. Retrieved from https://www.reuters.com/article/us-usa-prisons-computers/in-u-s-prisons-tablets-open-window-to-the-outside-world-idUSKBN1K813D

La Prensa. (2014). Blocking calls has reduced extortion in Honduras by 75%. Retrieved from https://www.laprensa.hn/honduras/tegucigalpa/476327-96/bloqueo-de-llamadas-ha-reducido-en-75-extorsiones-en-honduras

Law, V. (2018). Captive audience: How companies make millions charging prisoners to send an email. *Wired*. Retrieved from https://www.wired.com/story/jpay-securus-prison-email-charging-millions

Makuch, B. (2014). Canada wants to jam prison cell phones so inmates can't run drug cartels. Motherboard. Retrieved from https://motherboard.vice.com/en_us/article/8qxmyk/canada-is-thinking-about-using-cell-blockers-to-stop-prison-drug-dealers

Marques, P.R., & Voas, R.B. (2010). Key features for ignition interlock programs. (Report No. DOT HS 811 262). National Highway Traffic Safety Administration. Retrieved from https://www.nhtsa.gov/sites/nhtsa.dot.gov/files/811262.pdf

Marques, P., & McKnight, S. (2007). Evaluating transdermal alcohol measuring devices. National Highway Traffic Safety Administration.

Marzano, L., Fazel, S., Rivlin, A., & Hawton, K. (2011). Near-lethal self-harm in women prisoners: Contributing factors and psychological processes. *Journal of Forensic Psychiatry & Psychology, 22*(6), 863–84.

McKay, J. (2008). Prisons use RFID systems to track inmates. Government Technology. Retrieved from http://www.govtech.com/public-safety/Prisons-Use-RFID-Systems-to-Track.html

McKay, J. (2018). Interim report: Use of ion mobility spectrometers by Correctional Service Canada. House of Commons Canada. Retrieved from https://www.ourcommons.ca/content/Committee/421/SECU/Reports/RP9998633/421_SECU_Rpt25_PDF/421_SECU_Rpt25-e.pdf

McKenzie, V. (2018, April 19). Are cellphones really to blame for spike in S.C. prison violence? *CBS News*. Retrieved from https://www.cbsnews.com/news/south-carolina-prison-riot-are-cellphones-really-to-blame-for-spike-in-s-c-prison-violence

McKnight, A.S., Fell, J.C., & Auld-Owens, A. (2012). Transdermal alcohol monitoring: Case studies (Report No. DOT HS 811 603). Washington, DC: National Highway Traffic Safety Administration.

McVie, F. (2001). Drugs in federal corrections: The issues and challenges. *Forum on Corrections Research, 12*(3), 7–9.

Miles, C.A., & Cohn, J.P. (2006). Tracking prisoners in jail with biometrics: An experiment in a Navy Brig. *National Institute of Justice Journal, 253*. Retrieved from https://nij.ojp.gov/topics/articles/tracking-prisoners-jail-biometrics-experiment-navy-brig

Mothers Against Drunk Driving Canada. (2019). Fast facts. Retrieved from https://madd.ca/pages/about-us/what-we-do/fast-facts

Mulligan, P. (2018, September 19). Inmates at these jails were given tablets, but things went awry. *CBC News*. Retrieved from https://www.cbc.ca/news/canada/nova-scotia/inmate-jail-tablets-new-glasgow-pictou-jails-1.4828823

National Criminal Justice Reference Service. (2008). Evaluability assessment of trace detection technology. Retrieved from http://www.ncjrs.gov/pdffiles1/nij/tracedetection-technology.pdf

National Highway Traffic Safety Administration. (2017). Traffic safety facts 2016 data: Alcohol-impaired driving. U.S. Department of Transportation. Retrieved from https://crashstats.nhtsa.dot.gov/Api/Public/ViewPublication/812450

Office of the Correctional Investigator. (2014a). A preventable death. Retrieved from http://www.oci-bec.gc.ca/cnt/rpt/oth-aut/oth-aut20080620info-eng.aspx

Office of the Correctional Investigator. (2014b). A three year review of federal inmate suicides (2011–2014). Retrieved from http://www.oci-bec.gc.ca/cnt/rpt/oth-aut/oth-aut20140910info-eng.aspx

Office of the Correctional Investigator. (2016). *Annual report of the Office of the Correctional Investigator 2015–2016.* Retrieved from http://www.oci-bec.gc.ca/cnt/rpt/pdf/annrpt/annrpt20152016-eng.pdf

Office of the Correctional Investigator. (2017). *Annual report of the Office of the Correctional Investigator 2016–2017.* Retrieved from http://www.oci-bec.gc.ca/cnt/rpt/pdf/annrpt/annrpt20162017-eng.pdf

Olotu, M.K., Beaupre, M., & Verbrugge, P. (2009). File #394-2-68 Evaluation report: Electronic Monitoring Program Pilot. Correctional Service Canada. Retrieved from https://www.csc-scc.gc.ca/text/pa/empp/empp-eng.pdf

Ontario Ministry of Community Safety and Correctional Services. (2018). Electronic Supervision Program. Retrieved from https://www.mcscs.jus.gov.on.ca/english/corr_serv/comm_corr/elect_mon/elect_mon.html

Ontario Ministry of Transportation. (2019a). Ignition interlock program. Retrieved from http://www.mto.gov.on.ca/english/safety/ignition-interlock-program.shtml

Ontario Ministry of Transportation. (2019b). Reduced Suspension with Ignition Interlock Conduct Review Program. Retrieved from http://www.mto.gov.on.ca/english/safety/ignition-interlock-conduct-review-program.shtml

Outreach Smartphone Monitoring. (2019). Retrieved from http://www.osmnow.com/#brief1

Padgett, K., Bales, W., & Blomberg, T. (2006). Under surveillance: An empirical test of the effectiveness and consequences of electronic monitoring. *Criminology & Public Policy, 5*, 61–91.

Perreault, S. (2016). Impaired driving in Canada, 2015. Statistics Canada. Retrieved from https://www150.statcan.gc.ca/n1/pub/85-002-x/2016001/article/14679-eng.htm

Province of Alberta. (2014). Public fatality inquiry report on Edward Christopher Snowshoe. Retrieved from https://open.alberta.ca/dataset/d8bedb35-398a-4e24-befa-bef1d49531de/resource/2736fe62-60e2-4179-b919-eb4febbb93ed/download/2014-fatality-report-snowshoe.pdf

Rabuy, B., & Kopf, D. (2015). Prisons of poverty: Uncovering the pre-incarceration incomes of the imprisoned. The Prison Policy Initiative. Retrieved from https://www.prisonpolicy.org/reports/income.html

Raher, S. (2017). The wireless prison: How Colorado's tablet computer program misses opportunities and monetizes the poor. The Prison Policy Initiative. Retrieved from https://www.prisonpolicy.org/blog/2017/07/06/tablets

Renzema, M., & Mayo-Wilson, E. (2005). Can electronic monitoring reduce crime for moderate to high-risk offenders? *Journal of Experimental Criminology, 1*(2), 215–37.

Rhodes, A. (2012). Strengthening the guard: The use of GPS surveillance to enforce domestic violence protection orders. *Tennessee Journal of Race, Gender, & Social Justice, 2*, 129–44.

Riley, M. (2017, September 30). Southern prisons have a cellphone smuggling problem. *NBC News.* Retrieved from https://www.nbcnews.com/news/corrections/southern-prisons-have-smuggled-cellphone-problem-n790251

Riley, T. (2018). "Free" tablets are costing prisons inmates a fortune. *Mother Jones.* Retrieved from https://www.motherjones.com/politics/2018/10/tablets-prisons-inmates-jpay-securus-global-tel-link

Rivlin, A., Fazel, S., Marzano, L., & Hawton, K. (2011). The suicidal process in male prisoners making near-lethal suicide attempts. *Psychology, Crime & Law, 19*(4), 305–27.

Robbins, S. (2014). El Salvador blocks prison cellphones in attempt to cut extortion. *InSight Crime.* Retrieved from https://www.insightcrime.org/news/brief/el-salvador-blocks-cellphones-prisons-attempt-cut-extortion

Robertson, R. & Vanlaar, W. (2012). Canada's impaired driving framework: The way forward. Proceedings of the drinking and driving symposium. The Traffic Injury Research Foundation.

Robertson, R., Vanlaar, W., & Simpson, H. (2007). Continuous transdermal alcohol monitoring. Recovery Science Corporation.

Rockwell, M. (2018). Cellphone jammer targets illicit calls by prisoner. GCN. Retrieved from https://fcw.com/GIG/gcn/Articles/2018/06/19/cellphone-jammer-prison.aspx

Sawyer, W. (2017). How much do incarcerated people earn in each state? The Prison Policy Initiative. Retrieved from https://www.prisonpolicy.org/blog/2017/04/10/wages

SCRAM Systems. (2019). SCRAM Systems in Canada. Retrieved from https://www.scramsystems.com/scram-international/ca

Securus Technologies. (2018). Securus Technologies deploys AeroDefense drone detection solution at Georgia correctional facilities. Retrieved from https://securustechnologies.tech/securus-technologies-deploys-aerodefense-drone-detection-solution-at-georgia-corrections-facilities

Service Nova Scotia. (2019). Alcohol Ignition Interlock Program. Retrieved from https://novascotia.ca/sns/rmv/interlock

Shanahan, R., & Villalobos Agudelo, S. (2012). The family and recidivism. Vera Institute of Justice. Retrieved from https://www.prisonpolicy.org/scans/vera/the-family-and-recidivism.pdf

Sheldon, T., Smith, G., Doherty, S., Waddell, R., Donnelly, T., & Parker, A. (1998). Detection of concealed drugs on prison visitors: Realistic laboratory and field trials of six drugs trace detectors and passive dogs. Proceedings of the 32nd Annual International Carnahan Conference on Security Technology (pp. 234–7).

Solomon, R., Ellis, C., & Zheng, C. (2018). Alcohol and/or drugs among crash victims dying within 12 months of a crash on a public road, by jurisdiction: Canada 2014. Mothers Against Drunk Driving. Retrieved from https://madd.ca/

pages/wp-content/uploads/2018/05/Alcohol-and-or-Drugs-Among-Crash-Victims-Dying-Within-12-Months2c-by-Jurisdiction-Canada2c-2014_April-202c-2018.pdf

Sorenson, K. (2012). A study of electronic monitoring in the correctional and immigration settings. Report of the Standing Committee on Public Safety and National Security. House of Commons Canada. Retrieved from https://www.ourcommons.ca/DocumentViewer/en/41-1/SECU/report-6

Spanggaard, M., & Davidson, C. (2011). Remote alcohol monitor technology deemed reliable. *Journal of the American Academy of Psychiatry and the Law, 39*(1), 112–14.

Steele, P., Brydon, D., & Hare, T. (2012). GPS tracking. In S. Barton-Bellessa (Ed.), *Encyclopedia of community corrections*. Thousand Oaks, CA: SAGE Publications.

Stevenson, P.J., Fahy, S., & Dhungana Sainju, K. (2017). The use of GPS and RF devices to monitor defendants and convicted offenders in the United States." *Journal of Offender Monitoring, 29*(2), 4–6.

Stewart, S. (2017, September 5). How tablets are helping us clean up our prisons. *Washington Examiner*. Retrieved from https://www.washingtonexaminer.com/how-tablets-are-helping-us-clean-up-our-prison

sUAS News. (2018). Securus Technologies AeroDefense systems' AirWarden at Georgia Department of Corrections facility. Retrieved from https://www.suasnews.com/2018/06/securus-technologies-aerodefense-systems-airwardentm-at-georgia-department-of-corrections-facility

Thomas, P., & Krolowitz, B. (2010, December 31). Calling up hits: Cell phones used behind bars. *ABC News*. Retrieved from https://abcnews.go.com/US/cell-phones-call-hits-prison/story?id=12514648

Thurton, D. (2019, June 9). Corrections Canada turns to detection equipment to fight contraband drone drops. *CBC News*. Retrieved from https://www.cbc.ca/news/politics/corrections-canada-drones-drugs-prisons-1.5164531

Tison, J., Nichols, J.L., Casanova-Powell, T., & Chaudhary, N.K. (2015). Comparative study and evaluation of SCRAM use, recidivism rates, and characteristics. Washington, DC: National Highway Traffic Safety Administration. Retrieved from https://www.scramsystems.com/images/uploads/general/research/comparative-study-and-evaluation-of-scram-use-and-recidivism-rates.pdf

Turner, S., Chamberlain, W., Janetta, J., & Hess, J. (2010). Implementation and outcomes for California's GPS pilot for high risk sex offender parolees. Center for Evidence-Based Corrections. Retrieved from https://pdfs.semanticscholar.org/9a69/d681793a7fac0c3037f3f9d2a1a9c001bebd.pdf

US Department of Justice. (2018). Bureau of Prisons tests micro-jamming technology in federal prison to prevent contraband cell phones. Press release. Retrieved from https://www.justice.gov/opa/pr/bureau-prisons-tests-micro-jamming-technology-federal-prison-prevent-contraband-cell-phones

US Department of Justice. (2019). Aircraft sabotage. 18 USC § 32. Criminal Resource Manual. Retrieved from https://www.justice.gov/jm/criminal-resource-manual-2-aircraft-sabotage-18-usc-32

US News. (2018, August 2). Colorado inmates' tablets taken away for security reasons. Retrieved from https://www.usnews.com/news/best-states/colorado/articles/2018-08-02/colorado-inmates-tablets-taken-away-for-security-reasons

Van Der Meulen, E. "It goes on everywhere": Injection drug use in Canadian federal prisons. *Substance Use and Misuse, 52*(7), 884–91.

Waters, M. (2018). The outrageous scam of "free" tablets for the incarcerated. The Outline. Retrieved from https://theoutline.com/post/5760/free-tablets-in-prison-nightmare

Wakefield, J. (2018, November 5). Contraband, overdoses, death: Documents detail the flow of drugs into one of Canada's most advanced jails. *Edmonton Journal*. Retrieved from https://edmontonjournal.com/news/local-news/hundreds-of-overdoses-dozens-of-seizures-how-are-drugs-still-flowing-into-canadas-most-advanced-jail

Willis, C., Lybrand, S., & Bellamy, N. (2005). Alcohol ignition interlock programmes for reducing drink driving recidivism (review). *The Cochrane Database of Systematic Reviews, 18*(4), 6–10.

Wilson, J.D. (2013). Policy brief on electronic monitoring: Review and recommendations. St. Leonard's Society of Canada. Retrieved from http://www.stleonards.ca/wp-content/uploads/2014/10/SLSC-Policy-Brief-on-Electronic-Monitoring-Review-and-Recommendations.pdf

Wolff, K.T., Dozier, C.A., Muller, J.P., Mowry, M., & Hutchinson, B. (2017). The impact of location monitoring among U.S. pretrial defendants in the District of New Jersey. *Federal Probation, 81*(3), 8–14.

World Health Organization. (2007). Preventing suicide in jails and prisons. Retrieved from https://www.who.int/mental_health/prevention/suicide/resource_jails_prisons.pdf

Yune, H. (2015, June 1). Napa jail hits pause on inmate tablets, awaits security updates. *Napa Valley Register*. Retrieved from https://napavalleyregister.com/news/local/napa-jail-hits-pause-on-inmate-tablets-awaits-security-updates/article_40427cd5-b835-5ffb-b8a7-b3d9fb6777ec.html

Zakaria, D., Thompson, J.M., Jarvis, A., & Borgotta, F. (2010). Summary of emerging findings from the 2007 National Inmate Infectious Diseases and Risk-Behaviours Survey. Correctional Service of Canada. Retrieved from https://www.csc-scc.gc.ca//005/008/092/005008-0211-01-eng.pdf

Religious Services in Canadian Prisons

16

Davut Akca, Mehmet F. Bastug, and Nawal Ammar

Learning Objectives

After reading this chapter, you should be able to:

- Provide an overview of the historical nexus between religion and prisons in Canada.
- Understand how religious services in prisons are important for the well-being and rehabilitation of offenders.
- Describe the role of religious services in reducing recidivism rates.
- Explain the legal framework that governs the way religious services are delivered in Canadian prisons.
- Critically reflect on how Canadian correctional institutions address the increasing diversity in inmate populations and how minorities are affected by the particularities of the Canadian correctional system.

Chapter Overview

In an attempt to provide a landscape of the religious services in Canadian prisons, this chapter is organized into five parts. First, the historical context of religious services in prisons is discussed. The second part debates the essence of religious services within a context of punishment and incarceration. It asks what is so pressing about these services that make their delivery an important topic of discussion at all. The third part looks at the religious landscape of the incarcerated in Canadian prisons. What are the religious demographics of the incarcerated population? What religious services do they receive? How are religious services delivered, and how are they influenced by the particularities of the Canadian correctional system? The fourth part focuses on one specific incarcerated population requiring religious service delivery: Muslims. What services do they receive and what religious accommodations do they receive? How are their religious needs addressed? The last part of this chapter provides a summary, discusses the lack of research on the topic of religion in Canadian prisons, gives directions for future research, and provides some recommendations on how to proceed, both in terms of policy and research on religious service delivery in Canadian prisons.

Historical Context

Before addressing the contemporary issue of religious services in prisons in Canada, it is worth providing a short historical context of why religious services in prisons exist. This issue reflects on the larger theme of societal views on crime and punishment. While Canada was not created until 1867, ideas about reforming offenders were brought to the Americas in the late eighteenth century by the Quakers in Philadelphia's Walnut Street Jail (Correctional Service Canada (CSC), 2018b). Those ideas remained constant for centuries and motivated the pre-Confederation building of prisons in Kingston, St. John, and Halifax as well as those built after the establishment of the Confederation (Ekstedt & Griffiths, 1988).

Prisons at this early stage of their development were intended to be a rehabilitative setting for hard work, reflection, penitence, and religious guidance (Rothman, 1971). It is important at this juncture to acknowledge that a number of scholars (for example, Foucault, 1977; Scull, 1977; Takagi, 1975) argue against the idea that prisons became the principal form of punishment because of the concerns of reformists and instead see it as an attempt of the state to consolidate its power (Ekstedt & Griffith, 1988). However, the societal values embedded in the idea of prison as punishment followed the Quaker reformers' notion that prisoners can be rehabilitated through a system of productive labour during the day, solitary confinement, and the rule of silence at all times (Duckett & Mohr, 2015). These ideas continued to evolve in Canadian society, including Sir Walter Crofton's system of "inmate grades, earned remission, gradual release, open institutions and parole" (Solicitor General of Canada, 2002).

Why Do We Care about Religious Services in Prisons?

The influence of religious services and practices in correctional settings dates back to the initial establishment of prisons (Dammer, 2002b). Since the early years, correctional chaplains have been employed to provide education and counselling for prisoners. Almost all major religions endorse offender rehabilitation and recommend ways to facilitate re-entry into society and desistance from criminal and other antisocial behaviours (Stansfield, Mowen, O'Connor, & Boman, 2017). Religion can play an important role in the lives and well-being of offenders through rehabilitation, mitigating the adverse effects of imprisonment, and helping directly or indirectly prevent recidivism (Duwe & King, 2013).

During Incarceration

Imprisonment has several adverse effects on inmates, and religious support can help mitigate them and facilitate the inmates' adjustment to the prison by promoting "faith development, cognitive coping, purpose, and meaning making" (Stansfield et al., 2017, p. 113; see also Dammer, 2002a; O'Connor & Duncan, 2011; Sykes, 1958). Clear and Sumter (2002) found a significant positive relationship between inmate religiousness and psychological adjustment to prison. Some experts and volunteers who provide religious services or support in prisons suggest that the primary objective of these services is not reducing recidivism but guiding the inmates to preserve their dignity and humanity within the dehumanizing conditions of corrections (Clear, Hardyman, Stout, Lucken, & Dammer. 2000; Stansfield et al., 2017). This safeguard can be the result of increasing religiosity or joining a group of people

who have pro-social values. In a meta-analysis of 15 studies, Schaefer, Sams, and Lux (2016) found a moderate effect of religious programs on offender values and behaviours. Overall, faith-based interventions resulted in a significant shift in attitudinal dispositions and a decrease in inmate misconduct in corrections. Interestingly, they found that the influence of such programs on attitudinal shift is far greater than the decrease in criminal actions. That is, the attitudinal shift occurred thanks to interventions that partially led to desistance from crime. In another study, O'Connor and Perreyclear (2002) showed that the increase in the intensity of religious involvement of inmates leads to a decrease in the number of inmates with in-prison infractions.

Admission to a pro-social group in a prison environment provides inmates with protection against violence, especially from other inmates. Furthermore, being affiliated with a group can facilitate adapting to imprisonment because it provides psychological protection alongside physical protection (Hannah, Clutterbuck, & Rubin, 2008). Additionally, inmates can learn about and practise their religion upon joining a religious-oriented group. The supportive social network that faith-based interventions create might also provide opportunities for better social and family bonds, life skills training, educational and employment coaching, stable employment, safe accommodation, health services, and most importantly a sense of belonging to a community consisting of supportive and law-abiding people. Therefore, many inmates are inclined toward becoming members of such groups (Campbell et al., 2007; Farrall, 2002; Maruna & Immarigeon, 2004; Mowen & Visher, 2015; O'Connor & Duncan, 2011; Stansfield et al., 2017).

Rehabilitation

Religious support is used as a way of rehabilitation or as part of a broader intervention program in corrections. Religious programs in prison can provide opportunities to "channel inmates' energies in meaningful and beneficial ways" (Thomas & Zaitzow, 2006, p. 242) and alleviate their feelings of guilt (Hannah et al., 2008). Schaefer and colleagues (2016) suggest that faith-based programs can serve as a "hook for change" or "catalyst" (p. 617) to address the barriers that diminish inmates' motivation to change. Some theoretical frameworks can help us understand how religious support might improve the lives of inmates in prison and after they are released. Sykes's (1958) concept of the pains of imprisonment suggests that the disappearance of bodily suffering in prisons (beating, shackling, and caging prisoners) does not result in the vanishing of psychological and social pains of confinement. Indeed, it suggests that a "series of deprivations and frustrations in prison life" has led to "the destruction of the psyche [which] is no less fearful than bodily affliction" (Sykes, 1958, p. 64).

The pains of imprisonment and resulting adaptations are central organizing concepts in prison studies and can serve as tools to understand the role of religion in healing the harms of prison. According to the hellfire hypothesis of Hirschi and Stark (1969), religiosity promotes an inner mechanism of reward and punishment; thus, inmates who receive religious support could adhere to pro-social beliefs and behaviours, which could result in deterrence. With such a belief system, people might think that the costs of criminal involvement are higher than the benefits and stay away from reoffending, which is also the basic assertion of **rational choice theory** (Cornish & Clarke, 1986). Power, Ritchie, and Madill (2014) explain the inverse relationship between religiosity in correctional facilities and antisocial behaviours through **social attachment theory** (Bowlby, 1969) and **social learning theory** (Akers, 1998). Similar to other social institutions such as the family, schools, and employment, religion might have effects on life decisions of the inmates because, social attachment theory suggests, those who are attached to a major social institution are less likely to perpetrate a crime. Social learning theory, on the other hand, sheds light on how chaplains, religious volunteers, and other religious inmates can serve as pro-social role models for prisoners. Inmates can change their negative ways by learning through observation and positive reinforcement as they participate in religious programs and services in correctional facilities.

Dammer (2002a) studied why inmates get involved in religious practice in prison using participant observation and interviews with 70 inmates and correctional staff. The emerging reasons underlying such involvement (based on a thematic analysis of his qualitative data) were motivation, direction, and meaning that come from the practice of religion; the hope that religious beliefs give; the belief that being in prison is "God's will"; and some therapeutic goals, such as achieving a certain "peace of mind," altering the negative self-concept, and developing self-control

(Dammer, 2002a). In a larger analysis, a task force within the American Psychological Association (APA) combined the results of eight different meta-analyses of studies on "what works" in psychotherapy at the individual level and concluded that four individual characteristics are effective in adapting to psychotherapy: reactance/resistance, preferences, culture, religion/spirituality (Norcross & Wampold, 2011). Since these findings were released, the APA recommended psychotherapists to include religious support in their intervention programs (Norcross & Wampold, 2011).

Recidivism

Religion can play a significant role in the process of desistance from crime and antisocial behaviours. According to the **cognitive transformation** theory of Giordano and colleagues (2002), individuals who desist from crime first develop an openness to change. After they start to consider change as a possibility, they are exposed to particular "hooks" that may support them in persisting on the change path. Among other mechanisms such as employment, treatment programs, and family support, religion might be considered a powerful hook to change the way of life for released inmates.

The studies on the relationship between **faith-based intervention** and reduction in recidivism have found mixed results (see Duwe & King, 2013; Johnson, Larson, & Pitts, 1997; O'Connor, 2003; Sumter, 1999; Stansfield et al., 2017; Young, Gartner, O'Connor, Larson, & Wright, 1995). A systematic review of the literature on faith-based interventions for offenders revealed that religious services can promote positive outcomes, such as reduced institutional misconducts and other antisocial behaviours, and promotion of pro-social behaviours (Power et al., 2014). Duwe and King (2013) assessed the effectiveness of a faith-based prisoner re-entry program called InnerChange Freedom Initiative based on the recidivism rates of 732 male inmates who stayed more than 18 months in Minnesota prisons and were released between 2003 and 2009. Half of the inmates participated in the program while the other half who were eligible did not participate. The comparison of the recidivism rates of the two groups indicated that participating in the program significantly reduced re-arrest, re-conviction, and re-incarceration rates. However, those who dropped out the program (42 per cent) had the highest recidivism rates among all inmates. The lowest recidivism rates were seen in the offenders who met with mentors in prison and in the community after their release from prison. It is worth noting that the InnerChange program is an **evidence-based intervention** program that addresses criminogenic needs of offenders through a Christian perspective. Thus, Duwe and King (2013) concluded that faith-based correctional programs can reduce recidivism only if they apply evidence-based practices. These include but are not limited to "a behavioral intervention within a therapeutic community, addressing the criminogenic needs of participants and delivering a continuum of care from the institution to the community" (p. 813).

Johnson, Larson, and Pitts's (1997) assessment of a religious program conducted by the late Charles Colson's Prison Fellowship Ministries in four New York prisons showed there was no significant difference between the experimental group (those who were involved in the program) and the control group. However, the study did show that the intensity of the inmates' involvement in the program mattered. Those who were more active in Bible studies had lower recidivism rates. Johnson's (2004) replication of the same study with a longer follow-up period resulted in similar findings in terms of the differences in recidivism rates and the impact of the intensity of the Bible studies. In a longitudinal study, Stansfield and colleagues (2017) found that religious support for inmates led to a decrease in post-release substance use and unemployment, both of which are considered important predictors of long-term recidivism. Although, Stansfield and colleagues (2017) did not find any direct relationship between religious support and reoffending, they concluded that religious support may indirectly reduce recidivism by

facilitating and encouraging the process of re-entry to the community and increasing their "consciousness to prosocial life" (p. 136).

Religious Landscape and Religious Services in Canadian Prisons

What Are the Religious Demographics of Those Incarcerated in Canadian Prisons?

The corrections population in Canada has become more diverse in terms of religion and ethnicity. The proportion of Christian inmates (Catholic and Protestant) decreased from 50.8 per cent to 44.4 per cent between 2012 and 2017, while there was an increase in the proportion of inmates identifying as Muslim (from 5.0 to 5.9 per cent) and an Indigenous spirituality (from 4.8 to 5.2 per cent) for the same five-year period (Public Safety Canada, 2017). This change can be partially attributed to the rapidly increasing population of ethnic minorities. According to the 2011 census, the population rate of non-Christians (Muslim, Hindu, Sikh, and Buddhist) increased from 4.9 per cent to 7.2 per cent of the total population since 2001 (Statistics Canada, 2011a). However, there are also serious concerns regarding the overrepresentation of Indigenous peoples and other ethnic minorities, including Muslims, in Canadian prisons (Douyon, 2016; Office of the Correctional Investigator, 2018). Although there is not a comprehensive analysis of the reasons behind the overrepresentation of Muslims in Canadian prisons, evidence from other Western countries suggests

InnerChange Freedom Initiative

The InnerChange Freedom Initiative (IFI) was a privately funded program that provided educational, values-based services to prisoners on a voluntary and non-compulsory basis to help prepare them to re-enter the community. The program was based on Christian values but was open to prisoners of all faiths or no faith. Living in the same prison housing unit, participants were taught values and life skills for up to 18 months. Participants then received

guidance from a mentor and support from a local faith community for 12 months after they were released from prison.

IFI was first launched in Texas' Carol S. Vance Unit in 1997. Additional IFI sites opened in other states, including units for men and women in Minnesota. In 2016, the program was renamed the Prison Fellowship Academy.

Source: https://www.prisonfellowship.org

that the inherent socio-economic disadvantages of Muslim communities (Webster & Qasim, 2018), rising Islamophobic discrimination since 9/11 (Abbas, 2004), and increasing rates of conversion to Islam in prisons (Ammar, Weaver & Saxon, 2004; Kusha, 2015) are some of the causes.

What Religious Services Are Prisoners Entitled To?

The CSC provides religious services to inmates in federal correctional facilities in Canada. The official website of the CSC frames the purpose of religious services as helping offenders explore questions related to spirituality, religion, and life purpose; examine their behaviours and decisions; and discover new ways of living (CSC, 2012). The religious rights of inmates and chaplaincy services provided in Canadian prisons are guaranteed by national and international laws and regulations. Religious rights of prisoners are broadly protected by several United Nations conventions to which Canada is a signatory. One of those conventions is the Universal Declaration of Human Rights, in which Article 18 declares that every human being has freedom of thought, conscience, and religion. This freedom includes the right to change one's religion or belief and to manifest one's religion or belief in teaching, practice, worship, and observance.

The United Nations Standard Minimum Rules for the Treatment of Prisoners (Mandela Rules) is another international convention that Canada is signatory to, and section 41 indicates the necessity of employing full-time "qualified representatives" of each religion if there are "sufficient number of prisoners" of that religion kept in a correctional institution. Within this context, chaplains are allowed to provide religious services regularly by visiting the prisoners in private at proper times. Section 42 of the Mandela Rules specifically addresses how religious needs of prisoners should be met by stating that prisoners should be allowed to attend religious services within correctional institutions and to possess religious books.

The Canadian Charter of Rights and Freedoms and the 1982 Constitution Act guarantees freedom of conscience and religion, which is recognized in its fundamental freedoms section. Also, section 15 of the Charter provides the right to equally benefit from the protection of law and prohibits discrimination based on religion and other individual differences such as race, gender, age, and mental or physical disability.

Section 75 of the Corrections and Conditional Release Act states

> An inmate is entitled to reasonable opportunities to freely and openly participate in, and express, religion or spirituality, subject to such reasonable limits as are prescribed for protecting the security of the penitentiary or the safety of persons.

According to the Corrections and Conditional Release Regulations, inmates have the right to express their religion or spirituality and assemble for this purpose. In accordance with regulations 100 and 101, the CSC is responsible for providing the essentials needed for inmates to practise their religion or spirituality as long as they are "reasonably required" and do not fall under the category of "contraband" or other banned materials. The services mentioned in regulation 101 are "interfaith chaplaincy services, facilities for the expression of the religion or spirituality, a special diet as required by the inmate's religious or spiritual tenets, and the necessities related to special religious or spiritual rites of the inmate."

Religious and spiritual services are provided to inmates by the CSC based on the guidelines developed by the assistant commissioner of correctional operations and programs (CSC, 2012). The head of the chaplaincy services at the national headquarters of the CSC is responsible for ensuring all inmates have access to chaplaincy and assessing the consistency and quality of the services. Each correctional institution is responsible for determining the need and capacity for chaplaincy services and developing their annual chaplaincy delivery plan to ensure all inmates kept in the institution and the chaplains have access to each other as needed.

Also, this plan addresses the related resources required to deliver the services, the type of services that will be provided, and scheduling of use for sacred space. Religious and spiritual practices allowed in prisons are described by the CSC (2012) as "religious rites and spiritual rituals as prescribed by a recognized faith group." Inmates should be allowed to perform these practices as they do in their normal lives within the community. Within correctional institutions, there are sacred spaces established for the use of all inmates for religious needs, including but not limited to worship, celebration, meditation, prayer, and reflection. The warden of each correctional institution is also responsible for providing space for chaplaincy management and other related services. When needed, correctional institutions are also supposed to provide chaplaincy services to inmates when they are on escorted or un-escorted temporary absence, when they are hospital-ized, and when they are participating in parole hearings. Additionally, in cases of crises such as suicide attempts, death of family members, and other traumatic events in the lives of inmates, chaplaincy services are provided to help inmates heal from the harms of those events.

How Are Religious Services Delivered?

Religious services have been provided in Canadian pris-ons since the beginning of the penitentiary system itself. The roots and traditions of the chaplaincy system in Canadian prisons are based on the Protestant and Roman Catholic values, however, as society and the prison popu-lation have increasingly become more diverse, signifi-cant changes have been made to address emerging needs based on the ethnocultural and religious diversity. The Interfaith Committee on Chaplaincy (IFC) is a committee of the religious bodies of Canada and it acts as a liaison between faith groups and the CSC. The committee works based on the memorandum of understanding (MoU) signed between the committee and the CSC in 1982. Through this committee, the representatives of 24 major religious bodies delegated by their own faith groups vol-untarily coordinate, ensure, and support the delivery of religious services within the various correctional facili-ties. The group has an advisory role to the CSC director general for chaplaincy and the commissioner. The MoU signed between the CSC and IFC was later modified and the role of the IFC was defined as contributing to three major areas: providing advice on the development and application of policies about religious services, contribut-ing to the evaluation of these services, and facilitating the engagement of Canada's faith communities.

Until the changes in the prison chaplaincy system in 2012, the IFC had played a facilitator role in the contract model through which part-time chaplains from different faith groups were recruited. In 2012, the federal Conservative government decided to change the way chaplaincy services were provided and cancelled the contracts of non-Christian chap-lains at federal prisons (*CBC News*, 2012). The gov-ernment argued that with the help of volunteers from all faiths, Christian chaplains who are employed full time with the CSC could meet the religious needs of inmates from any religion (*CBC News*, 2014). There were roughly 70 full-time chaplains at that time and

almost all of them were representing Christian beliefs. This took place despite the duty of the CSC to accom-modate different religious faiths and beliefs and the increasingly diverse prisoner population. The Office of the Correctional Investigator criticized this change by pointing out that having permanent chaplains from only Christian belief systems will be ineffective "to provide multi-faith spiritual advice, religious counsel-ling and guidance" to the increasingly diverse offender population (Office of the Correctional Investigator, 2013). Besides, Christian chaplains are not qualified to deal with "languages, sacred writings, and trad-itions of other religions" (Dueck, 2012). It is suggested that the part-time chaplains will be replaced by a mix of volunteers, however, religious services might suffer from the lack of consistency and sustainability of a volunteer-based strategy. In response to mounting criticism, the government decided to privatize prison chaplaincy services. Two different companies have been contracted to deliver chaplaincy services since 2014 (Kairos Pneuma from March 2014 to March 2016 and Bridges of Canada from April 2016 to March 2020). Both companies are identified with Christian symbolism and are run by former Christian chaplains (Beckford & Cairns, 2015).

To formalize the administration of inmate reli-gious accommodations and explain the responsibilities and procedures for religious services, new guidelines were created in 2016 by the chaplaincy section of the Reintegration Services Division of the CSC in consul-tation with the IFC (CSC, 2016). According to these guidelines, the full-time chaplains are supposed to obtain requests for religious accommodations from in-mates and facilitate the relationship between inmates and their own faith communities to ensure their re-ligious needs are met. Inmates can access their "faith community resource person," who is accessible to them and who can also be called a volunteer chaplain. The guidelines identify the rules for scheduling the vol-unteer chaplain visits. The guidelines also regulate how religiously accommodated items and clothing will be dealt with. The faith community or the family of an inmate is allowed to donate religious items and resources with the approval of the head of the facility. The religious practices and necessities of the holy days and other special observances are required to be ac-commodated "to the fullest extent possible within the operational requirements of the safety and security of the institution."

The Particularities of the Canadian Correctional System

A comprehensive review of the religious and spiritual services in Canadian correctional facilities was conducted by the CSC in 2002 (CSC, 2007). The purpose of the review was to investigate (1) whether the religious and spiritual services and programs are available and accessible to inmates from all faith groups, (2) whether the standards are being consistently applied across the country within the legal and policy requirements, and (3) whether the spiritual needs of the inmates are properly assessed. In 20 different facilities across five regions, the review team of human rights and performance assurance experts interviewed inmates and correctional staff and administered questionnaires with 10 per cent of the offender population in each facility. Overall, the review team found positive outcomes regarding the availability of religious services. However, they noticed that the availability of religious services and resources was inconsistent across different facilities because of the dependence on part-time (contract) or volunteer chaplains for non-Christian faiths. Also, the team stated that there were few clear references made to non-Christian faiths in policy documents. For example, in the introduction to the Code of Professional Conduct for Chaplains the sentence "The full biblical concept of justice is the core of Chaplaincy ministry" is included, and this statement has not changed since 1993 (Beckford & Cairns, 2015).

The review also found a lack of criteria or standards for the evaluation of the services. The fact that the majority of the non-Christian chaplains are volunteers was one of the reasons for inconsistency in the quality of the services and lack of accountability. The incorporation of religious support into rehabilitation and reintegration programs was advised by the interviewed staff during the review process (CSC, 2007). The interviewed staff also stressed the need for raising the awareness of correctional staff about religion and spirituality, especially about minority faiths, through designated training programs.

The frequent changes and the complexity of the regulatory framework related to chaplaincy services impede correctional staff's understanding of their roles and responsibilities in the delivery of religious services (Beckford & Cairns, 2015). The most recent changes to the chaplaincy system of Canadian corrections (in 2016) did not resolve these issues. The private companies contracted by the government continued to hire contract chaplains; however, religious leaders from different faiths have increasingly complained about the lack of chaplains in prisons to meet the spiritual needs of inmates. Since the 2012 changes, the number of complaints filed by inmates to the Office of the Correctional Investigator and the Canadian Human Rights Commission about a lack of religious accommodation such as diets (kosher, halal, and so on), access to chaplains, and religious materials has critically increased (*CBC News*, 2017; Office of the Correctional Investigator, 2018; see Table 16.1).

The remand system in Canadian correctional facilities also creates some discrepancies and problems in terms of the consistency and sustainability of educational, rehabilitative, and other programs for inmates (Woods, Gopal, & George, 2014). Those who are sentenced to two years or more are kept in federal prisons, while individuals sentenced to less than two years and those who are remanded stay in provincial/territorial facilities. Remanded individuals are in the "accused" status, waiting for a further court appearance. Under Canadian law, they are innocent until they have been tried and proven guilty.

The remand population of Canadian prisons has significantly increased during the last two decades and

Table 16.1 Complaints Filed by Inmates about Religious Accommodations

	Religious Diet	Religious/Spiritual	Total
2009–10	30	N/A	30
2010–11	17	33	50
2011–12	15	31	46
2012–13	14	35	49
2013–14	12	36	48
2014–15	17	42	59
2015–16	20	43	63
2016–17	28	38	66
2017–18	36	36	72

Source: Based on data from the Office of the Correctional Investigator (www.oci-bec.gc.ca/index-eng.aspx)

it has now exceeded the sentenced population. Between the years 2005 and 2015, the remanded inmate population has increased fivefold relative to the increase in the sentenced custody population (Statistics Canada, 2017). The increase in remanded individuals has caused challenges in the delivery of correctional services programming, especially in provincial and territorial facilities because of uncertainty regarding the length of stay of an inmate (CSC, 2018a). In addition, the requirements of higher levels of security and more intensive supervision for remanded inmates as well as the frequent need for transportation limit the access of inmates to rehabilitative or recreational programs, including religious services (John Howard Society of Ontario, 2007).

Muslims in Canadian Prisons

In 2015–16, there were 40,147 adults in custody on an average day in Canada (Reitano, 2017). The data about self-declared religious preferences of offenders are available only about those who are under the responsibility of the CSC. According to Public Safety Canada's annual corrections and conditional release statistical overview report, Muslims who are either in custody or in the community under supervision accounted for 5.9 per cent of the total offender population of 23,045 in 2016–17. This amounted to a 1.5 per cent increase from 2010–11 (see Table 16.2). Muslims make up 3.2 per cent of the Canadian population (Statistics Canada, 2011b), so the percentage of Muslim inmates (5.9 per cent) is an indication of their overrepresentation in prisons.

Although the current number of Muslims compared to other religious groups in Canadian corrections does not appear to be high, it is on the increase annually—probably because of the growing Muslim population in the country. This is an alarming trend, because it is often neglected by policymakers. It is also reported that many inmates convert to Islam while they are incarcerated (Ammar et al., 2004). As suggested by Hamm (2009), "Islam is the fastest growing religion among prisoners in Western nations" (p. 667), and this pattern of growth of Muslim inmates is taking place in Canada. Muslims are also a religious group who require a considerable amount of religious services in prisons. Practising Muslims pray five times a day, attend one congregational prayer on Fridays, and on Muslim Eid days (major feasts) twice a year (Eid-ul Fitr and Eid-ul Adha). They observe certain dietary

Table 16.2 Muslim Inmates in Canadian Corrections

Year	n	%	Total Offender Population
2010–11	1,029	4.5	22,863
2011–12	1,091	4.7	23,156
2012–13	1,201	5.2	23,244
2013–14	1,228	5.3	23,154
2014–15	1,236	5.4	22,935
2015–16	1,288	5.6	23,057
2016–17	1,365	5.9	23,045

Source: Based on data from yearly Public Safety Canada "Corrections and Conditional Release Statistical Overview" (taken from reports of various years).

restrictions and fast during the month of Ramadan along with other practices. Chaplains or religious volunteers serving Muslims organize congregational prayers, notify the management about dietary restrictions, arrange for pre-dawn meals (*suhur*) and evening meals (*iftar*) during Ramadan, deliver a sermon during Friday and Eid prayers, teach religious duties and recital of the Koran, if asked by the inmate.

Research suggests that Islam has a moderating effect on inmates (Hamm, 2009). As noted previously, religion can provide a coping mechanism for some inmates in the prison environment. Clear and Sumter (2002) found a positive association between levels of religiousness and levels of in-prison adjustment. Some inmates may lean toward religion to cope with the negative impacts of incarceration and adjust themselves to the prison environment. As a result, they may need more religious services. Similarly, those who convert to Islam in prison also need more religious guidance, as they may want to learn more about their new religion. Despite the growing Muslim population in prison and the need for more Muslim chaplains, the Canadian government cut funding significantly to the chaplaincy program in 2012 and cancelled the contracts of part-time non-Christian chaplains the following year (Hussein, 2018). Today, religious services for Muslim inmates are offered mainly by volunteers (Beckford & Cairns, 2015). Interfaith chaplains can provide spiritual care for inmates from all religious backgrounds, including Muslim, but their religious guidance for Muslim inmates would be limited. Religious volunteers try to fill that need in prisons across the country.

Through interviews with Muslim prison chaplains conducted between 2010 and 2012, Beckford and Cairns (2015) compared the prison chaplaincy systems of Britain and Canada and how these countries have responded to the increasing numbers of Muslim prisoners. In contrast to the British system, where Muslim chaplains are full-time employees of the correctional organization, the contract-for-service model in Canada resulted in inconsistencies in training and recruitment of chaplains and a lack of clarity in the roles and responsibilities of the chaplains. Among the problems mentioned by the Canadian Muslim chaplains who were interviewed by Beckford and Cairns (2015) were feeling excluded from the corporate activities of the prisons, being stereotyped among staff and inmates, the lack of training for new chaplains, and the absence of a professional association for Muslim chaplains. One major problem mentioned was the lack of diversity in upper administration of chaplaincy services. Muslim chaplains are only represented in the practice phase of the services, such as conducting religious and pastoral activities with Muslim inmates and providing training about Islam to prison staff. The low ratio of the Muslim chaplains to the rising Muslim population in Canadian prisons causes several problems in accommodating their religious needs. The Muslim chaplains mentioned that Friday prayers, which are a duty in Islam that should be performed congregationally with the supervision of an Imam, often did not take place because of the lack of staff or space (Beckford & Cairns, 2015).

Although Beckford and Cairns's (2015) sample of Muslim prison chaplains identify themselves as religious authorities who had completed Islamic studies, and though there are opportunities to receive such training outside of the correctional organization, there is an obvious need for standardized training for Muslim chaplains serving in prisons across the country. There is also a lack of standards in the recruitment of Muslim chaplains. Other than a few exceptions, a formal interview process is not the general rule. The major method used in the recruitment of Muslim chaplains in the contract model is the community ties and recommendations made by other colleagues based on their "influential and respected position in the community" (Beckford & Cairns, 2015, p. 47).

Although there is not a formal training for chaplains within the CSC, there have recently been some efforts to provide training for chaplain candidates. The Emmanuel College at the University of Toronto offers a master's degree in pastoral studies, and students in this program are allowed to specialize in spiritual care with a special foci on Buddhist studies, Christian studies, and Muslim studies. Within the same stream, a certificate program on spiritual care is also offered that allows the graduates to serve as a chaplain in public institutions, including hospitals and prisons.

Conclusions and Directions for Future Research

In this chapter, we explored the issue of religion in Canadian prisons generally and prison chaplaincy of minority religions more specifically, using Islam as an example. Through the use of interdisciplinary mid-range theoretical perspectives, including pains of imprisonment, social attachment, social learning, cognitive transformation, and psychotherapy, we showed the positive impact of religious service delivery in prisons. Prisoners benefit from connecting with their religion on an individual level by reducing the pains of imprisonment, developing pro-social behaviours, alleviating their guilt, finding a supportive social group that helps them adjust and that protects them against violence, gaining spiritual growth, and developing a path to rehabilitation and change. At the institutional level, prisoners' connections with their religion decreases instances of misconduct and channels inmates' energies in a positive direction.

While there are many prisoners whose connection with their religion inside has helped them adjust when they re-enter society, the example often advanced as proof of the impact of religion is El-Hajj Malik El-Shabazz (Malcolm X). El-Shabazz was imprisoned at the age of 20 for a 10-year term. While in prison, he was introduced to the teachings of Elijah Muhammad and adopted the Black Muslim faith (Kusha, 2015; SpearIT, 2012). While Malcolm X's experience may not be typical, it nevertheless reminds us qualitatively of the importance of religion in rehabilitation inside the prison (since he served 6 years of his 10-year sentence) and of adjustment once released.

The chapter also summarized the various national and international laws and regulations that bind

Canada to providing religious services to incarcerated individuals. Within this legal and policy framework, we discussed the problems arising from the most recent policy introduced by the Conservative government in 2012 that centralizes chaplaincy mainly within the Christian denominations, making all other religious services voluntary and privatized. This creates multiple challenges for prisoners who adhere to non-Christian minority religions. More specifically, we examined the trials of the new system as it relates to Islam. Muslim prisoners have in the last few years increased in number (see Table 16.2), and they comprise the second-largest population of incarcerated individuals—and these numbers are bound to increase given the immigration trends of Muslims into Canada in the last decade. The Pew Research Center's Forum on Religion and Public Life (2011) notes that Canada's Muslim population is expected to nearly triple, climbing from 940,000 in 2010 to 2.7 million in 2030.

In addition to the increase in the number of incarcerated Muslims in Canadian prisons, we know from research conducted in the United States (Kusha, 2009) and United Kingdom (Beckford, Joly, & Khosrokhavar, 2016) that many inmates either convert to Islam or revert to Islam in prisons. As such, there is a need for consistent and regular follow-up with a Muslim chaplain to teach, guide, and interpret the religion in its moderate spirit and intent. The lack of good and appropriate religious guidance can be best seen in the Southern Ohio Correctional Facility riot (better known as the Lucasville riots) in 1993 (Lynd, 2004). This was one of the deadliest riots in Ohio, where nine inmates and a correctional officer were killed after Muslim inmates felt they were not taken seriously because they refused to take the mandatory tuberculosis testing and refused other services to fulfill their faith (Lynd, 2004). Insisting on an austere interpretation of Islam given to them by a volunteer chaplain, the Muslim inmates took matters into their own hands and began a riot (Ammar et al., 2004). The riot took on a different character after a number of other groups joined, and it lasted 23 days.

Finally, the chapter brings attention to the notion that under the best of circumstances practising Islam requires the provision of numerous services and guidance. It is a high-maintenance religion, and in a correctional setting it requires attention and responsiveness. A volunteer chaplain who comes for a few hours a week would not be able to provide required services adequately and safely. As such, full-time, paid minority chaplains in general and Muslim chaplains in particular must become a policy priority for correctional facilities. This would ensure the increase in standards of the service provided to Muslim inmates as well as the professionalization of Muslim chaplains.

Present Research and Future Directions

It is not difficult to notice that this chapter included little empirical or research data on the topic. While there has been scholarly (Coward, 1999) and public (Bramadat, 2008) interest in religion discussions for a long time in Canada, there has been little discussion as it relates to minority religions in correctional facilities. The meta-analyses and systematic reviews of the literature have shown that there are few studies that examine the impact of faith-based interventions on inmates, and those that have been conducted are inconclusive or methodologically weak because of a lack of random assignment and appropriate controls (Aos, Miller, & Drake, 2006; Power et al., 2014). The common suggestion that empirical studies and meta-analyses on this issue have made is that the findings on the effectiveness of religious programs in reducing recidivism are inconclusive, and more rigorous empirical research is needed to inform the policies on faith-based interventions (Aos et al, 2006; Duwe & King, 2013; Stansfield et al., 2017).

Power and colleagues (2014) concluded that the studies in the literature predominantly focus on interventions based on Christianity. Considering the diversity in the correctional system, research should focus on other religions as well and compare the impacts of programs based on different religions. Clear and Sumter (2002, p. 126) point out that in the twentieth century, scholars have provided a number of assumptions regarding the impact of religion on prisoners but added little empirical research. As a result, it is not surprising that our factual-based knowledge about Muslims in Canadian prisons is sparse. A research conducted by Zaidi and Ammar (2016) shows that a search of seven bibliographic online databases[1] that include titles, keywords, or abstracts that directly address Muslims in Canadian prisons for the years between 2009 and 2015 shows two published papers (see Loza, 2011, and Monaghan, 2015). Both papers are about radicalization—one focusing on the individual level and the other focusing on Canadian policy. None of those papers address the everyday lives of "normative"

Muslim inmates in prison. In other words, we know very little about Muslim inmates' prison "experience" in Canada. As Simon (2000) argues, it is ironic that in the age of hyper-incarceration, the classic studies of ordinary prison life, such as Sykes's *Society of Captives,* have largely disappeared. The political nature of the nexus between Islam and terrorism in general in the West has contributed to the sparsity of research on the daily lives of Muslims in North American prisons generally and Canadian prisons in particular. European researchers have remained diligent and have thus created a body of empirical knowledge that can help them in provisions of all services, including religious services (see Beckford, 2005; Beckford et al., 2016; Khosrokhavar, 2015; Spalek & El-Hassan, 2007).

Empirical research in Canada on religion in prisons generally and Muslims in particular is hindered by a number of issues. First, it is difficult to gain access to prisons to conduct research. Many researchers (either based at universities or in research institutes) face the various hurdles of institutional research requirements. Often, prison research requires full review by boards, and in some places prisoner advocates are part of the review, making the process long and tedious. For junior faculty or doctoral students, the relatively long time it takes to obtain approval to conduct prison research works against the tenure or graduation timelines imposed on them. Once the researcher gains access to the correctional institutions they will still face a range of methodological, ethical, and security issues and barriers. Methodological difficulties in measuring the impact of religious services on offenders include (1) many studies depend on non-random samples or a lack control groups; (2) the inmates who are eligible for faith-based interventions are generally low-risk offenders and highly motivated to change, which leads to self-selection bias in sampling; and (3) it is difficult to measure the success of such programs since they are more about internal spiritual transformation and their outcomes are subjective (Schaefer et al., 2016).

The prison researcher also faces ethical issues that are both practical and epistemological. Ethical issues pertain to affording the prisoners the required respect that all research participants require, despite all the prevailing norms among prisoners or prisoners and staff or issues of security (Ammar, 2015, p. 209). Other ethical issues relate to balancing the power issues between researcher–participants in a prison context, as well as the potential trauma that research can produce

with particular prisoners (Wakai, Shelton, Trestman, & Kesten, 2009).

One more issue that hinders social scientific research on the topic of Muslims in prison is the suspicion often expressed by criminologists and other social scientists of any mix of crime and religion (Ammar, 2001). Pepinsky (1991), in his classic work on peacemaking criminology, writes about this suspicion regarding another famous criminologist, Richard Quinney's use of Buddhist ideas in his writings after he had publicly declared his adoption of the tradition. He notes, "Richard (who has always been Richard and not a Marxist, or a Christian or a Buddhist alone) broke the ice and gave many of us criminologists the courage as we have dared ourselves to become avowedly religious—as seeker rather than purveyors of truth" (p. 303).

These suspicions become more compounded in prison research when the researchers interested in studying Muslims is Muslim themselves. Marvasti (2015) indicates that funding agencies, especially federal agencies, often prefer to give grants to non-Muslims to conduct prison research on Muslims. Quraishi (2015) also identified the challenges of increased scrutiny of researchers generally, but in his case as a Muslim researcher it called into question the legitimacy of his research.

It is difficult to be steadfast about any recommendations regarding directions for future research given that all and any research on religion in Canadian prisons will only add to the void that exists. However, the following are five areas where future research is needed, especially to guide policy:

1. *History of Islam in Canadian prisons:* We know very little about when and how Muslim inmates became a noticeable group in Canadian prisons and how their concerns evolved. In the United States, the works such as of Kusha (2009) and Moore (1995) have helped criminologists understand more about the origin, development, and evolution of Muslims in prisons. Who converts to Islam, how are their conversion patterns expressed, and why do they convert?

2. *The group nature of Muslim inmates in Canadian prisons:* It is difficult to find systematic works on various group elements, including sects of inmates, whether inmates convert or rediscover their religion, if Canadian federal

and provincial authorities impose a particular kind of Islam (for example, in the United States, neither Nation of Islam nor Wahhabi Islam are supported in prisons). Other research questions could include, What do Muslim inmates in Canada do that is different or similar to the general inmate populations? Does incarceration impact Muslim inmates differently, and if so, how? What are the contributions of practising Islam to the individual and group within prison?

3. *The challenges of conducting research on religion in Canadian prisons:* What are the logistical challenges in terms of research ethics requirements, ethical dilemmas of doing research with the incarcerated, and the insider/outsider dilemmas in terms of the researcher's identity?

4. *Service delivery to the incarcerated minority religious groups, including chaplaincy:* How are services generally (medical, exercise, leisure activities, educational opportunities, and religious activities) delivered, and how accommodating are these services to the needs of those groups that require them and to legal and policy regulations?

5. *The post-9/11 prison and the prison context for Muslim inmates:* How has 9/11 changed prison policy in Canada? How are Muslim inmates treated differently? How are these policy changes developed? What is the impact of US policy on Canadian prisons toward Muslim inmates?

All the above areas are fertile ground for further research and exploration. While on the one hand, and according to Statistics Canada (2011b), the second-largest growing religious faith in Canada is "nothing," on the other hand, a growing portion of the population reported belonging to religions other than Christianity (Stone, 2013). These growing religious affiliations were Muslims, Hindus, Sikhs, and Buddhists (Statistics Canada, 2011a). Stone (2013) reports on this growth by noting that Islam constitutes the largest growth (at 3.2 per cent of the population), followed by Hinduism (1.5 per cent of the population), Sikhism (1.4 per cent of the population), and Buddhism (1.15 per cent of the population). This increase in religious affiliations other than Christianity will in time (if not already) be reflected in societal institutions in Canada, including in prisons. However, research on religion in prison generally and the growing minority religions in prisons specifically remains sparse in the Canadian context (Zaidi & Ammar, 2016). Some of the areas suggested above have been explored by researchers in Europe and the United States (for example, see Ammar & Weaver, 2006; Ammar et al., 2004; Beckford, 2005; Beckford & Cairns, 2015; Beckford et al., 2016; Clear, & Sumter, 2002; Hamm, 2007, 2009; Spalek & El-Hassan, 2007). Systematic knowledge in this area is essential because, in its absence, biased opinions and stereotypes fill the gaps.

Policy Recommendations

It is difficult to make any policy recommendations that are based on empirical research or evidence-based evaluation. However, there is enough evidence to show that one important short-term recommendation is to advocate for faith-based services for minority religions in Canadian prisons to be seen as an essential service that requires attention and further research. Moreover, religious services should become part of therapeutic interventions for suitable inmates based on their special circumstances. Based on their meta-analysis, Schaefer and colleagues (2016) conclude that faith-based interventions should be tailored and individualized to each inmate because there is no effective one-size-fits-all program. They argue that faith-based interventions should be a component of a broader rehabilitation program because the programs that are congruent with the principles of effective intervention and which promote pro-social attitudes are the most effective ones in terms of changes in criminal attitudes and behaviour.

The issue of volunteer chaplains for minority religions is complicated by the economic pressures imposed on prisons. However, as always, decisions that adhere to strict economic cost–benefit considerations only work in the short run. The dominance of volunteer chaplains in US prisons has resulted in some of the most violent riots (for example, the Attica prison uprising in 1971 and the Lucasville riot in 1993). Making prisons safe places of reform must be a top priority for all correctional institutions. Having well-trained and professional Muslim and other chaplains whose focus is on rehabilitation and theological guidance—not on any political form of Islam and proselytization—would help create prisons as safe places (Ammar, 2015). There is also an obvious need for standardized training to improve the skills of chaplains from all faiths.

As Stansfield and colleagues (2017) stated, chaplains should aim to improve their skills "in order to have a greater positive impact on prisoners on the journey to desistance" (p. 138). Finally, evidence-based intervention programs similar to the InnerChange program for Christian prisoners (Duwe & King, 2013) should be developed for prisoners from minority religions to ensure the well-being of offenders, which should lead to fewer adverse effects of imprisonment and a reduction in recidivism rates.

Review Questions

1. What are the benefits of religion for prisoners both in prison and post-release?
2. What does research say about the role of religious services in reducing recidivism?
3. Does the distribution of inmate populations from different religions in Canada represent the general population of the country? What is the fastest-growing religion in Canadian prisons?
4. What are the main issues regarding Muslim chaplains and the delivery of religious services and practice?

Critical Thinking Questions

1. What should be done to address the limitations of the current system to ensure every inmate has equal religious rights during their incarceration?
2. Do you think further research on religion in Canadian prisons is necessary? Why or why not?
3. What could be the role of Muslim chaplains in preventing radical versions of Islam from taking hold in Canadian prisons?
4. How can faith-based interventions contribute to offender treatment? What kind of practices should be included in such interventions to ensure successful outcomes?

Multimedia Suggestions

Correctional Services Canada Chaplaincy Services
This website offers information on the chaplaincy services offered by the CSC: https://www.csc-scc.gc.ca/chaplaincy/index-eng.shtml

Interfaith Committee on Chaplaincy
This website offers information on the Interfaith Committee on Chaplaincy at the CSC: https://interfaithchaplaincy.ca

Bridges of Canada
Bridges of Canada is a not-for-profit organization that offers multi-faith chaplaincy services in both correctional facilities and community re-entry settings: https://www.bridgesofcanada.com

Crossroads Prison Ministries
Crossroads Prison Ministries is a Christian-based discipleship and advocacy ministry for prisoners and their families: https://cpministries.ca/chaplains

Buddhist Prison Chaplaincy Network of Canada
The Buddhist Prison Chaplaincy Network is a network of staff and volunteer Buddhist chaplains working in correctional facilities at both the federal and provincial levels: http://www.buddhismcanada.com/buddhist-prison-chaplaincy-network-of-canada

Pastoral Counselling: Becoming a Prison Chaplain
This website provides information on how to become a prison chaplain: https://www.pastoralcounseling.org/career/prison-chaplain

Association of Muslim Chaplains
The Association of Muslim Chaplains provides support for the professional development of Muslims who provide spiritual care as chaplains in the community, including in prisons: https://associationofmuslimchaplains.org

Note

1. Academic Search Primer, Applied Social Sciences Index and Abstracts, Criminal Justice Database, Humanities and Social Sciences Index and Retrospective, Religion Database, Sociological Abstracts, and Sociology Database.

References

Abbas, T. (2004). After 9/11: British South Asian Muslims, Islamophobia, multiculturalism, and the state. *American Journal of Islamic Social Sciences, 21*, 26–38.

Akers, R.L. (1998). *Deviant behavior: A social learning approach.* Belmont, CA: Wadsworth.

Ammar, N. (2001). Restorative justice in Islam: Theory and practice. In M. Hadley (Ed.), *The spiritual roots of restorative justice* (pp. 161–80). Albany, NY: State University of New York Press.

Ammar, N. (2015) Building better understandings of religion, corrections and society. In N.H. Ammar (Ed.), *Muslims in US prisons: People, policy, practice* (pp. 203–16). Boulder, CO: Lynne Rienner.

Ammar, N.H., Weaver, R.R., & Saxon, S. (2004). Muslims in prison: A case study from Ohio state prisons. *International Journal of Offender Therapy and Comparative Criminology, 48*, 414–28.

Ammar, N., & Weaver, R. (2006). Restrained voices: Female inmates and services in two Ohio women prisons. *Women in Criminal Justice, 16*(3), 67–89.

Aos, S., Miller, M., & Drake, E. (2006). *Evidence-based adult corrections programs: What works and what does not.* Olympia, WA: Washington State Institute for Public Policy.

Beckford, J.A. (2005). Muslims in the prisons of Britain and France. *Journal of Contemporary European Studies, 13*, 287–97

Beckford, J.A., & Cairns, I.M. (2015). Muslim prison chaplains in Canada and Britain. *Sociological Review, 63*, 36–56.

Beckford, J.A., Joly D., & Khosrokhavar, F. (2016). *Muslims in prison: Challenge and change in Britain and France.* Basingstoke, UK: Palgrave Macmillan.

Bowlby J. (1969). *Attachment. Attachment and loss: Vol. 1. Loss.* New York, NY: Basic Books.

Bramadat, P. (2008). Religion and public policy in Canada: An itinerary. *Studies in Religion/Sciences Religieuses, 37*, 121–43.

Campbell, M., Hudon, M., Resnicow, K., Blakeney, N., Paxton, A., & Baskin, M. (2007). Church-based health promotion interventions: Evidence and lessons learned. *Annual Review of Public Health, 28*, 213–34.

CBC News. (2012, October 5). Non-Christian prison chaplains chopped by Ottawa. Retrieved from https://www.cbc.ca/news/canada/british-columbia/non-christian-prison-chaplains-chopped-by-ottawa-1.1142212

CBC News. (2014, June 15). Privatizing the prison chaplain: A view from the inside. Retrieved from https://www.cbc.ca/news/canada/privatizing-the-prison-chaplain-a-view-from-the-inside-1.2673301

CBC News. (2017, December 23). Inmate complaints on the rise over access to religious services. Retrieved from https://www.cbc.ca/news/canada/nova-scotia/prison-religion-human-rights-commission-inmates-1.4401229

Clear, T.R., Hardyman, P., Stout, B., Lucken, K., & Dammer. H. (2000). The value of religion in prison: An inmate perspective. *Journal of Contemporary Criminal Justice, 16*, 53–74.

Clear, T.R., & Sumter, M.T. (2002). Prisoners, prison, and religion. *Journal of Offender Rehabilitation, 35*, 125–56.

Cornish, D., & Clarke, R.V. (Eds). (1986). *The reasoning criminal: Rational choice perspectives on offending.* New York, NY: Springer-Verlag.

Correctional Service Canada. (2007). Performance assurance. Retrieved from https://www.csc-scc.gc.ca/text/pa/ev-arsps-378-1-149/relig_spirit-eng.shtml

Correctional Service Canada. (2012). Chaplaincy services. Retrieved from http://www.csc-scc.gc.ca/chaplaincy/index-eng.shtml

Correctional Service Canada. (2016). Inmate religious accommodations. Retrieved from https://www.csc-scc.gc.ca/lois-et-reglements/750-1-gl-eng.shtml#d3

Correctional Service Canada. (2018a). Adult and youth correctional statistics in Canada, 2016/2017. Retrieved from https://www150.statcan.gc.ca/n1/pub/85-002-x/2018001/article/54972-eng.htm

Correctional Service Canada. (2018b). History of CSC. Retrieved from http://www.csc-scc.gc.ca/about-us/006-0007-eng.shtml

Coward, H. (1999). The contribution of religious studies to public policy. *Studies in Religion/Sciences Religieuses, 28*, 489–502.

Dammer, H.R. (2002a). The reasons for religious involvement in the correctional environment. *Journal of Offender Rehabilitation, 35*, 35–58.

Dammer, H.R. (2002b). Religion in corrections. In D. Levinson (Ed.), *Encyclopedia of crime and punishment (Vols. 1–4).* Thousand Oaks, CA: SAGE Publications.

Douyon, E. (2016). Ethnocultural minorities and the Canadian correctional system. Correctional Service Canada. Retrieved from https://www.csc-scc.gc.ca/about-us/006-4000-eng.shtml

Duckett, M.T., & Mohr, J.W. (2015). Prison. In *The Canadian Encyclopedia*. Retrieved from https://www.thecanadianencyclopedia.ca/en/article/prison

Dueck, L. (2012, October 12). One-size prison chaplains don't fit all. *Globe and Mail*. Retrieved from https://www.theglobeandmail.com/opinion/one-size-prison-chaplains-dont-fit-all/article4607354

Duwe, G., & King, M. (2013). Can faith-based correctional programs work? An outcome evaluation of the Inner Change Freedom Initiative in Minnesota. *International Journal of Offender Therapy and Comparative Criminology*, *57*, 813–41.

Ekstedt, J.W., & Griffiths, C.T. (1988). *Corrections in Canada policy and practice*. Toronto, ON: Elsevier.

Farall, S. (2002). *Rethinking what works with offenders: Probation, social context and desistance from crime*. Cullompton, UK: Willan.

Foucault, M. (1977). *Discipline and punish: The birth of the prison*. New York, NY: Pantheon Books.

Hamm, M.S. (2007), *Terrorist recruitment in American correctional institutions: An exploratory study of non-traditional faith groups*. Washington, DC: National Institute of Justice.

Hamm, M.S. (2009). Prison Islam in the age of sacred terror. *British Journal of Criminology*, *49*, 667–85.

Giordano, P.C., Cernkovich, S.A., & Rudolf, J.A. (2002). Gender, crime, and desistance: Toward a theory of cognitive transformation. *American Journal of Sociology*, *107*, 880–1064.

Hannah, G., Clutterbuck, L., & Rubin, J. (2008). *Radicalization or rehabilitation: Understanding the challenge of extremist and radicalized prisoners*. Santa Monica, CA: RAND Corporation.

Hirschi, T., & Stark, R. (1969). Hellfire and delinquency. *Social Problems*, *17*, 202–13.

Hussein, S. (2018, August 7). Islamic inmates need more religious support, say Muslim prison chaplains. *Global News*. Retrieved from https://globalnews.ca/news/4317151/muslim-prison-chaplains

John Howard Society of Ontario. (2007). Remand in Ontario. Second report to the Board, Standing Committee on Prison Conditions in Ontario. Retrieved from http://johnhoward.on.ca/wp-content/uploads/2014/09/remand-in-ontario-second-report-to-the-board-december-2007.pdf

Johnson, B.R. (2004). Religious program and recidivism among former inmates in prison fellowship programs: A long-term follow-up study. *Justice Quarterly*, *21*, 329–54.

Johnson, B.R., Larson, D.B., & Pitts, T. (1997). Religious programming, institutional adjustment, and recidivism among former inmates in prison fellowship programs. *Justice Quarterly*, *14*, 145–66.

Khosrokhavar, F. (2015). The constrained role of the Muslim chaplain in French prisons. *International Journal of Politics, Culture & Society*, *28*, 67–82.

Kusha, H.R. (2009). *Islam in American prisons: Black Muslims' challenge to American penology*. Burlington, VT: Ashgate

Kusha, H.R. (2015) Muslim history and demographics in and out of prison. In N.H. Ammar (Ed.), *Muslims in US prisons: People, policy, practice* (pp. 9–28). Boulder, CO: Lynne Rienner.

Loza, W. (2011). The prevalence of the Middle-Eastern extreme ideologies among some Canadians. *Journal of Interpersonal Violence*, *26*, 1388–1400.

Lynd, S. (2011). *Lucasville: The untold story of a prison uprising*. Philadelphia, PA: Temple University Press.

Maruna, S., & Immarigeon, R. (Eds). (2004). *After crime and punishment: Pathways to offender reintegration*. Devon, UK: Willan.

Marvasti, A. (2015). Policy responses and policy implications. In N.H. Ammar (Ed.), *Muslims in US prisons: People, policy, practice* (pp. 167–82). Boulder, CO: Lynne Rienner.

Monaghan, J. (2015). Criminal justice policy transfer and prison counter-radicalization: Examining Canadian participation in the Roma-Lyon Group. *Canadian Journal of Law and Society/Revue Canadienne Droit et Société*, *30*, 381–400.

Moore, K.M. (1995). *Al-Mughtaribun American law and the transformation of Muslim life in the United States*. Albany, NY: State University of New York Press.

Mowen, T.J., & Visher, C.A. (2015). Drug use and crime after incarceration: The role of family supply and family conflict. *Justice Quarterly*, *32*(2), 1–23.

Norcross, J.C., & Wampold, B.E. (2011). What works for whom: Tailoring psychotherapy to the person. *Journal of Clinical Psychology*, *67*, 127–32.

O'Connor, T.P. (2003). *A sociological and hermeneutical study of the influence of religion on the rehabilitation of inmates*. Ph.D. diss. Washington, DC: Catholic University of America.

O'Connor, T.P., & Duncan, J.B. (2011). The sociology of humanist, spiritual, and religious practice in prison: Supporting responsivity and desistance from crime. *Religions*, 590–610.

O'Connor, T.P., & Perreyclear, M. (2002). Prison religion in action and its influence on offender rehabilitation. *Journal of Offender Rehabilitation*, *35*, 11–33.

Office of the Correctional Investigator. (2013). *Annual Report of the Office of the Correctional Investigator 2012–2013*. Retrieved from http://www.oci-bec.gc.ca/cnt/rpt/annrpt/annrpt20122013-eng.aspx

Office of the Correctional Investigator. (2018). *Annual report of the Office of the Correctional Investigator 2018–2019*. Retrieved from https://www.oci-bec.gc.ca/cnt/rpt/annrpt/annrpt20182019-eng.aspx

Power, J., Ritchie, M.B., & Madill, D. (2014). Faith-based interventions: A systematic review of the literature (Research Brief B-56). Correctional Service

Canada. Retrieved from https://www.csc-scc.gc.ca/research/005008-b56-eng.shtml

Public Safety Canada. (2017). Corrections and conditional release statistical overview. Retrieved from http://www.publicsafety.gc.ca

Pepinsky, H.E. (1991). Peacemaking in criminology and criminal justice. In R. Quinney & H. Pepinsky (Eds), *Criminology as peacemaking* (pp. 299–329). Bloomington, IN: Indiana University Press.

Pew Research Center Forum on Religion and Public Life. (2011). The global Muslim population. Retrieved from http://www.pewforum.org/2011/01/27/the-future-of-the-global-muslim-population

Quraishi, M. (2015). Challenges in research. In N.H. Ammar (Ed.), *Muslims in US prisons: People, policy, practice* (pp. 47–61). Boulder, CO: Lynne Rienner.

Reitano, J. (2017). Adult correctional statistics in Canada, 2015/2016. Statistics Canada. Retrieved from https://www150.statcan.gc.ca/n1/pub/85-002-x/2017001/article/14700-eng.pdf

Rothman, D.J. (1971). *The discovery of the asylum.* Toronto, ON: Little, Brown.

Schaefer, L., Sams, T., & Lux, J. (2016). Saved, salvaged, or sunk: A meta-analysis of the effects of faith-based interventions on inmate adjustment. *The Prison Journal, 96,* 600–622.

Scull, A.T. (1977). *Decarceration: Community treatment and the deviant—A radical view.* Englewood Cliffs, NJ: Prentice-Hall.

Simon, J. (2000). The "society of captives" in the era of hyper-incarceration. *Theoretical Criminology, 4,* 285–308.

Solicitor General of Canada (2002). Working papers of the Correctional Law Review (1986–1988). Cat. No JS42-111/2002E. Retrieved from https://www.publicsafety.gc.ca/lbrr/archives/ke%209410%20c6i%202002-eng.pdf

Spalek, B., & El-Hassan, S. (2007). Muslim converts in prison. *Howard Journal of Criminal Justice, 46,* 99–114.

SpearIT (2012). Facts and fictions about Islam in prison: Assessing prisoner radicalization in post-9/11 America. Institute for Social Policy and Understanding.

Retrieved from https://www.ispu.org/wp-content/uploads/2012/12/ISPU_Report_Prison.pdf

Stansfield, R., Mowen, T.J., O'Connor, T., & Boman, J.H. (2017). The role of religious

support in reentry: Evidence from the SVORI data. *Journal of Research in Crime and Delinquency, 54,* 111–45.

Statistics Canada (2011a). Immigration and ethnocultural diversity in Canada. Retrieved from https://www12.statcan.gc.ca/nhs-enm/2011/as-sa/99-010-x/99-010-x2011001-eng.cfm

Statistics Canada (2011b). National Household Survey: Data tables—Religion. Retrieved from https://www12.statcan.gc.ca/nhs-enm/2011/dp-pd/dt-td/Rp-eng.cfm?LANG=E&APATH=3&DETAIL=0&DIM=0&FL=A&FREE=0&GC=0&GID=0&GK=0&GRP=0&PID=105399&PRID=0&PTYPE=105277&S=0&SHOWALL=0&SUB=0&Temporal=2013&THEME=95&VID=0

Statistics Canada. (2017). Trends in the use of remand in Canada. *Juristat.* Retrieved from https://www150.statcan.gc.ca/n1/pub/85-002-x/2017001/article/14691-eng.pdf

Stone, L. (2013, May 8). The second-largest religious faith in Canada? Nothing. *Global News.* Retrieved from https://globalnews.ca/news/544591/the-second-largest-religious-faith-in-canada-nothing

Sumter, M. (1999). *Religiousness and post-release community adjustment.* Ph.D. dissertation, School of Criminology, Florida State University.

Sykes, G.M. (1958). *The society of captives: A study of a maximum security prison.* Princeton, NJ: Princeton University Press.

Takagi, P. (1975). The Walnut Street Jail: A penal reform to centralize the powers of the state. *Federal Probation, 39,* 18–26.

Thomas, J., & Zaitzow, B.H. (2006). Conning or conversion? The role of religion in prison coping. *The Prison Journal, 86,* 242–59.

Wakai, S., Shelton, D., Trestman, R.L., & Kesten, K. (2009). Conducting research in corrections: Challenges and solutions. *Behavioral Sciences & the Law, 27,* 743–52.

Webster, C., & Qasim, M. (2018). The effects of poverty and prison on British Muslim men who offend. *Social Sciences, 7,* 184–97.

Woods, S., Gopal, T., & George, P. (2014). Look at my life: Access to education for the remand population in Ontario. *Canadian Review of Social Policy, 70,* 34–47.

Young, M.C., Gartner, J., O'Connor, T., Larson, D., & Wright, K.N. (1995). Long-term recidivism among federal inmates trained as volunteer prison ministers. *Journal of Offender Rehabilitation, 22,* 97–118.

Zaidi, H., & Ammar, N.H. (2016) Comparative analysis of the literature of Muslim inmates' radicalization in Canada and the USA. Presentation made at the American Society of Criminology Meeting, New Orleans, Louisiana, November 16–19.

Glossary

abolitionism (in relation to prisons) The belief that the criminal justice system is broken and that incarceration is a failed socio-political experience that harms criminalized people, their loved ones, and our communities. Abolitionists typically advocate for the end of the ritualized use of imprisonment, a host of alternatives to confinement, and greater community-based social support resources including affordable housing, access to mental health and substance-use treatment, and greater investment in the labour force.

Indigenous healing lodges Institutions that are designed to provide offenders with a correctional environment and programming that is responsive to Indigenous culture and spirituality.

actuarial prediction instruments Instruments based on longitudinal studies looking at offenders' characteristics associated with recidivism. The risk factors identified are translated into a scoring system, which produces a numeric score that can then be converted into a risk category.

administrative segregation The isolation of a prisoner in a single cell for 22 hours or more a day and without meaningful social interaction. Official reasons may include for the safety and security of the institution or the prisoner, at the prisoner's own request, awaiting adjudication of misconduct, if the individual would interfere with an investigation, or for medical isolation. Because this is an administrative decision, it does not have the same threshold for admittance as does disciplinary segregation, and the length of placement can be prolonged and indeterminate.

adverse childhood experiences (ACEs) Experiences during early childhood that have consistently been related to detrimental health outcomes across the lifespan.

aging/older prisoners In most prison research, 50 or 55 is considered to be the lower limit of seniority. It is lower than the community limit because an incarcerated individual tends to have the same health problems an individual in the community 10–15 years older would have. This process is known as "accelerated aging" and is often attributed to conditions of confinement and lifestyles prior to incarceration.

aiders or abettors Secondary offenders who assist with or encourage the commission of a crime.

argot roles A specific type of role prisoners take on as a coping response to the difficulties of prison.

assertive community treatment (ACT) Specialized community mental health teams that provide 24/7 access to mental health supports and services; these teams are typically composed of clinical staff (psychiatrists, forensic nurses) and in some cases police officers.

asylum A psychiatric hospital; institutions designed to treat and care for individuals with severe mental illness.

attachment An emotional bond between a parent and child that is involved in social, cognitive, and emotional development.

Bangkok Rules The UN Rules for the Treatment of Women Prisoners and Non-Custodial Measures for Women Offenders, also known as the Bangkok Rules. This set of 70 rules was adopted in 2010 as a response to the growing number of women prisoners facing unique challenges during imprisonment. It recognizes that many prison facilities and services around the world are designed primarily for male populations and that there needs to be a gender-sensitive approach for meeting the needs of women prisoners.

banishment Compulsory exile. Historically used in what is now Ontario, it was a court-ordered punishment, and it was used in all colonies as a condition of being pardoned from another sentence, usually the death sentence. Distinct from transportation, banishment involved ordering somebody to leave however they could arrange it and go wherever they wanted, whereas transportation, much less rarely used in Canada, involved being shipped to a penal colony under restraint and performing labour while there.

biometrics Technology that uses an individual's physiological data, such as fingerprints, retinal eye scan, facial features, or voice patterns, to verify and record an individual's identity.

Canadian Charter of Rights and Freedoms A federal statute entrenched in the Canadian constitution that outlines the legal rights and fundamental freedoms afforded to all individuals on Canadian soil.

carceral habitus An entrenched way of thinking and acting that permeates economic, political, cultural, and social relations by which imprisonment appears as a natural approach to dealing with conflict rather than a violent human experiment.

carceral retasking Instances where decommissioned penitentiaries, prisons, jails, and lock-ups are reconfigured into enterprises, like prison tourism destinations, which "continue to reproduce imprisonment as a dominant idea and/or material practice" (Ferguson et al., 2014, pp. 83–4).

clustered sites Institutions composed of two or more separate units or sites classified at different security levels that share a single property under one warden. Offenders classified at different security levels within clustered institutions are kept separate.

cognitive-behavioural therapy (CBT) A psychological intervention aimed at helping alleviate mental health problems by challenging and adapting unhelpful cognitive processes and behaviours.

cognitive impairment A variety of impairments that are often associated with deficits in decision making, concentrating, learning new things, and memory.

cognitive transformation A concept used to explain the change in the belief system of an individual that leads to desistance from crime. According to Giordano and colleagues (2002), there are four types of cognitive transformation in the desistance process: (1) openness to change; (2) exposure to (potential) hooks for change; (3) a shift in how one sees oneself; and (4) a shift in how one views deviant behaviour.

colonialism The practice of acquiring authority or political control over another population or country through settler occupation.

commissioner's directives A set of internal policies or rules that were created by the commissioner of the Correctional Service Canada that govern the daily operations of the CSC penitentiaries and cover areas including staff roles and responsibilities, inmate health services, complaints and grievances, intervention strategies, and protocols for female prisoners.

communication skills The ability to convey information to another person effectively and efficiently using verbal skills.

community corrections Sanctions or supervision programs provided to pre-trial defendants, convicted adults, or adjudicated youth within community settings.

co-morbidity The co-occurrence of multiple mental disorders or substance-use disorders.

conditional release A generic term for the various processes of serving the remainder of one's sentence in the community under state supervision. There are different forms of conditional release, including day parole and full parole.

Constitution Act The legislation that divided the correctional system into two entities, with the federal system overseeing offenders receiving a sentence of two years or more, and the provincial and territorial system responsible for offenders sentenced to a period of two years less a day or shorter.

continuous alcohol monitoring (CAM) device An alcohol-monitoring device worn as an ankle bracelet that detects the alcohol concentration level on the wearer's body by sampling perspiration on the skin.

contraband A prohibited item brought into a correctional facility illegally.

coroner's inquest A quasi-judicial public proceeding that reviews and determines the facts and circumstances of a death such as who, when, where, how, and by what means. In Ontario and Canada, for instance, all deaths occurring in custody-related operations, such as police lock-ups, prisons, and jails, come under the jurisdiction of a coroner's office. Coroner (or, in some provinces, the medical examiner) inquests often involve a jury of community members. Recommendations are made in the aim of preventing deaths from occurring in a similar manner in the future. Although not legally binding, the verdict and recommendations are often accepted and implemented by the respective institutions and agencies.

correctional functions carried out by government agencies that are involved in the state-sanctioned punishment, treatment, and supervision of people who have been convicted of crimes.

correctional officer role Officers are responsible for the custody, safety, security, and supervision of prisoners and the care, custody and control of prisoners in a closed-custody facility.

correctional plan An individual risk management plan created for each federal offender based on information about the offender and their offence.

Correctional Service Canada (CSC) The Canadian federal government agency responsible for the incarceration and rehabilitation of those convicted of a crime and sentenced to two years or more. Its mandate is laid out in the Corrections and Conditional Release Act (CCRA), a federal statute regulating prisoners' rights and various institutional procedures. The CSC reports to the minister of Public Safety Canada.

corrections An umbrella term for agencies that establish, maintain, operate, and monitor the punishment, treatment, and supervision of offenders. Corrections comprises facilities, government policies, and programs delivered by the government and community organizations that are designed to punish, treat, and supervise individuals convicted of criminal offences. This may take place in correctional institutions or in the community. Not-for-profit organizations and members of the public are part of the delivery of correctional services, both in custodial institutions and the community.

Corrections and Conditional Release Act (CCRA) Enacted in 1992, the legal framework governing the operations of the federal correctional system, including the mandates of the Correctional Service of Canada, the Parole Board of Canada, and the Office of the Correctional Investigator, as well as information on prisoner intake, prisoner rights, disciplinary processes, solitary confinement, and release. The CCRA is accompanied by the Corrections and Conditional Release Regulations (CCRR), which provide procedural details on the rights, obligations, and processes established by the Act.

Creating Choices The final 1990 report and policy document produced by the Task Force on Federally Sentenced Women.

criminal career The longitudinal sequence of crimes committed by an individual offender.

Criminal Code Federal legislation that lists and defines most crimes in Canada and includes their associated punishment.

criminal justice system A set of functions of related government agencies and institutions (that is, police, courts, and corrections) tasked with defining what acts are criminal, criminal penalties for committing those acts, adjudicating whether such an act has been committed and by whom, and enforcing those penalties.

criminalization   The process of identifying a person or act as a crime or a criminal by labelling and processing that person or action as in contravention of the criminal law.

criminogenic risk factors   Factors considered when making decisions regarding an offender's classification that have been found to influence the likelihood of future offending.

Crofton system   A prison regime in which inmates began their sentences in solitary confinement, and if they were well behaved they advanced through various forms of congregate work (working together) by earning credits, or "marks," for hard work and good behaviour. The system began in the 1850s and was named after Irish prison administrator Sir Walter Crofton.

CSC National Drug Formulary   The official list of medication available for prescription to federal prisoners. While the physician is free to prescribe medication off the list, the CSC has no obligation to make it available to the prisoner.

day parole   A form of conditional release that allows federal prisoners to serve a portion of their sentence in the community while returning at night to a halfway house or community correctional centre.

death in custody   A death occurring in a federal correctional facility.

de-escalation   The process of reducing the intensity of a conflict or potentially violent situation.

deinstitutionalization   The shift in providing care for persons with mental illness from institutional settings (such as psychiatric hospitals) to care in the community through health authorities and community-based agencies; individuals with severe mental illness were released into the community to be cared for in less restrictive and more humane settings.

dependent variable   A variable that is influenced by the effects of the independent variable.

deprivation model   One of the "classic" models of prison adjustment. Under this model it is believed that the depriving conditions of the prison environment itself cause the stress and difficulties associated with prison life and its coping mechanisms. See also *deprivation theory*.

deprivation theory   The belief that it is the depriving conditions of the custody environment itself that causes the stress and difficulties associated with life in custody and its coping mechanisms.

deterrence   The notion that a person will not commit an offence because of fear of being punished. There are two deterrence notions: Specific deterrence refers to the idea that a person will not commit an offence in the future because of the punishment inflicted on that person for a past offence. General deterrence relates to the idea that people in general will not commit offences because they fear they will be punished as they see or believe others have been.

developmental model of risk   A model that considers risk factors, which include biological and psychological characteristics identifiable in children and youth, that may increase their vulnerability to negative social and environmental influences over the course of development.

disciplinary segregation   The isolation of a prisoner in a single cell for 22 hours a day and without meaningful social contact as punishment for having been found guilty of institutional miconduct or serious offences. Admittance to this form of segregation can entail some measure of due process. As part of this form of segregation, other privileges might be revoked. Disciplinary segregation is imposed with a maximum amount of days; federally, it cannot exceed 30 days.

discrimination   The unjust treatment of different categories of people especially on a feature they possess rather than who they actually are.

disposition   A sentence for anyone 12 to 17 years of age.

drone   A pilotless, remote-controlled device that can be controlled via a smartphone app. Also known as unmanned aerial vehicles (UAVs).

dynamic factor   Factors related to recidivism that are associated with future behaviour that can change over time.

early release   The process through which an individual is released from prison before their sentence ends and serves the remainder of their time under supervision in the community. The main types of early release are day parole (where the individual is allowed into the community for a few hours at a time, and then returns to prison) and full parole (where individuals serve their remaining sentence fully in the community). Each individual must serve in prison various amounts of time, prescribed by the CCRA or the Criminal Code, based on their sentence. When the individual has served the required amount of time in prison, they reach their "parole eligibility date" and may file a parole application. Reaching the parole eligibility date and filing an application, however, does not guarantee release.

emotionality   The observable behaviour and psychological component of emotion.

emotional labour   The process of managing feelings and emotions to fulfill the emotional requirements of a job.

evidence-based intervention   Therapeutic interventions or treatments that are proven to be effective through scientific research.

exclusion zones   Unauthorized locations where an individual under supervision is restricted from entering.

executive functions   Higher-order processes that occur in the prefrontal cortex of the brain and are used to focus our attention, hold information, switch gears, and make decisions.

faith-based intervention   Therapeutic interventions or treatments designed for individuals belonging to a certain faith and that aim to create behavioural changes in those individuals through spiritual principles and practices.

faking   The voluntary suppression or expression of penile arousal.

federal correctional system   According to section 743.1(1) of the Criminal Code, people serving two years or more spend time in a federal penitentiary. Because of the long sentences, which include life sentences, the people serving time in these institutions are aging. This means that the consequences of an aging prison population disproportionately impact the federal correctional system.

fetal alcohol spectrum disorder (FASD)   An umbrella term used to describe a range of infant outcomes associated with maternal alcohol consumption during pregnancy.

follow-up period   Amount of time during which offenders are followed in the community after being released from prison.

full parole   A form of conditional release that allows federal prisoners to serve a portion of their sentence in the community under state supervision. Individuals are typically eligible for full parole one-third of the way through their sentence.

gender binary spaces   A physical space designed with only two genders in mind, thus supporting the notion that there are only two distinct and opposite genders rather than many genders that exist along a spectrum.

gender-responsive corrections   A correctional and rehabilitative approach that recognizes the unique histories and needs of female prisoners. It seeks to provide gender-informed interventions, tools, and training curriculums. In Canada, the Human Rights Act (federal and provincial/territorial) and the Charter of Rights and Freedoms provide the general legislative framework for gender equality and anti-discrimination. Many jurisdictions in Canada have corresponding legislation that mandates gender-responsive approaches to corrections.

***Gladue* report**   Special considerations made when sentencing Indigenous offenders that relate to unique cultural factors and personal histories.

global positioning system (GPS) devices   A location monitoring technology that tracks defendants and offenders in real time by sending, receiving, and triangulating geographical coordinates to and from GPS satellites and cellular towers.

halfway houses   Small-scale residential facilities that provide temporary housing, basic social services, and ongoing supervision to federally sentenced ex-prisoners on conditional release. Also referred to as community-based residential facilities.

historic crimes   An informal way of referring to crimes committed at least 30 years prior to being brought to trial.

hybrid offence   An offence for which the Crown can opt to prosecute the charge as either a summary or indictable offence.

ignition interlock   An in-car alcohol breath-screening device installed inside a vehicle that is connected to the engine's ignition system.

importation model   One of the "classic" models of prison adjustment. This model proposes that the manner in which prisoners adapt to prison is a function of adaptive patterns learned on the city streets and not related to the prison structure. This model presumes that it is what an individual walks into a prison with, such as past experiences, personal characteristics, and individual demographics, that predicts prison adjustment (rather than the prison environment). See also *importation theory*.

importation theory   The belief that a young person's adjustment to custody depends on what a young person brings into the custodial institution. It suggests that a young person's pre-custody experience in the outside world is what is critical. In this theory, it is a young person's external behaviour patterns that predict behaviour in custody—what one walks in with, such as past experiences, personal characteristics, and individual demographics.

incapacitation   Refers to the goal in sentencing that by holding a person in prison (incapacitating them), crime will be reduced because as long as the person is in prison, they simply cannot commit offences in the community.

incarceration   State-sanctioned confinement in a facility designated as a jail or prison.

inclusion zones   Predefined and authorized locations that a supervised individual can have access to during approved times.

independent variable   A variable that influences a particular dependent variable.

indeterminate sentence   A sentence that may be imposed on an individual classified by the court as a "dangerous offender." This designation may be given to an individual who has committed a violent offence and has shown a pattern of repetitive violent behaviour (s. 753(1) Criminal Code). Indeterminate sentences are akin to life sentences in that they never end and the portion that the individual must serve in prison is indeterminate. The individual is eligible to apply for parole at various intervals established in the Criminal Code, but, since the sentence never ends, they may spend their entire life in prison.

indictable offence   An offence that is considered more serious under criminal law for which the maximum penalty that can be imposed upon conviction is life in prison.

Indigenous   Existing in a place or country rather than arriving from another place. Indigenous refers collectively to the First Nations, Métis, and Inuit who live within what is now Canada.

institutionalized   A state in which a prisoner has become so used to life within the prison system that they cannot function in the outside world. Normally this would happen to prisoners that have very long sentences. See also *prisonization effect*.

integrated approach   A model used to describe the adjustment of prisoners that combines both of the classic models of prison adjustment: the importation theory of adjustment (what a person walks in with) and the deprivation theory of adjustment (the depriving environment of the institution). Under this model, prison adjustment is understood to be a combination of both the depriving conditions of the prison environment and the individual characteristics a prisoner brings with them into the prison.

ion mobility spectrometry (IMS) device A drug detection system used within correctional facilities to screen visitors, staff, and inmates for drug residue. Also called an *ion scanner*.

legitimacy theory A belief that there are conditions that make it more likely for prisoners to accept the authority of their custodians. A major determinant of legitimacy is an individual's perceptions of fairness in regard to the manner in which authority figures make decisions.

liberal–humanitarian The active belief in the value of human life, whereby humans practise treatment and provide assistance to other humans in order to better prisoners for moral and logical reasons.

Lifer Someone who has been sentenced to life in prison and will remain in prison until granted parole or until their death. In Canada, life almost always means life (that is, death in prison). Most Lifers have committed some sort of homicide (manslaughter, first or second degree murder), but this sentence can also be imposed for crimes including attempted murder, treason, and others. Parole ineligibility dates range from 7 years for non-murder offences and 10 to 25 years for murder. It cannot be overemphasized that there are no expiration dates for any life sentences.

Mandela Rules The UN Standard Minimum Rules for the Treatment of Prisoners, also known as the Mandela Rules in honour of Nelson Mandela, who spent 27 years incarcerated. Adopted in 2015, it contains 122 rules and is premised on basic principles of equal treatment and non-discrimination. Although not legally binding, these rules provide guidelines for international and domestic correctional and detention facilities. The rules are wide-ranging and cover discipline, pre-trial detention, the use of solitary confinement, staff training, gender considerations, vulnerable populations, access to medical care and legal representation, as well as complaints and investigations.

marginalized Existing in a condition peripheral to the mainstream or dominant group, usually in conditions of some disadvantage.

mature coping A model of coping with the psychological pains of imprisonment that is straightforward; not manipulative, deceptive, or violent; and which includes self-care and caring for others.

maximum security institution Federal institutions housing high-risk offenders; they are characterized by well-defined, secure, controlled perimeters and the strictly controlled and monitored movement of offenders.

mediator A variable that explains the relationship between an independent and dependent variable.

medium security institution Federal institutions housing moderate-risk offenders; they are characterized by well-defined, secure, controlled perimeters and the regulated movement of offenders that is usually monitored.

mental health court A specialized type of court for individuals with suspected or confirmed mental illness that recognizes the influence of mental illness on behaviour/criminal justice system involvement and through which individuals receive special consideration of their unique mental health needs and more individualized and holistic case management.

mental health A state of psychological and emotional well-being; the capacity to cope with everyday responsibilities and stressors and contribute to the community and society at large.

mental illness A condition that impairs a person's behaviour or thinking and negatively impacts their feelings and mood or their daily functioning; distinct from mental health.

meta-analysis A study looking at all previous studies conducted on a specific topic in order to evaluate the impact of a specific measure.

minimum security institution Federal institutions housing low-risk offenders; they are characterized by well-defined perimeters that are not controlled or secured with little monitoring of offenders, who are expected to interact pro-socially with other offenders.

multi-level institution Federal institutions with more than one security level on site within one institution overseen by one warden.

natural deaths Deaths that occur as a result of a health condition and are most often defined in contrast to non-natural causes, such as suicide, homicide, accident, or overdose.

neurodevelopment The brain's development of neurological pathways that help individuals develop skills to function across the lifespan.

not criminally responsible on account of mental disorder (NCRMD) As per the Criminal Code's definition, a mental disorder is viewed as a "disease of the mind." To be found NCRMD, there must be a mental abnormality (not caused by voluntary intoxication, temporary mental conditions, or uncontrollable urges) causing significant impairment to preclude the individual's understanding of their behaviour during the commission of an offence.

Office of the Correctional Investigator (OCI) Established in 1973, the correctional investigator is an ombudsperson for federally sentenced prisoners and fulfills the role of a prison monitoring mechanism. Mandated by the Corrections and Conditional Release Act, the OCI receives, investigates, and resolves individual prisoner complaints on a variety of issues related to their treatment and conditions of confinement. It also has the responsibility to conduct institutional visits, as well as to review and make recommendations about CSC policies and procedures. Through its annual reports and research activity, the OCI has identified various systemic issues and called for changes pertaining to a wide array of policies, practices, and culture in federal corrections. The OCI reports directly to the minister of Public Safety Canada.

open custody   (1) A community residential centre, group home, child-care institution, or wilderness camp or (2) any like place of facility. Open custody is less stringent and generally used for young people with less serious offences. Generally, open custody consists of several small residential facilities and a network of community homes. Youth in open custody facilities sometimes have access to community schools, recreation in the community, and local employment and treatment.

operational stress   Stressors involved in the content of a job.

organizational stress   Stressors involved in the context of a job.

pains of imprisonment   First proposed as part of the deprivation model, there are five pains of imprisonment associated with adjustment to prison. They include (but are not necessarily limited to) the deprivation of liberty, goods and services, heterosexual relationships, autonomy, and security.

pardon   A procedure (also called "record suspension") whereby a person can apply to have the effect of their criminal record limited or annulled such that they can indicate that they do not have a criminal record for which they have not received a pardon.

parole   A form of release from prison that is under the control of a parole board. Typically for those serving fixed length sentences (that is, not life sentences), people are eligible for *full* parole after serving one-third of their sentences. Day parole—where a person typically spends the night in a halfway house—is also under the control of a parole board and is typically used in anticipation of either full parole or statutory release.

Parole Board of Canada (PBC)   An independent administrative tribunal tasked with hearing and deciding upon early release requests from prisoners. Its mandate, including circumstances where prisoners may file early release requests with the PBC, are set out in the Corrections and Conditional Release Act and its regulations.

parole by exception   A special form of early release for which the eligibility criteria to apply are grounded in health reasons as opposed to the amount of time served.

peace officer   An officer appointed to preserve law and order, such as a police officer or correctional officer.

peer-on-peer violence   When a young person is exploited, bullied, or harmed by their peers, who are the same or similar age; everyone directly involved in peer-on-peer abuse is generally under the age of 18.

penitentiary   A secure correctional facility designated for people who have been convicted of serious crimes. In Canada, the term "penitentiary" refers to a correctional institution that is administered by the federal government and in which people serving sentences of two years or more are incarcerated.

phallometry   The recording of penile responses during the presentation of deviant and non-deviant sexual stimuli.

predictive validity   The extent that a score on a measure predicts future results.

prejudice   A preconceived opinion that is not based on reason or actual experience.

primary care   A primary care officer is the person who is most hands on with prisoners on a unit.

prison discipline   A movement that included sanctions for breach of prison regulations, but also encompassed the whole operational regime of the prison—the classification of inmates, the work regime, the division of the prison day into work and rest periods, uniform dress for inmates, and the rules determining how each inmate should interact with other inmates and guards.

prison fix   The way that governments turn to imprisonment (or carceral retasking) as a way to address fiscal, social, and political crises.

prison subculture   A term often used to describe the prison social system.

prison tourism   Tourism that takes place in decommissioned penitentiaries, prisons, jails, lock-ups, and other sites with the goal of entertaining or educating visitors through engagement with experiences that claim to be proximate to imprisonment. Examples of prison tourism sites include museums, restaurants, and hotels.

prisoner re-entry   An event signalling a person's return to community living as well as the informed continuous process of navigating the complexities of social life following incarceration.

prisoner re-entry organization   NGO-run organizations that act on ex-prisoners' lives during the early stages of prison release. They typically provide services and rehabilitative programming to former prisoners.

prisonization effect   The process by which an individual takes on the values and norms of the prison and the prison subculture. Prisoners are considered to be high or low on prisonization depending on how much they subscribe to the prison subculture.

professionalism   The competence, set of skills, conduct, aims, or qualities that characterize a professional person.

proportionality   The sentencing requirement (under s. 718.1 of the Criminal Code) that a sentence be proportional (or consistent with) the gravity of the offence and the degree of responsibility of the offender.

protective custody   A special unit of the prison reserved for inmates who cannot join the general population because of the nature of their crimes (such as sex offenders) or their past behaviour in prison (for example, informing on other inmates).

psy-carceral complex   The host of psychological, psychiatric, and medical discourses and practices that are mobilized to constitute criminalized subjects as irrational, mentally ill, and/or emotionally distressed and to monitor and manage their behaviour. This occurs both in correctional environments and in community-based supervision by way of parole release orders. In can include mandated forms of care, intervention, and treatment, including prescription psychotropic medication adherence.

psychosocial adjustment   A reflection of an individual's psychological well-being that is influenced by their experiences in the social arena.

public interest remedies   The Ontario Human Rights Code allows the Human Rights Tribunal to make orders and grant various remedies following a finding of human rights violations. In addition to financial or non-financial measures that benefit the applicant, the tribunal may issue public interest remedies that suit broader public interests. The rationale in issuing such remedies is to effect systemic change so that similar rights violations are prevented from occurring in the future.

radio frequency (RF) devices   A type of location monitoring technology that tracks an individual's location at a single fixed place.

rational choice theory   A criminological theory that suggests people commit crimes based on their self-interests through a rational decision-making process of determining the costs and benefits of alternative courses of action and choosing the one with the greatest perceived utility.

recidivism   Relapse into criminal behaviour.

regional treatment centres (RTCs)   Multi-level federal in-patient psychiatric institutions that are recognized as provincial hospitals or psychiatric hospitals and house prisoners who are unable to reside in federal institutions for reasons of disability or impairment. They deliver more intensive care and services for acute and chronic mental health issues and are a component of the CSC's mental health strategy.

regulatory capture   A multidimensional concept that is used to explain how regulatory mechanisms consistently fail to ensure legal and human rights compliance. Traditionally, regulatory capture referred to biased and imperfect oversight practices that were undermined by corruption and the "revolving door" of employment between watchdog agencies and the overseen industry. This concept is now used to explain profoundly compromised yet purportedly appropriate oversight practices whereby the overseen dictates how oversight occurs and its outcomes.

rehabilitation   The action or process of restoring an individual to health or normal life through training and therapy during or after a period of incarceration, addiction, or illness (the term is rather contentious).

remand custody   The detention of an offender who has been charged with an offence and has either not yet gone to trial or is awaiting their sentencing hearing following their conviction. People are placed in remand prior to trial for three reasons: because they are a flight risk, a danger to the public, or to maintain confidence in the administration of justice.

restorative justice   A collective approach to criminal justice that involves the offender, the victim(s), their families, as well as the community to acknowledge the harm that was done, ensure the offender is held accountable, and allow all parties to be involved in rectifying the issue.

risk assessment instrument   Used to assess a person's risk to recidivate based on identified risk and protective factors; this is based on indicators such as family-level factors, educational/vocational measures, substance-use measures, peer measures, and attitudinal measures.

risk-need-responsivity (RNR) model   A model used in offender rehabilitation that is based on three key principles. First, risk assessments should identify an offender's risk to recidivate. Next, they should establish the individual's criminogenic needs, or risk factors, and protective factors. Finally, they should assess the prisoner's prospective receptivity to treatment.

screening tool   Used to identify individuals with mental illness or mental health needs and to make appropriate service, programming, and treatment referrals.

secure custody   Any place designated by the lieutenant governor in council in a province for the secure containment or restraint of young people. Secure-custody facilities are what most people would think of as looking like a typical prison, albeit for young people. They are generally facilities where restrictions are continuously placed on young people by physical barriers, close supervision, and limited access to the community.

seg-like/lite   Various housing units/placements that are used as "alternatives" to segregation but entail similar movement and association restrictions. As such, these placements closely resemble segregation conditions of confinement. As these can be labelled alternative housing units, special needs units, mental health units, intensive support units, or gang ranges, they are difficult to track and monitor and are often without clear policies and procedural safeguards related to formal segregation.

segregation review   A review of the segregation placement in which the release or continued segregation of the individual is decided. Each jurisdiction has standard requirements for when, how, and by whom segregation reviews ought to be conducted. Reviews should consider various factors, such as the physical and mental health of the prisoner, the availability and appropriateness of potential alternatives, as well as strategies for the release of segregated prisoners. In many Canadian jurisdictions, segregation reviews function as a form of internal oversight.

self-harm   Deliberate self-inflicted bodily harm or disfigurement.

self-injurious behaviour   Harm that is deliberately incurred on the body but that does not indicate suicidal intent. Self-harm, alternatively, is a broader term incorporating self-injurious behaviour and other behaviours that impact one's health and body immediately or over time (such as health neglect, eating disorders, and substance abuse).

separate system   A penitentiary regime used first in Pennsylvania in the early 1800s in which prisoners were kept continually in solitary confinement, living and working alone in their cells.

sex offender   A person who commits a crime involving a sexual act.

silent system   A penitentiary regime used first in New York in the early 1800s in which prisoners were confined alone in single cells during the night but worked in groups during the day. At all times prisoners were supposed to remain silent, never communicating with guards or inmates unless ordered to do so. This regime of non-communication extended to more than silence, including prohibitions on looking at each other, making gestures, or engaging in any form of non-verbal communication.

social attachment theory   A social psychological theory that originally examined the developmental impacts of emotional connection between infant and caregivers on pro-social decision making. The theory has been used to understand how attachment to a major social institution, such as family, school, and employment, decreases the likelihood of offending.

social determinants of health   Social factors that influence the overall health of an individual by impacting health-related behaviours and access to health care, such as gender, culture, early experiences, home setting, education, employment, income, and social status.

social learning theory   A general theory of learning suggesting that people learn from one another via observation, imitation, and modelling. The implications of this theory in criminology show that both offending behaviour and desistance from crime can be learned from others through observation and reinforcement.

solitary confinement   Generally refers to the separation of the individual from the general population for 22 hours a day or more, without meaningful contact. In Canada, the legislation refers to this practice as "segregation" and can be of two types: disciplinary (as punishment, in response to a disciplinary offence, which is limited to 15 days at a time) and administrative (which covers any other reasons, including for protection, and currently has no time limit). Sometimes also referred to as "closed confinement."

specialization   The probability of repeating the same type of crime when next arrested.

static factor   Factors related to recidivism that are historical and unchanging.

status degradation ceremony   A ceremony that takes place upon entering a total institution and describes the moment when a person is stripped of everything that makes them an individual and turns them from an outsider to an insider.

statutory release   A form of conditional release that allows federal prisoners (those serving sentences of two years or more) to be released after two-thirds of their sentence and serve the remainder of their time in the community under state supervision, unless they have been sentenced for certain designated serious offences; in these cases the parole board can detain them until the end of their sentences.

stereotype   An overgeneralized belief about a particular category of people based on an assumed characteristic that is not grounded in fact or truth.

stigma   Negative stereotyping often associated with having a criminal record. Can lead to discrimination and exclusion for former prisoners in different domains, such as the labour market.

substance-use disorder   A mental disorder where the use of one or more substances leads to clinically significant impairment or distress.

summary offence   An offence considered to be less serious in criminal law for which the maximum penalty that can be imposed upon conviction is a $5,000 fine and/or six months in jail.

suspended sentence   The passing of a sentence which is then "suspended" and the person is released into the community (typically on probation).

temporary absences   Temporary absences (escorted or unescorted) are the most common mechanism through which an individual may access services in the community in person. Such absences require prior approval.

terminally ill   A term used to designate someone who has been medically assessed to have weeks or months to live. However, the term is not defined in correctional legislation or policy.

therapeutic jurisprudence   The identification and treatment of people with mental illness through holistic, collaborative responses.

total institutions   Institutions that have barriers to the outside world and have specific social arrangements. Within total institutions all aspects of daily life are conducted under a single authority, and all phases of the day are tightly scheduled with enforced activities. There is generally a split between a managed group and a smaller group of supervisory staff. Examples of total institutions include prisons, hospitals for the mentally ill, army barracks, and convents or monasteries.

transcarceral control   The extension of penal control, power, and regulation beyond the prison. Ex-prisoners experience penal control, for example, while serving the remainder of their sentence under state supervision.

trauma   the range of harmful emotional, psychological, and physical consequences a person can experience after living through a distressing event.

trauma-informed care   Practices that account for previous exposure to trauma, promote feelings of safety, avoid re-traumatizing, and support individuals' coping and ultimate recovery.

unfit to stand trial (UST)   When an individual is not fully capable of instructing counsel or understanding the nature and consequences of their trial.

use of force   The amount of effort required by correctional officers to compel compliance from a prisoner.

versatile   An offender engaging in various antisocial behaviours depending on the type of criminal opportunity arising.

victim surcharge   The requirement to pay a fixed sum of money (or a per cent of a fine, in cases in which fines are imposed as part of a sentence) that is supposed to fund victim services.

viewing time   The amount of time spent viewing a particular image or object.

vulnerable individuals   Incarcerated people with higher or different needs than the mainstream prison population. These needs place them at a higher risk of abuse, suicide, or other harms. Failure to address these needs acts as a barrier to their rehabilitation and reintegration into the community.

warn range   Blood alcohol concentration (BAC) levels between 0.05 and 0.08 per cent.

warrant expiry date   The end of a person's sentence.

wraparound services   Collaborative responses that address multiple aspects and diverse needs in an individual's life.

Youth Criminal Justice Act (YCJA)   The governing piece of legislation in Canada of youth from the ages of 12 to 17 who are suspected of committing a criminal offence.

Index